To
Phil,

with my best

wishes and

appreciation,

yours

Mohamed Ramady

Jan 2011.

The Saudi Arabian Economy

The Saudi Arabian Economy

Policies, Achievements, and Challenges

Second Edition

Mohamed A. Ramady

King Fahd University of Petroleum & Minerals

 Springer

Mohamed A. Ramady
Department of Finance
  and Economics
King Fahd University
  of Petroleum and Minerals
Dhahran 31261, Saudi Arabia
ramadyma@kfupm.edu.sa

ISBN 978-1-4419-5986-7   e-ISBN 978-1-4419-5987-4
DOI 10.1007/978-1-4419-5987-4
Springer New York Dordrecht Heidelberg London

Library of Congress Control Number: 2010930268

Printed on acid-free paper

Springer is part of Springer Science+Business Media (www.springer.com)

Your old men shall dream dreams: your young men shall see visions

Dedicated to my children Ali, Faisal and Layla and all the young men and women of the Arab world

Contents

Part III   The Financial Sector

Preface

The Saudi Arabian economy continues to evolve, driven by a palpable faster pace of economic and social reforms than at any other period since the Kingdom's establishment. Unlike earlier periods, when the decision to adapt and change was regarded as a luxury that could be accepted or delayed, the current pace of modernization and reforms has been thrust upon the Kingdom as a strategic necessity driven by globalization pressures and a willing political choice.

Since the first edition of this book in 2005, the characteristic of the Saudi economy has continued to change structurally. The social engineering that has also taken place has been no less significant in the field of education, opening up to the wider world and demonstrating a willingness to address pressing social issues which had hitherto been taboo or ignored.

Saudi Arabia's international economic standing has increased over the past few years and once again the Kingdom has demonstrated that, in the final analysis, it remains the global energy warehouse that is willing to play a moderating role to the benefit of both consumers and producers. The Kingdom is aware of the shift in global economic power and has embarked on forging its own independent, strategic economic and political relations with the BRIC economies – Brazil, Russia, India and China – particularly with China, which is now Saudi Arabia's second most important trading partner and a source of future strategic cooperation.

As this book highlights, the Kingdom is still having to diversify its economy fast enough to provide employment opportunities for its growing number of young educated citizens and ensure that the legal, educational and social reforms undertaken take root and are accepted by society at large. How this evolves will no doubt affect the economic well-being of many nations far away from Saudi Arabia's shores as well as the livelihood of a large number of foreign workers who call Saudi Arabia their home.

Dhahran, Saudi Arabia   M.A. Ramady
2010

Acknowledgements

Any book is a reflection of what others have contributed as accumulated knowledge before it, as well as the support given to the author by the many whose advice and suggestions have hopefully been incorporated in the final work. My grateful thanks go to His Excellency Dr. Khaled Al Sultan, Rector, King Fahd University of Petroleum and Minerals, and to the Dean and colleagues at the College of Industrial Management, and those at the Department of Finance and Economics for their constructive comments and suggestions. I appreciate their willingness to act as a valuable sounding board for ideas on issues affecting the Saudi economy and society at large, even when we disagreed.

Many thanks also go to the many friends and associates over the years in the banking, media, private and government sectors and who provided moral support, insightful comments and sharp wit when they were most needed. With apologies to all those not mentioned, my special thanks go to His Royal Highness Prince Turki bin Abdullah bin Abdulaziz, HE Dr. Ibrahim Al Assaf, HE Dr. Khaled Al Angari, HE Abdullah Al Hussayain, HE Dr. Mohammed Al Jasser, Sheikh Hamad Saud Al Sayyari, HE Dr. Abdulrahman Al Tuwaijri, HE Mr. Fehied AlShareef, HE Mr. Solaiman Al Hummayed, HE Dr. Bandar Al Aiban, HE Khaled Al Falih, Dr. Abdulaziz Al-Dukhayil, Abdulaziz Al Hashimi, Abdullateef Al Othman, Jamal Al Rammah, Motassem Al Ma'ashouq, Waleed Somali, Loai Mushaikh, Waleed Abal Khail, Abdulaziz Alayaaf, Abdulmohsen Al Saleh, Soliman Al Guwaiz and Mohammed Al Mansour.

From outside the Kingdom, my thanks to John Varley, Omar Selim, Karim Zahmoul, Ayman Sejiny, Dr. Thorsten Polleit, John Milne, Dr. Noel Brehoney, Gavin Shreeve, Dr. Robert Walker, Shaukat Aziz and Kevin Muehring.

Following in the tradition set for the first edition, I wish to recognize some of the many talented KFUPM students whom I have taught and in whose hands the future of the Kingdom lies as it moves forward to meet future challenges. They are Rashed Al Rashed, Majed Al Ahmad, Maan Nagadi, Hatem Tariq Jamal, Mazen Al Furaih, Nayef Al Athel, Abdullah Asiri, Tareq Qahtani, Khaled Al Moajil, Mohammed bin Saud bin Naif, Abdullah Al Dubaib, Bilal Choudhary, Khaled bin Saud bin Abdullah Al Faisal, Tawfiq Al Ibrahim, Rakan Al Otaishan, Abdulaziz Saja, Mohammed Al Guwaiz, Ahmad Baiyat, Abdelrahman Al Hussayain, Saud Al Moammar, Khaled Al Omran, Mohammed Al Modhayan, Fahad Al Farsy, Youssef Al Ibrahim, Tallal

Al Sulaim, Mohammed Yousef Al Dossary, Ibrahim Boumarah, Abdullah Al Waily, Fahad Al Saleh, Fahad Al Humaidah, Mohannad Al Alsheikh, Sh. Nasser Al Thani, Ayman Al Sayyari, Abdulrahman Al Hammad, Turki Al Jammaz, Abdullah Al-Towaijri and Mansour Al Akeel.

A special word of thanks and appreciation is due to the tireless efforts of the dedicated technical and secretarial staff, foremost among them Junaid Akthar.

Needless to say, I take full responsibility for any shortcomings and errors.

Finally I would like to acknowledge the support provided by KFUPM under project Number IN 100014 in the preparation of this book.

Abbreviations

AACSB	Association to Advance Collegiate School of Business
AAOIFI	Accounting and Auditing Organization for Islamic Financial Institutions
ABET	Accreditation Board for Engineering and Technology
ACH	Automated Clearing House
AMF	Arab Monetary Fund
ASEAN	Association of South East Asian Nations
Bear market	Falling market prices
BIS	Bank for International Settlement, Basle, Switzerland
BOO	Build Operate Own
BOOT	Build Operate Own Transfer
BOP	Balance of Payment
BOT	Build Operate Transfer
Bull market	Rising market prices
CAFTA	Central American Free Trade Agreement
CDS	Central Department of Statistics
ceteris paribus	Assuming everything else is equal
CIS	Commonwealth of Independent States
CMA	Capital Market Authority
CPO	Central Planning Organization
CRR	Cash Reserve Ratio
CSCCI	Council of Saudi Chambers of Commerce and Industry
Downstream	Processing of gas and oil for final product delivery
EC	European Community
EEC	European Economic Community
EFTA	European Free Trade Area
Emir	Ruler
EPCCI	Eastern Province Chamber of Commerce and Industry
ESIS	Electronic Share Information System
EU	European Union
FATF	Financial Action Task Force
FDI	Foreign Direct Investment
Fed (The)	Federal Reserve Bank, USA

FRNs	Floating Rate Notes
FTA	Free Trade Agreement
GAFTA	Greater Arab Free Trade Area
GATS	General Agreement on Trade in Services
GATT	General Agreement on Tariffs and Trade
GCC	Gulf Cooperation Council
GDBs	Government Development Bonds
GDP	Gross Domestic Product
GFCF	Gross Fixed Capital Formation
GNP	Gross National Product
GOSI	General Organization for Social Insurance
Hajj	Annual Muslim pilgrimage to Makkah
Hallal	permissible in Islam
Haram	forbidden in Islam
ICT	Information and Communication Technology
IDB	Islamic Development Bank
IMF	International Monetary Fund
IOC	International Oil Companies
IPO	Initial Public Offering
Iqama	Saudi residence permit for foreigners
IT	Information Technology
JIBOR	Jeddah Interbank Offer Rate
KAAU	King Abdulaziz University
Kafeel	Saudi sponsor of foreign labour
KFU	King Faisal University
KFUPM	King Fahd University of Petroleum and Minerals
KSA	Kingdom of Saudi Arabia
KSU	King Saud University
LDCs	Least-Developed Countries
LIBOR	London Interbank Offer Rate
Maaden	Saudi Arabian Mining Company
Majls Al-Shoura	National Consultative Assembly or Council
mbd	million barrels per day
MENA	Middle East and North Africa
MMBtu	One million British thermal units
MoF	Ministry of Finance
MoP	Ministry of Planning
NAFTA	North American Free Trade Agreement
NCB	National Commercial Bank
NCCI	National Company for Cooperative Insurance
NEER	Nominal Effective Exchange Rate
NGL	Natural Gas Liquid (or sometimes NLG)
NIEs	Newly Industrialized Economies
OBU	Offshore Banking Unit
OECD	Organisation for Economic Co-operation and Development

OEEC	Organization for European Economic Cooperation
OIC	Organization of Islamic Conference
OPEC	Organization of Petroleum Exporting Countries
ORR	Official Repurchase Rate
PIF	Public Investment Fund
PPP	Public Private Partnership
R&D	Research and development
Ramadan	Muslim month of fasting
REDEF	Real Estate Development Fund
REER	Real Effective Exchange Rate
Repo	Repurchase agreement
Reverse Repo	Reverse repurchase agreement
Riba	Usury interest
SAAB	Saudi Arabian Agricultural Bank
SABIC	Saudi Arabian Basic Industries Company
SADC	Southern African Development Community
SAGIA	Saudi Arabia General Investment Authority
SAMA	Saudi Arabian Monetary Agency
SAMBA	Saudi American Bank (until October 2004)
SARIE	Saudi Riyal Interbank Express system
SASO	Saudi Arabian Standards Organization
Saudia	Saudi Arabian airlines
SCB	Saudi Credit Bank
SCCI	Saudi Chambers of Commerce and Industry
SDR	Special Drawing Right
SEC	Security and Exchange Commission
SEP	Saudi Export Programme
SFD	Saudi Fund for Development
Sh.	Sheikh
Shariah	Islamic law
SIBOR	Saudi Interbank Offer Rate
SIDF	Saudi Industrial Development Fund
SIMAH	Saudi Credit Bureau
SIST	Saudi Individual Stock Traders
SLR	Statutory Liquidity Ratio
SMEs	Small- and Medium-Sized Enterprises
SPAN	Saudi Payment Network
SPRA	Saudi Pension and Retirement Agency
SR	Saudi Riyal
Status quo	Keeping things unchanged
STC	Saudi Telecom Company
Sunnah	Sayings of the Prophet Muhammad (pbuh)
SWCC	Saline Water Conversion Corporation
TADAWUL	Electronic share trading and information system
Takaful Ta'awni	Islamic cooperative life insurance product

TASI	*TADAWUL* All Share Index
T-Bills	Treasury bills
TCF	Trillion Cubic Feet (of gas)
UNCTAD	United Nations conference on Trade and Development
UNDP	United Nations Development Programme
Upstream	Production of oil and gas from wells
Wakeel	Saudi commercial agent of foreign companies
Wasta	connection, favour
WTO	World Trade Organization

Part I
The Setting

Chapter 1
Overview

We should never create by law what can be accomplished by morality.

Montesquieu

Introduction

The Kingdom of Saudi Arabia has witnessed a dramatic rise in the pace of economic and social change since the succession of King Abdullah bin Abdulaziz to the throne in August 2005. The country had been going through a transformation prior to the succession, but the pace and urgency was more evident in the domestic economic, social and educational sectors, as well as in Saudi Arabia's new-found confidence in establishing strategic economic alliances in the Far East.

This book builds upon the period covered by the first edition and examines the key factors of change that have taken place since 2005 and are continuing to shape the future destiny of the Kingdom on many fronts.

While the book covers some distinct groupings of chapters under a common theme, it becomes apparent that there are certain overriding issues that prevail in all chapters and often overlap. This is to be expected, as Saudi Arabia's economic development path is multifaceted and many factors affect the final outcomes, whether they are in education reform, economic restructuring or globalization. The key issues that remain facing Saudi Arabia include continuing to diversify the economic base and reduce the country's heavy dependency on hydrocarbons, managing expectations based on a narrow revenue base, coping with the needs of a young and growing population as well as rising youth unemployment for both males and females, empowering the private sector to become the engine of growth through meaningful Saudi national job creation and exports as well as meeting the Kingdom's new international obligations since accession to the World Trade Organization (WTO) in 2005. Many of these issues have remained the same since the first edition was printed, and this is necessarily so as fundamental changes affecting a nation take more than a few decades to be set on a right footing.

M.A. Ramady, *The Saudi Arabian Economy*, DOI 10.1007/978-1-4419-5987-4_1,
© Springer Science+Business Media, LLC 2010

This hurdle of simultaneous challenges would be a tall order for any nation to handle. For Saudi Arabia, it also includes reforming the educational system to be in line with market needs, establishing a knowledge-based economy, opening up to the rest of the world by a process of inter-faith dialogue, fostering a culture of moderation and dealing with other nations and cultures based on mutual respect. The country also seeks to meet the increasingly vocal aspirations of its female population through expansion of their participation in the economy and society at large, but without compromising on basic religious beliefs, customs and traditions.

Setting the Stage

The first broad themes are covered in Chapters 2 and 3. Chapter 2 addresses how economic planning was introduced and implemented in Saudi Arabia, and examines its evolution and whether it had managed to lay the framework for meeting future challenges. The chapter examines the strategic economic decisions Saudi Arabia made in the early boom era, the consequences of which are still apparent today. These consequences include investment in capital-intensive infrastructure and basic industries, reliance on cheap energy input, the use of subsidies and incentives to promote economic growth and the import of a large number of foreign workers. Planning during this period evolved from being directive to indicative, as the economy expanded and opened up to international trade. It also focused more on the private sector and started to set qualitative indicators, rather than the quantitative indicators of earlier planning periods. Chapter 2 points to Saudi Arabia's need for a more strategic and flexible short-term planning process that is better suited to a faster-evolving global economy.

The accelerated pace of key reforms in the economic, judicial and political sectors are examined, all of which are beginning to lay the foundation of a modern Saudi state. The empowerment of the consultative council or *Majlis Al Shoura* and the revamping of the judicial process are key measures that are helping to promote more transparency and accountability in the government system. The emphasis on increased education spending as a national priority stands out as a prerequisite for economic growth.

Chapter 3 assesses the Saudi budgetary framework and the urgent long-term need for a wider revenue base diversification. Recent high oil prices have moved Saudi Arabia back into a surplus position after nearly a decade of budget deficits and ballooning domestic debt, with the Kingdom now enjoying substantial foreign reserves. The chapter also discusses the possible crowding out of the private sector, which the government hopes will assume the future capital project funding needs of the Kingdom, estimated at around $400 billion over the next 20 years. It then examines the centrality of oil revenue and the lack of government control over nearly 90% of its revenue sources, pointing towards the need to adopt a new strategy to meet future fluctuating oil fortunes in order to move away from being a hostage to a *petrolized* economy.

Saudi Arabia is now a prominent member of the G20 group of nations and, by virtue of its economic size and holding the largest known reserves of oil in the world, Saudi spending and investment policies in key sectors such as oil have an important influence on world economies. The chapter explores the Kingdom's need to build true wealth rather than remain oil-dependent, for which end capital expenditure has been rising over the past few years.

The Financial Sector

We explore our second major theme in Chapters 4, 5 and 6, as we examine the evolving and, in some respects, mature financial sector of Saudi Arabia. Chapter 4 analyses the evolution of the Saudi de facto central bank – the Saudi Arabian Monetary Agency (SAMA). It looks at how SAMA has assumed a wide range of responsibilities and supervisory regulatory powers despite being constrained in the use of more traditional central bank policy tools, such as discount and interest rate instruments. However, SAMA has effectively managed the other range of monetary and exchange rate policy tools available to it in combating rising inflation in Saudi Arabia during 2007–2009, as well as ensuring that the Saudi banking system today is one of the most capitalized, liquid and profitable in the world. At the same time, SAMA has supervised the smooth transition of the Kingdom's foreign bank presence to joint partnerships, that is, a *Saudized* banking framework. This has turned out to be an effective partnership tool for transferring technology and management skills to the Saudi financial sector. The chapter also examines how SAMA has coped with the new wave of foreign banks operating in the Kingdom following Saudi Arabia's accession to the WTO, and how it managed to steer the Saudi banking sector safely during the global financial crisis of 2008/2009. Chapter 4 explores the growing sophistication of SAMA's use of *repos* and *reverse repos* as proxy monetary instruments, as well as SAMA's management of the national debt and foreign asset reserves. It also considers the rationale of SAMA's fixed exchange rate policy for the SR and the Kingdom's money supply creation process.

Chapter 5 further develops this theme and examines the broader financial markets that have evolved in the Kingdom, especially in the commercial banking sector and SAMA's supervisory process and results of such oversight in the Saudi banking sector. This sector is comprised of a mix of wholly owned "pure" Saudi banks, joint-venture *Saudized* banks, the newly approved foreign banks and other financial sector players, such as the specialized government financial institutions. The latter played a crucial role in providing long-term concessionary credit for Saudi economic development when most commercial financial institutions preferred to take short-term risks. Chapter 5 examines the core strength and market strategies of these various financial institutions and their financial performance. The emerging insurance sector is also discussed, as well as the growing role of Islamic financing in Saudi Arabia and how the Kingdom's financial sector hopes to cope with globalization threats and opportunities.

The focus on the financial sector concludes with Chapter 6, which analyses the Saudi capital market through a discussion of the evolution of the domestic capital market, the operating regulatory framework and the various obstacles. This is followed by an assessment of the new Capital Market Law and the establishment of an empowered Capital Market Authority (CMA), which has carried out a series of operational and supervisory reforms to make it one of the strongest capital market regulators in the Gulf. We explore the issue of ownership concentration and the lack of depth of the Saudi capital market, in contrast to the Kingdom's dominance of the Arab stock markets in terms of size and performance. This chapter analyses the sectoral composition of the Saudi stock market and the inherent weaknesses of having a thin market base. We assess investor behaviour, and take an in-depth look at the Saudi mutual fund market, the largest and most diverse in the Arab world, as well as the participation of foreign investors in the Saudi market through share swap facilities, and the opening up of the Saudi capital market to foreign investment banks and their impact. The Saudi government debt market's structure is closely examined, as well as the future evolution of the Saudi capital market in the face of ongoing liberalization and privatization.

The Heart of the Kingdom: The Hydrocarbon Sector

The third theme of the book revolves around the private sector and the challenges it faces, and Saudi Arabia's hydrocarbon and mineral sector – truly the heart of the Kingdom's revenue generation, diversification prospects and value-added job generation.

Chapter 7 critically examines the challenges for the Saudi private sector as it shoulders the responsibility of transforming the Saudi economy into a market-driven generator of wealth. It is important to assess whether an appropriate business environment exists in the Kingdom today, one that enables the private sector to take up these challenges. Therefore, we examine the legal, corporate and economic environments under which the private sector has to operate. We look, too, at the issue of foreign labour participation and current Saudi government pressure on the private sector to accelerate the process of *Saudization*. The role of the small- and medium-sized enterprises (SMEs), as well as the obstacles they face and how the government is trying to overcome these obstacles, is examined, given the importance of the SMEs to Saudi Arabia's goal of job generation and regional economic diversification. Chapter 7 also explores the role of the Saudi family businesses and their structures, and advocates for some changes to family businesses for enabling them to meet the future challenges of globalization following Saudi entry to the WTO, and some well-publicized family Saudi business problems.

This chapter also considers Saudi women and their growing importance in the national economy; we note the obstacles currently faced by women in managing their own businesses, and investigate how they are overcoming these barriers. During the past few years, there has been a greater momentum to generate more female job opportunities, to increase women's participation in economic nation-building and to open up more sectors for them. We analyse the potential impact of the ongoing Saudi "mega-city" projects on private sector participation with the government on a Private Public Partnership (PPP) basis and set out a model of private sector–government cooperation.

We look at the government's role as a planner, financing entity, buyer and seller, regulator and revenue collector. The issue of *Saudization* and how the private sector views it is examined in some detail, showing that the private sector and the government have divergent views. The private sector argues that *Saudization* can only succeed when a supply of skilled labour exists such that it meets market needs at competitive wage levels.

Chapter 8 discusses the oil and gas sectors and explores the opportunities that lie in the as yet relatively untapped non-carbon minerals sector. The importance of oil, its dominant effect on the Saudi economy and the Kingdom's pivotal role in this energy sector are highlighted. The chapter also thoroughly examines Saudi oil policy and its constraints. The record oil prices experienced during 2008, with oil prices reaching $147 per barrel on fears of supply shortages, underscored the Kingdom's importance as the major excess capacity producer of the world. Saudi gas, a new and important energy sector, is appraised in light of Saudi Arabia's attempts to attract foreign investment and technical partners to this field. Besides having a quarter of the world's proven oil reserves, Saudi Arabia also has the world's fourth largest gas reserves and is a significant natural gas liquid (NGL) exporter.

Chapter 8 also looks at the Saudi petrochemical industry, particularly as it could be the major beneficiary following WTO entry. Today the Saudi Arabian Basic Industries Corporation (SABIC) is a significant player in the world's petrochemical markets, with expanded operations both at home and abroad. For some products, SABIC's world share stands at around 18–20%, and it is a credit to the Kingdom that this was achieved in fewer than 20 years' time, literally created out of the desert. Saudi Arabia's evolving overseas energy markets are explored, as it has become evident that the export focus has shifted towards Asian markets for both crude and petrochemical products. Chapter 8 carries on exploring the Kingdom's mining sector and its potential to diversify the economic base and generate an integrated mining industry. If developed, the Kingdom's extensive mining resources could lead Saudi Arabia to rank as amongst one of the leading mining countries in the world.

The privatization of the Saudi Arabian Mining Company (*Maaden*) involves the restructuring of the company into separate units for gold, phosphate, bauxite, aluminium and other minerals. Foreign investors in the mining field will be encouraged to explore under planned new mining law concessions. Chapter 8 presents a new model of mining cooperation with foreign companies that will assist in taking the privatization forward. This model could help shield the Kingdom from fluctuations in basic commodity prices, such as oil, resulting in a narrow revenue base, despite the record 21-year-high oil prices seen during 2008 and the subsequent fall in oil prices triggered by the global financial crisis of 2008/2009. The chapter also examines Saudi Arabia's policy to develop alternative renewable energy solutions, especially solar energy, in order to meet growing domestic energy consumption and conserve oil reserves for future export revenue generation.

The Foreign Sector

Chapters 9 and 10 deal with the theme of Saudi Arabia's foreign trade relations and the impact of the Kingdom's accession to the WTO in 2005.

Saudi Arabia has embraced an open, market-based economy with few restrictions on goods and service, except for those that are in direct conflict with religious beliefs (including the import and consumption of alcohol and pork-related products). This liberal market policy is reflected in the Kingdom's trade relations with the rest of the world. Imports come today from virtually all continents, while Saudi exports flow to all major industrialized and developing countries. Saudi Arabia's major trading partners continue to be the United States, the European Union and the Far East; China is viewed as a major trading partner of the future and is now Saudi Arabia's second largest trading partner compared with negligible amounts only 20 years ago.

Exports from the Kingdom follow the same import trading patterns, and some effort has recently been made to ensure that Saudi exports become more diversified. Currently some 90% of total exports are made up of oil- and energy-related petrochemical products. It is this narrow export base that is worrying those who see potential problems for Saudi non-oil exporters post-WTO entry for the Kingdom. While Saudi Arabia has run relatively consistent trade surpluses, the Kingdom suffers from capital outflows due to large remittances by foreign workers, averaging around SR 60 billion per annum, as well as private sector capital outflows.

An analysis of Saudi Arabia's trade patterns reveals a shift in the type of products imported over the past three decades: during the earlier boom period, the imports were of capital goods, construction and machinery. Later these imports gave way to spare parts, food and consumer goods. The inter-Gulf Cooperation Council (GCC) trade still plays a small part.

Chapter 9 also discusses in detail Saudi Arabia's overall competitiveness and ease of doing business and finds that major advances have been made placing Saudi Arabia ahead of all the other GCC and Arab countries in terms of world competitiveness and ease of doing businesses, largely due to the activities of the Saudi Arabian General Investment Authority (SAGIA). However, some competitiveness obstacles still exist, with restrictive labour regulations being the most cited, besides an inadequately educated workforce.

Chapter 10 discusses Saudi Arabia's decision to join the WTO after 12 years of negotiations and its accession in 2005. The chapter explores the background to the establishment of the WTO and the benefits and costs of globalization for countries, as well as the various agreements that the Kingdom had to sign upon accession in the various trade, services and intellectual property areas. The Kingdom obtained several exemptions on WTO entry, including the prohibition of imports of goods in conflict with Islamic *Shariah*, as well as continuing with a policy of *Saudization* quotas for domestic and foreign companies operating in the Kingdom. Analysis of the potential impact of globalization on various Saudi manufacturing and service sectors revealed that some will be impacted, especially those with the highest levels of subsidies and tariffs, but that the petrochemical sector stood to gain the most from WTO accession. The chapter also examines the current Saudi legal system and its WTO conformity and the legal reforms that have been instigated by the Kingdom to ensure WTO compliance in certain areas such as arbitration procedures.

Meeting Future Challenges

The final theme involves analysing some key challenges faced today by the Saudi economy as it goes through painful structural adjustments. These challenges overlap, as they often do, since economic transformations do not occur in compartmentalized isolation, but rather react to one another in a dynamic fashion.

The challenge to the Kingdom's policy-makers is to try and identify key positive drivers operating in the economy that will lead the country forward towards set objectives while minimizing the negative consequences to society at large.

Under this broad theme, Chapter 11 examines the Kingdom's hopes and aspirations for foreign direct investment and the strategic option for liberalization and privatization. This chapter illustrates that Saudi Arabia's problem is not a lack of good intentions or of proper priorities, but rather that there is no matching consensus as to how much action is needed, and how quickly the Kingdom should act. Some tangible progress has been made through the establishment of the Supreme Economic Council, which has focused on developing the regulatory environment that will allow a successful privatization programme to emerge. The chapter examines the options for privatization and the sectors that have been targeted and the results to date, as well as analysis of private–public sector cooperation. Another positive development involves the enhancements of the Foreign Investment Law that offer a number of benefits, including a reduction in taxation levels to 20% on foreign companies' profits and which has now made Saudi Arabia one of the major recipients of FDI, after lagging at the lower end of the Middle East table for many years.

The critical issues of the moment – employment, *Saudization* and the structure and composition of the Saudi labour market – are dealt with in Chapter 12. With nationals accounting for just under 13% of the total private sector labour force, or around 829,000 Saudis, the government is making copious attempts to ensure that more jobs are found for nationals, either through creating new jobs or replacing foreigners through an invigorated *Saudization* programme. Planned versus actual *Saudization* results indicate that targets have not been met.

The government, however, can only push so hard. In the final analysis, Saudis with the appropriate market-driven skills will be employed. Others seeking jobs will realize that is necessary to change their mindset and to accept positions previously deemed to be either too menial or socially unacceptable. The "duality" of the Saudi labour wage structure is examined to explain wage differentials between Saudis and non-Saudis.

The mindset *is* changing, and some sections of Saudi youth are beginning to be more realistic in their job expectations as they compete with other new labour entrants, a result of one of the world's highest population growth rates.

Windfall gains arising from one or two years of higher than expected oil revenues, such as those experienced during 2007 and 2008, might produce a short-term "feel good" factor, but cannot solve such long-term demographic realities. This chapter also looks at the issue of female labour participation, since the Kingdom has one of the lowest female labour participation rates in the world.

Saudi female participation tends to be higher for those in the older age group, forcing younger Saudi women to prolong their entry in the labour market either by pursuing higher education or seeking less qualified jobs. Once again, the Saudi government recognizes these problems and the Saudi cabinet recently approved a nine-point plan to create more jobs and business opportunities for women, including the restriction of expatriate jobs in areas dealing with women-only services.

In any society, unemployment is a cause not only of social problems and of increased unemployment-related crimes but also of potential loss to national output and productivity. Chapter 12 calculates the cost of such a potential Saudi output gap. Using *Okun's Law*, this was estimated at around SR 1,021 billion for the period 1993–2008, based on fairly high levels of voluntary (or "natural") rate of unemployment for Saudi society. If this natural rate of unemployment was much reduced, then both the output gap and real rate of unemployment would be much higher using *Okun's Law* than those estimated in Chapter 12. The chapter also examines a new worrying trend for "educated unemployed" amongst Saudi nationals, both male and female, who are driven to seek higher education to enter the public sector or high wage resource-based jobs, and preferring to remain unemployed until such jobs are found. This differs from traditional developing countries' educated "brain drain," with educated nationals seeking jobs overseas and preferring to remain in transitory employment or unemployed until they find higher paid jobs overseas. In both cases – the Saudi model and the "brain drain" model – the success of those who seek jobs attracts others to obtain higher education to follow in their footsteps, except that in the Saudi model the number of new jobs in the public sector or in the high wage resource sector are limited.

Our analysis of earlier themes clearly marks the important role that quality education and the acquisition of market-related skills play in shaping Saudi economic development.

This issue is examined more closely in Chapter 13, which analyses the current Saudi educational structure's achievements and problems. Technological progress and the diffusion of scientific and technical innovations lead to higher productivity and improvement in all sectors of the economy. The ability of any society to produce, select, adapt and commercialize knowledge is critical for sustained economic growth and improved living standards. In relation to its population, size and undoubted quantitative educational investment, Saudi Arabia has produced negligible commercial patents compared with other developing countries such as Malaysia or Singapore.

Quality education output is now a key priority for the Saudi government. The 2008 and 2009 budget allocation for education showed that the Saudi government is beginning to direct resources towards higher education and vocational training institutions that are graduating students who meet labour market needs.

Saudi education had been driven by an "education-push" quantitative aspect in the early days of Saudi economic development, but over the past few years it has been driven by "jobs-pull" in the private sector. The Kingdom has also taken bold steps not to be left out of the global knowledge-based economy, and has established a world-class scientific research and teaching university – King Abdullah University of Science and Technology (KAUST) – to spur changes and reforms in other Saudi educational establishments. At the same time, a number of government and private sector higher education institutes have been established, with nearly all having international strategic alliances and cooperation to ensure that Saudi education remains relevant and up to date.

The Kingdom is not an isolated island. Regional developments, whether positive or negative, have profound consequences on internal stability, and on economic and social developments. Chapter 14 explores Saudi Arabia's multifaceted relationship with the five other members of the GCC, as developments within the GCC could have far-reaching economic consequences for the member states. This chapter examines why the GCC union was established in 1981 and discusses its developments to date, as well as Saudi Arabia's decision to establish new strategic relationships with the emerging economic giants of the 21st century – China and India – without disturbing traditional relationships and alliances with the USA and other European countries.

Chapter 14 aims to impart an understanding of the internal economic dynamics of the various GCC member states and of how far similarities and differences could accelerate or impede planned full monetary and customs union planned for 2010. The issue of a common currency and whether it will be implemented in light of two members of the GCC opting out of the plan (Oman and UAE) is examined in detail, as well as options for a GCC currency, whether pegged, managed or linked to oil, are explored. Economic diversification, generating employment for their young and growing populations, and economic integration is the destiny of the GCC countries. Oil is central to their well-being. Between them, the six GCC countries sit on some 45% of the world's total oil reserves, illustrating the magnitude of the region's importance. Chapter 14 shows that some success has been achieved, albeit on a modest scale, in the effort of individual GCC member states to diversify away from a narrow oil and gas revenue base. Dubai and Bahrain are leading the way, but the global financial crisis of 2008/2009 has also affected some countries of the GCC more than the others, particularly the Dubai emirate of the UAE, and most of the GCC countries are now refocusing on strengthening their domestic financial and capital market base to be able to withstand the global contagion.

Integration of various capital markets could be a first step in mobilizing domestic financial resources into large, economically viable inter-GCC or national projects.

Integration would also help facilitate a greater degree of inter-GCC job seeker migration and ease unemployment problems faced by some GCC countries while filling the job openings of other member states. In the long term, it is important to ensure that the GCC becomes open and accessible to its ordinary citizens so that they understand the objectives of the GCC, why it was established and how it affects their lives. It is only by doing this that the viability of the GCC's long-term future can be guaranteed, and that the "GCC family" survival as a stronger political and economic entity in the 21st century can be ensured.

Conclusions

Following these broad themes, Chapter 15 concludes by reviewing some key structural issues affecting the Saudi economy and highlighting some of the problems that need to be addressed going forward. There is a new sense of realism in the Kingdom amongst policy-makers, the private sector and the population at large. Despite domestic terrorism issues, there is a mood of determination to tackle pressing problems. Reforms and domestic changes are important, but they must not be seen as a competition between external and internal domestic reform agendas. Both need to progress at a comparable pace, without external pressure. Managing both expectations and the pace of reform will be a key challenge as things progress, as will be the management of the *Saudization* process and the maintenance of harmonious relations with expatriate labour.

Reforms, although implemented gradually, can be cumulative in effect. Gradual change may seem slow or less impressive to those outside the Kingdom, but if reforms are to endure and be effective, they have to respond to the needs, customs and mores of all society. Far too many experts have misjudged and underestimated the resilience of Saudi Arabia or the adaptability and creativity of Saudi society in meeting future challenges. Consensual change will be the means of change. The key will be a process of evolution and consensus-building, the hallmark of Saudi government, thus allowing for longer-term economic planning and stability.

Part II
The Development Process

Chapter 2
Reforms and Economic Planning

So many worlds, so much to do, so little done, such things to be.
Tennyson

Difficult Decisions Being Taken

In the space of a few years since the first edition of this book in 2005, the Kingdom has witnessed some fundamental changes having taken place, which few would have predicted to happen so soon. The entry of Saudi Arabia to the World Trade Organization in 2005 was probably one catalyst to speed up domestic economic and administrative reforms, but the momentum for change was already in the making, primarily driven by King Abdullah bin Abdulaziz. Upon succeeding to the throne in August 2005 following the death of King Fahd, the Custodian of the Two Holy Mosques (the King's official title), King Abdullah embarked on a series of domestic reforms, the outcome of which are not yet fully certain but which will determine the direction and pace of Saudi economic development over the next few decades. The outcome is not important just for Saudi Arabia but also for the wider world given the Kingdom's strategic geopolitical importance in the world and its enhanced role in such bodies as the G20 bloc and multilateral organizations like the International Monetary Fund and the World Bank. Saudi Arabia continues to play a significant role in energy matters, possessing around a quarter of the world's proven oil reserves.

Economic Diversification Remains Critical

Reducing dependency on oil revenues, however, remains a key government priority. This challenge exists for Saudi Arabia, which under a planned capacity output and production level of 12.5 mpbd, could theoretically cease to export in the next 50–60 years if global consumption continues to grow on a linear path. The solution seems clear enough: to develop an economy characterized by growing diversification of production and income, evolve inter-sectoral linkages and expand regional and

M.A. Ramady, *The Saudi Arabian Economy*, DOI 10.1007/978-1-4419-5987-4_2,
© Springer Science+Business Media, LLC 2010

global economic integration. Domestically, the Saudi government will continue to emphasize its core development goals of raising the standard of living of its citizens, improving the quality of their lives and enhancing their technical capabilities. The historical pattern of development plan allocations reflects the above goals. At the same time, the role of the private sector would be enhanced as a key development growth enabler. Economic diversification will not be easy. For the foreseeable future, the Kingdom would still heavily depend on hydrocarbon natural resources and its derivatives for economic output as well as public finances. This dependence has left fiscal policy at the mercy of cyclical and unpredictable developments in the world's oil markets. During the period 2005–2010, average oil prices fluctuated from the lows of $27 pb to the highs of $147 pb, creating uncertainties in Saudi budgetary planning. Notwithstanding the economic progress made by the Kingdom, and its relative resilience in the face of the 2008–2010 global financial crisis, some key challenges remain, especially in meeting the needs and aspirations of a fast-growing and young population. As such, the Kingdom, in common with other major hydrocarbon resource-based economies, has a limited window of opportunity which exists before some critical "crunch points" arrive when support from hydrocarbon production levels off, and eventually declines. Given the significance of Saudi oil reserves, the crunch point might be later than nearer. Compelled with rising global demand for clean and alternative energy sources, Saudi Arabia could be faced by competing environmental-led shifts in global energy demand towards coal, gas, biofuel and nuclear energy. For Saudi Arabia, such changing hydrocarbon energy balances will underpin the dynamics of the transition from a depletion-led development economic model to a sustainable development model. Structural economic reforms are key to this effort being successful.

Reforms at Centre Stage

A nation's economic transformation, as different models around the world from both the East and West illustrate (e.g. Malaysia, Singapore, Poland, Hungry, Chile, Turkey), depends on implementing appropriate regulatory and legal frameworks most suited to that particular country, and then allowing the competitive pressures of free market forces to determine the optimum allocation of resources needed by society. The excesses of the financial markets during the past few years have prompted international government intervention with the primary aim of strengthening regulatory oversight and reducing excessive risk-taking.

King Abdullah has recognized in public that governments must build not only their country's physical infrastructure but also a new social, civil and political infrastructure so that Saudi citizens can participate fully in creating towards and benefiting from a new economy. As such, opportunities are being made for the private sector to shape public policies that will help them to grow. Opportunities are also being created for the different regions of the Kingdom to express the socio-economic developments of their region through municipal elections. King Abdullah has also ensured that opportunities are also made for Saudi women to meaningfully participate in the development of society. If it is true that governments must change and be more responsive, it is equally true that civil society institutions must also change, and the King has publicly called for such reforms stating that "the Kingdom cannot remain frozen while the world is changing around us" and vowed to move ahead with political and economic reforms (Arab News, 2 April 2006). For economic reforms to take root and be sustained, some measures of political reforms are necessary. Once again King Abdullah has taken the lead to ensure that there is political stability in the case of leadership succession by issuing a new succession law in 2006 that would facilitate a smooth transfer of power and remove uncertainty caused by the inability of a King or a Crown Prince to run affairs of the State as a result of poor health. The new succession law went further than King Fahd's 1992 decree on succession, which had established the precedents that grandsons of King Abdulaziz, not only sons, were legitimate claimants to the throne, and also that the King had the prerogative to choose and to withdraw approval for the Crown Prince (Alfaisal, 2007). Under King Abdullah's succession law, a committee of senior princes would be appointed to select future generations of Kings and Crown Princes and this committee – called the Allegiance Committee – has powers to vote for choosing its own candidate for Crown Prince, and not that for the King (Saudi Press Agency, Oct. 2006). In effect, the new political reforms implied institutionalizing the succession process and bringing stability through an evolution of the role of consultation based on Islamic principles. The processes of change and reform in Saudi Arabia have picked up pace over the past few years and have opened the door for more participatory values in the Kingdom that are suited to its social structure, especially in the area of shared decision-making and checks and balances.

This has highlighted itself in two areas that affect the lives of Saudi citizens: the workings of the Consultative Council or "*Majlis Al Shoura*," and the judicial system. In the inaugural session of the new *Majlis Al Shoura* in March 2008, King Abdullah declared that no one in the country was above criticism, including himself, and stated that the Kingdom always respected responsible freedom, and encouraged the *Shoura* members to play their role to that end. The *Majlis* seemed to have taken this to heart and initiated a policy of inviting key Saudi ministers to address the council on matters of public interest, especially on economy and labour, to discuss issues such as the government's desire to increase the number of Saudis in the workplace or the so-called *Saudization* policy.

The *Shoura Majlis* profile rose even further during the aftermath of the flood disasters that overtook the port city of Jeddah in December 2009 when many people were killed following a flash flood. Public anger at perceived incompetence and corruption in project tendering prompted the *Majlis* to start hearings on the causes of poor infrastructure planning and to apportion responsibility and blame based on the direct instructions of the King (SPA, Jan. 2010). Grass-roots volunteer movements to alleviate the consequences of the Jeddah natural disaster were also a first for Saudi Arabia's civil society and established the foundations of direct citizen participation, something that had been lacking before.

Transforming the Judicial System

In February 2009, King Abdullah reshuffled the Kingdom's cabinet, changing four ministers and appointing for the first time a woman, Nora bint Abdullah Al Fayez, as Deputy Minister for girls' affairs at the Ministry of Education. Familiar faces such as the Ministers of Finance and Petroleum remained, but it was the judicial changes that attracted most attention, with the appointment of former *Shoura* Chief Bin Humaid as Chairman of the Supreme Judiciary Council and Abdulaziz Al Kelya as Chief Justice of the Supreme Court. A new Justice Minister was appointed–Mohammed Al Eissa and further changes were announced at the Court of Grievances and the Court of Appeal. The aim was to establish a more dynamic and proactive judicial environment by building up on the process of settling disputes through specialized commercial courts and appeals courts, and bring the Saudi legal system more in line with international practices. Civil courts would continue to handle family and personal conflicts. The judicial reforms were greeted positively by foreign companies who had previously complained at the lack of specialized commercial courts to hear disputes involving non-Saudi entities, and the lack of appeal to rulings. In March 2010, the Saudi Supreme Judicial Council decided to open commercial court branches in all major Saudi cities, and in a further land mark decision the Kingdom is set to bring in a new law to allow women lawyers to argue women cases in court for the first time.

Saudi Arabia also introduced significant reforms in the manner by which foreigners residing in the Kingdom were to be treated with respect to their labour law and human rights in general. King Abdullah appointed a well-respected *Shoura* member Dr. Bandar Al Aiban to head the Saudi Human Rights Commission in the February 2009 cabinet reshuffle, with powers for this commission to have the right to access to prisons and detention centres at any time and submit reports to the Prime Minister (the King) without the need to obtain official permission. The Saudi move on these fronts concerning relations with its foreign workforce, which constitutes a significant portion of the private sector workforce, is a recognition of the importance of adhering to international law concerning the treatment of labour and was in line with the King's directives to open up Saudi society to tolerance and moderation through national and international dialogue.

National Economic Planning: The Framework

According to observers, Saudi Arabia has some of the most sophisticated development planning processes of any nation in the developing world (Cordesman, 2003). The Saudi government utilizes the services of resident technical experts from the World Bank to advise on the development process.

It is often said that "the best government is the most invisible government." This means that "best" governments are those that establish regulatory and legal frameworks and then allow the competitive pressure of free market forces to determine the optimum allocation of resources needed by society. There are those who would argue that this is a utopian luxury that governments in the modern world aspire to, but few achieve in reality. The real world has witnessed a degree of planning and government control, ranging from central planning to what is termed mixed economies, where the government and private sector work together in partnership. Irrespective of which model of planning is adopted, the central goal seems to be the laying of a broad economic foundation for self-sustaining growth, with one or more key factors of production (land, labour, capital or managerial efficiency) creating the precondition for such growth (Rostow, 1960).

Saudi Arabia's economic development path has sometimes been characterized as one of the classical "rentier" economies (Chadhury, 1989, 1997, Auty, 2001). In this model, the government seeks to maximize its revenue from a natural resource – oil – and distribute the proceeds amongst various sections of the population. Some distinguish between a "rentier" economy and a re-distributive "welfare state", which derives its income through taxation and other means from one class of society and distributes it to other sections of society (Chadhury, 1989).

Since Saudi Arabia currently does not impose taxes on its citizens, although there has been some debate on introducing value-added taxation, the term "welfare state" is not technically correct for the Kingdom. The concept of "rentier economy" is a more accurate characterization of the early years of Saudi Arabia's economic development. According to some observers, an alliance developed between the State and certain business groups in the private sector that aimed to promote the national agenda at the expense of some excluded groups (Wilson, 2004, Champion, 2003).

During the early boom period of the Saudi economy in the 1970s and early 1980s, the large inflows of oil "rents" to the State created a momentum of its own, in which it seemed that the State's only function was that of a distributive agent and that the government sector became the exclusive motor of the economy (Chaudhry, 1997). The lack of administrative, educational, managerial and physical infrastructure led to absorbative capacity bottlenecks in those early boom days, with investment decisions being taken that had far-reaching consequences for the future (Mallakh and Mallakh, 1982).

The basic argument against "rentier economies" is that when a state's main source of private revenues is through government expenditures, the society thus supported does not instil a sense of initiative or entrepreneurship amongst its citizens. However, a state that is supported by society through one form of taxation or another will develop a more balanced relationship with its citizens, with both parties responding to the needs of the other (Ehteshami, 2003).

One further effect of the "rentier economy" was the emergence of powerful state bureaucracies which "orchestrated the States' development" (Ehteshami, 2003). The effect was to perpetuate the preference for government jobs in Saudi Arabia, which we shall examine in later chapters, at the expense of the private sector, since bureaucracy viewed the private sector in a subservient relationship instead of as a dominant force. This relationship between the government and private sector has affected the "institutional capacity to deliver" (Wilson, 2004). Surveys of attitudes of senior civil servants carried out in Saudi Arabia in the early 1980s showed deficiencies in "psychological drive, flexibility, communication, client relations and impartiality" (Hegelan and Palmer, 1999). According to some observers, there is little evidence that much has changed since those early days (Wilson, 2004).

Strategic Choices

In the early 1970s, the Saudi government along with its key planners and consultants grappled with strategic decisions on the direction the economy should be steered to. It was not an easy task, given the lack of planning experience, absence of data on the economy and raised expectations of Saudi nationals. Table 2.1 examines some of the strategic development options that were faced by Saudi planners and their potential positive and negative implications.

Table 2.1 Saudi Arabia: economic development options

Development option	Positive factors	Negative factors
Large oil production	• Large foreign investments and surplus financial resources • Balance of payment surpluses • No incentive to fund crude oil substitutes	• Economic dependency • International and domestic inflation • Rapid consumption of non-renewable national resources • Rentier economy
Oil production based on domestic needs	• Moderate investments abroad leading to paced development and equilibrium between domestic development needs and financial resources. • Large oil reserves for future generations	• World oil shortages • High international inflation and world recession • Strong incentive to find crude oil substitute and suppliers
Large-scale domestic industrialization and diversification of economic base	• Potential economic independence • Skills acquisition and new working habits • Exports potential • Technology transfer • Education base widened • Non-oil economic diversification	• Large imports • Need for expatriate labour increased • Balance of payments problems with a large element of exported salaries and profits • Domestic inflation • Institutionalized inefficiency due to subsidy policy (import substitution industry) • Mismatch between domestic labour supply output and market requirements

Each of the options set out in Table 2.1 has appealing positive factors, and these positive factors would have been paramount in the planning discussions – rather than the negative consequences. The country was in a rush to develop rapidly. There were few lengthy discussions or in-depth analyses of potential negative consequences of one strategic development objective or another (Farsi, 1982), although some commentators did raise early concerns (Bashir, 1977).

From all indications, what has actually transpired from the early 1970s to date is that Saudi Arabia opted for large-scale domestic industrialization and for diversification of the national economic base. The aim was to "transform the economy from overwhelming dependence on the export of crude oil into a diversified industrial economy," while admitting that dependence on oil revenues will continue for a considerable period of time (Farsi, 1982).

Depending on substantial crude oil production alone was not a long-term strategic choice, for it would have magnified the negative consequences of the "rentier economy" system discussed earlier. It would have meant a more rapid consumption of Saudi Arabia's major non-renewable natural resource; the only key decision facing the country would simply have been the rate of oil extraction and the price of oil.

Production of oil based merely on Saudi Arabia's domestic needs would have produced oil shortages, international inflation and world recession, along with a strong incentive to find other suppliers as well as crude oil substitutes. As we will explain in later chapters, Saudi Arabia is cognizant of its key role in world oil supply and has pursued moderating policies in its attempt to ease oil supply shortages. The most recent example was the Kingdom's decision in June 2008 to increase its production from 8.3 million barrels to over 9 million barrels per day in order to ease soaring prices of over $140 a barrel.

Adopting the large-scale industrialization and diversification option seemed then, on the surface, to have been the most viable option, with significant discernible advantages. The negative factors that have crept into this strategy over time are now causing the most concern. As will be discussed later, issues of mismatch between domestic labour supply and market needs, the continuing strain on balance of payments due to large expatriate labour remittances, institutionalized inefficiencies and, despite diversification, continuing reliance on oil and oil derivative exports are features of the Saudi economy today. Most of these problems are inherited from the earlier development plans.

The History of Saudi Planning

Saudi Arabia has undergone a substantial and fundamental transformation over the past three decades since planning was first introduced in 1970. Those who were involved in the First Plan admitted that, in essence, the First Plan of 1970–1974 was essentially "an exploration, theoretical and empirical," and that the biggest achievement was "the experience gained by Saudis in the field of development planning" (Farsi, 1982). Others are more critical of the whole planning exercise, arguing that the development plans demonstrated good intentions, but did not pave the road to major progress (Cordesman, 2003).

There are those who argue that Saudi Arabian planning has been more "a macroeconomic exercise than a form of detailed microeconomic management" (Wilson, 2004). The argument is that Saudi planning involves designing public expenditure programmes in the light of anticipated revenues and then executing these expenditures. If revenues are actually achieved, then all is well: projects are implemented and delayed projects restarted. Conversely, if anticipated revenues do not materialize, then the opposite happens: ongoing projects are delayed and new ones suspended.

Planning, however, can be carried out under various models and circumstances, ranging from setting targets for the economy as a whole and providing direction on how resources will be invested, to establishing targets for input resources and the desired output. The Saudi model has not established precise *qualitative* output targets but rather *quantitative* output targets. Planning can also follow an indicative direction on how and where the government wishes the economy to go, providing the necessary rules and regulations to allow the private sector to achieve those directions (Osama, 1987).

Planning exercises do not operate in a vacuum and it is important to analyse the administrative structure under which Saudi planning is carried out. The first planning exercises, in the late 1950s and early 1960s, depended heavily on external bodies and consultants such as the Ford Foundation, the United Nations Team for Social and Economic Planning and the World Bank. In 1961 a Planning Board was established in Saudi Arabia and in 1965 it was incorporated into the Central Planning Organization (CPO), which drafted the Kingdom's First Five-Year Plan in 1969.

In 1975 the CPO became the Ministry of Planning (MOP), reflecting the importance national planning was being assigned, although some argue that the Ministry of Planning in effect took a back seat to the actual implementation policies undertaken by the more powerful spending ministries such as Commerce, Industry and Electricity (Wilson, 2004).

Economic and social development in the Kingdom has been guided since 1970 by comprehensive five-year national development plans. As the economy expanded and grew more complex and diversified, the planning and fiscal management processes became ever more demanding and called for more sophisticated policy instruments, strong analytical capacities and diverse approaches to problem-solving and resolution. Furthermore, as the role of the private sector in the overall economy grew in size and importance, the planning process tracked this evolution by changing the planning paradigm from the *directive* to the *indicative*. This movement is expected to continue in the future as the government goes forward with its privatization programme and its role focused on providing the appropriate institutional, legal and regulatory environment most conducive to social and economic development, and for protecting the economically and socially disadvantaged.

To reinforce the importance of involving Saudi Arabia's key decision-makers in the planning and implementation process, the Supreme Economic Council (SEC) was established in August 1999. In November 2009 the SEC was reshuffled by King Abdullah, inducting Foreign Minister Saud Al Faisal and Prince Mohammed bin Naif, Assistant Interior Minister for Security Affairs, to this apex Saudi policy-making board, which has been dubbed a "mini-cabinet" by many. The 12-member panel includes the Ministers of Commerce and Industry, Economy and Planning, Water and Electricity, Labour, Petroleum and Minerals Resources and Finance. The SEC has taken a leading role in setting up specialized committees to discuss issues such as privatization, international relations and domestic security implications as signified by the new SEC-inducted members.

Plan Achievements

Actual and planned expenditures made by the Saudi government over the whole planning period from 1970 to date have been impressive, standing at around SR 3,135 billion or $836 billion. This is set out in more detail in Table 2.2 for each planning period, organized by broad expenditure categories.

From Table 2.2, it becomes evident how closely government expenditure patterns follow the fortunes of the Kingdom's oil revenues, with the current Eighth Development Plan (2005–2009) surpassing the peak "boom years" of the Third Development Plan period (1980–1984).

The expenditure trends of the Saudi development plans over time have become more evident: a focus on human resources development and education which accounted for 57.1% of the actual expenditures of the Seventh Development Plan (2000–2004) and reached 55.6% in the latest Eighth Development Plan (2005–2009). The Kingdom has recognized the fundamental importance of human development to the realization of sustainable economic and social goals. The Kingdom provides free education in its public schools, colleges and universities and, from the Seventh Development Plan, has made primary and secondary education compulsory with the aim of achieving universal primary education by 2015. According to the World Bank, adult literacy stood at 79% in 1999 and 88% in 2008. Another large sectoral expenditure item has been social and health development.

Social welfare and solidarity have been among the pillars of the development strategy of the Kingdom of Saudi Arabia. This important objective is pursued by ensuring that all citizens share the fruits of economic development across the various segments of society in all regions. Provision of public services and basic commodities at affordable prices has been one of the main components of this strategy. Furthermore, for segments of society at risk of being left behind or handicapped to equitably share the fruits of development, publicly and privately run programmes are in place to offer them the necessary help and assistance. Families and individuals in distress are assisted through a number of programmes conducted by the Deputy Minister of Social Affairs of the Ministry of Labour and Social Affairs.

Table 2.2 Expenditures during the Saudi development plans

Expenditures	Economic resources development		Human resources development		Social and health development		Infrastructure development		Total	
	SR Billion	(%)	SR Billion	(%)	SR Billion	(%)	SR Billion	(%)	SR Billion	(%)
First Development Plan: 1970–1974 (Actual)	9.5	27.7	7.0	20.6	3.5	10.3	14.1	34.1	34.1	100
Second Development Plan: 1975–1979 (Actual)	97.3	28.0	51.0	14.7	27.6	8.0	171.3	347.2	347.2	100
Third Development Plan: 1980–1984 (Actual)	192.2	30.7	115.0	18.4	61.2	9.8	256.8	635.2	635.2	100
Fourth Development Plan: 1980–1989 (Actual)	71.2	20.4	115.1	33.0	61.9	17.7	100.7	348.9	348.9	100
Fifth Development Plan: 1990–1994 (Actual)	34.1	10.0	164.6	48.0	68.0	20.0	74.2	340.9	340.9	100
Sixth Development Plan: 1995–1999 (Actual)	48.2	11.5	216.6	51.5	87.5	20.8	68.1	420.4	420.4	100
Seventh Development Plan: 2000–2004 (Actual)	54.4	11.2	276.9	57.1	92.6	19.1	61.4	12.6	485.3	100
Eighth Development Plan: 2005–2009 (Actual)	105.8	12.2	479.9	55.6	155.7	18.0	122.3	14.2	863.7	100
Ninth Development Plan: 2010–2014	227.6	15.7	731.5	50.7	273.9	18.9	211.6	14.7	1444.6	100

Source: Saudi Ministry of Planning, September, 2002, 2005, 2010

An important factor that contributes to a low incidence of extreme poverty in Saudi Arabia is one that is rooted in the culture and social traditions of the country. Strong family solidarity which permeates not only the nuclear family but also the larger and more extended family relations stretching as far as tribal boundaries in the rural areas helps protect those segments most at risk of poverty and need: the elderly, the orphaned and the young. Estimates of national poverty levels do not yet exist for lack of up-to-date survey data. No urban, rural or national poverty lines have yet been estimated.

It is important to analyse the different emphases placed during each planning period, reflecting national priorities. This is set out in Table 2.3, which captures key "planning indicators" for each plan, including the most recent Ninth Development Plan (2010–2014). It demonstrates that the planning focus has shifted towards allocative efficiency, human skill upgrading and private sector participation in economic diversification. The principal underlying themes of all plans continue to emphasize raising the standard of living of the people, improving the general quality of life and enhancing their skill capabilities. The Eighth Development Plan constituted a new methodological departure for Saudi Arabia, as it defined more precise targets quantitatively wherever possible and set out implementation schedules and assigned responsibilities for implementation agencies.

The Kingdom, in its Eighth and Ninth Five-Year Plans, has adopted strategic planning to complement the medium-term planning system and the shorter fiscal management process. This development has been motivated by the need to properly address some vital national issues that are characteristically of long-term nature such as resource development and utilization. Issues such as economic restructuring, human resource development, technology development (R&D), water and land management in a semi-arid environment and optimal utilization of the oil and gas resources, among others, all require long-term analysis and perspective.

As Table 2.3 indicates, one of the primary objectives over the last three plans has been an urgent insistence that the private sector play a greater role in the diversification of the economy. Saudi Arabia has realized that having rich natural resource endowments does not necessarily bring about sustained economic growth. In fact, other oil rich economies, such as Venezuela and Nigeria, experienced negative rates of per capita income growth between 1965 and 1996 (Gelb et al., 1998, Askari et al., 1997).

The importance of safeguarding Islamic values, cultural heritage and traditions continues to be emphasized at the outset of each plan. The intention was to promote economic development, but not "Westernization" – something which other traditional societies undergoing rapid development have found difficult to avoid. The Internet revolution makes maintaining a social *status quo* even harder, and Saudi society is no exception (Yamani, 1998, 2000, Rasheed, 2002). The recent advances made by Internet and global communication have broken down barriers; the IT revolution is one that few Saudi planners can ignore in the future. The impact of this flow of information has been researched in other Arab societies with social customs and traditions similar to that of Saudi Arabia; IT access has had a profound societal shaping effect (Masmoudi, 1998, Azzam, 2002).

Table 2.3 Saudi Arabia's national five-year development plans: key indicators

Overall national priorities	First (1970–1979)	Third (1980–1984))	Fourth (1985–1989)	Sixth (1995–1999)	Seventh (2000–2004)	Eighth (2005–2009)	Ninth (2010–2014)
• Safeguard Islamic values in conformity with *Shariah* • Improve standard and quality of life • Develop human resources, increase productivity and replace non-Saudis with qualified Saudis • Realize balanced growth in all regions • Diversify economic base and reduce dependence on production and export of oil • Provide favourable environment for activities of the private sector to encourage it to play a leading role in development	• Focus on provision of modern infrastructure, basic government services • Expansion of human resources and beginning of infrastructure growth • Starting hydrocarbon industries • Establishment of modern administrative infrastructure	• Expanding Infrastructure, economic resources • Human resources and educational base expansion • Hydrocarbon base expansion • Undertaking regional economic initiatives	• Concentration on operation and maintenance • Reconstructing the economy to allow more private sector participation • Human Resources and health expenditure rose • Shift from central planning projects approach to programme planning approach	• Human resources emphasis as well as social and health • Aiming for balanced budget • Reduction in foreign labour • Private sector expansion • Beginning of partial privatization • Reduction of subsidies	• Solving human resource problems • Diversify the economy • Increasing gas production • Consolidating efficiency in production, refining and distribution • Reducing State budget deficit • Increasing *Saudization* • Preparing for globalization, WTO • Privatization as strategic option	• Increase number of new entrants to labour market • Develop human resources and upgrade efficiency • Enhance national economic competitiveness and integrate into international economies • Enhance private sector participation • Develop science and technology system as base for economy • Reduce regional development disparities • Upgrade human capabilities and remove constraints that impede participation	• Raise standard of living of citizens • Diversify economic base • Move towards knowledge-based economy • Strengthen role of private and public sector cooperation • Continue institutional reforms • Develop SME sector • Bolstering human rights • Achieve balance regional development • Promote economic integration with GCC and other powers

Source: Ministry of Planning

The Ninth Development Plan makes gender equality and women's empower-ment issues more explicit, and Saudi Arabia has gone a long way to completely eliminate gender disparity at all levels of education. Expansion of female education has encouraged many Saudi females to join the labour force and seek employment and try to move away from the traditional sectors of education, health and social services. Expenditures during the latest Ninth Plan for the period 2010–2014 are forecasted at a record SR 1444 billion, more than the combined previous three plans, with around 50% allocated for human resources development.

The Performance of the Saudi Economy

Saudi Arabia's GDP is still dwarfed by the leading industrialized countries, as illus-trated in Fig. 2.1. The GDP figures for the various countries do not necessarily reflect the quality of life in each country, as only "economic" factors are included in GDP estimates, despite recent attempts to include qualitative measures. What Fig. 2.1 illustrates is that, despite massive government spending over the past three decades, the Saudi economy seems insignificant compared to the world's giants, such as the USA or Japan, and is in fact smaller than medium-sized industrialized countries such as Belgium or Switzerland.

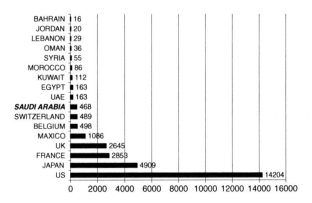

Fig. 2.1 2008 GDP comparison (US $ billions) (Source: World Bank, 2010)

It is sometimes noted that a GDP the size of the Saudi economy is *added* to that of the USA every 7–8 months when the U.S. economy grows at a real rate of 3% p.a. The basic reason for the lag in Saudi GDP growth is simple: the U.S. economy is diversified while Saudi Arabia's is not.

All of Saudi Arabia's economic reform efforts and development plans to date centre around the fact that its economy is essentially oil-driven, with the resultant strengths and weaknesses. The performance of the Saudi economy has been heavily influenced by two major factors: first the level and growth of oil revenues and second the government budgetary policies. The latter function as the main link between the

oil sector and the rest of the economy on one side, and economic growth in case of
reduced or increased oil revenue on the other.

The result has been identifiable major Saudi business cycles, each with its own
characteristic, as illustrated in Fig. 2.2.

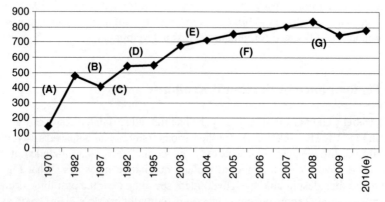

Fig. 2.2 Saudi Arabia: major business cycles GDP 1970–2010 (SR billions at constant prices
(1999 = 100) (Source: SAMA, 2009, Estimate 2010)

From Fig. 2.2 the following major business cycles are identified:

A. An oil boom cycle from 1970 to 1982
B. An oil bust cycle from 1983 to 1987
C. A recovery cycle from 1988 to 1992
D. A stagnation cycle from 1993 to 1995
E. A restructuring cycle from 1996 to 2002
F. An oil boom cycle from 2003 to 2008
G. A retrenchment cycle from 2009

Figure 2.2 indicates several distinct business cycles from 1970 to 2009. The first
cycle was characterized by high oil prices, rapid economic growth, elevated government expenditure on infrastructure, high per capita income and private sector
demand. The second cycle – the oil bust era – saw the Saudi economy take a dramatic downturn. Crude oil production declined from an average of 9.81 million
barrels per day in 1981/1982 to an average of 3.2 million barrels in 1985. Oil prices
dropped from peaks of $34 a barrel in 1981 to $11.5 a barrel in 1986. Government
revenues fell drastically to around SR 50 billion in 1986 compared to nearly SR
400 billion in 1981. As a result, imports fell and there was a reduction in investment expenditure by both the government and private sectors. The third phase –
or recovery business cycle – showed a reversal of fortunes due to improvement in
world oil markets, but was followed by a relatively stagnant business cycle affected
by declining oil prices and fiscal constraints.

The period between 1992 and 1995 was characterized by budget cuts across the board, a freeze on capital expenditure and a slowdown in government cash disbursements, which caused some problems to private contractors. From the oil bust cycle, the Saudi government started to draw down on its overseas liquid reserves, resulting in growing budget deficits and debt service payments, as shall be explored in more depth in later chapters.

The fifth cycle from 1996 to 2002 was a critical one, in which economic reforms and major restructuring efforts took place, with the government trying to ensure that the private sector becomes the main engine of growth. This cycle saw progress in the field of privatization, liberalization and capital market reforms, in order to attract FDI and Saudi capital held abroad.

The period from 2003 to 2008 was the second longest economic boom period in Saudi Arabia with real GDP growth increasing by an average of 5% a year, the strongest for a decade. Record oil prices and abundant liquidity characterized the period, with oil prices reaching $147 pb in mid-2008, but falling back to an average of $55–60 pb in 2009 and an average of $68–75 pb in 2010. The current cycle from 2009 can be viewed as another period of retrenchment and restructuring for the Saudi economy, which also witnessed the unfolding global financial and credit crisis. Although the Kingdom has been less affected by the direct impact of the global financial crisis of 2008/2009 and economic recession, the indirect impact affected the real economy through reducing government revenues, tighter credit and investor risk aversion in international markets to the Gulf region, leading to reduction of foreign capital and decline in local asset prices.

Economic Diversification: Realities

In order to assess the effectiveness of the Saudi economic diversification effort, we must analyse more closely the Saudi national accounts, which provide an insight into the structure of the nation's economy. An examination of these accounts helps one to decide whether the Saudi economy has unique characteristics compared to other economies.

The GDP is the sum of the value added by the various sectors of the economy – in other words, the market value of the total output of goods and services produced during a year. The Gross National Product (GNP) includes both the results of domestic activity within Saudi Arabia and the results of its economic relationship with the rest of the world. For Saudi Arabia, the government and the foreign sector play important roles as seen in Fig. 2.3.

Figure 2.3 highlights three important features of the Saudi Arabian economy. First, as the earlier analysis of the different business cycles showed, the model underlines the crucial role played by the government sector. The importance of oil and oil revenues ensures that the government, through its fiscal budgetary mechanism, is still in a position to influence both the level and structure of economic activity. These can be transmitted through direct expenditure on consumption and investment, as well as provision of "soft" long-term loans and subsidies.

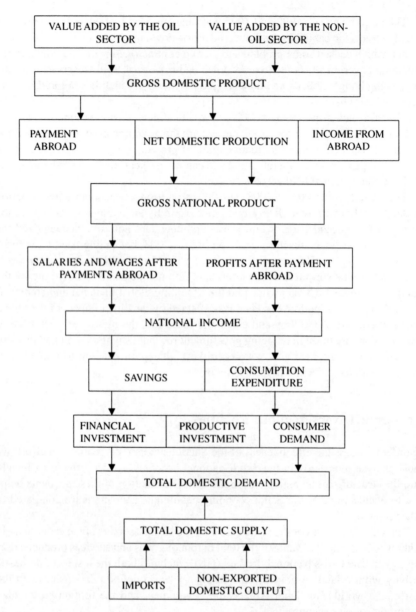

Fig. 2.3 Saudi Arabian model of economic flows (Source: Adapted from Cleron, 1978, p. 74)

The second feature of the Saudi model is the degree of interdependence with the rest of the world. This has risen dramatically as oil income has increased, with oil exports representing some 54% of GDP in 1979/1980, falling back to 40% levels in 1999/2000 and rising again to 60% levels in 2008. Imports from the rest of the world represented 55% of GDP in 1979/1980 and 12% in 2008 (SAMA, 2009).

The third striking element is the relatively large portion of the GDP that is paid for the use of foreign-owned resources – namely foreign labour working in the Kingdom as well as foreign-owned oil-related activities. As we will examine later, the campaign to reduce the number of outside workers and the dependency on foreign labour and to replace them with Saudi nationals – the so-called *Saudization* effort – has been partially successful. The size of remittances sent abroad by foreign labour continues to be a significant outflow as illustrated in Table 2.4.

Table 2.4 Remittances from Saudi Arabia (SR billion)

Year	GDP at constant prices (1999 = 100)	Private transfers
1970	148.0	0.81
1976	416.5	3.5
1982	480.5	18.0
1993	552.7	58.8
1995	557.6	62.2
1998	608.1	56.0
2000	632.9	57.7
2001	641.2	56.9
2002	647.7	59.4
2003	686.0	55.4
2004	722.2	50.8
2005	762.3	52.4
2006	786.3	58.5
2007	812.4	60.2
2008[a]	848.5	79.5

[a]Provisional
Source: SAMA, 2009

According to SAMA, the total amount of private remittances and transfers sent from Saudi Arabia for the period 1970–2008 amounted to a staggering SR 1,229 billion ($327 billion). Such figures prompt, from time to time, heated debates in the local media about the need to speed up the *Saudization* process or to impose curbs on remittances. Others argue that one way to reduce outflows would be to introduce a more investor-friendly climate in Saudi Arabia so that foreign workers can invest locally.

Comparisons are sometimes made with the United States, which has the world's largest immigrant population and yet records lower remittance outflows on a per capita basis compared to Saudi Arabia because of more favourable domestic investment opportunities for U.S. migrant labour. Whatever the arguments, the current level of remittances – amounting to around 10% of GDP and around 18% of private sector GDP – will continue to cause a serious balance of payment problem for Saudi Arabia in the foreseeable future.

Composition of Saudi GDP

The next set of figures and tables sets out in more detail the composition of Saudi GDP, from the pre-oil boom period to the "restructuring" era. It provides a closer examination of the "realities" of economic diversification and how far the private sector has taken over from the government in the key areas of consumption expenditure, investment and exports.

Figure 2.4 illustrates the historical GDP growth of the Kingdom from around $150 billion in 1980/1981 to around $300 billion in 2009.

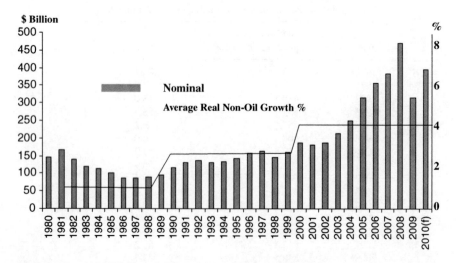

Fig. 2.4 Historical GDP Growth Developments (Source: SAMA, IMF, estimates)

The non-oil sector has been making steady progress and its contribution has been less erratic than the oil sector as Fig. 2.5 illustrates, although the non-oil private sector was also affected by the sharp fall in oil prices and reduction in crude oil production in 2009 as illustrated in Fig. 2.6.

A closer breakdown of the GDP by economic activity reveals the gradual rising value of manufacturing and the services sector in the Saudi economy since the modern economy started to take shape. This is illustrated in Table 2.5.

As a percentage share of the Saudi GDP, however, manufacturing continues to hover at around 10%, with petroleum refining and petrochemicals representing almost half of the manufacturing contribution to GDP. The service sector accounts for less than 30% of the GDP, with finance, insurance and real estate expanding their share, as well as the general trading sector. Construction activity seems to be affected by general business cycle movements but is still an important segment of the economy at around 8% of GDP. Agriculture, despite massive subsidy support in the early boom period, accounts for around 5% of the GDP, with Saudi Arabia a net importer of food products.

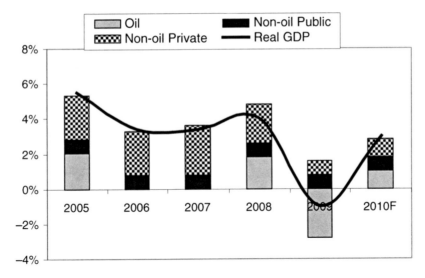

Fig. 2.5 Real GDP growth sector contribution (2005–2010) (Source: SAMA, forecast)

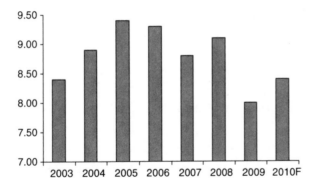

Fig. 2.6 Average Saudi crude oil production: 2003–2010 (Million barrels per day) (Source: OPEC, SAMA)

The data in Table 2.5 reflect the growing importance of wholesale, retail and restaurant activity. However, this activity consists largely of the marketing of imported goods and growth has been linked to Saudi demographic factors and changing consumer tastes and fashion. The community, social and personal services sectors, and the water and electricity sectors have also grown steadily, but have lagged behind population growth; however, the growth in the Saudi financial sector has been impressive and now accounts for around 13% of the GDP compared with 5–7% levels in earlier periods.

As will be analysed in later chapters, the accession of the Kingdom to the World Trade Organization and the liberalizing of FDI regulations has given the financial

Table 2.5 GDP by sectors and types of economic activity in producer's values (SR million)

	1969	1984	2000	2004	2009
Non-oil sectors	8,870	227,130	370,400	525,267	677,239
Producing sectors	3,790	85,280	150,400	178,250	234,214
Agriculture, forestry and fishing	990	11,620	35,570	38,005	44,399
Non-oil mining	50	1,860	2,520	2,723	3,982
Manufacturing	1,500	27,430	58,740	79,476	107,206
Petroleum refining	1,090	13,830	21,590	20,508	25,443
Petrochemicals	N/A	540	7,080	7,352	10,446
Other manufacturing	410	13,060	30,070	51,616	71,317
Electricity, gas and water	260	590	970	11,085	13,589
Construction	990	44,960	52,600	46,961	65,038
Service sectors	5,080	141,850	220,000	211,953	280,133
Trade hotels, etc.	990	30,390	39,250	57,299	73,980
Transport, storage and communications	1,230	23,850	34,780	36,674	52,727
Finance, insurance, real estate and business services[a]	950	25,830	24,060	90,724	121,103
Community, social and personal service	230	9,710	15,210	27,256	32,323
Government services	1,680	52,070	106,700	135,064	162,892
Oil product sector					
Crude oil and natural gas	7,740	120,300	269,320	196,696	225,049
Gross domestic product in producer's values	16,610	347,430	639,720	721,963	902,288
Import duties	270	3,970	9,620	7,063	7,122
Gross domestic production in purchasers' values	16,880	351,400	649,340	729,026	909,410

[a]Net of imputed bank services charges
Source: Ministry of Planning, 2004, SAMA, 2009

sector a boost, attracting foreign entry as well as added depth to existing market segments such as insurance.

The importance of these sectors contribution to the GDP is illustrated in Fig. 2.7, while Fig. 2.8 highlights GDP growth by expenditure.

On the expenditure side, investment and private consumption were the main sources of growth in recent years, which were supported by the range of economic reforms mentioned earlier in this chapter. Investment, both private and public, has steadily risen from around 20% levels of GDP in 2004/2005 to nearly 30% of GDP in 2008. Weaker oil prices in 2009 affected the level of both public and private investment to take it back to under 27%.

Saudi Arabian national income data are more difficult to obtain than GDP data. This is due to the high level of data aggregation. National data analysis will help explain who gets what of the national revenue. Intuition would suggest that the government obtains the major component of revenue through oil income. The rest is composed of profits made by business and wages and salaries as well as transfer payments for individuals.

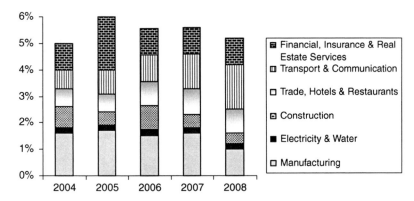

Fig. 2.7 Non-oil GDP growth and sector contribution (Source: SAMA)

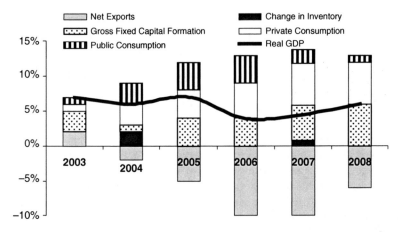

Fig. 2.8 Real GDP growth by expenditure (Source: SAMA).

In Saudi Arabia there is also a large element of "transfer payments" through the form of subsidies and subsidized products, especially agricultural products. Per capita income can, however, provide another proxy for how Saudi Arabian citizens have been doing over the past few decades, as per capita income, in which GDP is divided by population, is one measure of national income. Figure 2.9 illustrates GDP per capita over the period 1970–2009, and forecast for 2010.

The per capita income has mirrored the erratic oil revenue business cycles highlighted earlier in the chapter, to stand at roughly SR70,000 ($19,000) in 2008 compared with SR 5,000 ($1,500) levels in the pre-oil boom era of the early 1970s.

However, Saudi GDP per capita includes non-Saudis who, according to the latest data, accounted for 6.69 million or 27% of a total 2008 population of 24.81 million (SAMA, 2009, p. 298). If one takes into account inflation over the years since 1970, Saudi GDP per capita figures in *real terms* fell sharply to around SR 35,000 ($9,300), using 1999 as a base year.

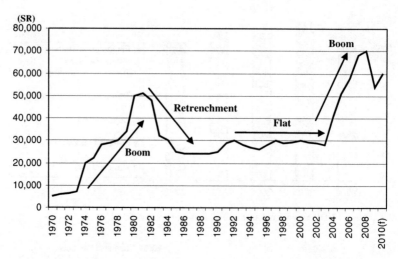

Fig. 2.9   GDP per capita (current SR) (f = forecasted) (Source: SAMA, 2009)

In analysing Saudi Arabia's national income data, the distinction between "stock" and "flow" of income becomes important. Saudi Arabia has what seems to be a flow of income, although erratic, from oil and oil-based revenues, but seems to be "stock income poor" compared to other developed economies. It takes time to convert "income flows" into "stocks of wealth," which include infrastructure, capital goods, technical skills and "quality" education output (Chenery, 1979). Social awareness, work ethics and civic participation are also other "intangibles" of a nation's stock of wealth, which, if nurtured, could produce a more sustained growth take-off.

In later chapters, we will examine the effects of such tangible and intangible factors on Saudi Arabia's economic development prospects, especially on education and employment objectives. While Saudi Arabia has made progress in many areas, the measures the government seems to have taken so far have "lacked the scale and speed" needed to restructure the economy at the rate required (Cordesman, 2003).

Economic theory stipulates the importance of capital accumulation in economic development, with special emphasis on both "capital deepening" and "capital diffusion." The former requires additional input of capital, while the latter involves changes in technology (Bernstein, 1973, Thirwall, 1994, Todaro, 1994). The large oil revenue surpluses Saudi Arabia amassed during earlier boom years allowed it the luxury of investing and expanding its capital stock.

With the rush to modernize and spend the windfall gains, Saudi planners appear to have neglected to take the time to ask essential questions about such concerns as the optimum rates of investment in domestic capital formation (Karl, 1997, Looney, 1989, Askari, 1990). Should these investments have been in tangibles – or intangibles such as quality education – so that a knowledge-based economy built on capital diffusion would become the engine of growth? Given the luxury of earlier capital surpluses, Saudi Arabia could seemingly have chosen both options, as evidenced from the previous analysis of budgetary expenditures on human resource development in the five-year plans. However, expenditures mask qualitative allocations and their economic effectiveness in the long run. The lack of disaggregated data on gross fixed capital formation (GFCF) makes it difficult to make a judgement, but as Table 2.6 highlights, the major element of GFCF has been in the construction sector. This is not surprising given the relatively young population of Saudi Arabia, but the expenditure on machinery and equipment has also been impressive as the Kingdom has built some large-scale hydrocarbon-based industries.

Table 2.6 Gross domestic fixed capital formation by sectors and type of assets in purchasers values

	1969	1974	2001	2005	2007
(a) By sector (Million SR)					
Oil sector	350	3,180	14,240	22,231	50,700
Non-oil sectors	2,350	9,650	111,855	173,401	235,543
Private	1,000	4,300	94,347	118,461	140,304
Government	1,350	5,350	17,508	54,940	95,239
Total (GDFCF)	2,700	12,830	126,095	195,632	286,243
(b) By type of assets (Million SR)					
Construction	2,100	9,520	57,909	93,620	138,627
Residential buildings	610	2,320	28,302	31,973	37,823
Non-residential	1,490	7,200	29,607	61,647	100,804
Transport equipment	290	1,470	21,004	28,804	35,168
Machinery and equipment	310	1,840	37,472	55,922	87,504
Total (GDFCF)	2,700	12,830	126,095	195,632	286,243

Source: SAMA, 2009

Oil sector GFCF has risen over the past few years to reach around 17–18%, but is still considerably below the 24% levels of the first Saudi oil boom infrastructure investment of 1974.

Given Saudi Arabian intentions to produce oil at an increased capacity to reach 11.5 mbpd as of 2011, as well as plans for expanding the gas sector, investment in these areas will have to involve either greater government expenditures or foreign investment to meet expansion plans. It is not a coincidence that Saudi Arabia has tried to attract international oil companies as partners and several large joint Saudi Aramco and foreign company projects were signed during 2008/2009.

The government data indicate *gross* investments and there are no reliable estimations as to actual *net* investments that the Kingdom is making after taking account of depreciation in the capital stock. The problem of depreciation accounting is well recognized in country GDP estimations, but it is also important to bear in mind that GFCF figures could provide an overly optimistic picture when the true net fixed capital formation figures are much lower. Given that the stock of Saudi capital formation is relatively new, having been built up over the period 1976–1986, the rate of depreciation might be lower compared to other countries. This, however, is offset by the relatively harsh environmental conditions under which Saudi projects operate, which could, in theory, accelerate both the rate of depreciation and replacement.

The Challenges Ahead

While some significant economic achievements have been registered by the Kingdom over the past four decades, meeting the needs of a fast-growing and young population with high expectations poses several challenges to the development process. The planning process that might have served Saudi Arabia in the past needs to be revisited. A more strategic and flexible short-term planning process is probably more suitable in a global economy that is evolving faster. It is worth highlighting that there has been some flexibility in this regard with the Eighth Five-Year Plan, which adopts strategic planning to complement medium-term planning, as well as shorter-term fiscal planning. Most observers of the Saudi economy agree that economic, social and structural reforms are now a necessity and not a luxury (Najem and Hetherington, 2003, Wilson, 2004, Champion 2003).

However, there are differences of opinion about the pace and scale of reform, as there are many different estimates of trends in the Saudi economy and how these interact with the most pressing issues of the moment, such as population and unemployment levels. In addition, these different estimations disagree about the level of problems that Saudi Arabia will face in the future. Added to this is a debate on the effectiveness of the economic assumptions of "Western" modernization theories that do not take into account non-Western cultures and customs (Najem and Hetherington, 2003, Abdeen and Shook, 1984). Saudi Arabia has made it clear that reforms will come at a pace that is driven by Saudi domestic considerations and this has been the hallmark of the reforms introduced by King Abdullah.

Table 2.7 explores some key conditions for Saudi economic growth and whether these conditions are of increased, decreased or neutral importance.

In the end, there can be no certainties in forecasting data for any country – developed or developing – regardless of the quality of data. Saudi Arabia is a case in point: observers of the economy seem to be either overly optimistic or overly pessimistic about the future, depending on the basic assumptions and trends one picks. The truth of the matter is that the Saudi economy lies somewhere in between, despite considerable "developed" country characteristics, which includes overdependence of the GDP and budget on petroleum revenues, lack of economic diversification and a high level of bureaucracy. However, some trends have emerged over the past few years that show Saudi Arabia can still effect meaningful change.

Table 2.7 sets out some necessary preconditions for growth that are sometimes used to assess a country's stage of development. Some of these factors are not based on hard data sources, but instead rely on perceptions. The table includes eight factors that assist growth without necessarily actively promoting growth (The Arab World Competitiveness Report, 2002–2003, p. 12). Poor performance would limit growth. From the table, we note that the Kingdom has preserved an open, international trading system, and is beginning to develop a more sophisticated financial system that is fairly solvent. In some areas the economy might seem to be under stress, such as inflation worries, but overall it is not one that is in crisis. Development of laws in support of a "new" economy is high, but the quality of government services as

Table 2.7 Saudi Arabia: necessary conditions for growth

Factor	Component	Saudi Arabian setting
Necessary conditions for growth		
• Macroeconomic stability		
	– Government deficits	↓
	– Inflation	↑
	– Exchange rate stability	→
	– Solvency of financial system	↑
• Deep financial markets		
	– Interest rate spreads	→
	– Developed equity markets	↑
	– Sophistication of financial system	↑
• Openness to international trade		
	– Low import tariffs	→
	– Low hidden import barriers	↓
• Quality of government		
	– Public expenditure not wasteful	↑
	– Subsidies improve productivity	↑
	– Senior management spend little time with government officials	↑
	– Admin. regulations burdensome	↑
• Infrastructure		
	– Road quality	↑
	– Efficient electrical generation	↑
	– High level of competition in provision of basic infrastructure	↑
• Education		
	– Years of schooling in population	↑
	– Perceived quality of education	↑
	– Companies invest in training	↑
• Rule of law		
	– Independent judiciary	↑
	– Ability to successfully litigate against government	→
• New economy		
	– Internet hosts	↑
	– Computers per capita	↑
	– Development of laws in support of new economy	↑

Note: ↑ refers to high importance, ↓ refers to low importance, → refers to neutral
Source: Adapted from the Arab World Competitiveness Report 2002–2003. pp. 10–11

they relate to interaction with the general public needs to be improved, as does the perceived quality of education.

"Engines of growth" are essential to start a virtuous cycle of economic growth. Table 2.8 includes the more dynamic factors that focus on these conditions for Saudi Arabia.

The lack of export diversification, a culture innovation and research and development is the key impediment to kick-starting some engines of growth.

Administrative barriers to start-ups are high despite loan availability and a non-existent taxation regime for Saudi individuals and corporations. The latter pay a

Table 2.8   Saudi Arabia: Engines of growth, current status

Factor	Component	Saudi Arabian setting
Engines of growth		
• Start-ups and entrepreneurship		
– Administrative barriers to start-ups		↑
– Venture capital availability		↓
– Loans available with low collateral		↓
• Capital accumulation		
– National savings rate		↑
– Investment rate		→
(Gross Fixed Capital Formation)		
• Taxation		
– Income tax rate		N/A
– Corporate tax rate (foreigners only)		↓
– Value-added taxes		N/A
– Tax system perceived to improve competitiveness		N/A
• Innovation		
– Highly rated research institute		↓
– Business conducts R&D		↓
– Close collaboration between universities and businesses		↓
– Government supports research		↑
– High expenditure on R&D		↓
• Transfer of technology		
– Foreign direct investment brings new technology		↑
– Licensing pursued to obtain foreign technology		↑
• Export diversification		
– Exports other than national resources		↓

Note: ↑ refers to high importance, ↓ refers to low importance, → refers to neutral
Source: Adapted from Arab World Competitiveness Report 2002–2003

2.5% *zakat* or religiously ordained levy on total assets, while foreign company corporate taxes were reduced to 20% in 2003. As discussed earlier, GFCF is still low despite a fairly high national savings rate, while non-oil-related export diversification has not matched national expectations.

Conclusion

As we will examine in later chapters, long-awaited structural changes and diversification efforts have not generated the necessary private sector jobs or produced a sustained "knowledge-based" economy. Expansion has been largely in the non-manufacturing services and construction sectors. The Saudi government has, to its credit, recognized a lot of these problems and is seeking ways to overcome them. The planning process has helped to identify key national objectives, but the emphasis going forward must be on *qualitative* rather than *quantitative* outputs.

The Saudi government, above all, must not waver in carrying through the necessary, harsh adjustments and reforms irrespective of temporary oil-related windfalls such as those that occurred during the period 2007–2008. Promised reforms in past Saudi development plans have been delayed or not fully implemented, particularly at times when the economy seemed to benefit from periods of relatively high world oil prices. It thus becomes easy to delay the economic and social costs of reforms when "windfall" government revenues are available; it takes long-sighted political skill and courage to continue with essential reforms, despite the temptation to ease back. The recent reform initiatives of King Abdullah on several key fronts are cognizant of time constraints and the need to act more quickly and decisively.

Summary of Key Points

- *Saudi Arabia has embarked under a more invigorated series of economic, social and political reforms since the accession of King Abdullah bin Abdulaziz as King in 2005, which is shaping the future direction of the Saudi economy.*
- *Saudi Arabia has put in place a system of sophisticated development planning since 1970 through implementing a series of medium-term five-year plans.*
- *The process of planning has evolved as the economic structure of the country has undergone transformation with the private sector assuming more importance in both consumption expenditure and GFCF.*
- *The strategic choices that early planners made to steer the economy from overwhelming dependence on oil are still being felt today in the area of continued foreign labour dependence, outward remittances and mismatch between domestic labour supply and market requirements.*
- *Planning is now shifting from a "directive" to an "indicative" role as the economy becomes more globalized and interdependent with the rest of the world.*
- *Precondition for growth as well as key "engines of growth" are examined as well as the obstacles that need to be overcome to support the emergence of a private sector-led economy.*

Chapter 3
Public Finance

Beware of little expenses; a small leak will sink a great ship.
Franklin

Overview

Counter-cyclical government spending is vital for Saudi Arabian growth and health of the national economy. Until the economic base is more diversified on a sustainable basis, government expenditures will remain the key driver of confidence in the domestic programme and investment plans. As such, any analysis of the Saudi Arabian economy must examine in depth the Saudi budgetary and public sector financing and how surpluses and deficits are invested and utilized. The state of a country's fiscal position has become even more important following the global economic and financial crisis of 2008/2010. The international financial markets are now demanding more transparency and fiscal accountability from countries that have opted for economic openness. The Kingdom is a significant member of global institutions such as the International Monetary Fund (IMF) and the World Bank.

As the Finance Minister of Saudi Arabia sits on the Board of Executive Directors of the IMF, Saudi fiscal policies and budgetary management have been influenced by the methods and practices of such organizations. During the global crisis of 2009/2010, Saudi Arabia was also a prominent representative of the developing world in the Group of 20 (G20) summits.

By virtue of its economic size in terms of spending, consumption and investment, as well its ownership of the single most valuable economic resource – oil – the fiscal policy of the government of Saudi Arabia directly affects the economic well-being of the country. One key economic policy tool at its disposal is the budgetary mechanism.

The Budget – A Barometer of the Nation's Health

Until 1986, the Saudi government scheduled its annual budget on the basis of the *Hejira* calendar, with the financial year beginning on the first day of *Rajab*, the seventh month of the *Hejira* year. In 1987, the budget implementation date was changed to the tenth day of the Capricorn zodiac sign, or January 1 on the Gregorian calendar.

M.A. Ramady, *The Saudi Arabian Economy*, DOI 10.1007/978-1-4419-5987-4_3,
© Springer Science+Business Media, LLC 2010

Each ministry and government sub-agency prepares its annual budgetary expenditures – and revenues where applicable – according to preset guidelines established by the Ministry of Finance. The national budget is then compiled by the Ministry of Finance. Once the budget receives royal approval, it is published in *Umm Al-Qura* – the Official Gazette – pursuant to a Royal Decree.

The publication of the Saudi budget for the forthcoming year attracts a lot of attention, both domestically and internationally. The principal reasons for this focus on the budget are that it provides the following:

- a forecast of expenditures to be made for the different economic sectors for the coming year
- signals regarding the intentions of government priorities in expenditures
- the composition of current versus capital expenditure, allowing businessmen to make plans for project bidding
- an indication of the likely forecasted, budgeted deficits or surpluses, thus suggesting whether the government might borrow domestically or internationally, as well as the likely impact on Saudi banking liquidity

The budget also contains quantitative and qualitative assessments of the preceding budget year in terms of actuals versus budgeted figures. In addition, it projects future economic prospects, especially on the expected price level of oil, as this is still the single most important revenue component of the Saudi budget.

By law, the Saudi budget must always be balanced. By accounting definition, the revenues and expenditures must balance on both sides of the balance sheet, but all that really means is that budgeted expenditures must equal budgeted revenues. In reality, the budget has rarely balanced, due to the unpredictable nature of budgeted revenues. However, in the earlier boom years, this concept of "balanced" was accepted as something workable, because of the large reserves built up (Johany et al., 1986).

Primarily because of significant declines and erratic oil revenues, as well as high population growth and the expanded economic base of the country, Saudi Arabia has begun to face both budgetary restraints and financial constraints. The matter of fiscal prudence and budgetary controls is now an important issue for Saudi Arabia which registered its first budget deficit in 2009 following record surpluses from 2002.

Government expenditures and the manner and direction of such expenditures play a vital role in every nation's economic well-being, as such expenditures have a significant impact on the private sector's activities and overall GDP via the so-called "multiplier" effect.

The multiplier measures the magnified change in aggregate production or GDP, resulting from a change in an autonomous variable such as government expenditures. The theory goes as follows: the basic multiplier process results because a change in production via the autonomous government expenditures on capital goods and services generates income, which then *induces* additional consumption, imports and investment expenditures. The resulting additional expenditures are also multiplied, as they are also expenditures on production and generate more income. The end result is a magnified, multiplied change in aggregate production, initially triggered by the change in autonomous government investment, but amplified by the change in induced expenditures. How these variables affect each other determines the rate of the multiplier, as do other factors such as the degree of economic openness, the level of remittances out of Saudi Arabia and the level of domestic confidence which can influence the rate of final consumption and savings. For Saudi Arabia, some of these variables can be important as will be explored later.

Government expenditures can also impact domestic liquidity using basic quantity theory of money relationships. The quantity theory of money relates output in the economy to velocity of money, the money supply and the price level. As we will discuss further in this chapter, inflation levels became an important issue in Saudi Arabia during 2008, subsiding in 2009, but remains a concern compared to the low inflation period of 1997–2007.

Oil Wealth versus Oil Poverty

Saudi economic growth has been fuelled by an increase in oil production and capacity, but at the same time the economy has become more dependent – like a hostage – to the fortunes of one commodity: oil (Gehb, 1998, Looney, 1990). This is illustrated in Table 3.1 which sets out Saudi oil output and oil revenues over the period 1970–2008. The erratic nature of oil revenue dependency can be seen during the various oil-related business cycles, especially during 1986–1992 period.

Table 3.1 Saudi Arabian oil production and oil revenues

	1970–1973	1974–1981	1982–1985	1986–1991	1992–1996	1997–2001	2002–2008
Oil Output (million barrels)	8.1	25.874	6.672	12.292	14.778	14.548	22.269
Oil Revenue (SR billion)	69.98	1374.6	540.3	478.3	571.6	742.5	2284.1

Source: SAMA, 2009

What Table 3.1 indicates is that, by the mid-1980s, Saudi Arabia had moved away from being a "capital-surplus" mineral economy that might evade growth problems through being a "rentier" economy – similar to smaller, mineral-rich economies such as Brunei, Kuwait and Abu Dhabi (Johany et al., 1986). The early boom period of Saudi economic history produced increased oil revenues that permitted the accumulation of financial reserves with which to lengthen the necessary structural adjustment of the economy to abrupt contractions of the "rental," or oil income stream, compared with capital-deficient oil-driven economies such as Indonesia or Mexico who have relied less on oil revenues (Auty, 2001). The "second" oil boom period for Saudi Arabia was in the 2002–2008 era, which also produced accumulation of financial capital leading to structural adjustments and emphasis on education and competitiveness of the Saudi economy. However, as we will examine later, despite the strong upturn in the oil boom era of the 2002–2008 period, robust oil revenues have also largely been saved, leading to a marked improvement in the Kingdom's external balance. One measure to assess the magnitude of expenditure changes is by looking at the change in the Saudi current account over the change in oil revenues, and estimate how much of the windfall revenue has been spent during different oil price shock periods. In economic terms, this is defined as the *marginal propensity to import*, which can be calculated as change in imports, net of non-oil exports, investments and transfers/change in oil exports.

The results are set out in Table 3.2 for the period 1973–2008, and Fig. 3.1 which illustrates the steady improvement in the Saudi current account balances from 2002 to 2008.

Table 3.2 Marginal propensity to import (MPI) out of oil revenues: Saudi Arabia 1973–2008

Period	1973–1974	1973–1975	1978–1980	1978–1981	2003–2005	2005–2006	2006–2007	2007–2008
MPI	0.23	0.45	0.28	0.41	0.21	0.66	1.31	0.47

Source: SAMA, IMF, National Commercial Bank, 2009

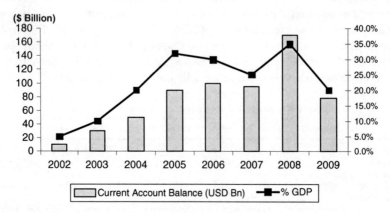

Fig. 3.1 Current account balances 2002–2009 (Source: Ministry of Finance, IIF)

The results from Table 3.2 seem to suggest that government spending had eased back during 2003–2005, surged again in 2006–2007 (even surpassing the extra oil revenues attained in 2007 by 31%) and declined again to 47% in 2008.

Record oil exports led to a record current account surplus of US$178 billion in 2008, a growth of nearly 60% compared to a drop of 4% in 2007. The 2009 current account surplus stood at around 38% of the 2009 nominal GDP, the second highest in 20 years. Even the 2009 current account surplus was a comfortable $76 billion at around 18% of nominal GDP despite sharply reduced oil prices in that year. The net results of the current account surpluses were that they translated to a surge in official reserves and an increase in the capital account deficit. Since Saudi Arabia does not possess a Sovereign Wealth Fund of any significance, official foreign assets are held by the Saudi Arabian Monetary Agency (SAMA). Such official reserves, which will be analysed later on, constitute a significant fiscal buffer against future oil price shocks, and they placed Saudi Arabia in a relatively stronger position to deal with a shortfall of capital inflows and limited access to international financing amid the global financial crisis of 2008/2009.

Saudi Windfall Gains and Losses

During the oil "windfall" era, Saudi strategy for deployment of this windfall exhibited a number of characteristics. First, the government captured the bulk of the oil rents through the nationalization of the production of oil and through appropriate taxation levels. It accumulated a substantial part of these oil revenues as reserves overseas, which some sources – IMF and World Bank – calculated as peaking at $170 billion levels in the early 1980s.

The second Saudi strategy seemed to have rejected the "rentier" option adopted in countries such as Kuwait (Auty, 2001) and to have embarked on an extensive diversification of the domestic economy. The result of this change was the overtaking of the oil sector by the non-oil GDP sector from 2002 onwards.

The third feature of the Saudi windfall strategy was the maintenance of an open economy. The economy was open not only for imported goods and services but also for foreign workers and international construction companies, in order to ease the boom period bottlenecks. The result of this third feature was to reduce the effect of the so-called "Dutch disease" during a resource boom (Auty, 1999, Balance et al., 2001, Sachs et al., 2001, Gylafson et al., 1999, Gehb et al., 1988). All these studies demonstrated that resource abundance may *reduce growth* by hurting domestic productivity growth. The opening up of the Saudi economy, through increasing the expenditure of foreign exchange on imported goods, helped to "sterilize" the Saudi foreign exchange from appreciating further, while reinforcing the sterilization role of the accumulation of financial reserves overseas. The bulk of imported goods in the early boom period was also primarily for infrastructure and capital-intensive projects. This helped to constrain domestic inflationary pressure in Saudi Arabia from the late 1970s to the mid-1980s, because the import of foreign labour and foreign construction companies helped to eliminate bottlenecks in Saudi absorptive capacity.

However, due to erratic world oil prices and other factors, the Saudi windfall deployment strategies that had seemed to serve it well in the boom years became a liability in the downturn periods that followed. The Saudi economy absorbed a sizeable amount of the windfall gains in current consumption, as opposed to fixed capital formation and domestic savings to sustain it in leaner years. This was only partially reversed during the period 2004–2008 when capital expenditure rose again.

A second flaw of the windfall strategy was that Saudi Arabia relaxed market discipline so that the windfall gains did not result in the competitive diversification of the non-oil sector. This was due to subsidy policies in agriculture and manufacturing. Suffice it to say that the subsidy policy adopted in those early periods of economic boom still linger in some form to date, and continue to have an impact on the Saudi government's fiscal policies, as well as on national productivity and resource allocation.

A third flaw of the windfall strategy was that the Saudi government did not deem it necessary to introduce a wider range of taxation systems, to broaden its revenue stream, nor was there an attempt to recover the costs of government services – utilities and others – at more economic rates. The provision of such services at subsidized prices, despite some attempts at recouping part of the charges, is still an inherent drag on Saudi fiscal policy today.

The fourth flaw of the windfall strategy was the sharp increase of employment in the public sector of the Kingdom, with Saudi workers choosing to work in the public sector, thus pushing the private sector to employ foreign workers. The consequence of this early Saudi rental deployment strategy will be more closely examined in the following chapters, but the effects have been to bloat government recurrent expenditures at the expense of capital investment, as well as to spawn an educational system that produces graduates geared for public sector jobs rather than promoting scientific and technical skills relevant to private sector manufacturing. The Saudi government has sought to counter this by initiating a comprehensive science-led university drive and an international scholarship scheme from 2007 onwards.

The phenomenon of public sector preference is not unique to Saudi Arabia. An earlier study (Chalk et al., 1997) compared capital-surplus oil producers of the Middle East with capital-deficient oil producers and some other OECD countries. It found that the capital-surplus oil producers expended a much higher percentage of their GDP on current expenditures, wages and salaries and subsidies than other countries.

Overdependence on Oil versus Building True Wealth

The Saudi Kingdom today is coping with rapid political, demographic and social challenges. A key economic objective is to move away from a state-driven economy that is largely dependent on oil wealth in order to create a more diversified, private sector-led economy. Saudi Arabia can no longer rely on oil wealth alone, and one or two years of oil revenues that exceed the forecast, temporarily building up the state's coffers, will not change the long-term need for building true wealth, in place of reliance on a single primary source of revenue.

This dilemma is set out in Fig. 3.2, which encapsulates in a simplified manner the main drivers of the Saudi economy during periods of increase and decrease in oil revenues.

With the exception of 2003–2008, the Saudi economy has recently been going through the adjustment phase, seen in the scenario illustrating the decrease in oil revenue, in Fig. 3.2. However, despite King Abdullah's statements that the oil "boom days" are over, some sections of Saudi society still see the oil boom days from the mid-1970s to the early 1980s, as exemplified by the "increase in oil revenue" section of Fig. 3.2, as being the norm rather than the exception. This is exemplified in the exaggerated public expectations of receiving large government salary increase during 2008 when Saudi inflation rose sharply. The public acts as if time and oil wealth will solve all problems in the future. This view postpones the needed hard

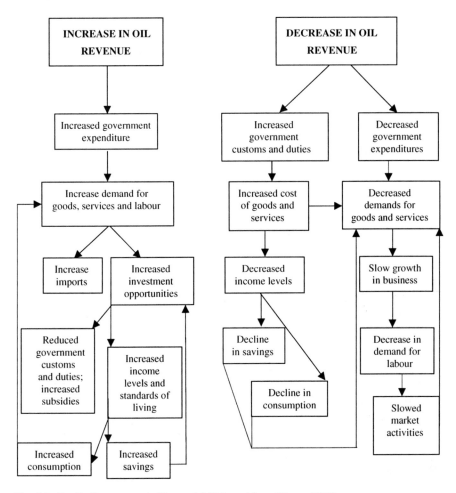

Fig. 3.2 Saudi oil revenue volatility model (Adopted from Cleron, 1978)

economic reforms and adjustments to spending patterns, under the misconception that little discipline is needed to restructure the economy. In essence, it is an unsustainable policy of "muddling through," based on the implication that the government will still play a dominant role in the Saudi economy. However, as we will discuss in Chapters 7 and 11, the government has already sent out signals about its intentions to disengage through a planned programme of privatization and let the private sector assume greater economic responsibility.

The problem facing many practising economists in Saudi Arabia is that there is no one way to calculate the precise scale and pace of reform that is needed to build "true wealth," because of differing estimates of the trends for the Saudi economy and how these interact with demographic and social pressures. These different scenarios vary in how they portray the problems that might lie ahead, as well as the pace

and direction of economic reform. Such issues increase the challenges that Saudi
Arabia faces in managing its national budget. However, the next section explores
the general macroeconomic spending trends that indicate that the government is
sending out signals as to its long-term spending intentions.

The Saudi Budgetary System: Signals versus Reality

Analysing projected or planned Saudi budget allocations and revenues might be considered an interesting academic exercise, in the sense that it serves as a guidepost to
Saudi government intentions about sectoral allocations. In reality, it is more important to analyse actual, ex-post Saudi budget results. Such an analysis graphically
illustrates two fundamental core issues facing Saudi fiscal authorities today: their
continued inability to have significant control over a large element of government
revenues, and their inability or unwillingness to curb and reallocate expenditures, a
problem which may be structurally inherent. This is illustrated in Table 3.3, which
sets out Saudi Arabia's actual versus budgeted revenues and expenditures for the
period 1981–2009. In every single year with the exception of one (1982), the budgeted revenues have always been underestimated, while actual expenditures have
consistently been higher than budgeted expenditures.

Table 3.3 Saudi actual versus budgeted revenues and expenditures comparison 1981–2009

Year	Budgeted revenue	Actual revenue	Realized revenue surplus/ deficit	Budgeted expenditure	Actual expenditure	Realized expenditure deficit/ surplus	Overall budget def/surplus
1981	340	368	+28	298	284.6	+13.4	+83.4
1982	313	246	(67)	313	245	−68.0	+1.0
1987	103	103.8	+0.8	159	173	−14.0	−69.2
1992	151	169.6	+18.6	181	211	−30.0	−41.4
1994	120	129	+9.0	160	163.7	−3.7	−34.7
1996	132	178.8	+46.8	150	198.1	−48.1	−19.3
1997	164	205.5	+41.5	181	221.3	−40.3	−15.8
1998	178	143	(35)	196	189	+7	−46.0
1999	121	147.5	+26.5	165	183.8	−18.8	−36.3
2000	157	248	+91	185	203	−18	+45.0
2001	215	230	+15	215	255	−40	−25.0
2002	157	204	+47	202	225	−23	−21.0
2003	170	295	+125	209	250	−41	+45.0
2004	200	392	+192	230	285	−55	+107
2005	280	564	+284	280	346	−66	+217
2006	390	673	+283	335	393	−58	+280
2007	400	642	+242	380	466	−86	+176
2008	450	1, 100	+650	410	520	−110	+580
2009	410	505	+95	475	550	−75	−45.0

Sources: Ministry of Finance, SAMA

Table 3.3 reveals that Saudi fiscal planners have, in general, tended to err on the conservative side when budgeting their revenues. With the exception of 1982 and 1998, this held true for all the years surveyed. The opposite seems to hold true when it comes to budgeted expenditures. Saudi planners tended to underestimate projected needs, with budgeted expenditures lagging behind actuals in all years, with the exceptions of 1981 and 1998. What has been the reason for this mismatch between planned revenues and expenditures, and actual revenues and expenditures?

Some argue that the Saudi Ministry of Finance has traditionally tended to be reactive rather than proactive, cutting current and capital expenditures after falls in oil prices and increasing them in better times (Wilson, 2003). According to this argument, no real attempt has been made to date to anticipate oil price cycles and steer the economy accordingly. Real power is effectively being held in the Saudi Ministry of Petroleum rather than in the Ministry of Finance, whose function is therefore relegated to control of disbursements (Wilson, 2003). Others have supported this argument (Askari et al., 1997, Gelb, 1998). However, in order to adopt flexible fiscal planning in the face of changing world economic and political factors that affect the movement and price of oil, Saudi Arabia would need to introduce several "minibudget announcements" during the fiscal year (akin to the UK's "autumn budget") which would take into account changed circumstances and would adjust accordingly for public expenditures. A key issue for Saudi fiscal planners has been the budgeted oil price benchmark for their revenue assumptions. Figure 3.3 illustrates the extremely conservative nature of such Saudi oil forecasts for the full budget year. From 2002 to 2008 the budgeted Saudi oil price was lower than the actual yearly average.

The 2010 forecast also illustrates that, despite a recovery in oil prices ranging from $65 to $75 a barrel since late 2009, the Saudi fiscal authorities were still using a nominal range of around $42 pb for their 2010 budget forecast.

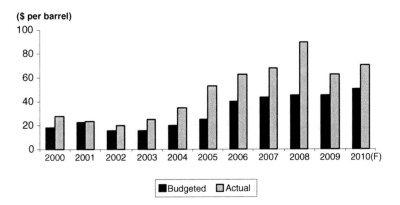

Fig. 3.3 Saudi oil revenue volatility model (Source: SAMA, BP, F = Forecast)

Budget Sectoral Allocations: Government Intentions Are Revealed

In announcing the yearly budget estimates, the Ministry of Finance sets out expenditures by broad economic sectoral categories and these often indicate the government's planned (as opposed to actual) expenditures and priorities. It serves as a signalling effect to the private sector and international companies wishing to do business in Saudi Arabia on the government's revealed preference ranking of expenditures. Table 3.4 sets out Saudi Arabia's historical budget allocations by broad economic sectors and it becomes clear that these are driven to meet a growing population, health and education needs.

Table 3.4 Saudi Arabia budgeted spending by sectors 1982–2010

	1982	1992	2002	2008	2009	2010
Sector	SR million					
A. Revenue						
Oil revenue	270,579	117,693	97,000	370,000	320,000	405,000[a]
Other revenues	42,821	33,302	60,000	80,000	90,000	65,000[a]
Total	313,400	151,000	157,000	450,000	410,000	470,000
B. Expenditures						
Human resource development	31,864	31,855	47,037	104,600	121,942	138,000
Transport and communications	32,535	8,452	5,464	12,143	14,642	24,000
Economic resource development	22,045	4,615	4,969	16,317	21,692	31,000[a]
Health and social development	17,010	13,534	18,970	34,426	40,426	61,000
Infrastructure development	11,705	2,090	2,693	6,384	7,762	15,000[a]
Municipal services	26,244	5,922	7,965	14,954	16,509	22,000
Defence and security	92,889	57,601	69,382	143,336	154,752	150,400[a]
Public administration and other government spending	44,586	49,176	39,316	63,031	79,148	80,000[a]
Government lending institutions	23,382	648	373	479	524	600[a]
Subsidies	11,162	7,107	5,831	14,329	17,602	18,000[a]
Total	313,400	181,000	202,000	410,000	475,000	540,000

[a]Estimates
Source: SAMA, 2009 Ministry of Finance 2010

From 2006 onwards, the government's planned expenditure intentions were clear: more for education and health, while trying to control unnecessary government recurrent expenditure. The public administration budget item has been kept in check at between 14 and 16% levels of total expenditures, as most of this item is wages and salaries in the public sector. Between them, health and education accounted for around 36–40% levels compared with 24–30% levels in earlier development eras. The emphasis on education will be examined in a later chapter, but Table 3.4 sets out the *quantitative* aspects of government spending in this sector. The *qualitative* questions of whether such expenditures are yielding an efficient economic and allocative output, especially in meeting Saudi Arabia's future skill needs, will be analysed later. Some items in Table 3.4 have been estimated as the 2010 budget announcement did not provide a breakdown for defence and security, but in 2008 this item accounted for around one-third of the budget and may well increase owing to tensions in the Yemen border and other sensitive border regions.

Capital Expenditure Assumes More Importance

After stagnating at between 12 and 15% as a proportion of total expenditures in the 1990–2002 period, capital expenditure has once more become a focus of government priority, although current expenditure will continue to dominate overall government spending. The increased capital expenditure is illustrated in Fig. 3.4.

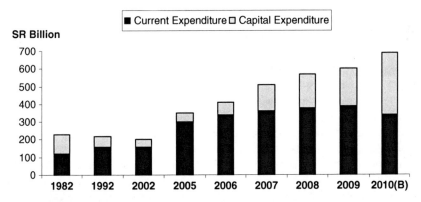

Fig. 3.4 Saudi government expenditure: capital and current outlays. Actuals 1982–2009, Budget 2010 (SR Billion) (B = Budget) (Sources: SAMA, 2009, Ministry of Finance)

The growth in capital expenditure has reflected the Saudi government's desire to help create opportunities for the private sector and keep the economy on a sustainable growth pattern, following the Kingdom's announced $400 billion infrastructure project programme through 2013. The 2010 budget for capital expenditure stood at SR 260 billion – an increase of SR 35 billion over the 2008 actual of SR 225 billion – which itself is the largest since Saudi Arabia embarked on its economic modernization strategy. Key spending in the new millennium has concentrated on water and energy sectors, as well as health and education infrastructure.

The Saudi government needs to keep the momentum going for increased capital investment to avoid the sharp drop evidenced in the 1990s to early 2002 era and falling into a widening gap between meeting the Kingdom's growing needs and future revenue shortfalls, as the budgeted 2010 fiscal deficit illustrates. As such, the government had placed great emphasis in the earlier consolidation phase of the economy on the private sector to build up the nation's capital stock.

The Saudi private sector of the 2010 era is a far cry from the private sector of the early development period. The overall effect of the "boom" and "adjustment" economic cycles ensured many businesses that entered the market during the economic boom era went bankrupt because of their failure to adjust to new market conditions. They had entered business without due proper planning, experience and cost control. The adjustment period was also one of the domestic bank loan crises, which forced Saudi banks to reconsider loan extension and tighten their credit policies (Dukhail, 1995). The global credit and economic crisis of 2008/2009 created a similar situation for the Saudi private sector.

On the positive side, however, many of the development strategies put in place towards the end of boom periods provided the basis for growth during economic adjustment eras. Of more long-term importance, those private sector companies that did survive adjustments and downturns did so on a sounder financial, managerial and planning footing, possibly enabling them to take up the challenge in filling the void of government services.

Limited Sources of Income Is Key Constraint

In more economically diversified countries, government revenues are derived from a variety of sources. In the USA and most western European countries, the bulk of government revenues are derived from the private sector in the form of direct and indirect taxes (IMF, 2002), with governments applying fiscal and monetary policies to either stimulate or dampen demand and output, depending on the state of the economy and the business cycle.

In Saudi Arabia, fiscal policy instruments are the chief means of controlling macroeconomic activity, but in practice this means government spending as opposed to taxes (Wilson et al., 2003). Oil revenue continues to be the main driver of the Saudi economy, despite attempts at economic diversification, and this major source of income is externally rather internally driven.

In essence, the Saudi economy has been described as having become "petrolized" (Karl, 1997). As seen earlier in Table 3.3, pendulum swings in fiscal fortunes are not conducive to sound national management in any sphere of the economy or society. In Saudi Arabia, there is no direct income tax on expatriates or Saudis. There was some debate about introducing a flat 10% tax on foreigners during 2003; however, the idea was abandoned (Arab News, 2003). Indirect and sales taxes have also been discussed but not implemented.

Besides oil revenue, current Saudi government revenues are mainly derived from corporate and business tax, *zakat*, customs and import duties, charges for government services, other "miscellaneous income" such as investment income as well as the sale of government assets. Overseas investment income is a hostage to international financial market conditions and the size of investments held. This became self-evident during the low-interest period of 2008–2010, when governments around the world reduced interest rates to stimulate recovery. Import duties do rise and fall in a pro-cyclical manner and could serve, to some extent, as automatic stabilizers

(Wilson et al., 2003). Income growth results in a rise in imports and a rise in duties and vice versa.

Thus, the price of oil remains of crucial importance to Saudi economic planning and, by extension, to the development of social projects such as health and education. Government spending then becomes the main instrument through which the Ministry of Finance exercises control over the economy, trying to restrain spending when oil prices fall, but allowing "budget overruns" when oil prices and, therefore, revenues rise. These Saudi fiscal policies seem to be at odds with traditional Keynesian macroeconomic policies, which call for government revenue injections during periods of economic slowdowns (lower private sector revenues) and higher government revenue collections during economic growth periods (larger private sector revenues).

The need to sustain and diversify Saudi sources of income is apparent from Fig. 3.5, which aims to correlate the trends in population growth and government revenues and expenditures from 1980 to 2010.

The figure illustrates the urgent need to diversify Saudi Arabia's sources of revenue in light of growing population needs. Despite the sharpest rise in Saudi revenues in the year 2008 to a record SR 1,100 billion, there are still indications of

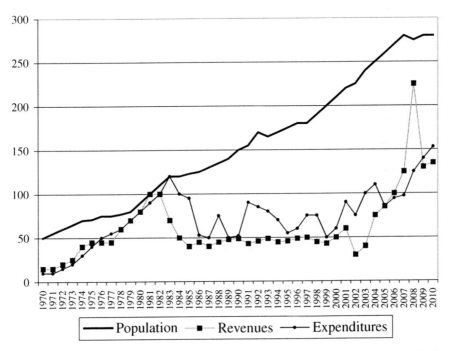

Fig. 3.5 Saudi Arabia population and government finances 1970–2009, Forecast 2010 (1980 = 100) (Note: Population and government finances data re-based to an index with the base year 1980 = 100. Lines represent relative change from the base year.) (Source: Adapted from SAMBA, 2002)

poverty levels in Saudi society. According to press reports, the number of Saudis claiming social welfare benefit rose to stand at 692,508 social security beneficiaries receiving around SR 1 billion a month, representing an average payment of around SR 1,350 per month (Arab News, 28 January 2010). Assuming a dependency ratio of two per claimant – a conservative estimate – the number of those in the population depending on social security benefits is around 2.1 million or nearly 11% of a Saudi population of around 18.5 million in 2010.

Compared to the other Gulf Cooperation Council (GCC) countries, Saudi Arabia's fiscal stimulus expenditure is higher than those of its GCC neighbours, as illustrated in Fig. 3.6, in terms of percentage of government spending to non-oil GDP.

This pattern of fiscal stimulus in Saudi Arabia has been a prevalent feature of the economy over the past decades, as illustrated in Fig. 3.7, which sets out government spending as a percent of Saudi non-oil GDP since 1997. It will be noted that this

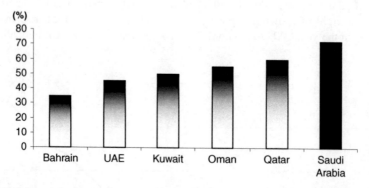

Fig. 3.6 Regional fiscal stimulus in 2009 (percentage of non-oil GDP) (Source: SAMA, GCC Central Banks)

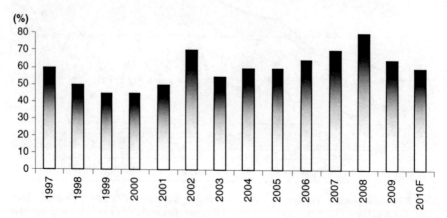

Fig. 3.7 Saudi fiscal stimulus: Government spending as percentage of non-oil GDP 1997–2010 (Source: Ministry of Finance, SAMA)

remained steady above the 45% levels over the whole period, reaching nearly 70% in some "boom" years such as 2002, 2007 and 2008.

Income Diversification Is Not Easy

Notwithstanding the steep drop in oil prices in 2009 and the gloomy outlook of world economies during 2010, the Saudi government seemed to categorically emphasize that it will continue to increase its spending irrespective of the expected contraction in government revenues during 2009 and 2010, and budgeted for deficits. As we will discuss later, fortunately for Saudi Arabia, such deficits are more than amply covered by the large surpluses amassed during the 6 years from 2002 to 2008 of high oil prices. As such, this still leaves the government with an important objective of diversification of its income sources. Figure 3.8 provides a snapshot of the breakdown of Saudi government revenues by hydrocarbon and non-hydrocarbon sources.

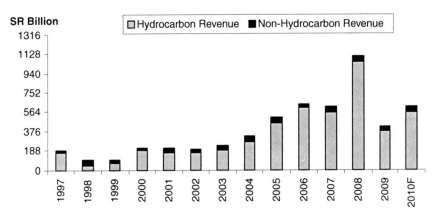

Fig. 3.8 Consolidated Saudi Government revenues by sources (SR billions) 1997–2010 (Source: SAMA, Ministry of Finance)

What becomes obvious is that despite major efforts to diversify its revenue base, the Kingdom is still largely dependent on and hostage to hydrocarbon revenue streams. Saudi Arabia can be best described as a "low-cost" but "high-needs" oil producer: low cost from the Saudi Aramco perspective of costing around $1.80–$2.00 per barrel to produce oil (Johany, 1982, Oweiss, 2000), and "high-needs" from the Ministry of Finance perspective of rarely receiving adequate revenues to balance the budget, except in bumper oil years.

This is illustrated in Table 3.5, which sets out in greater detail the *actual* budgetary revenues and expenditures outturns and provides some more information on the breakdown of non-hydrocarbon revenue sources and the likelihood of increasing this base. Given the lack of detailed budgetary breakdowns by the governments

Table 3.5 Saudi Arabia budgetary revenues and expenditures: actual outturns 1994–2009

	1994	1998	2002	2003	2007	2008	2009
Year	SR billions						
(A) Total revenue	129.0	141.6	213	293	642.8	1,100.9	505
• Oil	95.5	80.0	166	231	562.1	983.3	410[a]
• Non-oil	33.5	61.6	47	62	80.6	117.6	95[a]
Of which Non-Oil:							
- Investment Income	15.1	21.7	13.9	11.1	26.1	39.6	28.0
- Fees + Charges	10.1	21.2	23.0	24.0	26.8	27.0	27.5[a]
- Income Taxes	1.6	2.2	2.4	3.1	5.6[a]	6.8[a]	5.5[a]
- Custom Duties	2.7	4.5	4.0	5.5	6.4[a]	9.7[a]	7.3[a]
- Other (including *zakat*)	4.0	12.0	3.7	18.3	15.7[a]	34.5[a]	26.7[a]
(B) Total expenditure	163.7	189.0	233.0	257.0	466.2	520.0	550.0
By type current	161.3	168.3	203.5	223.6	347.2[a]	388.8	325.0
Of which:							
- Wage bill	87.4	99.8	117.0	120.5	126.5[a]	140.0[a]	155.0[a]
- Supplies/Services	22.1	19.4	22.9	27.0	31.5	38.4[a]	45.6[a]
- Subsidies	4.4	5.4	5.5	6.0	12.8	14.3	17.6
- Interest	15.3	25.4	34.5	35.5	23.5[a]	18.6[a]	12.5[a]
- Oper. & Maint.	17.4	18.3	23.6	26.0	31.5[a]	45.6[a]	47.6[a]
- Other	14.7	N/A	N/A	8.6	121.4[a]	131.9[a]	47.3[a]
By type capital projects	2.3	20.7	30	33.4	119.0	131.2	225
Budget balance	−34.7	−46.0	−20	+36	+176.5	+580.9	−45.0
Budget balance as percentage of GDP at current prices	−6.9%	−10%	−2.9%	4.5%	12.3%	33.0%	−3.3%

[a]Estimates
Source: Ministry of Finance, SAMA, IMF Staff Reports

for actual revenues and expenditures, Table 3.5 has used several official sources and also included author's estimates for some missing items in line with available data.

The actual "outturns" for Saudi non-oil revenues reveal that there has been a gradual rise in such revenue sources since 1994, from SR 33 billion to around SR 100 billion by 2009. The Saudi government has introduced a range of fees and charges for government-related services for the public, and such income has risen steadily to around SR 27 billion by 2009 or around 25–28% of non-oil revenues. Investment income has been erratic and is a function of the level of reserves held by the Kingdom and invested by SAMA, as well as prevailing rates on world money markets and erratic fixed income portfolios. The period 2008/2009 saw a sharp fall in global interest rates, and this has reduced Saudi investment income and portfolio returns.

Income taxes are mostly on foreign corporations operating in Saudi Arabia, while local *zakat* receipts are collected by the government but are not disbursed out of the government's general revenues but through the Ministry of Social Society and Zakat Affairs. Custom duties have tended to remain stable, and, despite the growth in Saudi economy, such receipts over time have tended to fall in line with Saudi import tariff reductions because of bilateral and regional tariff reduction agreements post WTO accession.

Analysis of the expenditure items reveals a steady rise in capital expenditure from a low of SR 2.3 billion in 1994 to SR 225 billion or nearly 41% of total expenditure in 2009. The current expenditure items have tended to be dominated by the wage bill and operations and maintenance over recent years. The government-announced objectives for incremental job generation have been pinned on the private sector to generate new jobs for Saudis and to try to curtail job growth in the government sector. According to government data (SAMA, 2009), there were around 828,000 Saudis, both male and female, employed in the government sector, as well as 70,000 non-Saudis. The comparable figures were 460,000 Saudis in 1994 and 652,000 in 2002. This has necessitated a rise in the government wage bill to around SR 155 billion in 2009 from SR 80 billion levels in 1994. The Saudi government in line with most other Gulf Cooperation Council member states introduced a package of salary pay rises during the high-inflation period of 2008. This was a 15% salary increase to be introduced in three equal stages, the last being a 5% pay rise in January 2009, and estimated to have added around an additional SR 10 billion to the wage bill.

Operation and maintenance expenditure has also grown as the Kingdom built up its surplus reserves during the period 2002–2008, and spending focus is now centred on enhancing physical and social infrastructure which had been neglected, especially in water and sewage networks and highlighted by the flooding in Jeddah in 2009. Interest payments have come down from peaks of around SR 35 billion in 2003 to an estimated level of SR 12 billion in 2009. This item reflected the interest paid by the government for its domestic public debt which will be analysed further below. The repayment of government debt reduced it to around 18% of GDP from a high of nearly 100% to GDP in 2002. At the same time, a low-interest-rate environment from 2008 also helped the government in its total interest payment obligations.

The subsidy item had remained steady at the SR 4–6 billion level but rose significantly from 2007 to reach around SR 18 billion in 2009. During that year, the Saudi government adopted a 17-point programme to offset the effect of rising inflation, and apart from the salary pay rise inflation allowance, the programme included a 10% increase in social insurance and subsidies for essential products such as rice, baby milk and barley. The government also approved an allocation of SR 10 billion towards building low-cost housing units for the poor during 2008/2009, and this is reflected in the "other" expenditure item.

The Saudi government was under heavy domestic public pressure to follow the lead of Qatar and the UAE, which increased public sector salaries by between 70 and 100% levels. In the end, the Saudi government opted for a more prudent salary hike of 15% in three stages mindful of fuelling domestic inflation through an increase in money supply. The overall increase in money supply for the period 2008–2009 from the salary increases is estimated at around 3.5%, which is a minimal increase and well below the reported rate of inflation of 9% levels for 2008 and 6% for 2009. One worry was that continued and large public sector salary increases run the risk of enticing Saudi nationals back to government jobs without a commensurate rise in productivity. At the same time, higher public sector salaries often send a signal to the rest of the economy and provide the private sector with a comparable benchmark, at least for Saudi nationals. As we will analyse in later chapters, the Saudi private sector is still largely dependent on expatriate labour and the impact of the Saudi public sector pay rises was minimal.

Despite Lower Oil Price, Bumper Expenditure Continues

The 2009 and 2010 budgets indicated that the Saudi government would continue to pump money into the economy to stimulate domestic growth and that stimulus packages would not be withdrawn prematurely, while at the same time they would not be expanded more than required so as to not to produce inflationary pressures. Analysis of budget expenditures for the Saudi semi-autonomous government institutions reveals an emphasis on educational expenditure, with 11 new universities being built and a boost in the budget for existing universities and the vocational training institutions. This is illustrated in Table 3.6.

Table 3.6 Saudi Arabia: budget allocations for semi-autonomous institutions

	2001	2003	2004	2008	2009
	SR million				
Saudi Arabian Airlines	10,384	11,280	12,580	17,400	19,503
General Sea Ports Authority	501	1,410	1,500	827	1,067
Grain Silos and Flour Mills Organization	980	1,034	1,168	914	935
Saline Water Conversation Corporation	3,296	2,245	2,350	5,053	7,645
Royal Commission for Jubayl & Yanbu	2,017	1,010	266	5,583	6,717
General Organization for Military Industries	598	716	774	1,036	1,206
King Abdulaziz City for Science and Technology	296	504	516	857	1,115
Saudi Red Crescent Society	243	295	340	630	1,399
Government Railroad Organization	217	145	143	823	1,147
Saudi Arabian Standards Organization	83	87	98	155	161
Telecommunications Authority		80	100	300	396
Saudi Arabian General Investment Authority	60	80	80	103	136
Supreme Tourism Council	45	125	150	347	384
Saudi Geological Survey	100	111	111	146	164
Institute of Public Administration	222	203	202	288	339
General Org. for Technical Education	1,396	1,540	2,880	3,433	3,735
King Saud University	2,257	2,403	2,420	3,698	5,698
King Abulaziz University	1,433	1,538	1,500	2,467	2,906
Imam Muhammed bin Saud University	1,255	1,250	1,170	1,866	2,192
King Faisal University	700	773	867	2,165	2,742
King Khalid University	356	422	469	1,398	1,974
King Fahd University of Petroleum and Minerals	547	574	622	822	921
Umm Al-Qura University	743	745	673	1,493	1,693
Islamic University of Madinah	277	288	310	431	493
Taibah University	–	–	–	890	1,150

Table 3.6 (continued)

	2001	2003	2004	2008	2009
	SR million				
Qasim University	–	–	309	1,096	1,296
Taif University	–	–	122	775	935
Jazan University	–	–	–	775	935
Al Jawf University	–	–	–	459	694
Hail University	–	–	–	480	588
Tabuk University	–	–	–	364	500.3
Al Baha University	–	–	–	323	445.9
Najran University	–	–	–	320	398.6
Riyadh Girls University	–	–	–	1,357	1,425.6
Northern Borders University	–	–	–	316	444.3

Source: Ministry of Finance, SAMA

The expansion in the new university programme has been impressive after a lag in the earlier decades to meet the growing Saudi population needs. The allocated budgets highlighted in Table 3.6 neither include expenditure on the newly authorized female university being constructed in Riyadh – Princess Noura bint Abdelrahman – and reputed to be the world's largest, with a planned enrolment of nearly 50,000 students, nor that on the world-class King Abdullah University of Science and Technology (KAUST), which opened in 2009 and has a separate endowment fund. The emphasis on education, and its hoped-for output, will be discussed in a later chapter.

Government intentions were highlighted once again: a drive towards a graduate market that is more science-based and oriented towards private sector jobs. These budgetary initiatives, if sustained on a qualitative basis, will contribute towards increasing real economic growth and the nation's productivity in the long run.

Financing Budget Deficits: Cyclical or Structural Deficits?

In 2009 and 2010, the Kingdom entered into a second phase of budget deficits after 7 years of surpluses. A question is raised on whether Saudi Arabia exhibits cyclical or structural deficit characteristics, as the latter is more fundamental and requires more painful economic readjustment.

Cyclical and structural deficits are illustrated in Fig. 3.9.

In the diagram in part (a), potential GDP is Y or 10. When real GDP is less than potential GDP (or 9), the budget is in a cyclical deficit. When real GDP exceeds potential GDP (or 11), the budget is in a cyclical surplus. This has been the mode of Saudi budget cycles to date. However, the situation seems to be approaching a structural deficit situation, as illustrated in part (b). Here potential GDP is Y_0 or 9 against real GDP of Y_1 or 10, and there is a structural deficit. But when potential GDP is Y_2 or 11, then there is a structural surplus. In theory, the government budget

Fig. 3.9 Cyclical and
structural surpluses and
deficits. (**a**). Cyclical deficit
and cyclical surplus. (**b**).
Structural deficit and
structural surplus

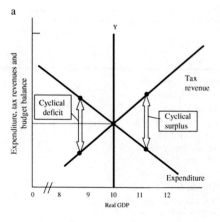

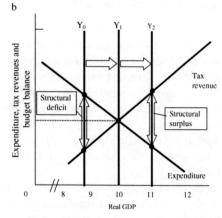

balance fluctuates with the business cycle. A temporary or cyclical surplus or deficit
varies when full employment returns. A persistent surplus or deficit requires government action to remove it. Structural deficits are the budget balances that would occur
at full employment, and when real GDP was equal to potential GDP. The cyclical
deficit is the actual deficit minus the structural deficit; that is, the cyclical deficit is
that part of the budget balance that arises purely because real GDP does not equal
potential GDP.

"Automatic stabilizers" are the mechanisms that stabilize real GDP without
explicit action by the government. These stabilizers operate like shock absorbers.
They make the deficits/surpluses less severe, because income taxes and transfer payments (revenues and expenditures) fluctuate with the real GDP. If real GDP begins
to decrease, tax revenues fall and transfer payments rise, and the government budget
deficit changes. To date, Saudi Arabia does not have such a range of fiscal tools and
hence there are no automatic stabilizers at work to ease deficit fluctuations.

Burden of Indebtedness and Debt-Led Growth

Until the Saudi government started to move into surplus from 2002, there was a debate among Saudi economists on what was termed a "debt-led" growth, and the threat that the Kingdom would hit a debt wall if it did not reverse this policy (Taher, 2003). Others pointed out long-term implications; they suggested that within 3 or 4 years, without fiscal reforms, lending to government will exceed private lending, which could lead to an internal debt service problem (Wilson et al., 2003).

The Saudi Arabian government has been cognizant of this issue and has tried to maintain some overall fiscal balance in its borrowings. As Fig. 3.10 shows, the level of government debt has steadily declined from a peak of around SR 675 billion in 2003 to under SR 225 billion by end of 2009.

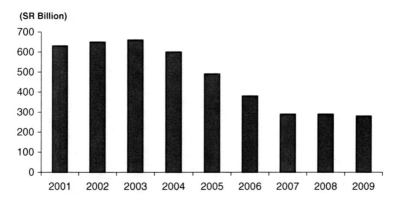

Fig. 3.10 Government debt (SR billions) (2001–2009) (Source: Ministry of Finance)

The Saudi government has been using its windfall oil gains to pay off outstanding debt, which is owed mostly to two pension funds, General Organization for Social Insurance (GOSI) and the Public Pension Agency, while the remaining is held at commercial banks. The 2008 and 2009 spending that Saudi Arabia embarked on, and which extends to the 2010 budget, is being done with no debt created, which was almost unique for any country within the G20 of which Saudi Arabia is a member. If we take into account the size of government deposits held with SAMA, the level of *net* domestic public debt is estimated to have reached around 45% of GDP in the government's favour in 2008, as illustrated in Fig. 3.11.

From Fig. 3.11, the implication is drawn that the Saudi government has more than enough reserves to pay off its entire domestic debt and has the enviable capacity to generate new debt to finance its expenditure plans in the coming years *should it decide to*. In the meantime, the Saudi government has started to draw down on its foreign reserves, as Fig. 3.12 illustrates, with the level of SAMA's net foreign assets peaking at $438 billion as of December 2008 and being around $383 billion as of August 2009. Figure 3.12 also illustrates the coverage ratio of foreign reserves to imports of goods and services, reaching a peak of around 260% in 2008, and being

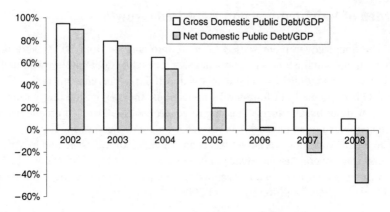

Fig. 3.11   Domestic public debt – Gross and net to GDP (Source: SAMA)

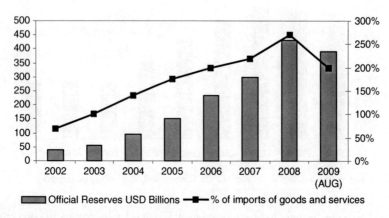

Fig. 3.12   SAMA's official reserves Source: (SAMA, Ministry of Finance)

around 190% in 2009. Whether the government decides to finance its deficit by drawing down on its foreign reserves or issuing domestic bonds will largely depend on the domestic liquidity situation and its implications for inflation in the long run.

Saudi Arabia reports minimal or virtually no direct sovereign state borrowing from the international capital markets, despite a first unsolicited sovereign credit rating by Standard+Poor's in June 2003. This rating assigned A+ to local currency short term and A–1 for long term, while foreign currency was A–1 for short term and A long term. Standard+Poor's raised the Kingdom's rating to AA– in 2009. Moody's upgraded the Kingdom to A1 in March 2009 from A2 in July 2007, citing the Kingdom's low government debt, high external liquidity, geo-strategic importance as the lynchpin of OPEC and prudential financial system regulation (Reuters, 2009). Moody's, however, provided the following rating constraints that could affect the rating:

- extended period of low oil prices resulting in prolonged reduction of economic growth
- unsustainable expenditure programme
- renewed large budget deficits and build-up of government debt
- heightened social or political tensions
- employment pressure from a relatively large population

"Crowding Out" the Private Sector

Moody's cautionary note raises the issue of a renewed rise in government debt and the so-called "crowding-out" effect on the private sector. The first budget deficit financing was in 1988 with an SR 42 billion issue of government bonds sold to the Saudi commercial banks and to other government semi-autonomous agencies, such as the GOSI and the Saudi Pension and Retirement Agency (Dukheil, 1995).

We have noted earlier how the Saudi government has been successful in reducing the level of public debt, but there is always a fear that government debt will "crowd out" the private sector as explored in Fig. 3.13.

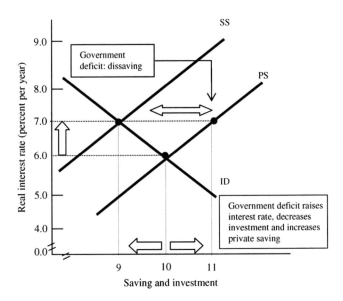

Fig. 3.13 A crowding-out effect

ID represents the investment demand curve of the private sector and PS is the private sector savings supply curve. It indicates the relationship between private saving and the real interest rate. SS shows the sum of private and government saving. At 6% in real interest rates, investment equals saving and the budget is balanced. A government budget deficit is negative government saving (dissaving). The effect of the budget deficit (government dissaving) is to decrease investment from 10 to 9, as interest rates rise from 6 to 7%. However, the higher interest rate level induces an increase in private saving from 10 to 11 as illustrated in the diagram. In reality, the increase in private saving might be small in the short term, but the increase in the government budget deficit is to decrease investments in the private sector or to "crowd out" the private sector investment demand.

Table 3.7 sets out the trend of government borrowing from the Saudi commercial banking sector to support or disprove the above "crowding-out" hypothesis. An indication that the Saudi private sector does not seem to suffer from "crowding out" in the most recent years is illustrated in Fig. 3.14, which indicates that government deposits with commercial banks have indeed been rising as the level of domestic debt has fallen.

As Table 3.7 indicates, the level of bank holding of government securities fell from around 25% in 2003 to under 15% in 2009.

Some might argue that there are few reasons for concern, as the government debt is translated back into the economy through government expenditure, and thus the working of the income multiplier outweighs the confidence and crowding-out

Table 3.7 Government and public sector security holdings by Saudi commercial banks (1996–2009)

	1996	2003	2008	2009(Aug)
	SR billion			
Government paper	65.266	148.346	241.986	200.742
Private securities	6.627	8.353	21.820	21.040
Total securities	71.893	156.699	263.806	221.782
Total bank assets	357.947	590.532	1,302.271	1,346.392
Government paper as percentage of bank assets	18.2%	25.12%	18.58%	14.91%

Source: SAMA, 2009

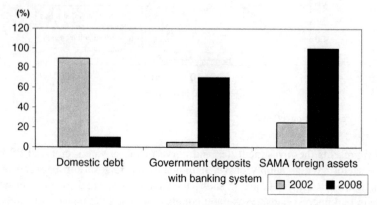

Fig. 3.14 Saudi Arabia key financial parameters 2002/2008 (% of GDP) (Source: SAMA)

effects. Others might argue that in a resilient and growing economy, debt is not a major concern as government borrowing merely absorbs excess domestic liquidity from the markets, which is then put to good use in socially productive programmes instead of creating price inflation and potential stock market bubbles and crashes. These arguments presuppose that government bases its borrowing on the golden rule *that governments borrow to invest rather than for short-term current consumption.* As discussed earlier, this has not often been the case in Saudi Arabia, and changes are required to the current budgetary system.

The growth in population, and specifically the young age profile of Saudi nationals, will necessitate continuing expenditures for health, education and basic infrastructure in future years. This has been the prime motivating force behind the Saudi government's drive to privatize the government sector, given the decline in Saudi capital expenditure patterns observed over the past few years, before the pick-up since 2006.

The implication is that in the absence of revenue diversification, the Kingdom's oil policy will be faced with the same two choices it has always faced: either pursuing a larger oil market-share policy at lower prices; or maintaining the current policy of defending firmer prices within a narrow, specified price band, and cutting back on production if the price band comes under pressure through non-OPEC production or changes in economic conditions and aggregate world demand for oil.

Neither option is particularly attractive in the long run. The first means larger government deficits today, and possible reductions in the future, as marginal oil producers are driven out due to Saudi Arabia's comparative cost-production advantage. The second option implies facing ongoing deficits of between SR 20 and SR 40 billion per annum for the foreseeable future.

Facing the Challenges: Short- and Long-Term Solutions

Despite the above issues, the Kingdom's future is not all bleak. As many commentators have pointed out, structural budgetary changes are possible. This will require both willpower and a commitment from the government to not be diverted from set goals. Many countries face similar budgetary structural issues as those faced by Saudi Arabia, in both economically developed and developing countries. The Kingdom is no exception and many countries would count themselves fortunate if their problems were only as severe as current Saudi problems. However, solving tomorrow's problems with today's solutions will not work. Saudi Arabia has been encouraged by both its own economists and the International Monetary Fund (IMF) to rethink its current fiscal strategies.

The Kingdom is not unaware of what needs to be done and the following steps are clearly spelled out in the Eighth and Ninth Development Plans:

- Increase non-oil government revenues
- Reduce budget deficits to lowest possible levels

- Finance deficit through the issue of development bonds
- Rationalize and reduce government non-investment expenditures
- Use government surpluses of oil revenues to reduce national debt
- Maintain strict adherence to approved expenditure limits
- Develop an adequate mechanism for attaining long-term fiscal stabilization in order to avoid the adverse effects of fluctuations in government oil revenues

These are all laudable policy objectives, but in reality few, if any, have been consistently followed, as illustrated earlier. Table 3.8 summarizes short- and long-term revenue sources and measures that could be implemented to overcome the current structural fiscal imbalances.

Table 3.8 Possible solutions for improving revenue base

Measures	Major issues
Short term	
(i) Revenue enhancement	
• *Zakat*	The 2.5% *zakat* on companies (Islamic levy on total assets) is earmarked for social welfare purposes. Better collection efforts could generate marginal increases
• Custom duties	Better collection of duties and tariffs will be offset long-term by inter-GCC tariff reductions and expected WTO entry
• Fees and charges	Increasing use of this revenue source has provided some fiscal certainty. Expand current base of fees on government service (expatriates and Saudis) as well as more market-based pricing for subsidized services
(ii) Measures	
• Budget adherence	Strict adherence to expenditure limits must be applied. Extra budgetary expenditures to be allowed only from other chapter allocations
• Reallocation of expenditure items to "best" economic use	Reallocation of expenditures to longer-term productive value-added, job-generating sectors and gradual reduction in wasteful subsidies. Close examination of defence expenditure while maintaining security needs
Long term	
(iii) Revenue sources	
• Taxation	Reintroduce personal income taxes on both expatriates and Saudis, after studies on poverty threshold levels
	Introduce sales tax on luxury goods and value-added tax on range of consumer durable goods
• Sale of government assets	Speed up sale of key government-owned industries starting with mature ones (banking), petrochemicals (SABIC) and telecommunications (STC). Revenue to be used for debt repayment and capital infrastructure investment
(iv) Measures	
• Civil service reforms	Needed as much as *Saudization* policy. Assess efficiency of current public sector expenditure and allocate according to productivity
• Privatization at fair market prices	Initiate full privatization of key sectors, but shape these around fair market prices to encourage Saudi private capital repatriation by the private sector

Table 3.8 (continued)

Measures	Major issues
• Studies on fiscal policies	Establish independent centre for fiscal studies to analyse economic effects of taxation measures on consumers, business and government revenue-generating impact
• Establish efficiency performance benchmarks	There is a lack of clear overall benchmarks for measuring adequacy of government efforts to meet needs of the public and Saudi economic development. Transparency is growing but more is needed on performance relative to public demand and need. This requires benchmarking through meaningful output measures
• Stabilization fund	Establish a "Revenue Stabilization Fund" to be allocated a specified percentage of annual revenues or surpluses and to be used for budgetary revenue stabilization under strict drawdown guidelines
• Regional/municipal level economic empowerment	Empower local municipalities and regional economic councils with budgetary allocations and responsibilities. This will result in local prioritization of economic resources and accountability for upcoming municipal elections
• Introduce "mini"-budgets	Current yearly budget announcement and planning is not proactive enough given fluctuating world economic conditions and oil prices. Introduction of bi-annual "mini-budget" announcement will adjust forecast of revenues and expenditures accordingly. Ministry of Finance will become more focused on fiscal stabilization programmes as well as more accurate macroeconomic production
• International borrowing	Reinforce financial discipline and obligations. Apply the "golden rule" – borrow to invest and not for the current expenditures. Less burden on domestic banks

The Time for Rhetoric Is Over

As Table 3.8 indicates, there are no easy options. Above all, no single measure can remedy the situation by itself, but a combination of short- and long-term measures can work. Structural reform is measured solely in macroeconomic success and never in intentions, plans, decrees or mere talk. Some of the measures can be implemented quickly, such as a more efficient collection of *zakat*, which, according to local reports, contributes only a small amount from an estimated *zakat* contribution potential of SR 15 billion on SR 900 billion private sector wealth in the Kingdom (Holayan, 2003). It is estimated that between SR 3 and SR 4 billion is currently collected from this source. Since *zakat* is paid towards charitable and social security transfer payments, some have argued that better collection will help in reducing unemployment-related crimes. A report by the Manpower Council suggested that crime rate among the unemployed rose by 320% in a 6-year period from 1990 to 1996, and was expected to rise further (Khazindar, 2003).

Taxation has been discussed by the *Majlis Al Shoura* but abandoned, and this was primarily focused on expatriate earnings above SR 5,000. The issue of taxation needs to be reintroduced, but for both nationals and expatriates, as the WTO and International Labour Office (ILO) would have deemed it discriminatory and reversed it if it applied only to foreigners. Saudi Arabia did impose a personal income tax before the oil boom era of the early 1970s. The current no-tax situation is an aberration from the norm in most countries, and Saudi economists are debating this option (Taher, 2003, Sheikh and Abdelrahman, 2003). However, some emphasize value-added and corporate taxes, rather than personal income tax, until a national consensus can be reached for lower income threshold levels and exemptions.

Privatization and proceeds from the sale of government assets would relieve the government from the burden of running state operations in an inefficient manner with a drag on fiscal resources. However, privatization needs to be carefully thought through and the appropriate regulatory and operating framework has to be in place prior to privatization taking place. The issue is divisive in many countries and some, especially Western, experts argue for this option, for the sake of privatization. However, some Saudi government planners tend to promote privatization for the sake of dumping the burden onto the private sector, and this is not an appropriate approach.

The recent increases in oil prices to over $140 pb and then sharp falls to under $40 pb also signalled the need for an oil stabilization fund. Among oil-exporting countries, the Kingdom is probably one of the few countries that does not possess a Sovereign Wealth Fund (SWF); instead, surplus assets are conservatively managed and held by SAMA. There was some debate in Saudi Arabia in 2009 on establishing such an oil stabilization fund, but it was downplayed given the collapse of global financial markets and asset prices. This has not deterred Saudi Arabia though from taking the first cautious steps as it approved the creation of an investment company known as "*Sanabel*" with an initial capital of SR 20 billion ($5.34 billion) to primarily invest in foreign and Saudi companies that add employment or technology transfer value to Saudi Arabia. There are hopes that as Saudi Arabia becomes more comfortable with managing *Sanabel*, there will be an opportunity to establish a larger oil stabilization fund that can assist the government's fiscal management policies in many respects.

First, there is the necessity of separating the role of monetary policy from fiscal policy. By establishing an oil fund, the central bank will be able to pursue an independent monetary policy to manage domestic liquidity. Second, a stabilization fund can lower the impact of volatile oil revenues on government budget plans, by saving during oil booms and dissaving when oil prices slump. Third, it can be used to diversify investments abroad and reduce the economy's reliance on oil as a source of growth. Finally, it can reduce currency revaluation/devaluation pressures resulting from fluctuations in oil export receipts. But aside from their long-term focus, SWFs in neighbouring countries have shown an important stabilizing role at times of financial distress. With the intensification of the global financial crisis, Kuwait, UAE and Qatar have utilized their SWF resources to inject liquidity, re-capitalize the banking sector and even invest in the local stock market to prop up confidence levels. In this way, an oil stabilization fund can support the domestic economy and restore financial stability while maintaining investments abroad. For the time being though, Saudi Arabia's official policy is to adopt a wait-and-see attitude for a more "adventurous" international investment policy.

Some have argued that domestic efficiency in state spending and obtaining value for money is just as critical in prudent fiscal policy. The Saudi General Auditing Bureau (GAB) certainly seems to believe so, as it accused some government departments of excess spending, delaying vital projects and negligence in collecting revenues when it presented its annual report to King Abdullah in January 2010 (Arab News, 11 January 2010). Lauding their efforts, King Abdullah encouraged them to continue in their financial auditing and performance monitoring. The issue of some government departments' misappropriation of state funds for vital projects gained added urgency following the Jeddah flash floods and acknowledgement by accused officials that embezzlement took place and projects not fulfilled up to required specifications. This aspect of Saudi fiscal expenditure monitoring will become a central feature of ongoing budgetary expenditure.

Hopeful Future

The outlook for Saudi Arabia seems more assured in 2010 compared with just a few years earlier. The sustained increase in public expenditure – especially in capital projects, infrastructure and education – as well as the government's readiness to run deficits after years of surplus will offer some confidence and support to the domestic economy. There could be reduction in overall economic growth, but the government will now encourage spending constraints by ensuring that projects undertaken are carried out more efficiently and thus reduce overall gross investment per capita.

As was pointed out earlier, Saudi Arabia is in a more advantaged situation than many countries, but the government must not ease up on the necessary long-term structural reforms, however painful these may be in the short run.

Summary of Key Points

- *The Saudi budget is a useful barometer of the financial health of the nation as it sets out quantitative and indicative directions as to government intention and priorities in expenditures and revenue forecasts.*
- *Saudi economic development has been fuelled by a rise in oil revenues which was unsustainable due to the inability of the government to control oil prices, while at the same time government expenditures seemed to be consistently overrun. As such budgeted plans never materialized.*
- *Overdependence on oil took place over building a true wealth-generating base for the economy, although there are some indications that the government is beginning to shift resources to market-required resources.*
- *Sources of revenues are being diversified away from oil dependency, but these are still limited and there are no direct or indirect taxation elements involved.*

As such, the Saudi budgetary system is evidencing a structural deficit situation, despite occasional bumper revenue years due to higher than forecasted oil prices.

- *The government has financed its deficits through internal borrowing, including from the domestic banks, which can give rise to "crowding out" of the private sector investment demand. Current total national debt level is around 25% of GDP.*
- *The government needs to introduce short- and long-term measures to diversify its revenue sources, restructure its expenditure patterns and consider taxation.*

Part III
The Financial Sector

Chapter 4
Saudi Arabian Monetary Agency (SAMA) and Monetary Policy

When I had money everyone called me brother.

Polish proverb

Learning Outcomes

By the end of this section, you would understand:

- *The organizational structure and functions of SAMA*
- *SAMA's evolving responsibilities in different financial areas*
- *Saudi monetary policy and instruments*
- *Effectiveness of monetary policy*
- *SAMA and exchange rate policy*
- *Money supply creation*
- *Process of financial deepening in the economy*
- *Inflation in Saudi Arabia*

Introduction

Sitting at the head of Saudi Arabia's financial system is the Saudi Arabian Monetary Agency (SAMA). Established by Royal Decree in 1952, it has now completed 58 years of service to the country. It has been an observer and key player in financial matters, and has seen its role expand with the evolution of the Kingdom's economy and financial system. The history and role of SAMA encapsulates the evolution of Saudi Arabia's banking and financial structures in the gradual institutionalization of the country's financial market. How SAMA operates and the tools and policies it adopts will have a great impact on all of Saudi society, not merely on the financial sector. SAMA has come a long way from those early days and proved a capable regulator during the global financial crisis of 2007–2010, ensuring that the Saudi financial sector was not affected by the global contagion and that Saudi banks remained relatively unscathed.

M.A. Ramady, *The Saudi Arabian Economy*, DOI 10.1007/978-1-4419-5987-4_4,
© Springer Science+Business Media, LLC 2010

As this chapter will explain, SAMA plays a leading role in the "financial deepening" of the markets, through the creation of new *financial instruments* and of the regulatory and legal framework within which such developments can occur. At the same time, these changes incorporate evolving public perceptions of monetary assets and increasingly active participation in the marketplace, while they create a higher level of sophistication leading to economic development (Azzam, 1997a). Although the Saudi financial and capital markets still have some way to go to reach the level of well-developed financial markets, SAMA has played a significant role in creating appropriate conditions for investors to mobilize resources domestically. Erratic oil revenues coupled with the needs of a young and growing population can only accelerate SAMA's efforts at financial development, and that in turn could encourage *capital inflows* for Saudi and foreign investors who seek better opportunities in the Kingdom.

Asserting Independence

The independence of a central bank to perform its mission without coming under undue pressure from governments is critical to the success of a central bank's policies and public confidence. Over time, SAMA has managed to acquire increased independence, which is a far cry from the original institution that was set up with technical assistance from the United States in 1952 to act as the country's de facto central bank within the confines of Islamic law.

SAMA is supervised by a Board of Directors that is headed by a Governor and Vice-Governor, both of whom are appointed by a Royal Decree by the King for terms of 4 years. These terms can be extended by Royal Decree for similar periods. SAMA's board also consists of three other members nominated from the private sector, who are also appointed by a Royal Decree to serve for periods of 5 years. The nominations and appointments of members of the Board of Directors, including the Governor and Vice-Governor, rest with the Minister of Finance and the Council of Ministers.

Senior SAMA managers have been in place for many years, providing stability and relative independence in decision-making, although they operate in close coordination with the Ministry of Finance. In February 2009, Dr. Mohammed Al Jasser was appointed as SAMA Governor after serving as Vice-Governor under the long-serving and well-respected Hamad Saud Al Sayari, who had been in the position of Governor since 1983 – making him one of the longest-serving central bank governors in the world. Dr. Jasser is an able international technocrat who had also served as Saudi Arabia's Executive Director to the International Monetary Fund (IMF) and is fully conversant and comfortable in dealing with global financial issues. His appointment as Governor could not have been better timed both to ensure a smooth transition at the helm and also to act as a steadying hand during the global financial crisis.

Following Dr. Jasser's appointment, several other senior-level management changes took place at SAMA and Dr. Abdulrahman Al Hamidy was appointed as

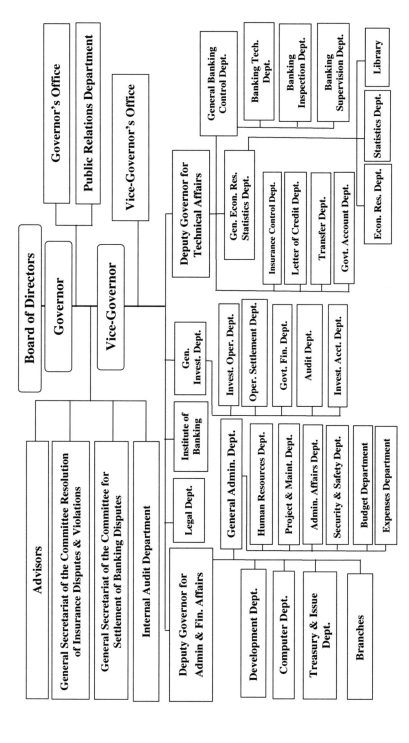

Fig. 4.1 SAMA's organizational chart (Source: SAMA)

Vice-Governor in August 2009, followed by Dr. Abdelrahman Al Kalaf as Deputy Governor for Technical Affairs and Mr. Ibrahim Abdullah Al Nasser as Deputy Governor for Administrative Affairs, both in November 2009.

Figure 4.1 illustrates SAMA's organizational chart.

Previous SAMA Governors served for various periods – George Bowlers (1952–1954), Ralph Standish (1954–1958), Anwar Ali (1958–1974), Abdulaziz Al-Quraishi (1974–1983) – and brought with them a blend of different management styles and professional backgrounds, mostly drawing upon Western central bank and IMF philosophies. Close technical and training cooperation is carried out with leading Western central banks and this has resulted in SAMA adopting a basically Western central bank approach in terms of bank supervision and risk management (Dukheil, 1995). While this might be true, it does not mean that SAMA does not have different policies from Western central banks, but that such differences can be explained by environmental influences based on the nature of the Saudi economy and of public perceptions and acceptance of this sector. The manner in which these particular environmental issues are handled will often determine the choice of organization that evolves. The growth of Islamic banking is one particular point, and SAMA, along with the Bahrain Monetary Agency (BMA), has been successful in regulating this fast-growing sector and ensuring that it operates under the same "fit and proper" banking supervisory regime that is imposed on conventional banking.

SAMA's Stated Functions

SAMA's 1952 founding charter stipulated that it would conform to Islamic law. It could not be a profit-making institution and could neither pay nor receive interest. There were additional prohibitions, including one against extending credit to the government, but this was dropped in 1955 when the government needed funds and SAMA financed about one-half of the governmental debt that accrued in the late 1950s (Abdeen and Shook 1984).

The introduction of the *Banking Control Law* in 1966 was a watershed in SAMA's history, as the new regulation clarified and strengthened SAMA's role in regulating the Saudi banking system (SAMA, 2004, Jasser, 2002). The Banking Control Law vested SAMA with broad supervisory powers and allowed the monetary agency to issue regulations, rules and guidelines regarding eight of the international supervisory developments that called for provision of capital adequacy, liquidity, *reserve requirements* and loan concentration ratios. The Banking Control Law supported the concept of a "universal banking model" that permitted banks to provide a broad range of financial services including banking, investments and securities through their branches.

SAMA sees its main roles as follows:

- issuing the national currency, SR
- acting as banker to the government

- supervising commercial banks operating in Saudi Arabia
- advising the government on the public debt
- managing the Kingdom's foreign exchange reserves
- conducting monetary policy for promoting price and exchange rate stability
- promoting economic growth and ensuring the soundness of the Saudi financial system

In addition to the above-stated goals, SAMA had also over time acquired for itself several other regulatory functions such as supervision of the insurance sector and any remaining money exchanges. Operationally SAMA carries out these functions through its head office in capital Riyadh and through its ten branches located in all major Saudi cities.

SAMA's Evolving Responsibilities

In order to better understand SAMA's current roles and responsibilities, one must also understand the historical trajectory of the monetary agency in order to better appreciate the significant developments that have taken place in the Kingdom's financial history in comparison with other nations. When analysing Saudi Arabia's current position, it is sometimes easy to forget just how fast and how far the Kingdom has had to travel in a short period of time, "learning by doing" along the way.

SAMA has had a colourful and unorthodox history since its establishment in 1952, and this has been well documented by others (Abdeen and Shook, 1984, Johany, 1986, Dukheil, 1995, SAMA, 2004). When SAMA was established, Saudi Arabia did not have a monetary system exclusively its own. Foreign currencies circulated in the Kingdom as a medium of exchange along with silver riyal coins. Saudi banknotes had not yet been issued and there were no national Saudi banks. Banking was conducted through foreign bank branches and specialized trading houses – the most famous being the Netherlands Trading Company, which later became the Saudi Hollandi (Dutch) Bank.

Major transactions had to be carried out using foreign gold coins, such as the popular "Maria Theresa" dollar, or large quantities of silver riyals. However, expanding oil production from the late 1950s increased national revenues and international payments due to expanded international trade, which necessitated a different financial system. Demand for cash and inter-regional payments grew substantially and the use of coins became almost impossible. An additional motive for financial institutionalization was the absence of a fixed exchange rate between the silver riyal coins and foreign gold coins, so that exchange rates varied widely.

SAMA almost died at birth, as its establishment coincided with acute government financial difficulties due to runaway spending and a near depletion of reserves. The introduction of the paper riyal was abandoned at that time. SAMA, however, assumed responsibility for maintaining the exchange rate of the Saudi silver riyal vis-à-vis the US dollar within a band set by the government. In essence, this was not much different from the current SAMA exchange rate policy.

In 1953 SAMA completed the country's indigenous monetary system by issuing Saudi Arabia's own gold coins and by eliminating the circulation of foreign currencies. In 1954 it began issuing so-called "pilgrim receipts" for relieving pilgrims of the burden of carrying heavy metallic currency; these receipts were acceptable for encashment throughout the Kingdom. Again, we can see the genesis of the use of traveller checks by modern pilgrims. The popularity of "pilgrim receipts" and the acceptance of a non-metal form of payment by the public paved the way for the issuance of the SR notes in June 1961. From that date, all gold and silver coins and all pilgrim receipts were de-monetized. It had taken nearly 12 years from the date of SAMA's establishment for a paper currency system to be accepted in Saudi Arabia.

According to SAMA, the last five decades can be classified into four broad eras, each characterized by distinctive features (SAMA, February 2004):

1960–1972: In this era, SAMA focused on establishing the basis for commercial banking regulations against a background of expanding domestic banking business and of Saudi Arabia's acceptance of full convertibility of the SR in March 1961, in accordance with Article VIII of the IMF Articles of Agreement.

1973–1982: During this period, SAMA was preoccupied with containing the inflationary pressures of a booming Saudi economy fuelled by the massive oil price rises of 1973/1974, and with managing the expansion of the banking system to cover most of the country. SAMA also saw itself catapulted into the international limelight through its management of substantial Saudi foreign exchange reserves, which built up during the boom period. These have been estimated at around $170–180 billion by 1984 (IMF, 1999). During this period, as the author can testify from his own personal banking experience, SAMA was the magnet to all international bankers hoping to "recycle" some of these "petro-dollars."

1983–2004: During this time, SAMA's priorities were to introduce financial market reforms and advise the government in managing the public debt. Both SAMA and Saudi commercial banking came of age with the completion of the so-called *Saudization* of the local branches of foreign banks operating in the Kingdom and the introduction of a wide range of new financial products domestically. The pros and cons of the concept underpinning foreign bank *Saudization* will be dealt with at length in the next chapter, but the issue of advising the government on the level of public debt was certainly of some concern to SAMA during the period 2000–2003, when the level of national debt rose to almost 100% of GDP.

During this period, SAMA took the lead in encouraging Saudi banks to invest in and use advanced technologies. Today Saudi banking is at the cutting edge of technology usage with automated cheque clearing systems, electronic fund transfer and "transaction plus zero" days share trading settlement system – probably one of the most advanced in the world.

2005–ongoing: Unlike the previous period, which was characterized by a global monetary easing triggered by the Internet bubble burst in 2000 and fears of deflation, the period from 2005 was a period of monetary tightening. SAMA raised its repo rates from 2.5% levels in early 2005 to 5.50% levels in 2007 and inflation considerations predominated the later years. SAMA set out commercial bank prudential guidelines to slow the pace of consumer and margin lending and raised the cash reserve requirements. Following the collapse of Lehman Brothers in September 2009, SAMA lowered its repo rate to around 2% in January 2009, and injected liquidity into the banks by lowering the cash reserve ratios. This period can be characterized as one that saw a more proactive interventionist stance by SAMA in ensuring that the Saudi banking system was not affected by the world's financial crisis and remained solvent. SAMA also oversaw the orderly settlement of some high profile Saudi corporate debt defaults and requested Saudi banks to take on appropriate reserves and strengthen their capital base. In this period, SAMA also oversaw the growth of the Saudi insurance sector and introduced a regulatory framework for the sector. The Saudi accession to the WTO in 2005 also presented SAMA with added regulatory oversight responsibilities for the "new wave" foreign banks that entered the Kingdom and which is still ongoing in terms of new licences applied.

Central Bank Monetary Policy

SAMA is vested with conducting monetary policy, and this includes exchange rate policy within a framework set by the government. How effectively has this been achieved and what are the major issues faced in the pursuit of these policies?

Generally, monetary policies, in conjunction with fiscal policies, are used to influence economic growth and inflation in an economy within desired limits. Both monetary and fiscal policies are called demand-management policies because they try to influence the economy's output indirectly through increasing or decreasing the economy's aggregate demand for goods and services.

In most countries, a *central bank* acts as the chief monetary authority and lender of last resort to the banking system. By "lender of last resort" we mean lending money to banks on an overnight basis or for longer periods when banks are unable to borrow money elsewhere at market rates. This function of a central bank as the last-resort lender provides a certain degree of stability to a banking system.

Central banks try to influence the economy by changes in interest rate levels and, therefore, the money supply. Various monetary tools are at the disposal of central banks to achieve intermediate and long-term goals. One such tool is the *discount rate*. This is the rate the central bank charges banks for borrowing funds from it. The central bank usually has the power to restrain commercial banks in their lending by raising or lowering the discount rate as needed, thus restricting or loosening credit conditions. This allows the central bank to control bank lending indirectly, and it is a signal to the market of central bank intentions. A central bank also tries to influence the level of interest rates and hence the pace of a nation's economic growth by adjusting the level of *reserve requirements*. This effectively reduces or increases borrowing rates through increasing and decreasing the level of statutory (obligatory) reserves a commercial bank must keep with the Central Bank, calculated on the basis of its non-borrowed deposit base. Another effective tool for a central bank is to increase or decrease bank reserves through *open-market operations* – the buying and selling of government securities in the open market. This action decreases or increases the pool of non-borrowed bank deposits, and hence money supply in the system.

In analysing SAMA's monetary policy in more detail, several factors have to be borne in mind about the economic environment that SAMA finds itself in. These can be summarized as follows:

* Saudi Arabia is an open economy with no restrictions on capital flows which makes capital control policies in effective.
* The bulk of economic activity and revenues are oil-driven and SAMA has not much control as to government inflows.
* Economic openness and oil dependency means vulnerability to external shocks.
* A fixed exchange rate regime against the US dollar which hampers SAMA's independent interest rate policies.
* A passive player in terms of the government's macroeconomic objectives of minimizing the impact of oil revenue swings through government-induced counter-cyclical measures, involving building surpluses in upswings and running deficits in downturns.

Structure of the Saudi Financial System

There is close cooperation and coordination between the major regulators of the Saudi economic and financial system. Figure 4.2 illustrates the major responsibilities of the regulators.

Figure 4.2 highlights several potential overlapping areas of supervisory jurisdiction such as the CMA's supervision of foreign investment banks and SAMA's regulation of foreign retail banking branches, the licensing of new corporates by the Ministry of Commerce, which includes foreign and Saudi financial entities, and the Ministry of Finance's supervision of the specialized government credit lending agencies, which lie outside SAMA's supervisory domain, but can impact monetary policy through their lending and money supply creation process. Over the past decade as the Saudi economy has evolved, the various government bodies have cooperated closely through "learning by doing," and there is a high degree of both informal and formal communication to ensure that policies are in harmony.

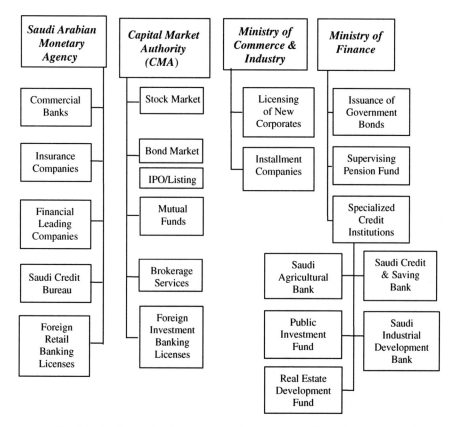

Fig. 4.2 Saudi Arabia financial and economic regulatory responsibilities (Source: SAMA, 2010)

Central Bank Monetary Policy: The Theory

Monetary policy can be broadly defined as the process by which central banks seek to influence the quantity of money in the economy to achieve certain macroeconomic objectives. These often include economic growth, low level of unemployment, inflation targeting, exchange rate targeting and monetary aggregates control. Monetary policy is often described as being expansionary when the level of interest rates is lowered and contractionary or tight when the level of interest rates is raised.

Central banks have to cooperate closely with the major spending bodies such as Ministries of Finance to ensure that their policies are not counter to each other, but in the final analysis central banks are independent to act on a discretionary basis as guardians of monetary policy, especially by influencing the quantity of money and hence the general price level within an economy. Figure 4.3 illustrates the sharing of economic and monetary responsibilities of a central bank and a Ministry of Finance as exemplified in Saudi Arabia.

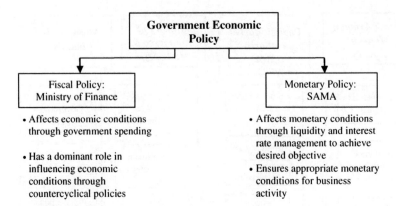

Fig. 4.3 Saudi economic and monetary policy responsibility

Saudi Monetary Policy in Practice

The key objectives of Saudi Arabian monetary policy are to stabilize inflation and the general level of prices, to maintain a fixed exchange rate of the SR against the US dollar and to allow free movement of currency and capital. According to SAMA officials (Al Jasser and Banafe, 2003), there are limitations to current monetary policies in Saudi Arabia "due to the openness of the economy, with the riyal effectively pegged to the US dollar since the suspension of the Special Drawing Right (SDR) riyal link in May, 1981." In practice this has resulted in riyal interest rates closely tracking dollar rates, with a small premium, a phenomenon we will further analyse below.

In line with other central banks in the region, SAMA is solely responsible for monetary policy formulation and implementation. It is free to select its operating procedures and to determine the choice of instruments as well as when to apply them. Only in a few cases prior approval is needed from the Ministry of Finance, such as when changing the statutory reserve requirements. To all intents and purposes, SAMA is relatively independent of government pressure.

SAMA relies on four-policy instruments in conducting monetary policy: cash reserve ratio/minimum reserve policy, repos and reverse repos, foreign exchange swaps and, finally, placement of public funds. Figure 4.4 illustrates SAMA's monetary policy framework in terms of overall strategy and implementation tactics and operating objectives and goals.

SAMA applies no direct controls, particularly with respect to the control of interest rates and foreign exchange. The first is due to SAMA's charter, which prohibits the payment and receiving of interest; furthermore, there is no discount rate policy. As such, interest rates play a subsidiary role, as they are predominantly affected by US dollar interest rates. However, SAMA has over the years successfully used the "repo" rate policy as a proxy for establishing an interest rate benchmark in the money market in lieu of a formal discount policy. As regards foreign exchange control, SAMA has adopted a regime of free movement of capital

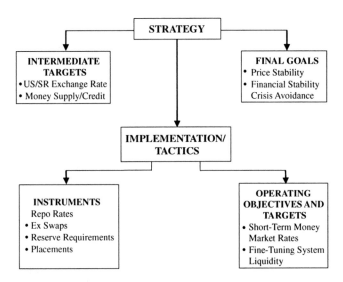

Fig. 4.4 SAMA's monetary policy framework

for Saudi Arabia. As part of monetary policy implementation, SAMA does not use other direct controls, such as credit ceilings. The monetary agency could, however, impose credit concentration ceilings on certain economic sectors, as well as overall loans-to-deposit ratios for Saudi commercial banks, in order to curb or expand bank lending.

Table 4.1 summarizes the major policy instruments that SAMA has, their recent use, and the rationale for using them as well as perceived effectiveness of such instruments in the Saudi financial sector.

Article 8 of the SAMA Banking Control Law prevents banks from lending more than 25% of their reserves and paid-up capital to any one entity, but at SAMA's discretion, this can be increased to 50%. A significant "secondary" monetary tool at SAMA's disposal is a maximum overall loans-to-deposit ratio that can be extended. While there is some leeway, the current maximum loans-to-deposit ratio stands at a conservative 75% for Saudi banks compared with 85–90% ratios for the US banking industry as a whole. Central banks sometimes use what is termed *moral suasion*, whereby a central bank attempts to influence commercial bank lending by *persuasion* rather than by direct means. In Saudi Arabia, this tool had not been particularly effective, especially in the early days of Saudi banking, because, when faced with a decision on lending in a booming era, the Saudi commercial banks chose profit maximization over SAMA "advise." This was compounded in the pre-*Saudization* banking era, when significant out-of-Kingdom forces and pressures were exerted on the foreign bank branches operating in the Kingdom. However, once *Saudization* of the Saudi banking system was completed in the mid-1980s, including the establishment of regular senior-level bank management meetings with SAMA, this policy tool became more effective. It will be interesting to see how SAMA will be able

Table 4.1 SAMA's monetary policy instruments: comparative analysis

Policy instrument tool	Rationale and operational usage	Effectiveness
Cash reserve ratio (CRR)	• To ensure banks have adequate liquidity to cover customer deposits • Raised twice in April and May 2008 from 7 to 9% and then 13% for first time since 1980 on current account and from 2 to 4% on savings account • Reduced to 7% on current account in November 2008	• Used for implementing structural changes in bank liquidity (credit creation control) and for fine-tuning short-term liquidity • Produces strong signal effects but infrequently used • Not imposed on inter-bank transactions
Statutory liquidity ratio (SLR)	• Banks required to maintain minimum amount of specified liquid assets equal to 20% of demand and time deposits	• "Free liquidity" at disposal of banks is reduced and can influence overall bank lending structure (short/long term)
Repos	• SAMA alters liquidity position of banks by dealing directly in the market to make temporary additions to bank reserves through short-dated repurchase agreements (overnight)	• Allows for short-term injection of reserves and automatic withdrawal upon repo maturity • Efficiency depends on SAMA's holding of securities and size and depth of market
Reverse repos	• Need for banks to place excess liquidity with SAMA through overnight matched sale-purchased operations	• SAMA can absorb rather than provide bank reserves • A definitive purchase of financial assets reversible at short notice not affecting prices in bond market; serves to regulate the money market
Foreign exchange swaps	• Intention to influence capital outflows, avoiding disruptions to monetary policy from foreign exchange markets • Used for liquidity management and currency speculation	• More flexible than repos/reverse repos in terms of their maturity and volume per deal • Affect liquidity but do not generally exercise influence on foreign exchange rate
Placement of public funds	• At SAMA's discretion to place governmental institutions' funds with selected banks	• A "rough tuning" instrument providing banks with long-term liquidity support • Can signal crisis management and problems in banks
Foreign exchange intervention	• At SAMA's discretion in times of acute speculation	• Rarely used to stabilize spot and forward market

Source: SAMA, Annual Report, 2003

to align the interests of Saudi Arabia with the interests of the "new wave" foreign-owned bank branches that were licensed to operate in the Kingdom post-2005 WTO accession.

Analysing the operational usage and effectiveness of the various policy instruments at SAMA's disposal in Table 4.1, we note the sudden and dramatic use of the cash reserve ratios (CRRs) that were used in 2008 for the first time since 1980. In 1980 SAMA reduced the CRR to 7% on current accounts and 2% on deposit accounts, but 28 years later it reversed policy by dramatically raising the CRR to 13% on current accounts and 4% on deposit accounts to send a strong "signalling" effect to the Saudi banking sector to curb back on lending. By the end of 2008, the CRR on current accounts had been reduced to 7%, but SAMA's intentions were taken on board by the Saudi banks. A consequent effect of raising the CRR is that such higher reserves will eat into bank profits even if sometimes they do not materially impact on lending growth. The reason of this "indirect bank tax" is that reserves at SAMA do not earn interest whereas other deposits through the reverse repo do. Another consequence of a higher CRR ratio is that banks might therefore increase the spread between the lending and deposit rates in order to maintain their previous level of profitability. Raising lending rates could also reduce lending growth.

Exchange rate targeting remains a plank of SAMA's monetary policy instruments through foreign exchange swaps and occasional foreign exchange intervention.

The Centrality of SAMA's Exchange Rate Policy

According to analysts, economic theory suggests that when a country fixes its exchange and interest rate and is subject to high capital mobility, it loses its ability to conduct an independent monetary policy. In terms of economic policy, this means that in Saudi Arabia, fiscal, not monetary, policy is the primary instrument for economic growth management. Fiscal policy – or more precisely government expenditures – can be used to increase or decrease GDP, while monetary policy is focused on fixing the exchange rate and interest rates (NCB, 2001, Abalkhail, 2002, Jasser and Banafe, 2003). Monetary policy is used to "fine-tune" the effects of fiscal policy. With the SR effectively pegged to the US dollar since 1981 at a rate of 3.75 to the dollar, there have been limitations to Saudi monetary policy on interest rate adjustments. In effect, the SR interest rates closely track dollar interest rates, often with a small premium. This is graphically illustrated in Fig. 4.5, which sets out US and SR 3-month deposit rates for the period 1994–2009. SR premiums reflect periods of sharp falls in oil prices, cuts in government expenditures and regional tensions.

In essence, Saudi interest rates – and by implication, Saudi monetary policy – are closely tied to that of an external central bank, specifically that of the United States. What might be prudent and necessary monetary policy in the USA (expanding or dampening the money supply) might not necessarily be the most appropriate interest rate level desirable for Saudi Arabia at the same period of time. A further concern for SAMA is that, under the adopted fixed exchange rate policy, if SR interest rates did not closely track that of the US dollar, an *arbitrage* opportunity would exist for either US or Saudi investors to borrow in the low-interest-rate currency and invest in the high-interest-rate currency, making a risk-free profit due to the fixed exchange rate, after allowing for inflation differentials between the two countries.

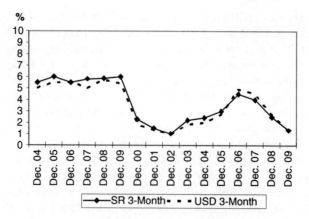

Fig. 4.5 US and Saudi interest rates 1994–2009 (Source: SAMA)

In Saudi Arabia, the exchange rate is central to monetary policy. SAMA's intervention under the fixed exchange rate regime is influenced by two factors: the level of foreign exchange outflow from the country and the level of dollar/riyal interest rate differentials. As such, SAMA's stated goals centre on internal price stability and balance of payments considerations. The monetary agency believes the fixed dollar/riyal peg has worked well due to the fact that "all of Saudi exports and most of its imports are denominated in dollars; the riyal is fully backed by foreign exchange reserves; such reserves are the result of oil revenues and investment income; the riyal is not a misaligned currency in terms of its nominal and effective exchange rates; and, finally, the stability of the dollar/riyal exchange rate sharply reduces risks for foreign investors." Table 4.2 sets out some of the major arguments for and against fixed exchange rate regimes that are applicable to Saudi Arabia.

Table 4.2 indicates that there are powerful arguments for both fixed and floating exchange rates. As far as Saudi Arabia is concerned, there is certainly some basis for reduction in investor risk due to a fixed rate policy. Saudi Arabia did not experience any of the upheavals seen in other countries during the East Asia and Mexican currency crisis of the mid- and late 1990s. However, there is some disagreement on the level of imported inflation and nominal and effective SR exchange rates, due to the SR being pegged to the US dollar. Disagreements on whether Saudi Arabia should adopt a fixed exchange rate pegged to one currency or to several currencies tend to arise as a result of the short- or long-term assumptions being made. Some argue that the fixed peg against the dollar has served Saudi Arabia well and will continue to do so in the long term with a minimal *devaluation* risk outlook as long as "there are no excesses . . . (and) government overspend, or external deficits surge . . ." (Azzam, 2002).

As stated earlier, Saudi Arabia has a pegged exchange rate regime, and monetary policy is geared to exchange rate targeting and pursuit of price and financial stability. In addition to its routine dollar sales to Saudi commercial banks, SAMA intervenes in the US dollar/SR spot and forward markets if need be to stabilize any signs of a

Table 4.2 Advantages and disadvantages of fixed and floating exchange rate regimes

Advantages	Disadvantages
Fixed exchange rate regimes	
• Maintains investors' confidence in the currency, thus encouraging domestic savings and investment and discouraging capital outflows • Reduces inflationary pressures associated with devaluation	• Does not allow the implementation of independent monetary policy • Exchange rates cannot be used to adjust for external shocks or imbalances • A fixed peg is also a fixed target for speculators
Floating exchange rate regimes	
• Allows pursuit of an independent monetary policy; when an economy suffers a downturn, monetary expansion can soften the impact • Allows a country to adjust to external shocks through exchange rates; that is, lower export prices and higher import prices would help the country regain external equilibrium	• Reduces investors' faith in the currency, thus discouraging capital inflows to avoid exchange risk • Floating rates can overshoot and become highly unstable, leading to speculation

Source: Adapted from Azzam, 2002, p. 98

volatile currency market condition resulting from speculative activity. In November 2008, SAMA for example, introduced unlimited swap arrangements for local banks, allowing them to exchange riyals for equivalent amounts of dollar.

SAMA's swap actions were important for several reasons. First, there had been a large outflow of speculative funds initially betting on an exchange rate revaluation once oil prices fell sharply in 2009 and the massive deleveraging in global financial markets. This had affected bank deposits and led to a shortage of US dollar denominated funds. Second, the rapid growth in loans in 2008 and shortfall in the growth of deposits contributed to a rise in the Saudi banks' loans-to-deposit ratios, which exceeded at one stage the 75% ceiling prescribed by SAMA and constrained the capacity of the banking sector to take new loans.

The fixed exchange rate policy of the Kingdom raises a number of challenges, sometimes rendering the monetary policy rather rigid. This occurred during a period of intense speculation on a possible revaluation or even a "depeg" away from the dollar during 2008. As the SR's peg to the US dollar meant that SAMA had to reciprocate any Federal Reserve cuts to prevent arbitrage opportunities, the Saudi macroeconomic conditions unsupportive of any domestic cut further strengthened the "depeg" argument. This was made evident in SAMA's repo rate cuts which ran contrary to the appropriate policies when Saudi Arabia was witnessing record high inflation levels and rising liquidity. The rate cuts as illustrated in Fig. 4.6 led to more severe negative real interest rates and fuelled inflation further.

SAMA however sees no permanent solution emerging from a revaluation of the currency. It was argued, correctly as it turned out in 2009, that revaluation might temporarily reduce inflation, but the pressure might still be stocked up by domestic

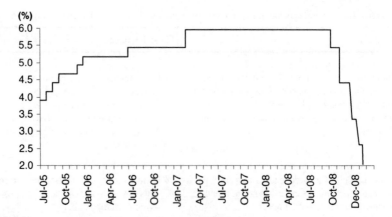

Fig. 4.6 Saudi Arabia: interest rate developments (Source: SAMA)

bottlenecks in supply. Revaluation might also have reduced the government revenues from oil and the value of SAMA's official reserves. As such, SAMA depended on the other instrument policies described earlier such as the easing of reserve requirements to free up liquidity.

Saudi Banks Have Ample Reserves

Saudi banks have built-up reserves well above SAMA's official CRR requirements as illustrated in Fig. 4.7 and Table 4.3.

From Table 4.3 we note that the average statutory deposit ratio with SAMA has ranged from 4.3 to 4.5% in the period to 2005, but rose to 5.3% levels by Q1 2009. To put this in historical context, the average deposit reserve ratio stood at 6.3% in

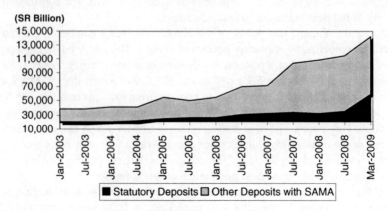

Fig. 4.7 Banks reserves well above requirement (Source: SAMA)

Table 4.3 Reserve position of Saudi banks (end of years)

	1999	2001	2002	2005	2007	2008	2009(Q1)
(A) Deposits with SAMA	SR Million						
Cash in vault	5,468	3,453	4,892	7.201	10,019	4,007	10,627
Current deposits	572	197	1,750	2238	3143	751	1259
Statutory deposits	10,504	12,599	14,270	21,039	36,142	44,297	46,414
Other deposits	1	2,874	7,732	2167	59,310	41,116	79,542
Bank reserves	16,545	19,122	28,643	32,646	108,614	97,171	137,842
(B) Ratios (%) to bank deposits							
Cash in vault	2.2	1.2	1.5	1.5	1.4	1.3	1.3
Current deposits with SAMA	0.2	0.1	0.5	0.5	0.4	0.1	0.1
Statutory deposits with SAMA	4.3	4.5	4.3	4.3	3.0	5.2	5.3
Other deposits with SAMA	–	1	2.4	0.4	8.3	4.9	9.0
Bank reserves (%)	6.7	6.8	8.7	6.7	15.1	11.5	15.6

Source: SAMA

1970, 11.5% in 1980 and 4.5% in 1986/1987. However, "other" reserve deposits held with SAMA peaked at SR 12 billion or 9.5% in 1986/1987 (SAMA, 2003), a reflection of SAMA's occasional requests for such "extra" reserves to be deposited by banks during periods of "extraordinary" banking activities. During 1986/1987, the Saudi banks, as shall be explored more fully in the next chapter faced some loan collection difficulties, and SAMA's request for additional reserves was a prudent measure to safeguard the banks' liquidity "safety net." Similarly, in 2002, Saudi banks witnessed private capital repatriation from abroad following the September 11, 2001 events and SAMA encouraged banks to place such funds with it in "other deposits" to avoid overheating certain sectors of the economy.

Inter-bank domestic market transactions are exempted from reserve requirements, but offshore banks' riyal deposits with the domestic banks are subject to CRR.

SAMA has always felt that Saudi banks should not be subject to sudden liquidity pressures due to local or regional uncertainties. As such, a relatively high level of statutory liquidity ratio (SLR) in comparison with banks in more developed economies is imposed on Saudi banks. A minimum amount of specified liquid assets equal to 20% of their demand and time liabilities is set, making Saudi banks fairly liquid, but imposing a "withholding tax" on lost potential earnings by Saudi banks.

Reliance on "Open-Market" Operations

As indicated in Table 4.1, SAMA has several other monetary policy instruments at its disposal, including *foreign exchange swaps*, *placement of public funds* and *open-market operations*. Placement of public funds with banks is entirely at SAMA's discretion and complements its efforts to fine-tune day-to-day liquidity instruments.

The placement of public funds is a way of "rough-tuning" the money supply; basically the Central Bank is seen to provide long-term liquidity support to a bank. In Saudi Arabia SAMA does this by placing the funds of semi-autonomous government institutions. SAMA has used this in the past to provide support to those banks facing liquidity problems or going through crisis management. The effect, however, is to reduce the returns of those government institutions whose funds are being placed at lower-than-market rates, but, more importantly, it sends a negative signal to the market about the state of health of the recipient bank.

Central bank support, unless it is a temporary measure to be followed by an asset and liability restructuring and by management changes, might induce banks to take more risks, creating a "moral hazard" situation. SAMA has used this type of support infrequently, aware that uncertainty about one bank could easily spread to the rest of the banking sector.

In common with most other developed central banks, SAMA has come to rely more on *repos* and *reverse repos* as the most flexible operating instruments of monetary policy, through the buying and selling of government bonds and securities in so-called "open-market operations." A central bank can alter the liquidity position of banks through dealing directly in the market by reducing liquidity (selling securities) or injecting liquidity (buying back securities), but the effectiveness of such operations depends on the size and depth of the capital market, specifically the number of institutional players who are buying and selling securities besides the central bank.

The Saudi *bond market* is still in its early stages, mainly restricted to SAMA, the Saudi banks and a few other institutions. The new Saudi *Capital Market Law* envisages broadening the range of instruments and players over time, as will be discussed in later chapters. In the short term, open-market operations are an effective and more precise tool in changing the money supply of the banking system through the buying and selling of government short- and long-term securities. These instruments are deemed to be "gilt-edged" or default-free, with other financial instruments priced above them to reflect liquidity and credit risk.

In 1986 the Saudi Arabian government introduced its first borrowing instrument – the Bankers Special Deposit Account or BSDA – as a means of financing growing budget deficits and as an alternative to drawing down on foreign assets to finance the budget deficits. Table 4.4 sets out the main securities that are currently offered by SAMA and it illustrates how far SAMA has come since those pioneering days.

Table 4.4 reveals an extensive "menu" of financial securities that are now on offer, ranging from very short term liquid instruments such as 1-week treasury bills to long-dated 10-year bonds. The introduction of floating rate notes (FRNs) in 1996 added a new dimension and provided a further rate risk-adjusted option for purchases of Saudi government securities. Pricing is competitive compared to other market instruments, with premiums added to longer-dated securities, especially for government development bonds (GDBs), which in turn are priced at a premium to comparable US bonds. Repo facilities are provided at 35% of total bank holdings of government securities and offered at Market Related Rates or MMRs. SAMA's official repurchase rate (ORR) is also available to banks seeking credit, up to the maximum limit of 0.5% of eligible securities. The ORR rate level is determined by

Table 4.4 SAMA: current securities offerings

Security issue	Currency denomination	Duration	Pricing	Offering	Observation
Treasury bills (T-Bills)	SR	1, 4, 13, 26 and 52 weeks	SR Interbank BID rate	Weekly basis	Replaced the 180 days Bankers Special Deposit Accounts
Floating rate notes (FRNs)	SR	5 and 7-year maturities	Saudi Interbank Offer Rate (SIBOR) Plus Margin	Monthly basis	Introduced in 1996 to provide rate risk hedging
Government development bonds (GDBs)	SR	2, 3, 5, 7 and 10-year maturities	Priced to reflect relative value in alternative investments (US bonds) plus 25–75 basis points premium	Quarterly basis	Issued on a fortnightly basis until 1996

Source: SAMA Annual Reports

SAMA. Given the extremely small amount of credit available to banks at the ORR, this serves more as a signal to the domestic money market in the absence of an official discount rate, than as a transactional influence. "Reverse repos" allow Saudi banks to deposit surplus funds with SAMA for a short period of time. The rate of investment is called the reverse repo rate (RRR) and is priced at below inter-bank bid rates.

Repos and reverse repos are thus automatic mechanisms for regulating the banking system's liquidity. According to SAMA's most recent annual reports, repo and reverse repo agreements entered into with commercial banks averaged SR 1.6 billion during the first quarter of 2009 compared with SR 1.4 billion in the corresponding period of 2008. The figures for reverse repo – banks placing excess liquidity with SAMA – were more staggering, averaging at SR 74.2 billion for first quarter 2009 compared with SR 78.4 billion for all of 2008. A significant factor was the placement of time deposits with domestic banks on behalf of government entities, but also indicated a risk aversion by Saudi banks to extending further credit to the Saudi private sector following the high-profile debt problems of Saudi corporate names such as the Al Gosaibi and Saad Groups during 2009.

Money Supply Creation and Monetary Policy

As analysed above, when exchange rate policy becomes the main plank of Saudi Arabia's monetary policy, it seems difficult to pursue a counter-cyclical monetary policy that is independent of the role of fiscal policy on Saudi GDP growth, money demand/supply and inflation. The major factors influencing monetary aggregates in the Kingdom are the government's fiscal operations and private sector balance-of-payments deficits.

In an oil-based economy like Saudi Arabia, the creation of money typically proceeds as follows. The Government maintains its accounts with SAMA. The receipt of oil revenues by the government, nearly all in US dollars, directly produces a rise in government deposits held in SAMA's international bank accounts. These foreign oil revenues have no immediate impact on domestic liquidity, since by definition domestic liquidity is held only by the private sector. Only when the government makes payments to contractors is the inflow of foreign exchange translated into domestic liquidity. When expenditures are made, the government draws checks on SAMA, which means SAMA's liabilities are shifted to the banks, thus facilitating credit creation by the banks.

SAMA effectively transforms the dollars held by it on behalf of the government into SRs, while still holding the dollars as backing for the "created" SR money supply. It is the private sector's transactions with the rest of the world that affect domestic liquidity. Given that the Saudi economy is an open economy, and that there are no capital restrictions, a large fraction of the domestic riyals received by households, contractors and foreigners operating in the Kingdom are converted into foreign currencies to pay for imported goods, remittances and investments abroad. This reverses the process of money supply creation, and partially offsets the money creation effects of the government. This is illustrated diagrammatically in Fig. 4.8.

The diagram is a simplified one, as it assumes that all government SR payments are converted into dollars and are transmitted as leakages out of the system. The net effect in this case is that while SAMA receives back all SRs through dollar sales to the Saudi banking system, it has in effect "extinguished" the available stock of SR money supply through its drawdown of foreign currency deposits.

In Fig. 4.8 the outflows from SAMA's foreign currency accounts exactly match the dollar leakages of the private sector. In reality, the amount of "leakage" is a function of the amount of remittances, the propensity to import and the amounts retained in the domestic economy by Saudi companies and individuals. The Saudi domestic money creation process seems to set it aside from other economies, where the quantity of money supplied responds to demand for the local currency through the banking system, through the selling of foreign assets or through the "printing of money." In the Saudi model, external government transactions also have no impact on domestic liquidity, as they represent bookkeeping entries in SAMA's foreign currency accounts.

Given the above, it is important to assess the causative factors for changes in Saudi Arabia's broad money supply, or M3, so as to work out the actual net domestic expenditure of the government and the balance of payments deficit of the private sector. This is set out in Table 4.5 for selected years from 1986 to 2009.

From Table 4.5, we note that the rate of monetary expansion M3 fluctuates over the period in question, reflecting a variety of factors. The positives include government expenditures during periods of regional tensions (such as the 1990/1991

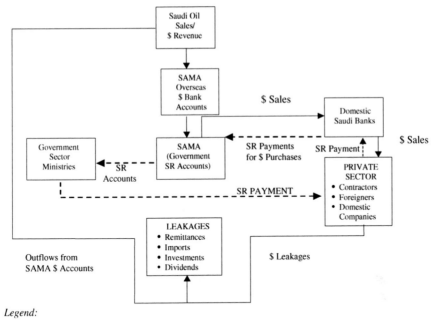

Fig. 4.8 Saudi Arabia: domestic money creation process

Table 4.5 Factors affecting changes in Saudi M3 (selected years)

	1986	1989	1997	2002	2007	2008	2009Q1
	SR billion						
Net domestic flows through government spending[a]	71.7	69.1	145.3	154.2	461.2	339.7	101.2
Commercial banks claims on the private sector	1.2	2.8	10.1	18.8	101.9	156.7	101.2
Net private sector balance of payments	−85.7	−96.0	−121.9	−161.0	−216.1	−344.0	−130.2
Net other items[b]	23.3	25.9	−24.2	37.1	−220.3	−7.7	61.1
Change in M3	10.5	1.8	9.3	49.1	129.2	139.4	131.6
Annual growth rate of M3 (%)	7.0	1.0	5.2	15.2	19.6	17.6	15.5

[a]Including net loans disbursed by government-sponsored credit institutions
[b]Includes payments for goods and services as well as capital outflow
Source: SAMA

Gulf War) as well as higher oil revenues (2007, 2008). Counteracting these positive developments are net private sector balance of payments outflows, which were
consistent for all the years. "Net other items" showed periods of capital outflows
(1991–1997), but was mostly a net capital inflow in 2002 following uncertainties
after 11 September 2001. Capital outflows were prominent in the high oil price
boom years of 2007 and 2008, but there was a net capital inflow in 2009 reflecting
uncertainties over international financial market events in 2008/2009.

Composition of Saudi Arabia's Money Supply

Evidence from many countries that have developed their financial markets seems
to suggest that people will gradually shift towards savings and other yield-bearing
instruments and away from cash and current accounts over time. A shift from a
cash-orientated society is taking place in Saudi Arabia, as illustrated in Table 4.6.

Table 4.6   Saudi Arabia monetary ratios (%)

End of year	Currency/M3	M1/M3	M2/M3
1972	44.4	73.3	88.8
1982	25.5	64.1	86.2
1997	16.8	51.9	80.3
1998	16.0	49.7	79.3
1999	18.3	52.0	80.4
2000	16.2	52.6	81.5
2001	14.9	54.3	82.1
2002	13.7	53.2	81.6
2003	14.2	54.4	81.8
2004	12.1	54.4	82.2
2005	12.1	51.2	81.3
2006	10.5	47.3	81.6
2007	9.3	48.6	84.4
2008	8.9	45.8	85.4
2009(1Q)	8.6	47.6	84.5

Source: SAMA

While Table 4.6 shows a downward trend in currency held outside banks over
time (currency/M3), seasonal fluctuations occur in Saudi Arabia each year around
the two major Muslim calendar events: the *Ramadan* month of fasting and the *Hajj*
or pilgrimage season. Demand for cash increases sharply during these periods, as
well as to a lesser extent during the summer school vacation, when currency outside
banks reaches its peak.

A key factor in the steady rise in demand deposits is the increase in such deposits
as bank customers feel more confident about the monetary stability of the country and the soundness of the banking system. The expansion of the use of credit,
debit and direct payment cards will also necessitate the use of such accounts to
satisfy the *transaction motive* for holding money. The growth in time and saving

accounts also indicates that the population's general reluctance and inhibition to receive interest payments due to religious reasons is somewhat diminishing, thereby increasing the *investment motive* for holding money. The increase in time deposits over the years has had a more significant effect on the Saudi banking industry, as this has encouraged Saudi banks to increase the maturity profile of their loans to longer periods and to improve the terms of such longer-term loans. They can more easily match their assets with a longer liability base, further monetizing the Saudi economy.

Financial Deepening of the Saudi Economy

"Financial deepening" is sometimes difficult to quantify, and different measures have been used for other Arab Gulf countries that can be applied to Saudi Arabia (Eltony, 2000). The measures used are as follows:

> K – Currency ratio (cc/M1)
> Z – Monetization ratio (M2/GDP)
> KK – Mobilizing longer-term assets (M1/GDP)

Table 4.7 shows the results of this financial deepening over the period 1971–2008, encompassing the pre-boom, boom and adjustment periods of the Saudi Arabian economy.

Table 4.7 Financial deepening in Saudi Arabia (%) 1971–2008

Year	K	Z	KK
1971	62.9	13.8	11.3
1973	52.4	13.6	11.7
1979	41.6	21.9	20.2
1986	44.3	39.0	16.1
1990	43.7	36.1	26.1
1997	32.4	35.3	22.8
2000	30.9	36.2	23.4
2001	27.3	38.8	25.6
2002	26.2	39.9	26.9
2003	25.4	42.4	28.2
2004	22.16	56.4	29.2
2005	22.67	53.2	37.1
2006	22.17	68.5	39.7
2007	18.82	82.0	47.2
2008	19.51	93.4	50.1

K – Currency ratio (cc/M1); Z – Monetization ratio (M2/GDP); KK – Mobilizing long-term assets (M1/GDP)
Source: SAMA

The currency ratio (K) reflects the degree of sophistication of the domestic financial sector. The monetization ratio (Z) reflects the size of the financial market, while KK is a measure of the extent of monetization and mobilization of long-term assets.

The Saudi data show that the currency ratio (K) followed a decreasing trend, similar to Kuwait data over the same period for the Eltony study. This signifies a high degree of diversification of financial institutions and greater use of non-currency forms of transaction media, such as other bank accounts. The ratio fell from nearly 63% in 1971 to around 20% in 2008.

The monetization variable (Z) also indicates significant improvements over the data period. This ratio has increased significantly from 14% levels in the early 1970 period to 50% in 2008, indicating further expansion in the financial market relative to non-financial markets. This in turn implies a faster accumulation of a wide range of financial assets, such as savings accounts. The KK ratio reflects the degree of sophistication of the financial market shown by the level of dependency on cash or liquidity preferences in the Saudi economy. This also has shown significant improvement over the study time period. In summary, the Saudi financial sector is showing substantial improvement in achieving financial deepening.

SAMA and Inflation Control Policies

According to SAMA, monetary policy continued to be "geared to the objective of maintaining domestic price and exchange rate stability." The considerable inflation witnessed by Saudi Arabia during the early "boom" years of 1974–1976, when inflation reached around 30% p.a., has been effectively tackled (Johany, 1986), but it became a major concern during the period 2007–2009 before subsiding again. Table 4.8 and Fig. 4.9 illustrate the sharp rise in the cost of living index in Saudi Arabia from almost negligible levels of under 1% in 2005 to nearly 10% by 2008. By end 2009, this had fallen to around 4.6% levels.

Table 4.8 Annual growth rates of selected indicators, including inflation (2005–2008)

	2005	2006	2007	2008
Non-oil GDP deflator (1999 = 109)	4.1	3.7	1.6	2.4
Cost of living index (1999 = 108)	0.7	2.2	4.1	9.9
Non-oil GDP (at constant prices)	5.2	5.1	4.7	4.3
Government expenditures	21.5	13.5	18.5	11.5
Money supply (M3)	11.6	19.3	19.6	17.6

Source: SAMA

Table 4.8 also summarizes the main inflation indicators as well as setting out the growth in money supply and Gross Domestic Product (GDP). In order to arrive at a better estimation for changes in the domestic economy and to isolate the impact of oil on the GDP, the non-oil GDP deflator is used. This is a price index that employs the current year's output mix for calculating a price index, using a base

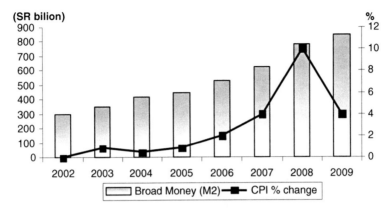

Fig. 4.9 Saudi Arabia money supply growth M2 and CPI % change (Source: SAMA)

year. Because GDP refers to the value added within Saudi Arabia during a year, the non-oil GDP deflator is a measure of domestic inflation. However, it is still an imperfect measurement as much of Saudi Arabia's GDP is produced by foreign-owned factors of production (labour) and the GDP deflator includes this element. What Table 4.8 also seems to indicate is that inflation has been impacted by the growth in money supply with M2 money supply growing rapidly from 2007. While there are other factors that account for Saudi inflation which will be analysed below, there is also some evidence that the quantity of money that the government was injecting was a factor rather than the velocity of money, which declined as illustrated in Table 4.9.

Table 4.9 Income velocity of money (non-oil sector) 1998–2008

Years	M1	M2	M3
1998	3.82	2.46	1.98
1999	4.12	2.64	2.11
2000	4.42	2.86	2.32
2001	3.94	2.60	2.13
2002	3.66	2.46	2.01
2004	2.11	1.14	1.14
2005	2.04	1.32	1.07
2006	2.09	1.25	1.02
2007	1.92	1.10	0.91
2008	1.67	0.96	0.80

Source: SAMA

Table 4.9 indicated that there was no positive correlation between Saudi money supply growth and the level of inflation. As such, the monetarist equation $MV = PY$ does not seem to hold, where M is money supply, V is velocity of money, P is the price index and Y is real income.

   The quantity theory of money relates output in the economy to the velocity of money, the money supply and the price level. Velocity of money is defined simply as the rate at which money circulates in the economy. If velocity is high, money is circulating quickly, and a relatively small money supply can fund a relatively large amount of purchases. On the other hand, if velocity is low, then money is circulating slowly, and it needs a much larger money supply to fund the same number of purchases. From the above figures, there seem to be other factors which also influenced inflation.

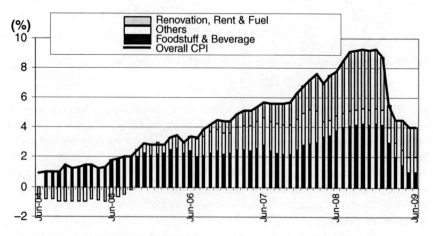

Fig. 4.10 Drivers of inflation (Source: SAMA)

   The pick-up in Saudi inflation was seemingly accentuated by the following factors, illustrated in Fig. 4.10, which sets out the key drivers of inflation:

- Supply bottlenecks in 2007/2008, especially in the real estate sector where residential demand for a young population was strong. The rental element of the consumer price index was a key factor. This is illustrated in Fig. 4.8; rent rose by 18.3% during 2008, impacting the CPI index due to the heavy weighting this item has in the index.
- During the oil-led boom of 2007/2008, Saudi Arabia and many of the Arabian Gulf countries suffered from shortages of skilled labour, causing salaries to rise, especially in the construction and finance sectors.
- Global food prices were a contributing factor during 2008, with the price of wheat and rice forced up by the shift in biofuels in some countries, restrictions on rice exports by some key exporting nations in order to combat their own domestic shortages and unusual global weather patterns affecting food production.
- Trading partners' inflationary pressure, with imports from non-dollar regions affecting Saudi imports from such regions.

By 2009, some of these strains began to unwind and price pressures subsided as illustrated earlier in Fig. 4.10.

The Economic and Social Impact of Inflation

Although Saudi Arabian inflation levels eased by 2009/2010 to 4.6–5% levels, there is some concern that the era of virtual low-or zero-level inflation in periods of induced economic growth was over, and inflation was a phenomenon that Saudi Arabia and others in the Gulf economies have to learn to live with. High rates of inflation can have several consequences on nations, as they tend to operate on different channels (Moody's, 2008):

1. *Fiscal* – Inflation, if unanticipated, can have a beneficial effect on a government's debt burden as the stock of local currency debt is eroded in real terms. This played a role in the past when some countries (e.g. some Latin American countries in the 1980s) attempted to "inflate their debt away." This effect is often offset over the longer term, however, by a range of negative developments. Governments can find it difficult to maintain fiscal discipline during inflationary periods as citizens demand compensatory increases in salaries, subsidies and welfare payments to offset their declining purchasing power. Governments' creditors can demand higher and more flexible interest rates. Inflation can also undermine confidence and cause an exchange rate depreciation which can swell the cost of servicing foreign currency debt in local currency terms.
2. *Political* – High rates of inflation often raise social tensions as the purchasing power of citizens, especially those on lower incomes, is undermined. Governments and public and private employers are sometimes reluctant to raise wages, subsidies and welfare payments quickly enough in order to offset this, partly because of a justified fear that such increases will exacerbate inflationary pressures and lead to further demands. The social impact of inflation can be particularly harmful if surging inflation damages the real sector and causes higher unemployment.
3. *Economic* – High rates of inflation can jeopardize growth by deterring productive investment, perverting market incentives and encouraging wage hikes. The free functioning of markets can also be hampered by the introduction of unorthodox economic measures such as price controls as governments attempt to stem inflation through alternative means.

Elements of all the above inflation control measures were introduced by Saudi Arabia in 2008/2009 and included cuts in custom tariffs on food such as foreign poultry, dairy products and vegetable oils from 20 to 5%, reduction in levies on building materials such as paints, electrical cables and plastic pipes to 5% and complete elimination of duties on wheat products. The government, besides introducing the staggered 15% salary rise for government employees, also introduced subsidies

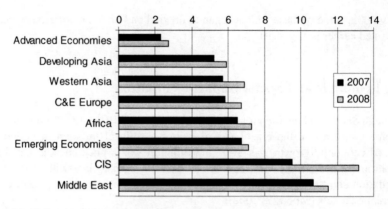

Fig. 4.11 Regional inflation rates (%) (Source: IMF)

on rice imports, other cost-of-living allowances and welfare payments (Saudi Press Agency, May, 2008). According to the IMF, the Middle East region experienced the highest level of inflation in 2007 out of any region globally and the second highest level in 2008 after the Commonwealth of Independent States (CIS) as illustrated in Fig. 4.11.

In 2007, the Middle East region inflation averaged at 10.4% and almost double the emerging market average of 6.4%, and was still higher in 2008. The last year in which the Middle East region's average inflation rate exceeded 10% was in 1995.

However, there is a broad variation in inflation rates among countries of the Middle East and in the Gulf Cooperation Council countries in particular, as illustrated in Fig. 4.12.

According to the 2008 IMF data, year-on-year inflation ranges from a high of 16.4% in Egypt to a low of 3.7% in Morocco. Saudi inflation rates are below those of

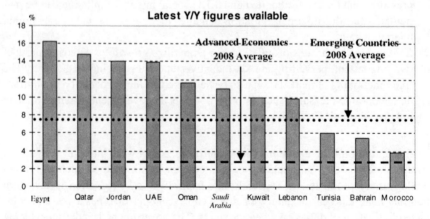

Fig. 4.12 Monthly inflation rates in Middle East countries (Source: IMF)

Qatar, the United Arab Emirates (UAE) and Oman, but slightly higher than Kuwait and much higher than Bahrain's, all members of the GCC.

Managing the Kingdom's Reserves

One important function that SAMA performs is managing Saudi Arabia's external reserve assets. While reserve assets have seen a sharp reduction from peaks in the mid-1980s due to government drawdowns to fund deficits, SAMA still considers this function an important means of diversification in its effort to improve the Kingdom's reserve portfolio.

In line with its evolution of financial instruments and risk management techniques, and in common with other central banks that manage national reserves, SAMA has made a more active use of a broad range of such investment instruments and has developed more performance benchmarks, compared to a mid-1970s investment strategy that was largely confined to bank deposits. Assets allocation then meant deposit allocation among major international banks based on their credit rating.

SAMA's Investment Committee is headed by the Governor and meets regularly to assess market conditions, asset allocation and market performance before deciding on investment decisions. The overall aim is still to preserve principal value with maximum liquidity and returns. As such, safety, liquidity and risk-adjusted returns are the driving goals. SAMA continued to apply these basic principles of investment guidelines during the global financial crisis of 2008/2009 and Fig. 4.13 illustrates SAMA's net foreign assets which reached a peak in October 2008 of around $430 billion before falling back.

The fall in SAMA's foreign assets in 2009 could be explained by several factors, including a rise in government deposits with Saudi banks, the repayment of around

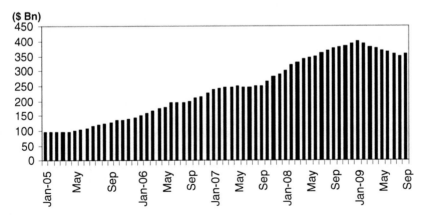

Fig. 4.13 SAMA net foreign assets (Source: SAMA)

$18 billion of Saudi bills and bonds held by Saudi commercial banks, and a Saudi transfer of around $10.2 billion to the IMF as part of the Kingdom's commitment to the IMF following the April 2009 G20 London meeting.

In its investment policy, SAMA also emphasizes portfolio benchmarking and performance measurement in order to evaluate internally managed and externally managed discretionary portfolios. In terms of current credit ratings for counterparty institutions, SAMA requires a minimum rating of "C" by the Fitch IBCA rating agency for bank deposits. Sovereign fixed income and supranational and corporate obligations have to be rated at AAA or AA by Moody's and S&P. The US dollar is used as the base currency and it dominates the currency composition of SAMA's portfolios, followed by other major currencies such as the Euro, Sterling and Yen. Currency allocations are not linked to trade flows according to SAMA. The benchmarks that SAMA uses reflect the monetary agency's diversity of assets and risk tolerance and include S&P 500 for the US equity markets, JP Morgan Global Bond Index for multi-currency bond portfolios, Morgan Stanley Composite Index for Europe and TSE for Japan. External fund managers are allocated funds and manage portfolios under SAMA-approved asset guidelines. Portfolio performance is measured on a total return basis with liquidation based on either poor performance or for reasons of asset allocation.

The global financial crisis that erupted in 2008 and affected many sovereign investors seemed not to have affected SAMA's investments as much as other GCC sovereign investors who had ventured into global equity markets for higher returns. Figure 4.14 sets out the size of assets under management by SAMA and other regional Sovereign Wealth Funds (SWFs) as of 2007 and 2008.

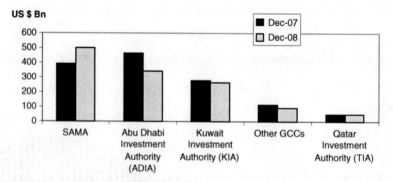

Fig. 4.14 Assets under management by SAMA and regional SWFs (Source: SAMA, IMF)

The conservative management of SAMA reserves has meant that savings have not been eroded by the collapse of global markets and asset prices at the end of 2008 and are in a relatively liquid form. The majority of SAMA's assets are estimated to be government debt, notably US bonds. SAMA is not expected to have seen the degree of losses estimated to have been realized by the funds for future generations or oil stabilization funds in other GCC countries. Although Saudi Arabia has indicated that it is setting up an investment fund in 2009 (*Sanabel*), it is expected to be only a very small portion of its assets (less than USD 6.0 billion), and SAMA is expected to pursue its current conservative capital preservation investment policy.

Future Development and Challenges

SAMA is faced by several domestic and international challenges in the years ahead that could test the monetary agency's ability to adapt to new circumstances. Table 4.10 summarizes SAMA's major challenges in the short, medium and long term.

SAMA has come a long way from those early exotic days of 1952 and, in essence, it is now a fully fledged central bank in all but name. It has tried to overcome the

Table 4.10 Challenges faced by SAMA

Short term	Medium term	Long term
• Control of money laundering and terrorism funding	• Establishing guidelines for Islamic banking supervision and regulation	• Effective participation through Islamic Banking Financial Services Board
• E-commerce application and internet banking	• Ensuring Saudi banks comply with new BIS capital adequacy ratios	• Effective participation in Gulf Cooperation Council Monetary Union and proposed single currency for GCC
• Ensure Saudi banks are adequately prepared following WTO accession	• Supervision and integration of newly licensed foreign banks into Saudi banking system	• Implement fine-tuning instruments for inflation targeting
• Overseeing effective *Saudization* of bank personnel	• Effective participation in international financial supervisory standards	• Supervision and regulation of cross-border Saudi bank mergers and acquisitions
• Establishment of data base and supervision of the insurance sector	• Supervision and regulation of non-bank financial institutions into the markets such as mortgage lenders	• Re-examine SR/US dollar fixed exchange parity policy and exchange rate targeting mechanism
• Completion of mergers of local money exchangers into one financial institution	• Develop secondary market instruments for capital market	• Apply lessons from 2008/2009 financial crisis in terms of vigilance on capital requirements and liquidity cushion
• Overseeing partial privatization of government-held bank shares in capital market	• Upgrade SAMA's Banking Training Institute to provide broader financial services expertise	• Ensure better risk management processes control and corporate governance
		• Initiate macroeconomic monetary policy forecasting models and publish minutes of policy meeting and decisions for private sector guidance

limitations imposed on it through its founding charter and has successfully introduced a range of innovative capital market instruments to add to the liquidity options of the Saudi commercial banks.

By its own admission, SAMA recognizes that in the years ahead it faces a range of domestic, regional and international challenges. Key objectives set out by SAMA include expediting the issue of regulations and legislations aimed at promoting and expanding the range of financial services in conformity with the "trends towards liberalization of international financial markets and WTO requirements" (SAMA, 2009). This, according to the monetary agency, requires the streamlining of operations of the capital and insurance markets and other financial services. SAMA also advocates changes to the current judicial system as it relates to commercial, financial and banking transactions and contracts, such as insurance and mortgages, as Saudi commercial banks do not currently possess the legal means to mortgage property in their own name.

The fact that the Saudi government is considering the introduction of a commercial mortgage law is a step in the right direction towards safeguarding Saudi financial institutions' rights while deepening the mortgage sectors' financing capability.

The list of challenges set out in Table 4.10 seems daunting, but SAMA has already started to confront some of the issues. A notable success has been the vigorous implementation of procedures to prevent money laundering and the funding of terrorism. SAMA received a clean bill of health on these matters from the Financial Action Task Force (FATF) in April 2004. The Kingdom was commended by FATF for taking several measures including freezing the accounts suspected of illegal dealings and requesting that all Saudi banks complete "know your customer" formalities or close accounts. Under SAMA's recommendations, the Saudi cabinet endorsed Saudi Arabia's first anti-money laundering law, which stipulated stiff penalties.

Saudization of bank personnel is proceeding apace with SAMA insisting that qualified Saudi personnel be appointed to key positions, based on appointment criteria focused on technical proficiency. To help upgrade local banking skills, SAMA's Banking Training Institute is running a wider range of training courses to meet future financial market needs, including those for the local insurance markets.

Islamic banking services and operations are becoming more important for SAMA, given the expansion of such services by most Saudi banks and the GCC countries. SAMA became a member of the Islamic Banking Financial Services Board in 2002, which will help in establishing new guidelines and rules to oversee this important market segment. Future development might necessitate a separate banking control law, targeting Islamic financial institutions and subjecting them to proper rules and supervision. This has been successfully achieved in nearby Bahrain, where Islamic banking supervision coexists side by side with "conventional" and investment banking activities. The new SAMA Governor Dr. Mohammed Al Jasser has been quoted in public that Islamic financing has an important role to play in the stability of the region's financial system as the 2008/2009 global financial crisis highlighted the apparent safety record of the Islamic banking sector versus the conventional banking sector. The key long-term issue is prudent supervision of this sector to avoid moral hazard, given the trust placed by ordinary investors when investing with Islamic institutions.

Other long-term issues that might need to be addressed include revisiting SAMA's 1966 Banking Control Law to allow the monetary agency to make more effective use of the full range of monetary policy instruments. In particular, there must be a wider use of the open-market operations, with outright sales and purchases of government securities by the central bank itself as a monetary tool, as opposed to the current policy of action initiated by Saudi commercial banks. This will add depth and breadth to the capital market.

Following the resurgence of inflation in the Gulf economies in 2008, SAMA's inflation control policies will become more important and mechanisms will have to be adopted and fine-tuned that sometimes gives SAMA the flexibility to act in a counter-cyclical manner to US monetary policy and reduce the effect of a pegged currency regime for the SR.

Managing the branches of foreign banks operating in Saudi Arabia post WTO accession in 2005 will also be an added challenge to SAMA in the medium and long term. With globalization of banking and financial services, the relationship between regulators and foreign banks or subsidiaries of foreign banks operating in their jurisdictions has come under greater scrutiny. The global financial crisis of 2008/2009 has added further urgency in the matter to avoid contagion to domestic institutions through systemic failures and risks emanating from the foreign banks' parent companies. SAMA seems to have adopted a "dual" regulatory approach. This includes a Saudi element as well as close coordination with the foreign banks' final home regulator.

In the long term, SAMA might face cross-border banking and other financial services mergers and acquisitions issues, with Saudi banks forming international strategic alliances and foreign banks acquiring interests in the Kingdom. This will test SAMA's cross-border regulatory and supervisory skills. SAMA will also need to supervise foreign-owned financial institutions in the Kingdom, whose objectives might be divergent from broader national considerations. This was the case in some instances in the 1970s, before the *Saudization* of foreign banks; it was one of the major factors for the *Saudization* drive to *align national* interests with those of the *Saudized* banks.

The issue of the GCC unified currency and monetary union seems to have taken a setback before the approach of the 2010 deadline. During 2010 it was decided that Riyadh would be the home of the envisaged GCC central bank, a decision which caused the UAE to withdraw from the planned GCC monetary union in protest. Oman had previously notified that it was not joining the proposed GCC currency, while Kuwait had opted for a managed exchange regime for its currency, instead of the peg against dollar favoured by Saudi Arabia, Bahrain and Qatar. Whether to opt for a unified GCC currency pegged to one currency – the US dollar – or to adopt a more flexible multi-currency peg will also be an important issue that SAMA will have to face. This could affect its current fixed parity rate policy.

SAMA will have to coordinate with these central banks on *economic convergence* and on internal harmonization of policies relating to inflation and budget deficit issues. This will require greater macroeconomic discipline by member states as well as central bank independence in voicing their concerns should target rates not be adhered to. SAMA acts, for all intents and purposes, as an independent central bank but its independent role must be further clarified to avoid undue influence by short-term economic measures based on political expediency.

SAMA now feels confident that it has gained sufficient experience from the *Saudization* era to be able to manage the new circumstances, helped by its active participation and membership in leading international multilateral bodies such as the IMF, the World Bank and the Bank for International Settlements (BIS), which SAMA joined in May 2009 and comprises 27 countries. The avoidance to date of any major financial crisis in Saudi Arabia compared to other economies world-wide attests to SAMA's regulatory and supervisory policies. The key is to ensure that Saudi Arabia's financial sector remains a vibrant and leading segment of the economy in the future.

Summary of Key Points

- *SAMA has evolved from being a monetary agency with a limited role into a fully fledged central bank with relative independence, a broad range of monetary tools at its disposal and with effective supervisory powers of the financial sector.*
- *Monetary policy is the primary focus of SAMA, whose key objectives are to stabilize inflation and the general level of prices, to maintain a fixed exchange rate policy against the US dollar and to allow a free movement of currency and capital.*
- *SAMA uses four main policy instruments in conducting monetary policy: cash reserve ratio/minimum reserve policy, repos and reverse repos, foreign exchange swaps and placement of public funds. It has increasingly relied on repos and reverse repos, the so-called "open-market" operations.*
- *Today SAMA offers a broad range and mix of securities on behalf of the government, ranging from short-term treasury bills (under 1 year) to 10-year government development bonds, priced at a premium to similar dated US Treasury bonds.*
- *SAMA's monetary policy assigns a high priority to its current fixed exchange policy as a means of controlling inflation, despite recent depreciation of the US dollar against major international currencies.*
- *Domestic money supply creation is a function of dollar reserves held abroad, domestic government spending and the effects of domestic purchases of foreign currencies for trade and remittances.*
- *There is evidence to suggest that the Saudi economy is going through "financial deepening" with a reduction in the level of currency ratio, increasing monetization and mobilization of long-term assets.*

- *SAMA is faced by future challenges including more effective participation in the GCC monetary union and the proposed single currency, developing a corporate bond market, the supervision and control of cross-border Saudi bank mergers and "new wave" foreign bank entry to the Saudi market, as well as overseeing the growth of Islamic finance and banking products in the Kingdom and combating inflationary trends.*

Chapter 5
The Financial Markets

When money speaks, the truth is silent.

Russian proverb

Learning Outcomes

By the end of this section, you would understand:

- *The role of the financial sector in Saudi Arabia's economic development*
- *The evolving structure of the Saudi banking sector*
- *SAMA and banking supervision*
- *The challenges faced by Saudi banking following the global financial crisis*
- *The performance of Saudi banks and non-bank players*
- *The Saudi insurance sector*
- *Growing importance of Islamic financing*

Introduction

The Saudi financial sector comprising commercial banks, the insurance sector and non-bank financing companies came out of the 2008/2009 global financial and credit crisis relatively unscathed, thanks to an accommodating policy of the Saudi Arabian Monetary Agency and a somewhat conservative Saudi banking sector compared to their international peers. Although some Saudi banks were forced to take large loan loss reserves to cover for possible domestic corporate defaults and exposure to some high-profile Saudi names, they are still in a better position when compared to the collapse of major banks and other financial institutions in the USA and Europe. Thus far only a limited number of Gulf banks have publicly admitted and quantified their exposure to the US subprime crisis. Only one Saudi part-government-owned Bahrain-based bank – Gulf Investment Bank – admitted to such exposure amounting to around $966 million and had to raise additional capital. In Saudi Arabia, SAMA was quick to announce that no serious Lehman Brothers exposure to Saudi banks existed, amid serious doubts that with time such exposure might well surface or

M.A. Ramady, *The Saudi Arabian Economy*, DOI 10.1007/978-1-4419-5987-4_5,
© Springer Science+Business Media, LLC 2010

might not be acknowledged. Some financial players in the Saudi market seemed to be directly affected though by events in the USA, and *Tawniya*, the leading Saudi insurance company, lost nearly two thirds of its market trading value in 2008, not because of any problems in its operating business but through possible exposure to dealings with the troubled US insurance giant AIG, which had to be bailed out by the US Treasury.

The most visible effects of the global financial crisis, thus, seem to have been caused not by direct exposure to troubled assets but in indirect form. Saudi Arabia and other GCC countries have seen some of their international cost of borrowing rise because of tightening credit, and this was also affected later by the events following the Dubai World loan standstill request, which will be analysed in fuller detail later in the chapter.

Notwithstanding current global uncertainties, the Saudi financial market stands at the threshold of a new era in its evolution, with the challenges of globalization affecting the sector. How it meets these challenges will be of critical importance, given the increasing significance of the financial sector and its intermediation role vis-à-vis the Saudi Gross Domestic Product, as illustrated in Fig. 5.1.

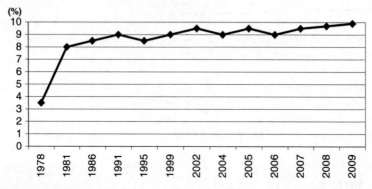

Fig. 5.1 Relative % contribution of finance and insurance sectors to non-oil GDP at current prices 1978–2009 (Source: SAMA)

By 2009, the finance and insurance sector contributed around 9.5% to the Saudi non-oil GDP, compared with around 3.5–4% in the 1970s. The opening up of the Saudi insurance sector to foreign companies and the entry of foreign banks have added an element of competition and depth to the Saudi financial sector. Implementing a Saudi mortgage law could also add depth to this sector by changing the way banks finance housing and introducing the possibility of adding non-bank mortgage financing companies into the Saudi market.

The Saudi Banking Sector

There are currently 20 banks operating in the Kingdom, a mixture of wholly owned Saudi banks and the so-called "*Saudized*" joint venture banks, which were obliged to dilute their ownership to allow majority Saudi ownership in the early 1980s, during the so-called bank *Saudization* phase initiated by SAMA. Table 5.1 lists the status of banks already operating in the Kingdom and those institutions that have obtained licences but are not yet operational.

Table 5.1 Status of banks holding licences to operate in Saudi Arabia (2010)

Bank ownership	Status
(A) Operational	• Wholly owned Saudi private sector: Al Rajhi, Al Bilad • Saudi private sector and government ownership: Riyad Bank, NCB, SAMBA, Al Inma • Joint venture banks: Saudi Fransi, Saudi British, Arab National, Al Jazira, Saudi Hollandi, Saudi Investment Bank • Foreign banks: Gulf International Bank, Bahrain, Emirates International Bank, Dubai, National Bank of Kuwait, Deutsche Bank, Muscat Bank, National Bank of Bahrain, J.P. Morgan Chase, BNP Paribas
(B) Licensed but non-operational	• HSBC, UK • National Bank of Pakistan • T.C. Ziraat Bankasi • State Bank of India

Table 5.1 shows that of the 19 operational banks, six are joint venture banks, three have some government ownership while three are wholly owned by the private sector. These banks operate on the universal banking model, which provides a broad range of products and services, brokerage facilities and derivative transactions, in addition to a variety of other consumer services such as credit cards, automated teller machines (ATMs) and point-of-sale transactions. In addition, Saudi banks offer and manage an increasing number of mutual funds.

Table 5.1 also highlights a diverse number of foreign banks that have obtained licences to operate in Saudi Arabia, despite problems related to domestic terrorism. This reflects a sense of optimism in the Kingdom's long-term economic development. SAMA has welcomed these international moves, hoping that they would contribute to activating competition amongst banks in Saudi Arabia. As of 2010 there were eight wholly foreign-owned banks operating in Saudi Arabia with a diverse ownership origin ranging from France, Germany and USA to other GCC countries. Banks from India, Pakistan and Turkey have obtained licences but are not yet operational. Their focus seems to be on capturing part of the remittance business of their fellow countrymen working in Saudi Arabia. There are some indications that given the closer economic and political relationships with the emerging economic giants of the twenty-first century such as China and Brazil, it will not be too long before there are bank representations from these countries in Saudi Arabia, and vice versa from Saudi banks, in order to intermediate in the increased trade flows between them.

Economic theorists on financial development and its impact on economic growth show some disagreement on whether financial institutions grow merely in response to the needs of society as their financial holding patterns evolve, or such financial institutions promote economic development per se by instigating changes themselves (Knight, 1998). There are suggestions in earlier literature on Saudi banking development that Saudi banking followed the passive or "demand-following" approach (Johany et al., 1986, Dukheil, 1995, Abdeen and Shook, 1984), but that more recently Saudi banks have been following a "supply-leading" approach, especially by introducing electronic banking and investment products (Abdullatif, 2002, Jasser, 2002, Fayez, 2002).

SAMA and Bank Supervision

The banking system in Saudi Arabia reflects the generally conservative social environment of the country, especially on issues relating to interest and perceptions of *riba* or usury. Under this environment, SAMA applies various rules and policies to regulate the financial markets, as we discussed in the preceding chapter. The main

Table 5.2 Saudi Arabia bank supervisory guiding policies

Guiding policy	Observation
• Maintain open and liberal financial market with minimal restriction on capital flow	• Effectively carried out, including minimal restrictions on capital flow
• Strong and healthy banking sector to maintain sustainable economic growth	• Saudi bank profitability is one of the highest in the world and its banking system has grown and adapted as the economy evolved
• Promote fair competition in financial and banking services	• More competition needed due to excessive bank concentration; foreign bank presence could promote more competition
• Benefit from participation of foreign banks and foreign shareholders so as to transfer technology, training of Saudi personnel and improve risk management practices	• Achieved with *Saudization* of banks in a smooth manner; Saudi banking personnel are in key positions and Saudi banks are positively rated by credit rating agencies
• Ensure Saudi financial markets are at cutting edge of communication and IT	• Achieved, for Saudi banking is one of the most technologically advanced in the world
• Pursue the adoption and implementation of global standards, principles and practices	• Achieved thorough SAMA supervision and the adoption of joint venture best banking practices
• Ensure availability of qualified Saudi finance professionals and training facilities	• Achieved through SAMA's Institute of Banking, which offers a wide range of finance training programmes including the opening of a Women's Training Centre in 2008. The institute has signed agreements with the International Finance Corporation
• Comply with latest BIS capital requirements	• Achieved and exceeded Basel capital requirements with Saudi banks averaging at 16% levels compared with prescribed 8% levels

thrust of the supervisory policies of Saudi Arabian banking throughout the evolution of the banking system to date seems to have been guided by certain objectives summarized in Table 5.2.

While there is general agreement on the relative success of the guiding regulatory principles, there is some debate on the issue of fair competition. Recent bank studies have shown that Saudi banks tend to price their products in an oligopolistic manner (Essayyad et al., 2003).

The Saudi banking sector has undergone significant evolutionary phases in a relatively short lifespan compared to other financial centres around the world. These evolutionary phases were instrumental in preparing the ground for the next evolutionary phases and have been well documented elsewhere (Dukheil, 1995, Jasser, 2002). The main features are recalled below.

The Early Years (1940s–1960s): Infancy Period

The few financial houses that existed in the pre-1950s era primarily served the pilgrim trade in Jeddah and Makkah, as well as imports and some export finance. The first branch of a foreign commercial bank, the Netherlands Trading Society (today the Saudi Hollandi Bank), was established in 1927 and concentrated on import and export finance from the city of Jeddah. These foreign banks were initially unpopular because of social and religious stigma, and there was strong resistance to paying and receiving interest. The result was effectively a *cash-oriented society* until the early 1970s. *Money-changers,* who carefully avoided the word "bank," flourished in those early days, and provided strong competition to foreign banks.

The newfound Saudi oil revenues of the 1950s brought a rise in government expenditure that resulted in an unprecedented escalation in demand for currency, outstripping supply. This oil wealth attracted foreign banks that soon opened branches in Jeddah: Banque Indochine, British Bank of Middle East, National Bank of Pakistan and Egyptian Misr Bank. The late 1950s saw yet more arrivals: Banque du Caire, First National City Bank and Banque Du Liban. In 1937, the Mahfouz and Kaki families successfully petitioned King Abdulaziz to establish the Kingdom's first locally owned bank, but it was not until 1953 that the Mahfouz-Kaki Company was transformed into what became the National Commercial Bank (NCB). In 1957, a second locally owned bank, Riyad Bank, was established.

The refusal of many depositors to receive interest meant that profits were sufficiently attractive for commercial banks to operate during this period. Banks were also able to provide loans with "service charges" being applied, without upsetting Islamic sensitivities. However, the bubble soon burst. The lack of available expertise led to incorrect loan processing and bad loan administration and some banks ran into trouble, including Riyad Bank. The government became a shareholder to restore confidence. This required more direct involvement from the de facto central bank (SAMA), which came of age in the 1960s and enacted the Banking Control Law in 1966.

The 1970s: The Adolescence Period

This was the beginning of the era of Saudi planned development with the first 5-year plan launched in 1970, as discussed in Chapter 2. The 1970s marked the start of the adolescence of the Saudi banking sector, with an increase in direct regulation and supervision.

Complementing the private sector banks, six major government lending institutions were also established during this period: the Saudi Arabian Agricultural Bank, the Saudi Credit Bank, Public Investment Fund, Contractors Fund, Saudi Industrial Development Fund and Real Estate Development Fund. Their aim was to provide medium- and long-term loans instead of the short-term loans extended by the commercial banks. Bank assets grew from SR 3 billion in 1971 to SR 93 billion in 1974. Deposits rose from SR 2 billion to SR 68 billion over the same period.

The year 1976 was a watershed year for the Saudi banking sector, as it was the year when the policy of *Saudization* of foreign banks operating in the Kingdom was first introduced, with far-reaching effects to this day. This policy required converting branches of foreign banks into publicly traded companies with majority Saudi ownership.

A primary reason for *Saudization* was that branches of foreign banks in Saudi Arabia were using policies drawn up by their foreign parent banks. These policies might not always be in harmony with local development plans, for they mostly concentrated on short-term foreign trade, with no priority for long-term loans. Foreign banks were also concentrated in Jeddah and Riyadh and provided no service in the under-banked rural areas. In addition, they were not reporting to SAMA as their final regulator, and their high profits were repatriated abroad.

Conflicts were bound to intensify as the Saudi economy expanded rapidly starting in the late 1970s, and the Kingdom saw a large part of the financial sector virtually outside its control. Given the enormous profits that foreign bank branches were making in the Kingdom – to which the author can attest from his service in this sector in those early days – there was little choice but to comply with *Saudization*, which was made palatable through long-term management contracts and tax breaks.

By 1980, *Saudization* of the major foreign bank branches had been completed. Citibank N.A. of the USA was the final one. The process boosted Saudi banks' capital base and branch expansion in other parts of the Kingdom; it also ensured an opportunity to benefit from foreign expertise and technology transfer.

The total number of bank branches rose to 247 from 145 by 1980. There were several other advantages flowing from the policy of *Saudization* of the foreign-owned bank branches. In competitive terms, the public had a wider choice of banks with which to deal, as well as receiving more competitive services at lower costs. *Saudization* helped to spread the country's new wealth among a wider section of its citizens through dividend payouts and stock ownership. This in effect laid the foundation for share ownership and its acceptance by the Saudi public.

A new and lucrative employment sector opened up for Saudis, with the opportunity to rise through the banks and manage such *Saudized* banks, as well as "cross-fertilizing" their banking skills with wholly owned Saudi banks. The increase in capital and reserves of the newly *Saudized* banks enhanced the banking sector's ability to lend large amounts to individuals and companies. As a result, offshore lending to Saudi Arabia, mostly from Bahrain-based "*offshore banking units*" or OBUs, was less effective (Bisisu, 1984). Finally, the broader national objectives of the Saudi economy would be harmonized with the banking policies of these *Saudized* banks. This alignment of interests was quite an improvement on the pre-*Saudization* era, when foreign banks' interests were more tightly tied to those of their home countries.

As seen earlier in Table 5.1, the Saudi banking system is today preparing to welcome back foreign banks to the Kingdom. This reflects the domestic banks' self-confidence in their capacity to effectively compete. It also reflects SAMA's ability to regulate these "new-wave" foreign banks. The situation facing the new foreign banks is different this time, with an extensive branch network, a sophisticated range of banking products and a cadre of well-trained Saudi banking professionals in place. It is likely that the new foreign banks will concentrate on niche investment and merchant banking activities such as *IPOs* and mergers and acquisitions, as well as positioning themselves to provide financing for the large infrastructure project the Saudi government has planned for the years ahead.

Coming of Age in the 1980s: Young Adulthood

This period proved to be the real test of strength and resilience of the Saudi banking system and of SAMA's supervisory skills. As discussed in earlier chapters, oil prices fell sharply from the highs of the 1981 boom era; the mid-1980s was a period of sharply reduced government revenues, which fell from SR 368 billion in 1981 to SR 104 billion in 1987.

The decline in government revenues meant significant pressure on the quality of bank assets, and several banks suffered non-performing loans (Dukheil, 1995). A judicial system that seemed to side with defaulters on interest payment issues did not help either (Wilson, 1983). In 1982, SAMA successfully overcame supervisory and regulatory challenges brought about when irregularities appeared in the operations of Saudi Cairo Bank. These irregularities involved unauthorized trading in bullion, with the bank concealing accumulated losses that exceeded its share capital (Suhaimi, 2002). A new share capital was issued which was taken up by the government-owned Public Investment Fund (PIF) and this helped to restore confidence and liquidity to Saudi Cairo. This bank eventually merged with the United Saudi Commercial Bank (USCB) in 1997 to form the United Saudi Bank.

The 1980s were characterized by bank mergers. USCB itself was born in 1983 of a merger of the branches of foreign banks, namely United Bank of Pakistan, Bank Melli Iran and Banque due Liban et d'Outremer (In 1999, United Saudi Bank merged with Saudi American Bank.).

During this period, SAMA came of age and employed a number of measures in reaction to the problems the sector faced (Dukheil, 1995). SAMA required prior approval for declaration of bank dividends, extended the tax holiday period for banks, introduced tax breaks to encourage provisioning of doubtful debts and insisted on improvement in corporate governance. Finally, the monetary agency created an unofficial "blacklist" of defaulting clients through the creation of a banking disputes settlements committee.

Other significant policy changes were also introduced in this period, including legislation to control the activities of the money exchangers. Since 1982 SAMA had required that they obtain a licence to operate and that they maintain specified capital and reserves, and that they do not take deposits and issue loans. This followed the spectacular collapse of the Al Rajhi Trading Establishment in the Eastern Province in 1984 due to silver speculation.

In addition, the Saudi government, through SAMA, introduced the first public borrowing instrument – the *Bankers Security Deposit* Account (BSDA) – later replaced by bonds and treasury notes. Further, SAMA advised that prior permission was needed for Saudi commercial banks to invite foreign banks to participate in SR loan syndication. Finally, equity trading on the Saudi stock market could be conducted only through the local commercial banks.

By the end of the decade, bank branches rose from 247 to 1,036 and employees from 11,000 to 25,000 (Suhaimi, 2002). Total assets rose to SR 253 billion by 1989, a 150% increase over 1979. Saudi banks also ventured onto the international stage, with branches opened in London, Bahrain, Geneva, Beirut and Istanbul.

The 1990s and the Period of Maturity

This era started traumatically for the whole Gulf. The Iraq–Kuwait crisis of 1990–1991 was a severe external shock to the banking system, characterized by outward capital flight. SAMA, however, once again proved adept at crisis management and reacted by providing domestic banks with adequate liquidity in the form of foreign exchange swaps and deposits. Confidence was restored to the financial sector.

Following the resolution of the 1991 Gulf crisis, there was a boom in the Saudi economy. Banking activity picked up, showing its resilience despite the foreign exchange crisis sweeping other parts of the world, notably the 1994 Mexican and the 1997 South East Asian currency crisis. The 1990s saw Saudi banks begin to reap the benefit of their large investment in technology, which had been introduced in the late 1980s as an antidote to the insufficient number of qualified Saudi banking personnel. The impact of the use of new technology to deliver banking services has been enormous, the most popular being the use of ATMs for cash withdrawal and other consumer transactions such as utility payments, account transfers and general enquiries.

This period also saw the rapid spread of the use of debit cards, credit cards and stored-value cards (point of sale), and Saudi banks competed fiercely in this new market segment. The cash-oriented society seemed to be gradually changing its transaction habits.

The technological advances made by the Saudi banks have been remarkable compared to the 1950s when the public was reluctant to use anything but silver riyal coins and foreign gold coins. Under the guidance of SAMA, Saudi commercial banks now enjoy a number of sophisticated payment and settlement systems. In 1997, the Saudi Riyal Interbank Express (SARIE) system was introduced, which is a gross settlement electronic fund-transfer system, operating in real time. It is the backbone of the Saudi payment infrastructure between banks. Other advances included the Automated Clearing House (ACH) and Saudi Payment Network (SPAN), which supported the ATMs and point-of-sales terminals, as well as the Electronic Share Information System (ESIS).

All of these systems have been linked to SARIE, enabling banks to make and receive payments directly from their accounts with SAMA on a real-time basis and to credit beneficiary accounts with transfers of funds on the same day. Another electronic share trading and information system (*TADAWUL*) has recently been enhanced to provide T+0 (transaction plus zero days) settlement capability and to permit the trading of government bonds, treasury bills and mutual funds in addition to corporate shares (Suhaimi, 2002). Few countries in the developing or developed world can boast of such an array of sophisticated payment systems.

Such technological developments have contributed significantly to improving the level and quality of consumer services, reducing costs, enhancing efficiency and strengthening banking control. The Saudi banking sector had a solid base on which to meet the challenges of information technology in the new millennium.

2000 Onwards

The Saudi banking sector entered the new millennium on high hopes but major events characterized this period, bringing about some significant challenges. The new millennium saw Saudi banks faced with competitive pressures from regional and international banks who began to market the Saudi market more aggressively following the turnaround in Saudi Arabia's fiscal fortunes from 2002 onwards. At the same time, competition from foreign banks was brought nearer to home as some significant global foreign banks opened branches in the Kingdom post WTO accession in 2005, forcing some Saudi banks to reposition themselves in a more focused manner in the Saudi market. At the same time, the international environment of low interest rates in the later part of the decade affected Saudi banks' margins as the cost of funds fell faster than lending rates, eroding lending margins.

Saudi banks began to search for non-interest investment income and to diversify their product range to reduce dependency on interest income (or commission income as it is termed in Saudi Arabia). Domestic banks also faced the prospect of losing out on their lucrative brokerage commission fees, acting as brokers from share trading, as the Saudi Capital Market Authority (CMA) started to license both local and foreign brokers and investment management companies in the later part of the decade, thus putting pressure on Saudi banks' earnings. Some reacted by creating their independent brokerage and investment advisory companies under names such as SABB Securities Ltd. Company, SAMBA Capital, Riyad Bank Capital, NCB Capital, Fransi Capital, Saudi Hollandi Capital, Al Rajhi Financial Services, Arab National Investment Company and so on.

With foreign licensed banks eyeing the investment income market in Saudi Arabia, the domestic banks realized that they needed to develop more expertise and deliver more products if they are to effectively compete in this market segment in the future. The current period was also characterized by the growth in Saudi Islamic banking services from existing market participants, as well as the entry of two new Saudi Islamic *Shariah*-compliant banks – Al Inma and Al Bilad – to cater to this fast-growing market segment. Al Bilad was the result of the amalgamation of the Saudi money brokers into a new bank and brings to a close the long history of this rather exotic money broker segment. At the same time, most Saudi banks either converted some of their retail branches to offer *Shariah*-compliant products or opened "Islamic" windows. The new millennium also saw the complete *Saudization* of SAMBA to a full Saudi ownership after Citibank sold its remaining share in the Saudi American Bank joint venture entity and forego its management licence. *Saudization* had indeed come a full circle, at least for SAMBA, indicating that local bankers and senior management felt more confident in running their banks without direct technical support from overseas joint venture partners, although many Saudi banks continue to draw upon technical, IT and training cooperation from foreign counterparts.

The period also witnessed the venturing abroad of some Saudi banks either through acquisitions or direct branch openings, the most visible being Al Rajhi Bank's acquisition in 2007 of a Malaysian bank's 12-retail-branch network to enable Al Rajhi to enter the profitable Malaysian financial market and to have access to the latest Islamic finance market instrument developments, given Malaysia's lead in this area. As of 2010, the Al Rajhi network in Malaysia increased to 20 branches. Table 5.3 illustrates the current Saudi bank's international presence.

Table 5.3 Saudi banks' international branches (2010)

Bank	Country location
• Al Rajhi	• Malaysia, Kuwait (Licence obtained)
• National Commercial Bank	• Turkey (60% of Turkiye Finans Bankasi), Singapore
• Arab National Bank	• London
• Riyad Bank	• London, Houston, Singapore
• SAMBA	• London, Dubai, Pakistan, Qatar
• Saudi Fransi	• Banque BEMO Saudi Fransi, Syria (60%)

Source: Bank annual reports

Saudi Bank Shareholder Concentration and Ownership

The issue of shareholder concentration is one of the major concerns for the Saudi banking sector, as it is for most other publicly listed Saudi joint stock companies (Dukheil, 1995, Abdullatif, 2002). From late 1980s to date, there has been a significant concentration of shareholders in the banking sector, as shown in Table 5.4.

Table 5.4 Shareholder concentration for selected Saudi banks

Bank	1981	1986	1998	2001
Saudi British Bank	8,008	5,100	15,155	11,846
Saudi Hollandi Bank	2,850	2,600	1,033	685
SAMBA	102,594	45,000	15,171	44,600
Saudi Fransi Bank	95,600	73,000	9,668	8,185

Source: Author's survey based on bank annual reports and Bank Investor Relations Units

The increase in the number of shareholders for certain years, such as witnessed for the Saudi British Bank in 1998, was tied to capital increases, while for SAMBA in 2001 it followed the merger with United Saudi Bank in 1999. The trend towards far fewer shareholders is unmistakable and there are several implications. First, holding a higher concentration of shares in fewer hands might enable some business groups to influence day-to-day operations and bank management through board representation. Second, the concentration of shares in a few hands with block votes "de-democratizes" the role of annual general meetings in joint stock companies. Concentration eliminates transparency and leads to joint stock companies operating like partnerships.

The issue became a concern to the regulators in 2009 following the default of two prominent Saudi family groups – Saad Group owned by Maan Al Sanei, and the Al Gosaibi Group, which had large exposure to Saudi and international banks, some of loans were seemingly extended on a "name lending" basis from banks where both groups held significant share holdings. SAMA moved quickly to reinforce existing regulations that requested more transparent bank corporate governance and disclosure in cases of direct and indirect shareholder loans.

A survey was carried out by the author on the size of Saudi family ownership of "core" share blocks in the various Saudi banks using available public information from annual reports, as well as share register information and bank sources. This information is displayed in Table 5.5.

The concentration level shown in Fig. 5.4 is also reflected in other "wholly owned" Saudi banks such as Riyad Bank and the National Commercial Bank (NCB) through government major ownership participation in these banks.

Since 1961, the Saudi government has held a 38% stake in Riyad Bank, and 80% of NCB since January 2003. In 1999, the Public Investment Fund (PIF), the Saudi government's domestic investment vehicle, acquired 50% of the privately owned National Commercial Bank from the Mahfouz and Kaaki families. The PIF went on to sell 10% of its share to the government-owned General Organization for Social

Table 5.5 Saudi commercial banks major ownership holdings by number and percentage (2000)

Institution	Private individuals or groups				Government or foreign ownership
	Under 2%	3–5%	6–9%	Over 10%	
National Commercial Bank (NCB)	1	1	1	–	80% (Government PIF)
Saudi British	2	2	1	–	40% (HSBC)
SAMBA	2	2	1	2	40% (Government institution)
Saudi Hollandi	6	3	2	1	40% (ABN-AMRO)
Al Rajhi	–	2	1	2	
Saudi Investment	2	1	3	–	25% (Various foreign institutions)
Saudi Fransi	2	3	1	–	31.5% (Credite Agricole-Calyon)
Riyad Bank	–	3	2	–	45% (Government)
Arab National	2	3	–	1	40% (Arab Bank)
Al Inma Bank	4	2	1	1	30% (Government-GOSI, Public Pension Agency, Investment Fund)

Source: Author's survey

Security (GOSI) in 2001. GOSI went on to acquire Citibank's share in 2007 when that bank sold out its participation. The issue of large government ownership in banks raises concerns of possible "*moral hazard*" arising whereby banks with substantial public ownership might be tempted to take on a greater risk, knowing that they will always be bailed out. In Saudi Arabia there has been no evidence of systemic banking crises and bank failures over the last few decades, but this is due to mainly the application of either a "purchase and assume" policy of mergers and acquisitions of one institution with another (such as Saudi Cairo with United Saudi Commercial Bank when the former was having difficulties), or government direct participation in the Arab world's largest bank, the National Commercial Bank.

Table 5.5 reveals that, of the original *Saudized* banks, only the *Saudi British, Saudi Hollandi* and *Arab National banks* have maintained their original 40% foreign joint venture partner shareholding, with others, such as Saudi Fransi, Saudi Investment and Saudi American, either selling part of their holdings or being diluted through new capital increases.

The table also indicates that major shareholder concentration is more pronounced within Saudi Hollandi, SAMBA and Al Rajhi banks, with Saudi British the least concentrated of the three. Historical reasons explain the high level of Saudi bank concentration, especially for the joint venture banks. These banks usually started life through a founding group of investors who were granted a certain percentage of the founding share capital, with the remaining shares distributed between the foreign joint venture partner and the general public. Because there were few shares distributed to the smaller investors, over time they sold out to the larger investors and founding shareholders. This also happened for the latest Saudi banks to be floated – *Al Inma* bank issued 1.5 billion shares valued at SR 15 billion, 70% of which were sold to the public in 2007. By 2010 an estimated 40% of the original shareholders had sold their shares.

The Saudi government is aware of these issues, and is encouraging wider share ownership by planning a partial privatization of its own bank holdings, especially in the Kingdom's largest bank, the National Commercial Bank (NCB). According to press reports, the government is planning to sell up to 50% of its current holding in NCB, which, if it happens, would give a large boost to the Saudi capital market.

This partial privatization sale would provide both short- and long-term benefits to the government, which would still retain a major stake in NCB. In the short run, the flotation proceeds could be used to repay part of the government's outstanding debt, while in the long run the government would see its share value appreciate on the capital markets once NCB shares are listed, while continuing to receive future dividends from NCB. No plans have been announced for selling part of the government's holdings in Riyad Bank, and it will be interesting to see what the government wants to do with its newly acquired 20% shareholding in the profitable SAMBA.

Performance of the Saudi Banks

Although some Saudi banks have been affected by the global financial crisis, specifically in some of their domestic loan portfolio, they are still in a better shape compared to many others in the world.

As we will analyse below, core banking income remains solid and has increased for many of the banks; total assets continue to grow and profitability ratios remain satisfactory with return on average assets (ROAA) standing at around 2.3% and return on average equity (ROAE) at around 18%. Furthermore, Saudi banks enjoy high levels of capitalization with their Tier 1 capital adequacy ratios at around 16% for year-end 2009, well above the 8% minimum recommended by Basel II guidelines. Table 5.6 provides a snapshot of the key banking ratios and potential risk indicators.

Potential risk remains for Saudi banks following the global and regional financial crisis of 2008/2009, some of which is reflected in Table 5.6. To the extent that some Saudi banks might have exposure to international debt and derivative markets, any further fall in asset prices might prompt banks to increase provisioning to safeguard their balance sheets. This will result in lower profits and the higher perception of financial risk, in turn manifest in tighter bank lending measures, coupled with a weakening business environment and rising non-performing loans. This was noticeable in 2009 when non-performing loans (NPLs) rose to 1.5% compared with 1.4% in the previous year, which is still far lower than the 2.3% level of 2004. Saudi banks' NPL coverage ratio is still fairly high at around 150% level and the Saudi banking sector entered the global financial crisis in a strong position with high capital adequacy ratios, ample liquidity and an enviable demand deposit ratio of around 40%, comparable with under 5% for most European banks.

Table 5.6   Saudi banking sector: key sector indicators (2004–2009)

Bank	2004	2005	2006	2007	2008	2009
Loans-to-deposit ratio (%)	72.0	89.1	80.5	80.5	86.8	78.1
Minimum risk assets/total assets (%)	33.9	28.4	28.9	29.8	25.6	26.3
Cash and cash equivalents/total assets (%)	4.4	3.8	5.4	8.1	5.8	5.6
Tier I capital adequacy ratio (%)	13.5	17.8	21.9	20.6	16.0	15.9
Non-performing loan (NPL) ratio (%)	2.3	1.7	1.6	1.6	1.4	1.5
NPL coverage ratio (%)	231.4	179.0	176.7	158.0	145.0	148
Bank reserves to total bank deposits (%)	7.3	6.7	8.8	15.1	11.5	15.6
Demand deposits to total deposits (%)	42.6	39.6	36.8	39.4	36.9	39
Total assets (SR Billion)	655.3	759.0	861.0	1,075.2	1,303.2	1,370.2

Source: Bank annual reports

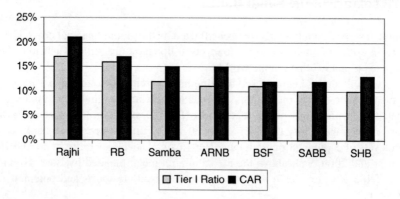

Fig. 5.2   Saudi banks: capital adequacy ratios (CAR) (Source: SAMA, Credit Suisse 2009)

Figure 5.2 sets out the capital adequacy ratios and Tier I Basel capital ratios for some selected Saudi banks.

It is noted that all seven Saudi banks maintain healthy capital adequacy ratios (CARs), with Al Rajhi Bank and Riyad Bank (RB) being the most capitalized. The Saudi Hollandi Bank (SHB) is the least capitalized bank with a Tier I ratio of 9.8%. With total assets of SR 1,370 billion as of December 2009, the Saudi banking sector is estimated to be the second largest in the GCC, just behind the UAE, growing from SR 655 billion in 5 years, or nearly 110% growth.

Of the 12 local banks that make up the Saudi banking sector, 11 are listed on the *TADAWUL* stock market with an aggregate market capitalization (excluding *Al*

Inma Bank) of SR 268 billion ($77 billion) as of December 2009, down from SR 405 billion ($108 billion) as of December 2007.

The total distribution network of the Saudi banking sector extended to 1,430 branches and 9,258 automated teller machines (ATMs) in December 2009, up from 1,060 and 1,400, respectively, as of December 1994. The growth in both is illustrated in Fig. 5.3, which demonstrates the increased popularity of ATMs.

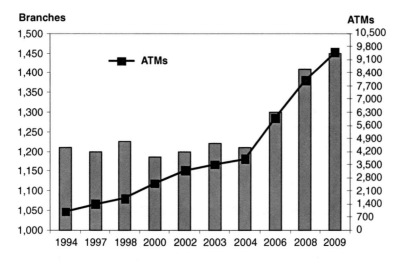

Fig. 5.3 Evolution of branches and ATMs 1994–2009 (Source: SAMA)

Most Saudi banks have found it more cost-effective to install ATMs rather than invest in a brick-and-mortar branch network. They had bet on Saudi society's acceptance of electronic banking and ATMs and points of sale becoming more accepted in what had traditionally been a cash-oriented society. Their strategy seems to have been correct, as Fig. 5.4 illustrates. While the number of ATMs has increased, so has

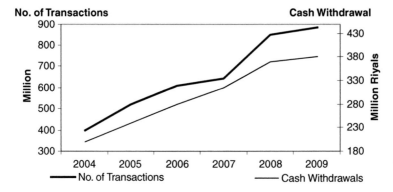

Fig. 5.4 ATM Transactions and withdrawals: 2004–2009 (Source: SAMA)

the number of transactions and point of sales over the period 2003–2009 to reach nearly 1 billion transactions in 2009, compared with under 200,000 for 2003, while the value of cash withdrawn reached SR 380 million for 2009.

The above trend has been helped by the heavy investment in technology in the financial sector since the late 1980s. Under SAMA's auspices, the Saudi banking sector is one of the world's most technologically sophisticated using advanced inter-bank clearing house operations in SAMA's regional branches, and *SARIE* or Saudi Arabian Riyal Interbank Express payment system introduced in 1997. SARIE's systems at SAMA and the banks have been replaced and upgraded in stages to cope with increasing volumes of payments from the existing and newly licensed banks and also to ensure compatibility with new technology. This is particularly important in such areas as information security, network technology and applications of software systems. Bill payments can now be made in Saudi Arabia using the *"SADAD"* payment system, which entered operation in 2004 and is a central system for presenting and paying of bills and other payments electronically. All forms of outlets such as ATMs' telephone banking and the Internet can be used to make *SADAD* payments.

Concentration Ratios Are Worrying for Competition

An analysis of Saudi bank performance must also address the issue of competition. Such competition has not been significant in the past, primarily because Saudi banks have experienced high profit ratios in terms of net return on assets and equity compared to other banks worldwide. Barriers to entry – at least before the new foreign bank licences were granted in 2004 – and the low cost of funds due to the large element of current/non-interest-bearing accounts help to explain this. The lack of external entry and competition has led to a high banking industry concentration level in Saudi Arabia. Table 5.7 summarizes the level of Saudi bank concentration for the periods 2001 and 2008. It is noted that three banking groups have around 50% of the banking market in both periods.

In 2001 and 2008, the same three banks, NCB, SAMBA and Al Rajhi, dominated, although Riyad Bank came a close fourth. Despite new entrants into the Saudi banking sector, the top three continued to dominate, the only erosion being seen in their loan and asset share.

Table 5.7   Saudi Arabian bank concentration levels in 2001 and 2008

Year	Number of banks	Concentration levels
2001	9 commercial, 1 Islamic	3 groups (NCB, SAMBA, Al Rajhi) have 54% of loans, 51% of deposits, 49% of assets and 50% of branches
2008	10 commercial, 2 Islamic	3 groups (NCB, SAMBA, Al Rajhi) have 48% of loans, 49.8% of deposits, 43.2% of assets and 54% of branches

Source: Bank annual reports 2001, 2009

The effects of such concentration levels have been researched for the Saudi market (Essayyad et al., 2003). Studies conducted in the area of bank concentration and economic efficiency indicate that a high concentration ratio may induce banks to charge borrowers with higher interest rates than when there is a low banking concentration.

According to Saudi studies, the non-interventionist policy of SAMA in this area of bank regulation could hamper the growth of companies, particularly small- and medium-sized industries, due to more restrictive credit conditions by the banks within a system of imperfect competition (Essayyad et al., 2003). The scope of the problems faced by small- and medium-sized enterprises (SMEs) in Saudi Arabia, discussed later in Chapter 7, confirmed this finding.

The Rush to Segmentation

Competition in Saudi Arabia amongst banks is along various segmentation lines, and each of these is further segmented by gender. Segmentation by gender means that "ladies-only" banking operations were developed as a niche market, either in separate branches or in ladies sections within the same branch. This has proved to be both successful and profitable, and all Saudi banks today operate "ladies-only" branches.

In Saudi Arabia, segmentation also seems to follow asset size and class, like the various prestige-level card awards of hotels or airlines (blue, silver, gold, platinum). Saudi banks seemed to realize that traditional "old wealth" private banking clients (with their emphasis on wealth preservation) are not as numerous as the larger affluent segments for whom wealth creation is the main objective. The former clients seem to be the domain of international private banking financial institutions, while the latter are those who created wealth in the Saudi stock and real estate markets.

Market surveys indicate that consumer preferences are determined not by individual bank strengths, but rather by the national origin of the bank. Important too is the family tradition in dealing with "Islamic"-oriented banks or "conventional" banks, even though each Saudi bank has used the media to portray different strengths, reputations and allegiances.

While it is difficult to generalize, Table 5.8 attempts to capture the main marketing strengths and public perceptions of the different Saudi banks, which could partly explain their varying performances in separate market segments.

The perceived strengths in each bank's niche markets are also partly reflections of the different management styles, philosophies and orientations of the pure "Saudi" banks, such as NCB and Riyad Bank with their "domestic roots" on the one hand, and those with foreign affiliation and management control on the other hand. The concentration of joint venture banks, such as Saudi Fransi, Saudi Hollandi, Saudi British and Arab National Bank, on core corporate business, investment and treasury products meant that they left the consumer loan mass-market and small business lending to the "pure" Saudi banks, in order to concentrate on "big-ticket" corporate

Table 5.8 Saudi commercial banks: perception of key strengths

Institution	Perception – strengths
• Saudi British Bank (SABB)	• Electronic banking, investments, treasury products, international links, medium-term facilities to Saudi corporate, part of an international HSBC network and global image
• SAMBA	• Corporate banking, treasury and investment products, electronic banking, high net worth clients, international links, syndications
• Riyad Bank	• Consumer loans, trading activities, investments, government accounts, oil and agricultural sector, syndications, small business
• Al Rajhi	• Islamic investments, foreign exchange, trading activities, "safety first"
• Arab National	• Electronic banking, mutual funds, consumer banking, small business, treasury products
• Saudi Fransi	• Corporate banking, investments, treasury products, loan syndication
• Saudi Hollandi	• International trade, medium corporate loans, international capital markets, off-balance sheet products
• Saudi Investment Bank	• Corporate finance medium-to long-term loans, international trade, treasury products, syndications
• National Commercial Bank	• Consumer banking, small businesses, Islamic products, Corporate and government lending, foreign exchange and treasury, large ticket items
• Al Bilad Bank	• Expertise in FX and remittance, SME-friendly
• Al Jazira Bank	• Islamic investments, innovation in capital market *sukuk* products
• Al Inma Bank	• Islamic investments, "people's bank", strength through government participation

loans. The increasing popularity of Islamic banking bas forced many to consider this target market segment and two new banks – *Al Bilad* and *Al Inma* – focus mostly on this segment, while *Al Jazira* has tried to convert most of its banking operations to *Shariah*-compliant ones. SAMBA which became a fully owned Saudi bank still concentrates on the core corporate market but has tried to differentiate itself in the investment banking sector.

The differences between national Saudi banks' and joint venture banks' "efficiency" measured in terms of loans and deposit volumes per branch is illustrated in Fig. 5.5.

The differences between joint venture banks (JVs) and the national banks go deeper than their origins and ownership structures. Their underlying banking philosophies differ, with the joint ventures targeting the upper wealth segment, both corporate and individual, and the national banks targeting the lower segments, although each national bank also has a segment for its high net worth clients.

Because of these differences, the national banks operate a larger branch network, as seen in Fig. 5.5, but joint ventures enjoy a higher loan-to-branch and deposit-to-branch ratio. The brick-and-mortar branch network of Saudi Fransi Bank and SABB has proved to be the most effective amongst local peers, although SAMBA as the latest "national" bank has done extremely well, beating all other banks as illustrated in Fig. 5.5. Such high efficiency levels indicate consistent management

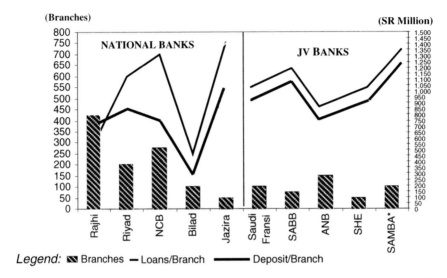

Fig. 5.5 Comparison between Saudi national banks and joint venture banks by branch loans/deposits (2008) (SAMBA became national in 2007) (Source: Bank annual reports)

efforts and investments in optimizing alternative delivery channels to maximize sales performance and provide access to a wider client base.

While joint venture banks might seem to be efficient in terms of the amount of loans and deposits per branch, the Saudi national banks tend to generally have a lower cost of funds due to their bigger demand deposit ratios and larger branch network, often in rural areas where the taking of interest-is not as widespread as in urban areas. This is illustrated in Figs. 5.6 and 5.7.

From the above figures, Al Rajhi bank which represents the Saudi national banks has the lowest funding costs compared with the joint venture banks, owing to its high

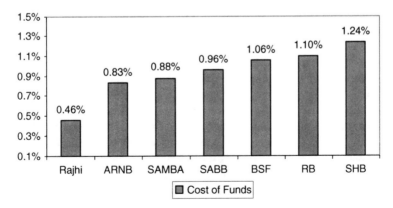

Fig. 5.6 Saudi: cost of funds (2009) (Source: Bank reports)

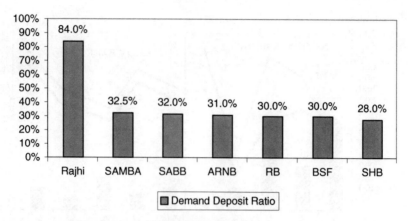

Fig. 5.7 Saudi: Demand deposit ratio (2009) (Source: Bank annual reports, Credit Suisse)

demand deposit ratio of nearly 85%, while the joint ventures averaged around 30%, with Saudi Hollandi Bank the lowest at 28%. As such, this bank had the highest funding cost at 1.24%. Over time, as we explored in the previous chapter, the relative ratio of current accounts to total deposits will come down, further putting pressure on Saudi banks to seek alternative revenues from interest-bearing products.

Saudi Banks' Lending Profile

Saudi banks have traditionally a low loans-to-deposit ratio and thus more liquidity compared to other Western institutions (Azzam, 2002, NCB, 2001b). SAMA maintains a 65% loans-to-deposit ratio level due to its requirement that commercial banks maintain liquid reserves of at least 20% of their deposit liabilities in the form of cash, gold, Saudi government bonds or qualifying assets that can be converted into cash within a period of no less than 30 days (SAMA).

During the period 2007–2008, the Saudi banks' loans-to-deposit ratio rose significantly to reach nearly 91% level by October 2008, as illustrated in Fig. 5.8, and then easing back as SAMA started to introduce monetary tools such as reserve requirements to curb on lending described in the previous chapter.

By the end of 2009, the loans-to-deposit ratio had declined to just under the 80% level as illustrated in Fig. 5.8, while Fig. 5.9 sets out the ratio for individual major banks. We note that the two largest Saudi national banks, NCB and Riyad Bank, had different ratios, with NCB being more conservative at 63% and Riyad Bank at 92%, and the joint venture banks also being more aggressive lenders.

Although SAMA's conservative ceiling on loans-to-deposit ratio has shielded the Saudi banking sector in times of global downturn, such a strict measure could undermine the industry's growth moving forward. This could be one option for SAMA as it reconsiders the effect of Saudi bank lending policies during boom periods, as

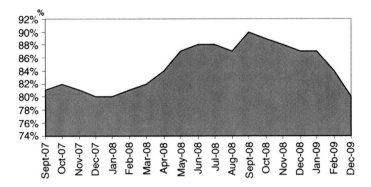

Fig. 5.8 Loans-to-deposit ratio in the Saudi Arabian banking system (Source: SAMA)

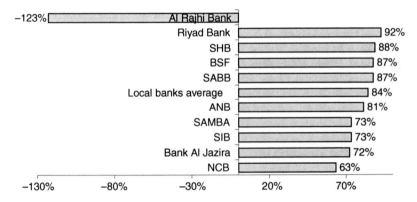

Fig. 5.9 Loans-to-deposit ratio per bank as of December 2008 (Source: SAMA, bank reports)

was the case during 2007/2008, in order to ease a liquidity pressure in the Kingdom, without having the government to pump in liquidity as a fiscal measure.

While this high-liquidity cushion of Saudi banks might be looked upon favourably from the regulatory aspect of a central bank, it raises some other issues. First, the low ratio imposes a restriction on domestic lending opportunities, and excess liquidity is absorbed through the acquisition of foreign deposits or local investments. This could be profitable when foreign interest rates are higher than domestic rates, and if domestic investment opportunities are positive. The downturn in international interest rates, specifically US dollar interest rates, as well as uncertainties in the international stock markets has prompted some repositioning of lending to the domestic markets. However, the majority of bank lending was of less than 1 year's duration.

This type of lending structure is not conducive to long-term industrial investment and planning. Filling a need for long-term investment capital was the prime reason for the Saudi government's establishment of its own lending agencies. It will be interesting to see if some of the newly licensed foreign banks spot a market niche and establish long-term credit relationships with Saudi corporations.

By all accounts, 2009 was a watershed year for Saudi banks which saw bank credit to the private sector fall for the first time since 1990 during the tension of the Second Gulf War. This is illustrated in Fig. 5.10, which sets out the annual change in bank lending.

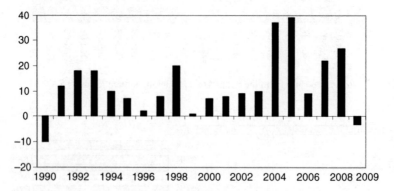

Fig. 5.10 Bank credit to the private sector (% annual change) (Source: SAMA)

Asset-Liability Management Is a Problem

Saudi banks, similar to other GCC markets, suffer from widening asset-liability maturity mismatch, raising major concerns about banks' liquidity risk as well as credit risk. Adverse global and domestic market conditions can also affect the asset-liability mismatch by having depositors opt for shorter maturities. Figure 5.11

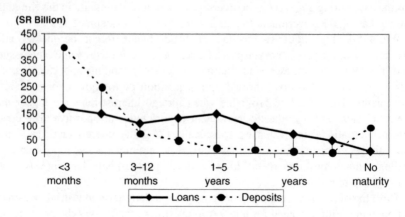

Fig. 5.11 Loans and deposits maturity gaps (December 2008) (Source: SAMBA)

highlights the significant gap between medium- and long-term loans and matched bank deposits.

The above loans and deposits maturity gap is a major impediment to the Saudi banks' ability to fulfil medium- and long-term commitments that are funded primarily by short-term deposits. Given this current reality, Saudi banks can either tap into medium- and long-term debt markets by issuing bonds, or use inter-bank liabilities as liquidity buffers to meet medium- and long-term obligations.

Due to the Saudi banks' market constraints, and cognizant that some of the major Saudi projects, especially in the basic industries and petrochemical sectors, will require long-term funding, the government-owned Public Investment Fund (PIF) announced new measures in 2008 to increase funding to such projects. The PIF raised the cap on lending for each project in which it participates from 30% to 40% of its value, and extended the loan duration from 15 to 20 years (including a 5-year grace period). Of more significance, the PIF announced raising its lending limit on each project from the current level of SR 3.8 billion (just over $1 billion) to SR 4.9 billion ($1.6 billion).

It has not only been the PIF, the Ministry of Finance's investment arm, but also other specialized government financing institutions that were set up to provide much-needed longer-term financing sources. Table 5.9 examines the outstanding loans disbursed by the five major Saudi specialized credit institutions which went a long way in assisting the modern Saudi economic infrastructure to be built up.

Besides the PIF, the largest disbursements have been carried out by the Real Estate Development Fund (REDF) and the Saudi Industrial Development Fund (SIDF). The REDF was established to provide long-term personal home-building assistance for Saudi citizens, with grants of SR 300,000 being given on 20-year terms at virtually nil interest rates. This amount remained unchanged since REDF's establishment but was raised to SR 400,000 in 2009 due to inflationary pressures and rising construction cost, but still remains insufficient to meet the needs for building an average Saudi villa which costs around SR 800,000–1,500,000. The possible introduction of a Saudi mortgage law and mortgage financing through Saudi banks

Table 5.9 Government specialized credit institutions – outstanding loans

	1987	1993	2002	2006	2008
Institution	SR billions				
Agricultural Development Fund[a]	11.7	8.7	9.4	9.5	9.5
Saudi Credit and Saving Bank	0.5	0.7	0.8	1.3	9.8
Public Investment Fund	43.0	31.9	25.5	17.8	28.7
Saudi Individual Development Fund	42.0	5.2	9.2	11.1	17.2
Real Estate Development Fund	69.4	66.7	68.7	71.2	75.4
Total	166.9	113.2	113.6	110.9	140.6

[a]Formerly Saudi Arabian Agricultural Bank
Source: SAMA

aims to release funding to this sector. The SIDF provides loans to Saudi industries, joint venture companies and foreign entities operating in Saudi Arabia under the liberalized foreign direct investment laws on concessionary basis based on a project's business viability and ability to repay. SIDF is run by professionals, many of whom had completed the much sought Chase Manhattan Bank intensive credit evaluation course. SIDF applies rigorous credit evaluation procedures and standards and has a very low rate of loan default, often self financing itself from loan repayments as Table 5.9 illustrates. The recent rise in disbursements of the Saudi credit and savings bank – popularly known as the "marriage" bank for giving out marriage loans to Saudis – was due to extending loans to Saudi small- and medium-sized enterprises (SMEs), as part of the government's strategy to support the SMEs due to perceived lack of traditional bank financing and interest in this market segment.

Saudi Banks Sectoral Lending: Consumer Lending Takes Off

Table 5.10 illustrates the sectoral allocation of bank lending from 1999 to 2009 and reveals the growing importance of consumer lending.

Consumer loans represented around 27% of all private sector loans, compared with 38% in 2009. According to SAMA, the majority were for financing motor vehicles and "other" unspecified personal loans; real estate and credit-card financing remained steady. This situation is unlikely to change in the foreseeable future, at least not until Saudi banks feel they have more legal certainty over extending real estate loans. At present they cannot hold mortgages. Credit-card facilities are normally backed up by appropriate cash collateral – mostly time deposits. Given such uncertainties, foreign banks are not likely to be competing in this market segment in Saudi Arabia.

Table 5.10 Bank credit to private sector by economic activity

Sector	1999	2003	2004	2008	2009
	SR billion				
Agriculture/fishing	1,458	2,549	2,638	10,980	10,681
Manufacturing	23,753	26,604	26,149	70,333	79,090
Mining/quarrying	1,799	650	614	4,265	4,613
Electricity/water	1,454	1,837	2,038	10,629	12,631
Building/construction	19,373	21,955	21,647	54,371	52,641
Commerce	38,966	51,886	50,811	176,858	179,741
Transport/communication	6,858	12,803	11,491	37,814	43,312
Finance	6,469	11,877	17,128	16,812	13,968
Services	9,891	8,839	9,627	32,324	37,230
Miscellaneous	41,955	82,124	91,550	289,351	274,047
Total	151,976	221,123	233,692	712,737	707,953

Source: SAMA

What is more worrying for Saudi manufacturing growth prospects is the relative decline in the share of lending to this sector, which has registered a drop from around 15% in 1999 to 11%, for current years, as set out in Table 5.10. This fall, combined with the short-term nature of lending in Saudi Arabia, is a matter of concern if the Saudi private sector is to be able to meet the challenges of diversifying the economic base of the country.

In order to protect Saudi banks from potential consumer loan losses based on asymmetrical information from borrowers – the withholding of information by borrowers from banks – the Saudi government has encouraged financial institutions to share credit information through a common credit reference bureau. In 2002, the Saudi Credit Information Company (SIMAH) was established under the supervision of SAMA. By 2008, SIMAH credit information had membership not only of the Saudi banking sector but also the automobile financing sector, telecommunications, and foreign banks operating in Saudi Arabia, besides government disbursing agencies. Insurance companies joined in late 2008 and SAMA has received applications from many other potential members and studies each request rigorously in order to protect both creditors and lenders. SIMAH has been enhanced and introduced a credit rating or "scoring" system based on the assessment of an individual's solvency and potential credit risk, while the creation of the Commercial Credit Bureau of SIMAH aims to provide the banking sector with a more scientific risk weighted assessment on lending to the medium- and small-sized companies or SMEs. Further developments included a register of checks returned without sufficient funds, and identifying risks of companies with no previous credit history.

All the developments in the Saudi financial sector points to a gradual maturing of the industry given the mix of domestic and international players, as well as the sophistication of the operating framework. At the same time, Saudi Arabia seemed to have adopted a non-interventionist free-market approach, but the approval of new foreign bank licences implies that the government is also encouraging more competition in the domestic market. Table 5.11 summarizes the emphasis of SAMA's overall regulations concerning Saudi commercial banks.

As the above table points, there was a lack of formal Saudi government safety net for bank depositors until October 2008, such as that of the US Federal insurance deposit scheme which guaranteed the first $100,000 of bank deposits but which was raised to $250,000 at the height of the 2008/2009 global financial crisis.

The Saudi move in 2008 was also in response to the acute global financial crisis and followed the action of the other GCC member states. SAMA's decision sent a strong signal that it was standing behind the Saudi financial system to restore confidence, while reiterating the soundness of the industry's liquidity situation and SAMA's willingness to pump extra liquidity into the system. SAMA had acted before to support the Saudi financial sector, and, despite no formal guarantee, it acted as a bank of "last resort" when it intervened to avert banking crisis from developing, such as those with Riyad bank in the 1960s and Saudi Cairo and NCB in the 1980s and 1990s. A major regulatory deficiency seems to be in the area of restrictions on bank holdings, as reviewed earlier in this chapter.

Table 5.11 Saudi banking regulatory checklist

Category	Availability	Non-Availability	Observations
• Government safety net[a]	• Available		• No formal deposit insurance scheme existed until October 2008
• Restriction on bank holdings		• Not available	• No restrictions, large concentration in few hands
• Capital adequacy requirement	• Available		• Basle BIS capital adequacy ratios exceeded
• Disclosure requirements	• Available		• Large loans need SAMA approval
• Chartering and bank examination	• Available		• SAMA makes on-site and off-site audits and approves new bank licences
• Consumer protection	• Available		• Maximum SAMA-imposed commissions and charges
• Restriction on competition		• Not available	• No formal regulatory restrictions exist as to branch network numbers or to type of banking activities to be carried out

[a]Since 2008
Source: Essayyad et al. (2003)

The Emergence of the Insurance Sector

One of Saudi Arabia's hopes for deepening the financial market lies in the insurance sector. The insurance industry in Saudi Arabia is relatively new, as the country's insurance activities in the past were mainly focused on imports and there were only foreign players or their agents in the market. Social and religious reluctance to engage in insurance activities also played a role, due to perceived restrictions imposed by Islam. In 1983, the Saudi market saw the emergence of an insurance concept called "cooperative insurance," which was Islamically acceptable.

The concept of *cooperative insurance* was based on the principle of joint and several liabilities among the insured persons who participated in compensating any of the insured individuals, and thus the insured persons within this cooperative system are the participants or owners of the insurance operations. They have a right to receive surpluses after allocations are made for reserves.

This concept is different from commercial insurance where policyholders do not share profit; it is more akin to the Lloyds of London "Names". The cooperative insurance concept was implemented by the Saudi government in 1996 through the establishment of a publicly owned joint stock company called the *National Company for Cooperative Insurance* (NCCI). The insurance market in Saudi Arabia is at its infancy stage compared to other more mature markets worldwide but has been growing the fastest over the years since WTO accession in 2005.

Despite the recent growth in the Saudi insurance sector, it is still in its infancy compared to other mature markets as Table 5.12 illustrates.

Table 5.12 Saudi and world insurance market indicators 2008

	Life premiums (US$ Billion)	Non-life premiums (US$ Billion)	Total premiums (US$ Billion)	Total premium per capita ($)	Premiums as % of GDP
Industrialized Countries	2,219	1,538	3,757		
United States	578	662	1,240	2,570	8.49
Canada	48	57	105	1,543	7.37
Japan	367	106	473	3,896	11.87
United Kingdom	343	107	450	2,930	11.22
Germany	111	132	243	2,800	11.94
France	181	92	273	2,203	10.3
Italy	83	58	141	1,740	8.4
Australia	43	28	71	1,926	9.12
Emerging markets	272	241	513		
Brazil	22	25	47	173	2.6
Russia	1	38	39	N/A	N/A
China	96	45	141	N/A	N/A
India	49	7	56	N/A	1.95
Africa	38	17	55	22	1.2
World	2,490	1,779	4,269		
Saudi Arabia	0.16	2.75	2.91	118	0.62
Saudi Arabia % of world	0.01	0.15	0.07	–	–

N/A = Not Available
Source: Swiss Re, 2009, SAMA

The table indicates that the premiums paid per capita in Saudi Arabia are still far lower than those in advanced countries and even below Latin American levels. The penetration ratio of insurance, defined as the level of insurance premiums to GDP, is also very low at around 0.62% in 2008, up from 0.53% in 2007 and 0.40% levels in 2002. The averages for advanced economies are over 8% levels.

Despite the small share in world market, the growth in the Saudi insurance sector has been very impressive as demonstrated by Fig. 5.12, which tracks the growth in gross premiums paid over the period 1995–2008.

In terms of premiums by type of insurance in the Saudi market, general insurance premiums represent 51% and health insurance 44%. Health insurance has grown rapidly due to the application of the compulsory health insurance regulation issued by the government on employees of the private sector. Car insurance has also risen sharply and ranks second to health insurance, also spurred on by the government's compulsory car insurance regulations for third party liability.

According to reports from NCCI, there are more than 5 million cars registered in Saudi Arabia, and demand for motor insurance has been increasing as the country suffers from one of the highest traffic accident rates in the world. According to the Saudi Ministry of Interior, there were 2.2 million accidents in the Kingdom over a 10-year period to 2005, and the situation has not improved since then with nearly 40,000 people losing their lives. In terms of economic loss to the country, the

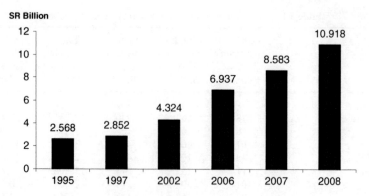

Fig. 5.12 Saudi insurance gross premiums 1995–2008 (Source: SAMA, NCCI)

Ministry studies indicate that accidents, loss of life and property as well as treatment charges cost Saudi Arabia around SR 21 billion annually (Arab News, 20 September 2004).

In order to ensure that only financially fit companies operate in this sector in Saudi Arabia, the *Majlis Al Shoura* passed legislation in September 2002, specifying that insurance companies intending to provide cooperative insurance services should have a minimum capital of SR 100 million. This amount was raised to SR 200 million for companies providing re-insurance (SAMA, 2009). Life insurance remains low due to religious beliefs, which frowns on taking out this type of insurance, but it has been growing over the past few years.

The significant insurance event of the past decade concerned a mandatory scheme of medical insurance for some 7 million expatriates and their families working and living in Saudi Arabia. According to reports, the Saudi Ministry of Health was giving employers up to 3 years to introduce this scheme from 2003, depending upon the number of employees. Because the impact of these decisions on the Saudi private sector would be to make the cost of hiring expatriate labour more expensive, there were attempts to postpone their implementation for smaller Saudi companies. The Kingdom is planning to introduce private sector health insurance scheme for Saudis 3 years after the completion of health sector insurance for expatriates from 2007. This could boost the Saudi insurance sector to around SR 18 billion within the next 5 years.

The implication for the Saudi economy is much wider. First, the medical insurance law will help to ease pressure on the Kingdom's budgetary outlays in the medical sector, as the Saudi government provides free medical services for all citizens and non-citizens alike, and this budgetary item had been increasing each year, as pointed out in Chapter 2.

Second, the boost in insurance services has encouraged the introduction in December 2001 of an interest-free Islamic insurance system, with some of the local banks such as Al Jazira Bank pioneering the launch of Islamic insurance or *Takaful*, and introducing *Takaful Ta'awni* or an Islamically acceptable life insurance product.

This product is the only *Shariah*-compliant insurance product approved by SAMA to date (SAMA, 2003). Recognizing the importance of this Islamic insurance market, the Saudi government endorsed a new Islamic insurance law in July 2003, and it is expected to boost the market's turnover according to reports.

A third important factor is the ability of the insurance sector to provide long-term investment funding to the Saudi capital market due to the gradual rise in liquid assets available for investments after claims are paid. Life and general insurance companies in the developed world are important players in their capital markets. The Saudi insurance sector can also play such a role by providing depth and long-term investment outlook, compared to the individual investor volatility experienced in the Saudi stock market today, which is examined in the next chapter.

Foreign Participation in the Insurance Sector

As a result of its accession to the WTO, Saudi Arabia agreed to open its insurance sector to foreign investors and to allow foreign insurance companies to operate branches in the Kingdom. Amongst foreign companies having a local Saudi presence through joint ventures or in their own names are Allianz, Bupa, Ace and AXA.

By April 2010 there were 31 licensed insurance companies operating in Saudi Arabia employing around 5,500 staff, of whom 45% were Saudis in this new financial sector. To ensure that the sector had qualified employees, SAMA's Institute of Banking designed and conducted courses specifically for the insurance market and there was coordination with King Saud University in Riyadh to introduce a Bachelor programme in Actuarial Science as well as diploma courses.

Some major obstacles for insurance companies remain, however, in complying with Saudi Arabian government requirements for insurance providers to form incorporated cooperative joint stock companies. Saudi Arabia has declared that a commercial presence will be permitted for insurance companies which operate according to the cooperative insurance system and have a paid-up starting capital of not less than SR 100 million ($26.6 million). The government is also requiring insurance companies to allocate 20% of their annual profits to be added to their reserves until the reserves equal the entire paid-up capital. Because of these conditions, all operating insurance companies in the Kingdom are in the process of transforming their business operations and structures, while some are also exiting the market.

The government is giving a 3-year transition period to existing foreign insurance companies to either convert to a Saudi cooperative insurance company or to a direct branch of a foreign insurance company. During this transition period, existing foreign insurance providers will be allowed to continue business operations, as well as to offer new products and to service new clients.

WTO accession allowed for cross-border foreign insurance companies to continue providing insurance to Saudi-based clients, especially for large ticket insurance and re-insurance premiums, which the smaller capitalized Saudi insurance companies cannot cover. The benefits from greater foreign insurance participation in the domestic market is also claimed to bring the following:

- improvement in customer service and value,
- transfer of technological and managerial "know-how,"
- additional external financial capital,
- improvement in the quality of insurance regulation by applying international best practices, and
- creation of beneficial domestic spillover in terms of more and higher-quality local jobs.

These recent rapid developments in the Saudi insurance sector are one of the more promising features of the domestic financial market. Some commentators estimate that this liberalized and invigorated sector could create as many as 10,000 jobs, mostly for Saudis, and reach an annual turnover of SR 50 billion in another 5 years (AFP, 15 July 2003).

Islamic Finance in the Kingdom

Islamic financing, and a rapid increase in both Islamic and "conventional" institutions offering Islamic products and services, attests to the growing popularity of this market segment (Archer and Karim, 2002, Faroqui, 2002, Abdeen and Shook, 1984). The Saudi market is no exception, as evidenced by the remarkable market share that Al Rajhi Bank currently enjoys, and the conversion of a large number of the branches of the National Commercial Bank to "Islamic branches," as well as the licensing of two new *Shariah*-compliant banks – Al Bilad and Al Inma Bank.

Despite the lack of the word "Islamic" in the title of any Saudi financial institution, there is widespread support and encouragement for Islamic financing in the Kingdom. This support is manifested in the establishment of the Jeddah-based Islamic Development Bank (IDB), with the Kingdom contributing 25% of the $8 billion capital of the largest Islamic financial institution owned by all the members of the Organization of Islamic Conference (OIC). In addition, the Islamic Investment Company (IIC), a subsidiary of the Geneva-based *Dar Al Mall* Group, has nearly 20 branches in the major cities of Saudi Arabia, operating under a "quasi-legal" status through the personal sponsorship of HRH Prince Mohammed Al Faisal Al Saud, the late King Faisal's son. As we saw in Chapter 4, SAMA has been closely monitoring the experience of other GCC central banks in relation to controlling and supervising Islamic financial institutions.

The Bahrain Monetary Agency seems to have been the most successful one, as it served as a model of "coexistence" of conventional and Islamic banks under one regulator. SAMA's increased confidence about regulating this sector has been mirrored by the granting of more product licences and approvals for the launch of Islamically complaint mutual funds. There were 19 *Shariah*-compliant mutual funds listed on the Saudi stock market as of January 2010.

It is in the area of project finance that Islamic-oriented institutions such as Al Rajhi could play a developmental role in the economy. Currently, because of interest considerations, unlike other Saudi banks, Al Rajhi does not purchase government bonds or treasury notes to finance government budget deficits. However, Al Rajhi has successfully funded government projects on Islamic financing principles (lease financing, buy and sell, or buy, operate and lease) such as school construction and electricity projects. They are considering other government-related project financing. The success of such Islamically acceptable financing will open up a large market segment for the Saudi government, using Al Rajhi and other Islamic financing entities to fund the large capital projects the Kingdom needs over the next few decades. During 2004, one of the world's largest Islamic financing transactions was announced when a consortium of Saudi and Gulf banks (Al Rajhi, NCB, Abu Dhabi Islamic House, Emirates Bank, Citi group and SAMBA acting as arranger bank) concluded a \$2.35 billion *murabaha* financing for Ettihad Etisalat Company, which had been awarded the second GSM licence in Saudi Arabia (Ghazanfar, 27 September 2004).

Market reports indicate that Al Rajhi is going one step further in identifying new Islamic financing instruments and is considering underwriting a multi-billion riyal Saudi government Islamic bond programme. This would represent Saudi Arabia's first Islamic bond, and would follow on the footsteps of Bahrain's successful issue of similar Islamic leasing bonds of \$450 million. Such Islamic instruments would undoubtedly add breadth to the new Saudi capital market and provide Saudi investors with the choice of participating in Islamically acceptable products and, in the process, further deepen the Saudi financial system.

Conclusion

The Saudi banking sector's recent performance attests to its financial strength and efficiency. Management, risk control and cost efficiency have greatly improved, which to some extent explains the milder impact of lower oil prices on the Kingdom's financial institutions compared to previous periods of oil price downturns. The banking sector has seen a dramatic change in its operating environment, especially in the use of non-traditional banking services through the use of electronic means. The Kingdom of Saudi Arabia, after lagging behind many regional Arab countries in the use of the Internet, has seen the number of Internet users rise to about 7.7 million at the end of 2008 compared with around 1 million in 2001. The penetration ratio for the population stood at 31% for 2008 – higher than the global average of 23.5% and the Arab world average of 14% (SAMA, 2009). Such fundamental changes are forcing Saudi banks to rely on more technological delivery and "smarter" service out of home. The expansion of the insurance sector and its wider acceptance compared to earlier decades is another significant development, but it is the wider penetration of Islamic financing that will become a major revenue source for the local banks as they compete with the new-wave foreign licensed banks. Islamic banking by its nature had avoided the high-leverage and structured packages of conventional loans and investments in such offerings, and seemed to have escaped the worst excesses of the global financial turmoil.

In the process of financial globalization, there is increased pressure for consolidation between local banks and for cross-border alliances of choice. This chapter has illustrated how some Saudi banks have begun to venture abroad, and the trend to open branches or acquire overseas banks will become more noticeable in Asia, as Saudi Arabia develops a stronger economic relationship with the Far East.

The Saudi banking sector faced some serious challenges in the first decade of the new millennium, mostly arising from deteriorating global macroeconomic conditions and financial crisis. The Saudi banks had minor exposure to Western "toxic" assets and they faced the crisis on the basis of strong capitalization ratios.

The main source of risk for Saudi banks remains credit risk and high concentration, and possible exposure of some banks to the private corporate sector and family-owned businesses, highlighted by the debt repayment difficulties of some prominent Saudi family conglomerates. The local regulator, SAMA, has acted prudently and quickly to ensure adequate liquidity is available and guaranteed local depositors but the emphasis going forward is strengthened corporate governance and transparency at bank board level to avoid lax lending standards and "name lending" from rising up again. Other challenges faced by the Saudi banking sector include the mismatch in their maturity profile of assets and liabilities, and both domestic and foreign banks will have to come up with some innovative new capital instruments to reduce the imbalance in asset-liability maturities.

The Dubai bond repayment standstill announcement in November 2008 sent shock waves globally, and although Saudi banks were not exposed to the bonds, the consequence was that credit quality assessment of sovereign and semi-government entities in the region were bound to be affected in the medium to long term. The belief however is that global investors will end up differentiating between Gulf economies who are more highly leveraged, and those like Saudi Arabia that have managed to reduce the level of their domestic debt and have raised the level of their international reserves. The Saudi financial sector has come of age and seems more than capable to meet emerging challenges, reflected by the reaffirmation and credit upgrading of some of its institutions as well as sovereign credit rating by Standard & Poor and Moody's. The stability and maturity of the Saudi financial sector has played a large part in this perception.

Summary of Key Points

- *The Saudi banking sector is one of the financially strongest and most profitable in the world, with high capitalization in excess of international required levels, advanced automation and a diversified range of banking services delivered to well-defined target market segments.*

- *Banking supervision is through SAMA control. The transformation of previously wholly owned foreign bank branches into "Saudized" banks, passing on technology and management skills, has been of benefit to the banking sector.*
- *The Saudi financial markets passed through several phases of evolution, each laying foundation for the next phase. Currently the banking sector is going through a phase of consolidation and mergers, preparing to face globalization threats following WTO accession as well as the granting of banking licences for wholly owned foreign banks to enter the Saudi market.*
- *Saudi banks are characterized by a high degree of shareholder concentration levels, which could be counterbalanced by partial privatization of government-held shares in some Saudi banks.*
- *Saudi banks, lending policies are still limited by their small capital base as well as SAMA-mandated loans-to-deposit ratios, but consumer lending has become a major growth sector.*
- *The insurance sector will add some depth to the financial sector because of foreign entry and government-mandated insurance laws in health and vehicle insurance.*
- *Islamic finance has acquired more importance, and both Islamic and non-Islamic banks have entered this market segment.*
- *Saudi banks have escaped relatively unscathed during the 2008/2009 global financial crisis but certain lessons have been learned, especially the centrality of credit extension.*

Chapter 6
The Saudi Capital Market

A fool and his money are soon parted.

George Buchanan

Learning Outcomes

By the end of this section, you would understand:

- *Role of capital markets in economic development*
- *The historical development of the Saudi capital market*
- *Functions of the Capital Market Authority*
- *Performance of the Saudi capital market, and its international comparisons*
- *Sectoral performance of the Saudi capital market and new listings*
- *Analysis of Saudi investor behaviour*
- *The Saudi mutual fund industry*
- *Deepening of the capital market*

Introduction

The role of capital markets in economic development has increasingly been empha-sized as an important tool of financial intermediation. Saudi Arabia has been endowed with enormous wealth, gained in a short period of time. An efficient cap-ital market structure could help in recycling capital surpluses, especially those held by the private sector. There is no doubt that Saudi Arabia possesses such capital surplus.

The development of a broader and deeper capital market will lead to other bene-fits, encouraging the creation of new risk management instruments (such as interest rate hedging, futures and options) while widening the scope of central banks to allow them to conduct monetary policy through open-market operations (Azzam, 2002). It is also recognized that a well-developed capital market, especially a stock market,

M.A. Ramady, *The Saudi Arabian Economy*, DOI 10.1007/978-1-4419-5987-4_6,
© Springer Science+Business Media, LLC 2010

performs at least three other functions. It is a signalling mechanism to managers regarding investment, a source of finance and a catalyst for corporate governance.

In principle, stock markets are a useful tool for economic development. Efficient stock markets pool private funds, and allocate them for corporate investment. This gives firms access to cheaper capital than traditional bank finance and also helps them to mitigate financial risk. Stock markets also encourage efficiency through the prospect of takeover: if management does not maximize shareholder value, then another economic agent could take control of the firm and introduce more efficient practices and personnel.

Academic research indicates that various measures of stock market activity are positively correlated with stronger economic growth and productivity improvement across countries and that the association is particularly strong in emerging markets.

Establishing a National Stock Market Carries with It Risks and Responsibilities

For example, very liquid stock markets might negatively influence corporate gover- nance: with share prices rising, investors might be tempted to take a relaxed view of management practices, in the knowledge that they can sell their shares at any time and for a profit. This seemed to have occurred during the period 2005–2006 in Saudi Arabia when the stock market increased by virtually 100% a year or more before crashing in 2006. Markets also tend to favour big firms over smaller ones, often with little regard to efficiency. Thus, large inefficient firms are more likely to take over and/or absorb small efficient firms without any improvement in their own man- agement practices. For a market to thrive, it also needs to have robust supporting architecture, such as good-quality institutions and a well-functioning supervisory structure.

A key question is whether stock market prices affect investment, independent of fundamentals of the economy and the financial health of companies, causing a misallocation of capital, which can lead to considerable damage at the sectoral level (Bolbol and Omran, 2004). As will be discussed later in this chapter, the Saudi capital market has seen sharp volatility due to several factors, necessitating the need for an efficient regulator.

Saudi Capital Market Developments: A Historical Perspective

Plans for establishing a formal Saudi stock market have been in the making since the early 1980s (Abdeen and Shook, 1984). It is interesting to note some of the major concerns raised then regarding elements that might be a hindrance to the smooth functioning of a Saudi stock market, and to assess whether the same "prob- lems" continue to exist in the new millennium. According to earlier observers (Dukheil, 1995, Abdeen and Shook, 1984), the first problem related to the lack of an "organized legal framework for a stock exchange," with three sources of official directives controlling the stock market. A second problem concerned the "non-specialist" offices that emerged to deal with shares. A third difficulty was the "ownership of a large percentage of shares by board members and founders." A fourth challenge was that "most Saudi citizens have little understanding of stock market operations and transactions." Such transactions were based on rumours, because of a lack of analysis of companies' financial positions, profitability or other financial considerations. Another problem, according to the early market observers, was that citizens from "other Gulf countries invested in Saudi stocks via Saudi agents."

Even in those early days, there were recommendations for overcoming such problems. These included the "assigning of one government body responsible for share companies; establishment of an effective set of regulations for the organization of stock operations and transactions"; and the imposing of limits on individual stock ownership. A final plea was made for increasing the number of publicly held companies in the Kingdom in order to "increase the potential number of issues and shares." In 1983, Saudi Arabia could only boast 38 publicly listed companies, while Kuwait had 48 (Abdeen and Shook, 1984, Nashashibi, 1983).

Until the Saudi Capital Market Law (CML) was passed in 2003, the Kingdom was slow to restructure its stock market to encourage private domestic investment. The Saudi stock market remained more a "government-controlled banking consortium" than a real stock market (Cordesman, 2003).

From 2003 to date a determined effort has been made to structure the operational and regulatory capability of the Saudi Capital Market Authority (CMA), as the benefit from such a determined reform can contribute to the economic development of the Kingdom, fuelled by the provision of risk capital. Transparent, efficient and well-regulated markets can add to the general level of investor confidence, and can reverse capital flight as happened during the periods 2002–2004 and 2008–2009 owing to fear of investing in falling Western assets and global financial instability.

A new capital market law, although essential to market reform, dragged on for many years. The Capital Market Law, which was approved by the cabinet and passed into law in November 2003, was only implemented in July 2004. The pace of change had more to do with the conservative regulatory approach adopted by the Saudi Arabian Monetary Agency (SAMA), the financial market supervising authority. However, the intention for reform seems to address most of the issues and problems highlighted by observers of the early stock market.

Saudi Capital Market Operation

Before analysing the new Capital Market Law and the Capital Market Authority (CMA), it would be useful to examine the stock market structure that this new law replaced. By examining the deficiencies in the previous system, we can assess

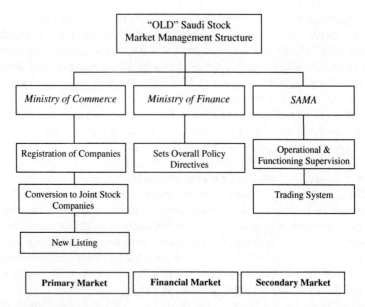

Fig. 6.1 "Old" Saudi stock market

whether the new law has rectified outstanding operating concerns. Figure 6.1 illustrates the workings of the "old" stock market structure.

As noted from Fig. 6.1, the "old" Saudi stock market structure operated under three masters. The Ministry of Commerce was directly responsible for the formation of new companies, the conversion of firms to joint stock companies and IPOs. In essence, it was the primary market function. The second regulator was the Ministry of Finance, which set the overall policy directives and objectives of the stock market. Finally, SAMA controlled the operational and functional management of the Saudi stock market. This was the secondary market function. Share trading activity was executed through Saudi commercial banks that were responsible for the settlement of transactions between buyers and sellers against a maximum 1% commission. Figure 6.1 highlights the absence of an exchange bourse and of independent market makers. Under the old regulations, forward trading of shares and acceptance of post-dated checks to settle transactions were prohibited, no doubt influenced by what happened during the Kuwaiti *Souk Al-Manakh* 1982 stock market crash.

In 1985, SAMA introduced certain operational improvements in the share-dealing process. First, it established the Saudi Shares Registration Company (SSRC) and limited its shareholding to banks. However, share ownership was based on a physical documentation exchange. In 1990, SAMA introduced an electronic trading system called Electronics Securities Information System (ESIS), through which all the buy and sell orders placed at individual banks are transferred from bank computers to a central system at SAMA for matching. This fostered market liquidity and increased trading volume. The overall price movement in the Saudi stock market was tracked by the *Bakheet* and CCFI stock market indexes, which were the most widely quoted Saudi indexes, similar to the Dow Jones index for the USA.

In 2001, an automated trading system called *TADAWUL* was launched which enabled trading to be carried out through the Internet. By virtue of its ease, transparency and speed in processing, *TADAWUL* gave yet another boost in trading volumes for the Saudi stock market. It is no exaggeration to state that as of 2004, the Saudi stock market trading system became one of the most technologically advanced system in the world, with *T + Zero* delivery – transaction plus zero days. The establishment of *TADAWUL* enabled a new stock market index to emerge called *TASI* or *TADAWUL All Share Index* and it is currently quoted as the official Saudi stock market index.

Participation in the Saudi stock market was initially restricted to Saudi citizens, Saudi corporations and Gulf Cooperation Council (GCC) citizens. Foreign participation was initially allowed in the banks' mutual funds, with the first closed Saudi mutual fund (SAIF) introduced by the Saudi American Bank in 1997. In 1999, the stock market was opened for foreign investment through a wider range of Saudi bank mutual funds. In 2006, there were further significant developments, as the Kingdom announced that it would also allow foreigners resident in Saudi Arabia to invest directly in the stock market in order to strengthen the bourse, a move welcomed by many as it provided more investment choice rather than through mutual funds. In August 2008, the CMA approved new rules that allowed non-Arab foreigners to participate in share trading through "swap" arrangements with local CMA approved and licensed intermediaries in the hope of adding depth to market participants, especially foreign institutional investors. In March 2010, the CMA advised that it planned to start its first exchange-traded fund (ETF) and will allow non-resident foreign investors to trade in it.

The New Capital Market Law

After deliberation by the *Majlis Al-Shoura* or Consultative Council of Saudi Arabia in December 2002, a new Capital Market Law composed of 67 Articles was passed by the Council of Ministers in June 2003, with the law taking effect from November 2003 after publication in the Official Gazette.

At first glance, the new law seems to address some of the more glaring shortfalls of the "old" stock market structure, which had no independent brokerage firms, no investment advisory and custodial services and little or no market-making capabilities. Above all, the "old" law lacked an independent financial market regulator. The "new" law establishes an independent Saudi Arabian Securities and Exchange Commission (SEC), which later became the Capital Market Authority (CMA), the sole regulator of the stock market, with the objective of protecting investor interests, ensuring orderly and equitable dealing in securities and promoting and developing the capital markets. The CMA had the power to license non-bank financial intermediaries and to authorize the offering of securities to the public.

It also established the first ever national securities depository centre. In terms of management, the CMA was to be governed by five commissioners appointed by Royal Decree, one of whom will be nominated as Chairman and another as Vice Chairman. As Fig. 6.2 illustrates, the head of the CMA reports directly to the Prime Minister – the King of Saudi Arabia – to ensure that maximum freedom of power is given to the sensitive position of head of CMA.

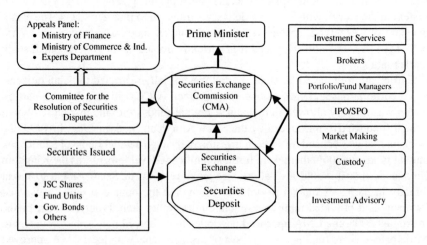

Fig. 6.2 The new Saudi capital market regulatory structure

In July 2004, a Royal Decree was issued naming Jammaz Al Suhaimi as Chairman with ministerial rank, Mohammed Al Rumaih as Vice Chairman as well as the other three members of the commission. The appointment of the Chairman was widely welcomed because of the continuity it brought. Mr. Suhaimi was the Deputy Governor of the Banking Control Department at SAMA and had been closely involved in the "old" Saudi stock market operations. In May 2006, Dr. Abdulrahman Al Tuwaijri was appointed as acting Chairman of the Capital Market Authority and was later confirmed as Chairman by Royal Decree in May 2009 along with a new Vice Chairman Abdulrahman Al Rashid, with Mazen Al Romaih and Abdulrahman Al Barrak as new commissioners. Mr. Mohamed Al Shumrani retained his position as Commissioner in the CMA reshuffle. Before that, in 2007, the Saudi government approved the establishment of the Saudi Capital Market Company with a capital of SR 1.2 billion, converting *TADAWUL* into a joint stock company fully owned by the Public Investment Fund, a decision that seemed to go in line with international stock market operations. Future plans call for part of the new company's share to be floated for public subscription.

While there is a large degree of autonomy for the CMA, there is also some measure of close cooperation with other government bodies.

Figure 6.2 highlighted the "Committee for the Resolution of Securities Disputes," which can use the services of an appeal panel composed of members from the Ministry of Finance, Ministry of Commerce and the Experts Department.

A novel feature of the Capital Market Law was the establishment of a Securities Exchange or "bourse" which incorporated the National Securities Depository. The exchange will be a private sector company, with a board of nine members, three from the government (Ministries of Finance and Commerce, as well as SAMA) and six from shareholders of the exchange. It will be the only stock exchange operating in the Kingdom, and its wide powers include the following:

- Ensuring fairness and transparency of the market
- Admitting members (brokering and clearing)
- Listing new companies
- Promoting high ethical standards amongst members, employees and market participants
- Promoting high standards of corporate governance
- Ensuring timely and accurate dissemination of market information
- Establishing and operating a nationwide system for securities trading, settlement clearing and depository service

The above seems laudable and could reduce deficiencies in corporate disclosure under the old law. The new Capital Market Law also sets out in some detail (Articles 35–64) the type of penalties and punishment for wrongdoing, which could be an important deterrent.

However, some could argue that the imposition of a maximum fine of SR 100,000 for each violation committed (Article 59(b)) was too lenient, given that no jail sentences are specified in the new law, especially for "insider information" trading, which has been a flaw in even developed and regulated capital markets.

The CMA has been aware of this, and over the past few years the level of fines and public disclosure of those committing them have been increasing, especially the latter, in a society which is sensitive to name disclosure of wrongdoers. The recent publicly reported actions taken by the CMA include the following decisions:

- *October 2005* – Suspension of an investor who sold large quantities of shares in two companies after publicly praising their prospects but quietly selling them after price manipulation.
- *October 2005* – Investigation and suspension of a trader for not declaring a stake of more than 5% built up in *Mubarrad Services Company.*
- *June 2009* – Imposing a fine of SR 100,000 on one of the Saudi market's top five retail investors after an appellate body affirmed that he had conducted insider trading in shares of Saudi Hotels Company based on his membership of the company's board, and was ordered to pay $3.37 million profit that the CMA said he had made in trading the shares.
- *October 2009* – Fining board members of the Saudi Chemical Company SR 50,000 each for allegedly approving an acquisition in which the Chairman had a vested interest, but failed to consult shareholders.

- *December 2009* – Imposing sanctions and fines on five people for insider trading and stock market manipulation, ranging from SR 450,000 to SR 250,000, and ordered to reimburse back around SR 3 million between them.
- *December 2009* – Fining the listed company National Industrialization Company (Tasnee) SR 50,000 for not disclosing the resignation of a senior finance and investment executive.

Over the period 2008–2009, according to the CMA, the supervisory body had revoked the licences of a dozen brokerage firms for violating market laws and regulations. Commendable in terms of boosting investor confidence and improving market transparency was that the above CMA actions were imposed on a wide range of individuals and corporations without fear or favour, to send out a strong signal about the CMA's vigilance and deterrence intentions.

Organization Structure and Operations of the CMA

According to the CMA, its vision is to raise the efficiency of the Saudi capital market and to enhance its competitive strengths by building on the best international standards and practices (CMA, 2009). Figure 6.3 sets out the CMA organizational chart which illustrates the depth of specialization that the CMA has at its disposal today compared to the pre-2004 Saudi stock market organization structure.

Over the past few years, the CMA's enforcement and market supervision functions have become more prominent, as incumbents in these positions gained experience and confidence in pursuing cases brought to their attention or through

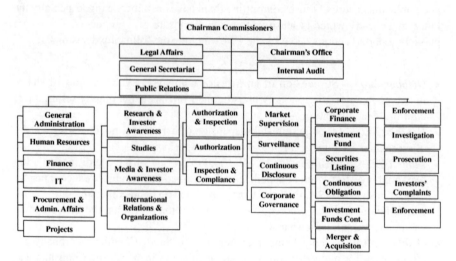

Fig. 6.3 Saudi CMA organizational structure (Source: CMA)

Table 6.1 Parties subject to CMA control and supervision

Party	Definition
1. *TADAWUL* Saudi stock exchange	• *TADAWUL* is the sole entity authorized to carry out trading in Saudi Arabia in securities trading and responsible for all operations of the exchange
2. Authorized persons	• Legal entities authorized to carry on securities business and only persons holding a valid licence issued by CMA are allowed to perform this function
3. Listed companies	• Companies whose securities are traded in the Saudi capital market *TADAWUL*
4. Traders	• Entities representing the public who trade in securities in the Saudi capital market

Source: CMA, 2009

inspection. At the same time, investor awareness programmes have become an important CMA tool to try and stabilize market speculation, as we will note later on in the chapter when analysing Saudi stock market behaviour.

The key players that are subject to CMA supervision and control are set out in Table 6.1.

Since its formation, the CMA has issued the basic guiding regulatory frameworks for those operating in the Saudi capital market, and an array of "implementation regulations" and regulatory decisions are available for authorized persons and others to refer to as guidance. Table 6.2 summarizes the main implementation regulations issued by the CMA since 2004.

The CMA regulations also comply to international best standards, as the CMA has established close cooperation with Western regulators such as the UK's Financial Services Authority (FSA) and the USA's Security and Exchange Commission (SEC).

On the operations side, the CMA has sought to enhance its capability, especially in systems that could detect stock trading manipulation. In 2006, the *TADAWUL* signed a contract with OMX, a leading supplier and operator for stock exchange trading that originated in Sweden which soon became the largest in the Nordic countries before being taken over by NASDAQ in the USA in 2007. The implementation of new systems now allows the CMA to obtain real-time reports and analyses of unusual trading activities and pinpoint violations, hence the pick-up in trading violations detection since 2008, illustrated in Fig. 6.4 by category of violations.

The CMA has also been active in issuing new directives at market participants and some of the key directives are summarized as follows:

- *2006* – prohibiting listed Saudi joint stock companies to buy and sell securities for themselves unless these financial activities are explicitly stated in the participating companies' codes and regulations.
- *2006* – drafting of regulations for the issuance of *sukuks* or Islamic bonds.
- *2007* – the introduction of "book-building" for new initial public offerings (IPOs) in Saudi Arabia to determine the price of shares for new listings. As such, market

demand and supply forces would determine the price of new IPOs and not financial advisors or the company. The change to book-building came on the heels of the spectacular crash of the Saudi stock market in 2006 which had left individual investors losing out after purchasing new share offerings during an equity boom in the previous 2 years, and paying prices set by the companies on flotation and not through market demand and supply forces.

- *2009* – establishing a market for debt securities including *sukuk* bonds helping to add depth to the Saudi capital market.

Table 6.2 Major Saudi CMA implementation regulations and regulatory decisions (2004–2009)

Year	Regulation type	Key aspects covered
2004	• Market conduct regulation	• Sets out key guiding principles in terms of prohibition of market manipulation, insider trading, untrue statements and authorized persons' conduct
2005	• Securities business regulation	• Defines the securities business scope and carrying out security business, exclusions from authorizations and established procedures for securities advertisements
2006	• Real estate investment funds regulations	• Establish the operating framework for the real estate investment funds in Saudi Arabia, fund management disclosure, fund asset requirements, custody of assets and the functions of the fund managers as well as valuation and custodian services for such funds
	• Investment funds regulations	• Establish the authorization process and offer of launching of such funds, the required level of disclosure to the public, the organization of investment funds and the role of fund managers, fund governance and the methods of offers and redemption of funds
	• Listing rules	• Set out the role of the financial advisor, conditions for admission and listing, admission to the official list and compliance with listing rules and the continuing obligations after listing
2007	• Merger and acquisition regulations	• Set out the steps for announcements and takeover timetable for M&As, independent advice and restrictions on dealings, acceptance conditions and compliance of the offer with competition law, documentation on display and the method of profit and asset valuation precast
2008	• Anti-money laundering and counter-terrorist financing rules	• Establish the principles of AMT/CTF procedures, beneficial ownership, business relationships, clients and counterparties as well as dealing with non-profit organizations and politically exposed persons
	• Offers of securities regulations	• Set out the general provisions on offers of securities in Saudi Arabia, public offers and private placements, as well as the liability for incorrect documents
2009	• Corporate governance regulations	• Establish the rights of shareholders and the role of the general assembly, the level of disclosure and transparency and the role and responsibilities of the board of directors

Source: CMA

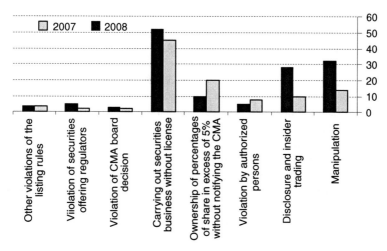

Fig. 6.4 CMA – Total number of investigations into suspected violations by type (2007 and 2008) (Source: CMA, 2009)

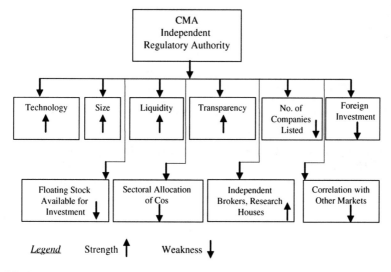

Fig. 6.5 Assessment of current strengths and weaknesses of the Capital Market Law

Given all the above developments in the "new" Saudi capital market structure, what are the remaining areas of weaknesses of the CMA going forward? Figure 6.5 identifies the perceived areas of current strengths and weaknesses of the CMA and the Capital Market Law.

Figure 6.5 points to strengths in independence, technology, transparency, size, independent brokers and researchers and liquidity. Weaknesses, however, remain in the areas of the number of companies currently listed, the limited participation of foreign investment despite some progress on this and the low level of floating stock available for investment due to the high level of shareholder concentration.

One of the major drawbacks of the Saudi stock market had been the small number of listed companies in relation to the size of the Saudi economy. In 2002, there were 68 listed companies with share capital of SR 38 billion compared to 121 registered joint stock companies, with SR 81.3 billion share capital (SAMA, 2003). There were another 6,000 limited-liability Saudi companies operating in the Kingdom and 1,400 joint venture companies (Saudi and non-Saudi), with a combined SR 85.5 billion of share capital.

By December 2009 the number of listed companies had risen to 134 with a share capital of SR 596 billion. At the same time, the number of registered joint stock companies were 400 with SR 470.2 billion share capital, with another 16,908 limited-liability and joint venture companies with a combined SR 155.6 billion in share capital (SAMA, 2009). The increase in listed companies on the Saudi capital market is illustrated in Table 6.3 for the period 1990–2009.

Table 6.3 Saudi listed companies and number of shares issued (1990–2009)

Year	Companies listed	Total shares issued (Million)
1996	70	3,921
1997	70	3,983
2002	68	9,807
2006	86	19,328
2007	111	30,728
2008	127	39,728
2009	134	41,223

Source: CMA

Despite the increase in the number of listed Saudi companies over the 7-year period, there was still a large potential for more IPOs and expansion of the stock market. According to some analysts, current Saudi listing requirements have been onerous and could explain the slow pace of new IPOs and listing (Najjar, 1998, Dukhayil, 2002, Azzam, 2002, Cordesman, 2003).

According to the Saudi Ministry of Commerce regulations, the procedure to convert into a joint stock company involves several necessary conditions. The major requirements are listed in Table 6.4, which sets out both the old listing requirements and those that were introduced in 1999 by the ministry.

Besides the requirements listed in Table 6.4, there was another, rather unspecified condition relating to the management of a joint stock company. That provision set that the company was to have "able administrative and efficient internal controls." Until the level of corporate transparency rises and the quality of regular reports is raised to higher standards, in the immediate term, the Kingdom's regulators well err on the side of caution to protect investors from "rushed" IPOs and public listing, as it is felt that the threshold levels for company conversions to a Saudi joint stock company had already been significantly reduced in the 1999 Ministry of Commerce requirements.

Table 6.4 Rules for company conversion into a Saudi joint stock company

Parameters	Pre-1999	Post-1999
• Net assets	• SR 75 million	• SR 50 million
• Return on shareholders' equity	• 10% for the last 5 years to be maintained for next 5 years	• 7% for the last 3 years to be maintained for next 3 years
• Public subscription	• 51%	• 40%
• Company age	• 10 years	• 5 years

Source: Ministry of Commerce, Riyadh, 2002

Regulatory Supervision and Inherent Biases

However well-intentioned a regulator, sometimes there are flaws arising due to ingrained systematic biases that can lead to systematic errors as opposed to random errors which tend to cancel each other out. Such potential CMA biases can be summarized as falling under the categories shown in Table 6.5.

Table 6.5 Potential CMA regulatory biases

Regulatory bias	Cause and effect
A. Supervision bias	
1. Focusing observation and trustworthy biases	*Cause*: CMA could suffer from focusing too much on recent and immediately available information. As such, the CMA is too quick to see a pattern in a series of events that are random. CMA may suffer from observation bias, by placing too much weight on probability of past events that actually occurred, relative to those that did not. CMA might also have an "attribution" bias, leading investigators to overestimate the influence of perceived outlook (e.g. fraud) in explaining behaviour while overlooking the influence of the person's particular circumstances in any given situation
2. Seeding effect	• *Cause*: This may lead the CMA to act vigorously in cases to avoid possible investor losses or erosion in CMA's own authority. Many of the CMA's regulatory initiatives were launched shortly after either large investor losses or threat of diminished CMA authority
B. Operational bias	
1. Overconfidence bias	• *Cause*: CMA may be overconfident in their policy prescriptions leading to errors and regulatory overreach. Example is CMA's decision of reduction of repaying commissions from banks to investors before April 2006 market crash. CMA officials were confident that decision taken would reduce speculation but investors took this as a signal that stock prices were overvalued and caused massive selling

Table 6.5 (continued)

Regulatory bias	Cause and effect
2. Confirmation bias	• *Cause*: Once regulations are on the books, regulators may feel the need to justify their worth instead of critically evaluating their effects. Evidence that does not discredit regulation unambiguously will be ignored. CMA regulators that focus on the success of the Saudi securities markets may become "locked in," making future changes to regulations difficult
3. Group think bias	• *Cause*: Cognitive biases within the CMA could be magnified by organizational "group think," which occurs when individuals come to identify with the organization in an uncritical manner, deferring to consensus. The CMA is known for its strong organizational culture and the mission of investor protection is taken to heart by CMA staff which could reduce the range of potential hypothesis that an organization considers when faced with a problem
C. *Regulation bias* 1. Bounded rationality bias	• *Cause*: The CMA receives vast amounts of information ranging from registration statements for IPOs, periodic filings for public companies and filings for the secondary market transactions. Through its enforcement arm, the CMA receives daily intelligence on market manipulation and potential fraud. Dealing with such a multitude of factors, regulators often develop a "tunnel vision" and stick to known regulatory schemes and are unable to assess all market risks and prioritize them due to the "bounded capabilities" of the regulatory staff

To its credit the CMA has become aware of many of the possible regulatory biases that can affect its operations and CMA staff are provided with extensive refresher on- and off-site training courses to ensure that they recognize and deal with emerging complex financial oversight and control. This will become even more important as the Saudi capital market deepens in terms of the range of securities offerings and the number and type of market players expand internationally, and when one day Saudi companies will be able to have dual listing of their shares in other major international bourses, thus adding to the complexity of CMA supervision.

The Saudi Capital Market: Arab World's Largest

Over the past decade, the Saudi capital market has overtaken all the other Arab capital markets to becoming the largest as illustrated in Table 6.6.

From the table, Saudi Arabia not only dominates the rest of the Arab world's bourses in terms of market capitalization and the value of shares traded, but also in

Table 6.6 Arab capital market indicators (2008)

Country	Market capitalization ($ Billion)	Value of shares traded ($ Billion)	Number of listed companies	GDP at current prices ($ Billion)	Market depth %[a]	Turnover ratio %[b]
GCC Region						
Saudi Arabia	*246.5*	*523.4*	*127*	*465.6*	*53*	*212.3*
Kuwait	70.1	133.6	204	148.4	47.3	190.4
Bahrain	19.9	2.1	51	18.6	107.1	10.5
Oman	15.2	8.7	122	46.4	32.6	57.4
Abu Dhabi	68.8	63.1	65	240.4	28.6	91.7
Dubai	63.1	83.1	65	240.4	26.3	131.7
Qatar	76.6	48.2	43	95.8	80.0	62.9
Other Arab						
Egypt	85.9	87.9	373	159.2	54.0	102.4
Morocco	65.7	14.0	77	87.0	75.6	21.4
Jordan	35.8	28.6	262	20.1	178.4	80.0
Tunisia	6.3	1.7	50	38.9	16.2	26.8
Algeria	0.09	0.3	2	152.3	0.1	0.3
Palestine	2.1	1.2	37	6.2	34.2	58.1
Lebanon	9.6	1.7	13	28.3	33.9	17.8

[a]Market depth = Ratio of market capitalization to GDP
[b]Turnover ratio = Value of traded shares to market capitalization of shares at end of period
Source: SAMA

terms of market depth and trading turnover. The second largest GCC capital market is Qatar's followed by Kuwait's, but the turnover ratio for Kuwait is three times that of Qatar. From the non-GCC countries, Egypt, with almost triple the population size of Saudi Arabia, has the second largest Arab market capitalization. Algeria's market activities are negligible for the country's GDP size, with only around 4% of Algeria's GDP, and is surpassed even by Palestine's stock market.

In most developed economies, the turnover ratio generally exceeds the total market capitalization. This has been rising for Saudi Arabia but it picked up sharply after 2004, before subsiding following the market crash of 2006 as illustrated in Table 6.7.

Besides the above measures, sometimes it is also valuable to examine the degree of liquidity and riskiness measures of stock market volumes. While market liquidity is measured by the annual turnover ratio and Table 6.7 indicates that the Saudi market has generally been very liquid, the level of market risk can also be measured by *annual volatility*. The annual turnover-to-volatility measure relates price swings to value-traded swings, and Table 6.8 examines this for the major GCC and Arab markets.

Analysis of Table 6.8 reveals that in terms of turnover ratio, the Saudi market is the most liquid of all the Arab markets. All the Arab markets, however, exhibited stable and non-volatile conditions in 2009 as they were all below 1.0, above which

Table 6.7   Saudi Arabian share market indicators (1993–2008)

Year	Value of shares traded (SR billion)	Market capitalization (SR billion)	Turnover ratio (%)	Market capitalization as % of GDP
1998	51.5	159.6	32.2	29.3
1999	56.6	228.6	24.8	37.9
2000	65.3	255.0	25.6	36.1
2001	83.6	275.0	30.4	39.4
2002	133.8	280.7	47.6	40.4
2003	596.5	589.9	48.0	48.9
2004	1,773.9	1,148.0	154.3	122
2005	4,138.7	2,438.2	169.7	206
2006	5,261.9	1,225.9	429.19	91.7
2007	2,557.7	1,946.4	131.4	135
2008	1,962.9	924.0	212.4	53

Source: SAMA

Table 6.8   Arab stock market volatility (2009)

Country	Turnover ratio	Annual volatility (%)	Annual turnover/volatility ratio (%)
GCC countries			
Saudi Arabia	*1.01*	*0.44*	*2.30*
Abu Dhabi	0.26	0.47	0.54
Dubai	0.79	0.50	1.58
Qatar	0.28	0.52	0.53
Kuwait	0.71	0.32	2.25
Oman	0.29	0.36	0.81
Bahrain	0.03	0.24	0.12
Other Arab			
Egypt	0.59	0.35	1.66
Morocco	0.14	0.25	0.56
Tunisia	0.13	0.17	0.75
Lebanon	0.05	0.36	0.14

Source: Riyad Capital, 2010

markets are classified as being volatile (unstable if above 1.8 levels). Analysis of the annual turnover-to-volatility ratio is an important factor in assessing the measure of market liquidity. The higher the turnover-to-volatility ratio is, the more liquid is the market and such markets should be able to handle swings in volumes of trading without large price swings. From Table 6.8, both Saudi Arabia and Kuwait seemed to have the most ability to absorb large swings in trading volumes without large swings in price and volatility. In the non-GCC Arab countries, Egypt had the most ability to absorb large swings in trading volumes.

Free Share Float Is an Issue

Being liquid is one matter. Having enough "free float" shares available for trading is just as important to enable markets to operate efficiently without distorting prices based on trades in a few shares. Earlier studies on the Saudi stock market (Azzam, 1997a) had estimated the level of free float to be around 47.7% for 1995. By the end of 2009, according to *TADAWUL*, the level of free float had fallen to just under 38% for the whole market as illustrated in Table 6.9, but with significant sectoral differences.

From Table 6.9 one observes that the lowest free float was in the multi-investment sector at just 8.4% while the highest level of free float was in the retail services and

Table 6.9 Saudi Arabia shares outstanding and those held by the public as free float (2003–2009)

Sector	2003[a]			2009		
	Total out-standing shares (mil-lions)	Shares held by public free float (mil-lions)	Free float as % of total shares outstand-ing	Total out-standing shares (mil-lions)	Shares held by public free float (Million)	Free float as % of total shares outstand-ing
1. Banking and financial services	378.9	226.8	60	8,903.9	4,711.5	52.9
2. Petrochemical industries sector	455.7	186.8	41	8,664.7	3,533.7	40.8
3. Cement	118.9	80.8	68	828.0	569.9	68.8
4. Retail services	177.5	127.8	72	302.5	215.8	71.3
5. Energy and utilities	765.7	290.9	38	4,241.6	766.9	18.0
6. Agriculture and food	36.0	30.6	85	939.4	666.2	70.9
7. Telecommunication	300.0	249.0	83	4,200	1,400	33.3
8. Insurance sector	N/A	N/A	N/A	661.0	254.3	38.5
9. Multi-investment sector	N/A	N/A	N/A	6,616.6	552.4	8.27
10. Building and construction	N/A	N/A	N/A	666.2	447.6	67.2
11. Real estate development	N/A	N/A	N/A	3,136.2	1,427.6	47.2
12. Transport	N/A	N/A	N/A	476.3	339.5	71.3
13. Media and publishing	N/A	N/A	N/A	155.0	91.8	59.3
14. Hotel and tourism	N/A	N/A	N/A	79.3	46.5	58.8
15. Industrial investment sector	N/A	N/A	N/A	1,352.4	586.5	43.4
Total sectors	2,232.7	1,192.7	53.4	41,223.1	15,660.2	37.9

[a]By 2007, the CMA had introduced 15 sub-sectors compared with 7
N/A: Not available as not segregated
Source: SAMA, CMA

transport sectors at around 71%. The prime reason for the low float in the multi-investment sector was the fact that only 5% or 315 million shares were available for trading out of 6,300 million issued by Kingdom Holding Company owned by Prince Al Waleed bin Tallal bin Abdulaziz. This skewed the sector average considerably, but the energy/utilities, telecommunications and insurance sectors had low free float shares. As noted earlier in the chapter, there is a need to list more Saudi companies on the exchange to enable a larger float of shares and so avoid undue market price movements due to trades in a few shares of closely held sectors affecting the overall market.

Saudi Capital Market Performance

The Saudi stock market is relatively higher than global and other emerging markets in terms of dividend yield, reflecting the preference for high dividends not only in Saudi Arabia but also amongst the other GCC countries. This is illustrated in Fig. 6.6 as well as in Fig. 6.7, which sets out the price/earnings ratios for Saudi Arabia *TADAWUL* TASI index and other markets.

Despite the volatility and underperformance of the Saudi TASI in 2009, the price/earning ratio is relatively at the same level with other emerging economies such as Brazil, Russia as well as the S&P 500 index. The Saudi P/E ratios, however, are higher than GCC peers which range from 7 to 11, compared with a Saudi P/E ratio of nearly 18, causing some concern that another asset price bubble might be developing in Saudi Arabia, but traditionally Saudi P/E ratios are at these high ranges. The Saudi capital market though has had a roller-coaster experience, especially during the period 2005–2009 as illustrated in Fig. 6.8 for volatility in the Saudi

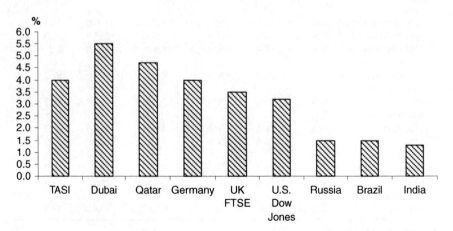

Fig. 6.6 Dividend yield: Saudi TASI and other selected markets' indexes (January 2010) (Source: CMA, Bloomberg)

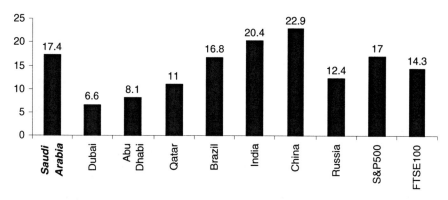

Fig. 6.7 Price earnings ratios: Saudi TASI and other selected markets' indexes (January, 2010) (Source: Bloomberg)

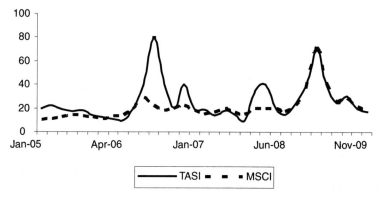

Fig. 6.8 Saudi TASI and MSCI-EM: volatility comparison 2005–2009 (Source: Bloomberg)

TASI in comparison with the Morgan Stanley Capital Index (MSCI) for emerging markets.

The greatest period of volatility compared to the MSCI was during the period 2006–2007 when Saudi P/E ratios reached a high of 67 in February 2006, and in some cases exceeded 100 for a few companies. Expected corporate profit growth began to be ahead of actual results, compounded by some annual company reporting showing that many companies had invested heavily in the stock market and booked unrealized stock exchange earnings. It was this asset bubble build-up and companies entering into non-core financial transactions activities that forced the CMA in 2006 to introduce directives prohibiting listed companies from buying and selling securities of listed companies for themselves, unless these are explicitly stated in their company codes and regulations. By 2006 there was sign that the Saudi market was overheating when the *TADAWUL* index touched the 21,000 level in February 2006 and then started its sharp fall to close at the 7,000 levels. The Saudi year-end

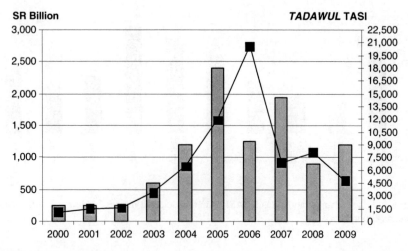

Fig. 6.9 Saudi market index year ends and *TADAWUL* TASI highest levels reached, 2000–2009 (Source: SAMA, CMA, *TADAWUL*)

market capitalization and the highest levels reached by the *TADAWUL* TASI index are set out in Fig. 6.9. By 2009 the Saudi index and market capitalization were once again at the levels of 2004, and in May 2010 the TASI touched 5,750.

Sectoral Performance of the Saudi Market

Like any other stock market in the world, the Saudi TASI composite stock market index masks sectoral differences. The Saudi stock market has 15 sectors and, in order of size, finance and basic materials are the dominant sectors, together accounting for just under 70% of market capitalization, with the two biggest companies Saudi Arabian Basic Industries (SABIC) and Al Rajhi Bank accounting for around 11% of the market. Figure 6.10 illustrates the Saudi market capitalization for year-end 2009 by the different sectors.

What is of some concern for the Saudi capital market is that while some of the smaller sectors have a larger number of companies, they only account for a smaller percent of the market capitalization. As such, a small movement in the highly capitalized sectors will unduly influence the whole market index.

This is demonstrated in Fig. 6.11, which sets out the sectoral activities for 2009 in terms of value of shares traded, the volume for the year and the number of transactions. Volume indicates how many trades took place for a security on a given day, with high trading volume an indicator of high investor interest.

What is noticeable is that the largest value of share trading was in petrochemicals followed by insurance and then banking and financial services. The number of transactions was lower for banking compared to insurance and around the same for industrial investment and building construction, but the value for banking was far higher indicating the sensitivity of price movement in this sector.

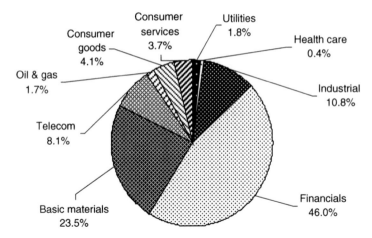

Fig. 6.10 *TADAWUL*: Market share by sector (percent of market capitalization, December 2009) (Source: *TADAWUL*)

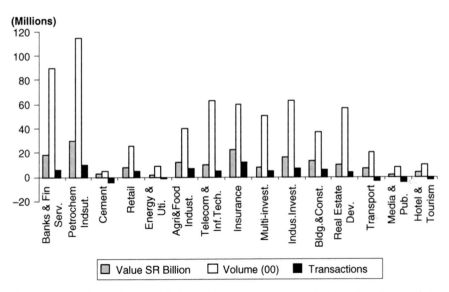

Fig. 6.11 Sectoral activities Saudi stock market 2009 by value, volume and number of transactions

Investor Behaviour: Irrational Exuberance and Herd Mentality

While extensive analysis has been carried out on the actual results and price movements of the Saudi stock market, far less research has been carried out on investor behaviour of current players in the Saudi market compared to other markets which have tried to understand what drives investors, particularly individual investors. The effect of "herd mentality" – with investors driven to act in the same direction irrespective of underlying market fundamentals – has been observed in many markets including the GCC markets (Chang et al., 2000, Dahel and Labbas, 1999, Devenow and Welch, 1996, Hammoudeh and Choi, 2006). A principal aim of such research is to test whether "efficient market" hypothesis exists and under what circumstances the hypothesis does not operate.

The efficient market hypothesis (EMH) asserts that financial markets are "informational efficient" or those prices on traded assets, e.g., stocks, bonds, or property, already reflect all known information and therefore are unbiased in the sense that they reflect the collective beliefs of all investors about future prospects.

The efficient market hypothesis states that it is not possible to consistently outperform the market by using any information that the market already knows, except through luck. Information or news in the EMH is defined as anything that may affect stock prices that is unknown at present and thus appears randomly in the future. This random information will be the cause of future stock price changes. The efficient market hypothesis requires that agents have rational expectations; that on average the population is correct (even if no one person is) and whenever new relevant information appears, the agents update their expectations appropriately.

There are three common forms in which the efficient market hypothesis is commonly stated:

Weak form efficiency: It asserts that all past market prices and data are fully reflected in securities prices. In other words, technical analysis is of no use.

Semi-strong form efficiency: It asserts that all publicly available information is fully reflected in securities prices. In other words, fundamental analysis is of no use.

Strong form efficiency: It asserts that all information is fully reflected in securities prices. In other words, even insider information is of no use.

From evidence presented earlier in the chapter, it is certainly correct to assume that "strong form efficiency" does not completely exist in Saudi Arabia today given the number and range of CMA violations listed. Anecdotal evidence suggests that the Saudi stock market is currently driven by irrational exuberance and herd-like mentality characterized by rumours and bouts of buying followed by panic selling as the *TADAWUL* TASI index had earlier highlighted. Over time, with investor experience and CMA investor awareness programmes, such type of investment behaviour could change towards a long-term investment outlook and asset holding. It is important to highlight that there are differences in Saudi individual investors behaviour based on education, gender and age. Field research results carried out (Koshhal, 2004) showed some interesting differences amongst Saudi Individual Stock Traders (SISTs), indicating the following:

- The level of financial and technical knowledge among the SISTs were below average; 80% had no formal training in stock trading.

- The majority of SISTs were risk-takers who believed that they would continue to make high profits on the Saudi stock market, despite falls.
- In picking stocks, some 40% of SISTs depended on technical analysis, some 32% depended on financial analysis while 25% depended on other people's opinions and Internet forums. Only 3% went with their personal "feelings."
- The 25–35 age groups seemed to make the most profit on the Saudi stock market, which the research survey correlated to higher levels of education and formal course training.
- The lowest level of profits were found amongst those who depended on others' opinions, while the highest was achieved by those who depended on technical analysis.
- Respondents with the highest education levels (masters and doctorates) depended on financial analysis and made medium to high profits. Those with lower levels of education depended on others' opinions and made the lowest profits.
- Respondents with lower risk aversion depended solely on financial information in their decision-making and realized medium profits.

Research conducted for other developed markets seemed to corroborate the above Saudi field research findings (Ackert et al., 2003), but such findings have important implications for the future development of the Saudi stock and capital market, concerning how to widen the number of players (foreign and domestic) and type (institutional or individual). Figure 6.12 illustrates that the individual retail investor still dominates the market with an average of over 87% of the monthly traded value.

In larger European bourses such as London's, institutional investors tend to account for around 90% of the transactions value. While the Saudi data indicate the sizeable contribution of individuals to total value added, analysis of net investment flows for each investor category indicates that they are not the sole drivers of the market, but that the Saudi corporate sector is the main driver as illustrated in Fig. 6.13.

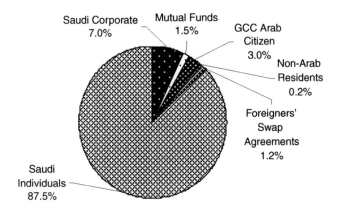

Fig. 6.12 Average monthly contribution to Saudi stock market trades by category of investor and % of value traded (2009) (Source: *TADAWUL*)

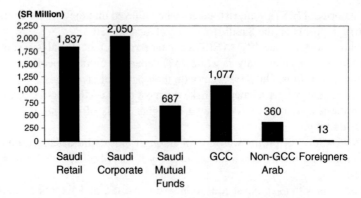

Fig. 6.13 Average monthly net investment in absolute terms per category of Saudi investors (2009) (Source: *TADAWUL*)

From Fig. 6.13 it is interesting to note the increasing importance of non-Saudi investors such as those from the GCC, non-GCC Arabs resident in Saudi Arabia and foreigners in terms of net investment flows. However, the fact that Saudi retail investors dominate in terms of value, while Saudi corporates dominate in terms of net flows, indicates that they could balance each other out to some respect in terms of market price movement. This is illustrated in Fig. 6.14, which indicates that, except for one month (May 2008), retail and corporate investors seemed to work in a *contrarian* manner.

However, it is important to analyse deeper to assess whether the various participants also move in the same direction when the market direction changes and shed some light on the earlier findings on Saudi individual investor behaviour. Figure 6.15 highlights some interesting but surprising findings, especially concerning the Saudi corporate investor sector.

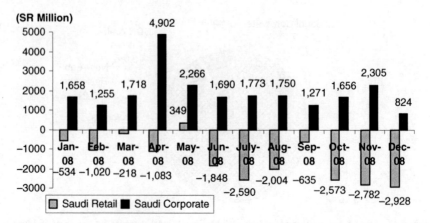

Fig. 6.14 Average monthly net investments (2008) (Source: *TADAWUL*, SHUAA Capital, 2009)

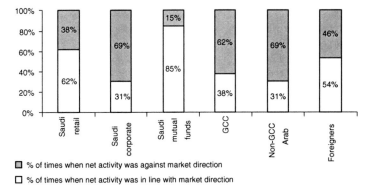

Fig. 6.15 Saudi market trends and participants correlation % of times (2008) (Source: *TADAWUL*, SHUAA Capital 2009)

While the Saudi corporate sector dominated the net monthly inflows, they seemed to do poorly when it came to forecasting market direction compared to individual investors, mutual funds and foreigners. Saudi corporates were on average 31% of the times in the same direction as the market, while individual investors were 62% , mutual funds 85% and foreigners 54%.

As such, the corporate investors in Saudi Arabia seem to play a significant net monthly investment role, but more a balancing role when it comes to market movements. What Fig. 6.14 indicated is that other participants in the Saudi market are playing an increased role in balancing market movements, and these are mutual funds and non-resident foreigners.

Boosting Foreign Participation

The Saudi regulatory authorities have recognized the potential contribution of widening institutional participation, particularly from foreign entities, but at a controlled pace to avoid the sudden injection and outflow of so-called "hot-money" investments as seen in other open emerging markets, especially during the 1998 Asian currency crisis. The argument for more foreign participation lies on assumptions such as having foreign participation reduces the potential volatility in the market by buying stocks when they are undervalued and withdrawing when valuations become overstretched. Foreign investment firms' focus on technical research also might discourage price bubbles from developing by promoting more vigorous fundamental analysis of the emerging market and helps to promote corporate governance.

Since 2005, the CMA has awarded investment banking licences to a number of foreign banks, which have also been allowed to provide brokerage services. Consequently, the quantity and quality of corporate research has improved markedly, and many investors are now better informed than previously. Regular analysis of individual shares of major companies is now available, providing valuations based on internationally recognized models such as discounted equity cash flow, dividend discount and peer-based valuations, as well as buy, hold or sell recommendations.

This has encouraged the Saudi authorities to open up the local market to foreign investment and in 2008 the CMA opened the *TADAWUL* exchange for non-resident foreign investors, whether individual or institutional, as long as the Saudi stocks are acquired by an authorized Saudi intermediary. These were the so-called "total returns swap" (TRS) agreements, which operated under the conditions that the authorized local intermediary will have the legal ownership of the stock and the foreign non-resident investor will have exposure to the stock's economic gains or losses.

In further developments, the CMA also imposed some restrictions on the TRS, such as a maximum term of 4 years for the agreement. The authorized entity, however, has voting rights on the stock under swap agreement. Finally, the CMA required the authorized persons to avoid any credit risk by receiving 100% of the funds from the foreign investor.

The move, although not fully opening the Saudi market to all forms of investors, was a major step towards the integration of the *TADAWUL* with the global market. For whatever the limitations might be, the CMA, by doing away with the restriction on foreign ownership limits, has rendered the Saudi market, on this specific issue, more open than other GCC markets (with the exception of Dubai), which are still bound by such restrictions.

The result of the gradual opening up of the Saudi capital market has been a steady volume in swap activity, as illustrated in Fig. 6.16.

It will still be some time before the current swap facilities are replaced by outright ownership of Saudi stocks by non-resident foreigners but the experience gained by both sides has been beneficial to the Saudi capital market, making the CMA consider other changes. In 2009, the CMA indicated it was considering the possibility of allowing exchange-traded funds (ETFs) and agreed to this in March 2010. Such ETFs can be bought and sold like shares, have lower costs than mutual funds and

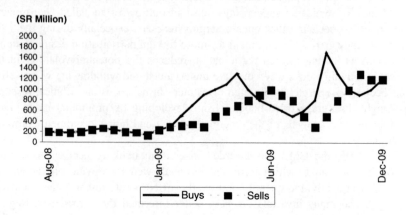

Fig. 6.16 *TADAWUL* foreign swap volume August 2008–December 2009 (Source: *TADAWUL*)

can give investors exposure to a wider selection of stocks then individual shares. Such an introduction would also create an international market for "shadow" Saudi stock market indexes, unlike the current swaps. In July 2009, the Dow Jones Indexes of the USA became the first international index provider to offer indexes on the Saudi *TADAWUL*, and Dow Jones currently provides four Saudi indexes based on real time data and prices from Saudi Arabia. This has encouraged other international companies such as Standard & Poor's and Bloomberg to consider Saudi indexes.

Once again the CMA has demonstrated that "learning by doing" approach benefits Saudi Arabia, and during 2009 the CMA granted licences to launch indices tracking the performance of *Shariah*-compliant companies listed on the Saudi exchange, catering to the strong demand for Islamic financial products, especially following the global financial crisis of 2008/2009 which hit traditional investment banking hard.

Saudi Mutual Fund Market Growth

As illustrated earlier in Fig. 6.15, the Saudi mutual funds sector seemed one of the few that correctly moved in line with market direction, adding to some stability to market prices in times of volatility despite its smaller net monthly investments. This could be due to the fact that mutual funds are managed by professional and authorized fund managers and are closely regulated to ensure compliance with the terms of the fund structure and investment guidelines.

The mutual fund market has exploded in size and diversity of products all over the world and now constitutes a large and important segment of the financial and capital markets. The US market, the largest in the world, saw the market share for mutual funds reach $5.8 trillion in 2005 from $371 billion in 1984, according to the number one US fund manager, Fidelity, which handled around $550 billion in its institutional retirement group alone (Fidelity, 2006).

The history of the Saudi mutual funds market has been equally impressive and today Saudi Arabia has the largest mutual funds industry in the Arab world. Mutual funds were first introduced in the Saudi market by the National Commercial Bank (NCB) through its "open-ended" *Al Ahli* Short-Term Dollar Fund in 1979. It was aimed at the smaller investor, particularly the expatriate worker, and it quickly became a success with this market segment due to the fund's low service charges, ease of entry and redemption.

Over the years, public interest and demand for this financial product has risen to a peak of SR 137 billion in 2005 before falling back in later years, as the figures in Table 6.10 show, with assets under management in all mutual funds standing at SR 77.2 billion by the end of first quarter of 2009.

Table 6.10 indicates Saudi investors moved out of the mutual funds sector to try direct investing in the stock market during the boom year of 2005/2006 and reverting back to mutual funds in 2007 following the crash of 2006, as explained earlier in this chapter. The table also shows the switch towards domestic assets from 1995 onwards.

Table 6.10   Growth in Saudi managed mutual funds (1995–2009)

Characteristics	1995	2005	2006	2007	2008	2009[a]
Number of funds	71	199	214	252	262	253
Number of subscribers	33,051	568,282	499,968	426,085	374,975	375,097
Assets under management (SR Billion)						
Domestic	5.5	115.6	61.3	79.8	61.3	64.5
Foreign	7.2	21.3	27.7	25.2	13.6	12.7
Total SR billion	13.0	136.9	84.0	105.0	74.9	77.2

[a]First Quarter, 2009
Source: SAMA, CMA

The causes of the switch towards domestic assets are many, including the sharp rise in Saudi share prices compared to international equity markets, the growth of Islamic mutual funds and the growing expertise over time amongst Saudi banks in managing such funds by themselves.

The reasons for investing in Saudi mutual funds are also varied. Only a decade ago, most Saudis looked to their employers – whether in the government or private sector – to provide them with a pension, but an increasing number of Saudis (and expatriates living in the Kingdom) have now invested in these funds as a form of retirement hedging. The attraction of holding mutual funds is apparent: pooling the resources of small investors and sharing risk in many diversified stock/bond portfolios while minimizing transaction costs and information costs. Mutual funds also provide greater liquidity, meeting investors' need for cash.

As mentioned earlier, the growth of mutual funds in Saudi Arabia has been impressive over such a short period of time. Initially, the focus was on select high net worth or "private bank" clients, but all Saudi banks have now expanded their target market to include the professional middle-income and top-tier expatriates. Competition has been fierce amongst banks and some have developed in-house expertise to manage their funds, whereas others have established strategic alliances with international fund managers to design funds exclusively for their Saudi clients. Those Saudi banks with foreign affiliation and part ownership such as Saudi British Bank, Saudi Fransi and others had a head start over the "pure" Saudi banks such as NCB and Riyad Bank. However, the local banks have gained mutual fund management experience, especially in the domestic equity market, and have created a niche market in Islamic mutual funds, which now account over 50% of the total assets under management and nearly one fifth of the number of funds as illustrated in Table 6.11.

What is noticeable from Table 6.11 was the decline in investment in international equities following the 2008 global financial crisis, mirrored by a fall in domestic equities, but a sharp rise in *murabaha* Islamic mutual funds.

According to NCB, there is a growing desire among Saudi investors to participate in Islamic-based mutual funds that are *Shariah*-compliant and are consistent with the principle of equity participation and risk-sharing. For the Saudi economy, this

Table 6.11 Saudi mutual fund sector by assets under management and type of funds (2007–2008)

Type of fund	2007		2008	
	Number	Assets (SR Billion)	Number	Assets (SR Billion)
Local equity	35	43.7	45	16.5
GCC equity	13	3.8	16	1.6
International equity	74	14.8	74	6.7
Debt instruments	11	0.8	7	0.1
Murabaha	49	33.9	57	43.0
Real estate	4	1.6	4	2.3
Fund of funds	33	2.3	34	1.8
Other	14	4.2	25	2.8
Total	233	105.1	262	74.8

Source: CMA

type of funds not only improves market liquidity but also provides risk diversification opportunities in medium- to long-term maturity structures, although most of the Islamic mutual funds started through low-risk and modest-return instruments such as *murabaha* (short-term secured commodity trade finance) and *ijarah* (structured medium-term leasing).

According to a survey carried out by the same bank, most participants in mutual funds are Saudi males, the majority of whom have college degrees. Nearly half of the female investors were in the 18–25 age group. According to the survey, the most important objective for investing in the mutual funds was to secure a comfortable retirement. About 38% of those surveyed said they would not tolerate any risk, while 40% were prepared to take some risk, suggesting that a very small proportion of Saudi mutual fund investors are ready for higher risk (NCB, 2000).

The risk profile seems to be different from those investing directly in the equity markets, which we examined earlier, but given that a large number are investing in the mutual funds for long-term retirement pension objectives, this risk aversion is not surprising.

Based on the data in Table 6.10, the average investment per person is around SR 400,000, reinforcing the fact that mutual funds are mostly investment instruments for the upper-income groups, while lower- to middle-income groups depend mainly on bank deposits or individual share purchases to grow their savings.

In conclusion, the outlook for the Saudi mutual market looks bright, with growth anticipated in total assets, especially for *Shariah*-compliant funds.

Conclusion

While significant strides have been made in the development of the Saudi capital market over recent years, some further changes are needed to make the Saudi market even more attractive to both domestic and international investors. Countries are competing for investment capital; either they constantly try to improve or they will

Table 6.12   The changing face of the Saudi capital market

1970s	1980s	1990s	2010 onwards
• No disclosure	• Regulatory regimes improving	• Technology utilization	• Commercial paper and bonds
• External funding on selective basis	• External funding	• Specialized funds	• Family businesses going public
• Poor regulatory and legal structure	• Government soft loans	• Government debt increasing	• Mergers and acquisitions
• Commercial bank funding on secured basis	• Syndicated loans	• Islamic financing	• More disclosure and transparency
• Dominance of family companies	• Some disclosure available	• Foreign ownership on joint venture basis	• Foreign inward investment
		• Non-recourse finance	• Privatization
			• Foreign participation
			• IPOs
			• Securitization
			• Islamic financing

be left behind. Saudi Arabia, while blessed with a national private sector capital surplus, needs as well to attract international investments in order to establish a better investment, financial and regulatory environment that will maximize their potential to attract investment. Table 6.12 summarizes the changing pace and face of the Saudi capital market.

The Saudi capital market took off during the 1990s, with the beginning of domestic economic reforms in the field of privatization and liberalization, especially when the country opened up to the outside world for inward investments. The post-2010 era requires an even bolder capital market reform programme to address several key issues highlighted in this chapter.

First, the government should vigorously encourage and support listings of new companies on the Saudi stock market. The Ministry of Commerce can re-examine some of its stringent guidelines, procedures for listing and the laborious documentation that accompanies conversion to joint stock companies. The current number of listed companies and their narrow sectoral basis cannot be sustained.

The passing of the Saudi Capital Market Law has gone a long way in convincing the Saudi private sector and the international community at large that policy-makers in the Kingdom are serious about implementing reform strategies aimed at economic liberalization, competition and market efficiency. Time and again, commentators have said that while the intentions of the Saudi government and policy-makers were sound and well-meaning, the problem has been the speed of implementation.

The Saudi authorities have sent robust signals that the way forward for the economy lies in decentralized, private market-based activities, and the new capital market would play a vital role in the following areas. As a priority, Saudi Arabia can attract back Saudi capital resources held abroad. A deeper and more dynamic Saudi capital market has the potential to draw back Saudi resources invested abroad, which could contribute towards the financing of the non-oil sector.

In the past, the liquidity, safety and dependable market infrastructure of overseas markets have attracted private Saudi wealth. There are varying estimates as to the size of this overseas investment, ranging from a conservative $480 billion to a generous $900 billion according to various bank sources (NCB, 2000, SAMBA, 2003), although this figure could have decreased following the turmoil in the global financial markets in 2008/2009. Whatever the actual figures, these are substantial sums, and the response to the latest IPOs shows that the public is ready to invest locally. However, for this capital repatriation to be sustained, a new Saudi capital market must build solid investor confidence.

Second, development of the domestic Saudi capital market will contribute directly to the growth of the non-oil sector by promoting the financial services industry. A market-based expansion of contractual savings to service pensions, insurance and diversification needs will create a demand for institutional investors, such as pension funds, insurance companies and mutual funds. They will be in a better position to satisfy the economy's demand for long-term resources and to assume the role now played by specialized government credit agencies. Since the early "boom" days of the mid-1970s and early 1980s, government financing has been made available for manufacturing enterprises at zero interest rates. This encouraged reliance on the state, institutionalized operating inefficiencies and promoted a business culture of relying on commercial bank debt financing and soft loans from the government, rather than equity financing.

Third, a well-developed capital market will improve risk management practices. In previous chapters, we showed that the volatility of oil prices leads to volatility and unpredictability in Saudi government revenues, resulting in a magnified effect on other sectors of the economy. Financial market developments can contribute to better risk management in the economy; for example, the introduction of derivative instruments (hedging) can help domestic market participants manage the effects of oil price volatility on their activities. This can lead to greater macroeconomic stability, thus improving the investment climate and growth in the non-oil sectors.

Fourth, a well-developed local capital market can respond to the demand of infrastructure services. With the Saudi government signalling its disengagement from public investment and announcing its ambitious privatization programme, infrastructure finance will be at risk if international capital markets lose their appetites for taking risks on emerging countries. Furthermore, international capital is more likely to flow when there is evidence of private domestic capital in the projects they are called to finance. As such, limited recourse finance needs a diversified menu of financing instruments that can expand without relying on government guarantees. Only a capital market that is liquid, transparent and diversified could help in this process.

Above all – and this must be emphasized continuously – the Saudi Capital Market Authority must carry out its regulatory responsibilities vigorously. Capital markets that function well offer their investors the twin virtues of transparency and protection. Through transparency, investors will be able to see exactly what is going on inside the listed companies; they will feel protected if they see that their money is safeguarded from intermediaries. Such changes in attitude and regulatory frameworks take decades to achieve. The omens are good as evidenced by the vigorous actions of the CMA over the past few years. The road that Saudi Arabia has taken could be a long one, but the Kingdom has achieved much in the development work already. If this is now put into practice, the Capital Market Regulatory Authority in Saudi Arabia will become one of the leading regulators in the world, and the Saudi capital markets will become one of the most productive developments that Saudi Arabia has witnessed.

Summary of Key Points

- *Efficient capital markets can play an effective role in recycling capital surpluses and promoting economic growth. The Saudi private sector has demonstrated that it has the liquidity to participate in any deepening of the current capital market.*
- *The Saudi capital market has evolved from the formal establishment of a stock market in the 1980s to the passing of the Capital Market Law in 2004, which created an independent Securities Exchange Commission (SEC) and later the Capital Market Authority (CMA) to oversee the stock market.*
- *The establishment of the CMA has helped to overcome some of the previous obstacles in expanding the capital market, namely an increase in the number of listed companies, increase in the number of shareholders, expansion of brokerage and investment advisory services and licensing of non-bank financial institutions.*
- *The benefits of the Capital Market Law could be felt in several areas: potential to draw back Saudi resources invested abroad, growth of non-oil financial services sector, improvement in risk management practices and response to the infrastructure services demand.*
- *In terms of performance, the Saudi capital market dominates the rest of the Arab world in size and has registered impressive performances, especially during 2003–2004, when it outperformed most international market indexes but saw sharp retreats after 2006. The Saudi market has improved in terms of turnover ratio and market capitalization as % of GDP.*
- *The total "free float" shares for trading is around 50% of all listed shares. This could benefit from additional planned government privatization sales and private sector IPOs.*
- *The capital market is still characterized by a high degree of sectoral concentration and the dominance of banking, electricity and telecommunications, with six companies accounting for nearly 70% of the total market capitalization.*
- *The Saudi capital market has made some progress in opening up to foreign investors through swap facilities and there are some developments in expanding the use of exchange-traded funds (ETFs) and index funds.*

- *Investor behaviour in the capital market is characterized by a mixture of sophisticated technical analysis and those with no formal training in stock trading who depend on opinion and make the lowest profits.*
- *The Saudi mutual fund market is now relatively mature with a broad range of investment vehicles catering to middle-income Saudi investors. A discernible growth in demand for Islamic investments has been noted.*

Part IV
The Domestic Sector

Chapter 7
The Private Sector: Globalization Challenges

It is not the crook in modern business that we fear, but the honest man who does not know what he is doing.

Owen D. Young

Learning Outcomes

By the end of this section, you would understand:

- *The growing responsibility placed on the private sector to diversify the economic base*
- *The operating framework under which the private sector works (legal, corporate, economic)*
- *Foreign participation in the private sector*
- *The importance of small- and medium-sized enterprises (SMEs)*
- *Saudi family business structures*
- *Saudi women and the national economy*
- *Government and business relations in Saudi Arabia*
- *Promotion of private sector growth*

Introduction

In spite of tangible past accomplishments, Saudi Arabia faces future challenges that, if not addressed, will be difficult to overcome. One key objective is for the private sector to take the lead in reducing its reliance on oil revenues and in diversifying its economy. As we will explain in the chapters that follow, the Kingdom has not yet created a sufficient number of jobs for its Saudi population, nor has it adequately diversified its economy, although some progress has been made in expanding the non-oil GDP base.

The Saudi government signalled its intent to gradually "disengage" from the economy and let the private sector assume a greater share of the economic

M.A. Ramady, *The Saudi Arabian Economy*, DOI 10.1007/978-1-4419-5987-4_7,
© Springer Science+Business Media, LLC 2010

transformation when it announced in mid-November 2002 its massive privatization plans through opening up of 20 sectors to the private sector (Saravia, 2002). The increased reliance on the private sector to generate jobs and create a sustainable economic base has also been further emphasized in the recent economic development plans. To assume this responsibility, the private sector faces both a unique historical challenge as well as potential opportunities. It must come of age in order to transform itself into the dominant economic sector and to provide self-sustaining, steady economic growth. A viable state–private sector relationship is essential to attaining this objective. How these two sectors cooperate is vital to the private sector's success in taking the lead economic role.

The aim of this chapter is to assess the inherent strengths and weaknesses of the private sector in meeting the challenges and responsibilities that the Saudi government is devolving to it. An important aspect of the present study will be to assess whether an appropriate business environment exists in the Kingdom to enable the private sector take up these challenges.

The Operating Framework

Modern commercially oriented societies operate under certain frameworks that enable the private sector to carry out its function with a degree of certainty. A successful government–private sector partnership depends on some key services being provided by the state to enable the private sector to flourish. These are an effective bureaucratic framework, a clear legal regulatory system and appropriate infrastructure to deliver the necessary goods and services. The overall aim is for the private sector to be able to produce desired goods and services in the most efficient and cost-effective manner, compared to the public sector, thus freeing the government to concentrate on providing the most suitable operating environment for the private sector (Awaji, 1989).

The Legal Setting

As in other Islamic nations, the fundamental source of law in Saudi Arabia is Islamic law or *Shariah*. The *Shariah* consists of the Holy Koran, the teachings of the Prophet Mohammad *(Pbuh)*, called the *Sunnah*, and the writings of renowned Islamic legal scholars. Several other sources of law elaborate on the *Shariah* and govern commercial relations. Decrees are adopted by the Saudi Council of Ministers and provide broad rules for particular areas, such as commercial law, labour law and taxation. These laws are published in the Saudi Official Gazette, *Umm Al-Qura.*

In the past, potential new laws covering commercial activities, not generally open for discussion, were considered by ad hoc ministerial committees and legal experts before being promulgated by Royal Decree. Other, less important regulations were developed within relevant ministries. Interpretations and enforcement of these regulations were executed at ministerial levels, as were elaborations and provision of more specific requirements. Such interpretations could vary which is not conducive to long-term private sector business planning.

If a dispute arises, a company may sue – or be sued – in Saudi court. As such, both Saudi and non-Saudi businessmen should be aware of how potential disputes are settled in the Kingdom. This issue becomes more important following the Kingdom's accession to the World Trade Organization (WTO) in 2005 and the encouragement of foreign direct investment (FDI) as part of the ongoing liberalization initiatives. If a dispute arises between a foreign company and a Saudi party, the case may be heard in Saudi Arabia, unless specified otherwise by both parties. Saudi law prohibits government agencies from disputing a contract in another country. Table 7.1 sets out the main legal and commercial systems for settling disputes operating in Saudi Arabia.

One issue that the Saudi government has recently addressed is *precedence* in commercial disputes and judgments in *Shariah* courts. Unlike the Board of

Table 7.1 Saudi Arabia: legal, commercial and dispute settlement system

Legal system	Observations
• Judicial System	• Supreme Judiciary Council created in 2008. Consists of both general courts and specialized tribunals. Courts may consist of a combination of judges and non-judges. Decisions can be quick or lengthy. Decisions may be appealed
• Jurisdiction	• *Shariah* courts are courts of general jurisdiction. *Shariah* judges preside over almost any disputes, unless Saudi law provides otherwise. *Shariah* judges apply Islamic law to decide a case. Decisions may be appealed
• Board of Grievance	• Has exclusive power to decide disputes over Saudi government contracts and may decide some types of commercial disputes. Unlike *Shariah*, the board observes a system of *precedent*. Decisions may be appealed. System reformed in 2008 to strengthen right of appeal. Specialized commercial courts established to bring Saudi legal system with international practices
• Civil Rights Directorate	• Responsible for enforcing judgment of Saudi courts or tribunals
• Negotiable Instruments Committee	• Decides on cases involving bills of exchange, promissory notes and checks
• The SAMA Committee	• Resolves disputes between banks and clients
• Conciliation Committee	• At the Saudi Chambers of Commerce, assisting in problems between foreign partners and Saudi companies, especially in agency matters
• Preliminary Committee for Settlement of Labour Disputes	• Hears all matters related to labour and employee relations
• Human Rights Commission	• Strengthened and reshuffled in 2009 and given wider powers of access to government bodies without official permission to investigate cases

Grievance, which observes a system of precedence in reaching a judgment, the *Shariah* system allows individual judges to pass down judgments based on their personal interpretations, rather than precedence for similar cases. As such, under the old Saudi judicial system, it becomes hard for specialized *Shariah* courts and judges to evolve into ones that can handle more complex commercial cases, especially involving multinationals from different countries. However, as discussed in Chapter 2, and illustrated in Table 7.1, the Kingdom reformed the appeals courts in 2008 and established specialized commercial courts to hear disputes, with judgments based on precedence. Over time this system will be tested as to efficiency and comparability with international arbitration standards.

Saudi Arabia has ratified several international legal agreements, the most important being the Convention on the Settlement of Investment Disputes between States and Nationals, and the Convention on Foreign Arbitral Awards. In July 1995, an agreement on legal protection for guaranteed foreign investment between the Multilateral Investment Guarantee Agency (MIGA) and Saudi Arabia was signed (Sheikh and Abdelrahman, 2003).

The Corporate Setting

Saudi law recognizes nine different forms of business organization structures. Three involve limited liability structures, while the others do not. Firms that are owned entirely by Saudi citizens may either be limited partnerships or joint stock companies; in addition, more than one such company may enter joint venture agreements or form cooperative societies. Table 7.2 sets out by legal structure the cumulative number of companies operating in Saudi Arabia as of 2002 and 2008.

From the table, it is evident that the corporate base of Saudi Arabia has expanded rapidly with issued share capital reaching SR 640 billion by 2008 or over 270% increase since 2002, while the number of companies increased by around 86% over the same period. What is noticeable is the increase in the number and capital of foreign joint ventures and wholly owned foreign companies, given a boost post WTO accession in 2005 and a more liberalized FDI regime, which will be examined in more detail in later chapters.

Establishment of joint stock companies in the Kingdom requires ministerial or sometimes even a Royal Decree. The formation of the other types of companies is less complicated, involving registration of partnership deeds with a notary public. The creation and registration of the new company must be advertised in the Companies Register at the Ministry of Commerce.

Foreign firms wishing to carry out business in Saudi Arabia have a number of options, ranging from the appointment of local agents, or *wakeels*, to the formation of partnerships with Saudis. Table 7.2 indicates that this was the favourite route of local companies, as 2,974 joint venture limited liability companies were operating with a combined capital investment of SR 55.2 billion as of 2008. Since 2001, when the Kingdom started to encourage FDI, wholly owned foreign companies began to

Table 7.2 Total outstanding number of companies operating in Saudi Arabia by legal structure (2002 and 2008)

Type of companies	2002		2008	
	Number	Capital SR Million	Number	Capital SR Million
1. Joint stock companies	121	81,305.6	400	470,273
2. Limited liability partnerships	7,816	83,567.3	16,908	155,623
Saudi	6,159	52,238.6	13,123	90,996
Joint venture	1,421	29,896.9	2,974	55,125
Non-Saudi	236	1,431.8	811	9,502
3. Joint liability partnerships	2,630	3,747.6	3,139	4,136
Saudi	2,593	3,714.8	3,103	4,104
Joint venture	19	15.7	35	27.3
Non-Saudi	18	17.1	1	5.0
4. Mixed liability partnerships	1,054	2,747.1	1,241	10,770.1
Saudi	1,043	2,709.7	1,231	10,733
Joint venture	8	21.9	8	21.9
Non-Saudi	3	15.5	2	15.2
5. Mixed liability partnerships by shares	1	0.5	4	209
Total	11,622	171,368.1	21,692	640,805

Source: SAMA

operate legally under their own name without a local *wakeel* or partner (SAGIA, 2002). Table 7.2 shows that between them, joint stock companies and limited liability partnerships account for almost 96% of company capital. However, joint stock companies represent around 2% of companies and 73% of total capital. It is from amongst these 400 registered joint stock companies that the most recent IPO listings on the Saudi capital market came, a total of 13 in 2007 and 9 in 2009.

The Economic Setting

We have to analyse the structure of the operating companies by economic activity in terms of employment, efforts towards *Saudization* and contribution to the national economy to better understand whether the private sector has achieved some of the diversification objectives the government set for it. Table 7.3 sets out the key economic indicators by major productive sectors.

Table 7.3 highlights several important characteristics of present-day Saudi economic sector activities. Concerning the employment pattern of the private sector, the trend has been for more, rather than fewer, foreigners employed, contrary to government development plan objectives. During 2001, the number of Saudis

Table 7.3 Private sector economic indicators (2001–2008)

Indicator	2001	2008
*Employment total	2,376,974	6,221,947
– Saudis	540,817	829,057
(A) Male	N/A	777,606
(B) Female	N/A	51,451
– Non-Saudis	1,836.157	5,392,890
*GDP (SR billion)	686.3	1,746.0
*Non-oil GDP	275.1	440.0
– % Contribution	40.0%	25.2%
*Non-oil GDP by economic sector (SR billion)		
– Agriculture & fishing	35.7	39.9
– Manufacturing (Incl. oil refining)	69.2	102.5
– Public utilities	8.9	14.0
– Construction & building	43.2	58.8
– Whole sale & retail trade	49.8	70.7
– Transport & communication	30.6	55.6
– Finance & insurance & real estate business	78.8	105.9
*Gross final consumption (SR billion)	448.4	841.4
– Government	188.9	359.8
– Private	259.5	481.5

N/A = Not Available
Source: SAMA

employed by the private sector represented around 23%, while in 2008 this had fallen to around 13% despite the Saudi economy generating an additional 3.8 million new jobs over the period 2001–2008. The issue is a particularly sensitive one between the government, represented by the Ministry of Labour, and the private sector, represented by the different regional Chambers of Commerce, and will be analysed in greater detail in a subsequent chapter. The implication is clear though: private sector growth over the past decades seems to have been built on cheap imported labour. The objections to current *Saudization* policies will be examined in more detail from the private sector perspective in a later chapter dealing with the structure of the labour market in the Kingdom. Leading Saudi companies emphasize the principle of employing productive Saudi employees at a reasonable cost for the job categories in which they are hired. They stress that *Saudization* is not about raising a company's Saudi employee headcount (Zamil, 2003).

The non-oil GDP contribution has gone up to around SR 440 billion in 2008 at current prices compared with SR 275 billion in 2001, but as an overall percentage of Saudi GDP, the non-oil GDP contribution fell to 25% in 2008 from 40% level in 2001, no doubt affected by the exceptional oil-led boom year of 2008, which has been analysed earlier. What is more significant is that the amount of non-government gross final consumption expenditure of the private sector has exceeded the government sector final consumption, and represents around 58% in 2008, about the same level for 2001.

On analysis of the non-oil private sector contribution, one notices a steady level for agriculture, forestry and fishing over the years, but a rise in manufacturing (which includes oil refining), wholesale trade and services and the finance, insurance and retail estate sectors. The pattern has remained the same over the period 2004–2009 as illustrated in Fig. 7.1, which sets out the growth rate for the major non-oil economic sectors over the period 2004–2009.

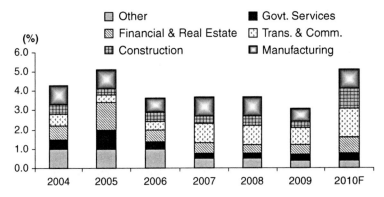

Fig. 7.1 Drivers of the non-oil Saudi real GDP growth (2004–2009, 2010 forecast) (Source: SAMA)

Government National Strategy for Industry

The government has set out a specific national strategy for domestic industry to serve as a blueprint for the private sector. This national strategy up to the year 2020 is built around four key goals and eleven strategic foundations listed below.

Strategic goals:

1. Triple the national industrial base by 2020 as measured by the level of industrial value added.
2. Induce significant structural transformations in the ways of how to support value added in the industrial sector.
3. Activate the role of the national industrial sector in international trade group and raise the export share of industrial production as well as the share of high-tech-based exports.
4. Make a quantum leap in the percentage of Saudi manpower in the industrial sector.

To realize the above strategic goals, the government is adopting the following foundations to implement the vision:

1. Support industries that rely on the comparative advantages available to the Kingdom.

2. Direct industrial products towards high value added.
3. Promote high-tech and knowledge-based industries.
4. Provide and develop necessary infrastructures.
5. Adopt and support a balanced national development process.
6. Adopt a pattern of industrial clusters.
7. Enhance the role of small and medium enterprises.
8. Raise the competitiveness of national products.
9. Effectively contribute to the establishment of a national system of creativity and innovation.
10. Develop the business environment, including laws, procedures and policies.
11. Develop human workforce needed for the industrial sector.

The above are laudable goals and objectives but the results have not been consistent across all objectives, as witnessed by the low level of Saudi manpower employment rate. What has been more noticeable over the past decade has been the gradual creation of a more *favourable environment* for the development of Saudi industry in general and the encouragement of market-led policies. These have centred around developing laws and regulations which encourage industrial investment, both domestic and foreign; the promotion of industrial clusters to raise the productive capacity and competitiveness of Saudi national industries; developing the small- and medium-sized enterprises (SMEs) and their operating environment; improving and developing the national system for industrial innovation; and finally enhancing the adequacy and experience of human resources working in the industrial sector. As we will analyse later in this chapter, the results have been more advanced in some areas, but lagging in many other areas.

Foreign Participation

Ever since the beginning of Saudi Arabia's development process, the Kingdom has welcomed foreign participation in the transformation of the country's economic structure. The relationship with the outside world has been ambivalent at times. On the one hand, the Kingdom has welcomed the transfer of technology, skills and know-how, but on the other hand it has sought to shield itself from "cultural pollution" out of fear of impacting deep-rooted cultural traditions and customs. The transition to a society with all the trappings of a modern state has been difficult at times, with pressure being exerted on those same traditions and customs (Abir, 1988, Khalaf, 2004, Yamani, 2000, Qusti, 16 July 2003).

The wave of terrorism in the Kingdom during 2003 and 2004 highlighted the mutual dependency between the Kingdom and its foreign labourers. Saudi authorities expressed their utmost determination to protect foreign workers and to maintain the continued presence of foreign investments in the country. A more frank and sympathetic public debate on the importance and value of the foreign workforce to the Kingdom's economy began to emerge, as well as a greater respect for the human

rights of such workers (Rasheed, 2002). At the same time, these debates acknowledged the need to speed up the educational and economic reforms that would enable
Saudi citizens to assume the tasks currently undertaken by foreigners. These issues
will be addressed in later chapters.

The most popular or preferred form of Saudi and foreign collaboration at the
corporate level seems to be the appointment by a foreign distributor of a local Saudi
commercial agent or a *wakeel*. According to SAMA, the number of new commercial
agencies registered by the Ministry of Commerce and Industry during 2008 alone
was 430, representing various nationalities, the largest being US (59), German (32),
British (32), Italian (27), French (21) and Indian (20). By 2008, the total number of
agencies registered in Saudi Arabia was 10,318, broken down by different categories
in Table 7.4.

Table 7.4 Foreign trade agencies in Saudi Arabia by categories as of 2008

Category	Number	%
Distribution agencies	9,225	89.4
Concession agencies	557	5.4
Commercial agencies	310	3
Service agencies	226	2.2
Total	10,318	100

Source: SAMA, Ministry of commerce

By far, the most popular foreign association was in distributorship agencies,
nearly 90% of all agencies granted, followed by the franchise concessions at around
6%. According to the Ministry of Commerce data, nearly 80% of all agencies
granted to Saudi representatives were from developed countries, with Egypt and
China showing a strong presence. The apparent bias towards agencies from the
developed countries could be attributed to the desire of Saudi consumers, with their
new-found "oil boom" wealth and subsequent conspicuous consumption, to obtain
Western goods and services, especially after they had become familiar with them
while studying in these countries, as well as making contacts on behalf of their families. Some of the agencies might only involve a distributorship on behalf of the
foreign company against agreed-upon commission on sales.

Franchising became popular in Saudi Arabia as a form of doing business. Most
Saudi cities and towns today boast an array of world-famous franchise brand names,
with the USA accounting for around 35–40% of the current franchise market in
Saudi Arabia. This began with the introduction of a Saudi Franchise Law in 1992
(US Saudi Arabian Business Council, 2003). The accession of Saudi Arabia to the
WTO in 2005 has not significantly altered the number of trade agencies given by
foreigners to Saudi Arabian companies, but there has been a noticeable shift in the
manner through which larger service companies, especially in the oil sector, have
now established a presence in Saudi Arabia under their own name without the use
of a local agent or *wakeel*. This is illustrated in Table 7.5, which reveals that while

Table 7.5   Saudi Arabia foreign establishments by economic activity (2008)

Economic sector	Joint ownership	Wholly foreign ownership
Agriculture/fishing	3	6
Mining and petroleum	26	49
Manufacturing	220	275
Electricity	27	42
Construction	650	128
Trade/hotel	1,240	85
Transport/communications	370	110
Financing/real estate	293	89
Community/social services	188	30
Total	3,017	814

Source: Ministry of commerce, Central Department of Statistics

foreign wholly owned companies are to be found in all sectors of the economy, the main concentration is in manufacturing, mining and construction.

A primary aim of such foreign investments is the transfer of appropriate technology and skills. The private sector joint venture technology transfers were mostly in the form of franchises and other less comprehensive technology transfer mechanisms, with the exception of some joint venture investments in the petroleum and finance sectors.

The Small and Medium Enterprises – SMEs

As discussed earlier in this chapter, the government has now emphasized the importance of the SME sector in its national industrialization strategy, and after years of secondary attention to SMEs, today Saudi Arabia is committing both resources and attention to the sector. The reasons are many, and key ones include the pressing need for job creation, the reduction of foreign labour force and dependency, increasing economic diversification on a sustainable basis, and increasing the level of general scientific and technological capability of this sector.

According to SAMA, there are currently around 763,000 individual proprietorships in Saudi Arabia, spread throughout the country, with the majority located in the major cities as illustrated in Fig. 7.2.

Figure 7.2 shows that the Riyadh, Makkah/Jeddah and Eastern Province accounted for nearly 73% of the SMEs. Some estimates claim that around 5 million people depend on them for their livelihood. As such, this sector has come to assume a major socio-economic importance in Saudi planning (Radwan, 2002, Sugair, 2002, Malik, 2004).

What these figures for proprietorship do not tell us, however, is how many enterprises survive and how many close their business for different reasons. It is important that Saudi authorities collect such information so as to assess the obstacles faced by SMEs and the efficiency of these enterprises in meeting national

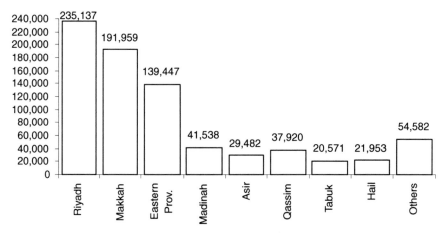

Fig. 7.2 Individual proprietorships in Saudi Arabia 2008 (Source: SAMA)

goals. From such studies one can then draw appropriate conclusions about the necessary private sector adaptations to new economic conditions that are facing them, following the Saudi government's retrenchment from its dominant role in the economy.

Saudi businesses of all sizes face issues or problems particular to their sector, and SMEs are no exception (Sugair, 2002, Sajini, 2004). Part of the problem lies in the development path that Saudi Arabia chose in the early days, as we have already discussed. The modern Saudi economy took off in the oil boom of the 1970s with massive investment in both infrastructure and capital-intensive industries, such as petrochemical and basic industries. The establishment of large-scale manufacturing enterprises, whether Saudi-owned or joint venture, received substantial preferential treatment in the form of subsidized financial assistance from the Saudi state and input subsidies. In the rush to industrialize, the SMEs were neglected, not because of any ill-will towards them by the bureaucracy, but because they were not "glamorous enough" or organized managerially, and state bureaucrats preferred to handle the needs of larger corporations. The past lack of attention to this sector was compounded by the feeling that SMEs were not a priority segment in the "oil boom" era, that SMEs relied on non-Saudi labour and that they did not have a role to play in the wider economy (Sugair, 2002). This perception is gradually changing, with studies indicating that for every 1 million SR invested in large companies, one additional job was created, while a similar amount invested with SMEs created around 28 new jobs (Radwan, 2002).

SMEs can also offer political and economic diversification, which encourages a more sustainable consumer base for the Kingdom, given their diversified spread in the Kingdom, which we saw earlier in Fig. 7.2. Table 7.6 demonstrates that the Saudi private sector today *is* the SME sector in terms of Saudi employment.

From the table, and analysing Saudi-only employees by different economic categories and employee segmentation, the majority of Saudi employees are in

Table 7.6   Economic sectors by employee segmentation (2008)

Employee segment	Wholesale and retail	Real estate	Manufacturing	Construction	Restaurants and hotels	Electricity, gas, water
1–9	120,600	19,600	32,750	8,200	75,400	1,200
10–49	75,200	15,850	29,600	58,250	48,600	950
50–99	18,400	2,300	17,400	60,219	1,300	1,900
100+	10,003	3,009	21,312	101,000	247	9,450
Total	224,203	40,759	101,062	227,669	125,547	13,500

Source: CDS, SAMA

wholesale and retail, construction and restaurant and hotel sectors and predominantly in the under-50-employee segmentation. This fits in with the generally accepted norm for an SME in Saudi Arabia.

Based on the definition of SMEs used by the Saudi Chambers of Commerce, they employ 64% of the total workforce. This identifies SMEs according to employee and asset size. "Micro" companies have fewer than 10 employees and less than SR 200,000 in assets; "small" companies have 10–25 employees and SR 1 million in assets; "medium" companies employ 25–100 workers and have assets of SR 5 million. It is obvious from Table 7.6 that SMEs are concentrated in the wholesale and retail sector, and that they make up the bulk of the real estate and restaurant and hotel business. Given the prominence of growing youth unemployment in Saudi Arabia, the government is paying close attention to SMEs and is assisting them to overcome perceived obstacles, with the Ninth Five-Year Plan addressing SME concerns. According to observers, SMEs seem to suffer in their access to finance (short and long term) from an inappropriate business environment, lack of development service and managerial inadequacies as well as an underdeveloped IT structure and insufficient market data (Kurdi, 2002). A position paper on SMEs prepared by the Saudi Arabian General Investment Authority (SAGIA) pointed to the sector's "low quality, high prices and inadequate marketing skills ... compounded by lack of modern technology, experience and constant problems with cost and raw material purchases..." (SAGIA, 2004).

The entry of the Kingdom into the WTO will add further pressure on the SME sector according to some observers (Sajini, 2004). The argument is that SMEs will be swamped by the entry of cheaper and higher-quality imports, with technology transfer through foreign-owned companies adding more pressure. Others argue that competition will force those SMEs that are particularly inefficient out of the market, so that in the long run the sector will be better off in terms of competition and high-quality products. This is a big "if" and a lot needs to be done to ensure that the SME sector flourishes in the face of WTO entry. To its credit, the Council of Saudi Chambers of Commerce and Industry (CSCCI) have started to take some concrete measures to help the SME sector. According to CSCCI, and following detailed studies conducted with the help of financial institutions with experience in this field such as the UK's HSBC, the following measures have been recommended:

- Creation of an office for the development of SMEs called Saudi Small Business Agency (SSBA), which is a single umbrella organization sponsored by the government for the small firms, but with autonomous private management.
- Establishment of a loan guarantee fund for the SMEs.
- Establishment of business incubation centres for SMEs in the various regional Chambers of Commerce and Industry.
- Establishment of training and advice centres at the chambers for SMEs through Business Support Centres (BSCs).
- Provision to the SME sector of the full support and attention of the government by giving the director of the SSBA access to different ministers.

The studies of the CSCCI indicated that for the SME sector as a whole, fewer than 20% of the firms set up conducted feasibility studies, fewer than 33% kept financial records, fewer than 20% prepared annual budgets and 33% had no separate bank accounts. To reinforce the need for intensive management training for this sector, the CSCCI noted that "typical" SMEs could not correctly assess assets and liabilities, insolvency, profitability and how finance was to be raised or used.

Besides the above initiatives, the SME sector needs a clear source of financing, unencumbered by bureaucracy and burden of collateral and excessive guarantees. According to the Ministry of Finance, a special programme to finance SMEs through Saudi banks and the State was set up with an equal contribution of SR 100 million, to be disbursed through the Saudi Industrial Development Fund (SIDF). In a further development, the Saudi Credit Bank expanded the scope of SME lending, and raised the current lending ceiling to SR 200,000 (Sugair, 2002).

In order to extend "soft loans" to the larger category of the SME sector, especially those employing more than 50 employees, the Saudi government has introduced such a lending programme through the Ministry of Finance, specifically for establishing hotels, tourist resorts, hospitals, dispensaries, bakeries, date factories and agricultural projects. Table 7.7 summarizes the total number of loans granted, as

Table 7.7 Saudi large SME soft loans programme (2008)

Type of loan	Number granted	Value (SR million)
Hotel and tourism	103	2,358
Health projects	118	2,195
Agricultural projects	19	332
Press and misc. projects	45	197
Bakeries	68	258
Contractor financing	64	167
Cooling warehouses	44	179
Dates factories	6	59
Educational establishments	46	862
Total	513	6,607

Source: SAMA

well as the value of disbursements made which totalled SR 6.6 billion, the majority of loans being in the hotel and health sectors.

SME Model for Growth

In line with other country experiences that have successfully focused on the SME sector as a vital engine of growth, the Saudi government needs to realign its traditional approach, not just for the SMEs but also for the private sector as a whole, along the following lines:

Traditional approach	New path
• Public sector is the main economic driver	• Private sector delivery of goods and services
• Subsidized inputs	• Market-based pricing
• Supply-driven	• Market demand-driven, commercially viable
• Unsustainable allocation of resources	• Long-term sustainability

The above approach will help to enhance the survivability of the SMEs and the private sector by focusing on their areas of weaknesses and enhancing their areas of strength, as illustrated in Fig. 7.3.

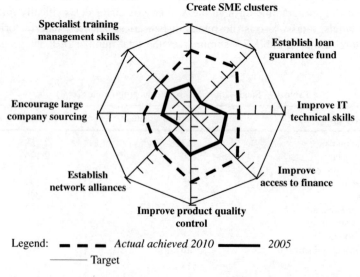

Fig. 7.3 Enhancement of SME survival and growth in the Saudi economy (actuals 2005 and 2010)

Figure 7.3 sets out an "optimum" path for SME enhancement in Saudi Arabia in light of the current strengths of each of the identified "enhancements." The figure plots the actual progress made over the two periods 2005 and 2010 in the target areas. Some will take longer to achieve, especially in the area of management training, IT skills and quality control. Others can be established sooner and produce more immediate results, including establishing and fostering SME "clusters", improving access to finance, networking alliances and, above all, encouraging the larger Saudi companies to source local tenders for goods and services from SMEs. This has worked elsewhere, notably in the Far East and Japan, and could be a model for cooperation in Saudi Arabia. Above all, the Saudi government, because it also recognizes that SMEs constitute an important economic segment, it is adapting some of its lending and regulatory policies to help this sector to survive, flourish and grow in a more dynamic environment (Radwan, 2002). Altogether, by 2010, the Saudi SME sector has improved, especially in the target areas of loan guarantees, access to finance and creating SME clusters thanks to awareness programmes initiated by the Saudi Arabian General Investment Authority (SAGIA) and the Chambers of Commerce SME units. The Japanese have been particularly supportive of the Saudi SME sector given the large role that is played by SMEs in Japan, especially in so-called business clusters. Given Saudi Arabia's dominant role in the energy sector, one such obvious business cluster model for Saudi SMEs in the upstream and downstream energy sector would be as set out in Fig. 7.4.

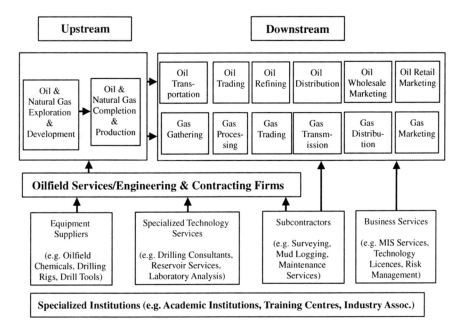

Fig. 7.4 Saudi SME energy cluster development (Source: Porter, 2010)

From Fig. 7.4, one can observe that Saudi SMEs have a broad range of opportunities to add value in various upstream or downstream activities in the energy sector so long as they are technically proficient and meet required standards. To achieve this, Saudi Arabia needs to continue investing in SME capabilities for:

- upgrading the quality and efficiency of SME products and services,
- upgrading local industry clusters,
- building clusters around strong multinational or national corporations, and
- developing related clusters that can cross-benefit from each other and broaden existing clusters including those that are resource-based such as oil.

Given the success of some SME participation in Saudi mega projects in specialized and high-skill areas such as in energy for Saudi Aramco, the Saudi Ministry of Defence also decided in 2010 to allow Saudi firms to bid to supply basic materials, excluding armaments, with the aim of encouraging a domestic military industry. The move will involve, according to the Ministry of Defence, some 15,000 items that range from plastic to pipes, covers for jet engines and batteries; a "central committee for local industrialization" was set up to develop local capabilities and ensure speedy delivery and reduce costs. This move was a breakthrough for Saudi companies, and SMEs in particular, as all military-related purchases were internationally tendered or brought from abroad by local suppliers. The decision no doubt was influenced by the outbreak of hostilities against intruders from Yemen into Saudi Arabia in late 2009, which increased the military purchases.

Saudi Family Businesses

Much has been written about the role of family businesses in the Arabian Gulf and Saudi Arabia, with most writers highlighting the significant economic impact of such family businesses on domestic economies in terms of investment, employment, international agency alliances and capital flows (Field, 1985, Fahim, 1995, Holden and Johns, 1981, Wright et al., 1996, Carter, 1984). In 2009, there were 45 family-owned Saudi entities in the top 100 Saudi companies. More recent writers have stressed the problems faced by such family businesses, and the need to transform them into joint stock companies to enable them to survive global competitive pressures and liberalization moves by national governments (Azzam, 2002, Speakman, 2002).

In Saudi Arabia, family businesses are estimated to hold around SR 250 billion in domestic investments, with 200 family companies dominating commercial life in all sectors of the economy (Daghsh, 2004). An examination of any of Saudi Arabia's trade directories will reveal that the majority of franchises and agencies highlighted earlier in Table 7.4 are owned by no more than 100 of the top Saudi family businesses.

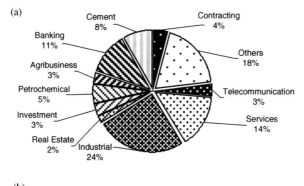

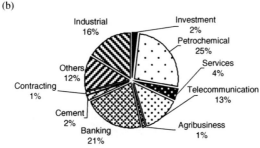

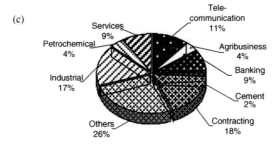

Fig. 7.5 Top 100 Saudi family companies (2007), **a** By economic sector, **b** By revenue source, **c** By employees (Source: Top 100 Saudi Company Surveys, Saudi Research and Marketing, 2007)

How significant a role they play is illustrated in Fig. 7.5, illustrating their impact in the diversity of economic sectors, their employment contribution and revenue generation from various economic sectors.

Given this prominent impact on the nation's economy, the Saudi government has encouraged family businesses to examine their current structure and to try to address the potential problems that might affect both the family business and the national economy. Several high-profile forums have been held to discuss issues of concern, such as the need for separating business and family loyalties, hiring only the most competent family members as managers in the business and giving serious consideration to taking family businesses public. The issue of succession, or more precisely of *competent* succession, in the Kingdom's family businesses has been brought into the public discourse following some high-profile cases of family business break-ups due to succession problems. The key is either to agree upon a succession plan or to separate management from ownership (Malik, 2004).

Mergers and acquisitions are other options for like-minded family businesses, but these have been rare in Saudi Arabia. They have mostly been concentrated in the banking sector and some allied food industries led by Prince Waleed bin Tallal bin Abdulaziz, such as the *Savola* and *Panda* groups and in 2008 of the merger of the Geant Stores with Panda/Savola group. In a society where mergers and acquisitions imply social and managerial failures, there is reluctance to sell to "outsiders," leading some family businesses to continue to operate despite significant financial losses. The preferred option in the Arabian Gulf seems to be "informal" family-related alliances through marriage or bloodline (Field, 1985, Wright, 1996).

To an outsider, it would be difficult to discern who is related to whom by marriage or blood affiliation, but for those operating in the Kingdom this is more transparent and it influences how business is carried out.

Such alliances could influence the efficient management of family businesses, whereby decision-making could be constrained by ethical considerations of whether to act independently or in line with external socially driven factors. This is illustrated in Fig. 7.6, which sets out the social and ethical environments in which Saudi Arabian family businesses operate.

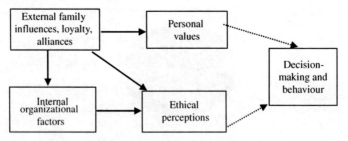

Fig. 7.6 Decision-making and ethical dilemmas in family-run businesses (Adapted from Morris et al., 1996)

Figure 7.6 describes the external environmental factors that affect internal organizational factors, which in turn impact upon ethical considerations and decision-making. If moral conduct and ethical behaviour conflicts with the larger interests of the country, then increased government regulation will result (Ostapski et al., 1996).

In Saudi Arabia, the government has not yet reached the stage of imposing regulations on family-run businesses, preferring instead internal reforms of such family groupings. The recent high-profile cases involving prominent Saudi family businesses such as the Saad and Al Gosaibi groups and the public dispute between them involving alleged fraud and corporate mismanagement has caused some concern in the Kingdom and the Gulf as to the future of family businesses, and whether they can continue to operate in their current structure given the impact on national financial institutions and the wider economy such disputes had generated. Analysts say family businesses have been reluctant to go public as they want to keep control of their companies and avoid exposing their operations to outsiders as required by disclosure rules. The public disputes of the prominent Saudi family groups mentioned above very much centred on the lack of transparent disclosures on the manner of some of their activities and decision-making processes.

To face future challenges, the Saudi family business management structure has to be changed. A centralized decision-making "power culture," in which tasks are assigned downward by the chief executive or owner and strict hierarchy is tempered by heavy doses of paternalism, is not the way forward (Azzam, 2002). Under these conditions, family companies are more likely to provide clients with the kind of goods that are already available, rather than customized goods that meet clients' needs. Obsession with balance sheet size, rather than size and growth of market share, becomes a feature, which explains the enormous interest shown by Saudi family businesses in being included in the *Saudi Top 100 Companies* surveys published by local media (Saudi Marketing and Research, 2007). While some companies provide data on assets, turnover and sales, as well as capital and employee numbers, they give little information on their profitability and market share.

Table 7.8 outlines the areas of changing management structure to which some family businesses are adapting. Others will need to address such structural issues.

Table 7.8 reveals how fundamental a shift in mindset the Saudi family businesses need in order to proceed into the next "new structure" age. Above all, the

Table 7.8 Family businesses: changing management operating structures

Characteristic	Current structure	New structure
• Organization	• Pyramid, strict hierarchy	• Horizontal, delegation
• Focus	• Balance sheet growth, agencies and franchises	• Profitability, maximizing shareholder value, production
• Ownership	• Family, affiliated groups	• Publicly listed joint stocks
• Financial structure	• Internal raising of capital	• External funding, IPOs
• Resources	• Physical assets	• Human capital
• Competition	• Between family groups	• Between brands, services and products
• Expansion	• Using influence, family alliances and "*wasta*"	• Productivity and achievement
• Financials	• Internal, annual, not audited	• Quarterly, audited financials
• Leadership style	• Top-down, paternalistic, dogmatic	• Bottom-up, inspirational
• Workers	• Mere employees	• Shareholders, participatory, critical, professional management delegation
• Job expectations	• Look for security, obedience	• Personal growth, satisfaction

Source: Adapted from Azzam, 2002

paternalistic top-down leadership style has to change to a bottom-up, inspirational leadership approach, which might still remain in the hands of the younger, educated and technically proficient family members, aided by independent professional managers with a stake in the family business (Yamani, 2000). Instead of having employees with a civil service attitude, only mindful of rank and title and rewarded for obedience to the family hierarchy, true empowerment of professional talent must be emphasized. Whatever the eventual outcome, the family business model is under stress, and it is doubtful that many will continue to survive in their present structure for years to come.

Saudi Women and the National Economy

During the past few years, women-related issues have moved to the forefront in Saudi Arabia. Social customs and traditions came under passionate social debate and many old taboos were broken. As we will discuss in a later chapter, the Kingdom has made a great effort to provide Saudi females with all levels of education. It may surprise many to learn that females outnumber males in higher education. However, some have argued that while such education is valuable as an end in itself, the returns are lowered by minimal participation of Saudi women in the formal workforce (Wilson, 2004). Higher education, international travel, access to the Internet and gender developments in nearby Gulf Cooperation Council (GCC) countries have all ensured that the subject of more effective participation of Saudi women in society at large will continue to be an important issue. Over 85% of the estimated 272,000 working women in Saudi Arabia were employed in the public sector in education, health care and government work in 2001 (Doumato, 2001) and the situation had not changed much by 2008 as illustrated below. The private sector is expected to be the major employer of female Saudi job-seekers, theoretically putting pressure on male job-seekers. In reality, Saudi social custom precludes women from entering employment where they can openly mix with men. Ways have to be found, therefore, to employ Saudi women in an environment that respects local customs and traditions, but which allows them to contribute more fully to the country's economic development.

Table 7.9 illustrates the number of employed Saudi females by all categories as of 2008.

From Table 7.9 we note Saudi women employment in manufacturing and construction. However, this relates to women-only assembly line employment processes. Table 7.9 does not provide a total picture about the effective employment participation rate of Saudi females in the national economy. Latest SAMA data indicate that female Saudi employment represented a mere 0.8% of the total Saudi labour force in the private sector, and 33% in the government sector because of female employment as teachers in the education field.

However, as we already mentioned, social taboos and stereotypical perceptions about Saudi women are being broken. A female Saudi television

Table 7.9 Saudi female employment by economic sectors (2008)

Economic sector	Number	%
• Government sector/education	275,128	84.88
• Agriculture/fishing	203	0.06
• Mines, oil	694	0.22
• Manufacturing	3,254	0.99
• Electricity, gas, water	74	0.03
• Construction/building	6,243	1.92
• Wholesale/retail	8,708	2.67
• Transport/communication	190	0.06
• Finance, insurance, real estate	2,969	0.98
• Community, social and personal	28,757	8.82
Total	326,240	100

Source: SAMA

presenter – Buthaina Al Nasr – made history by becoming the first Saudi woman to read the opening news bulletin of the Kingdom's all-news satellite channel, launched in January 2004 (Arab News, 13 January 2004). Despite criticism from some quarters, the TV presenter is now accepted as a feature of the new channel. Another landmark was achieved when Hanadi Hindi become the Kingdom's first commercial female pilot. Some female Saudi commentators lament the fact that while the oil boom era brought great changes to the GCC societies in material terms, it did little to alter "fundamental attitudes towards women" (Hafni, 2003).

Officially the Saudi government has been sympathetic to women's issues, and, while King Abdullah advised patience, the leadership has encouraged continued national dialogue on women's issues under the forum of the King Abdulaziz National Dialogue Centre, set up by the then Crown Prince Abdullah. Several such dialogue forums were held in *Makkah* and *Madinah* during 2004, and by all accounts there were some heated debates and disagreements on the direction of change (Akeelg, 15 June 2004). Some social commentators were disheartened by the outcome, stating that what happened at the dialogue forum "yet again illustrated our incapability to solve our own differences and problems" (Qusti, 16 June 2004).

Saudi women's issues have been addressed not only in domestic forums but also in international forums such as the various Jeddah Economic Forums. The Chairperson of the 19-member Women's Business Committee at the Jeddah Chamber of Commerce and Industry was no less than King Abdullah's daughter Princess Adela bint Abdullah. She stated that it was important to support qualified Saudi women by giving them the opportunity to actively participate in key social and economic activities (SAGIA, 18 January 2004).

Because of their need to help support the family by working, Saudi Arabian women are motivated to change facts on the ground. They have become a formidable presence in the economy. They are not afraid to take on jobs that were previously considered "menial," such as factory work. There was astonishment when 1,500 women applied for 400 positions at a major dairy factory outside Riyadh in

2003, proving that the search for jobs was not limited to university graduates alone (Ahmad, 2004). Unfortunately, the pioneering dairy farm decided not to proceed with the hiring, but other Saudi businesswomen have initiated women-only assembly line employment.

The demand for this type of female labour has encouraged Saudi businesswomen to petition for "women-only" industrial cities and, according to the Saudi Arabian General Investment Authority (SAGIA), such women-only industrial cities are planned for Riyadh and Jeddah (SAGIA, June 3, June 13, 2004). Apparently a 600,000 m^2 site has been allocated for this purpose in Riyadh and a site of similar size has been allocated in Jeddah, which would accommodate 83 factories. It is said that "two foreign firms will operate the city and train 10,000 women for two years" (SAGIA, June 3, 2004). Despite some good intentions, there has been little significant achievement in reality concerning these ideas, illustrating once again the polarization of Saudi society concerning women's issues.

Progress has been made, however, on women's issues since King Abdullah acceded to the throne in 2006. The King has made it a point meeting and honouring outstanding Saudi female academics and businesswomen in public, and has ensured that Saudi businesswomen accompany him abroad as part of Saudi Arabia's official delegations such as the one he made to China, India and other Far Eastern countries in 2006. While there are no full Saudi female cabinet ministers, the appointment of the first Saudi female Deputy Minister for Girls' Education in 2009 was widely welcomed, as was the appointment of the first two Saudi female members to the Eastern Province Chamber of Commerce and Industry in January 2010. Saudi businesswomen have also been appointed to the Board of the Saudi Management Association, which has some 2,400 members across the Kingdom, of whom 21% are professional women. Saudi corporations have began to be more active in recruitment of Saudi females, especially in the banking and insurance sector which today employs around 3,000 professional females ranging from female-only branches to credit analysts and call centre operators. The more widespread use of IT has also allowed Saudi women to carry out tasks out of their homes, or women-only business centres, and the trend is growing for such outsourcing support services. Government ministries have been encouraged to employ Saudi females and the Ministries of Foreign Affairs and Commerce have either set up women-only sections or started to employ female professionals for international assignments.

Estimating the Size of Saudi Women's Investments

Data on the economic status of women in Saudi Arabia are somewhat sketchy, with varying estimates given, but all point to substantial economic involvement in the country. According to a study carried out by King Abdulaziz University in Jeddah in 2004, Saudi women hold nearly 30% of the bank accounts in the Kingdom with deposits worth SR 62 billion, hold 20% of corporate shares and own 15% of the private companies and 10% of the real estate sector (Abdul Ghafour, 4 June 2004). The same study states that women have a 34% stake in private businesses in Riyadh,

25% in Jeddah and 6% in Makkah, and that there are an estimated 5,000 business-women in Riyadh and 4,000 in Jeddah. Not to be outdone, the Eastern Province Chamber of Commerce and Industry (EPCCI) set up a joint committee of Saudi businesswomen at the chamber with the aim of encouraging women to participate and invest in different projects. This was followed by a "women-only wing" of the Riyadh Chamber of Commerce and Industry.

Other studies report that Saudi women own 40% of private wealth (which might have been passively acquired due to Islamic inheritance laws), and approximately 15,000 commercial establishments or 10% of private businesses in Saudi Arabia (Doumato, 2003). To better service this lucrative market segment, all Saudi banks have opened women-only branches, and one of them, Saudi British Bank (SABB), went one step further and inaugurated a women-only centre for financial and invest-ment consultancy for lady clients. Even SAGIA decided to offer its services to Saudi businesswomen and to establish a "one-stop" service centre for women only, staffed by professional female experts who will be able to provide full-fledged services to both Saudi and foreign businesswomen intending to invest in the Kingdom, while ensuring their privacy. SAGIA was encouraged by the response of Saudi women, for apparently a large number have applied for investment licences. Almost all for-eign banks and investment companies operating in Saudi Arabia have employed Saudi females in high-value professional positions, opening up another employment segment for Saudi females.

When it comes to types of businesses set up by women, Saudi businesswomen certainly seem quite innovative (Akeel, 2003, Doumato, 2001). Besides the usual tailoring shops, beauty and hair salons, jewellery and clothing, Saudi women are now running businesses in marketing, public relations, event management, Web design, programming and recruitment consultation. In addition, Saudi business-women have invested in industries such as iron and steel, furniture, plastic products and solar cell technology (Doumato, 2003). Women now work as architects and journalists and there is great interest in nursing, after this sector was previously frowned upon by society as being a less-than-acceptable job. Many jobs avail-able for women continue to be filled by foreigners in Saudi Arabia. Some 600,000 foreign women work as nurses, nannies, secretaries and housemaids. This huge for-eign workforce holds jobs that Saudi women cannot fill because either they are not qualified or they reject the job as low-prestige or unsuitable for women, such as sec-retarial work in a mixed-sex environment. However, some companies are now using segregated female secretarial pools, and nursing is beginning to be more acceptable but in a female-only environment.

Some analysts who follow the issues of Arab and Gulf women have noted, how-ever, that there is a danger that current reform moves are being headed by "elite" female groups – women who are not representative of society at large (Hijab, 1988, Khoury et al., 1995, Sanabary, 1994, Doumato, 2003). When one notes the distin-guished academic credentials of most Saudi women participants at such forums, one sees the validity of this argument. At the same time, one is convinced by their claim that as compared to men they are more in tune and can better articulate what Saudi women in general wish to achieve. However, informal contact following the most recent national forum with a wide range of Saudi females of all ages revealed some disappointment amongst younger Saudi females. Some felt that superficial issues were discussed, and others had not heard of the forum discussions at all. Saudi businesswomen have come a long way in a short period, and it is only a matter of time before some of the more onerous bureaucratic impediments before them are removed so that they can play a more effective role in the Saudi economy. Table 7.10 lays out the status of some of the current issues which are being faced by Saudi businesswomen.

Table 7.10 indicates that both the government and the various Chambers of Commerce and Industry are trying to facilitate the operating needs of Saudi businesswomen. The key is to pursue this momentum while ensuring that society at large is willingly accepting the changes taking place, without affecting basic Islamic beliefs and traditions.

Towards dealing with this difficult and multifaceted challenge of women-related issue in the Kingdom, education policies labour market policies and other related

Table 7.10 Saudi businesswomen's operating barriers

Barriers	Status
• Difficulty for businesswomen to accomplish official business in person without using male intermediary	• Government has now allowed women to submit applications directly without intermediary
• Lack of training organizations and specialist women-related business programmes	• Chamber of Commerce establishing training programmes
• Difficulty in obtaining required market information	• Special sections of Chamber of Commerce set up to provide data
• Difficulty in qualifying for loans	• Government lending institutions instructed to handle female loan applicants on equal basis
• Limited allowable investment sectors	• Industrial zones planned and special investment advisory service from SAGIA set up
• Unavailability of women's sections in major government ministries	• Some progress in this field and some ministries have established women-only sections
• Clarification of legal rights of businesswomen with government agencies	• Steps are being taken to ensure that women can correspond directly in their own legal capacity without intermediaries
• Limited networking groups for businesswomen	• Businesswomen's associations established to facilitate networking
• Travelling in Kingdom unescorted by male relatives or spouses	• More flexibility and acceptance now to allow mobility in Kingdom based on written approval from next of kin without male chaperones
• Ban on hiring trained female staff from abroad	• Case-by-case submission to ensure that qualified Saudi females can be employed for position but in Kingdom mobility for Saudi females is still an issue

administrative policies have been put under ongoing review in order to reach a satisfactory resolution to this important social and economic issue bearing in mind the conservative social structure of Saudi Arabia.

Government and Business Relations in Saudi Arabia

The centrality of governmental interaction with the private sector in Saudi Arabia has been undeniably demonstrated throughout the preceding chapters. A successful public–private sector dialogue and ongoing cooperation will bring about a business environment that will allow the private sector to flourish, while the government continues to play a supportive role. This has become a central policy goal of the Saudi Arabian government and is clearly set out in the latest development plan and government statements. Over time, there has been a gradual evolution in the manner by which the Saudi private sector and the government have interacted depending on perceived government priorities. Figure 7.7 illustrates this changing relationship.

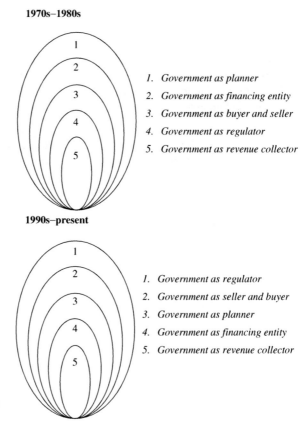

1970s–1980s

1. *Government as planner*
2. *Government as financing entity*
3. *Government as buyer and seller*
4. *Government as regulator*
5. *Government as revenue collector*

1990s–present

1. *Government as regulator*
2. *Government as seller and buyer*
3. *Government as planner*
4. *Government as financing entity*
5. *Government as revenue collector*

Fig. 7.7 Saudi Arabia: Evolving government–private sector relationships

In the Kingdom, as in many other developing nations, governments assume the responsibility of setting goals and guiding the discharge of both public and private resources to achieve the objectives of development. Previously, we examined the various development processes adopted by the Kingdom and what the government had hoped to achieve over the past three decades. In the section that follows, we will analyse the development process from the private sector's perspective, before assessing a suitable model for public–private sector cooperation. We will look at the roles of the government in relation to the private sector in five key areas and how these have evolved over time. Within each of these five roles, there are different mechanisms that the government might use to influence the degree of participation of the private sector in the national economic development process. Figure 7.5 is based on the five relationships between the public and private sector throughout the 1970s and 1980s, and then from the 1990s to date. The five areas of public–private sector cooperation and mutual dependency are

- government as planner,
- government as financing entity,
- government as buyer and seller,
- government as regulator and
- government as revenue collector.

As Fig. 7.7 illustrates, there has been a noticeable shift in emphasis over the two periods in question, with the first ranking indicating the most important emphasis, and the fifth ranking indicating the lowest emphasis. The rankings in between show other levels of emphasis and priorities for the different periods.

> *One: The government as a planner.* The crucial fact of economic development since 1970 has been the Saudi government's comprehensive planning for the short- and long-term activities of the public and private sectors. Over time, there was less emphasis on direct planning and indicative planning was introduced in order to promote the state's objectives of economic diversification and greater private-sector, value-added industrial investment. The government had used earlier oil revenue surpluses to build up capital- and energy-intensive industries. The private sector in general knows that it is assuming this new national economic responsibility, but it is also arguing for a more effective government–business relationship to implement it. Research indicated that despite some praise for the government on what it has done to date, the private sector was still critical of the business environment, which the private sector felt did not yet meet their needs (Malik, 2004). The government needs to involve the private sector in a closer dialogue from the outset, before committing itself to far-reaching decisions. The entry of the Kingdom into the WTO is one case in point where the private sector feels that there was not enough preparation and consultation between the government and the private sector on the economic ramifications of entry.

Two: the government as a revenue collector. The significant increase in oil revenues in the 1970s eliminated the need for Saudi Arabia to introduce direct or indirect taxes. The government hoped that the resultant limited fiscal collection role would promote a stimulating climate for Saudi industrial and business activities, with the 2.5% *Zakat* or religious prescribed levy being the only one imposed on Saudi companies. This rate is considered low by international corporate tax standards and it is doubtful that the government will raise Saudi corporate taxes. What might be introduced are indirect taxes that could be placed on luxury consumer goods in line with some other GCC countries. However, as a result of this low tax environment, the business sector in Saudi Arabia took the situation for granted, and government attempts to remove subsidies on certain basic utilities such as electricity met with such resistance that they were cancelled. This reinforces the Saudi business sector's perception of the government's role as being a *provider* rather than a *partner,* although the inevitability of the introduction of some form of taxation is accepted by some businesses, probably under the guise of WTO equalization regulations. Foreign companies operating in the Kingdom, whether wholly owned or in partnership, pay a corporate income tax of 20%, following a reduction from a top tier of 45% in order to attract foreign direct investment. How Saudi Arabia will be able to maintain this dual tax policy towards foreigners and nationals after WTO entry will be of major interest to both parties.

Three: government as a buyer and seller. As both buyer and seller, the Saudi government is a key economic player in a Keynesian macroeconomic sense of managing aggregate demand. The government is a de facto seller through its use of subsidies. In the early 1970s, the Saudi government became the provider of a wide range of free and subsidized goods and services. These actions had long-term negative effects on economic development efforts, by underestimating the true cost of production and thereby encouraging some resources to be over-utilized (Nazir, 2002, Saravia, 2002, Trivedi, 2002). Subsidies currently stand at around SR 15 billion per annum or 3% of total expenditures, up substantially over early periods, when subsidies were at SR 10–11 billion levels in 1981/1982 or 4% of total expenditures (SAMA). The Saudi government is aware of the cost of this support and has, over the years, taken some steps to rationalize its subsidy policies by cancelling some, such as the wheat subsidy in 1995, but reintroduced some to support local consumers during the period of higher inflation in 2007–2009. Of more long-term significance for the private sector is the government's strategic decision to rationalize its use of resources by selling part of its share in the huge industrial projects in *Jubail* and *Yanbu,* including its holdings in the Saudi Arabian Basic Industries or SABIC. This trend will accelerate with the implementation of the government's multifaceted privatization programme (Nazir, 2002, Speakman, 2002). Figure 7.7 demonstrates how the role of the government as a buyer and seller will increase in the current period due to this privatization strategy.

In most countries, the government is the private sector's major purchaser of goods and services, and the degree to which the government is effective in using this tool often determines the size and growth of existing private sector industries and future private sector investments. The private sector–government experience of buying and selling in Saudi Arabia has been mixed. The Saudi government has gradually passed numerous decrees insisting that government contracts stipulate a domestic input of goods and services, but these are not always adhered to and foreign goods are imported instead. The government complains of the lack of response from the private sector to government tenders and its lack of professionalism in meeting tender specifications, while the private sector complains in turn that government agencies lack an understanding of what is currently available in the market and impose unrealistic specifications (Nazir, 2002, Wright, 1996). Others argue that the system can sometimes lack transparency, with government tenders linked to favours and whom you know or *wasta*, especially for large government tenders (Malik, 2004).

Some progress has been made in Saudi Arabia in this regard, with a more transparent bidding system and discussions on the required specifications. More effort, however, is required in order to better understand each sector's needs, including resolving the issues of late government payments and late private sector delivery. How long the Saudi private sector can obtain favoured supplier status from the Saudi government for its contracts remains to be seen following entry into WTO, but Saudi companies who have established themselves on such contracts will need either to diversify or to become even more competitive, should foreign companies be allowed to bid openly for government contracts, which they are entitled to under WTO accession, although government tenders still specify a certain "local content" input from foreign companies.

Four: government as a financing entity. One of the key focus in developing the state's ability to finance industrial enterprises has been the creation of specialized loan institutions to make funds available to industry on terms more favourable than those offered by commercial banks. As Fig. 7.7 indicates, this was an important function in the 1970s and 1980s, but has been relegated to a lower level since the 1990s. To meet its development objectives, the Saudi government established several funding institutions and Fig. 7.8 sets out the level of disbursements and repayments of loans made by the Saudi government credit institutions.

What is noticeable from the table is that government loan disbursements picked up from 2005 when the oil revenues of Saudi Arabia increased, but had depended on loan repayments in the earlier period to replenish the government credit institutions lending base.

Each of the government financing institutions that were created filled a niche in its respective area, with the Saudi Industrial Development Fund (SIDF) concentrating on medium- to long-term loans for industrial investment, the Saudi Agricultural Bank providing loans for agricultural

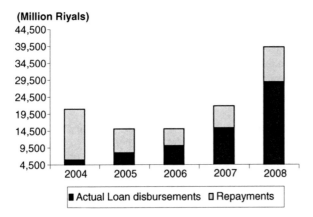

Fig. 7.8 Actual disbursements and repayments of loans of specialized credit institutions (2004–2008) (Source: SAMA)

farm projects and mechanization, and the Real Estate Development Fund (REDEF) granting personal as well as commercial housing loans. The Saudi Credit Bank (SCB) filled a gap by lending to the smaller businesses and artisans, as was noted elsewhere in this chapter, and today SCB is the vehicle for SME funding along with the SIDF.

Five: the government as a regulator. Notwithstanding the free-market ideology stated in all Saudi development plans, the Saudi government regulates the marketplace to some extent, and in Fig. 7.7 we have assumed that this role will receive the highest priority going forward. On the financial side, the government controls currency prices by fixing the price of the SR against the dollar. The government also intervenes to regulate both safety at the workplace and the environmental effects of production. The government is still the major supplier and regulator of the education sector, and is now encouraging more private sector universities and colleges to ensure that the private sector will have the skilled manpower they require. The government is still the regulator in terms of establishing the overall commercial and legal regime within which the private sector can operate, although according to a sample survey of Saudi businessmen, there was some dissatisfaction with the status of the legal system (Malik, 2004), which was taken into account when the legal system was reformed in 2008/2009.

The Saudi government, to its credit, has gone to great lengths to meet some of the challenges and issues raised by the private sector, including its requests for a less burdensome bureaucracy, more predictability of regulations and a legal system conducive to business, which adapts to deal with the realities of modern international business. E-commerce and e-government are being seriously studied, and according to a 2004 survey carried out by the Economist Intelligence Unit (EIU) and IBM, Saudi Arabia was ranked 45th in terms of "e-readiness" amongst the world's 60 largest economies

(EIU/IBM Survey, June, 2004). Since that earlier survey, the Kingdom's
e-commerce application has been significantly enhanced through several
measures including the launch of "smart-city" initiatives, where communication broadband is provided to retail and business sectors, and ensuring that
all government services are available for Internet users. There is a five-year
plan to 2015 under the so-called "*YUSUR*" e-Government Interoperability
Programme, whereby 150 public services will be connected to collect payments and fees, and apply electronic government procurement systems, as
well as a national centre for digital validation for electronic signatures and
increased security of electronic transactions will be set up.

Promoting Private Sector Self-Sustained Growth

This chapter has already established that fostering diversification and competitiveness in the Saudi private sector in order to enable it to meet future challenges
requires a multi-programme and long-term process of adjustment. It will entail
measures that private firms, industries, regions, the labour force and the government will consciously have to adopt, promote, maintain and increase, despite any
short-term setbacks or disagreements between the government and the private sector.
This was illustrated during 2004 when the Kingdom decided to establish a separate
Ministry of Labour, after having split off the Ministry of Social Affairs from it, as
well as abolishing the Manpower Council (Saudi Press Agency, 23 March 2004).
A veteran Saudi minister, Dr. Ghazi Al Gosaibi, was appointed to head the Labour
Ministry. The Manpower Council was absorbed into this new ministry, which was
charged with dealing with labour disputes, employment in the private sector and
visa issues. The Ministry of Labour issued bans on recruiting workers from overseas and stopped issuing visas for small Saudi companies, some of which they
accused of "trading in visas" and helping to compound the domestic unemployment situation. Debate on this action raged in the press, and in the end there were
compromises on the ban deadline, but the minister made it clear that tackling unemployment would now be a "national policy" rather than a government "concern"
(Bashir, 4 June 2004). The Ministry of Labour took more drastic steps to stem foreign worker mobility in the Kingdom. It banned the transfer between employers of
visa sponsorship for low-skilled workers, limiting such transfers to professionals
with university and technical degrees. At the same time, the SME sector with fewer
than 20 employees, which had previously been exempted from certain *Saudization*
quotas, are now required to apply the same *Saudization* regulations. The issue of
Saudization will be dealt with in more depth in a later chapter, as well as the debate
on whether to liberalize existing workers' sponsorship rules, especially following
the abolition of private sector workers' sponsorship in Bahrain and allowing free
labour mobility under a new government sponsorship role in August 2009.

   In the past, the Saudi private sector has shown it can adapt itself to the
changed economic fortunes of the country. However, with greater globalization

Table 7.11 Private sector challenges and solutions

Challenges	Opportunities and solutions
• Promoting government–business dialogue and collaboration	• The private sector has to engage the government in a dialogue on competitiveness and impediments to improving productivity
• Internal business environment and international competitive comparisons	• Up-to-date information on local and international market opportunities made available as well as comparing relative costs and efficiency with international standards
• Expansion of the privatization policy	• Private sector must engage in dialogue to ensure that transfer is done on a transparent basis with no "hidden" costs and commitment; flexibility in hiring and firing
• Paying attention to scientific research that might serve the production sector	• Poor communication between the productive sectors and research centres must be overcome through R & D funding, and developing science park/incubator concepts
• Increasing investment locally	• Better coordination with SAGIA and Chambers of Commerce to create business and investor-friendly environment; update and harmonize business regulations; create a demand-driven economy
• Reduce national unemployment	• Short-term "fix" through expatriate labour reduction vs. long-term solution of employing productive Saudis; ensure that the market knows of the skill needs of the private sector

and international competition, the private sector needs to be even more resilient. Table 7.11 summarizes some of the challenges to be faced.

In Table 7.11, we find the first steps that the private sector ought to take if it wishes to continue conducting an effective partnership with the government in the years to come. The beginnings of a fruitful dialogue already exist. The government cannot afford to see the private sector fail, given the Kingdom's free mobility of capital and the fact that nearby GCC countries are an attractive alternative location for any sections of the Saudi private sector that feel pressured by unacceptable demands or are frustrated by bureaucracy and outdated regulation (Abdulaziz, Al Waleed bin Tallal, 9 July 2003). Over the past few years a more vigorous public–private sector dialogue has emerged, with the private sector raising questions such as the validity of pegging the SR only to the US dollar as well as the reduced level of bank lending to the private sector following the 2008/2009 global financial crisis.

Despite the crisis, Saudi Arabia continues to forge ahead with a multifaceted investment programme that provides both short- and medium-term opportunities for the private sector, especially in gross fixed capital formation. Saudi Arabia has made public a $400 billion investment programme over the period 2010–2015 which involves expanding the productive base including oil, gas and downstream, as well as significant investment in the water desalination and power sectors. Other areas targeted are transportation, education and housing. In 2010 the government-owned

Public Investment Fund (PIF) agreed to contribute 20% of the SR 2 billion capital of a new home finance company called Islamic Corporation of the Private Sector (ICD), representing the single largest investment in a mortgage company in the history of the PIF. According to market estimates, the demand for new housing in Saudi Arabia is 150,000 units per year over the next 10 years and private–public sector participation is crucial to meet this growing demand, as according to the Saudi Home Loans Company, an Islamic mortgage lender, only 30% of Saudi nationals owned their homes, one of the lowest in the GCC.

After 20 years of under-investment and strong national population growth, such investments are required and Fig. 7.9 illustrates the planned and awarded Saudi projects.

(a)

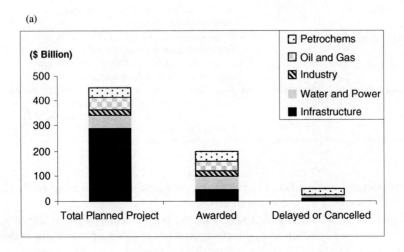

(b)

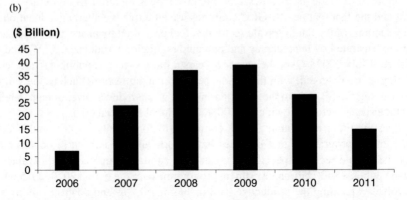

Fig. 7.9 Saudi investment programme **a** Investments by project sectors and **b** Awarded project workload (Source: MEED Projects)

Despite the global economic downturn, Saudi Arabia continues to show robust project activity and the value of construction contracts awarded in the first 3 months of 2009 exceeded the total awarded in the boom year of 2008 according to MEED Projects, which tracks such contract projects in the region.

The development of the various Saudi "economic cities" will also give a boost for Saudi private sector participation and is an important component of the country's plans and will drive investments in the foreseeable future.

Looking Ahead: A Model for Cooperation

Despite some element of mistrust on both sides, there is a genuine desire to see the private sector succeed. Figure 7.10 sets out a business relationship model between Saudi Arabia's private and governmental sectors that captures the main relationship flows between the parties in the context of external forces, such as the World Trade Organization.

By its own admission, the quality of the civil service in Saudi Arabia needs improvement and lags behind the private sector by as much as a decade, according to some (Janoubi, 2002, Khemani, 2002, Nazir, 2002). This is the "glass ceiling"

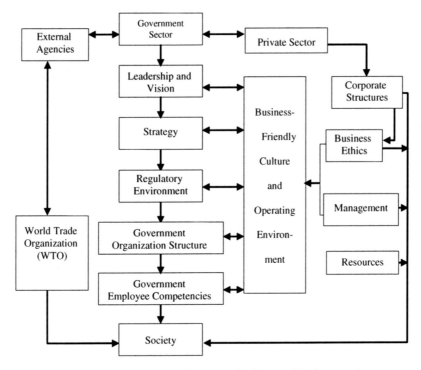

Fig. 7.10 Saudi Arabia: A government–private sector business model of cooperation

under which the private sector has to operate, but fortunately both the private and government sectors are seeking solutions.

In summary, the private sector has to learn to take charge of its own economic life and move forward, requesting that the government provides the necessary business-friendly environment under which the private sector has to operate. The lower the "glass ceiling," the less effective the private sector will be. All indications are that the government is happy to improve the business environment although the speed at which this is being done has caused some concern.

Summary of Key Points

- *The private sector is being urged to assume a greater degree of responsibility in national developing in the areas of job creation, economic diversification and international competitiveness.*
- *The Saudi private sector is currently having to operate under multiple legal settings, corporate structures as well as government pressure to accelerate the pace of Saudization of the labour force.*
- *Foreign participation is still important to the Saudi economy whether through the provision of labour and key management or through foreign joint ventures. Franchising and agency distribution was the preferred method of cooperation, but with globalization the Saudi private sector has to find new ways of foreign participation and cooperation.*
- *The small- and medium-sized enterprises (SMEs) dominate private sector economic activity but face particular problems which need addressing, particularly in the field of financing, training, advisory and dedicated business centres in the chamber of commerce and industry. The concept of clusters to promote inter-industry linkages for the SMEs is an important goal for Saudi industry.*
- *Saudi family businesses play a prominent role in the nation's economy. With globalization and international competition, it becomes urgent that they adapt internally to meet these challenges. Such adaptation can take the form of publicly listing family businesses, hiring of external professional management and delegation of authority. Recent high-profile family business problems have highlighted the need for more transparency and possible regulatory oversight.*
- *Saudi women are beginning to play a more visible role in society at large, and in the economy in particular. Estimates as to the size of their investments and corporate ownership varies but it is substantial. To take account of their effective participation, initiatives have been taken by the various Chambers of Commerce and Industry to meet their concerns and try to overcome some of the operating obstacles facing them. The government has been sympathetic to their issues and has encouraged an open dialogue on women's role in society, bearing in mind Islamic principles and social customs.*

- *The relationship between the government and the private sector and how it has evolved over time in the areas of planning, financing, regulation and revenue collector is examined, as well as the important role of the government as a purchaser and seller to the private sector. The relationship is still evolving. It is expected that regulatory issues will predominate in the foreseeable future as the government "disengages" from the economy and allows the private sector to assume greater responsibilities. A model of government–private sector cooperation is examined.*

Chapter 8
The Energy Sector

Business is like oil. It won't mix with anything but business.
J. Graham

Learning Outcomes

By the end of this section, you would understand:

- *The important role energy plays in Saudi economic development*
- *The centrality of Saudi Arabian petroleum sector to world output and demand*
- *Saudi oil policy and constraints*
- *Saudi oil and GDP contribution*
- *The growing importance of the Saudi gas sector*
- *Saudi petrochemicals and their role in economic diversification*
- *The Saudi mining sector and its future development*
- *Alternative energy solutions*

Introduction

Energy is a necessary and vital input to economic activity throughout the world. Oil plays a key role in this regard; crude oil is today one of the most highly valued commodities in international trade. While some might consider oil as a homogeneous commodity that should carry the same price worldwide, in reality price differentials among regions of the world exist due to market conditions, shipping distance and political factors. Saudi Arabia remains the dominant force in oil, accounting for around 13% of the world's production and 20% of global exports. The country possesses around 25% of the world's reserves at around 260 billion barrels of oil, has the fourth largest gas reserves in the world and enjoys the largest spare production capacity at more than 2 million barrels a day (mbd). Saudi Arabia has indeed been called the "central bank" of world oil, or its oil warehouse. Oil fuels the Saudi economy by financing the government budget as well as large infrastructure projects,

M.A. Ramady, *The Saudi Arabian Economy*, DOI 10.1007/978-1-4419-5987-4_8,
© Springer Science+Business Media, LLC 2010

providing the country with ample liquidity and driving its robust consumption. The surplus generated by the oil industry has also allowed the country to accomplish an ambitious development of its industrial sector, and to capitalize on the synergies and subsidies available to sectors such as the petrochemicals. While the hydrocarbon sector has brought about undoubted material benefits to the Kingdom over the past 30 years, it has also brought great responsibilities and limitations on how far Saudi Arabia can go in pursuing its own energy interests, unlike marginal oil producers that wish to optimize on current revenues, knowing that their reserves will run out in the short run.

The government's recent emphasis on *economic diversification* encompasses energy-based manufacturing and the exploitation of gas and mineral resources, both for domestic consumption and for the establishment of a new export market. However, despite efforts at diversification away from oil, the hydrocarbon sector will continue to be at the heart of the Kingdom's economic well-being for some time. Given the Kingdom's low-cost production, which gives it a comparative advantage estimated at between $1 and $3 per barrel for extraction compared to other high-cost energy producers, it is not unreasonable to assume that future private sector-led economic diversification will somehow be associated with energy-related products.

Oil-Based Economies: A Theoretical Analysis

One major characteristic of developing economies is the so-called "dualistic" nature of their economic structure whereby a modern industrial base sits alongside a traditional sector. Dualistic models of economic development analyse the differences and structural relationships between the two sectors to explain the development process and the obstacles faced, especially by the traditional sector as it copes with the challenges of the modern sector and its needs. According to some economists (Ranis and Fei, 1988), the main focus is on how to shift the overall economy's "centre of gravity" from traditional-based economic production such as agriculture to the modern industrial sector, and, in the process, the traditional sector becomes an appendage of the modern sector.

The result is that dualistic economies are soon characterized by modern "industrial enclaves." Oil-based economies such as Saudi Arabia, which depend to a large extent on this natural resource, are different from the above model. The basic problem for economies like Saudi Arabia is not one of shifting the economy's centre of gravity from a traditional static sector (non-oil) to a dynamic (oil) sector, but using the growth-led effects of the dynamic sector throughout the traditional non-oil sector. The key factor here is that the dynamic sector for oil producers represents an exhaustible and non-renewable finite resource that generates flows of income at the cost of its own depletion unlike manufacturing enclaves. This type of development model creates a dilemma for oil producers: conserve oil resources and grow at your own pace, or deplete at a faster rate and develop the traditional sector built around a dynamic sector. In the latter, the dynamic sector acts as the leading sector and growth engine contributing to the entire economy, but unlike generally accepted Western models of economic development, the oil-based dynamic new sector is essentially an alien sector superimposed on the traditional sector and how the two interact will be the measure of success or failure in the future. For all practical purposes, the linkage between the traditional and oil-based dynamic sector is the indirect capital flows derived from resource sales in the short run, which can be translated to effective direct linkages in the long run if the output of this sector is widened from just extraction and sales into a value-added chain. Should such linkages become strong over time, the dynamic sector may ultimately become integrated into the domestic economy and lose its dominant position to the static sector (Yamani, 1994). For this to be successful, a government of an oil-based economy must be willing to channel the receipts from the dynamic sector into development projects in which the country enjoys a comparative advantage, made possible by the low-cost supply of raw materials input by the dynamic sector.

The above encapsulates the current Saudi energy policy and its diversification into high-value petrochemical projects to create and integrate the dynamic sector into the traditional sector of the Saudi economy. Under such a model, the government's fiscal and expenditure role plays a predominant role, unlike traditional Western development models where the generating force of development is provided by private sector entrepreneurs. The benefit of an entrepreneurial led economic development is that they can act quickly, unlike governments which can influence the pace and tempo of innovation assimilation, capital formation and consequently the flow of resources from the dynamic to the static sector and thus affect the pace of development (Yamani, 1994). As examined in earlier chapters, the Saudi government has quickened the pace and tempo of the major causative factors that promote economic development.

The Saudi Petroleum Sector

Oil reserves of Saudi Arabia are controlled by the state-run Saudi Aramco company. Saudi Aramco has maintained its first ranking for the consecutive 23rd year to 2010, as the largest oil company in the world according to Petroleum Intelligence. As of 2010, the Saudi Aramco Board of Directors were Oil Minister Ali Al Naimi, Minster of Finance Dr. Ibrahim Al Assaf, Dr. Abdulrahman Al Tuwaijri (Chairman, CMA), Dr. Khaled Al Sultan (Rector KFUPM), Dr. Mohammed Al Suwaiyel (President of KACST), Mr. Peter Woicke (former Managing Director of the World Bank), Sir Mark Moody-Stuart (former Chairman of Royal Dutch/Shell), David O' Reilly (former Chairman of Chevron) and from Saudi Aramco, Mr. Khaled Al Falih (CEO), Mr. Salim Ayedh (SVP), Amin Nasser (SVP) and Abdulaziz Al Khayyal (SVP).

When it surveys the future of the oil market, Saudi Aramco can claim many favourable factors, including massive reserves, low production costs, high production capacity and a well-skilled labour force that has one of the highest *Saudization* ratios in the entire Kingdom. According to Saudi Aramco, the total number of the petroleum sector employees stood at just under 55,000, 87% of which were Saudis.

Fig. 8.1 Saudi Aramco: number of employees in the year-end 2008; (**a**) Saudi and expatriate employees, (**b**) Expatriates by major global regions (Source: Saudi Aramco)

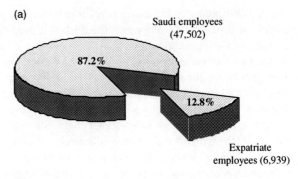

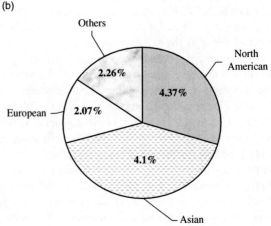

This is illustrated in Fig. 8.1, which also gives the breakdown of the expatriate labour by nationality.

There is a historical explanation for the relatively high number of North American expatriates working for Aramco in comparison with other nationalities. The Saudi company enjoyed a close relationship with the founding US oil companies which had formed the Arabian American Oil Company (Aramco) that was later renamed Saudi Aramco when it was nationalized by the Saudi government. The high percentage of skilled technical and administrative Saudi staff in the most economically critical and sensitive of Saudi industries is reassuring, especially if some foreign workers decide not to renew their contracts with Saudi Aramco due to the wave of domestic terrorism in Saudi Arabia which particularly targeted Western expatriates during 2004.

According to Saudi Aramco, the Kingdom contains 259.9 billion barrels of proven oil reserves including 2.5 billion barrels in the Saudi-Kuwait "neutral" zone (Saudi Aramco, 2009). This represents one quarter of proven, conventional world oil reserves. Around two thirds of Saudi reserves are considered "light" or "extra light" grades of oil, commanding a higher pricing premium, with the rest either "medium" or "heavy." Although Saudi Arabia has around 80 oil- and gas-fields (and over 1,000 wells), more than half of its oil reserves are contained in only eight fields, including the giant *Ghawar*, the world's largest oilfield, with estimated remaining reserves of 70 billion barrels, and *Safaniya*, the world's largest offshore oilfield with an estimated reserve of 35 billion barrels.

By 2010, Saudi Arabia had raised its production capacity to 12.5 million barrels per day (mbpd) but was producing around 8.5 mbpd in 2010 compared with 9.5 mbpd in 2008 at the height of the global oil price rise to nearly $147 pb, as illustrated in Fig. 8.2.

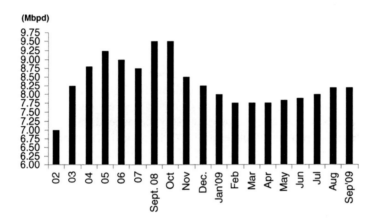

Fig. 8.2 Saudi crude oil production (2002–2009) (Source: Saudi Aramco)

A key challenge for Saudi Arabia in maintaining a high production level is the estimated "decline rate" for existing fields, which, as some have conservatively estimated, is at between 2 and 10% for the major fields (Petroleum Intelligence Weekly). The implication is that Saudi Arabia needs to add around 500,000 to 1 million bpd in new capacity each year to compensate for the declared decline rates, which some analysts like US-based Simmons and Company have disputed as being underestimated, leading to an even larger depletion rate and requirement of new reserve finds.

Saudi Arabia's long-term goal is to further develop its lighter crude reserve finds and Saudi Aramco has been successful in this respect, as the number and quantity of new finds summarized below show:

- *Shaybah field* – Located in the empty quarter near the UAE border; is now producing 500,000 bpd of Arabian extra light crude oil and the production capacity is set to rise to 750,000 bpd.
- *Khurais development* – the largest oil project in Saudi Aramco's history is producing 1.2 million bpd of Arabian light crude. To put this new production into perspective, *Khurais* produces as much as all of Angola's production, with

Angola being the latest African country to produce oil in sizeable quantities like Sudan and Chad.

- *Khursaniyah* programme will add another 500,000 bpd of Arabian light crude from the oilfields of *Abu Hadriya, Fadhili* and *Khursaniyah*.
- *Nuayyim* field added another 100,000 bpd of super light crude oil and the off-shore *Manifa* project added 900,000 bpd of Arabian heavy crude oil as well as 90 million scfd (standard cubic feet per day) of associated gas.
- The *Haradh* 3 project has already come onstream and added another 300,000 bpd besides producing significant volumes of non-associated natural gas.

The above new Saudi finds, as well as reports of massive new offshore and onshore oil finds in Brazil and Venezuela, have not settled the so-called "oil peak" debate, which will be discussed in detail later in the chapter. According to a US assessment of Venezuela's oil reserves, the new finds could give that country double the reserves of Saudi Arabia or an additional 500 billion barrels of "technically recoverable" oil in the Orinoco belt, based on oil recovery rates of 40–45% (BBC News, 23 Jan 2010). Others remained more sceptical about the new find and doubted if the Venezuelan recovery could exceed 24% levels and that much of the new find would not be economic to produce; however, Venezuela holds the largest oil reserves outside the Middle East.

By all accounts, Saudi Arabia and possibly Iraq have the lowest cost of production amongst the major producers for oil extraction and Fig. 8.3 illustrates the relevant estimated "oil price benchmark" for new oil projects to be viable for selected producing countries.

As noted from Fig. 8.3, Venezuela's oil industry threshold barrier is around $114 fully loaded costs per incremental barrel compared with around $20 for Saudi Arabia.

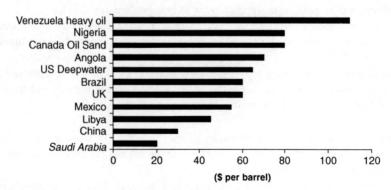

Fig. 8.3 Minimum oil price benchmark needed for new oil project profitability. Selected oil producers (Source: CERA)

The Opportunity Cost of Maintaining Spare Capacity

Saudi Aramco has planned to invest around $130 billion during the period 2008–2012 to expand the production capacity to 15 million bpd by end of 2012 from the current 12.5 mbpd. This new capacity will bolster what is already the largest excess capacity in the world, and position the Kingdom to any increases in demand without any lag in supply.

Following the slump in oil prices in 2009, the Organization of Petroleum Exporting Countries (OPEC) agreed on production cuts designed to halt further falls in oil prices, and Saudi Arabia reduced its production to around 8.1 million bpd from peaks of 9.5 million bpd in 2008. Sustaining such an idle capacity entails a very high opportunity cost for the Kingdom in terms of lost revenues and ongoing investment upkeep and oilfield maintenance. Some analysts estimate the income foregone from such an idle capacity in 2009/2010 at around $53 billion a year based on current oil prices of $70–75 pb (BSF, 2009).

Ironically, the reduced oil prices and slowdown in global demand will carry positive implications for Saudi Arabia in the medium term. The scarcity of financing and low oil prices in the current conditions will discourage further oil explorations and efforts to find alternative sources of energy, the two factors that were fast becoming a concern for the oil producers in the recent high-oil-price environment. At the same time, as demand picks up in the future, Saudi Arabia will find itself best-positioned to meet the increases based on its largest excess capacity and the cheapest cost base. Aramco estimates that 70% of the projected global demand growth will be met by capacity expansion in Saudi Arabia alone. As such, the dominance of Saudi Arabian oil in the global economy will continue in the upcoming years.

"Oil Peak" Debates: Sooner or Later?

Peak oil is the simplest label for rapid energy resource depletion without compensating new oil reserves, leading to a peak in global oil production. The rate of oil production is a function of its derived demand. Those supporting peak theories extrapolate rising demand levels with known reserves, and a peak in production is arrived at. According to many researchers, the world reached its oil peak in the 1970s, the 1990s, a range between 2000 and 2010 and so forth. Such gloomy scenarios fail to take into account the evolving advances in oil engineering technology, environmental pressures, the exploration of new areas and the fact that demand for oil need not be a linear projection exercise. Perceived scarcity, economic cycles and taxation policies could alter such forecasts, and appropriate energy pricing will allow market forces to produce a solution. In the short term, a seeming "peak-oil" problem is with us – world demand went from 79 million barrels a day in 2002 to 84.5 million in 2009. At the same time, the world needs to open up enough new fields to pump an additional 6–8 million barrels a day – at least 2 million to meet rising demand and 4 million to compensate for the declining production of existing fields.

The bone of contention lies in the reliability and availability of oil industry statistics or "data transparency." Some accuse National Oil Companies (NOCs) of not being transparent, and that a lot of reserves are merely "phantom reserves" that have been jacked up for a variety of economic and geopolitical reasons (Alsahlawi, 2009).

Estimating oil reserves involves political manipulation and bargaining by either OPEC or/and major consumers such as the United States. OPEC reserves estimates are used to negotiate quota allocation among the members. On the other hand, the United States tends to overestimate the world oil reserves to imply lower oil price. The most reliable reserve estimates were usually provided by International Oil Companies (IOCs) in the past and for the areas they are currently developing. The reserves-to-production (R/P) ratio is one measure for estimating the remaining life of oil reserves and it indicates when oil production is peaking. As presented in Table 8.1, the R/P ratio for the world is 46 years; it increased by 40% from 1970 to 2007.

Table 8.1 World reserves-to-production ratio by region (1970–2007)

Region	Years				
	1970	1980	1990	2000	2007
North America	12.4	10.1	10.1	10.2	10.9
Latin America	13.8	36.3	48.6	35.8	37.5
Eastern Europe	23.1	15.1	14.2	34	29.4
Western Europe	37.4	16.6	11.3	8.3	9.5
Middle East	66.51	54.3	112.2	88.6	90
Africa	23.1	25.1	26.7	37.8	36
Asia and Pacific	31.4	18.8	14.8	14.9	14.3
Total world	32.9	30.2	45.4	45.2	46

Source: OPEC Annual Statistical Bulletin, 2007

Table 8.1 also indicates that on current production levels, it is only the Middle East region that has the longest R/P ratio of 90 years, making it the strategic energy reserve centre for the world, and the fastest depletion rate for traditional oil reserves being North America and Western Europe, of around 10 years.

What is interesting though from Table 8.1 is that despite an increase in the absolute total of world oil demand, the world average of R/P ratio has been going up rather than down.

The differences between the "peak oil" optimists and the pessimists seem to centre on the type of assumptions they are each making. Most pessimists seem to assume that technology will not advance by much to tap more difficult or currently uneconomic oil reserves, that oil demand management does not take place under increasing price pressures and that nuclear energy might not play an increasingly important role. Optimists believe that economic growth is unbounded for all nations and for all times, and, finally, that environmental taxes are not introduced.

Disagreements occur because maybe it is truly impossible to fully measure oil with extreme precision, as it is a liquid and it moves.

The above disagreements do not take into account discontinuities, or events that beat the trend. These discontinuities make face value predictions and forecasting extremely difficulty. Examples of discontinuities include the 1974, 1979 and 2008 shocks, the nuclear accidents of Three Mile Island in the USA and Chernobyl in Russia, the nationalization of oil sectors and, on a more mundane but significant level, the introduction of the combined gas cycle turbine technology which reduced energy production costs. Future discontinuities could very well be privatization of the same national oil sector, leading to desired oil reserve data transparency, and an advance in technology to ensure that non-conventional renewable energy plays a more dominant role.

Such discontinuities seem to postpone reaching peak oil – the facts seem to indicate otherwise. Recovery rates of oil have increased from 22% in 1980 to 35% today, thanks to new technology. The ratio between proven oil reserves and current production has been constantly adjusted upwards as seen in Table 8.1 despite erratic and sometimes low oil prices, when conventional wisdom dictates that the search for proven oil reserves should have declined.

Maybe it is not that important to discuss when a peak may happen as much as a realization that a peak *will eventually happen*. There will never be 100% accurate oil data.

Saudi Arabia, OPEC and "Fair" Pricing

The history of oil, specifically that relating to the formation of the so-called "oil cartel," the Organization of the Petroleum Exporting Countries (OPEC), in 1960, has been extensively reviewed elsewhere (Johany, 1982, Newberry, 1981, Parra, 2004, Kuwaiz, 1986, Farsi, 1982). However, it is relevant to examine the negotiating strength of the oil cartel and assess whether OPEC contributes to oil price stability in the world markets. Based on basic economic principles of demand and supply, if OPEC is to affect the price of oil, it must affect the quantity. Table 8.2 illustrates the latest world demand and supply for oil.

In 2002, world demand for crude oil was just under 80 million bpd, with the Organisation for Economic Co-operation and Development (OECD) countries consuming around 50 million bpd or over 63%. By 2009, this had fallen to around 55% or 46.7 million bpd due to production efficiency and alternative energy uses. In the interim, demand from China and Asia grew, and today they represent around 22% of global consumption as illustrated in Fig. 8.4, which also shows in the estimated global demand growth in Fig. 8.4(b) that demand growth forecasted for 2010 will primarily come from Asia, the Middle East and some African countries, with smaller recovery in demand from the other regions.

Table 8.2 also illustrates the supply of global crude oil by major producers and by OPEC. The share of OPEC in world production has fluctuated around 36–39% levels since 1987, and was at 39% for 2009, but is coming down substantially from

Table 8.2   Average world demand and supply of crude oil (2006–2009)

	2006	2007	2008	2009Q1
	Million barrels per day			
(A) Demand				
• North America	25.4	25.5	24.3	23.7
• Western Europe	15.7	15.3	15.2	14.7
• Pacific Countries	8.5	8.3	8.0	8.3
OECD countries	*49.6*	*49.1*	*47.5*	*46.7*
Non-OECD				
- Foreign USSR	4.1	4.1	4.2	3.9
- China	7.2	7.5	7.9	7.7
- Eastern Europe	0.7	0.8	0.8	0.8
- South America	5.3	5.6	5.9	5.8
- Other Asian	9.0	9.3	9.4	9.4
- Middle East	6.2	6.5	6.9	6.9
- Africa	3.0	3.1	3.1	3.2
Total non-OECD	35.5	36.9	38.2	37.8
Total world demand	85.1	86.0	85.7	84.5
(B) Supply				
OPEC	*34.34*	*35.41*	*36.92*	*33.02*
OECD	19.97	19.85	19.33	19.42
Other major non-OPEC producers				
- Former USSR	12.25	12.77	12.75	12.69
- USA	7.34	7.47	7.54	7.82
- China	3.67	3.73	3.79	3.89
- Canada	3.19	3.32	3.24	3.35
- Mexico	3.68	3.48	3.17	3.05
- UK	1.66	1.66	1.56	1.48
- Norway	2.78	2.56	2.47	2.35
Total world supply	85.43	85.55	86.08	83.91

Source: SAMA, Aramco

the 60% levels seen in the mid- and late 1970s (Perra, 2004). The Middle East has by far the world's largest known and proven oil reserves, representing around 62% of global reserves as illustrated in Table 8.3.

What is noticeable from Table 8.3 is that while world proven oil reserves have increased over time, somewhat contradicting imminent peak theory depletions, there has been a noticeable decline in North American proven reserves but substantial new reserves found in Africa, Latin America and the Middle East. The 2007 Latin American figures do not include the new large finds discovered in Venezuela discussed earlier. Table 8.3, however, masks the world's largest proven oil reserve countries and this is illustrated in Fig. 8.5, which demonstrates the significance of Saudi Arabia's oil reserves amongst the seven largest oil reserve countries of 2009.

Out of the seven countries with the largest conventional crude oil reserves, five are to be found in the Middle East region, and all five are members of OPEC, as

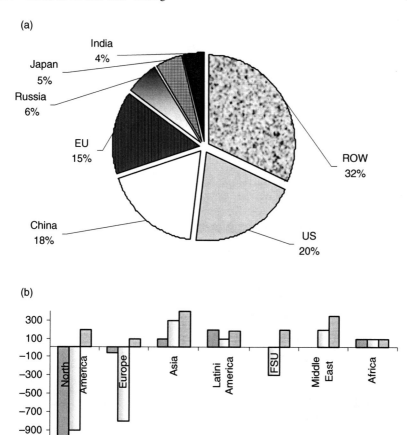

Fig. 8.4 Global primary energy consumption by region 2008 and global demand growth forecast by region 2010. (**a**) Global primary energy consumption 2008; (**b**) Global demand growth ('000 bpd) (Source: BP and IEA)

well as Venezuela, which is a non-Middle East OPEC member, while Russia is not an OPEC member but an observer in the organization. Table 8.4 illustrates the current contribution of OPEC to world oil production and its relative share, which has ranged between 31 and 40% of total world production. Saudi Arabia's production level has ranged from a low of 6.6% in 1987 to around 10% of the world's total production and around 27–28% of the total OPEC production.

OPEC has often been loosely termed a "price cartel." According to the above data, characterizing OPEC as setting the price of oil without regard to market forces needs some further explanation. To label OPEC a "cartel" does not really convey much economic information. The world "cartel" implies that OPEC members cooperate to restrict output and generate higher world oil prices. But cartels come in

Table 8.3   World proven oil reserves by region: 1970–2007 (Billion barrels)

Region	1970	1975	1980	1985	1990	1995	2000	2007
North America	49.8	39.78	36.61	34.2	31.84	27.25	26.9	25.41
Latin America	26.2	36.07	74.03	118.53	122.8	132.47	122.23	134.7
Eastern Europe	61.01	61.9	66.9	64.6	58.92	58.36	95	124.05
Western Europe	6.93	19.5	15.31	14.7	16.9	21.12	19.02	15.11
Middle East	336.22	387.1	365.24	431.43	662.1	655.4	694.6	741.6
Africa	51.12	59.1	56.01	56.22	58.6	70.97	93.4	119.3
Asia and Pacific	17.26	33.31	33.9	37.1	34.1	35.54	39.52	38.3
Total world	548.45	636.7	656.73	756.7	985.03	1,011.10	1,090.62	1,204.20

Source: OPEC/Annual Statistical Bulletin, 2007

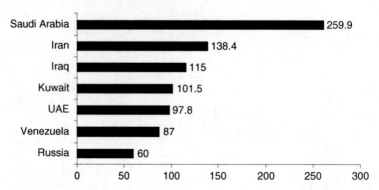

Fig. 8.5   Conventional crude oil reserves (billion of barrels) of seven largest reserve countries (January, 2009) (Source: Saudi Aramco, Oil and Gas Journal)

Table 8.4   Saudi oil production as share of world and OPEC oil production (Million barrels/day)

Year	World production	OPEC production	Saudi production	Saudi share of world (%)	Saudi share of OPEC (%)	OPEC as % of world production (%)
1987	62.4	19.7	4.1	6.6	20.9	31.5
1994	68.6	27.4	8.1	11.7	29.4	39.9
1999	74.1	29.4	7.6	10.2	25.7	39.6
2004	83.7	32.9	8.9	10.6	27	39.3
2006	85.4	34.8	9.21	10.8	26.8	40.1
2008	86.6	36.9	9.2	10.6	24.9	42.3
2009[(E)]	84.5	28.7	8.1	9.6	28.2	33.9

(E) Estimate
Source: SAMA, IEA

different forms and change form over time. Others characterize OPEC as a "loosely co-operating oligopoly" (Adelman, 1995). According to this viewpoint, OPEC has tended to move between two different modes of operation. The first is a "full cartel" mode, in which all members operate together to change output so as to control a share of the market. The second is a "residual supplier" mode, in which only certain key producers take responsibility for controlling the market price by playing a "balance wheel role."

The history of OPEC from 2000 to 2004 seems to confirm both modes of operation. The period 2000–2003 was characterized by OPEC's greater determination to stick to agreed-upon production quotas, while in 2004 and again in 2008, Saudi Arabia acted as the price "balancing wheel" by producing more oil to counteract higher oil prices, which touched over $147 per barrel in June 2008.

For OPEC to operate like a cartel and control prices, a number of conditions must be met (Johany, 1982). These are summarized in Table 8.5, where it is clear that OPEC does not meet a "full cartel" characterization.

Table 8.5 Cartel characteristics and OPEC: A score sheet

Characteristic	OPEC reality	Comment
• Small number of members	• Meets the condition	• Members vary from smaller producers (Qatar 500,000 b/d to Saudi Arabia 11.5 million b/d)
• Secret price cuts observable	• Does not meet	• Difficult to monitor "discounts"
• Offending members subject to punishment	• Does not meet	• Voluntary membership in OPEC
• Entry barriers must exist	• Does not meet	• Other oil producers enter the market outside OPEC
• Market demand and cost conditions stable	• Does not meet	• Cost conditions change with technological advances outside OPEC's control

If OPEC wished to expand its market share, theoretically it should not have any problem based on its oil reserves. While OPEC's share of the world's output is under 40% as seen earlier, this becomes less significant when compared with the size of the reserves of OPEC member countries in relation to the rest of the world.

What is of interest is that OPEC does have a sustainable production capacity of around 36.4 million barrels per day compared to current production levels of 28 million barrels per day as illustrated earlier in Table 8.4. OPEC's sustainable production capacity and spare capacity is set out in Table 8.6.

Clearly, OPEC nations in general are using their proven reserves much less intensively than other countries that are producing the 60% of world output from 25% world reserves. Some suggest that these OPEC output restraints are meant to maintain "cartel-like" high oil prices, rather than reflect a lack of "need" for revenue or a conservationist concern about future energy supplies (Mettale, 1987, Gelb et al., 1998). However, this is another generalization, for different OPEC members have different needs and some smaller OPEC members exhibit higher production-to-reserves ratios than others. While Iraq's current production is around 2.6 million bpd, there were reports that Iraq was aiming to produce 10 million bpd by 2020, adding significant capacity to OPEC production.

Table 8.6 OPEC crude production sustainable production capacity and spare capacity (2009)

mb/d*	Sustainable production capacity	Spare capacity vs. supply	OPEC quota
Saudi	*12.5*	*4.4*	*8.01*
Nigeria	2.6	0.7	1.7
UAE	2.85	0.56	2.23
Kuwait	2.65	0.38	2.22
Iran	4	0.35	3.33
Libya	1.77	0.22	1.47
Angola	2.1	0.19	1.5
Venezuela	2.4	0.16	2.01
Algeria	1.4	0.16	1.2
Iraq	2.6	0.13	N/A
Qatar	0.9	0.12	0.73
Ecuador	0.5	0.04	0.43
Total	36.37	7.11	24.83
GCC	19.0	5.46	13.19
GCC % of total	52	73	53

*Million barrels per day
Source: IEA, December 2009

Saudi Oil Policy

The Kingdom has never expressed a single unified policy statement regarding its crude oil. This is probably wise, given the complex and changing external issues affecting world oil markets (Ali Sheikh, 1976, Mettale, 1987). What has been noticeable however in 2009 and 2010 is Saudi Arabia becoming more explicit about what was considered to be a "fair" price for oil in the international markets at $70–75 levels, first announced by King Abdullah and then reiterated by Oil Minister Ali Al Naemi. This explicit price statement has had a significant impact on market sentiment as will be discussed later.

Table 8.7 sets out Saudi Arabia's *implicit* and *explicit* oil policy objectives as announced by the relevant authorities in the Kingdom.

The information in Table 8.7 confirms that, overall, Saudi oil policy has been a relative success. The primary concern, however, has been to ensure oil prices which provide the Kingdom with "sufficient" income to meet its revenue needs. As discussed in earlier chapters, with the exception of a few years during which oil prices were driven higher than budgeted, the Kingdom had run persistent budget deficits, which were only reversed in the period 2003–2008 but then fell back to a deficit. Of greater concern is the fact that, despite record oil prices of $45–50 per barrel during 2004 and $147 in 2008 in *real terms*, the purchasing power of the Kingdom's oil prices has fallen due to inflation and depreciation of the dollar's value. The historical decline in the real value of Saudi oil export prices has not been fully compensated by recent higher world oil prices, as illustrated in Fig. 8.6.

Table 8.7 Implicit and explicit Saudi oil policy objectives

Policy objectives	Observations
• Reasonable oil prices which give producer sufficient income	(a) OPEC price band of $22–28 per barrel has been maintained until 2003/2004 when it overshot the range, and again in 2008 when prices reached $147 per barrel and then fell to $40. The Kingdom called for a price range of $70–75 pb in 2009 as a "reasonable" level for consumers and producers (b) In real terms, the price of oil exports per barrel has fallen sharply
• Sufficient supplies to satisfy market needs at all times, including maintenance of excess capacity	(a) Achieved to a large extent; Saudi Arabia increased output to 11 million b/d in 2004 to meet world demand and 9.5 mb/d in 2008 and expanded capacity to 12.5 mbd
• High level of cooperation among oil producers	(a) Achieved to a large extent during the period 2000–2004, and 2008/2009 including non-OPEC members such as Russia, Norway and Mexico
• Close communication with oil-consuming nations	(a) Achieved to a large extent with dialogue at highest national levels
• Recognition that oil is important to the health of the world economy	(a) High oil prices can cause rise in inflation, restrict economic growth and cause political damage in oil-consuming nations (b) Saudi Arabia argues for conciliatory approach in OPEC
• Commitment to protect the environment	(a) Kingdom applying latest world environment protection standards
• Maintaining a robust oil industry ready and able to supply future energy needs	(a) Saudi Aramco investing in future capacity and new energy fields both onshore and offshore and committing around $190 billion in new investments over the period 1998–2012
• Stability and predictability in the oil market to ensure Saudi and global economic growth	(a) Saudi Arabia's investment plans are known as they involve large number of foreign oil service companies in exploration and drilling. Oil production is used to smooth market forces as exemplified by Saudi 300,000 bpd increase in 2008 to meet global needs
• Promoting concept of "reciprocal security" among producers and consumers	(a) Consumers are assured of a steady and uninterrupted supply of oil at reasonable market prices and producers to be given open and free access to markets without discriminatory taxation against oil

As can be seen from Fig. 8.6, it was only over the period 2004–2008 that the average real price of North Sea Brent oil rose to reach the level of 1980 and partly compensated oil producers for the losses incurred in the purchasing power of their dollar revenues.

Although there was some marginal gains in terms of trade for the US dollar, the impact of the dollar's depreciation on the real value of OPEC's export earnings are

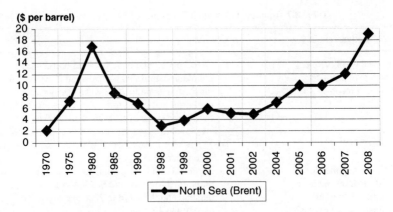

Fig. 8.6   Real oil prices (base year: 1970) (1970–2008) (Source: SAMA)

evident as illustrated in Fig. 8.6. This has caused the issue of pricing oil in US dollars or alternative currencies to be subject of debate (Alsahlawi, 2009), although Saudi official policy has been adamant about remaining pegged to the US dollar and continuing to denominate oil export revenues in dollars (SAMA, 2008). Despite Saudi Arabia's adamance on this matter, other non-Middle East and Middle East OPEC members, such as Venezuela and Iran, have discussed the issue of whether to continue pricing oil in US dollars, as several factors seem to be at work in determining oil prices and dollar movements. These include inflation, the dynamics of oil supply and demand, the role of OPEC in setting oil prices (especially during the 1970s and 1980s), capital flows and the development of the oil futures markets. Yet, the interaction among those factors cannot be ignored and might offset each other. For example a dollar depreciation is going to reduce the oil price in domestic currencies – if those currencies are not pegged to the dollar – and to increase their demand for oil, which contributes eventually to a long-run rise in oil prices.

This process would be operated by the dynamics of oil demand and supply through price and income elasticities. Furthermore, dollar depreciation will increase inflation and decrease the purchasing power of oil-exporting countries that are linked to the dollar, and oil supply will decline as a result of reductions in investments in exploration and production because of lack of required capital. However, it is found empirically that oil prices are affected by inflation more than by the movements in the value of the dollar (Dailami, 1982, Alsahlawi, 1995, Beck and Kamps, 2009). On the other hand, the demand and supply of oil are influenced by the price, world economic growth, the institutional framework and geopolitical risks in the oil-exporting areas. Another important development that reshaped the oil market and complicated the dollar and oil price relationship is the emergence of the futures market for oil since the early 1980s (Bassan Fattouh, 2010).

Considerable debate remains over the impact of financial sector "investors" on oil prices. The analysis of recently released disaggregated oil trading data from the US Commodities Futures Trading Commission (CFTC) is not conclusive, but has been used by some to argue that such activity has a major bearing on price developments, especially the spike in mid-2008. Certainly there appears to be a consensus that prices during 2009 have been considerably buoyed by investment in the oil futures markets and OPEC has argued that a major component of high oil prices was due to financial investor speculation.

Pricing oil in US dollars is a key element in supporting the value of the dollar and, ultimately, US economic and political power. However, the current (2009) US fiscal debt and its high government budget deficit, along with the global financial crisis, have raised some doubts about the sustainability of the US dollar as an international reserve currency although the 2010 euro crisis provided some relief for the dollar.

The alternatives have varied from pricing oil in a basket of currencies, such as SDRs, to euro pricing as a potential world currency. The decision to change or not to change the dollar-dominated pricing depends, to a large extent, on strategic implications and trade relations, which indicate that the United States remains a major oil importer and, moreover, a special political alliance with key OPEC oil states in the Middle East, especially Saudi Arabia. Furthermore, the decision to move away from the dollar will have an impact on the foreign assets of oil exporters, which are denominated in US dollars as we have analysed earlier. Recognition of the historical and functional relationship between oil price and the dollar will not lessen the direct trade and capital impacts of such a relationship. Any pricing scheme of a single currency or dual currencies or a basket of currencies based on trading patterns necessarily will need to assess the importance of the traded crude and of the future value and distribution of foreign assets.

Dilemma of High and Low Prices

OPEC and Saudi Arabia face dilemmas in facing both high and low oil prices as follows:

(a) higher oil prices creates a dilemma: should they defend higher oil prices with no growth in production volumes or revenues year after year, or
(b) should they let prices drop to discourage non-OPEC oil production in order to capture a larger market share for future years?

Both options have negative revenue implications for Saudi Arabia. Defending higher oil prices means gradually increasing government deficit in the long run, while non-OPEC producers benefit from higher prices and continue to produce more oil, potentially causing a market share loss for the Kingdom. The second option might bring substantial short-term revenue shortfalls and growing deficits, in the hope of capturing a higher market share and greater future revenues.

In the face of new production realities from non-members, OPEC decided to shift its strategy from strict price fixing, which could not be defended without massive "production balancing wheel" scarifies by countries such as Saudi Arabia, to an

OPEC strategy of quantity fixing and trying to defend a wider price band (Oweiss, 1990, Parra, 2004, Cordesman, 2003). OPEC members have bitterly complained that high oil prices were the result of forces other than supply and demand, and of new players in the oil market that had not been a factor only a decade earlier. The developing countries' nationalization of oil resources at the upstream stage – the production or recovery stage – meant that the "oil majors" who had controlled such upstream production no longer controlled large volumes of petroleum within vertically integrated channels, from production to refining to distribution. The oil majors were transformed into major buyers of oil, and an active spot and forward commodities market was developed by oil brokers.

By the 1990s, the spot and futures oil market accounted for over 60% of oil sales, compared with less than 5% in the 1960s (Parra, 2004, Oweiss, 1996). These new market players were reactive to day-to-day variations in demand and supply, supported or exaggerated by real events or rumours in the market. Figure 8.7 provides a snapshot at how oil prices have performed over a short period of time from 2002 to 2010, rising from $20–25 levels to $140, before falling to $30 levels in 2009, and becoming steady again at the $70–75 per barrel.

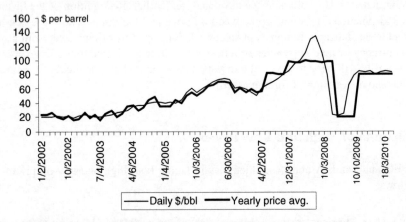

Fig. 8.7 OPEC reference basket price 2002–2010 (Source: Bloomberg)

The relative price stability around the $70–75 range has been somewhat remarkable, as it represented a new paradigm recognition of the global nature of energy security and growing interdependence between various stakeholders – consumers and producers, both of whom seemed to accept King Abdullah's proposition that the $70–75 range for oil was a "fair price" that met the following objective:

• oil consumers focusing on *reliable* and *affordable* supply and
• oil producers focusing on stable and *remunerative* markets.

The new emerging consensus on what is deemed to be a "fair price" for both producers and consumers may undercut the economic asymmetry between the two groups evidenced in the past and translated into the erratic oil price movements illustrated in Fig. 8.6. Until 2009, explicit oil prices ranges or targets have not been announced; rather implicit targets have caused tensions between the two groups.

Empirical evidence suggests that oil consumers are differently affected by higher oil prices and have different coping potentials. This may explain why, as a group, they have been intentionally vague about their price preferences. In contrast, and as examined further below, the producers have been forthcoming in revealing their own preferences, following Saudi Arabia's statement on what constitutes an acceptable price. This is probably due to their relative economic similarities and disproportionate vulnerability to international oil prices.

Table 8.8 explores these differences between consumers' and producers' coping potentials.

Table 8.8 IEA and OPEC macroeconomic coping potentials on similar oil price ranges

2008 estimates		IEA countries	OPEC countries	Saudi Arabia
Average oil prices ($/bbl)	($/bbl)	97.19 cif	94.45 fob	
Share of energy imports in total energy	%	20.5	1.4	0.3
Share of energy exports in total exports	%	10.1	84.5	95.9
Share of energy trade in GDP	%	6.8	43.7	63.5
Share of petroleum taxes in budget revenues	%	7.1	72.3	89.7

Source: APICORP Research (2009)

At the heart of the economic asymmetry between producers and consumers are several macroeconomic anomalies related to the structures of trade, GDP and budget receipt, which is explored in Table 8.8. In the International Energy Agency (IEA) countries, for instance, energy imports represented about 21% of total imports in 2008, and energy trade (both imports and exports) represented some 7% of aggregate GDP. By stark contrast, in OPEC countries, petroleum exports (crude oil, oil products, natural gas and NGLs) represented about 85% of total exports and petroleum trade represented some 44% of aggregate GDP. Similarly, despite the fact that the IEA countries get much more revenues from taxing final petroleum consumption than OPEC countries get from taxing primary production, the share of these respective revenues in total budget resources was 7% for the IEA and 72% for OPEC. For Saudi Arabia, the impact was much higher than the average for OPEC on petroleum revenues and share of energy in total exports and share of energy trade in GDP.

Looking forward, it is more than likely that Saudi Arabia will continue with its current oil-pricing strategy within OPEC, while at the same time trying to ensure that new production capacity is added to the oil industry, through using the latest technology and lowering costs. Saudi Arabia unquestionably has always had very low *recovery costs*, at $0.30 per barrel in the 1960s to between $1.80 and $2.80 a barrel in the 1990s (Johany, 1986, Cordesman, 2003) and around $8–15 for current new fields. This gives the Kingdom a comparatively large advantage over other high-cost oil producers. Industry experts attribute this advantage to the high pressure of oil wells in Saudi Arabia, which eliminates the need for pumps to bring oil to the surface, as well as to the high production "flow" rate of these wells. By way of comparison, fewer than 1,500 wells in Saudi Arabia yield current production levels of 8.2 million barrels per day, in contrast to a US production of 6.4 million barrels per day from around 590,000 wells (IEA, 2008).

In the long term, relatively "fair" oil prices are needed to compensate oil producers in real terms for their current production. It is to its credit that Saudi Arabia continues to invest billions of dollars to expand capacity in today's dollar's real terms, to produce oil that will give them less and less in future real oil prices. "High" oil prices are needed to sustain the massive level of future investments needed to develop existing and new oil reserves. Global figures of $900 billion are said to be needed by 2013 to develop existing fields, and some estimates reach levels of $250 billion a year that need to be spent by 2030 for exploration and production costs. Producer countries are faced by volatile oil prices, large population growth and managing expectations – all of which adds pressure on their fiscal position in the long term. "High" oil prices might affect the developing countries in the short run, but in the long term both they and the advanced economies will learn to conserve on energy costs.

Over time, the energy consumption-to-GDP ratios of advanced countries have reduced due to energy efficiency. While they stood at around 15% levels during the 1970s, they are now in the range of 7%. At the same time, the per capita income of most of the industrialized countries is more than that during the 1970s. Even the Chinese are expected to follow the pattern of the OECD, as their industries become energy-conscious. Who will bear the future costs of investment in the energy industry? This is where interdependence and partnerships between National Oil companies (NOCs) and International Oil Companies (IOCs) will become more important. Already the oil producers of the Middle East are allowing the IOCs more exploration concessions in return for joint venture investment partnerships.

The oil producers are also having to face up to the growing environmental pressures to utilize more "environmental friendly" energy sources, and there has been a perceptible reduction in the share of oil in total energy consumption worldwide as illustrated in Table 8.9.

Table 8.9 Share of oil in total energy consumption (%)

	1985	1995	2003	2006	2008
World	37.9	39.8	37.2	35.8	34.8
OECD	42.8	43.0	41.1	40.7	39.6
USA	40.2	39.0	39.7	40.4	36.5
Japan	55.1	54.6	49.3	45.2	43.7
Russia	32.5	23.4	19.0	18.2	18.2
China	13.8	19.3	22.1	20.6	18.8

Source: SAMA

The combination of more energy efficiency use and alternative energy utilization to oil is also of some concern, especially to countries such as Saudi Arabia, which is undertaking substantial long-term capital investment in oil capacity expansion. The issue of alternative energy and its potential impact on Saudi Arabia is discussed later on in this chapter.

Oil and Saudi GDP Contribution

The oil and energy sector is still a significant contributor to the Saudi GDP as illustrated in Table 8.10, which sets out a snapshot of key energy indicators.

Table 8.10 Saudi Arabia: Hydrocarbon sector indicators (1972–2008)

Index	1972	1982	1992	2002	2008
• Oil production (Million barrels)	2,201	2,366	3,049	2,588	3,366
• Oil exports (Million barrels)	1,992	2,058	2,408	1,928	2,672
• Oil revenues (SR billion)	13.4	186.0	128.8	166.1	983.3
• World export market share (%)	2.6	4.7	3.25	2.57	4.2
• Refined production (Million barrels)	222	310	541	582	722
• Refined export (Million barrels)	208	195	473	362	386.3
• Natural gas liquids (Million barrels)	19.8	156.7	227.7	292.4	402.2
• Nominal oil prices ($/barrel)	3.61	33.42	19.33	25.03	97.3
• Real oil prices (at 1970 prices $/barrel)	3.28	12.19	4.79	4.93	16.69
• GDP at current prices (SR billion)	38.3	524.2	510.4	705.8	1,758.0
• Oil sector GDP at current prices (SR billion)	22.4	254.7	199.8	261.8	1,001.7

Source: SAMA

The oil sector contributes on average around 40% of Saudi GDP, but this rose sharply to around 55% in 2008 due to exceptionally strong oil prices as seen in Table 8.10. Non-oil GDP growth has been on a steady increase since 1982/1983 and the Saudi government is encouraging this trend, but oil revenue and oil-related products continue to be the major source of government revenue. What has been noticeable though is the increased capacity for refined oil products, which more than tripled from 222 million barrels in 1972 to over 720 million barrels in 2008. The amount of natural gas liquids (NGLs) has also risen sharply, as will be discussed later.

While the composition of the Saudi GDP was changing over time, so too were the trading links of Saudi Arabia's petroleum and other energy export sectors. Today, the Far East, South East Asia and emerging economies of Africa are the prime customers of Saudi petroleum products, as Fig. 8.8 demonstrates.

It is interesting to note from Fig. 8.8 how few refined products are imported by European and US markets from Saudi Arabia, with around 9% of total exports in this category. The existence of domestic petrochemical refining industries in Europe and the USA coupled with accusations of "unfair" or low-priced Saudi feedstock inputs has ensured that Saudi Arabia seeks alternative markets in the Far East. China is fast becoming a major trading partner for Saudi Arabia. As Fig. 8.9 shows, China today

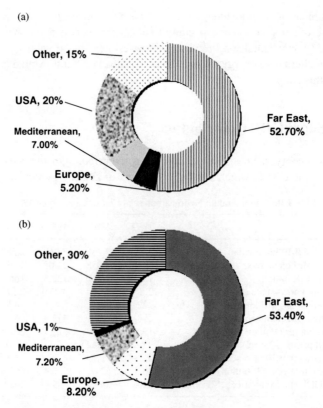

Fig. 8.8 Saudi petroleum and other hydrocarbon exports by destination (2008): **(a)** crude oil; **(b)** refined products (Source: Aramco)

is the third largest importer of oil, after the USA and Japan. Chinese economic growth rates of around 7–9% p.a. over the past few years have kept commodity prices – including oil – relatively high in the face of weaker European and US economic growth rates during 2003/2004 and the global economic crisis of 2008/2009.

Figure 8.9 shows the falls experienced in some countries worst affected by the global economic and financial crisis of 2008/2009, namely the USA, Europe, Japan and South Korea to some extent. The worsening oil market demand has hinged on the hope that China's demand will offset any slowdown elsewhere, but even China's growth forecast for 2010 is minimal at around 50,000 barrels per day according to IEA forecasts.

The disproportionate energy consumption of the USA, relative to its population size, together with the expected depletion of domestic oil reserves in around 11 years at current production levels, highlights future problems for the USA. Identifying and securing a stable source of oil is paramount for the USA, as is the search for alternative fuel sources. Saudi exports of oil to the USA account for around a quarter of all

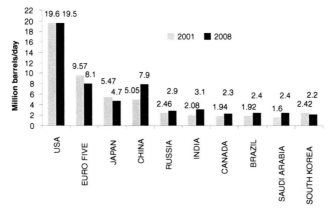

Fig. 8.9 Top ten oil-consuming countries (Million barrels/day), 2001, 2008 (Source: SAMA, Saudi Aramco)

daily US oil imports and underlines the close economic and strategic relationship between the two countries in terms of energy policies.

What is interesting from Fig. 8.9 is that Saudi Arabia has become a major oil-consuming nation, with an average 2.4 million barrels used in domestic consumption. An increased population, a speeding up of domestic projects' hydrocarbon and non-hydrocarbon base as well as a continued subsidy on refined gasoline has led to this increased demand, which is consuming around 30% of total Saudi daily oil production and diverting this production output to domestic as opposed for export revenue generation. At some stage, Saudi Arabia has to reconsider its domestic subsidy policy on gasoline and other consumer fuels, but given the high level of inflation seen in the Kingdom during 2007 and 2008, there is little likelihood that a substantial increase in domestic gasoline prices will be introduced by the government.

Maintaining the Far East Pricing Premium

The Far East energy market is not only becoming a larger volume player, but is also a more profitable one for Middle East producers.

It is not generally known that different regions of the world have different pricing formulas for the same crude oil exports. Saudi Arabia adopted "formula pricing" since the late 1980s, which involves the use of three indices for sales of Saudi and other Middle East oil to various regions around the world. These indices or "markers" are as follows:

- West Texas Intermediate (WTI) as a benchmark for sales to the North American markets (until November 2009), thereafter ASCI or Argus Sour Crude Index.
- IPE Brent crude prices for sales to Europe.
- Dubai and Oman averages for sale to the Asian markets.

The selling price formula is then calculated applying a discount or premium to the price of the "marker" indexes. The cost of freight is an essential element in the calculation of the final pricing. Currently the Saudi market prices the different regions through the following formulas:

European market = IPE Brent – Discount
American market = WTI–Discount (from November 2009 ASCI–discount)
Asian market = Average Oman/Dubai + Premium

This explains the steady growth in sales of Saudi crude to the Far East as it enjoys a premium, while sales to the European and US markets suffer a discount to the "marker price." Further, Russia's proximity to the European market has ensured that Russian oil export strategy in the short term will concentrate on obtaining a greater European market share at the expense of Middle East producers. In the long term, Russia could also pose a potential competitive threat to Saudi's Far East oil exports, as Russian oil companies are planning to commission different pipeline systems through Central Asian and Far East countries to reach the main Chinese and Japanese markets. Should this be successfully completed, the current Saudi Arabian premium on Far East sales could be eroded. Given the logistics of building these pipelines, crossing many different nations, it could take the Russians some time. The main worry for Saudi Arabia in the short term is further loss in the already-discounted European market.

In November 2009, Saudi Arabia announced its decision to switch away from West Texas Intermediate (WTI), the key US benchmark oil blend that is traded at the New York Mercantile Exchange (NYMEX) futures exchanges as US Light Sweet Crude, to Argus Sour Crude Index or ASCI, a price index of Gulf of Mexico crudes published by Argus (Aramco, 2009). The reasons were many, but seem to be based on the fact that Saudi crude exports to the USA have been declining, and that Saudi physical crude is not actually traded on the NYMEX, but carried out separately through contracts between countries and oil companies, and Saudi Arabia had based its North America prices on the WTI index. The Kingdom had been voicing its concern for a number of years that global oil prices are not properly reflected. Of more significance, Saudi Arabia wanted oil to be treated as a tangible and physical commodity reacting to fundamental demand and supply forces and not a paper product or index for financial traders in the USA hedging against a weak US dollar as highlighted earlier in this chapter. The new Argus ASCI is based on a weighted average of actual prices paid for three crudes pumped out of the Gulf of Mexico – Mars, Poseidon and Southern Green Canyon – and these are primarily "sour" or high sulphur crudes, more like Saudi Aramco's Arab light, and thus a better price match. Venezuela has indicated that it might follow Saudi Arabia's move to switch to ASCI.

The Saudi decision to drop WTI was one sign of the consequences of the global financial and economic turmoil of 2008/2009.

It is also a sign that after years of dominance of the established oil benchmarks – the WTI in the Americas, Brent in Europe and Africa and Dubai and Oman in Asia

– changes are now on the horizon. The backing of the world's biggest oil exporter gave new clout to the ASCI benchmark, and to the Mexican Gulf Coast market where the oil tracked in the Argus index is delivered.

Aramco's move may also well be an indication that further changes in the world's oil benchmarks, and indeed in the overall crude markets, could well be in the offing. A potentially more critical yardstick change is likely to take place in East Asia. Virtually all crude sold from the Middle East Asian markets, including China, is benchmarked from two Middle East crudes: Dubai and Oman. The Argus and Oman benchmarks also bring some diversity to the oil market by tracking sour crude.

Some have argued that one possible non-dollar oil-pricing alternative is crude benchmarking with indexes other than WTI, as this is denominated in US dollars only (Noreng, 2006, Samii et al., 2004). For example Brent is more traded in Europe and Africa or through the London International Petroleum Exchange (IPE). Brent offers pricing information alternatively in Euros based on the physical trading of oil by spot or futures. Dubai crude also can be the price marker in Japanese yen for the Middle East and Asia. On the other hand, OPEC's reference basket of crudes could be an oil-pricing benchmark, even though WTI and Brent affect its price. The current basket, introduced in June 2005, is composed of 12 crudes: Algeria's Sahara blend, Angolas Girassol, Ecuador's Oriente, Iran's heavy, Iraq's Basra light, Kuwait's export, Libya's Es Sider, Nigeria's Bonny light, Qatar's Marine, Saudi Arabia's Arab light, United Arab Emirate's Murban and Venezuela's Merey. However, a currency mix reflects the currencies of these crudes, some of which are dollar-pegged, but it might be considered suitable if the mix would satisfy the internationalization, stability and neutrality requirements for any designed oil-pricing currency. The Saudi Arabia move has certainly caused many to consider long-term non-dollar oil-pricing alternatives that reflect more truly the physical output and actual market demand.

A New Energy Star: The Gas Sector

The Kingdom's gas sector made the headlines during 2003 and 2004, first for the announcement of the cancellation of major gas projects and then for the signing of replacements with new partners of choice. As noted earlier, Saudi Arabia has the world's fourth largest gas reserves of around 263 trillion cubic feet and is also a significant exporter of natural gas liquids (NGLs). Figure 8.10 illustrates the top ten largest gas reserve countries as of 2008.

Unlike nearby Qatar, whose gas is mostly "non-associated" – extracted without producing oil – roughly two thirds of Saudi Arabia's proven gas reserves consist of "associated" gas, mainly from the onshore *Ghawar* field and offshore *Safaniya* and *Zuluf* fields. Most of Saudi Arabia's natural gas was flared or burned off, when oil was produced prior to the start-up of the Kingdom's master gas system, which was completed in 1982. This system cost some $13 billion and was created to meet domestic demand and to provide most of the 0.7 million barrels per day of NGL. By

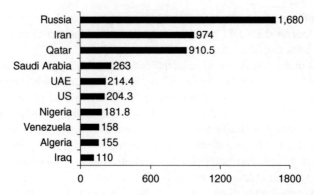

Fig. 8.10 Natural gas reserves (trillions of cubic feet) in top 10 countries (2008) (Source: Saudi Aramco)

all accounts, gas production has done much to meet domestic energy needs and to reduce domestic demand for oil, which is easier and more economical to export than liquefied natural gas. Gas requires large onshore investments for gas liquefaction and then it requires transportation in specialized container vessels. Domestic oil consumption is not insignificant, and accounted for around 25% of total Saudi oil production in 2002 as seen earlier in Table 8.9.

Foreign Interest in Gas Projects

Unlike crude oil production, the Kingdom of Saudi Arabia signalled its intention early on to invite foreign companies to participate in the development of its large gas sector. In 2000, ten International Oil Companies (IOCs) noted their interest in participating in the ambitious plan to develop upstream gas and processing facilities. Plans for three integrated gas projects were submitted by the Saudi government: the *Haradh* gas development project, the *Rabigh* integrated refinery and petrochemical projects and the *Kidan* and *Shaybah* gas development projects. Saudi Aramco was to be a partner in all three projects. In May 2001, Saudi Arabia selected a mix of eight IOCs to participate in the huge $25 billion "Saudi gas initiative," as it was to be called. This Saudi gas initiative was to develop an *integrated* gas sector comprising upstream gas development (production), with "downstream" (processing) petrochemicals, power generation and desalination plants. The IOCs involved in the bidding were the elite of the energy industry, including Exxon Mobil, Royal Dutch Shell, BP and Conoco Phillips. It is useful to closely examine the major factors that drove the great gas initiative, as well as the reasons for the breakdown of discussions with the initial group of IOCs.

First, the initiative was launched during a time when oil prices were falling, sharply reducing Saudi oil revenues. The need for outside investment was probably felt more severely than during a period of higher oil prices, such as the years

2003 and 2004. The IOCs probably sensed this earlier Saudi need and held out for more concessions in terms of a larger gas acreage.

Second, it is not always true that foreign investors will bring a cheaper source of capital to Saudi Arabia. Saudi Arabia can still borrow on relatively good terms in its own name, as the reaffirmation of its long-term credit rating of AA by Standard & Poor's in 2009 confirms. Moreover, there is no guarantee that a foreign IOC will pass on the full benefit of such cheaper international borrowing to Saudi Arabia; in fact, it might add an additional country risk premium for carrying out Saudi projects.

Third, some argued that foreign companies would transfer appropriate technology to Saudi Arabia. This is not a convincing argument (Mabro, 2002, Cordesman, 2003). There is no technology for upstream development that Saudi Aramco does not possess or is unable to acquire from sources other than IOCs. The irony is that, by their own admission, IOCs are *not* specialists in power generation or water desalination plants, which were one of the key components of the "great gas initiative."

Fourth, the management aspects of these large integrated projects were put forward as justification for IOC participation. There is some merit to this argument, if an IOC itself was to handle all the integrated components through upstream development and transmission infrastructure, as well as constructing and running plants of different sizes for final users of gas. As it stands, this challenge can probably not be met with the present resources of Saudi Aramco. However, the alternative is to break the project into smaller parts and subcontract to industry specialists, with Saudi Aramco retaining overall project management control.

In the final analysis, what the IOCs were really seeking was an involvement in Saudi Arabia's upstream *oil* industry and this clashed with Saudi Aramco's desire to remain in total control of this strategic sector (Mabro, 2002).

In short, the oil companies wanted an involvement in a sector that Saudi Arabia does not really want to grant, even if it agreed on some concessions, while Saudi Arabia wanted IOC investment in sectors which were not of real interest to the oil companies, even when they had expressed a conditional interest to do the job. There was no commonality of interest, so it was no surprise the talks broke down.

New Partners Step In

Given Saudi Arabia's energy position in the world, it was not surprising that other international oil companies would step in to replace the consortiums that withdrew. In March 2004, Saudi Oil Minister Ali Al Naimi announced the signing of gas exploration contracts with companies from Russia (Lukoil), China (China Petrochemical Company Sinopec), Italy (ENI) and Spain (Repsol YPF) (Hassan, 6 March 2003). Under the agreements, nearly 122,000 km^2 of land was assigned for gas exploration to these foreign companies. Saudi Aramco maintained a partnership in all the ventures planned, and held 20% of the stake in each of the three projects.

According to press reports, the contracts will run for a maximum of 40 years and are expected to generate around 35,000 additional high-value jobs for Saudis in this new energy sector. The entry of the Chinese into the Saudi hydrocarbon sector attracted much positive interest and seemed to further cement growing trade relations between the Kingdom and China. The Russian participation was also significant, as it may herald a closer relationship between the world's two largest oil producers, raising the possibility of joint ventures inside and outside the Kingdom. This was discussed during the historic visit of the then Crown Prince Abdullah to Russia, mentioned earlier, when the two countries signed a 5-year oil and natural gas agreement, which Russian officials said could lead to deals worth up to $25 billion (Saudi Press Agency, Reuters, 27 January 2004).

The strategic move towards the East seems to have paid off as Saudi Arabia currently exports nearly 46% of its natural gas liquids (NGLs) to the Far East as illustrated in Fig. 8.11, mirroring the crude oil sales to the Far East.

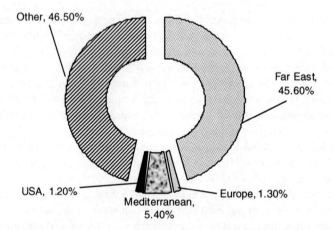

Fig. 8.11   Saudi natural gas liquid sales by region (2008) (Source: Aramco)

Outlook for Saudi Gas Sector

Saudi natural gas is processed to produce several types of feedstock. These range from clean fuel (methane or sales gas) to feedstock (methane, ethane, propane, butane and natural gasoline). Both methane and ethane are consumed entirely in the Kingdom's utilities and petrochemical industries and the excess propane, butane and natural gasoline (also known as natural gas liquids or NGLs) that are not used in Saudi petrochemical projects are exported as set out in Fig. 8.11. Saudi Aramco estimates that the Kingdom's demand for gas will continue to grow at around 5% per year given the Kingdom's ongoing industrial diversification programme, as well as generating electricity, fuel gas and feedstocks for petrochemicals, desalination and supporting oil and gas operations. Aramco's plan calls for increasing gas processing capacity to 12.5 billion standard cubic feet per day (SCFD) from 9.3 billion SCFD.

The expansion will come from the following operations:

- *Hawiyah* NGL Recovery Plant – capacity to process 4 billion SCFD of sales gas to yield 310,000 NGL bpd.
- *Khursaniyah* Gas Plant – processing capacity of 1 billion SCFD of associated gas.
- *Hawiyah* Gas Plant – 800 million SCFD of non-associated gas additional raising capacity to 2.4 billion SCFD.
- *Karan* Gas Field – Saudi Arabia's first non-associated offshore gas field with projected output of 1.8 billion SCFD by 2012.

These developments in the Saudi gas sector augur well for the Kingdom, as not only does it allow for energy diversification so as to compete with other gas producers, but also it enables entry into the more environmentally friendly energy sector which gas represents.

Petrochemicals: Adding Value

Only a couple of decades ago, Saudi Arabia seemed a most unlikely location for a major industrialization drive. The great "oil shocks" of the mid-1970s opened up vast new opportunities for the Kingdom's planners to deploy large revenue sources for industrial and economic diversification and to move away from being a primary energy supplier. Industrialization, especially in hydrocarbon energy-related industries where Saudi Arabia enjoys comparative cost advantages, remains at the heart of Saudi development plans and strategies. The earlier emphasis on state ownership and expenditure might be giving way, in the new millennium, to public–private partnerships or pure private sector initiatives, but the petrochemical sector remains one of the more promising ones for the future.

Petrochemicals are certainly making their impact felt worldwide. The scope of products manufactured from petrochemicals is broad, ranging from insulators, cable wraps, sockets, tires, plastic and rubber parts, to everyday items such as home furnishings, bedsheets, typewriters, ribbons, book covers, clothes, soap and detergents. The modern world's mass consumption of goods would be greatly hindered without the final output of the petrochemical industries.

Today, Saudi Arabia is home to 21 large, modern petrochemical complexes located in the two industrial cities of *Jubail* (on the eastern coast of Saudi Arabia) and *Yanbu* (on the western coast). Eighteen of these complexes are owned by affiliates of the Saudi Basic Industries Corporation (SABIC). The remaining three are private sector joint ventures with international companies such as Shell and Exxon Mobil. Of the eighteen SABIC petrochemical affiliates, two are wholly owned by SABIC, five are SABIC partnership with Saudi private investors and the remaining eleven complexes are joint ventures with international companies. *Jubail* hosts fourteen of the SABIC-owned complexes, three are in *Yanbu* and one is in *Dammam* in the Eastern Province. The engineering projects to transform the desert to their current status have been on a monumental scale. As an illustration, some 270 million cubic meters of earth was moved to prepare the *Jubail* site alone, which is enough to build a road around the world at the equator 1 m deep by 7 m wide (Royal Commission for Jubail and Yanbu, 2004).

In 2002, the then Crown Prince Abdullah bin Abdulaziz inaugurated the cornerstone for further expansion of a second industrial city at *Jubail* at a cost of SR 131 billion. It is forecasted to employ an additional 55,000, mostly Saudi, workers.

Such petrochemical-based industries create an economic multiplier effect in the Saudi economy. The value chain travels down further rather being exported as natural gas liquids. The associated business opportunities and range of products touch all aspects of modern life ranging from cans, bottles, plastic bags, household goods, toiletries and cosmetics to consumer electronics.

Alongside upstream oil and gas production, the Saudi petrochemical sector was the single largest industrial sector contributor to the Kingdom's GDP, especially in the years when oil prices rallied to new record highs as in 2008. Due to the high correlation of basic petrochemical products such as ethylene prices with oil and natural gas prices, Saudi petrochemicals stand to gain when oil prices rise and this is also reflected in the value of the shares of petrochemicals companies listed on the Saudi TASI *TADAWUL* stock market index. There are 13 listed petrochemical companies on the TASI index with a weighting of about 20% of the total index and the petrochemical sector is the second most important sector in the index in terms of weight. This compares to their combined market capitalization representing about a quarter of the index market capitalization. The 13 listed companies generated close to SR 187 billion ($50 billion) in revenues and a combined market capitalization of around SR 240 billion ($64 billion) in 2009.

The basis of this profitability lies in feedstock advantage for Saudi petrochemical producers. Primary feedstock for manufacturing of petrochemical products is oil and naphtha derivative and natural gas. During a process called "cracking," the feedstock is transformed into so-called olefins and aromatics which are at the core of the petrochemical industry. "Olefins" include products such as ethylene, which represents around 40% of the global petrochemical volume, propylene and butylenes, while "aromatics" are made of benzene, toluene and xylene. Both the olefins and aromatics are then processed to produce the plastics, detergents, synthetic rubber and synthetic fibres that consumers are familiar with.

The capability of the Saudi petrochemical companies to achieve a higher profit margin than their European, US or Asian competitors gives them a global competitive advantage, which is supported by new and substantial capacity expansion programmes. This provides an impetus to expand on a larger global market share as Table 8.11 illustrates for the 2007 installed ethylene capacity and estimated 2012 capacity.

Such a competitive advantage and a healthy profit margin have enabled Saudi Arabia to venture abroad and acquire other petrochemical companies not only to expand geographical market penetration but also to acquire new technology and R&D processes. The acquisition of Dutch group DSM, Huntsman and GE Plastics

Table 8.11 Saudi installed and planned ethylene capacity and global market share (2007, 2012)

	2007	2012 (Forecast)
• Saudi Ethylene Capacity (Mtpa) (Million ton per annum)	7.4	19.7
• Global Ethylene Capacity (Mtpa)	122.9	174.2
• *Saudi Market Share (%)*	*6.0*	*11.3*

Source: SABIC

(both of the USA) are such examples of international acquisitions by SABIC. By 2008, Saudi petrochemical output represented around 55% of the total output of the Middle East North Africa (MENA) region, with SABIC output representing around 85% of the Saudi output and the rest coming from private sector petrochemical companies such as Sahara Petrochemical Company and Saudi International Petrochemical Company (Sipchem).

Not to be outdone by SABIC, Saudi Aramco has also entered the petrochemical high-value supply chain and commissioned the giant "Petro Rabigh" joint venture with Sumitomo Chemical Company of Japan, and marked a first for Saudi Aramco when it listed Petro Rabigh on the Saudi *TADAWUL* Stock exchange by raising SR 4.6 billion ($1.223 billion), with the offering three times oversubscribed. The second Saudi Aramco petrochemical venture is the "Ras Tanura Integrated Project" joint venture with Dow Chemical company, completed in 2008, with an initial public offering also contemplated for the project.

Generating Secondary Industries

Of more long-term importance to the Kingdom is SABIC's ability to promote a second-generation industrial linkage with the rest of the Saudi private sector. To some extent this has been successful, for there are currently 12 secondary industries and 115 light and supporting industries serving the SABIC complexes. Some have argued for more labour-intensive industries, such as textiles and clothing, besides traditional plastics (Wilson, 2004). The emphasis on secondary industries will grow with the completion of the second *Jubail* industrial city, where plans for smaller, more labour-intensive projects are being developed. However, given Saudi labour costs, which tend to be higher than foreign labour, enterprises that might be established must try to achieve comparative cost competitiveness in the international market. This is due to the close proximity and competitively priced feedstock of gas and oil products to Saudi industries. It is no coincidence that the *Jubail* industrial city is located very close to its primary source of energy input in the Eastern Province of the Kingdom, thus reducing the cost of transportation of its feedstock. It is this availability of low-cost feedstock, along with excellent infrastructure support and low utility costs in the industrial cities of *Jubail* and *Yanbu*, that has attracted international joint venture partners to Saudi Arabia's petrochemical industries. The

Saudi government has also extended attractive financing facilities through the Saudi Industrial Development Fund (SIDF) to joint venture operations at low rates. The degree of interest, both Saudi and international, in developing the industrial sector is a far cry from the earlier days of basic industry infrastructure, when it was observed that "no private investors are financially capable of undertaking such basic industries" (Johany, 1986). There were also doubts about the profitability of the hydrocarbon-related basic industries as discussed earlier. Today, petrochemicals make a sizeable contribution to the Saudi GDP.

The results of the Saudi petrochemical industries have been impressive over such a short period of time; today they account for around 10% of the world's total petrochemical output and about 8% of global exports. In composition, about 52% of Saudi petrochemicals are in basic products, 26% in intermediates and 22% in final products. Saudi Arabia is aware that it needs to diversify its production line into a broader mix, preferably in intermediate and final products.

Future Challenges

SABIC success has made it a natural target for domestic and international investment, and the commercial track record could make any further government sales of its share in SABIC an assured success. The Saudi government has already announced that it plans to reduce its current ownership in SABIC from 75 to 25% through sales to the Saudi public. The initial government sale of 25% to the public in 1987 was a success in terms of investor confidence and of market acceptance of such partial privatization moves. However, there are several challenges facing SABIC in the future.

First, SABIC and all those entering the petrochemical sector have to ensure that their future feedstock demand is met. The availability of cheap feedstock derived from gas and NGL will be a main preoccupation for Saudi Aramco, which might have difficulty in meeting supply commitments for the upcoming new projects. Increased production of gas, particularly non-associated gas, is crucial for the petrochemical industry's future prospects and puts into perspective the recent international gas deals signed by the Kingdom. The two go together.

Further, Saudi Arabia had to prepare itself for WTO entry and strategize around how that affects the petrochemical sector. While it was argued that WTO accession for Saudi Arabia could provide greater market access and improved trade security, some members of the WTO, particularly those in the European Union (EU), are likely to resist *Saudi petrochemical* exports to the EU, arguing that Saudi Arabia affords an unfair competitive advantage to its petrochemical industries through cheap or subsidized feedstock. The Kingdom is aware of these issues and is committed to removing subsidies on its feedstock prices. During 2002, the price of feedstock was raised from $0.5 one million British thermal units (MMBTU) to $0.75 MMBTU; that brought Saudi domestic prices into line with others in the Gulf Cooperation Council. However, the problem lies in the domestic market, where there is a large differential in liquefied petroleum gas (LPG), sold at a nearly 30% discount on international prices. This appears to be in conflict with WTO rules, although Saudi Arabia has now successfully concluded its bilateral trade agreement with the EU.

Another factor is the relative inefficiency of the system for marketing SABIC products. Despite great advances made in this regard over the years, the primary approach seems to have been built around the hope that SABIC's foreign joint venture partners would assure market access to the joint venture products in their home countries. Unfortunately, with the exception of the Japanese and Taiwanese markets, this approach has been disappointing. To address the situation, SABIC is now pursuing a policy of direct sales and of establishing a manufacturing presence in its primary markets or through acquisitions to strengthen its marketing presence as illustrated earlier.

In order to sustain the long-term success of the petrochemical industries, SABIC must remain at the cutting edge of petrochemical research. To achieve this, there needs to be growth in the internal dynamics of SABIC, especially with regard to qualified human resources and to building the internal research and development capability. The establishment of advanced R&D facilities in the Kingdom and in SABIC's Houston-based operations, along with associations with the Kingdom's leading science-based universities, is a step in the right direction.

The Mining Sector: A Hidden Gem

After being assigned a low priority in both government planning and public expenditure in the 1970s and 1980s compared with the hydrocarbon sector, the Saudi mining industry now has a more prominent place in the Kingdom's strategy to diversify its economic base, as evidenced by the privatization of the state-owned mining company *Maaden* in 2008. Following privatization, *Maaden* will be restructured into separate units of gold, phosphate, bauxite, aluminium and minerals.

In terms of its long-term strategic goals, *Maaden* aspires to be a premier global producer and marketer of phosphate fertilizers and has established joint ventures with SABIC in Saudi Arabia to develop the phosphate reserves of the Kingdom's Northern Borders to produce 3 million tons of phosphate fertilizers. *Maaden* is also expanding its aluminium production capability to utilize Saudi Arabia's bauxite to produce aluminium for local and international markets and has established a joint venture with Alcoa, the world leader in the production and management of primary aluminium, with Alcoa taking a 40% stake in 2009, although later reduced to 25.1% in 2010. Table 8.12 illustrates the wide range of mineral ores that are extracted in Saudi Arabia, besides precious metals.

According to *Maaden*, there is an extensive discovery programme for gold and there is an estimated 8 million ounces and confirmed reserves of 2 million ounces of gold in the five previous mines that it owns. The company is planning to raise its gold reserves to 10 million ounces by 2010 (*Maaden*, 2009).

Table 8.12   Saudi Arabia major mineral ore and precious metal extraction (2004–2008)

Types of exploited ores ('000 tons)	2004	2006	2008
(A)			
Limestone	31,000	30,500	35,000
Mud	4,000	3,800	4,000
Salt	1,430	1,752	1,600
Silica sand	592	782	900
Crusher materials (pebbles)	156,000	217,000	248,000
Sand	33,000	34,000	26,000
Iron sands	495	584	642
Gypsum	2,553	2,200	2,300
Marble for industrial purposes	680	810	832
Marble masses	83	85	85
Granite masses	716	962	1,100
Limestone masses	409	308	308
Kaolin	2	4	44
Barite	15	23	30
Feldspar	42	42	73
Basalt	43	53	–
Boslan	277	400	784
Dolomite	532	550	465
Shiest	663	722	608
(B) Precious metals			
Gold ('000 ounces)	265.8	166.6	146.0
Silver ('000 ounces)	466.0	411.2	265.0
Copper (tons)	652.0	730.0	1465.0
Zinc (tons)	–	983.0	3,663.0
Lead (tons)	–	–	347.0
Kaolin (tons)	–	–	22.0

Source: *Maaden*, SAMA

It may come as a surprise that Saudi Arabia is home to a wide and rich resource base of mineral deposits – the largest in the Gulf region.

The Saudi Arabian government, through its privatization of *Maaden*, is moving away from the old policy of mere mineral extraction to a policy aimed at creating a well-integrated mining industry over the next two decades. Some of the Saudi mining industry's current operating framework has been reassessed, however, to bring industry policies in line with international practices (Marboli, 2002, Dabbagh, 2002).

The legal framework has been addressed. The current framework under which the Saudi mining industry operates was established more than 30 years ago with comparatively little expenditure in the mining sector – a total of around SR 9 billion over all these years. Expenditures were mostly for basic surveys, exploration activities, laboratories and basic infrastructure support. The level of government attention did not encourage either domestic or international mining company investment in the mining sector, with local Saudi company participation confined to providing building material, crushers and quarry supplies.

The government concluded that, in order to open up the mining sector, it needed to carry out the following steps:

- Modernize the *mining code*
- Formulate a Saudi geological survey
- Formulate a comprehensive strategy for the mining sector
- Construct a railway network

During 2001, the Ministry of Petroleum and Minerals started discussions with the Ministry of Finance about reviewing the mining code. It forwarded the code to the Council of Ministers for ratification. The Saudi cabinet approved the new mineral investment law in September 2004 (Saudi Press Agency, 14 September 2004). The key point of the mining code ratification was ensuring that the Kingdom was competitive with other international mining investment regimes. According to Article 14 of the Saudi Basic Governing Law, all resources that lay under or over the ground within the perimeter of the land or offshore of the Kingdom belong to the State. The problem for the mining industry in Saudi Arabia is how to reconcile this with the international practice of "licensing concessions" to the private sector. The amendments before the Council of Ministers will allow for such licenses to be issued by the Ministry of Petroleum and Minerals.

The other major changes to be introduced by the new mining law included:

- All permits, licences and leases classified as "licences"
- Principle of "first come, first served" introduced
- Removal of requirements for technical and financial qualifications of exploration licences
- No limit to number of licences applied
- Introduction of the right to explore all minerals in the licensed area
- Requirement for advance payment removed
- Bank guarantees for exploration licences removed
- Exploration work programme replaced by mining exploration expenditure
- Investment incentives introduced
- Total tax liability not to exceed 25% of profits.

The above, once fully implemented, will supply a major boost to the Saudi mining industry, so that the government can achieve one of its desired objectives: to broaden the economic base of the country and create new employment opportunities through high-value jobs. It has been estimated from mining countries' experiences that for every dollar spent on mining, the net return is $8 to the national economy (Marboli, 2002). The establishment of a viable and integrated Saudi mining industry will also ease Saudi Arabia's *balance of payments*, as today the Kingdom *imports* around 5 million tonnes of raw minerals every year. Import substitution of these minerals could be effective if it is conducted on an economic, cost-efficient and scientific basis. These imports cost Saudi Arabia around SR 8–9 billion per annum (CDS, 2003). One key area that needs addressing, whether by the government or through a public–private partnership, is the construction of an integrated railway network to service the diverse mineral-producing regions, and in 2008/2009 there was a major initiative taken in starting plans for a trans-Saudi rail network. It has been estimated that such a network will cost around $1.5 billion over a 5-year period and bids from international companies, mostly Japanese, were submitted during 2002 and 2003, but finally signed in 2009.

Establishing a Model for Mining Cooperation

Foreign participation in the Saudi mining sector is considered essential due to the relative lack of experience in this field, in contrast to the petroleum sector where Saudi technical skills exist in all work areas. However, in order to attract foreign investment and concession sales, certain issues will need to be clarified. While the new mineral code law addresses many problems faced by the industry, there are other questions about the timing and process of obtaining mineral concessions, the Saudi government's right to a specified percentage of net profits, the State's rights to participate in private mines management and clarification of the exact role of joint venture equity policies.

Figure 8.12 sets out a model of mining cooperation between the private sector and the government and it incorporates many of the mining law's proposed changes.

Figure 8.12 sets out a vision for the future of mining in Saudi Arabia. There are already expressions of interest from countries with rich mining experience, such as Canada, Australia and South Africa, to become involved with Saudi Arabia's "hidden" treasures. In a couple of decades, mining could be playing a role in the Saudi economy like the one oil played two decades ago.

The Challenge of Alternative Energy

While many would agree that oil as a source of energy still has a substantial future as developing nations expand their economies, there is a growing debate concerning the use of alternative energy sources. Oil producers such as Saudi Arabia argue that more can be done to reduce the level of global greenhouse emissions through increasing oil use efficiency than through using renewable energy sources to conserve oil supplies. The Organization of Arab Petroleum Exporting Countries (OAPEC) has forecasted that by 2030 there will be a 40% increase in energy use, 70% of which would derive from oil fossil fuels, but renewable energy sources in the same period are expected to grow by 58%. OAPEC forecasts that although the share of oil in the energy mix would decrease from 34% in 2007 to 30% in 2030, in absolute terms oil would increase from 85 million barrels a day to 105 million barrels a day in the same period. The majority of increase would come from countries such as China and India, but can this type of assumption hold for the long term?

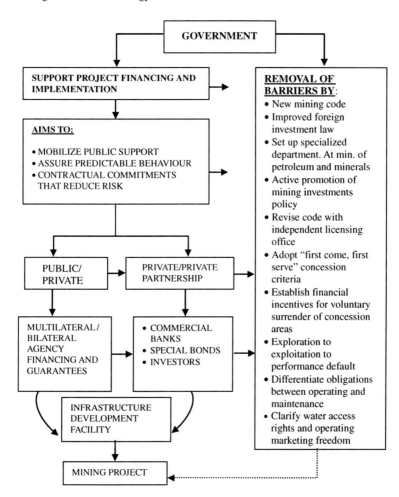

Fig. 8.12 Model for mining cooperation

Will the Chinese and Indian economies continue to grow at phenomenal rates year in, year out? Will their seemingly insatiable demand for oil keep growing at the same rate? Countries will, by necessity, become more energy-conscious, their industries will become more efficient and consumer demand for oil will follow other industrialized country patterns. As countries develop economically, the demand for oil decreases and energy from gas, electricity and piped gas increases. The demand for oil flattens, and China and India will follow the same path. This can bend current oil projections for both countries and cause a discontinuity in oil demand. Both countries could also follow OECD practices and raise energy taxes under a cloak of environmental necessity. Climatic change and ozone depletion could also put both governments under pressure to introduce oil demand management and seek non-oil energy sources such as nuclear fuel. Demand management could be given

Table 8.13 Share of alternative energy consumption in total energy consumption 1980–2008 (%)

Region/energy source	1985	2000	2005	2008
(A) Natural gas				
• World	20.1	24.2	23.6	24.1
• OECD	19.9	22.7	23.1	24.6
• USA	24.7	26.1	24.5	26.1
• Japan	9.9	13.3	13.6	16.6
• Russia	34.7	43.4	54.2	53.3
• China	1.8	2.9	2.6	3.6
(B) Coal				
• World	30.7	23.6	27.8	29.2
• OECD	22.5	20.9	21.0	21.3
• USA	24.6	24.6	24.4	24.6
• Japan	19.9	19.2	23.2	25.4
• Russia	26.3	16.7	16.6	17.2
• China	80.3	59.4	69.9	70.2
(C) Nuclear				
• World	4.5	6.5	5.9	5.5
• OECD	7.4	9.5	9.6	9.4
• USA	5.8	7.8	7.9	8.4
• Japan	9.2	14.0	12.7	11.2
• Russia	2.6	4.6	5.0	5.8
• China	0.0	0.5	0.8	0.8
(D) Hydrogen energy				
• World	6.7	6.8	6.3	6.4
• OECD	7.4	5.8	5.3	5.2
• USA	4.6	2.7	2.6	2.5
• Japan	6.0	4.5	3.8	3.1
• Russia	3.9	5.9	5.9	5.2
• China	4.1	7.2	5.6	6.6

Source: Aramco

further urgency by perceived oil supply security concerns from their Middle East suppliers, although Saudi Arabia has made it clear that it will honour any long-term commitments made.

There has been a perceptible shift towards alternative energy as illustrated in Table 8.13, and the shift has not been confined to one region of the world only, but seems widespread globally.

What is noticeable from Table 8.13 is the rise in nuclear energy despite the nuclear mishaps of Chernobyl in Russia and Three Mile Island in the USA and public opposition to nuclear energy sites. In 2010, the USA announced its intentions to open up its first new nuclear energy facilities since the 1970s and throughout the world nuclear energy has begun to take on more prominence, not least in the Middle East, which sees this energy sector as meeting domestic needs and releasing fossil oil for exports and revenue generation.

Solar energy is also another environment-friendly source and Gulf countries, including Saudi Arabia, are launching solar power initiatives. The Riyadh-based

King Abdulaziz City for Science and Technology (KACST) has begun building a desalination plant using solar power with a 10 MW capacity, and the newly established King Abdullah University of Science and Technology (KAUST) has established advanced solar energy research centres in collaboration with end-users such as Saline Water Conversion Company (SWCC) and the electricity authorities. Saudi Arabia's domestic energy demand is expected to grow to more than 60,000 MW by 2020 from around 40,000 MW current capacity. A strategic decision was taken through the establishment of the King Abdullah City for Atomic and Renewable Energy in 2010 to embark on a civilian nuclear programme.

Conclusion

The hydrocarbon and mineral industries will remain at the heart of the Saudi economy for a long time to come, despite diversification attempts into non-hydrocarbon areas. Saudi Arabia is blessed by an abundance of oil, gas and mineral resources and, with luck and far-sighted planning, it can position itself to become a major player in all three sectors. Economic cycles will mean that as demand for one diminishes, it will rise for the other. The Kingdom must also continue to pursue its current policy to add value, whenever possible, to its exploration of these raw resources, rather than settling with mere extraction and sale. The Kingdom has applied both vertical integration and horizontal integration and both need to be constantly reviewed and amended as circumstances change. The vertical integration has been the expansion of the petrochemical sector, which implies lower government fiscal revenues from oil but a more stable long-term revenue factor from the primary and secondary processing of petrochemicals and employment generation in subsidiary industries. The Saudi horizontal integration has centred around involving more industry clusters and increasing local content and transfer of technology. It is only through this economic approach that economic integration, diversity and skill-building can be achieved in order to shield the Kingdom from fluctuations in basic commodity prices.

Summary of Key Points

- *The petroleum sector has played a significant role in Saudi Arabia's economic development. Rising world oil prices and Saudi Arabia's response to meet world demand by increasing its output levels have once again demonstrated the Kingdom's importance as the world's leading oil supplier.*
- *Saudi oil policy attempts to meet national goals while taking into consideration consumers and environmental interests. At the same time, Saudi Arabia plays an important moderating influence within OPEC and tries to establish working relationships with non-OPEC oil producers.*
- *The oil sector currently contributes around 45% of GDP compared with 60% levels in the early 1970s. The majority of oil and oil products are currently*

exported to the Far East, with the North American and European markets next in importance.

- *Saudi Arabia has the world's fourth largest gas reserves and is the world's largest exporter of natural gas liquids (NGLs). Most Saudi gas is "associated" (gas-produced when oil is produced), but new "non-associated" gas fields are being developed with foreign partners.*
- *The petrochemical industries are located in the industrial cities of Jubail and Yanbu and Saudi Arabia is a major petrochemical producer accounting for around 10% of the world output. Plans are underway to expand the petrochemical production base through international acquisitions by SABIC and the establishment of secondary and support industries in Jubail and Yanbu. These are expected to be carried out by the private sector, be more labour-intensive and create value-added products and jobs for the Saudi market.*
- *The mining industry has a lot of future potential, as Saudi Arabia holds large quantities of mineral resources which have not yet been exploited. The passing of new mining laws, opening this sector to domestic and international investments, should enable further economic diversification to the economy.*
- *Alternative energy usage worldwide will create a challenge for Saudi Arabia's fossil oil exports, and the Kingdom is also trying to develop alternative energy sources such as solar and nuclear energy in order to conserve on its oil resources.*

Part V
The Foreign Sector

Chapter 9
Foreign Trade: Changing Composition and Direction

Commerce is the equalizer of the wealth of nations.

Gladstone

Learning Outcomes

By the end of this section, you would understand:

- *The need to trade for Saudi Arabia*
- *The composition and evolving patterns of imports*
- *The changing origins of imports*
- *The importance of the export sector*
- *The dominance of the oil sector*
- *The need for efficiency and competitiveness in the export market*
- *Saudi Arabia's trade and balance of payments*
- *The need to establish trade competitiveness best practices*

Introduction

Saudi Arabia leads the Arab world in exports and imports, and ranks among the top five in the Islamic world, along with Malaysia, Turkey, Indonesia and the UAE (Wilson, 2003). This chapter discusses the various aspects of foreign commerce, principally imports and exports; we will look at how the composition has changed over time as well as their impact on the Kingdom's balance of payments. We will closely examine Saudi exports to assess the success of the economic diversification programme to date, as well as to analyse Saudi product export competitiveness. The final section of the chapter sets out model guidelines for a more effective export promotion programme to help the private sector achieve the country's economic diversification goal.

Why does Saudi Arabia need to trade? Economic theory postulates that countries trade with each other based on either absolute or comparative advantage. In trade,

M.A. Ramady, *The Saudi Arabian Economy*, DOI 10.1007/978-1-4419-5987-4_9,
© Springer Science+Business Media, LLC 2010

countries specialize in exporting commodities where specialization gives them cost-of-production advantage. Saudi Arabia, with large, homogeneous and low-cost oil fields, undoubtedly has a comparative advantage over other high-cost oil producers. But it does not have an absolute advantage, for the Kingdom never had to make the choice of producing non-oil products, and as such there was no opportunity cost or alternatives forgone (Wilson, 2003). There was no trade-off between oil and non-oil production, but rather a positive relationship between oil exports and revenues and imports, with imports rising during oil booms and remaining static or declining in oil depressions. The next major challenge for the Kingdom is the expansion of Saudi Arabia's export base into other finished and semi-finished products not directly related to oil. It will be based on production efficiency and specialization, in competition with similar products produced worldwide. This will not be easy. According to the World Trade Organization (WTO), the Middle East and North African countries have seen their share of global trade diminish. This is illustrated in Table 9.1 for the period 2005–2007.

Table 9.1 GDP and merchandise trade by region, 2005–2007 (Annual percentage change at constant prices)

	GDP			Exports			Imports		
	2005	2006	2007	2005	2006	2007	2005	2006	2007
World	3.3	3.7	3.4	6.5	8.5	5.5	6.5	8.0	5.5
North America	3.1	3.0	2.3	6.0	8.5	5.5	6.5	6.0	2.5
United States	3.1	2.9	2.2	7.0	10.5	7.0	5.5	5.5	1.0
South and Central America	5.6	6.0	6.3	8.0	4.0	5.0	14.0	15.0	20.0
Europe	1.9	2.9	2.8	4.0	7.5	3.5	4.5	7.5	3.5
European Union (27)	1.8	3.0	2.7	4.5	7.5	3.0	4.0	7.0	3.0
Commonwealth of Independent States	6.7	7.5	8.4	3.5	6.0	6.0	18.0	21.5	18.0
Africa and Middle East	5.6	5.5	5.5	4.5	1.5	0.5	14.5	6.5	12.5
Asia	4.2	4.7	4.7	11.0	13.0	11.5	8.0	8.5	8.5
China	10.4	11.1	11.4	25.0	22.0	19.5	11.5	16.5	13.5
Japan	1.9	2.4	2.1	5.0	10.0	9.0	2.5	2.5	1.0
India	9.0	9.7	9.1	21.5	11.0	10.5	28.5	9.5	13.0
Newly industrialized economies[a]	4.9	5.5	5.6	8.0	12.5	8.5	5.0	8.5	7.0

[a]Hong Kong, China; Republic of Korea; Singapore and Chinese Taipei
Source: WTO Secretariat

Exports from North America declined, as did those from Europe, but imports rose for the Middle East and India.

The Causes of Trade

From an economic perspective, the case for freer trade rests on the existence of gains from trade and most economists typically agree that there are gains from trade. In recent years, however, free trade has increasingly come under fire and it is not uncommon to hear trade sceptics say that economists' arguments in favour of free trade and in particular comparative advantage may have been valid at the time of Ricardo (in the early 19th century) but that they are no longer valid in today's globalized world. Most trade models are designed to answer two closely related questions: what goods do countries trade and why?

The idea that there are gains from trade is the central proposition of normative trade theory. The gains from trade theorem states that if a country can trade at any price ratio other than its domestic prices, it will be better off than in *autarky* – or self-sufficiency. More generally, the basic gains from trade propositions are that (i) free trade is better than autarky; (ii) restricted trade (i.e. trade restricted by trade barriers) is better than autarky; and (iii) for a small country (i.e. a country too small to influence world prices) free trade is better than restricted trade. Samuelson (1939) showed that there are potential gains from trade for small countries provided world prices diverge from autarky prices. Kemp (1962) showed that restricted trade is better than no trade. He also extended the argument to the large country case, proving that free trade is potentially superior to autarky, in the case when there are many commodities and factors and with variable factor supplies. As noted by Deardorff (1979), most treatments of the gains from trade say that if trade could potentially benefit all members of a country's population (assuming their preferences and income were identical), it is regarded as benefiting the country because some form of income redistribution among the country's consumers is assumed to be feasible.

These basic propositions about the gains from trade, however, are not the end of the story. First, as pointed out by Corden (1984), the divergence between autarky and free trade prices is only an approximate explanation of the gains from trade. A full explanation of those gains should link them to the causes of trade – that is, to the elements that give rise to divergence between autarky or self-sufficiency and free trade prices. Those elements are the ones that lie behind the sources of comparative advantage. They would include differences in technology or differences in endowments. Second, economic theory points at other forms of gains from trade that are not linked to differences between countries. In particular, countries trade to achieve economies of scale in production or to have access to a broader variety of goods. Also, if the opening up of trade reduces or eliminates monopoly power or enhances productivity, there will be gains from trade additional to the usual ones. Finally, trade may have positive growth effects.

Table 9.2 provides a simplified summary of some of the basic characteristics of different trade models to illustrate the diversity of opinions on the subject.

Traditional trade theory emphasizes the gains from specialization made possible by differences among countries. The main contribution of this strand of thought is that opportunities for mutually beneficial trade exist by virtue of specialization on the basis of relative efficiency – a country does not have to be better at producing something than its trading partners to benefit from trade (absolute advantage). It is sufficient that it is relatively more efficient than its trading partners (comparative advantage). This insight explains why so many more opportunities to gain from trade exist than would be the case if only absolute advantage counted. More recent theories point to other sources of gains from trade not linked to differences among

Table 9.2   Trade model theories

	Traditional trade theory Ricardo, Heckscher–Ohlin	New trade theory Krugman	Heterogeneous-firms model Melitz
Gains from trade (causes)			
Specialization	Yes	No	No
Economies of scale	No	Yes	Yes
Pro-competitive	No	Yes	No
Variety	No	Yes	No
Aggregate productivity (through selection/ reallocation	No	No[a]	Yes
Trade patterns			
Inter-industry	Yes	No	No
Intra-industry	No	Yes	Yes
Exporters and non-exporters within industries	No	No	Yes
Distribution			
Trade liberalization affects relative factor rewards	Yes	No	No

[a]In the Krugman model, "productivity" in the integrated market also increases in the sense that the same total amount is produced at lower average cost due to exploitation of scale economies. However, the Krugman model is silent about which firms remain in business, since it does not include differences among firms. Once firms are distinguished according to their productivity level, as in the Melitz model, the exit of less productive firms itself leads to improvements in overall industry productivity
Source: WTO

countries, such as economies of scale in production, enhanced competition, access to a broader variety of goods and improved productivity.

International trade can affect the growth process through its effects on the accumulation of capital and on technological change. In a standard "neoclassical" growth framework, where technological change is determined externally (*exogenously*), international trade affects factor and product prices and, through this channel, incentives to accumulate capital. Within this framework, the effect of international trade on growth depends on the nature of trade taking place (Grubel, 1967, Porter, 1990).

Many studies that have focused on how trade might stimulate firms to innovate have uncovered several new mechanisms that could associate trade liberalization with higher growth rates. Examples of such mechanisms include increased market size, knowledge spillovers, greater competition and the improved quality of the institutional framework. Several studies have pointed to possible offsetting effects resulting from differences in human capital across countries, imitation of foreign technologies, a worsening of policies affecting trade and so on.

Nevertheless, many studies focusing on knowledge spillovers and firm productivity demonstrate a high correlation between growth rates and trade volumes. But this does not necessarily imply that trade leads to growth. Does trade cause faster growth or do economies that grow quickly also trade more (Cohen and Levinthal, 1989, Hoekman et al., 2004b)?

An alternative strategy is to estimate the importance of international knowledge spillovers, which are crucial for the realization of dynamic gains from trade. Recent studies point to the presence of "direct" (i.e. bilateral) research and development (R&D) spillovers, which are related to the level of R&D produced by the trading partner, and "indirect" knowledge spillovers, which result from participating in international trade more generally (Branstetter, 2001, Bottazzi and Peri, 2007, Young, 1991).

Finally recent studies that use firm-level data find that trade liberalization has a positive effect on firm productivity and that "learning by exporting" effects (externalities) exists in several emerging market economies (Gould and Gruben, 1996, Falvey et al., 2006a).

Studies that focus on international knowledge spillovers find that knowledge developed in one country has positive effects on other countries through trade. Trade leads to the spread of international technology for three major reasons. First, technologically more sophisticated intermediate goods become available for production. Second, the technological specifications of intermediate and final goods developed abroad can be studied and the intrinsic knowledge can be acquired. Finally, trade favours person-to-person communication as an important vehicle of knowledge transfer (Branstetter, 2001, Hoekman et al., 2004b). This type of international learning by doing was examined in the previous chapter in relation to the wide range of foreign companies operating in the Saudi energy sector.

Studies have emphasized several factors determining whether technology is successfully absorbed across countries. These factors are associated with the idea that a country needs to have certain types of skills (e.g. human capital) and institutions in order to be able to adopt foreign technological knowledge (Ventura, 1997).

Policies to improve a country's ability to adopt technological innovations must be targeted at its educational system as well as its business and regulatory environment. One particular problem related to the transfer of technology is that innovations produced in advanced economies may not respond to the needs of developing countries (Bhagwati and Brecher, 1980).

Such a mismatch may result from insufficient property rights protection. This suggests a role for international organizations in promoting international technology diffusion through adequate property rights enforcement. Other areas where international organizations can help include the coordination of development aid to build infrastructure and human capital (Young, 1991).

Saudi Industrial and Export Strategy

Since the launch of Saudi Arabia's industrialization strategy in the early 1970s, the key debate was on what type of strategy to adopt: an import substitution strategy or an export-led strategy (Johany, 1986). While both are not mutually exclusive and can coexist for a certain period of a nation's economic development, both have some inherent appeal for national planners, as follows:

- *Import substitution strategy*: This type of strategy can be characterized as being an industrial development policy whose aim is to encourage investment in both the private and public sectors so as to establish a viable domestic industrial base that gradually replaces foreign imports. The perceived advantages of following such a policy are a reduction in the amount of foreign exchange outflow and pressure on the balance of payment current account; the chaneling of investment opportunities domestically instead of capital outfows; the creation of new jobs in such import substitution industries and the building up of an expertise in the labour force; reduction in foreign country dependency, especially for strategically deemed products, and enabling a higher degree of self-sufficiency in such products.

  There are some disadvantages associated with a prolonged import substitution policy. These centre around the opportunity cost of a continued protection policy for so-called "infant industries," which might become powerful domestic business lobby groups demanding continued government subsidies and protection against foreign competition. Also, the successful establishment of an import substitution industrial base might shift and change the structure of imported goods and services from consumer goods to one dominated by raw materials and highly specialized capital goods and foreign labour. Such import substitution policies usually do not succeed if the domestic demand base is small and fragmented.

- *Export-oriented industrial strategy*: This type of policy is more proactive and involves fundamental structural, administrative and capacity changes in the domestic economy for it to succeed. The aim of such a strategy is to encourage the production of competitive industrial domestic goods and services to be exported to other countries on equal terms. As discussed earlier, for this strategy to be successful, a country primarily focuses on the production of goods and services in which it has a comparative advantage. Similar to the import substitution strategy, the export-oriented industrial strategy has imbedded advantages and disadvantages. The advantages relate to the reduction of foreign currency outflows and replacing this with foreign currency inflows helping to build up current account surpluses; an effective export-oriented policy will help to promote domestic competition and efficiency as higher standards are often required for export goods to meet internationally accepted International Organization for Standardization (ISO) benchmarks. Finally, a high-quality export-led industrial policy may open up new foreign markets for the domestic producers owing to economies of scale, instead of relying on a more limited domestic demand and market.

The disadvantages of an export-oriented industrial policy can also be significant and relate to the intensity and level of international competition for initial market entry and if the foreign companies react by "dumping" their products at lower prices in the developing countries' market in order to kill off competition. Also, this export-led strategy may lead to increased levels of imports for high-value capital goods and reliance on foreign skilled workers to run the newly established export industries, causing a deterioration in the balance of payment position in the short run, as well as dependence on foreign skilled labour and foreign technology dependence and know-how in the long run.

Over the next few chapters, we will examine how Saudi Arabia tried to overcome these constraints and balance both objectives and whether they have been successful to date. In summary, some of these obstacles are set out in Table 9.3.

Table 9.3 Obstacles facing Saudi industrial sector development and solutions

Obstacles	Possible solution
• Skilled manpower shortage at both technical and managerial levels	• Expansion of specialized vocational and technical institutions, development of market-led courses at universities, international scholarships for areas deemed to be of national priority, on-the-job training
• Transfer of technology and its continuous application, and maintenance of such new technology	• Establishment of joint venture companies with access to foreign companies' R&D processes, establishment of internal R&D centres and specialized research institutions at universities, supports for commercialization and new patent applications
• Potential dumping of foreign goods	• Application to international bodies such as WTO for redress and imposition of penalties on such foreign companies

Saudi Arabia's Trading Patterns: Exports

From a humble beginning in the early 1970s, Saudi Arabia's imports and exports have risen dramatically over the past decades as illustrated in Table 9.4.

What is noticeable from the above table is that while oil exports tended to fluctuate, there was a gradual increase in non-oil exports to around SR 120 billion by 2008, compared with under 1 billion in 1970. The driving force for exports has been

Table 9.4 Saudi trading patterns 1970–2008 (SR billion)

Year	Imports	Total exports	Non-oil exports
1970	3.197	10.907	0.800
1975	14.823	104.412	1.160
1981	119.298	405.481	4.635
1991	108.934	178.636	15.328
2001	116.931	254.898	30.182
2005	222.985	677.144	71.263
2007	338.088	874.403	104.468
2008	431.753	1,175.354	120.182

Source: SAMA

Table 9.5   Composition of Saudi exports 1984–2008 (SR billion)

Composition	1984	1993	2000	2008
• Foodstuff	0.166	1.656	1.700	8.875
• Petrochemicals	1.489	8.348	15.930	62.738
• Base Metals	0.185	0.869	1.982	10.503
• Electrical Equipment/Machines	0.008	0.460	0.951	6.388
• Construction material	Nil	1.273	2.357	10.206
• Re-exports	2.505	1.527	1.886	21.472
• Total	4.353	14.134	24.806	120.182

Source: SAMA

the petrochemical sector, which now accounts for around 52% of total exports in 2008 as broken down in Table 9.5.

Besides petrochemicals, there has also been noticeable success in non-energy-related Saudi exports in the foodstuffs sector and general machinery and construction material. These are the results of the establishment of modern agro-business enterprises such as the Saudi Al Marei group, which is the largest in the Middle East, and the various Saudi cement companies and other industrial groups. This non-oil export trend was assisted by several initiatives that the Kingdom undertook to assist the private sector, by creating a number of entities such as the Saudi Exports Programme of the Saudi Fund for Development, the Saudi Export Development Centre and the Saudi Exports Development Authority. Each is analysed in Table 9.6.

Table 9.6   Saudi export assistance agencies

Agency	Function
• Saudi Exports Programme of Saudi Fund for Development (SFD)	• Established in 1999 to provide finance and insurance for non-oil exports. Helps Saudi exporters to receive export proceeds due to importers' inability to pay, by providing 90% non-payment risk. In 2008 the programme provided SR 838 million in export finance and SR 3.525 billion in guarantees
• Saudi Export Development Centre (SEDC)	• Established in 1985 under the auspices of the Chambers of Commerce and assists exporters by making proposals and studies, conducting research on export potential and new markets, assisting with marketing plans and assisting with internal and external trade missions, as well as providing import regulations of designated target countries to Saudi members
• Saudi Exports Development Authority (SEDA)	• Established in 2007 by the Council of Ministers. The SEDA's objectives are in setting the State's policies of developing non-oil exports, increasing the export sector's competitive capacity, developing policies and legislation and improving the export environment and providing incentives. SEDA also prepares studies on export opportunities and organizing symposia and conferences

Import Diversity

Imports saw the largest sustained rises, with this sector growing at an annual compounded rate of over 33% during the first boom period of 1974–1982 (Johany, 1986). Even more striking are the marked changes in the composition of imports and their points of origin, along with relative changes in sectoral demands. Table 9.7 illustrates the evolution of the composition of imports for the period 1970–2008. Imports of goods and services are virtually unrestricted to the Kingdom, with the exception of those goods and services that are deemed *haram* or forbidden by Islam (such as pork and alcohol products), as well as immoral or security-related commodities. Goods from countries that the Kingdom is still boycotting, such as Israel, are also forbidden.

Table 9.7 Saudi Arabia – imports by major commodity groups (1970–2008) (SR billion)

Commodity group	1970	1984	2000	2006	2008
• Machines, appliances	0.590	28.410	24.982	67.302	117.318
• Foodstuffs	1.011	18.739	20.258	35.547	62.199
• Chemicals	0.355	11.625	14.716	33.394	53.039
• Textiles/clothing	0.157	3.605	7.573	10.281	13.875
• Metals and their products	0.300	14.183	8.895	38.626	66.012
• Wood and jewellery	0.416	7.790	8.769	4.256	8.355
• Transport equipment	0.428	15.916	19.996	50.453	77.619
• Other goods	0.042	3.716	3.072	21.543	33.336
• Total SR billion	3.299	103.984	108.261	261.402	431.753

Source: SAMA

In 1970, the import of foodstuffs accounted for around 31% of total imports, but the oil-led boom of the mid-1970s changed the composition of imports, with machinery, transport equipment and mineral and chemical products becoming nearly 60% of imports until the mid-1980s. With the decline in government capital expenditure, discussed in earlier chapters, the private sector increasingly drove import demand. Today, in addition to foodstuffs that account for around 15–16% of total imports, textiles, machinery and vehicle imports account for a significant portion of imports that meet domestic and expatriate consumer needs.

Despite the growth of the domestic petrochemical industry as analysed in previous chapters, Saudi Arabia still imports significant amounts of chemical products, representing around 12% of total import value for 2008, with such chemicals being final consumption items to meet shortfalls in domestic production.

As Saudi Arabia's industrial base expands and matures, the composition of imports will move towards intermediate and fixed assets as illustrated by Fig. 9.1. For the year 2005, fixed assets made up around 18% of total imports, with final and intermediate consumption goods at 39 and 43%, respectively, as illustrated in Fig. 9.1(a).

Figure 9.1(b) illustrates that raw material imports average around 5%, while the bulk of imports (72%) are composed of finished products in value terms. Semi-finished products stood at around 24% of total imports. This high proportion

(a)

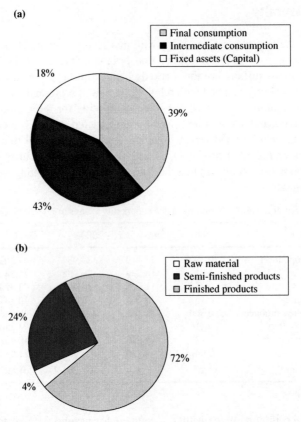

(b)

Fig. 9.1 (**a**) Import by utilization of items, 2008 (SR billion); (**b**) Imports by nature of items (Source: SAMA)

of finished product imports for the Kingdom is a function of the open economy. It also reflects the degree to which consumer demand has been influenced by international consumption habits. Relatively sophisticated local advertising and marketing campaigns have also developed brand awareness, especially for high-value luxury items.

Saudi Arabia now has large, flourishing shopping malls, catering to a younger generation. We have seen earlier that non-oil GDP has been gradually rising over the past few decades, contributing to some import demand stability. Earlier studies carried out on the level of the Saudi marginal propensity to import (MPM) indicated a fairly high level of MPM, almost 75% (Bashir, 1977), as well as a high level of correlation between imports and non-oil GDP. By marginal propensity to import, we mean the fraction of each increment or addition to income that is spent on imports. In the earlier research, 0.75 of each additional 1 riyal income was spent on imports. It will be interesting to note whether, in the long run, this high-level MPM will continue in the face of domestic Saudi manufacturing expansion, especially in the food sector, where Saudi products have established brand recognition and international standards.

Origins of Imports Are Changing

It is not just the composition of imports that has changed over time for Saudi Arabia, but also the origins of these imports. This reflects an interesting mixture of economic relations, consumer taste and political realities. Figure 9.2 sets out the share of total imports accounted for by the top six exporting nations to Saudi Arabia for the years 2000 and 2008.

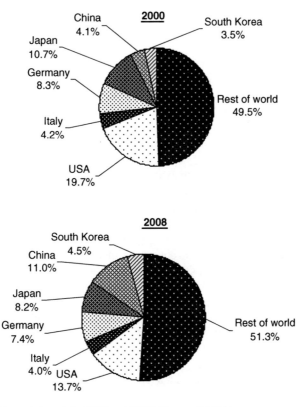

Fig. 9.2 Saudi imports by origin (2000 and 2008) (Source: SAMA)

On the whole, the Kingdom's trade direction is largely determined by the private sector; it is based on commercial relations, the agencies held and the level of comfort in dealing with their international counterparts, rather than being based on political considerations. While some government-to-government lobbying does certainly exist to obtain government-related contracts, such contracts have become less important over time as the Saudi government has emphasized the role of the private sector in economic decisions.

Figure 9.2 shows the pre-eminent position of the USA as the Kingdom's major import trading partner. This is not surprising, considering that the USA is, in turn, the largest importer of Saudi oil. Following the September 11, 2001 events, the premier position of the USA has been eroded to around 14% in 2008, down from 20 to 21%. Political sensitivities and travel problems to the USA for Saudi citizens have also been issues. What the figure further demonstrates is that Saudi Arabia's import relations are mainly carried out with non-Arab and non-Muslim countries. This supports our earlier observations that Saudi buyers are generally knowledgeable of, and sensitive to, market conditions, especially when it comes to the import of "quality" or "brand name" items that are lacking in the wider Arab or Muslim world (Johany, 1986).

Currently, imports from all the Arab and Muslim countries account for around 11% of the total imports. The presence of Lebanon in 1972 amongst the top five exporting countries to the Kingdom is an interesting historical aside. It came about because of Lebanon's position as a trans-shipment centre in the early 1970s for Saudi goods; Saudi Arabia used Lebanese ports because of its own limited port facilities in that early boom era. In 1970, the handling capacity of the combined Saudi ports stood at around 2000 tons, rising to 3,700 in 1974. By 2000, Saudi port capacity had risen to 252,000 tons. It is interesting to note the rising market share from China, with imports accounting for around 4.1% of total imports in 2000 and rising fast.

The almost doubling of Chinese exports to Saudi Arabia in a decade to become the second largest importing trading partner after the USA by 2008 is a reflection of the sharp increase in Saudi oil exports to that country, raising China's importance to the Kingdom as a major trading partner for the future. As noted from Chapter 8, 2008's high oil prices have been largely underpinned by strong demand from China. This is expected to remain robust over the next few years according to oil industry analysts. Over the next decade, the origin of Saudi imports could continue to shift towards the Asian markets, given that Japan has also been the second most consistent exporter to Saudi Arabia, while imports from the USA could see further volatility, despite competitive U.S. product prices, due to the fall in the value of the U.S. dollar during 2007–2009.

Most Saudi imports are financed by Saudi commercial banks through letters of credit opened in favour of overseas beneficiaries. The major financing is applied to motor vehicles and foodstuffs, followed by textile and clothing, as illustrated in Fig. 9.3.

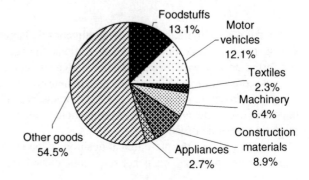

Fig. 9.3 Private sector imports financed through commercial banks 2008 (Source: SAMA)

Overall, around 65–70% of total imports are financed through banks. The remaining imports use different forms of direct payments or supplier credit arrangements. With the growth of local Saudi industries and a wider manufacturing base, the level and composition of future imports to Saudi Arabia could yet undergo fundamental change. There could be more machinery, spare parts and raw material imports, and fewer imports in foodstuffs, appliances, construction material and textiles.

The Export Sector: Oil Is Still King

Despite efforts to diversify the country's production base, and specifically its export base, oil exports continue to dominate the Kingdom's foreign export trade. As such, any overview of Saudi Arabia's exports is much simpler than that of its imports.

The lack of meaningful export diversification could have implications for the Kingdom following entry into the World Trade Organization (Azzam, 2002, Husseini, 2002). According to the WTO, the Arab world in general has fallen behind in the export race relative to world growth in exports; one key reason is the lack of diversification of export products.

From a peak of around 12% of total world exports in 1980, the Arab world's share is now fluctuating between 5 and 8%, despite a 300% increase in world export value over the period 1980–2008.

Significantly, the expansion of exports in the Arab world has not kept pace with world export growth, but rather it has mostly correlated with changes in oil prices.

Crude oil exports currently account for around 75–80% of total Saudi exports, down from 94 to 96% during the period 1979–1984, but still giving a one-dimensional emphasis on a single commodity. If one adds petroleum-related finished and semi-finished products, exports from this sector accounted for around 95% of the total in 2008 as illustrated in Table 9.8.

Table 9.8 Oil-related merchandise exports 1979–2008 (SR billion)

Export segment	1979	1984	2005	2008
Total exports	213.183	132.220	677.144	1,175.354
• Crude petroleum	200.225	127.867	513.939	926.613
• Refined products	0.600	1.750	91.942	127.119
• Petrochemicals	1.939	1.489	42.055	62.464
Oil-related exports	202.764	131.106	647.936	1,116.196

Source: SAMA

Saudi Arabia's other petroleum-related product exports are important sources of revenue, especially refined oil products, including bunker fuel.

Saudi manufacturing and processing industry is slowly coming of age, with steady export rises in foodstuffs, equipment and base metals, in addition to plastic and construction materials. The Saudi government aims to ensure faster growth of such exports so that they will constitute a larger share of overall Saudi exports, achieving diversification within non-oil-based economic structure (Zarouk, 2002, Khemani, 2002). This will be a long-term task. In the meantime, the Kingdom will continue to be primarily a raw material, intermediate consumption goods exporter (goods which still need value-added input), as illustrated in Fig. 9.4(a) and (b).

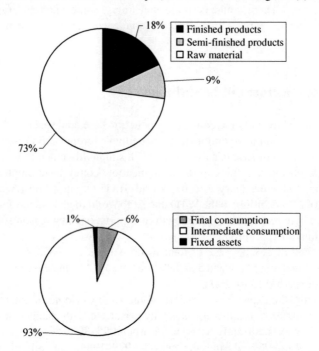

Fig. 9.4 (a) Export by nature of items (2008); (b) Export by utilization of items (2002) (Source: SAMA)

In 2008, according to Fig. 9.4(a), some 73% of Saudi exports were composed of raw materials, with finished products accounting for 18% and semi-finished for 9%. It is the second category that needs to be encouraged to grow, as it is a high-value export category. Similarly, Fig. 9.4(b) points out that only 1% of total exports were in fixed assets and 6% in final consumption goods. An increase in finished product exports will assist in the growth of exports in the value of final consumption goods, that is, goods that have final use. Developing these export sectors will reduce the instability of export earnings that result from oil dependency.

Asian Exports Predominate

Saudi Arabia's main export market is Asia, which accounted for some 51% during 2008 as illustrated in Fig. 9.5.

These were followed by North America and Western Europe, while the GCC states took 7% of exports. Saudi exports to other Arab countries were a meagre

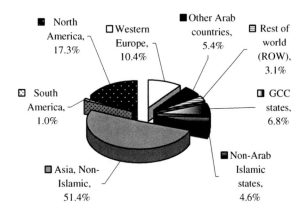

Fig. 9.5 Geographic distribution of average Saudi exports 2008 (Source: SAMA)

5%, and the non-Arab Islamic states took 4%. Once again, it was the predominantly industrialized Western and Asian economies that received the bulk of Saudi oil exports and petroleum-related products.

Given the strong performance of primarily Asian countries such as China and India during the 2007–2009 financial crisis, the trend for Saudi exports to Asia is set to grow.

Saudi Arabia's relatively narrow export base is also a reflection of the government's development strategy during the first planning periods, discussed in Chapter 2. This strategy emphasized import substitution as an explicit goal, as well as investment in petrochemical-related industries. The result of import substitution policies was the creation of protected domestic manufacturing industries that looked to the lucrative domestic consumer market as their first choice for expansion and sales (Jalal, 1985). An export-oriented, non-oil manufacturing base was not emphasized, and Saudi Arabia is now trying to find its niche in this competitive sector to create some stability in exports, as compared with oil. This could take several decades, and significant steps have been achieved, and it is not impossible, given the financial resources that are available to the private sector as evidenced from earlier chapters. This leads us to a discussion on the required change in the operational environment of the non-oil export sector.

Efficiency and Competitiveness

Over the period 2006–2010, the Saudi investment environment and private sector operating framework has benefited from significant progress from the structural reforms examined in Chapter 2, which involves liberalization, greater transparency and the reduction of red tape and bureaucracy. The result has been a gradual improvement in Saudi Arabia's global ranking in the World Bank's "ease of doing business" index, which is illustrated below and has placed the Kingdom in 16th position, ahead of some western European countries.

Saudi Arabia: Ease of doing business World Bank ranking

	2006	2007	2008	2009
Global Rank	35	38	23	16

This improvement in Saudi Arabia's global ranking has largely been driven by the Saudi Arabian General Investment Authority (SAGIA), which was created to overcome red tape and bureaucracy and make Saudi Arabia an "investment-friendly" destination for foreign and domestic companies. SAGIA's objective is even more ambitious – to rank Saudi Arabia in the top 10 countries of the world in terms of competitiveness by the end of 2010, through SAGIA's so-called 10×10 vision (SAGIA, 2009).

Aspiring to be in the top 10 countries is one thing, while achieving it is another, as it involves some fundamental structural changes in the competitiveness-enabling environment. There are many methods for enhancing a nation's competitive position, and we summarize the main concepts below.

Competitiveness can be broadly defined as the ability of a nation to create sustainable value through its enterprise, and to maintain a high standard of living for its citizens. In addition, countries are placed in three broad categories:

- *Factor-driven*: relying heavily on natural resources and basic production.
- *Investment-driven*: increasing investment to make production more efficient and enabling the economy to move up the "value chain" from basic manufacturing towards product design, distribution and marketing.
- *Innovation-driven*: producing unique goods and service that demand high prices on the global market.

As analysed in the previous chapters, Saudi Arabia's competitiveness has been primarily factor-driven, but with more emphasis now on investment-driven, due to the emergence of a high-value petrochemical sector.

Whichever competitiveness measures are taken, there is one common factor that drives competitiveness, i.e. productivity or the level of output per unit of input used to produce something of value. The main drivers of a nation's prosperity and hence its competitiveness vis-à-vis other nations are as follows:

- The proportion of the labour force engaged in productive economic activity
- The efficiency with which goods and services are produced
- The value these goods and services can demand on the world markets

A nation's competitiveness depends on its ability to capitalize on these three factors to create new sources of wealth over time. However, Saudi Arabia must ultimately define competitiveness for itself that suits its own unique operating environment as there is no single standard or blueprint for success and such strategies need to be tailored to reflect a country's unique character. For example, natural resources such as oil may bestow Saudi Arabia with an "inherited prosperity" that makes generating a momentum for change that much more challenging compared with other less favourably nature endowed countries but which seek out new challenges to give them a competitive edge. The example of Singapore in the latter category suffices.

Achieving Competitiveness

More than one factor is essential to achieve a sustained level of competitiveness. These involve broad strategic issues such as

  (i) the quality of macro-economic, social, political and legal policy;
 (ii) the quality of the business environment and
(iii) the sophistication of company strategy and operations.

The overall macroeconomic, social, political and legal policies create the potential for greater company productivity by providing access to capital and foreign markets. However, actual wealth generation takes place at a microeconomic level through the creation of unique and innovative goods and services that can demand high prices on world markets. Wealth can be inherited, whether for individuals, or through endowed factors such as oil for a country like Saudi Arabia, but ultimately it needs to be created to achieve sustainable prosperity. Competing on cost or low wages or an abundance of natural resources is not a basis for a sustainable competitive advantage.

Countries that have high rankings and/or have shown significant gain have done so by showing consistently superior performance in key macro- and microeconomic areas:

- *Macroeconomic environment*: high budget surpluses, low government waste, strong country credit rating, low inflation
- *Strong public and private institutions*: absence of corruption, business and governmental transparency, judicial independence, enforcement of property rights
- *Technology and innovation*: high spending on research and development (R&D), aggressive adoption of new technologies, university and industry research collaborations, active use of technology
- *Education and training*: high educational enrolment rates, excellent educational establishments, skilled labour force

The World Competitiveness Report (World Economic Forum, 2009) has identified 12 "pillars" of competitiveness and Fig. 9.6 sets them out by groupings relating to the factor-driven, efficiency-driven and innovation-driven economies.

How has Saudi Arabia performed against the above pillars and what are the perceived obstacles achieving a higher level of competitiveness in the Kingdom?

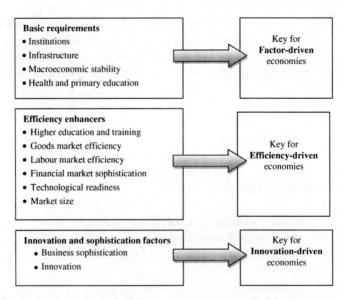

Fig. 9.6 The 12 pillars of competitiveness (Source: Global Economic Forum (2009))

Saudi Competitiveness Performance

Saudi Arabia has steadily improved its world ranking in both ease of doing business as discussed earlier, and also in the global competitiveness index as illustrated in Table 9.9, which indicates that Saudi Arabia's rank as 28 out of 133 surveyed countries.

Table 9.9 Global competitiveness index: Saudi Arabia ranking

	Rank (out of 133)	Score (1–7)
GCI 2009–2010	28	4.7
Basic requirements	30	5.2
1st pillar: Institutions	28	4.8
2nd pillar: Infrastructure	36	4.6
3rd pillar: Macroeconomic stability	9	5.9
4th pillar: Health and primary education	71	5.4
Efficiency enhancers	38	4.5
5th pillar: Higher education and training	53	4.3
6th pillar: Goods market efficiency	29	4.8
7th pillar: Labour market efficiency	71	4.3
8th pillar: Financial market sophistication	53	4.4
9th pillar: Technological readiness	44	4.2
10th pillar: Market size	22	4.9
Innovation and sophistication factors	33	4.2
11th pillar: Business sophistication	35	4.6
12th pillar: Innovation	32	3.7

Note: Score 1 defines the lowest and 7 defines the highest rankings
Source: Global Economic Forum (2009)

(a) Saudi Arabia

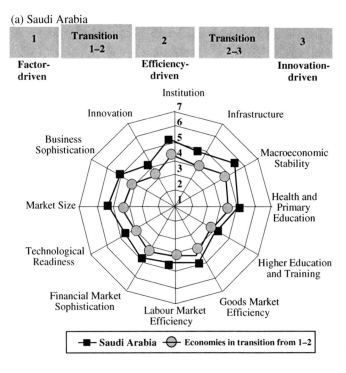

(b) BRIC and OECD average scores

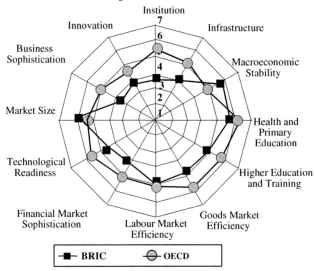

Fig. 9.7 Stages of development across 12 pillars of Global Competitiveness Index (**a**) Saudi Arabia; (**b**) BRIC and OECD average scores. Source: Global Economic Forum (2009)

Table 9.9 reveals varied differences in the competitiveness index pillars for the Kingdom. Saudi Arabia's macroeconomic stability ranked it 9th out of 133 countries, and the Global Economic Forum gives the Kingdom special praise about progress being made with respect to upgrading its public institutions, which were ranked at 28 for 2009. According to the Global Economic Forum, Saudi Arabia is in a state of transition from being a factor-driven economy towards an efficiency-driven economy, but still has some way to go before being an innovation-driven economy. This is illustrated in Fig. 9.7, which compares Saudi Arabia to similar economies in transition as well as with the Organisation for Economic Co-operation and Development (OECD) countries and the so-called BRIC (Brazil, Russia, India and China) economies.

From Fig. 9.7(a) we note that Saudi Arabia has done relatively better for all 12 pillars compared to other similar transition countries, especially in macroeconomic stability, institutions, market size and business sophistication, but does less well on labour market efficiency and health and primary education. Saudi business sophistication is also ranked higher with its peers. Analysis of Fig. 9.7(b) illustrates that the BRICs do well in terms of market size in comparison with the OECD block, as well as receive a high score for labour market efficiency, macroeconomic stability and health and primary education. Comparing Saudi Arabia with the BRIC economies, the Kingdom does well on most scores with the exception of innovation. There seems to be a correlation between countries with a higher efficiency and innovation-driven economy than those in the factor-driven phase. Figure 9.8 maps out a global prosperity index using purchasing power parity (PPP) adjusted GDP per capita and growth of real GDP per capita for the period 1998–2007.

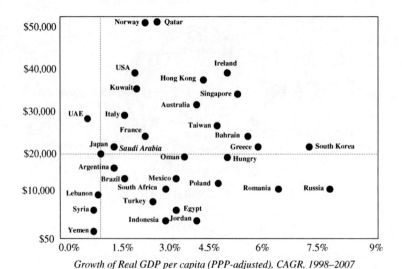

Fig. 9.8 Global prosperity performance growth of real GDP per capita adjusted in PPP terms (1998–2007) (Source: EIU (2008), Porter (2010))

From Fig. 9.8, we note that Saudi Arabia, although doing better than most Arab and other developing countries in terms of PPP adjusted GDP per capita growth, did not outperform the other GCC member states and was slightly ahead of Oman. From the GCC block, Qatar was the highest at $73,000 ahead of the USA and on par with Norway, while Saudi average was around $22,000.

Reducing Competitiveness Obstacles

Despite the progress noted above, obstacles still remain in achieving higher competitiveness levels for the Kingdom. These can be measured in the manner by which businesses operate and the relative ease of doing business and by asking respondents to list the factors they feel the most problematic for doing business. Both issues are illustrated in Figs. 9.9 and 9.10.

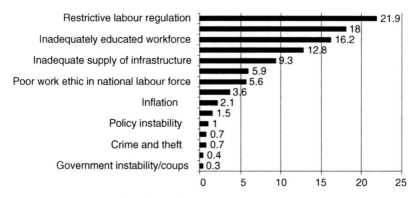

Fig. 9.9 The most problematic factors for doing business: Saudi respondents (2009). Note: From a list of 15 factors, respondents were asked to select the five most problematic for doing business in their country/economy and to rank them between 1 (most problematic) and 5 (least problematic). The bars in the figure show the responses weighted according to their rankings (Source: Global Economic Forum (2009))

According to respondents, Fig. 9.9 indicates that most agree that Saudi competitiveness is hampered by restrictive labour regulations, followed by access to financing. The labour issue will be covered in a later chapter, but the high negative response concerning restrictive financing reflects the generally tighter credit terms imposed by Saudi banks in general following the 2007–2009 global financial crisis as discussed in a previous chapter. An inadequately educated labour force was also listed as a high impediment, as well as inefficient government bureaucracy, despite the higher positive rating given by the Global Economic Forum survey to Saudi Arabia for institution building examined earlier in Fig. 9.7(a). Analysis of Fig. 9.10 seems to confirm some of the respondents' unfavourable findings in obtaining credit, but employing workers in general seems to get a higher positive rating.

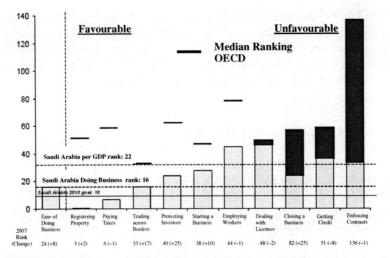

Fig. 9.10 Saudi Arabia ease of doing business (2008) (Source: World Bank Report: Doing Business (2008))

Figure 9.10 sets out the OECD median ranking for most favourable ease of doing business benchmarking, and the Saudi ranking changes over the period 2007 and 2008. The most positive changes have occurred in trading across borders, protection of investors, starting a business and closing a business as well as general ease of doing business. All these factors had been targeted by SAGIA as discussed before, and seem to demonstrate the relative success of that government organization in reducing bureaucracy. The factors which saw unfavourable rankings were in employing workers, dealing with licences, getting credit and enforcing contracts. All these factors involved government legislation and laws and lay outside the direct control of institutions such as SAGIA, but within legislative decision-making bodies. As discussed in Chapter 2, there has been some movement towards legislative and legal reforms, but more is needed if Saudi Arabia aspires to reach OECD levels.

Saudi Arabia's Competitive Advantages

Saudi Arabia needs to adopt a new export promotion strategy that focuses on efficiency and competitiveness and which encompasses both oil- and non-oil-related products (Nojaidi, 2002, Richard, 2002). Broad macroeconomic data such as export volumes or values do not reflect individual sectors' export performance based on competitive efficiencies. The *Arab Competitiveness Report of 2008* has conducted intensive studies in this area and has ranked 16 countries of the Arab world amongst 100 exporting countries based on their Trade Performance Index (TPI). The composite rankings of the TPI were supposed to capture many dimensions of export performance for various commodities based on competitiveness and efficiency.

Trade Performance Indexes were classified as *current TPI* and *change TPI* and countries were ranked from 1 (the most efficient and competitive) to 100 (the least efficient and competitive).

The findings of the report established that the Kingdom has five sectors in which it competes with mixed results on the international level, including oil and gas, plastic, chemical products and processed foods. Figure 9.11 sets out these areas of dominant Saudi export portfolios.

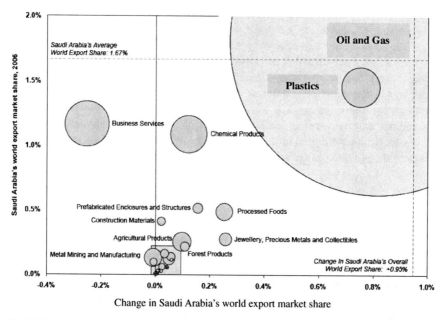

Fig. 9.11 Saudi Arabia's "Champion" export cluster portfolios (Source: UNCTAD, IMF, Global Economic Forum, Porter 2010) (1998–2006)

Figure 9.11 illustrates the overwhelming dominance of the oil and gas sector and the increase in market share in this cluster but also the decrease in Saudi business services over the period 1998–2006.

Trading based on advantages in resources will lead to depletion of such resources in the long run and make a country hostage to fluctuations in world commodity prices. What should the strategy be then? In practice, it is not necessary to move away from resource-based exports completely, but it is important to build alternatives, especially high-value-added export alternatives. In order to achieve a higher level of sustainable growth, Saudi Arabia needs to shift from trading on resource-based advantages towards trades based on products, skills, processes, quality and innovation. This requires improved productivity, upgrading existing technology and increasing the efficiency of the use and allocation of resources. It is only in this manner that countries like Saudi Arabia can meet the challenges of gaining an increasing share of a growing world export market.

Foreign Sector Trade Development

The Kingdom is conscious of the wealth-generating effect of export promotion; the world has observed the remarkable growth in the GDP of the so-called "Asian Tiger" economies, as well as that of China in more recent years. Studies have indicated that the traditional development strategies of import substitution that were adopted by many developing countries in the post-Second World War period have been ineffective for long-term sustained economic growth (World Bank, 1993, Solow, 1970, Romer, 1994). A shift towards export-led growth has taken place, with many developing countries seeking to establish supremacy over competitors in niche areas, based on productivity and efficiency. Saudi exporters face both opportunities and challenges, evidence of which is the broad range of products exported by the Saudi Arabian Basic Industries Corporation (SABIC).

However, there are some areas of institutional support that are needed to make Saudi exports more competitive, as in the final analysis it is firms that compete, and not nations, and the focus of the Kingdom should be to assist individual exporters as they tackle concrete problems of market entry, while protecting them from unfair competition and dumping practices. This support can take different forms:

Direct Assistance for Exporting Firms

As exporting is generally new to the Saudi Arabian private sector, exporters might require assistance at each stage of the export process, including customer and market identification, product development and client adaptation, pilot testing in the target market and finally developing a detailed marketing strategy. Further stages involve process development, productivity and quality improvement, production launch and sales. There needs to be follow-up performance analysis and modification of the marketing strategy.

Very few Saudi private sector companies have carried out all or some of the above processes. Instead, they have concentrated on the domestic market, securing sales through "net-back" discounts and special offers. It was left to the government-owned and joint venture companies in the petrochemical sector, along with well-established and well managed Saudi private sector companies, to enter the export market. There have been some notable private sector successes in this field. Table 9.10 lists some selected private sector companies operating in the export sector that have also established an international presence.

Table 9.10 highlights the major emphasis on food products by Saudi exporters with the majority of companies concentrating on the nearby Gulf Cooperation Council (GCC) markets due to shorter communication routes, logistics and GCC trade harmonization policies. A few companies such as Al Zamil, Amiantit and Fakieh have ventured into Europe, Asia and North America. On the whole, Saudi exporting experience has been confined to tried and well-tested regional markets.

Table 9.10 Selected prime Saudi private sector exporting companies

Group	Product range	International presence
Al Babtain	Household appliances	No
Amiantit	Pipes, storage tanks	Yes
Halawani	Food products	No
Al-Qahtani Pipes	Coated pipes, equipment	Yes
Savola Snack Food Co.	Snacks, general confectionary	No
Abdulateef Jameel	Car accessories	Yes
Al Zamil	Air conditioners, steel fabrication, aluminium, plastics	Yes
Arasco	Fertilizers, feedstock	No
Abdulhadi Qahtani Co.	Oilfield equipments, machinery	No
Al Marai	Dairy products	No
Al Rajhi	Foodstuffs, juices, shrimps	No
Bahrawi	Cosmetics, perfumes, food	No
Al Jomaih	Beverages, cans	No
Nissah	Bottled water	No
Jeraisy	Smart cards, PC equipment	Yes
Fakieh	Poultry, fast food	Yes
Hail Agriculture Dev. Co.	Food product	No
Saudi Cement Co.	Cement	No
Saudi Cable Co.	Cables, electrical wires	Yes
Fitaihi	Jewellery, perfumes	Yes
Savola Group	Ghee, edible oils, foodstuff	Yes

Source: Top 1000 Saudi Companies, 6th Edition, 2000–2001, IIT Publishing, Khobar

Assist All Sizes of Firms to Export

Most of the Saudi company names listed in Table 9.10 belong to the top-tier family businesses, often in the top 100 companies of the Kingdom. For exports to succeed at the national level, neither size nor ownership should be criteria. The Saudi government should be able to assist those smaller companies that are willing to help themselves enter the export market, if they are willing to take the associated risks. Resources of like-minded smaller companies could be pooled to share export risks and the government could be more generous in providing financial support in the form of larger export guarantee insurance to this sector.

Establish Institutional Development Programmes

An export development agency will be able to develop strategy and coordinate amongst members, besides having a powerful "lobbying" voice to discuss specific export issues of concern with the government.

Develop International Trade in Services

During the past two decades, the provision of services has become the major economic activity of many countries in the world. Within the region, the economies of Bahrain and Dubai in the United Arab Emirates have shifted towards international and domestic services, whether in the transportation of goods and people, banking and insurance services, communications, leisure industry or entertainment. Other economies have established expertise in legal services, education and health. For Saudi Arabia, the service sector accounted for around 28.0% of GDP in 2008 (SAMA). The Saudi government has begun to make some serious plans to expand its domestic tourism industry so as to attract year-round visitors to the holy Muslim sites of *Makkah* and *Madinah* and to other tourist areas of interest. While the overall Saudi GDP percentage of services is lower than that of the USA, which stood at around 75% in 2001, in Saudi Arabia the service sector accounted for 78% of the labour force compared to 71% for the USA. If in the future the provision of services becomes a more "knowledge-based" activity, with information and ideas as the most precious resources, the Kingdom would have to adapt accordingly if it is not to be left behind in this sector (Zarouk, 2002).

Adopt Best Practices

Nations do not need to "reinvent the wheel" as there are many best practice models available around the world to draw upon and to adapt to domestic conditions. Saudi Arabia can benefit from the experiences of those countries that have transformed themselves to outward-looking, export-oriented economies, and can choose models that best suit the Kingdom's current human, technological and capital resources. The aim is to give Saudi exporters some comparative advantage over competitors by adapting selected "best practices." Table 9.11 outlines a best practice export promotion programme for Saudi Arabia that draws upon the experiences and practices adopted by countries such as Malaysia, Ireland, Singapore, India and Tunisia (Khemani, 2002). Table 9.11 also highlights the current Saudi status in implementing such a proposed programme. In some areas the government has taken action, especially in funding and lead agency assistance, but so far the assistance has not been wide enough to make a significant impact.

The promotion of Saudi exports and opening of new markets can be very beneficial to Saudi Arabia in terms of revenue diversification and job creation. According to reports, it estimates that every SR 1 billion of new exports will generate some 25,000 new jobs (Saudi Commerce and Economic Review, February 2003). In the final analysis, however, government support is needed not only to ensure market access and market development but also to create an integrated trade support programme that deals with the central issue of export *competitiveness*. Export promotion should not be conceived in isolation. The creation of new supervisory institutions, however good, cannot alone bring about needed institutional change

Table 9.11 Saudi Arabia: An export promotion programme model

Programme	Required action	Current status
Marketing	Market promotion, strategies, internet marketing, market development	Internet marketing is still not fully developed; market research tends to be product-driven rather than customer-driven
Technological	Quality assurance, product and technology development, skills development, information technology, tooling, productivity	Uneven quality assurance and internal R&D development, productivity low
Investment and working capital	Export credits and guarantees, bonded warehouses, marketing finance, seed capital, R&D finance/incentives, export insurance cover	Available but limited in amount and only recently extended to non-oil exports. Limited bonded warehouses, limited R&D finance from commercial banks and government
Collective promotion programmes	Research, marketing and trade missions, group promotional programmes, comprehensive system of marketing, information collection, global sourcing	Effected through the regional chambers of commerce and industry, some national trade missions; comprehensive database at national level not yet developed, global sourcing on a pooled basis
Funding and cost sharing	Government funds, 50% cost sharing	Saudi export credit programme exists, using the Saudi Fund for Development (SFD)
Lead agencies	Export promotion authority; export centres, industry associations and insurance corporation	Export non-payment risk coverage exists through SFD using the French COFACE as partner; amounts are limited; no national insurance corporation

in an export climate that involves all organizational sectors of society: universities, research institutes and government departments. There is a need for dedicated and qualified personnel, databases and an entrepreneurial spirit to venture into new markets.

Conclusion

Saudi Arabia is a country with an unusually large foreign sector and a particular reliance on exports from a narrow commodity base to fund its developments needs. The composition and origins of its international trade have changed over the past three decades and Saudi Arabia today stands on the eve of new trade relationships.

The accession to the World Trade Organization by Saudi Arabia, preceded by bilateral trade agreements with WTO member states, has created a new set of internal dynamics. There is now a greater sense of urgency to position the Kingdom's trading relations on more competitive terms than ever before.

WTO entry is expected to benefit the Saudi petrochemical industry, whose exports to western European markets in particular have been hit by an imposition of tariffs against Saudi petrochemical products. WTO entry would ensure a fair and level playing field for Saudi exports in this market. Similarly the private sector is also beginning to position itself for greater competition following Saudi accession, despite some reservations from vested interests that saw WTO entry as a threat to their domestic markets.

It is not that Saudi Arabia has limited experience in establishing multilateral trade partnerships. The Gulf Cooperation Council (GCC) has achieved some success in harmonizing the six member countries' trading policies with a reduction in tariffs to 5% in January 2003, and with duty-free access to products originating in the GCC, if 40% of value added is from the GCC region.

It is no wonder that Saudi exporters have tended to concentrate on the GCC market, as we explained earlier, but the size of the GCC market is small compared to the potential economies of scale for Saudi exports to larger non-GCC markets. The Kingdom is also a member of the *Greater Arab Free Trade Area* (GAFTA), which extends from the Gulf to North Africa and includes 18 member states. It was established in 1997 with the objective of eliminating all tariffs and taxes but with specific items exempt from tariff reduction in health, security and religious areas.

Summary of Key Points

- *Saudi Arabia is the Arab world's leading exporter and importer and trade plays a vital role in the economic development of the country.*
- *Imports have risen in quantitative terms since the early 1970s, fuelled by oil revenues, but the composition of imports has changed over the past decades. Imports are now more diversified towards consumer goods orientated compared to equipment, machinery and infrastructural demand of the earlier period. Import origins have also begun to change, with China becoming a major trading partner.*
- *Exports are still dominated by oil and oil-related products which account for around 90% of total exports despite attempts at export diversification. Foodstuffs and chemical products are the major non-oil exports followed by base metals and electrical equipment.*
- *Saudi Arabia, in common with other exporting nations, is focusing on efficiency and competitive advantage for its exported products.*
- *Saudi Arabia has made significant strides in global ranking in areas such as ease of doing business and global competitiveness, but obstacles still remain in areas such as labour issues and access to finance by the private sector.*

- *Saudi Arabia is moving from being a factor-driven (resource-based) economy towards an efficiency-driven economy.*
- *Foreign sector trade development could benefit from several institutional programmes. These include direct assistance for exporting firms, establishment of institutional development programmes through an export development agency, development of international trade in services sector and adoption of best practices.*

Chapter 10
Saudi Arabia and the WTO

*The world is like a board with holes in it, and the square men
have got into round holes, and the round into the square.*

Bishop Berkeley

Learning Outcomes

By the end of this section, you would understand:

- *Globalization and the evolution of the WTO*
- *The key challenges facing Saudi Arabia's economy*
- *The WTO option and the opportunities and threats to Saudi Arabia*
- *Financial globalization as a test case for world economic integration*
- *Meeting globalization challenges*
- *Saudi Arabia's legal structure and WTO compliance*

Key Challenges

In the new millennium, the Kingdom of Saudi Arabia has set itself the objective of reducing the economy's vulnerability and heavy dependence on oil market fortunes, and has opted for decentralized, private market-based economic activities (Auty, 2001). The Kingdom aims to achieve this through different approaches. A strategic decision was made by the Kingdom to join the World Trade Organization (WTO) to enable a bigger Saudi world market share and this was achieved in December 2005. Other strategic options which will be examined in the following chapter involved the initiation of domestic privatization programmes of core government services and using foreign direct investment (FDI) to foster technology transfer and domestic economic stimulus (Najem and Hetherington, 2003).

M.A. Ramady, *The Saudi Arabian Economy*, DOI 10.1007/978-1-4419-5987-4_10,
© Springer Science+Business Media, LLC 2010

Globalization: The Theoretical Arguments

While there is no universally agreed definition of globalization, most economists typically use the term to refer to international integration in commodity, capital and labour markets. Over the past hundred years, there have been waves of globalization, with the first wave ending before the commencement of the First World War, and the second major wave beginning after the end of the Second World War and continuing to date. The lesson from history is that globalization has not been a relatively smooth process but has been marked by periods of accelerated integration and sometimes reversals due to emerging political and economic power blocs and conflicting interests. The main forces that have driven global integration have been technological innovations, broad political changes within and between nations and economic policies. In the case of technological innovations, chief among these driving forces of globalization were inventions that improved the speed of transportation and communication and lowered their costs. These included the development of the jet engine, massive investment in road infrastructure around the world and the revolution in information and communication technology. New products such as the microprocessor, the personal computer and the cellular phone have contributed to significant socio-political and economic transformation (UNCTAD, 2009).

Changes in production methods created new tradable products such as petrochemical plastics, or expanded global production in food through the so-called green revolution. The large switch from coal to oil and gas by the major Western industrialized economies since the Second World War was also an important step towards globalization, providing a large and relatively cheap source of energy to power global economic growth and in the process integrating the oil-exporting countries such as Saudi Arabia into the global economy.

The link between political developments and globalization has been far more complex, but the world has gone through cycles of empires, cold war and global crisis, the fall of the Soviet Union and the emergence of the European Union and Far Eastern countries such as China as major powers. A key driver in the above has been economic policy which has resulted in deregulation and the reduction or elimination of restrictions on international trade and financial transactions, although the global financial crisis of 2007/2009 reversed some of the trend and reinstated more government control and ownership in this sector.

Table 10.1 summarizes the major events affecting or influencing globalization.

Before the 2007 global financial crisis, the trend had been for currencies to become convertible and balance of payments capital controls to be relaxed. In effect, for many years after the end of the Second World War, it was currency and payments restrictions rather than tariffs that limited trade the most. The birth of the eurodollar market was a major step towards increasing the availability of international liquidity and promoting cross-border transactions in western Europe. Beginning in the 1970s, many governments deregulated major service industries such as transport and telecommunications. Deregulation involved a range of actions, from removal, reduction and simplification of government restrictions to privatization of state-owned enterprises and to liberalization of these industries so as to increase competition.

Table 10.1 Globalization main events

Time	Economic	Political	Technological
1940s	• Establishment of the Bretton Woods system, a new international monetary system (1944–1971) • Establishment of GATT (1947) entering into force in January 1948 • Soviet Union establishes the Council for Mutual Economic Assistance (CMEA) for economic cooperation among communist countries (1949–1991)	• Foundation of the United Nations (1945) • Launch of the Marshall Plan (1948–1957), a European recovery programme • Founding of the Organization for European Economic Cooperation (1948) • Decolonization starts (1948–1962)	• Expansion of plastics and fibre products • Discovery of large oil fields in the Middle East, especially in Saudi Arabia (1948)
1950s	• Treaty of Rome establishes the European Community (1957). EC and the European Free Trade Association (1959) favour west European integration • Major currencies become convertible (1958–1964)	• Korean war (1950–1953) • Suez crisis (1956) • Decolonization in Africa (15 countries become independent between 1958 and 1962)	• Increased use of oil from the Middle East in Europe and Japan • Increasing usage of jet engines in air transport (1957–1972)
1960s	• Foundation of the Organization of the Petroleum Exporting Countries (OPEC) (1960) • Development of the eurodollar market in London, which contributed to the expansion of international liquidity • Kennedy round, sixth session of the GATT (1964–1969) • Rapid spread of automobiles and highways in the North accelerates demand and shift in fuel consumption (from coal to oil)	• Erection of Berlin Wall (1961) and Cuban missile crisis (1962)	• Integrated circuits become commercially available (1961) • Offshore oil and gas production developed • Green Revolution – transforming agricultural production in developing countries (1960s onwards)
1970s	• Departure from US dollar exchange rate gold standard (1971) • Tokyo round of the GATT (1973–1979) • Rise of Asian newly industrialized countries • China's economic reform (1978)	• 1973 war helps to trigger oil price hike • EU enlargement to nine members (1973)	• First single-chip microprocessor (Intel 4004) is introduced (1971)

Table 10.1   (continued)

Time	Economic	Political	Technological
1980s	• Developing country debt crisis • Mexico starts market reforms and joins the GATT in 1986 • Louvre Accord promotes stabilization of major exchange rates (1987)	• Enlargement of the EU to 12 members • Establishment of the Gulf Cooperation Council (GCC) 1981 • Fall of the Berlin Wall (1989)	• IBM introduces the first personal computer (1981) • Microsoft Windows introduced (1985)
1990s	• Indian economic reforms launched in 1991 • Establishment of the North American Free Trade Agreement (1994) • Asian financial crisis (1997) • Establishment of the WTO (1995) following Uruguay round (1986–1994) • Adoption of the euro by 11 European countries (1999)	• Dissolution of the Soviet Union (1991) leads to the formation of 13 independent states • Maastricht Treaty (formally, the Treaty on European Union) signed (1992)	• Eurotunnel opens in 1994, linking the United Kingdom to continent • The number of mobile phones increases due to the introduction of second-generation (2G) networks using digital technology • Invention of the World Wide Web by Tim Berners-Lee (1989); first website put online in 1991. Number of Internet users rises to 300 million by 2000
2000s	• Dotcom crisis (2001) • China joins WTO (2001) • Saudi Arabia joins WTO (2005) • Global financial crisis 2007/2008	• Enlargement of the EU to 27 members	• Container ships transport more than 70% of the seabome trade in value terms • Number of Internet users rises to 1.8 billion in 2008 • 3G technology introduced

In case of trade, liberalization was pursued multilaterally through successive General Agreement on Tariffs and Trade (GATT) negotiations. Increasingly, bilateral and regional trade agreements became an important aspect of (preferential) trade liberalization as well. However, many countries still undertook trade reforms unilaterally. In the case of developing countries, their early commercial policies had an inward-looking focus. Industrialization through import substitution was the favoured route to economic development. The subsequent shift away from import substitution may be owing partly to the success of a number of Asian newly industrializing countries that adopted an export-led growth strategy, but also partly to the debt crisis in the early 1980s, which exposed the limitations of inward-looking policies.

Benefits and Costs of Trade Liberalization

The integration of any country into the global economy brings benefits and challenges not only to consumers and businesses but also to the public sector, and the debate is fierce from both proponents and opponents of globalization. For some countries with few endowed natural resources, tariff reductions are an element of trade liberalization which might be of particular concern due to the negative impact on lower tax revenues. For Saudi Arabia this issue was not a particular concern, as custom duties were a very small element in the total Saudi government budgetary revenues discussed in earlier chapters. For many developing countries though, this matters, as it has been estimated by the WTO that in the mid-1990s tariff revenues exceeded 30% of the government's total tax revenue in more than 25 developing countries, compared with around 2% for high-income developed economies (Devarajan et al., 1999).

It is the adjustment period and costs associated with trade liberalization that cause some uncertainty. There will always be industries in which foreign competitors are more efficient than domestic producers and when import barriers on the products of those industries are lowered, the foreign producers will be able to attract domestic consumers with lower prices. This could lead to economic losses, job losses and perhaps company closures in the domestic markets. The overall economy suffers if the newly liberalized economy does not compensate for losses by expanding into new growth dynamic industries and sectors, especially in knowledge based sectors (Burtless et al., 1998). We shall examine the potential "losers" and "gainers" from Saudi WTO accession later on in this chapter.

The World Trade Organization

The World Trade Organization (WTO) is the only international body dealing with the *rules of trade* between nations. At the heart of the WTO are the agreements that are negotiated and signed upon accession to the WTO by member countries. These documents and agreements are the binding legal ground rules for international commerce and the reference point for trade dispute resolutions. There is sometimes confusion about who "owns" the WTO. Unlike other multilateral organizations such as the IMF or World Bank, the WTO is run by its member governments and all major decisions are made by the membership as a whole, either by each country's ministers (who meet at least once every 2 years) or by trade officials and WTO representatives (who meet regularly at the WTO headquarters in Geneva). Decisions are normally taken by consensus. In the WTO, power is not delegated to a board of directors unlike the World Bank or IMF, and the bureaucracy has no influence over an individual country's policies. Figure 10.1 illustrates the WTO governing structure.

When WTO rules impose discipline on countries' policies, that is generally the outcome of negotiations among WTO members and such rules are only enforced by the members themselves under agreed procedures that they have negotiated.

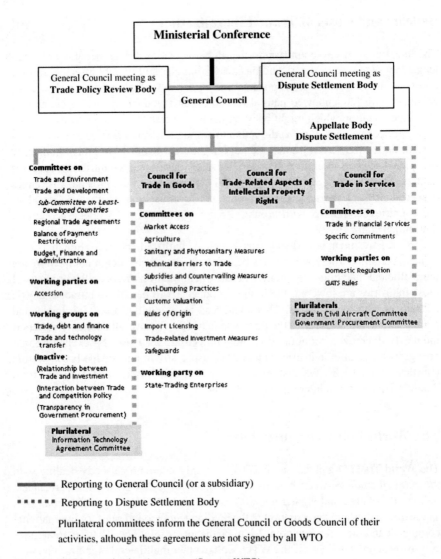

Fig. 10.1 WTO organizational structure (Source: WTO)

Sometimes enforcement by the WTO of its agreements produces the threat of sanctions, but these sanctions are imposed by the member countries and not the WTO as an organization. As Fig. 10.1 illustrates, the WTO has grown to a large size with many specialized committees and policy reviews, and reaching decisions by consensus among the 153 members as of 2010 can be difficult, leading to calls for the creation of a smaller executive body. For the foreseeable future the WTO will remain as a member-driven and consensus-based organization.

According to the WTO's basic operating principles, stated as follows, the trading system should be

- *Without discrimination* – a country should not discriminate between its trading partners (they are all, equally, granted "*most-favoured-nation*" or MFN status), and it should not discriminate between its own and foreign products, services or nationals (they are given "*national treatment*"). Each member treats all the other members equally as "most-favoured" trading partners. If a country improves the benefits that it gives to one trading partner, it has to give the same "best" treatment to all the other WTO members so that they all remain "most favoured."

  MFN is so important that it is the first article of the *General Agreement on Tariffs and Trade* (GATT), which governs trade in goods. MFN is also a priority in the *General Agreement on Trade in Services* (GATS) (Article 2) and the *Agreement on Trade-Related Aspects of Intellectual Property Rights* (TRIPS) (Article 4), although in each agreement the principle is handled slightly differently. Together, those three agreements cover all three main areas of trade handled by the WTO.

  Some exceptions are allowed. For example, countries within a region can set up a free trade agreement that does not apply to goods from outside the group. Or a country can raise barriers against products from specific countries that are considered to be traded unfairly. And in services, countries are allowed, in limited circumstances, to discriminate. But the agreements only permit these exceptions under strict conditions. In general, MFN means that every time a country lowers a trade barrier or opens up a market, it has to do so for the same goods or services from all its trading partners – whether rich or poor, weak or strong.
- *Freer* – with barriers coming down through negotiation.
- *Predictable* – foreign companies, investors and governments should be confident that trade barriers (including tariffs, non-tariff barriers and other measures) should not be raised arbitrarily, and more tariff rates and market-opening commitments are "bound" by the WTO.
- *More competitive* – by discouraging "*unfair*" practices such as export subsidies and dumping products at below cost to gain market share.
- *More beneficial for less developed countries* – by giving them more time to adjust, greater flexibility and special privileges.

Historical Overview of GATT and WTO

The WTO provides the institutional and legal foundation for the new multilateral trading system that came into being on 1 January 1995. But despite its short history, the WTO had a predecessor the General Agreement on Tariffs and Trade (GATT). GATT evolved from 1948 to 1994 through a series of trade rounds (Havana, Annecy,

Table 10.2   The GATT trade rounds

Year	Place	Subjects covered	Countries
1948	Havana	Tariffs	23
1949	Annecy, France	Tariffs	13
1951	Torquay, UK	Tariffs	38
1956	Geneva	Tariffs	26
1960–1961	Geneva (Dillon)	Tariffs	26
1964–1967	Geneva (Kennedy)	Tariffs and anti-dumping	62
1973–1979	Geneva (Tokyo)	Tariff and non-tariff measures, framework agreements	102
1986–1994	Geneva (Uruguay)	Tariffs, non-tariffs, rules, services, intellectual property, dispute settlement, textiles, agriculture, creation of WTO	123
1994–to date	Doha round	All plus financial services	147

Source: WTO

Torquay, Tokyo, Uruguay, Montreal, Brussels and Marrakesh) with the aim to establish a strong and prosperous multilateral trading system that became more liberal
through these trade negotiations. Table 10.2 summarizes the various GATT trade
rounds and the subjects they covered and the growth of membership in trading
partners.

From Table 10.2 we can note that the establishment of the WTO in 1995 did not
come overnight, but it represented the biggest reform of international trade since
after the Second World War. Up to 1994, the global trading system had operated
under GATT, but by the end of the 1980s the system needed a thorough overhaul
due to the emergence of non-physical trade between nations, especially in services.
GATT tried to take such changes into account as exemplified by the "Kennedy
round," which brought anti-dumping issues, and the "Tokyo round," which tried
to tackle non-tariff barriers such as quotas. The last completed round, the so-called
"Uruguay round," was the most extensive and tried to tackle a wide range of issues,
including intellectual property rights (IPR) and dispute settlement services, and led
to the creation of the WTO. Figure 10.2 summarizes in a nutshell the basic structure
of the WTO agreements.

As illustrated from Fig. 10.2, the basic principles have been expanded to include
intellectual property rights and trade in services, and ensuring that market access
commitments are adhered to by members.

Even before the formal establishment of the WTO in 1995, there were cracks
appearing in the GATT pillars. One key issue was regionalism or "regional
integration agreements" (RIAs) or trading blocs. There were many reasons why
RIAs were formed. The collapse of the Soviet Union led to many ex-Soviet umbrella
states to seek RIAs with the European Economic Commission (EEC). The USA led
its own regionalism bloc in its hemisphere by forming the North American Free
Trade Association (NAFTA), and Asian countries followed suit by the formation
of Association of Southeast Asian Nations (ASEAN). Not to be outdone, the Arab

	Goods	Services	Intellectual Property	Disputes
Basic principles	GATT (General Agreement on Tariffs and Trade)	GATS (General Agreement on Trade in Services)	TRIPS (Trade-Related Aspects of Intellectual Property Rights)	Dispute settlement
Additional details	Other goods agreements and annexes	Services annexes		
Market access commitment	Countries' schedule of commitments	Countries schedule of commitments (and most-favoured-nation exemptions)		

Fig. 10.2 Structure of WTO agreement areas (Source: WTO)

Gulf countries formed the Gulf Cooperation Council (GCC), while Africans formed the SADC or Southern Africa Development Community.

The reasons were many for such regional groupings, ranging from "like-minded" governments getting together to implement their own trade accession on a faster pace, to seeing RIAs as a mechanism for domestic policy reforms and to signal such commitment to domestic and international investors. Sometimes RIAs drive foreign policy and national security concerns and the GCC is one such RIA. In this scenario, some regional problems and issues which are shared by a few countries and neighbours can be better resolved on a smaller regional, as opposed to a larger multilateral, basis.

As discussed earlier, accession negotiation to join the WTO needs the consensus of all the existing members and can be time-consuming. An RIA involves fewer countries than a multilateral trade agreement and therefore is much easier to achieve. Many RIAs – as illustrated by those from Americas, Asia, Africa or the GCC – involve similar countries with income or endowment or resource levels and they can introduce trade agreements that suit their own particular circumstances.

There are drawbacks however with RIAS, as they could be detrimental by inducing a shift away from the most efficient non-member supplier to a higher-cost regional member and thus reduce international trade flows. There is also the growth of political economy lobby groupings that try to maintain the external protection of RIAs, and consumer interests might be harder to defend in an RIA whereas producer interests are more likely to be strengthened in regional organizations.

Unlike current WTO rules, participation in an RIA is an option that is allowed, as also under GATT. Although to some conditions multilateral disciplinary action is not enforced and multilateral surveillance is limited, the WTO secretariat has no mandate to monitor the trade value or term-of-trade effects of RIAs.

In conclusion, RIAs may embody many good practices and some may go beyond WTO trade agreement requirements in terms of liberalizing market, with the European Union (EU) being a good example. Within the EU there are no tariffs, no safeguard mechanisms, but full binding of policies. However, this only applies to EU member states. RIAs then represent both a challenge and an opportunity for the WTO-based multilateral system, but some RIA member countries use them as an "experimental laboratory" for cooperation on issues not yet resolved by multilateral trade agreements. The challenge arising from RIAs is to control the discrimination that is inherent in such preferential regional trade agreements.

What Next for the WTO?

Since its establishment in 1995, the WTO has been involved in more intensive global reform of its agenda under the so-called "Doha round," which started in Doha, Qatar, in 2001 with the aim of removing trade barriers and subsidies, particularly in agriculture, by 2013. This has since failed to achieve agreement in several rounds of talks which collapsed in 2008 in the face of resistance from India, China, Brazil and other major agricultural countries who wanted more measures to protect their own vulnerable agricultural industries from a flood of cheaper European and U.S. exporters, and before opening up their own markets to services from these advanced economies. To revitalize the talks, a so-called 19 member Cairns Group was established, whose members account for 25% of the world's agricultural trade, but to date no new progress has been made, and the matter was not assisted when both the European Union and the USA reintroduced dairy export subsidies, further alienating countries such as India and Brazil.

Agriculture has become the most important and controversial issue. The first proposal in Qatar, in 2001, called for the end agreement to commit to substantial improvements in market access, reductions (and ultimate elimination) of all forms of export subsidies and substantial reductions in trade-distorting support.

The United States is being asked by the European Union (EU) and the developing countries, led by Brazil and India, to make a more generous offer for reducing trade-distorting domestic support for agriculture. The United States is insisting that the EU and the developing countries agree to make more substantial reductions in tariffs and to limit the number of import-sensitive and special products that would be exempt from cuts. *Import-sensitive products* are of most concern to developed countries like the European Union, while developing countries are concerned with special products – those exempt from both tariff cuts and subsidy reductions because of development, food security or livelihood considerations.

Given also the rise in global agricultural prices during 2008/2009, most countries feel that food security is now a critical issue and it will be some time before an agreement on agriculture will be reached between developed and developing countries in this sector.

Saudi Arabia's WTO Accession: A Long and Hard Road

The Kingdom made a strategic decision to enter the WTO given its prime trading position in the world as the largest oil exporter, the 22nd largest importer and the largest economy in the Middle East. Saudi Arabia was a true global trade power. On 11 December 2005, the Kingdom acceded to the WTO and became the 149th member after over 12 years of on–off negotiations. In 2010, only Russia was the last remaining world economic power to remain outside the WTO, along with Belarus, Kazakhstan and some smaller nations.

To become a member of the WTO, Saudi Arabia had to make major commitments on several trading issues and domestic reforms, as WTO accession carries with it both opportunities and threats to countries that are not prepared. Entry required transformation of existing domestic market structures into more competitive systems to enable the Kingdom to comply with the "global rules" of the game. Saudi Arabia made commitment to reduce tariffs, open the services sectors of the economy to greater foreign participation and, above all, implement all WTO rules upon membership without recourse to transition periods, unlike those granted to other developing countries. This meant that when Saudi Arabia became a member, it committed immediately to the following steps:

- Reducing import tariffs from around 15 to 7% levels, with further decreases in the future, with only a few exceptions
- "Binding" tariff levels on individual products to a guaranteed ceiling beyond which they cannot be increased
- Phasing out government subsidies to the private sector and agriculture
- Applying non-discriminatory treatment to the goods and services of other WTO members
- Enforcing intellectual property rights
- Guaranteeing "predictable and growing" access to the Kingdom's financial markets
- Allowing majority foreign ownership of investment projects
- Treating foreign and local investors equally (equal tax treatment, removal of local sponsorship agents or "*wakeels*," allowing foreigners to own real estate)
- Opening up the services sectors such as banking, legal, insurance and capital markets to greater foreign participation

The Saudi government indicated that it will also take a phased approach to the following issues:

- Establishing new trademark and intellectual property laws
- Removing technical barriers to trade by easing travel visa requirements
- Signing the Information Technology Agreement and phasing in tariff-free trade in information technology equipment
- Phasing in the Basic Telecommunications Agreement to allow competition in telecommunications services

- Changing competition laws to provide anti-trust protection and consumer protection in accordance with WTO rules

Before WTO accession in 2005, the Kingdom carried out an enormous amount of preparatory groundwork that involved the following:

- Provided 94 basic laws, regulations and decrees (7,000 pages of documents)
- Had 13 working party meetings for clarifications and Saudi WTO commitments
- Engaged in 314 rounds of bilateral market access negotiations
- Replied to 3,400 questions from WTO committees on its trade regime
- Signed 38 bilateral agreements prior to WTO accession with key countries, including the USA in 2005
- Approved 42 new regulations domestically, in conformity with WTO rules

Prior to WTO accession, there had been some disquiet within some sections of the business community and the general public on what the accession will bring for some key issues, but in the final accession agreement the Kingdom was successful in the following safeguards:

- It does not require the importation of religiously banned or *haram* products such as pork, alcohol or pornographic material into Saudi Arabia.

Essentially, other issues arising under the *Shariah* or Islamic ruling were also recognized by the WTO such as Saudi Arabia's continuing right for Saudi businesses to continue paying their *zakat* tax obligations, and as a WTO member Saudi Arabia was at liberty to maintain a differential income tax scheme for foreign and domestic businesses (Bhala, 2004). Saudi Arabia also successfully argued that it will continue to apply a voluntary non-trade regime with Israel and the latter has accepted its legal inability to combat a voluntary, private sector boycott of trade relations.

What the final WTO agreements also did not cover was any requirement to changes to Saudi Arabia's *Saudization* policies, human rights issues or weakening of Saudi product standards or food safety standards, nor did they require the Kingdom to charge higher domestic prices for energy and petrochemical feedstock – a major concern for Saudi private sector investors in this sector. The WTO agreements also agreed that only GCC citizens can invest directly in Saudi real estate and that domestic companies continue to use the loan subsidies of the specialized Saudi government credit lending institutions such as the Saudi Industrial Development Fund (SIDF), Real Estate Development Fund (REDF) or the Public Investment Fund (PIF).

In terms of benefits to the Kingdom, WTO accession was deemed to bring about the following strategic benefits:

- Protects the Kingdom from discriminatory trade policies of other nations
- Involves Saudi Arabia in settlement procedures to resolve trade disputes through a formal WTO process

- Saudi Arabia was no longer subject to anti-dumping practices or countervailing duties except within WTO guidelines
- Saudi exports to WTO members will be granted most-favoured-nation (MFN) status
- WTO membership will accelerate privatization and domestic economic reforms and make Saudi Arabia a more attractive destination for foreign direct investment
- WTO membership could also institute greater domestic efficiency and cost-cutting measures in the economy

However, the impact of globalization can be viewed from short- and long-term perspectives. Table 10.3 sets out a brief summary of the potential impact of globalization on the Saudi economy, based on field research for different Saudi business sectors carried out by the author.

Table 10.3 indicates a mixed score sheet of positives and negatives. As far as the private sector was concerned, their major worries centred on the loss of export markets. Of even greater significance was the loss of the lucrative and discriminatory government contracts, for which only Saudi companies could bid, resulting in the institutionalization of local industrial inefficiencies. Some Saudi service and manufacturing enterprises were designed and set up to function in a secure environment protected by high tariffs and monopoly agency agreements.

Having to operate under WTO rules might put them out of business, as opening up the economy to foreign multinationals and imports will threaten profit margins and the monopoly of commercial agencies. The insistence of the industrialized countries on fully implementing these changes was one of the prime causes for failure of the Cancun 2003 WTO talks.

The WTO Agreements: Implications for Saudi Industry

The concerns of some sections of Saudi business about the potential negative impact of globalization on their sectors are not misplaced. Table 10.4 examines the potential impact of globalization on selected key Saudi industries against the various formal commitment agreements that Saudi Arabia signed upon WTO accession. The analysis indicates that few Saudi industries would be able to withstand long-term international competitive pressures following the Kingdom's WTO accession.

Table 10.4 illustrates the whole range of complex agreements that the Kingdom had to sign on accession to the WTO in 2005. Some of these commitments need to be examined further.

The manner by which some trade in goods takes place changed after WTO accession. One aspect related to what was termed "importers of record," whereby foreign companies could now import into the Kingdom without having a commercial registration or investment presence in Saudi Arabia. As such, foreign companies could theoretically import goods into a Saudi port and notify their Saudi distributors that the products are available at point of import, but not yet cleared of customs, and sell these products. Such type of "importers of record" could affect smaller

Table 10.3 Impact of globalization on Saudi Arabian economy

Impact	Short-term impact	Long-term impact
Positive	• Lower-priced imported inputs • Higher multinational investment in local industry with implementation of international patent laws	• Shift from exporting primary products to exporting value-added industrial products • Local firms' restructuring • Formation of international strategic alliances with brand name manufacturers • Development of specialized expertise in range of products • Higher multinational investment in local industry with implementation of international patent laws • Wider variety of technology transfers
Negative	• Encouraging more imports to Saudi Arabia, with balance of payment implications • Weaker local producers under competitive strain • Govt. procurement policy giving local priority will be scrapped, making some local firms unable to effectively compete against foreign competition • Export sales may not go up due to quality considerations • Growth in some sectors could slow down, with unemployment consideration • Implementation of international patent laws will have impact on certain sectors, such as pharmaceuticals and chemicals • Less efficient service providers in insurance, banking and telecommunications will be negatively affected by competition	• Questions about the ability of some Saudi industries to meet modernization challenges and adjustment costs • Potential structural unemployment • Exit of some industries due to reduction of subsidies, subsidized loans and tariff protection • Foreign ownership of certain strategically deemed sectors (e.g. communications)

Source: Author's survey, Eastern Province Chamber of Commerce, 2006

Saudi licensed distributors and existing commercial agents for similar products. The impact on smaller Saudi importing companies dealing with foreign agencies could be significant, as upon its accession, Saudi Arabia agreed that minimum capitalization requirements and commercial registration were *not* necessary to become an "importer of record" or to *re-export* from Saudi Arabia. Relevant laws, regulations and requirements would permit foreign firms *not resident* in the KSA and wishing to be importers of record to engage in these activities *without limitation on equity or requirement to invest in* Saudi Arabia. The Kingdom, however, maintains the right

Table 10.4 Saudi Arabia's WTO agreements and potential impact on economic sectors

Sector	Agreements	Impact on Saudi Arabia
(A) Agriculture	■ Saudi Arabia will "bind" *over 90% of all agricultural tariffs at 15% or lower*. Although some reductions are implemented over 5 years, the majority of bound rate commitments will be in effect *upon accession* ■ Approximately 75% of agricultural exports to KSA will have access at the low rates (corn, rice, barley, corn oil, soybean meal, almonds, apples, raisins, cheese, potato chips, frozen fries, bakery goods and processed foods) ■ *After implementation*, the average bound goods will be 7% tariffs	■ *Major* impact on Saudi agricultural/dairy industry ■ Subsidies range from 30% cash subsidy on poultry equipment, plus SR 160 per ton on imported feedstock equipment, plus SR 160 per ton on imported feedstock ■ 20% custom duties exist on agricultural imports ■ Edible oil industry will face less pressure as it is fairly cost-efficient and export-orientated in some areas. There are 11 operating units with capacity of around 380,000 tons. Current market demand around 300,000 tons. Industry investment around SR 500 million ■ Dairy industry enjoys up to 30% of total cost subsidies and SIDF loans. An SR 12 billion industry with domestic demand around 1.4 million tons p.a. 61 operating units employing 8,000 workers
(B) Sanitary and phytosanitary measures	■ Saudi Arabia is committed to applying science-based sanitary and phytosanitary standards to all agricultural goods, including grains, meats and fruits/vegetables ■ Saudi Arabia will eliminate its prohibition on importing beef and other meat products from animals treated with growth-promoting hormones ■ Saudi Arabia will facilitate U.S. meat and poultry exports by recognizing an official USDA Food Safety and Inspection Service Export Certificate	■ Could cause concern amongst Saudi consumers relating to hormone-treated products ■ Saudi poultry industry is around SR 6 billion with two companies having 50% of the market. Another 450 companies operating in this sector could be damaged ■ Industry is subsidized (30% cash subsidy on poultry equipment, plus SR 160 per ton on imported feedstocks) 20% custom duties

Table 10.4 (continued)

Sector	Agreements	Impact on Saudi Arabia
(C) Industrial goods market access	■ General Agreement on Tariffs and Trade (GATT). KSA will take on the obligations of GATT 1994 plus: ■ Tariff Reductions: Cuts in Saudi tariffs on industrial goods. Some reductions are implemented over 5 years; the majority are in effect upon accession. Saudi Arabia will bind its tariffs on over three fourths of exports of industrial goods at an average rate of 3.2%, many other key exports at less *Specifically* ■ Participation in the Information Technology Agreement with elimination on tariffs on computers, semiconductors and other information technology products. These to be eliminated by 1 Jan 2008. ■ Eliminate all tariffs on pharmaceuticals and trade in civil aircraft upon accession ■ Saudi Arabia will implement the tariff rates required by the WTO's chemical tariff harmonization agreement. This covers nearly 1,100 products and harmonization will be in effect for the vast majority of these on accession ■ For a small number, harmonization will be in two phases with final effect on 1 Jan 2010	■ Those Saudi industries with heavy custom duties protection will suffer (e.g. aluminium – shielded at 20% custom duties; steel and base metals will be affected as protection exists for 116 items out of 740 lines, with 20% custom on imports) ■ There are around 215 projects in steel and base metals, employing around 25,000 workers and investment of SR 8 billion. Annual demand 2.5 million tons. 16 of the Saudi projects are joint ventures. There are 26 aluminium operating units with capacity of 120,000 tons with 4 units producing 95,000 tons. No aluminium smelters yet in Saudi, reliant on imported aluminium imports. The furniture industry is an SR 5 billion market with 65% imported. There are 125 large units operating and 7,000 small units. Tariffs set 12% on imports plus 20% protected each ■ Refrigeration will suffer (SIDF loans at 50%); technologies will be affected given the short period for tariff elimination ■ Furniture industry will suffer (tariffs set at 12% on imports plus 20% on protected items) ■ Pharmaceuticals will be affected. This is an SR 6–8 billion market and growing. However, major producers are Saudi–foreign joint ventures and could assume smooth transition for many ■ Annual demand now around 2.5 million tons for whole GCC with Saudi share growing

Table 10.4 (continued)

Sector	Agreements	Impact on Saudi Arabia
(C) Industrial goods market access	*Removal of non-tariff barriers* ■ Non-tariff barriers will be removed, to allow for free trade in commercially traded information technology products such as cell phones, computers and cameras ■ KSA has agreed to bind all other duties and charges on industrial goods at Zero on accession ■ KSA has also agreed to charge fees for customs and port services on imports based on the *cost of services rendered* and terminate certificate of origin authentication and customs certificates by Saudi consulates ■ KSA committed to remove its export ban on all scrap metals prior to accession and will not apply export duties to these products *Import licensing* ■ Commits to principles of "national treatment" and non-discrimination ■ Import licences not conditioned on performance requirements of any kind, such as local content, export performance, technology transfer or research and development or whether competing domestic suppliers exist	■ Will affect Saudi industries who are receiving discriminatory national treatment in supplying "local content" for government-related projects. The removal of technology transfer and R&D requirements will hit Saudi Arabia's need for such items
(D) TRIPS (Trade-Related Aspects of Intellectual Property Rights)	■ Saudi Arabia fully committed to implement TRIPS upon accession without any transition period ■ Saudi Arabia committed to protecting pharmaceutical and agricultural chemical test data submitted to obtain marketing approval against unfair commercial use for a period of 5 years and will not register a generic form of a pharmaceutical when a patent application is on file	■ No major impact as Saudi Arabia has already established stringent TRIPS regulation and Ministry of Commerce inspections ■ Pharmaceutical and chemical test data are not sufficiently strong domestically to be affected ■ Significant progress made on TRIPS since WTO accession and in 2010 Saudi Arabia removed from USA copyright watch list owing to progress in enforcement of intellectual property rights

Table 10.4 (continued)

Sector	Agreements	Impact on Saudi Arabia
(E) Services market access	*1. Banking and securities* ■ Immediately upon accession, foreign banks will be able to establish direct branches to be regulated on the basis of worldwide capital. Foreign equity can increase from current 40 to 60%. KSA also provided assurances regarding management control ■ Cross-border market access commitments are comparable or superior to those of OECD countries. Foreign firms are afforded non-discriminatory treatments or "national treatment" across all financial services sub-sectors ■ Asset management and financial advisory services may be provided through banks or non-bank financial institutions. Foreign financial institutions will be permitted to provide pension funds supplementary to public pension schemes at the same time that Saudi financial institutions are permitted to do so *2. Insurance* After accession SAMA will issue operating licences to foreign insurance companies as follows: ■ Allow direct branching by foreign insurance providers. Foreign insurance can also establish a cooperative insurance company in KSA with up to 60% equity stake ■ A company may keep 90% of the profits and redistribute 10% to the policyholders ■ Foreign insurance companies will receive national treatment ■ Existing foreign insurance company providers in KSA are allowed to continue operations without disruption and offer new products and services to new and existing customers until April 2008, after which they must convert to either a branch of a foreign insurance company or a Saudi cooperative insurance company	■ Foreign wholly owned bank licences are already granted. Issue is whether Saudi market can absorb more foreign bank entry, but foreign banks can now operate under "cross-border" basis without local presence ■ Pension fund management is a big untapped market and this is where Saudi banks have not developed expertise and could lose market share ■ Large-scale foreign entry into this market forecasted, aided by government regulation to impose mandatory health and car accident insurance ■ The amount of foreign profit repatriation is quite high and not much will be left for domestic recycling or long-term investment

Table 10.4 (continued)

Sector	Agreements	Impact on Saudi Arabia
(E) Services market access	■ Foreign insurance providers may now solicit and sell reinsurance and a number of product lines for large sophisticated customers on a cross-border basis without establishing in KSA	■ Will take away business from Saudi companies, especially for those bidding for mega projects
	3. Telecoms	
	■ Committed to market access without limitation for cross-border supply and consumption abroad	■ Saudi Telecom Company market share will be further eroded and profitability could be dented
	■ By end of 2008, there will be 70% foreign equity ownership allowed	■ Since WTO accession, three other foreign telecom providers have entered the Saudi market
	■ Commitments include basic telecommunication services and value-added telecom services through any means of technology	
	■ KSA to establish an independent regulator and obligations to prevent anti-competitive behaviour by dominant supplier	
	4. Audio-visual services	
	■ KSA commitment for motion picture and home video entertainment distribution services includes video tapes and DVDs, while leaving open the door to new home entertainment technologies in the future	■ Not much impact as this industry is in infancy or non-existent for radio and TV production in private sector, as mostly government-controlled
	■ Commitment for radio and TV production and distribution services covers both the production of radio and TV programmes and their distribution	■ However, there is a domestic CVD/ home video cassette production industry
	5. Energy Services	
	■ Allows for energy services companies to compete on level playing fields in areas of oil and gas exploration and development, pipeline transportation of fuels, management consulting, technical testing and analysis and repair and maintenance of equipment	■ Foreign pipeline transportation could cause current Saudi operators to lose out on "local content" mandated business as well as some Saudi energy services companies, unless they have already established foreign joint ventures or partnerships
		■ Since WTO accession, there has been some major wholly owned foreign company entry in this sector

Table 10.4 (continued)

Sector	Agreements	Impact on Saudi Arabia
(E) Services market access	**6. Express delivery** Unrestricted delivery of documents, parcels, packages and goods and other items through all relevant modes of supply, and guarantee that foreign express delivery service operators will receive treatment no less favourable than that accorded to the postal office	■ Will impact current Saudi sponsors of international brand names (Fed Ex, DHL, etc.) who could now operate independently plus see other names come into the market in the long term, but so far local joint venture agreements operating
	7. Transportation services KSA will open its markets for maintenance and repair of aircraft and computer reservation systems	■ Nascent Saudi aircraft maintenance companies such as Al Salaam will be hit by competition
	8. Business service ■ KSA will provide improved market access for professional and business service providers (lawyers, accountants, architects, engineers, consultants, advertising marketing executives and veterinarians) ■ KSA guaranteed the rights of the these service companies to hold up to 75% equity in firms established in Saudi Arabia while it would be 100% in the computer and related services	■ Local law firms and other professional bodies who already have foreign association could see these associations loosen and new foreign independent operating names appear ■ Will hit hard all emerging Saudi IT and computer-related industries unless carried out on joint venture basis
	9. Distribution services ■ KSA will liberalize the wholesale, retail and franchise sectors. Foreign service providers may establish joint ventures and retain 51% share. Three years after accession, the foreign equity limitations can be increased to 75%	Major foreign wholesale and retail names already exist but under agency agreements. These could be re-examined and new foreign retailers may appear without sponsors; this has been evident since WTO accession with foreign brand names operating independently
	10. Environmental services ■ KSA will liberalize their environmental market. U.S. service providers may provide a wide range of services (sewage services, noise abatement) without limitation on market access or national treatment	■ Limited impact on Saudi environmental service providers, as these are not yet well established

Table 10.4 (continued)

Sector	Agreements	Impact on Saudi Arabia
	11. *Hotels and restaurants* ■ KSA will open its market to encourage increased foreign investment in the Saudi hotel industry as well as opening opportunities for foreign hotel management companies ■ KSA will comply with all obligations under the WTO agreement on technical barriers to trade from date of accession without recourse to any transition period ■ KSA has to enact new legislation and establish new institutions and procedures to ensure transparency and non-discrimination as follows: – Establishment of Ministry of Commerce and Industry as the authority responsible for making notifications to the WTO – Establishment in SASO of a single point for information and mandate to follow the code of good practice for preparation, adoption and application of standards – Establishment of a non-discriminatory and cost-based fee structure for assessing the conformity of products – The application of national treatment and non-discrimination with respect to products	■ Pressure on Saudi Hotel and Resorts Company and other private hoteliers if new brand names come in or existing management contracts re-negotiated. Some foreign brand names now operating independently since WTO accession ■ Already in process and established by Ministry of Commerce ■ SASO has high standards ■ Non-discriminatory fee structure could be a problem
(F) Agreement on technical barriers to trade	■ Ensuring that state-owned or controlled enterprises or those with special or exclusive privileges will make purchases and sales of goods and services based on commercial considerations, and that firms from WTO members will be allowed to compete for sales to, and purchase from, these Saudi enterprises on non-discriminatory terms	■ This is potentially one of the most damaging clauses of the new agreements as substantial business is generated by Saudi companies receiving discriminatory national treatment

Source: WTO, SAMA, Ministry of Commerce

to require such importers of record to provide information in customs declarations on the *further disposition* of goods entering the Kingdom and existing Saudi laws on import licensing procedures were to be *amended*.

Table 10.4 noted the Kingdom's commitment on *"sanitary and phytosanitary (SPS) measures,"* which deal with food safety measures. Sometimes countries used SPS measures to restrict foreign companies' imports and create an "uneven" competitive field. In its WTO agreements, Saudi Arabia committed to applying a science-based SPS standard to all agricultural goods, including grains, meats, fruit and vegetables, and eliminated its prohibition on importing beef and other meat products from animals treated with growth hormones, which was a key U.S. bilateral agreement demand prior to WTO accession. Saudi Arabia also removed its ban on imports of live (i.e. day-old chicks) and also made changes to shelf-life restrictions. The Kingdom would henceforth accept "internationally recognized" manufacturer-determined "use by dates," with the exception of those on certain perishable foods and baby foods (WTO, 2005).

Saudi Arabia *committed* to reconcile some inconsistencies between domestic legislation and WTO SPS agreement, so that all Saudi laws and regulations are consistent with the WTO SPS agreement. Saudi Arabia also committed that SPS measures would be published in advance of their application and the Saudi Arabian Standards Organization (SASO) will be the main information vehicle for SPS notification.

In the "franchising" sector, Saudi Arabia committed to foreigners being able to set up their own franchises in the Kingdom, without having a local sponsor or *wakeel*. Under the WTO accession agreements, the rules were changed to allow foreigners to establish such franchises and own 51% of company equity, with the maximum equity raised to 75% by 2008. However, a foreign franchiser had to be authorized in his own country to practise franchising or be a partner in an authorized company of no less than 5 years without interruption to avoid operationally and financial inexperienced franchisers operating in the Kingdom. The result was a boom in fast food franchises following WTO accession.

As mentioned in Table 10.4, Saudi Arabia made commitments on Trade-Related Aspects of Intellectual Property Rights (TRIPS), and by 2010 this had achieved significant success in curtailing unauthorized intellectual property rights violation. Upon WTO accession in 2005, Saudi Arabia committed to fully implement TRIPS without any transition period.

The Kingdom has completely overhauled and modernized its *legislative* framework and administrative infrastructure for the protection of intellectual property rights. *Three main categories covered by TRIPS are as follows:*

(a) *Copyrights* are exclusive rights granted by a government for a limited time.
(b) *Patents* are a set of exclusive rights granted by a government to an inventor for a limited time, preventing others from using or selling the invention.
(c) *Trademark* is a distinctive sign (logo) of some kind which is used by a business to uniquely identify itself and its products to consumers, and to distinguish itself from the products of other businesses.

The implication domestically is that such regulations and safeguarding measures will encourage local companies' R&D and investment in TRIPS-related activities. The Kingdom enacted a whole range of legislation prior to WTO accession, the key ones being, according to the Saudi Ministry of Commerce, as follows:

- Copyright Law (30 August 2003)
- Copyright Law Implementing Regulations (29 May 2004)
- Law on Patents, Layout Designs of Integrated Circuits, Plant Varieties and Industrial Designs ("New Patent Law") (17 July 2004)
- "New Patent Law" Implementing Regulations (26 December 2004)
- Trademarks Law (7 August 2002)
- Trademarks Law Implementing Regulations (2005)
- Rules of Protection of Trade Secrets (2005)

Saudi Arabia has also committed to protecting pharmaceutical and agricultural chemical test data submitted to obtain marketing approval against unfair commercial use for a *period of 5 years from the date of approval.* The Kingdom will not register a generic form of a pharmaceutical when a patent application is on file, unless the invention in the application is *not* patentable.

Copyright violations are a serious impediment to international service trade and Table 10.5 illustrates the extent of global software piracy for 2008.

Table 10.5 illustrates the major improvement the Kingdom has made in combating software piracy compared to other countries in the Middle East; the Kingdom

Table 10.5 Global software piracy 2008: Top 10 countries and selected Middle East countries

Rank	Country	Rate (%)	Rank	Country	Losses $ Million
(A) Highest piracy rates			(B) Highest piracy losses		
1	Georgia	95	1	United States	$9,143
2	Bangladesh	92	2	China	$6,677
3	Armenia	92	3	Russia	$4,215
4	Zimbabwe	92	4	India	$2,768
5	Sri Lanka	90	5	France	$2,760
6	Azerbaijan	90	6	United Kingdom	$2,181
7	Moldova	96	7	Germany	$2,152
8	Yemen	89	8	Italy	$1,895
9	Libya	87	9	Brazil	$1,645
10	Pakistan	86	10	Japan	$1,495
Other Middle East					
■	*Saudi Arabia*	*52*	■	*Saudi Arabia*	*$7*
■	Bahrain	55	■	Bahrain	$27
■	Egypt	59	■	Egypt	$158
■	Kuwait	61	■	Kuwait	$69
■	Lebanon	74	■	Lebanon	$49

Source: Business Software Alliance, IDC, 2009

has successfully reduced software piracy-related losses to around $7 million, down from $120 million in 2003 (Business Software Alliance, 2009).

WTO and Dispute Settlement

One of the key benefits attributed to WTO membership is having access to WTO's dispute settlement process. As stated earlier, the WTO provides the agreed channel for dispute settlement and only a member state of the WTO can take another member to its dispute resolution mechanism. However, as illustrated in Table 10.6, the procedure can be quite lengthy and cases can take more than 1 year if not resolved amicably between members.

Table 10.6 Duration of dispute settlement cycle at WTO

Duration of dispute-settlement – WTO	
60 days	Consultations, mediation, etc.
45 days	Panel set up and panellists appointed
6 months	First panel report to parties
3 weeks	Final panel report to WTO members
60 days	Dispute Settlement Body adopts report (if no appeal)
Total = 1 year	(without appeal)
60–90 days	Appeals report
30 days	Dispute Settlement Body adopts appeals report
Total = 15 months	(without appeal)

Source: WTO

Even when a case has been arbitrated and decided, a lot more is involved before penalties in the form of trade sanctions are imposed. In its accession agreements, Saudi Arabia committed to introduce WTO-consistent legislation on anti-dumping, countervailing measures and safeguards. As it is incumbent for the private sector of WTO member states to initiate an anti-dumping dispute case, and for the government to take it up at the WTO, the process can be costly, sometimes reaching over $1 million, and very cumbersome. The proof of dumping is put on the importing country; dumping must have occurred over many years and not one-off trade transactions or promotions; the goods in question must be identical in all respects; the case must meet minimum national industry injury criteria (that is affecting a minimum segment of the industry and not just one company); and finally the goods must not be sold at below the export price in the originating country. The amount of data collection to support an anti-dumping case can be substantial, and this sometimes puts off frivolous claims being made against legitimate competitors. The WTO imposes an anti-dumping "two-test" pass rule before they can accept a case for dispute settlement. These are as follows:

- *First*, the domestic procedures *supporting the application* must collectively account for more than 50% of the total production of the like product produced by that portion of the domestic industry expressing either support for or opposition to the application.

- *Second*, domestic producers *expressly supporting* the application must account for *at least 25%* of *the total production* of the like product produced by the domestic industry.

Since its accession, Saudi Arabia's private sector has not initiated any anti-dumping case with the WTO, but there have been some lodged by China against the Kingdom, especially against Saudi petrochemical products. In June 2009, China began a dumping investigation on petrochemical products from Saudi Arabia, Indonesia, Malaysia and New Zealand (Arab News, July 2009). The Saudis strongly denied that its methanol was subsidized and that no protective fees were imposed on the estimated 70,000 tons of methanol to China every month, out of a total 6.2 million tons production.

The Hydrocarbon Sector and WTO Accession

Saudi Arabia has placed great hopes on its hydrocarbon sector following WTO accession. There are two components in the hydrocarbon equation: oil and petro-chemicals. The principles of the international trading system, as spelled by the WTO agreement, are explicit on many sectors and commodities and not explicit on others. Among the latter is crude oil. Crude oil was not explicitly addressed by the GATT 1949 or its subsequent round of negotiations, since it had not been considered as an ordinary economic commodity but as a strategic one. In addition, when the GATT negotiations started in 1947, most of the petroleum fields in the world were under the control of multinational companies, which were mostly owned by nationals of the main contracting parties to GATT such as the U.S., Britain, the Netherlands and France. These countries wanted to avoid new tensions over the control of resources through renegotiating the terms governing the pricing and production of oil. For these reasons, it is believed that there was an unwritten agreement involving an understanding among the initial signatories of the GATT not to discuss petroleum issues in the initial negotiation and its subsequent negotiating rounds. Another factor is the special nature of oil as an exhaustible natural resource, and its uneven geographical distribution resulting in reducing the impact of tariff and non-tariff barriers, which were the main concerns of GATT and its subsequent rounds of negotiations, as an instrument of trade policy. Finally, the fact that major oil-producing and -exporting countries in the Middle East were not contracting parties to GATT was an additional good reason for not addressing crude oil explicitly.

Influenced by the aftermath of the two major upward adjustments in oil prices in the 1970s and 1980s, some industrialized countries, with an initiative from the U.S., included the subject of exports restriction and dual-pricing practice in petroleum in the Tokyo round and then in the Uruguay round. The two rounds, however, failed to conclude an agreement in this respect. Since the launching of the WTO multilateral trading system, following the conclusion of Uruguay round, concerned organizations like the WTO and UNCTAD have confirmed on different occasions that trade in crude oil is not excluded from the rules and regulations of the Uruguay round agreements, although it was not explicitly addressed.

Oil and oil products, however, are listed on WTO commodity schedules and are subject to the provisions of market access agreements. However, a limited group of GATT members, about 12, managed to exclude oil and oil products from their original commodity schedules. As a member of the WTO, Saudi Arabia can conduct negotiations directly with members of the group, in an effort to have such exceptions cancelled and replaced by bound tariffs or tariff ceilings on oil and oil products. As a practical matter, however, there are very low or zero tariffs on crude oil imports around the world. Also of concern to Saudi Arabia is the issue of high taxes on refined products, especially in European countries, with tax rates reaching nearly 70% in the UK and the USA, and the mid-60 levels for most other European countries (U.S. Department of Energy, 2009). Taxation, however, is not a WTO issue as the tax is not a tariff on cross-border trade in oil, but a domestic tax applied to all sources of oil, whether domestic or foreign. A central principle of the WTO is "national treatment," the concept that foreign players in a market should receive the same treatment as nationals of the country. In the case of these taxes, the principle of national treatment applies, as the tax is applied regardless of the source of the oil. So, for example, oil refined and sold as petrol in the UK has taxes levied on the final sale of the petrol whether that oil comes from the UK sector of the North Sea or from a foreign source such as Saudi Arabia. Such domestic taxes are WTO-compliant as long as they are applied equally to all sources of oil, foreign or domestic.

Since WTO accession, Saudi Arabia has been relying on bilateral talks and international energy meetings to try to change such tax policies in oil-consuming countries, but without much success to date.

Petrochemical industries in the GCC countries, including Saudi Arabia, are primarily export-oriented. Thus, they are highly sensitive to developments in the international markets. The benefits of petrochemical industries in the region from the price and income effects resulting from tariff reduction on chemicals, and higher level of growth generated by liberalized trade, depend on certain facts. Among them are development in the structure of production, market access and unchallenged comparative advantage of access to cheap feedstock.

Petrochemical products from the GCC countries have duty-free entry to the EU market. However, the same products are subject to high tariff and non-tariff barriers in the U.S. and Japan as well as in South East Asian countries. Countries in Asia are becoming increasingly more important markets for petrochemical exports from the GCC countries as seen in an earlier chapter.

As far as Saudi petrochemicals were concerned following WTO accession, there seemed to be two advantages accruing to Saudi petrochemical production. First, the Kingdom made no commitment to change the pricing of feedstock, and second, the "chemical tariff harmonization agreement" substantially lowered tariffs globally on chemical imports, which included all of the 64 chemicals exported

Table 10.7 Chemical harmonization tariffs (%)

	1995	2000	2010
■ Ethylene bi glycol	8.0	5.5	5.5
■ Ethylene	0.0	0.0	0.0
■ Ethylene glycol	13.0	9.25	5.5
■ Melamine	8.5	6.5	6.5
■ Methyl *tert*-butyl ether (MBTBE)	7.4	5.5	5.5
■ Methanol	13.0	9.25	5.5
■ Propylene	0.0	0.0	0.0
■ Styrene	6.0	0.0	0.0
■ Polyethylene LDPE-LLDPE-HDPE	12.5	9.5	6.5
■ Polystyrene and polyvinychloride (PVC)	12.5	9.5	6.5

by the Saudi Arabian Basic Industries Corporation (SABIC)-affiliated companies. Table 10.7 summarizes the new chemical harmonization tariffs.

According to Saudi experts, the removal of trade barriers and reduction of chemical tariffs will allow Saudi petrochemical producers to offer lower prices to tariff-protected markets such as the E.U., USA and Japan (Al Sadoun, 2005). As illustrated from Table 10.7, it will be difficult for high-cost producers in these economies to meet the lower market prices caused by the tariff reductions, and in the long run high-cost producers in these economies will exit the industry or form strategic alliances with countries such as Saudi Arabia, as we noted from SABIC's petrochemical acquisitions in Europe.

Thus, Saudi petrochemical manufacturers will retain a substantial cost advantage over their foreign competitors while gaining better market access to foreign markets as tariffs decline globally. Saudi Arabia may also use the WTO dispute mechanism to challenge the protective tariffs imposed by some countries on petrochemical imports.

The issue of Saudi pricing of feedstocks for petrochemical production was one of the most important and toughest negotiating points in the accession process. The European Union took the view that feedstock prices were unfairly subsidized, but in the end Saudi Arabia was not required to commit to a change in the pricing regime. The pricing is as follows:

Natural gas (ethane and methane) is sold by Aramco to consumers at a fixed price of SR 2.81 ($0.75) per million BTU. The current price of natural gas in the USA for comparison is over $14 per million BTU, giving Saudi companies using natural gas a strong cost advantage over foreign competitors. Natural gas is not sold for export due to the high cost of gas export infrastructure. Previously, gas was flared as a waste by-product of crude oil production. Based on a combination of commercial and environmental concerns, the Kingdom now sells the gas for domestic use in power generation, water desalination, cement manufacture and petrochemicals production.

The pricing for natural gas liquids (NGLs) – propane, butane and natural gasoline – is set based on a more complex formula of adjustments to international market prices established in 2002. These products are also exported, so trading partners raised a concern about "dual pricing" of NGLs – a lower price in Saudi Arabia than the Kingdom charges for exports of the same products. In actuality, these products are sold domestically at a discount to the international price for naphtha, a common global petrochemical feedstock. According to a SAMBA study, the current pricing formula for NGL prices is based on international market price for naphtha and adjusted downward for the following:

- Cost savings in infrastructure. The expensive export infrastructure for NGLs is not necessary for domestically consumed NGLs.
- Cost savings in marketing. Domestic customers are committed to long-term off take agreements, whereas foreign sales would require marketing costs.
- Commercial advantage associated with long-term contracts. There is a lack of long-term contracts in the export market of NGLs.
- Commercial value of reduced volatility. The export market is also characterized by large seasonal demand and price swings, as exported NGLs are primarily used as fuel rather than petrochemical feedstock.
- Commercial value of large-volume purchases. Domestic purchasers commit to much larger volumes than do purchasers under short-term export contracts (SAMBA, 2005).

In response to a concern from one trade partner, Saudi Arabia made assurances that taking these adjustments into consideration the commercially negotiated price of NGLs as petrochemical feedstock in Saudi Arabia would still be based on full recovery of production costs and at a reasonable profit. Both natural gas and NGLs are sold domestically without discrimination between Saudi- and foreign-owned firms. Currently, the price for NGLs in Saudi Arabia is about 30% below the naphtha price on the international market (Al Sadoun, 2005).

The implication for the petrochemical industry in Saudi Arabia is that the Kingdom's position on this issue preserves the benefit of low-cost feedstock. The petrochemical plants, both existing and planned, in the Kingdom have based their economic viability on the presumed continuation of low-cost feedstock throughout the life of the plant. The WTO commitments preserve these assumptions (SAMBA, 2005).

WTO and "*Saudization*"

There was some concern prior to WTO accession that the Kingdom would be forced to open up its labour market to free movement of workers. It soon became apparent that, following accession to the WTO, there was no alteration to the structure of the Saudi labour market and accession did not impact the government's so-called *Saudization* plans to increase the percentage of Saudis in the national labour force. Labour matters do not fall within the WTO's mandate, except insofar that labour issues affect traded goods and services across borders. The WTO, however, was concerned with the degree to which foreign companies operating in the Kingdom are treated equally with national companies. This is the so-called WTO "national treatment" concept. The issue of *Saudization* was the one area where Saudi Arabia successfully requested that it is given "national treatment" exemption. With this exemption, Saudi Arabia imposed some *Saudization* requirements on foreign companies entering the services sectors of the country such as finance, insurance and legal services.

The Labour and Workers Regulations require that for any enterprise, Saudi- or foreign-owned, the percentage of the Saudi workers not be less than 75% of the total workforce and receive at least 50% of the total payroll. Under the same regulations, the Minister of Labour has the authority to reduce the required percentage in circumstances where qualified Saudi workers are not available and this exemption has been applied in some critical services.

In addition, regulations require that certain job categories in a company be reserved for Saudis, including personnel and recruitment officers, receptionists, cashiers, civilian security guards and transaction follow-up clerks to government departments. This requirement applies to both foreign and local firms.

Expatriate workers will still need a work visa to work in Saudi Arabia. The sponsorship system will remain unchanged. A release letter is still required for an expatriate's transfer of employment from one employer to another within Saudi Arabia. In its services commitments to the WTO, Saudi Arabia stipulates that business visitors into the Kingdom will enter the country for no more than 180 days. Intra-corporate transferees (an employee of a multinational company transferred to work in Saudi Arabia) can stay in the Kingdom for 2 years, after which his contract can be renewed for 1-year extensions. If a company with no commercial presence has obtained a service contract in Saudi Arabia and the presence of its employees is required, then a renewable 6-month visa will be issued for a variety of professions, except *Umra* and *Hajj* tour operators and travel agents.

The WTO and Saudi Legal System

Saudi Arabia's WTO accession seems to have given an impetus to carry out both legal and judicial reforms to comply with international agreements. The Kingdom had earlier acceded to the "Vienna Convention" on the Law of Treaties 1969. As a general rule, under the Vienna Convention, should Saudi Arabia's laws contradict international treaties or agreements, then the Kingdom would bring its laws into conformity with such international treaties. There were exceptions, however, and these were if such international agreements or treaties were in conflict with the Kingdom's fundamental Islamic or religious principles.

Saudi Arabia has an established framework for making and enforcing of legal policies and is based on the following framework:

Basic Law of Governance 1992. Establishes the law concerning the political authority in Saudi Arabia.

– *Basic Law* states that the King is Chairman of the Council of Ministers.
– *Law of Council of Ministers* – Lays down powers of Council of Ministers (CoM)
   regarding internal/external policies.
– *Consultative Council Law* (CoC) – resolutions are passed by CoC to the Chairman
   of Council of Ministers for consideration.

In practice, when *both* councils – Council of Ministers and Consultative Councils
– agree, a law is then enacted by the King. When there is *difference* between the two
councils, the King is free to approve what is considered most appropriate. Laws
and international agreements are approved and implemented by Royal Decrees,
after the consideration by both councils. Royal Decrees are the legal instruments
by which international agreements are implemented into domestic law. The question then arises as to which laws take precedence, for example the WTO Agreement
or domestic laws.

In principle, international agreements do not take precedents over the provisions
of domestic law, *nor* do other provisions of domestic law take precedence over international agreements. What is the solution then? Inconsistencies between domestic
and international provisions are resolved in accordance with the same *rules of interpretation* that are applied to domestic legislation, i.e. the *more recent laws take
precedence over older laws*.

The rules of interpretation are also set out in Saudi Arabia. For example, international agreements could *not* override a rule of *Shariah* Islamic principles such as
the importation of pork and alcohol.

Given *inconsistencies* between domestic/international, *the text* of each would be
interpreted so as to *avoid conflict.* Where text *did not resolve* conflict, recourse could
be had to the *intent* and *purpose* of the agreement and domestic law. If conflicts did
still exist, then this could be resolved following the rule that *a new law or international agreement to which Saudi Arabia has agreed was superior to previous laws
or international agreements (with Shariah exception).*

Concerning the implementation of Saudi Arabia's WTO laws and rules, again
these follow a distinct path in the Kingdom. New WTO-related laws and regulations originate in the Saudi Ministry having authority over the subject matter of the
law, e.g. Ministry of Labour, Health, Commerce, etc. If Consultative Council law
and legal expert opinions have been sought, and a Council of Ministers approval
obtained, the King then issues a Royal Decree and the new law is published in
the Saudi government Official Gazette, *Umm Al-Qura.* Once the Royal Decree is
passed, the law is returned back to the ministry that drafted the law, and that ministry now has the responsibility for the "implementation" regulations. As such, any
new laws, when enacted, *dealt with any conflicts with older laws and superseded
them.*

In implementing WTO-related legal issues, Table 10.8 sets out the key Saudi
supervisory bodies relating to WTO matters and sectors.

Table 10.8 indicates the broad depth of Saudi supervisory agencies involved with
WTO-related matters. At the same time, the Saudi government established a WTO
grievance and redress procedure for dispute resolution. In summary, an aggrieved

Table 10.8 Key Saudi supervisory bodies relating to WTO legal issues

Saudi supervisory body	Related area
■ Ministry of Commerce and Industry	■ The principal government agency concerned with formulation and conduct of trade policies. It implemented the laws and regulations relating to trade – the Companies Law, the Law on Commercial Registration and the Law on Commercial Agencies
■ Ministry of Finance	■ Concerned with formulation and conduct of financial and fiscal policies and with international economic issues. It is also the parent ministry of the Department of Custom, Department of Zakat and Income Tax
■ Ministry of Petroleum and Mineral Resources	■ Formulates and implements the oil policies of the Kingdom and supervises concessions in the oil and mining sectors
■ Ministry of Agriculture	■ Formulates and implements agricultural policies and was responsible for matters relating to sanitary and phytosanitary measures
■ Ministry of Health	■ Responsible for supervising the health industry and for matters related to the import and sale of medicines and medical supplies
■ Ministry of Information and Culture	■ Responsible for implementation of the Copyrights Law and matters relating thereto
■ The King Abdulaziz City for Science and Technology KACST	■ Responsible for implementation of the Patents Law and matters relating to it
■ The Saudi Arabian Standards Organization (SASO)	■ Established and approved the voluntary standards and mandatory technical regulations for imported and domestically produced goods
■ The Saudi Arabian Monetary Agency (SAMA)	■ Acts as the central bank of Saudi Arabia and is responsible for the monetary and exchange rate policies and the supervision of banking and cooperative insurance

Source: Ministry of Commerce WTO Agreements, 2005

party has a final right of appeal against *all* administrative decisions in matters of trade to the Saudi Board of Grievance. This board is an independent tribunal to which appeals are made against all government administrative decisions. The board's decision could be challenged and appealed to the Appeals Court (Scrutiny Commission) within the board. This Scrutiny Commission could confirm or reverse the appealed decisions. The appeals commission's decisions are final. Since Saudi Arabia's WTO accession, the Kingdom's laws provide for a right of appeal on matters subject to WTO provisions to an *independent tribunal* in conformity with WTO obligations. In this regard, the Ministry of Commerce and Industry continues to oversee and coordinate within the Saudi government all matters relating to the WTO, including implementation and interpretation issues. Saudi Arabia has also confirmed to the WTO that *only* the Saudi central government has authority over matters covered by the WTO agreements. It has also confirmed that the central government was superior in authority to sub-central government bodies. Furthermore, Saudi Arabia committed that where WTO provisions are *not* properly applied – or not applied in a uniform manner – the Saudi Arabian central authority would act to correct the situation and to enforce the WTO provision without requiring further legal proceedings.

Conclusion

The accession to the WTO in 2005 has brought the Kingdom into the mainstream of a global multilateral trading system after many years of negotiations. Saudi Arabia is now in a position to shape and influence trade policies from the inside and protect its trading interests while hoping to increase its global competitive trading position in certain key commodities such as petrochemicals. WTO accession is also a means to generate domestic economic, legal and structural changes and induce domestic efficiency to meet international competitors who are now free to enter the Saudi market. As analysed, there are both gains and potential losses to some industries, but the Kingdom felt, on balance, that WTO accession was worthwhile for the long term.

Summary of Key Points

- *Saudi Arabia has opted for a decentralized, market-based economy to be achieved through joining the WTO*
- *The Kingdom acceded to the WTO in 2005 and has taken the necessary steps to fulfil certain accession requirements, especially in tariff reduction, phasing out subsidies, enforcing intellectual property rights and allowing majority foreign ownership of investment projects and services, including in the banking and insurance sectors.*
- *The potential impact of WTO accession and globalization on the Saudi economy is not yet certain. In the short term, the negatives could outweigh the positive factors before long-term structural adjustments bring about desired benefits. The petrochemical industry is set to make gains.*
- *Legal reforms have been established to meet WTO Agreement obligations and central government agencies have been empowered to act on WTO-related matters.*

Part VI
Key Challenges

Chapter 11
Privatization and Foreign Direct Investment

The art of taxation consists in so plucking the goose as to obtain
the largest amount of feathers with the least amount of hissing.
Colbert

Learning Outcomes

By the end of this section, you would understand:

- *Privatization's theoretical function*
- *Privatization as a strategic goal of the state and the initiatives taken*
- *Public and private sector partnerships (PPP)*
- *Privatization results to date and consequences*
- *Foreign direct investment (FDI) as a principal tool of economic reform*
- *The positive and negative effects of FDI*
- *FDI flows to the Kingdom by source and sector*

Introduction

There is a consensus amongst Saudi economic observers and practitioners that the Kingdom truly needs to make economic reforms work and it can only do so by strengthening the private sector, finding other sources of investment and encouraging repatriation of Saudi capital in viable domestic projects. What then are the obstacles? It is not that Saudi Arabia lacks good intentions or has not set the proper priorities. Rather, there is *no matching consensus* as to how much action is needed and how quickly it should act. While different economists and government planners might assign different priorities and values to the urgency of the effort needed, most would agree that success will depend on far more progress being made in the following areas:

- Privatizing key public assets
- Attracting more effective foreign direct investment (FDI)

M.A. Ramady, *The Saudi Arabian Economy*, DOI 10.1007/978-1-4419-5987-4_11,
© Springer Science+Business Media, LLC 2010

- Strengthening the private sector in a meaningful manner
- Repatriating Saudi capital into domestic projects
- Creating meaningful and value-added jobs for the Saudi economy

Some have argued that implementing some or all of the objectives can no longer be postponed (Cordesman, 2003), due to a multitude of challenges faced by the Kingdom. Amongst these are a wide range of external forces that shape the value of the Kingdom's petroleum revenues in ways it cannot control. These forces include serious problems in planning budgets and 5-year plans, because of an inability to predict cash flow. There also has been low productivity in many subsidized and sheltered sectors. In addition, the pace of structural change has been slow, so that despite all the measures of diversification away from oil, the private sector still only accounts for a base of around 35% of the GDP. Diversification efforts have also had a limited productive impact, and the economy has neither generated sufficient number of jobs for Saudis nor induced a "knowledge-based" society.

Taking the First Steps for Privatization

Until it announced its wide-scale privatization programme in late 2002, the Saudi government had run core services itself or through the private sector via operation contract method, whereby government services are carried out on a contract basis by the private sector. The decision to privatize government services and transfer them wholly to the private sector is an implicit acknowledgement that both the operation contract method and the use of direct government services have failed. This failure can be traced back to the government's inability to deliver on its commitments in the face of increased domestic demand, and to the inherent conflict of interest created by the fact that the government was judging its *own* performance.

Countries worldwide are redefining the roles of government and the private sector. As they rely more on the private sector for the provision of infrastructure and public utility services, which in many cases are exposed in the short and medium term to little or no competition, there is also a need for economic regulation.

Economic regulation is required to protect consumers from monopoly or from the abuses of limited competition and, at the same time, to give the private sector the necessary incentives for short- and long-term efficiency. On the other hand, there is some evidence to indicate that, in their zeal for regulation, this could have an adverse effect on economic growth (Speakman, 2002).

Regulators must therefore play the important role of an independent and impartial referee who balances the interests of government, consumers and private sector providers of infrastructure and services. For most countries that do not have a regulatory tradition, the establishment of entities that are responsible for economic regulation poses major challenges, as is the case for Saudi Arabia.

While there are some disagreements on approaches to be taken, most experts would agree that "good" economic regulation should aim to maximize the overall welfare of societies, otherwise changes will only add to confusion and lack of direction (Saravia, 2002). The key tasks are the design of regulatory institutions and of processes that are seen to be independent and accountable, as well as transparent and consistent.

To its credit, the Saudi Arabian government is aware of all these issues. Despite the then Crown Prince Abdullah's declaration in 2000 that privatization is a strategic choice for the Saudi economy, the Supreme Economic Council, which has been mandated to implement economic policies, has attributed the slow progress on privatization to the nature of structural changes that are required (Saudi Press Agency, 2002). The council has focused its efforts on developing the regulatory environment, without which the outcome and direction of the new economic liberalization will be beneficial in terms of sustained structural economic diversification.

Privatization: Key Concepts

Since its first appearance in England in the late 1970s under Prime Minister Thatcher, privatization has been, by far, the most controversial instrument of economic policy of the past two decades. Economics, politics and ideology have punctuated the debate on privatization and have polarized opinion, but do not diminish the importance of privatization as a policy instrument and as a process shaping the economics of the twenty-first century. As we highlighted earlier, the rulers of Saudi Arabia have publicly stated that privatization is a strategic goal of the state and which has been reiterated in the latest Ninth Five-Year Plan.

Privatization is an instrument of economic policy through which there is a transfer of property or control of assets, usually owned by the state, to the private sector. Thus, in its purest form, privatization encompasses the privatization of management and ownership.

A broader definition describes privatization as the abolition of barriers to private sector provision of services or to the infrastructure necessary for their delivery. This broad definition usually applies to privatization of a sector (telecommunications, electricity, gas, water, etc.) and it often requires a restructuring of the whole sector rather than just one firm. It also requires legal and regulatory mechanisms to ensure that private providers do not overlook the public dimensions and responsibilities of the services they are licensed to deliver, and to ensure they meet the pre-agreed upon targets and policy objectives, such as coverage to certain areas and access for the public. It is this issue – the regulatory framework – that has kept the Saudi privatization process from advancing more rapidly than hoped for, given the political statements of support.

Different economies and countries have adopted privatization for different ends. Thus, for example, the former Socialist economies of Eastern Europe used privatization to increase the role of the private sector in the economy. Some Arab economies going through transition and change, like Egypt and Algeria, are striving to move from a state-controlled and dominated economy to a market-based economy where the private sector plays a much greater role.

The oil-rich countries of the Gulf Cooperation Council (GCC) have used privatization as a means of diversifying their economic base, moving away from

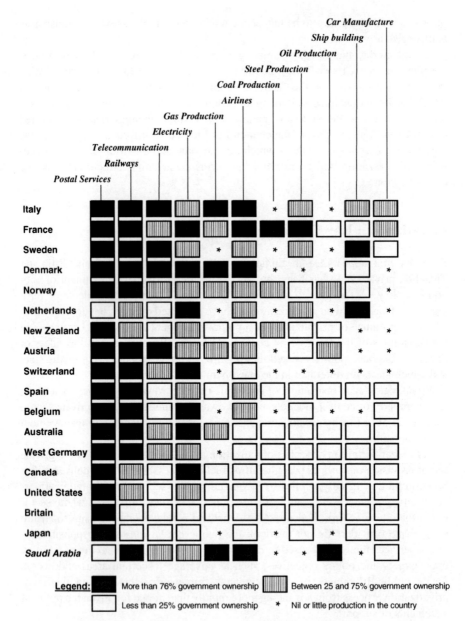

Fig. 11.1 Privatization pattern – industry ownership in selected OECD countries and Saudi Arabia (1998) (Source: Adapted by Author from OECD Privatization Database, 2000)

a heavy reliance on the oil sector (Al Bazai, 2002, Seznec, 2002). It is also fortunate that the earlier adoption of privatization in many countries will make it possible for Saudi Arabia and others in the GCC to learn from these experiences and to draw important lessons that are relevant to their own economic structures.

Figure 11.1 compares the status of Saudi privatization with those of selected Organisation for Economic Co-operation and Development (OECD) countries in 1998. It is interesting to note that, with the exception of Britain, Japan and the USA, the majority of OECD countries have yet to privatize many state industries. It is worthwhile noting that Saudi Arabia's nascent car manufacturing industry is entirely in private sector hands, like all other OECD countries (with the exception of Italy and France). Saudi car production, though, is more of an assembly line operation for trucks, buses and other specialized cargo vehicles carried out through a Saudi–German partnership of the Jeddah-based *Juffali* group with Mercedes Benz and the Riyadh-based *Al Jomaih* group with General Motors.

Routes to Privatization

Privatization follows many different routes, from a minimal or low level of private ownership to total private ownership, as Fig. 11.2 illustrates.

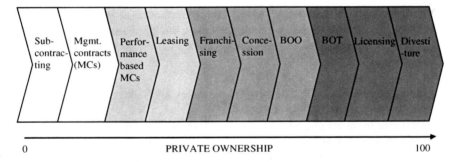

0   PRIVATE OWNERSHIP   100

Fig. 11.2 Privatization scales

Each public–private partnership noted here entails a different set of agreed commercial and operational elements, as well as a specified period for the privatization. The subcontracting and management contracts (MCs) are of shorter duration than the leasing contracts, franchising, etc., until total divestiture (sale) of the public asset. As discussed in earlier chapters, the MCs and subcontracting have been the main methods of operation of the Saudi government to date in involving the private sector. Other countries in the region, especially Turkey, pioneered the concepts of build-operate-transfer (B-O-T) and build-own-operate (B-O-O) as part of their privatization strategy.

The political push for privatization as a strategic choice is necessitated by the forecasted capital expenditure needs of the Kingdom in key areas. Current estimates of such capital expenditures over the next 20 years are around $540 billion or SR 2,025 billion for education, electricity, oil, gas, mining, water and agricultural projects (National Commercial Bank, 2003). The government cannot meet these needs, so it must either borrow or turn over key sectors to the private sector to operate on a profitable and cost-efficient basis.

In November 2002, the Saudi Arabian government announced plans to privatize 20 economic sectors, including telecommunications, civil aviation, desalination, highway management, railways, sports clubs, health services, municipality services, water and sewage, highway construction, airport services, postal services, grain and flour silos, hotels, seaport services and industrial city services. Privatization would also cover state share sales in the Saudi Electricity Company (SEC) and the Saudi Arabian Mineral Company (*Maaden*), as well as local petroleum refineries. Both SEC and *Maaden* have been partially privatized since the announcements.

It was a staggering list in both size and diversity, and one of the most ambitious privatization announcements of any country in the world over the past few decades.

Experiences of privatization elsewhere, including pioneering Britain, showed that government revenue maximization through privatization is not necessarily the best option. It is the method and quality of privatization that is of more importance, specifically the management and technical capabilities of those new operating owners who will be answerable to shareholders. The checks and balances through independent industry regulators are also important, especially for utilities such as water, electricity and gas.

Because privatization can take many forms, governments around the world have used different methods to achieve their objectives, and the most common methods to implement privatization programmes have been as follows (Dagdeviren, 2006, Clarke 1994, Clarke et al., 1995):

- *Share issue privatization,* whereby the government sells part or all its shares on the local or international stock market
- *Asset sale privatization,* whereby the government sells the entire corporation or part of it to a strategic investor, usually by public auction
- *Voucher privatization,* whereby the shares of ownership are distributed to all citizens, usually free or at very low prices

Share issue privatization is the most common type of privatization and is the route taken by Saudi Arabia. The benefit of such an approach of share issuance is that it can broaden and deepen domestic capital markets, boosting liquidity and potential economic growth (Kemp, 2007, Clarke, 2005), and this was evidenced when STC and SABIC shares were listed on the Saudi stock market. Sometimes developing countries adopt the asset sale privatization route for strategic reason that involves international foreign partners to capitalize on their expertise, R&D and efficiency gains. Voucher privatization has been rare, but has been used in the transition economies of Central and Eastern Europe, such as Russia, Poland, the Czech Republic and Slovakia (Dagdeviren, 2006).

As noted earlier, privatization raises opposing arguments, and the key arguments are summarized in Table 11.1.

As noted from the various arguments for and against privatization, there is no clear consensus as both sides have some valid arguments. The decision to undertake a privatization programme is not an easy one for any government, given the opposition it generates primarily based on "social justice" and equity as opposed to

Table 11.1 Arguments for and against privatization

For	Against
• Private market factors can deliver goals and services more efficiently owing to market competition, leading to lower prices, improved quality, more choice and quicker delivery. Governments have few incentives to ensure enterprises are well run. Lack of benchmark comparison with state monopolies • State-run industries tend to be bureaucratic and changes only happen when they become politically sensitive • Managers of privately owned companies are accountable to stakeholders and consumers while managers of public enterprises are accountable to political stakeholders • Investment decisions are governed by market interest rates instead of cross-subsidizing of government entities with overall credit risk of the country • Governments may bail out poorly run state businesses often due to sensitivity of job losses when economically it may be better if such enterprises are curtailed • Successful market-led enterprises generate new jobs, stimulate R&D and create wealth for society. As such subsidies are reduced, and fewer taxes are raised by governments to maintain state corporations	• Governments are proxy owners of state enterprises and as such they are answerable to the people and will lose elections or popularity if state enterprises are not managed well • Society should be sheltered from some elements of more "ruthless" market forces that do not take into consideration social responsible services such as health and education • The government mission is for social support whose primary aim is delivering affordable and quality services to society • Governments can raise funds in the financial markets more cheaply than private companies and re-lend to state-owned enterprises • Governments have chosen to keep certain sectors or companies under public ownership because of their strategic or national interest and which cannot be turned over to the private sector to manage • Government-owned companies in essential utilities such as water or electricity provide such services to all regions and would not cut off regions or households less able to pay • Government corporations often take a long-term view of their operation unlike a short-term conflict between profitability and service level of private companies

efficiency. For Saudi Arabia, the decision to privatize has been based on efficiency criteria as the critical factors explored below show.

Saudi Arabia's Basic Privatization Objectives

In June, 2002, the Supreme Economic Council (SEC), under the Chairmanship of the then Crown Prince Abdullah bin Abdulaziz, approved the privatization strategy for Saudi Arabia (Saudi Press Agency, June 2002). The strategy consists of eight basic objectives, each of which requires the adoption of a number of policies. These are as follows:

Objective 1: Improving the capacity of the national economy and enhancing its ability to meet the challenges of regional and international competition.

Objective 2: Encouraging private sector investment and effective participation in the national economy and increasing its share of domestic production to achieve growth in the national economy.

Objective 3: Expanding the ownership of productive assets by Saudi citizens.

Objective 4: Encouraging local investments of domestic and foreign capital.

Objective 5: Increasing employment opportunities, optimizing the use of the national workforce and thus ensuring the equitable increase of individual income.

Objective 6: Providing services to citizens and investors in a timely and cost-efficient manner.

Objective 7: Rationalizing public expenditure and reducing the burden of the government budget by giving the private sector opportunities to finance, to operate and to maintain certain services that it is able to provide.

Objective 8: Increasing government revenues from returns on the sale of assets to be transferred to the private sector.

While these are laudable objectives for any government to pursue, the Supreme Economic Council also recognized when setting these objectives that, in order for them to be successful, a regulatory framework had to be in place for the privatized industries. In addition, they needed to prepare and restructure the sectors and public enterprises to be privatized. They also indicated that one option was to pursue foreign strategic partners to provide capital, share risks provide advanced technical and management expertise and assist in creating a suitable climate for a successful privatization programme. What have been the accomplishments to date?

Privatization Efforts by Sector: Mixed Results

The Saudi government's actions to date have been partly characterized as market-driven and partly as an effort to shift current and future investment burden away from the government. They do not seem like a serious effort to privatize functions now operated by the state sector on a commercial basis. The eight broad privatization objectives set out so clearly by the Supreme Economic Council seem to intuitively recognize that privatization, in the Saudi Arabian context, can only have the required impact on growth and reform if it means conversion of state-held functions to truly competitive private enterprises. These enterprises can charge market prices and, by extension, reduce labour and overhead costs so as to become more productive and profitable.

Until recently, the economic regulation of infrastructure and utility services was not an issue in the Kingdom, as most of these services were provided directly by government entities (Al Bazai, 2002, Khemani, 2002). As such, issues related to policy, ownership and operation of assets for the provision of the services were interconnected and any regulation that existed was primarily in the form of self-regulation. To date, the government of Saudi Arabia has not (with the exception of the postal services) totally privatized – and therefore economically regulated – any major sector of services or industry. It has only sold part of its shareholding to the public in companies such as the Saudi Arabian Basic Industries Corporation (SABIC), Saudi Telecom Company (STC) and Saudi Arabia Mining Company (*Maaden*).

Recognizing the need for such a regulatory framework, the Saudi government approved the Telecommunications Regulations in 2001 and, in the same year, established the Saudi Telecommunications Authority. This built upon the experience of the Electricity Services Regulation Authority set up in 1998 (SAMA, 2003).

From 2006, however, the pace of privatization-led initiatives has picked up in Saudi Arabia, no doubt assisted by the favourable turnaround in the Kingdom's fiscal position due to high oil revenues as explored in earlier chapters. The key initiatives are summarized below by sector.

The Saudi Basic Industries Corporation (SABIC): SABIC is one of the pillars of Saudi industrialization policies and represents the Middle East's largest non-oil hydrocarbon-based industrial company. The government currently owns 70% of SABIC, and 30% is owned by the private sector. SABIC shares are actively traded on the Saudi stock market. To date, there has been no sign of further government sales of SABIC shares to the public, despite a cabinet approval in principle to sell three-quarters of its 70% share. The success of SABIC's share flotation and Saudi Arabia's relative comparative advantage in petrochemical products has encouraged other private sector companies to enter the petrochemical field, and this would not have been done at the level of investment undertaken if the government had not partially privatized SABIC.

The Saudi Electricity Company (SEC): SEC is the merger of the previous four separate Saudi Electricity Companies (SCECO) in the east, west, centre and south. These supplied around 85% of the Saudi power supplies, and in 2000 the various SCECOs and ten private power companies were all merged into the SEC. The government share in SEC is 74.15% and the private sector holds the remainder. The restructuring of the SCECO system was intended to lead to a more efficient streamlining of the Saudi power sector base, with the expectation that SEC would develop three separate sector companies for generation, transmission and distribution. The government has established an Electricity Services Regulation Authority to assist with the privatization programme and is considering alternative forms of private sector participation in this sector through BOO, BOT and even build-own-operate-transfer (BOOT) schemes. According to SAMA, the financial requirement for the power sector through 2023 is estimated at SR 341 billion or $90.9 billion (SAMA, 2009).

The partial privatization of SEC encouraged the company to initiate some public and private sector partnerships (PPPs) with the aim of attracting investors in the area of power generation for several mega projects including *Rabegh*, a project with a capacity of 1,200 MW to be operational in 2012, and *Alqariah*, a 2,000 MW project to be operational in 2014.

SEC also participated on a 50/50 basis with the Saline Water Conversion Corporation (SWCC) in establishing the Water and Electricity Limited Company, provided that SEC would be the sole buyer of water and electricity; production projects were awarded on the basis of BOO principle.

Saudi Telecom Company (STC): A 30% stake of STC was sold to the private sector in December 2002, in one of the largest government sales of shares; it raised around SR 15 billion or $4 billion. Following the sale, the STC became the Saudi stock market's second largest listed company in terms of capitalization, after SABIC. Work has progressed to create a specialized body with the administrative and financial autonomy to organize the telecommunications sector and provide rules and regulations to ensure fair competition amongst private firms. Following STC's partial privatization, and the Kingdom's accession to the WTO in 2005, several other telecom providers have entered the Saudi market, notably *Mobily* in 2006 and *Zain* in 2008, creating competition with STC for its mobile and Internet services. According to STC, Saudi Arabia has 21 million mobile users generating annual profits of around SR 14 billion and STC holds 85% of the market share, with *Mobily* at 10% and *Zain*, the new entrant, the remaining market share. Due to the competition it faced following partial privatization, STC has diversified its portfolio, targeting specific segments of society, mainly youth between 18 and 25 years old. New third-generation (3GP) services offered by STC include mobile TV, Internet access over mobile and video calls. Some argue that all this would not have occurred without privatization competition.

Saudi Arabian Airlines (Saudia): The first pronouncements on privatizing the national airline Saudia were mooted as early as 1994. In 2000, SAUDIA's board of directors invited investment banks to prepare bids for the privatization of the company. Some significant developments have taken place since those days and by 2010, the following actions were taken: a privatization implementation programme was approved by the Supreme Economic Council (SEC) in 2006 to convert Saudia's non-basic sectors into commercial units in the catering, ground services, cargo, aviation academy and real estate divisions. At the same time, the privatization directive of the SEC was to restructure the basic core sector of aviation and convert it into a strategic unit. These Saudia privatization initiatives prompted some new entrants to compete against Saudia in its core aviation business. New Saudi private airlines, SAMA (literally meaning to "rise high") and NAS were granted licences in 2006 and 2007 to compete on domestic routes, operating on the global model of budget or low-cost airlines. Once again, the strategic intent for privatization attracted private sector entrants, and Saudi consumers now enjoy alternative choices for domestic flights, especially on the more lucrative Riyadh and Jeddah routes; Saudia is still studying the partial flotation of its core aviation business. In March 2010, the Director General of SAUDIA, Mr. Khaled Al Molhelm, announced that the organization's core aviation unit would be privatized within 2 years and that the privatization of the maintenance service unit would be completed by 2011. Financial observers believe that SAUDIA's financial position has improved, given the taking over of virtually all its debt by the Public Investment Fund, to allow for a successful privatization.

General Railway Organization (GRO): Currently, the GRO operates a railway system connecting the Eastern Province with Riyadh. Saudi Arabia has always sought to expand this railway network by linking Riyadh to *Makkah, Madina and Jeddah*. Other plans call for establishing a rail network to link the mining regions in the north-west of the Kingdom to Riyadh, and to continue on to the *Jubail* industrial port. The World Bank was asked to make detailed studies, the results of which were submitted to the Supreme Economic Council, and, according to SAMA, "the project of expanding the railway network will be put out for execution by floating a tender to specialized companies on the basis of BOT." Bids were invited in late 2009 on that basis. To date the private sector has executed a number of projects and services for the GRO in engineering, maintaining the rail network and developing the electronic booking system, as well as operating and managing the dry ports of Riyadh and *Al-Dammam*.

Saudi Post Corporation: This sector is one of the most advanced in terms of privatization, with just under 95 private sector operating agencies providing a full range of postal delivery services by the end of 2008. Express mail was separated from mail parcels sector and a general directorate for this sector was formed as a preliminary step for its complete privatization in the future. Work is under way to convert the Saudi Post Corporation into a holding company with a number of subsidiaries operating in the post services sector in the Kingdom.

General Port Authority: The Saudi government started to involve the private sector by granting 10-year lease contracts to operate general port services on an income-sharing basis, through which the port assets are owned by the state but are operated by the private sector. Besides the shorter-term contracts, some 20-year contracts were also awarded. All eight Saudi ports have such private sector involvement ranging from general goods to containers, bulk grain, roll-on cargo, chilled and frozen food.

Grain Silos and Flour Mills Organization (GSFMO): In 2002, the Council of Ministers approved a list of targets for GSFMO to make conversion of the organization into a private enterprise on a commercial basis. External consultants were hired to propose alternative options, and these were finalized in 2009 and included converting the organization into a fully commercial enterprise, or separating all silos from mills while bringing together silos in a company subsidiary to the state. The final decision of the Supreme Economic Council is awaited.

Saline Water Conversion Corporation (SWCC): Demand for water in the Gulf has grown exponentially fuelled by energy revenues and consumer and industrial demand. This increased demand has necessitated countries in arid regions such as Saudi Arabia to embark on ambitious plans to achieve self-sufficiency in water production through desalination projects, often at great cost because of subsidized water distribution. The GCC accounts for around 50% of the world's desalination plants and Saudi Arabia has the largest share at round 41% of the GCC total. Saudi Arabia has 30 desalination plants of varying ages and technologies, operating either on thermal or membrance processes with a daily production of more than 3 million m^3 and generating 5,000 MW of electricity, as some plants are dual use. These provide about 70% of the daily drinking water supplies and 20% of the power generation of Saudi Arabia (SWCC, 2009). It has been forecasted that around $24 billion will be required by 2020 in both capital and operating expenditure for the existing plants and six new major projects. As such, the Kingdom has decided to privatize SWCC as a central strategy to meet both the funding and efficient supply distribution challenges.

It is estimated by the Water Ministry that Saudi consumers on average use 221–250 L of water a day, compared to between 150 and 200 L a day internationally. Wastage is also significant, with an estimated 20% of water production wasted through spillage in the Kingdom.

The privatization strategy hinges on transforming the SWCC into a state-owned joint stock holding company that has multiple subsidiaries consisting of current and future planned production companies. The aim is to invite private sector investors and developers to tender for the production companies.

The Saudi privatization plans are novel; they consist of separating production from transmission, and maintaining these as well as older operating plants and the Research and Desalination Technology Institute under the holding company. This is different from the "full" water privatization models adopted by other countries.

Under Saudi privatization plans, private sector investors and developers will not bear the burden of transmission, which is exorbitant given the huge landmass of Saudi Arabia that has to be covered to deliver water from coastal desalination plants. The percentage of the private sector's participation in each of the newly proposed production affiliates to the holding company shall be in accordance with the investment attractiveness, provided that the private sector's participation is no less than 60% in each production subsidiary. At the same time, costly research and development will be assumed by the new SWCC holding company. Hopefully, what emerges is a more realistic but "tiered" water tariff level to consumers, compared with current subsidized pricing that induces waste on a massive scale.

SWCC has now completed its strategic privatization studies and submitted its findings based on expert consultant advice, and is awaiting the final implementation decision from the Supreme Economic Council to initiate the SWCC conversion into a joint stock holding company fully owned by the state with an option to float shares at a later stage.

Saudi Arabian Mining Company (Maaden): Maaden offered 50% of its shares for an IPO which was oversubscribed 200% and which injected SR 10.956 billion to the company in 2008. This will help to assist *Maaden's* strategic expansion plans to open up the Saudi mining sector to private investments. Encouraged by the public's response to the first IPO, *Maaden* has sought approval from the Council of Ministers to increase its capital to SR 9.25 billion with 50% again being offered for public subscription.

Privatization of education services: During 2008, the Saudi Ministry of Education made several initiatives in privatizing some educational support services such as leasing of its unused land for private developers, signing contracts for recycling of paper waste and unused school books, school transportation, school cafeterias and canteens and allowing the private sector to bid for the building of new schools and maintaining current schools.

Besides the above key privatization initiatives, the Saudi Arabian government has also signalled its willingness to enter into a public and private partnership (PPP) to encourage the private sector to participate in the development and construction of the "mega cities" being established in the Kingdom. Four such mega cities are being constructed in Saudi Arabia, and Table 11.2 summarizes the major characteristics of these projects with the aim of establishing a reinvigorated regional economic diversification and more equitable wealth creation for Saudi citizens.

By 2020, it is expected that the major phases of the economic cities will have been completed and the forecasted impact on the Saudi economy are far-reaching. According to the Saudi Arabian General Investment Authority (SAGIA), some 1.3 million new jobs will be created, with the economic cities adding $150 billion to the Saudi GDP. They will attract over $100 billion of new investments domestically and from abroad, and their population will be three times that of Dubai, with an area four times that of Hong Kong. The Government of Saudi Arabia is forecasting that

Table 11.2 Saudi economic cities: major characteristics

Characteristic	King Abdullah Economic City	Prince Abdulaziz bin Mousaed Economic City	Knowledge Economic City	Jazan Economic City
Location	Rabigh, Red Sea coast, north of Jeddah	Hail, Northern Saudi Arabia	Madinah	Jazan, Southern Saudi Arabia
Project size ($ billion)	80	23	7	30
Project area (million m^2)	168	156	8	110
Project details	Largest Saudi private sector development	30,000 residential units	Focus on knowledge-based industries	Heavy industries (aluminium, refinery, steel, power)
	260,000 apartments and 56,000 villas	180,000 residents	30,000 housing units	Secondary industries (fisheries, pharmaceuticals, tech parks)
	To generate 1 million new jobs	New airport	20,000 new jobs	500,000 new jobs
	Promoting energy- and transportation-related industries	250,000 new jobs	150,000 residents	
	Seaport of 13.8 million m^2 handling 300,000 pilgrims	Agro-industry and mineral exploitation services	4,000 multipurpose commercial units and hotels	
Expected completion date	2020	2018	2020	2013 Phase 1; 2023 Phase 2; 2037 completion

a staggering $800 billion will be invested in these economic zones and other mega projects, including those by Saudi Aramco and SABIC over the next 20 years.

We can see that progress has taken place and that there is the political will to pursue a meaningful privatization programme. This political will is made doubly urgent by the forecasted estimates of future investment costs and capital needs if privatization is ignored or delayed.

Obstacles to Privatization

Within the Saudi Arabian context, there has been some debate amongst economists on the various problems and impediments that might arise out of the current desire to privatize a large element of government entities, and some of these potential obstacles are highlighted in Table 11.3.

Table 11.3 Saudi privatization: possible obstacles

Obstacles	Rationale
1. Fair book value for public assets	• A wide gap could arise between the fair book value and the market price. There could be limited availability of information concerning government operations and future risk factors, thus affecting the valuation method
2. Rigid pay structure	• Government employee pay scales are higher than in the private sector, and sometimes are not related to productivity. There is the problem of adjusting wages and reducing employment numbers, and of allowing the private sector to strike a balance between wages and productivity expectations
3. Government subsidies	• The removal of government subsidies on basic services such as utilities or health care could cause social problems. At the same time, artificially imposing low price levels will affect the most efficient allocation of private sector resources. Other forms of income support for those who are less well-off will have to be found
4. Lack of regulatory framework	• The government needs to address this major concern to ensure consumer protection and a degree of competition after privatization. Major progress has been made since the privatization process picked pace and experience has been gained
5. Updating public sector accounting standards	• These need to be updated so as to allow prospective investors to evaluate the true worth of these privatized public corporations
6. Financial resources	• There is a lack of depth in the current capital market structure that will make it more difficult to transfer public to private ownership. However, the growth in the numbers of new IPOs as well as their size indicates that this might not be such a critical impediment • Domestic banks have an aversion to long-term risk capital and there is an uncertain commercial/legal framework
7. Employment	• Potential unemployment becomes an issue, as the government faces pressure to reduce current unemployment levels

The list of possible obstacles to privatization in Saudi Arabia highlights one fundamental point that structural reform should precede privatization and that the benefits accruing from privatization are most sustainable when competition is free, the economy stable and the regulatory sector strong. Privatization remains more of a politically driven goal, albeit driven by a fear of the unknowable consequences of selling strategic state companies that have been supported for years by government assistance and protection. For those countries that have embarked on this unknown journey, the results have, in general, been more positive for industries and services after privatization than before. Studies for both industrialized and developing countries (Bourbakri, 1997, D'Souza and Megginson, 1998, Megginson et al., 1994) have indicated that, on average, there are improvements on all counts of productivity and efficiency measures as set out in Table 11.4.

What is interesting to note from the empirical studies carried out and documented above is that employment considerations post-privatization were not as bad as feared by some opponents of privatization. They worried that the policies would contribute to a greater level of unemployment in the long run, as highlighted earlier in Table 11.3.

Table 11.4 Consequences of privatization

Concept	Measure	Countries	Source	Median 3 years before sale	Median 3 years after sale
Profitability	Net income/sales	(IC)	= MNR	5.5%	8.0%
		(DC)	= BC	4.3%	11.0%
		(IC)	= DM	14.0%	17.0%
Efficiency	Sales/number of	(IC)	= MNR	0.96[a]	1.06[a]
	employees[a]	(DC)	= BC	0.92[a]	1.17[a]
		(IC)	= DM	1.02[a]	1.23[a]
Investment	Capital	(IC)	= MNR	12.0%	17.0%
	expenditure/	(DC)	= BC	11.0%	24.0%
	Sales	(IC)	= DM	18%	17.0%
Output	Sales adjusted by	(IC)	= MNR	0.90[a]	1.14[a]
	CPI	(DC)	= BC	0.97[a]	1.22[a]
		(IC)	= DM	0.93[a]	2.70[a]
Employment	Number of	(IC)	= MNR	40,850	43,200
	employees	(DC)	= BC	10,672	10,811
		(IC)	= DM	22,941	22,136
Leverage	Debt/assets	(IC)	= MNR	66%	64%
		(DC)	= BC	55%	50%
		(IC)	= DM	29%	23%
Dividends	Dividends/sales	(IC)	= MNR	1.3%	3.0%
		(DC)	= BC	2.8%	5.3%
		(IC)	= DM	1.5%	4.0%

[a]Ratio in year of sale set to 1.00 to avoid large differences among industries
IC = Industrialized countries; DC = Developing countries; MNR – Source: Megginson, Nash and Van Randerborgh (1994); BC – Source: Bourbakri and Cosset (1997); DM – Source: D'Souza and Megginson (1999)

Foreign Direct Investment (FDI): Theoretical Basis

Foreign direct investment (FDI) is an investment of foreign assets into domestic structures, equipment and organizations. It does not include foreign investment into the stock markets. FDI is thought to be more useful to a country than investments in the equity of its companies because equity investments are potentially "hot money" which can leave at the first sign of trouble, while FDI is durable and generally useful whether the economy is doing well or badly (Aitken et al., 1997, Liu et al., 2000). An example of this is the 1988/1989 Asian financial crisis that resulted in a deficiency of short-term debt finance, but did not have a significant impact on the level of foreign direct investment in the Asian region. Also, the return to direct investment is dependent on profitability, unlike debt finance where the capital and interest must generally be repaid, regardless of performance (Helpman et al., 2004).

When analysing FDI, it is important to know what the strategic drivers are for organizations to invest in other markets. According to some analysts, there are two main patterns of internationalization, the first being firms who want to move production to foreign countries in order to reduce their overall production costs. This type of FDI is referred to as vertical FDI and is generally influenced by differences in labour costs (Buch et al., 2005). Vertical FDI is beneficial to the organization investing by achieving a reduction in costs but also beneficial to the country receiving the investment. Not only is there infrastructure and capital being invested into the economy of the developing country, but more importantly there are specialist skills and knowledge that the organization must transfer to their local workforce that will spill over to be shared within and between industries in the local market (Kugler, 2006).

The second type of FDI identified by Buch, Kleinert, Lippioner and Toubal is horizontal FDI, and this is where organizations invest in other countries as a means to gain better access to foreign markets, get closer customers and avoid trade costs. The majority of FDI between developed nations is predominantly some form of horizontal FDI in order for multinational organizations to operate efficiently in a global context (Buch et al., 2005).

There are also political factors that can influence a firm's decision to invest as FDI, including the avoidance of trade barriers as well as economic development incentives that may be available from governments wishing to build up infrastructure in their country (Fisher et al., 2006).

Foreign direct investment is a major component of today's global business environment and a clear way for large multinational companies to achieve strategic advantages. This can occur through vertical FDI, where the benefits are mainly reduced costs, or horizontal FDI, where the benefits are mainly access to new markets. There is evidence to show that FDI into a nation has a wide array of benefits for both the organization and the country being invested in, which also equates to knowledge and productivity spillovers (Aitken et al., 1997, Harrison, 1997).

The global financial crisis of 2008/2009 has affected net private capital flows, but with different aspects as illustrated in Table 11.5 for the period 2006–2009.

Table 11.5 Net capital flows to emerging and developing markets 2006–2009 ($ billions)

Region	2006	2007	2008	2009
Africa: Total	35.2	33.4	24.2	30.2
Net direct investment	23.4	32.1	32.4	27.6
Net portfolio investment	17.6	9.9	−15.8	0.9
Other net investments (outflows)	−5.7	8.3	7.9	1.8
Middle East: Total	−50.0	11.0	−120.9	−29.5
Net direct investment	14.9	4.0	11.4	17.6
Net portfolio investment	−25.7	−31.0	−12.3	−14.4
Other net investments	−39.2	38.0	−120.1	−32.7
Emerging Asia: Total	31.8	164.8	127.9	−46.9
Net direct investment	94.3	138.5	222.6	161.6
Net portfolio investment	−107.2	11.2	−65.9	−192.1
Other net investments	44.6	15.2	−28.7	−16.3
Commonwealth of Independent States	55.1	127.2	−127.4	−119.0
Net direct investment	20.7	26.6	44.4	17.3
Net portfolio investment	12.9	14.5	−36.8	1.6
Other net investments	21.5	86.1	−135.1	−137.9

Source: SAMA, IMF, World Economic Outlook

An analysis of Table 11.5 seems to confirm the volatility of portfolio capital flows discussed earlier, compared with the relative stability of net direct foreign investment. "Other net investment" flows in the above table relate to residents' investment outflows to other markets and their inflows to their home markets. Given the significance of such global investment flows, what measures has the Kingdom adopted to attract FDI and what have been the results to date?

Saudi FDI: Establishing the Operational Framework

Saudi Arabia's WTO accession in 2005 helped to bring changes to the Kingdom's investment environment under the Agreement on Trade Related Investment Measures (TRIMs). However, prior to WTO accession, the Kingdom had been taking some measures to attract FDI and a new Foreign Investment Law was enacted in 2000 to replace and liberalize the 1979 Foreign Investment Law. The 2000 law established the Saudi Arabian General Investment Authority (SAGIA) as responsible for approving foreign investment projects; SAGIA also serves as the enquiry point on laws, regulations and procedures relating to foreign investment, and the Governor of SAGIA, currently Dr. Amr Al Dabbagh, holds the status of a cabinet minister.

Reflecting the impact of WTO negotiations on Saudi legislation over the past several years, Saudi Arabia confirmed to the WTO that the 2000 Foreign Investment Law is fully consistent with the WTO Agreement on TRIMs and that Saudi Arabia would not apply any measures prohibited by that agreement.

This agreement recognizes that certain investment measures can have trade-restrictive and distorting effects. TRIMs state that no WTO member shall apply a measure that is prohibited by the provisions of GATT Article III (regarding national treatment) or Article XI (regarding quantitative restrictions). An example of inconsistent measures includes local content requirements. The agreement contains transitional arrangements allowing members to maintain TRIMs for a limited time following the entry into force of the WTO (2 years in the case of developed country members, 5 years for developing country members and 7 years for least-developed country members). The agreement also establishes a committee on TRIMs to monitor the operation and implementation of these commitments (SAMBA, 2006). Table 11.6 summarizes the main features of the new law and the old law it replaced.

As can be noted from Table 11.6, the 2000 law and other subsequent actions made considerable changes to the Kingdom's foreign investment regime in order to make the country more business-friendly and open to FD1. The old law favoured joint ventures over 100% foreign-owned projects. Under the new law, foreign investors are no longer required to take local partners. The new law provides equal treatment for non-Saudi firms. The repatriation of profits and capital are guaranteed. It offers foreign licensed companies the right to buy property for the purposes of the company and allows them to sponsor their own non-Saudi employees, previously denied. The new law streamlined the investment process by committing to respond within a specified amount of time to an investment application from the date of receipt.

Other related laws and regulations in the past have added to the more liberal environment. Saudi Arabia also reduced the maximum income tax rate for foreign firms to 30% (from 45%) in April 2000, and in January 2004 a new tax law reduced the rate to 20%. Business travel into the Kingdom has become more relaxed with less onerous requirements for business visas.

Table 11.6 Comparisons of main features of the new and old Saudi foreign investment laws

Feature	New law	Previous law
Tax holiday	• No reference is made to tax holidays and dividend taxes	• If the Saudi share in the company is greater or equal to 25%, foreign investors will not pay taxes during the first 10 years for industrial projects, or 5 years for services and agricultural projects
Taxing scheme	• If the corporate profits of a company are: • less than SR 10,000; they are taxed at the rate of 20%; the rate rises to 30% if corporate profits are more than SR 100,000. The new law reduced the tax brackets from four to just two	• If the corporate profits of a joint venture company are: – less than SR 100,000, the tax rate is 25% – more that SR 100,000, but less than SR 500,000, the tax rate is 35% – more than SR 500,000, but less than SR 1,000,000, the tax rate is 40% – more than SR 1,000,000, the tax rate is 45%

Table 11.6 (continued)

Feature	New law	Previous law
Financial losses	• There is no limitation on the number of future years that financial losses can be allocated to	• Financial losses can only be allocated to next year's operations
Loans from the Saudi Industrial Development Funds (SIDF)	• Companies fully or partially owned by foreigners can apply for subsidized loans from SIDF and can now enjoy all of the incentives and privileges offered to local projects	• For company to apply for SIDF loans, the Saudi share in equity has to be at least 25%
Real estate ownership	• Full ownership of the project is granted to the licensed firm (including land, buildings and housing for employees)	• There must be a Saudi partner/sponsor who would own the land • Foreign ownership prohibited
Sponsorship	• No Saudi sponsor is needed for the foreign investor. The licensed company will be the sponsor for the expatriate workers	• The Saudi partner will be the sponsor for the foreign investor and for expatriates working in the joint venture company
Investment guarantees	• Foreign investor has the right to transfer his share derived from selling his equity or profits out of Saudi Arabia. Not subject to expropriation (nationalization) except in public interest and in exchange for equitable compensation	• None were specified
Penalties for violation	• A petition against any penalty may be brought by foreign investor before Board of Grievance. Possible penalties include: withholding incentives, imposing fines not exceeding SR 500,000 and cancelling a licence	• Kingdom could cancel licence or deny incentive after investor received warning from Ministry of Industry and Electricity to correct violation within a certain period. Investors could appeal to Board of Grievances within 30 days
Administration	• SAGIA Investor Services (one-stop shop) was focal point for investors and comprises representatives of nine investment-related ministries	• Several ministries and government agencies
Type of investments	• 100% foreign-owned project in addition to joint ventures	• Favoured joint ventures over 100% foreign
Period of approval of licences	• Maximum 30 days	• Not specified
Investment fields open to investors	• All fields open for investments except those on "negative list"	• To be approved under national development plan
Possibility of more than one licence	• More than one licence allowed in different fields	• Restricted and had to be in the same field

Source: SAGIA

To ensure compatibility with WTO rules, in April 2005 Saudi Arabia removed the minimum foreign requirements for foreign investors, which had been SR 25 million for agricultural projects, SR 5 million for industrial projects and SR 2 million for services businesses. Technology transfer was not a condition for investment under the new law.

However, as Table 11.6 also indicates, there are still some restrictions placed by the new FDI law on certain investment fields that foreigners can enter, the so-called "negative list."

Since 2000, the number of activities prohibited to foreign investors has been reduced to exploration, drilling and production of petroleum, manufacturing of military equipment and uniforms and civilian explosives. In the service sector, foreigners are not allowed to invest in military catering, security or real estate in *Makkah* and *Madina* nor can they invest in real estate brokerage television and radio stations, advertising and public relations, recruitment and employment services and transport.

Excluding the negative list, all sectors are now open to foreign investment in Saudi Arabia, including the lucrative insurance services, wholesale and retail trade, air and train transport and communication services, including satellite transmission services.

Saudi FDI: A Score Sheet

By all accounts, FDI can be a critically important ingredient to *long-term* sustainable growth for developing countries, especially if the FDI is channelled into neglected productive sectors, or internationally underperforming, but potentially profitable sectors. FDI can play an important "spillover" effect as demonstrated by other countries' experiences (Aitken et al., 1997). Table 11.7 examines an FDI "score sheet" of positive and potential negative factors and their Saudi Arabian applicability in light of the new FDI law and the recent structural and economic changes that have taken place in the Kingdom.

As Table 11.7 illustrates, there seems to be little reason for concern as far as potential large-scale negative factors affecting Saudi Arabia from encouraging more FDI are concerned. This is due to the large and varied industrial and manufacturing base that has been recently built up, most of which is of a new technology and on par with international standards, unlike other developing countries which often see foreign "enclave economies" arise through FDI investments.

Saudi FDI Flows: On the Rise

After many years of languishing at the lower end of Middle East FDI league tables, Saudi Arabia is fast becoming the attraction of both Arab and non-Arab FDI destination. For example, FDI by the UAE in the Kingdom stood at nearly $5.8 billion in

Table 11.7 Foreign direct investment: Saudi Arabia score sheet

FDI factors	Analysis	Saudi Arabia applicability
Positive factors		
1. Capital formation	• This is more stable than other forms of investments. Essentially it is an equity investment – profits are repatriated when projects yield returns and part of the profits is reinvested in the host country • Risks are borne by foreign shareholders • FDI will not lead to debt crises (like bank lending) that require bailouts	• Applicable: In Saudi Arabia investments are in either Saudi majority-owned companies, or, now, 100% foreign-owned companies
2. Productivity growth	• A new understanding of the growth process treats technological changes as endogenous growth. This also involves the "soft" side of technological advances (organizational structure, managerial practices, etc.) that contribute to productivity growth • Rather than reinvent technological advances, developing countries can benefit from best practices in standards, embodied technology and markets of parent company	• Applicable: This is the main reason why SABIC established international joint venture affiliates as examples as well as entry of new telecom companies such as Mobily and Zain
3. Economic linkages	• The impact of FDI on domestic economic growth depends on spreading out best practices through backward linkages with local producers and distributors, horizontal linkages with local competitors and linkages with local institutions such as universities and research institutes	• Applicable: Local sourcing is an important stimulant to domestic companies. Linkages to universities are also important (e.g. science parks) • More is needed on backward linkages with local suppliers, but this varies with the industry
4. Employment and labour standards	• Employment can be created via three areas: (a) direct employment in operations, (b) backward and forward linkages in enterprises that are suppliers, subcontractors and service providers and (c) employment in sectors not directly related to FDI projects • Quality of labour standards is improved in the domestic economy, through good labour practices, superior working conditions and positive career prospects • Adopting international global labour management practices that are different from host country and ensuring that practices are of international standards	• Applicable: The quality of labour employment and the creation of best employment practices have been more important to date than the quantitative aspect of employment and Saudi companies are adapting best HR practices from leading international companies now operating in Saudi Arabia
5. Environmental standards	• FDI can lead to higher environmental controls and procedures	• Applicable: Saudi Arabia insists on the latest environmental-friendly technology

Table 11.7   (continued)

FDI factor	Analysis	Saudi Arabia applicability
Negative factors		
1. "Crowding-out" effect	• FDI may remove investment opportunities of the domestic firms and drive them out of business (e.g. in financial markets) • If FDI borrows locally, interest rates could rise if there are scarce resources, making borrowing for local firms uncompetitive • FDI could pre-empt entry into the market of some types of production, especially if the foreign company employs aggressive marketing practices	• There is not yet any evidence of this in Saudi Arabia, as most FDI has been capital-intensive and the joint venture majority is Saudi-owned
2. Balance of payments problem	• FDI profits could be repatriated, constituting financial outflows to be set against net annual FDI inflow. This is important for countries with exchange controls	• This is not an issue for Saudi Arabia as no exchange control regime exists
3. "Enclave economies"	• FDI investments could be narrowly based with a limited overall impact on domestic economy and benefiting only a small group of population. Examples are in mining natural resource extraction or "export processing zones," whereas if mining is only for exports, then it will not generate secondary industry employment. Neither would repackaging of goods in a duty-free "export processing zone"	• Not applicable as oil sector is in state hands and no foreign-owned exclusive zones exist

2008, the largest FDI flow by an Arab country, as per figures released by the Inter-Arab Guarantee Corporation (IAIGC). The UAE investment in Saudi Arabia was more than double the total FDI channelled by the UAE into other Arab countries in 2008, and nearly 45% of the total investments received by Saudi Arabia from other Arab League nations.

Until 2005, the Kingdom had not seemed to match inward investments with its undoubted economic size and potential compared to other Arab and Islamic countries. The reasons were obvious – sluggish bureaucracy, uncompetitive incentives and taxation regime, multiple layers of governmental approvals and seeming inflexible labour and sponsorship laws. The general feeling in Saudi Arabia was that the domestic market had ample surplus liquidity, unlike other "capital-poor" Arab countries. Continued government spending on mega projects would make up for any capital shortfall. This rosy picture could not last forever in the face of persistent budget deficits during the period 1983–2001, the advent of privatization as a strategic tool for private sector participation and the Kingdom's accession to the World Trade Organization (WTO) in 2005. The time for change had arrived and a fresh perspective had to be found to attract foreign investors.

From 2005, the Kingdom's FDI took off as illustrated in Fig. 11.3, with inflows of $12.1 billion recorded in that year, compared with a meagre $245 million on

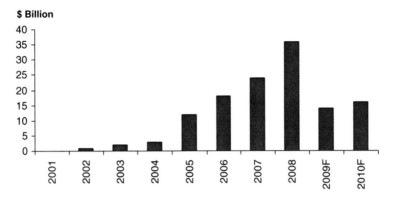

Fig. 11.3 Saudi FDI inflows (2001–2010) (Source: UNCTAD) ("F" stands for "forecast")

average per year for the period 1990–2000. By 2008, the net inflow had reached $38.2 billion as illustrated in Fig. 11.3.

In line with global trends seen earlier in Table 11.5 the net FDI inflow to Saudi Arabia was forecasted to fall to around $15 billion in 2009, but is forecasted to rise in 2010 on the basis of higher oil prices for the region (averaging at more than $70 p.b.). According to UNCTAD however, Saudi Arabia came eighth among the top 10 recipients of FDI in 2009 with inflow of $36 billion, making Saudi Arabia the tob Middle East FDI destination. What is also significant is that FDI is now making a larger impact on the national economy and the relative size of FDI to GDP has been rising as illustrated in Fig. 11.4.

In 2007, Saudi Arabia's inward FDI flow as a ratio to GDP was 6.4%, but this had risen to 8.1% in 2008, despite the record oil revenues of that year which saw GDP rise to $465 billion levels. An analysis of FDI flows into the Kingdom by country of origin reveals that the top-ranked investing countries are primarily non-Arab,

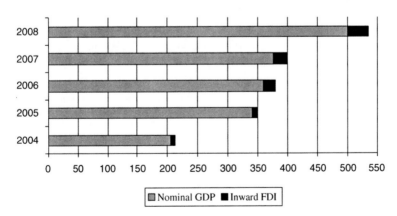

Fig. 11.4 Saudi Arabia's FDI vs. GDP (US$ bn) (Source: SAMBA, UNCTAD, World Investment Report, 2008)

Table 11.8 Net cumulative FDI flows into Saudi Arabia – top 10 countries 1999–2005

Country	1999 ($Million)	Country	2005 ($Million)
1. USA	2,252.5	1. Japan	12,906
2. Japan	576.8	2. USA	4,979
3. Bermuda	312.3	3. France	4,035
4. Netherlands Antilles	219.9	4. UAE	3,930
5. Jordan	214.7	5. Germany	3,351
6. France	198.3	6. Lebanon	1,292
7. UK	147.1	7. Canada	1,069
8. Panama	107.6	8. Bermuda	1,043
9. Italy	100.7	9. Cayman Islands	981
10. Switzerland	97.1	10. UK	780

Source: National Centre for Economic and Financial Information, 1999, SAGIA, 2006

with the recent exception of the UAE's investment into Saudi Arabia, especially in the mega economic city projects. Table 11.8 illustrates this by analysing the top 10 cumulative FDI contributors by country of origin for 1999 and 2005.

From Table 11.8, we note that while the USA was the largest equity investment partner in 1999, it had been overtaken by Japan in 2005 in a significant way, with the large petrochemical joint projects at *Petro Rabigh* on the Red Sea Coast of the Kingdom accounting for a large portion of the investment by the Japanese Sumitomo Corporation. In both 1999 and 2005, countries such as Bermuda, Netherlands Antilles, Panama and Cayman Islands appear on the FDI list, but the countries of origins of those registering in these offshore tax havens are not known. They represented a significant portion of investment source in 1999 but less so by 2005, probably due to stricter "know-your client" rules by the Kingdom, especially following the September 11, 2001 events and tighter international control over finance movements.

Analysis of FDI by sector of investment reveals that the industrial and service sectors take the overwhelming bulk of investments, with agriculture being the least attractive either for fully foreign-owned licensed projects or for joint venture licensed projects. This is illustrated in Table 11.9, which sets out the cumulative FDI stock in Saudi Arabia by 2005.

Table 11.9 Total cumulative FDI finance by ownership and project sector 2005

Investment sector	Fully foreign licensed		Joint venture licensed	2005 ($million)
	Number	Value (SR billion)	Number	Value (SR billion)
• Industrial	782	21.392	464	100.057
• Services	1,271	22.19	586	7.898
• Agriculture	5	0.125	4	0.366
Total	2,058	43.707	1,054	108.321

Source: SAGIA

By 2005, the cumulative FDI stock was around $40 billion, but this had risen to $115 billion by 2008 for both fully foreign licensed and joint venture projects. To put the 2008 data in perspective, the total world FDI stock in 2008 was $14,909 billion and Saudi's share represented less than 1%. Similarly, Saudi Arabia's record inflow of $38.2 billion FDI inflow in 2008 represented around 2.2% of the world's total of $1,697 billion, according to the United Nations Conference on Trade and Development (UNCTAD).

Sometimes the driving force behind FDI is not new projects or joint venture projects but rather cross-border mergers and acquisitions of existing companies. In the developed world, mergers and acquisitions (M&As) have become the primary mode of entry of FDI, while in the developing world their importance is small but growing. In the developed countries, one regularly hears of mega deals such as the acquisition of Mannesmann of Germany by Vodafone (UK) for $200 billion in 2000 and of Voice Stream (USA) by Deutsche Telecom (Germany) for $24.6 billion in 2001 or the 2010 acquisition of the Asian subsidiary of AIG by the UK's Prudential for $35.5 billion in 2010.

Cross-border M&As in the Arab countries are very small in comparison. Table 11.10 sets out the ten largest deals during the period 1997–2010.

Table 11.10 The ten largest cross-border M&A deals in the League of Arab States, 1987–2010

Acquired company	Target country	Acquiring company	Acquiring country	Year	Value in million dollars
Zain	Kuwait	Bharti	India	2010	10,700.0
Telecommunication Corporation of Jordan	Jordan	Investor Group	France	2000	508.0
Assiut Cement	Egypt	Cemex	Mexico	1999	373.0
Societe Marocaine de L'Industrie	Morocco	Corral Petroleum Holding AB	Sweden	1997	372.5
Societe des Cimens de Gabes	Tunisia	Secil (Semapa – Sociedade)	Portugal	2000	251.0
Al Ameriya Cement Corporation	Egypt	Lafrage Titan	France	2000	249.0
Societes des Ciments de Jbel	Tunisia	Cimpor – Cimentos de Portugal EP	Portugal	1998	229.9
Alexandria Portland Cement (EG)	Egypt	Blue Circle Industries PLC	United Kingdom	2000	196.0
Al-Sharif Group	Egypt	Investor Group	Saudi Arabia	1993	177.3
Societes des Ciments d'Enfidha	Tunisia	Uniland Cementera SA	Spain	1998	169.1
Credit Libanais (Lebanon)	Lebanon	Investor	Saudi Arabia	1997	163.0

Source: UNCTAD, Cross-Border M&A Database, 2002

The low level of M&A activity could be due to several factors. One factor is the type of company structures in the Arab world, which often tend to be closed, family groupings with no intention of selling to outsiders. Another factor is the lack of suitable publicly listed corporations that meet foreign investors' criteria in terms of market share, profitability and management structure (Field, 1985, Fahim, 1995, Wright, 1996).

The ten largest M&A Arab deals highlight the fact that the majority of such large deals are carried out by *non-Arab investors*. Unspecified Saudi investors participated in two deals in Lebanon and Egypt. The largest deal was $10,700 million, with Indian investor interests acquiring Zain telecom of Kuwait in 2010. The table also illustrates that those Arab countries with the longest experience of privatization, such as Egypt, Tunisia and Morocco, have led the way in cross-border M&A deals. However, the key implication of this table is that Arab capital, by and large, *prefers to migrate to non-Arab opportunities*. The exception to this is the international Saudi investor Prince Al Waleed Bin Tallal Bin Abdulaziz, who has diversified his holdings in both Western and Arab countries, particularly in Egypt, Jordan, Lebanon and Syria (Abdulaziz, Al Waleed Bin Tallal, 2003).

Continuing investor perception of a lack of development in the Arab world's general legal framework governing foreign investment, such as labour laws, company laws, bankruptcy laws and intellectual property laws, is a contributory factor to this negligible Arab cross-border activity. Knowing that they are being left behind in the FDI race, most Arab countries are taking steps to amend existing legislation and laws and to introduce new ones that are more foreign investor-friendly.

The high oil prices and larger revenue flows to several Gulf Arab countries such as Saudi Arabia and the UAE during the periods 2006 and 2007 have led to some significant cross-border acquisitions for these countries, as illustrated in Table 11.11.

While other regions such as Asia were active in both cross-border sales and purchases/acquisitions, other countries such as Turkey were more active in sales but not in acquisitions, unlike the Arab Gulf countries such as Saudi Arabia and the

Table 11.11 Cross-border merger and acquisition overview, 1990–2008 (millions of dollars)

Region/ economy	Sales (net)				Purchases (net)			
	1990–2000 (Annual average)	2006	2007	2008	1990–2000 (Annual average)	2006	2007	2008
Saudi Arabia	15	21	125	102	536	5,398	12,730	1,450
Turkey	78	15,340	16,415	11,628	42	356	767	1,313
United Arab Emirates	12	53	1,230	1,225	111	23,117	15,611	4,384
Asia and Oceania	8,970	65,130	68,538	64,730	10,488	70,714	91,250	89,006
Developing economies	25,860	89,028	96,998	100,862	13,900	114,119	139,677	99,805
World	257,070	635,940	1,031,100	873,214	257,070	635,940	1,031,100	673,214

Source: UNCTAD, World Investment Report, 2009

UAE who were more active in purchases and acquisitions than in sales. During 2006 and 2007, the UAE's purchases amounted to around $40 billion as compared to Saudi Arabia's $18.2 billion for the same period. However, while the majority of Saudi acquisitions were carried out by the private sector, the UAE's acquisitions were mostly the result of the country's Sovereign Wealth Funds such as Abu Dhabi Investment Authority (ADIA).

Conclusion

Most neutral observers commend the Kingdom's recent economic reforms, including the adoption of the new Foreign Investment Law allowing foreigners to own land, and the introduction of a comprehensive and inspiring privatization strategy. Most observers also agree that the pace of reform in the privatization and the FDI areas has been impressive, leading to tangible movement on both fronts, more so on the FDI sector where Saudi Arabia is now an attractive FDI destination. The Saudi WTO accession in 2005 has spurred this reform, but Saudi Arabia is also an attractive target for international investors which felt that the Kingdom had not been widely affected by the 2008/2009 international financial crisis and that the Arab world's largest economy and its ongoing mega projects were an attractive investment proposition.

Summary of Key Points

- *Privatization was officially launched in 2002, and planned to encompass all spheres of economic activities in the Kingdom. First steps have already been taken through the establishment of various regulatory agencies under which the privatized entities would operate.*
- *Privatization is an instrument of economic policy whereby there is a transfer of property or control of assets owned by the state to the private sector – both management and ownership. To date, Saudi Arabia has carried out "partial privatization" through the sale of shares of government-held corporations, such as SABIC, SCECO and SEC. More are being planned.*
- *Certain obstacles need to be overcome before privatization could become effective. These relate to assessing the fair book value of public assets, overcoming rigid pay structures of the privatized labour force, reduction of government subsidies and updating public sector accounting standards.*
- *Saudi Arabia has now been successful in attracting sizeable FDI to the Kingdom due to the size of its economy, market depth and more recent enhancements to the Foreign Investment Law, such as a reduction to 20% in foreign corporate profit tax. Cross-border mergers and acquisitions are still not common in the Middle East. Investor perception is that more is needed to enhance the legal and operating frameworks such as labour, company and bankruptcy laws.*

Chapter 12
Population and Demographics: *Saudization* and the Labour Market

> *Everyone now works for the government – either on the payroll or on the tax roll.*
>
> German Saying

Learning Outcomes

By the end of this section you would understand:

- *Saudi demographic trends and their economic impact*
- *Government* Saudization *policies and results to date*
- *Private sector and* Saudization
- *Expatriate labour in the Saudi economy and its impact*
- *Trends in the Saudi labour market*
- *The issue of rising Saudi youth unemployment*
- *A model for Saudi labour participation*
- *Measurement of potential GDP losses due to unemployment*
- *An examination of current and planned structures of the Saudi labour market*
- *Duality of Saudi and foreign labour market structure*

Overview

There are a multitude of reasons – economic, social and political – for the Saudi Arabian government's serious approach to the current state of the labour market and to Saudi unemployment issues. Unemployment means less output, a lower standard of living and a high and worrying dependency rate. Some studies have put the number of Saudi dependents as high as 56 per 100 Saudi workers, 2.4 times the world average (Al Sheikh, 2003). Thus, any major decline in income per worker, or a total lack of work, could have a dangerous effect on living standards and social cohesion. A worrying rise in juvenile crime rates connected with unemployed youth has now been widely reported in the local Saudi press and this adds further pressure on the government.

M.A. Ramady, *The Saudi Arabian Economy*, DOI 10.1007/978-1-4419-5987-4_12,
© Springer Science+Business Media, LLC 2010

But, as we will soon see, the Saudi government's effort is hampered by two factors. First, Saudi Arabia has a relatively young population age structure, with increasing numbers of new labour market entrants; this is coupled with one of the highest birth rates in the world. Second, there is a continuous flow of foreign workers into the Kingdom. However, the system does not seem to match available jobs with the skills of existing foreign workers, but merely compounds the problem by bringing in additional foreign workers under the Saudi private companies' sponsorship scheme, known as the *Kafeel* system.

The Saudi government has adopted a programme of *Saudization* directed at gradually replacing expatriate workers with Saudi employees. The private sector is being steered towards increasing the proportion of nationals in employment through a policy of inducements and punishments, with charges for work permits or *Iqamas* and exit/re-entry visas raised substantially. This makes it more expensive to hire expatriate workers. Foreign labour visa issuance is also being more vigorously enforced. However, as we will discuss, the process of *Saudization* should not take place at the expense of efficiency and productivity in the national economy. The government is emphasizing improved education and training to provide Saudi graduates with the skills and the quality of education demanded by the private sector.

Saudi Arabia's accession to the WTO in 2005, while allowing the government to pursue its *Saudization* policy, yet also allowed foreign companies to hire their own skilled foreign labour and granted them the right to sponsor their own employees without having a Saudi sponsor.

Population and Demographics

An evaluation of a country's labour market and its characteristics would be somewhat meaningless without an understanding of the underlying demographic trends and composition of the population. Such an analysis will provide an insight into the potential problems that might arise in the future, based on current government labour policies. By its own admission, Saudi Arabia is amongst the fastest growing nations in the world in terms of population growth (SAMA, 2008). The Kingdom's population grew threefold from 7.3 million in 1975 to 24.8 million in 2008. The high growth rate of the Kingdom's population, currently put at around 2.3% p.a., is due to a number of demographic transformations in the structure of Saudi society. These changes resulted from great improvements in living, health and social conditions over the past three decades. Some analysts have argued that there is no way to be sure of the true size of the Kingdom's demographic challenge, as no comprehensive census has been taken, until recently (2010). Despite this, there is some agreement that the population data used by the Saudi Ministry of Planning to forecast current and future population trends probably errs on the conservative side (U.S. Census Bureau, 23 March 2003).

The age composition of the population is a major worrying point for future labour market entrants. Countries can be characterized as either having an "ageing" or "young" population structure, with most countries of western Europe falling in the

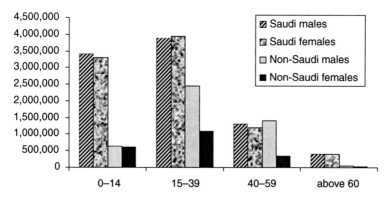

Fig. 12.1 Saudi Arabia's population by age groups, gender and nationality (2008) (Source: SAMA)

first category and Saudi Arabia in the second. This is illustrated in Fig. 12.1, which shows that, as of 2008, the age groups below 40 years account for 78% or 19.4 million of the population.

The Saudi population under 15 years constitutes 8 million or 32% of the total population. This reinforces the dependency ratio explained earlier, without adding those over 60 to the ratio.

Table 12.1 sets out demographic trends for Saudi Arabia compared with other Arab countries, as well as the developing countries, the Organisation for Economic

Table 12.1 Demographic trends: A comparison of Saudi Arabia and the world

Description	Year (period)	Saudi Arabia	Arab countries	Developing countries	OECD	The world
Total population (million)	1975	7.3	144.4	2,972.0	928.0	4,076.1
	2005	23.1	313.9	5,215.0	1,172.6	6,514.8
	2015	29.3	3,804.0	59,566.0	1,237.3	7,295.1
Annual growth rate	1975–2005	3.9	2.6	1.9	0.8	1.6
of population (%)	2005–2015	2.1	1.9	1.3	0.5	1.1
Urban population (ratio	1975	58.3	41.8	26.5	66.9	37.2
to total population)	2005	81.0	55.1	42.7	75.6	48.6
	2015	83.2	58.8	47.9	78.2	52.8
Population below 15 years	2005	34.5	35.2	30.9	19.4	28.3
(ratio to total population)	2015	30.7	32.1	28.0	17.8	26.0
Fertility rate (infants	1970–1975	7.3	6.7	5.4	2.6	4.5
per woman)	2000–2005	3.8	3.6	2.9	1.7	2.6
Life expectancy (years)	1970–1975	53.9	51.9	55.8	70.3	58.3
	2000–2005	71.6	66.7	65.5	77.8	66.0
GDP per capita (in US $	2003	9,745	5,685	4,359	25,915	8,229
based on purchasing	2004	11,111	5,680	4,775	27,571	8,833
power parity)	2005	13,645	6,716	5,282	29,197	9,543

Source: Central Department of Statistics and Information, Ministry of Economy and Planning and Human Resources Development Report of 2006, UN Development Programme, SAMA, 2009

Co-operation and Development (OECD) and the rest of the world. It immediately highlights the high Saudi population growth rate, young population profile and high fertility rate compared to the other blocs mentioned.

Regardless of whether Saudi or non-Saudi estimates are absolutely correct, it is extremely clear that rapid population growth is taking place in Saudi Arabia. What was largely a rural society 50 years ago has become a relatively urbanized one. According to the World Bank, roughly 49% of the total population was urbanized as early as 1970, and 12% of the population was living in cities with a population of 1 million or more (World Bank, World Development Indicators, 2002). By 2005, the percentage living in cities was 83%, with 35% of the population living in cities of 1 million or more.

This urbanization trend will undoubtedly affect the numbers of Saudis seeking jobs in cities as opposed to agricultural work, with the percentage of those employed in agriculture dropping from 45% in 1970 to fewer than 8% in 2008 (SAMA, 2009).

The Saudi population was not only one of the fastest growing, but also one of the most fertile; the proportion of infants per woman was considerably higher than in other regions of the world.

These current *population growth* trends have sharply widened the gap between the population and Saudi government finances over the years, especially from the end of the 1980s' "boom years". The erratic revenue pattern over the past decades and sharp population growth reinforce the government's determination to diversify the base of the Saudi economy in order to create more private sector jobs. As countries economically develop and urbanize, the demographics shift towards a lower birth rate, as seen earlier in Table 12.1, especially as women enter the labour force and economic pressures lead to smaller families. According to a recent study conducted amongst Saudi females, 22% of Saudi mothers wanted "a maximum of six children." Only one in 10 women wanted fewer than four children (Arab News, 24 April 2003). The study revealed some changing social customs. Younger women between 20 and 29 felt freer to discuss this subject than those older than 29, and 35% of married women discussed family size with their husbands.

So far the impact of such shifts in social attitudes on Saudi Arabia's population growth has been limited. Saudi population figures provide an insight into future trends. According to SAMA, the total population (Saudi and non-Saudi) could rise to 29.3 million by 2015 and 33.4 million by 2020, assuming an average annual growth rate of 2.1%.

These estimates show the extent of the impact Saudi population growth will have on internal social cohesion, economic wealth and development (Kanovsky, 1994, Abdelkarim, 1999). In turn, population growth will determine the size of the labour force and the degree to which a policy of *Saudization* will ease *unemployment*. It will also indicate the level of investment needed for infrastructure and education.

There are no figures on the distribution of income within Saudi Arabia. As such, Saudi per capita income data are not of much value in providing a meaningful analysis of real wealth. The published official figures seem to indicate, however, that because of higher population growth and erratic revenues, Saudis are still behind GDP per capita for the OECD countries, as illustrated in Table 12.1.

Human Resources and Employment: Theoretical Analysis

Despite its key role within economic development, human resources remain a fundamental challenge for most Middle East countries. The literature on this subject is varied but it is widely accepted that human resources development is an important factor in economic growth and for influencing changes in economic structure (Arthur, 1994, Barney and Wright 1998, Kuruvilla, 1996, Heneman et al., 2000). It is argued that human resources development can be a more realistic, reliable and pervasive indicator of economic development than any other single factor since it is invariably a necessary condition for all kinds of growth. Economic growth of a country requires both financial and human resources, and as analysed in earlier chapters, financial resources have not been a critical issue for Saudi Arabia, while obtaining sufficient level of qualified manpower for industrialization and economic growth is a more problematical one that needs to be overcome through the development of a better educated and training programme that will be explored in the next chapter.

The Saudi government is aware of the importance of manpower development, and the Ninth Five-Year Plan (2010–2014) sets out the following national labour force development objectives:

- Optimum utilization of the national labour force. Encourage Saudi nationals to join the productive work in all economic sectors.
- Ensure harmony between educational and training programmes of Saudis and the labour market requirements.
- Provide more employment opportunities to Saudi nationals in the private sector; this includes new openings as a result of natural employment growth as well as replacement of existing foreign workers.
- Rationalize the recruitment of foreign workers and limit it to actual requirements. Enforce decisions and regulations related to *Saudization*. Restrict employment in certain job categories to Saudi nationals.
- Provide more employment opportunities to Saudis, and in particular to women. Adopt appropriate policies that enhance women's participation in the labour market in the positions that best suit the skills of women and do not contradict with *Sharia* principles.
- Reduce unemployment levels of Saudis and recommend solutions that address unemployment.
- Encourage investment in productive and service activities that use high technology with high value added but also generate job opportunities for skilled Saudis.

In order to implement the above broad objectives, the following implementation mechanisms would be initiated by the government in partnership with the private sector, according to the Ministry of Planning:

- Arrange for close coordination and integration between the private sector and the agencies responsible for national workforce policies.

- Encourage and expand the scope of private sector initiatives in the areas of training that end up with generating actual employment by utilizing the training capacities of the private sector to prepare the technical and professional skills required of the national workforce and make it equipped for work in the new economy sectors.
- Intensify the efforts to improve the productivity of the national workforce and expand training programmes that qualify Saudi nationals to take advantage of the available employment opportunities through natural growth or replacement of foreign workers.
- Continue to update and develop the education curricula compatible with labour market requirements. Provide a broader supportive role to the appropriate sectors and relevant agencies concerned with labour force issues.
- Expand the opportunities of sending suitably qualified students to study abroad so as to build a Saudi cadre with the requisite skills and qualifications in areas of priority.
- Take advantage of bilateral agreements with industrialized countries to establish in Kingdom-specialized training centres. Send more Saudi trainees to attend advanced specialized training courses overseas.

The above are very laudable goals and objectives, but to achieve them is another matter, and as we will discuss later, the results have been uneven to date. In order to better assess Saudi employment prospects it is essential to analyse the structure and composition of the Saudi labour market in more detail.

Structure of the Saudi Labour Market and Trends

Table 12.2 sets out the national employment structure as of 1999 and 2009 as per the Seventh and Eighth Development Plans. The government's clear aim was to ensure

Table 12.2 Structure of the forecasted labour market in the Kingdom – Saudis and non-Saudis (1999–2009)

	1999		2009	
	Number of workers ('000)	% distribution	Number of workers ('000)	% distribution
Total labour force	7,176.3	100.0	9,221.3	100.0
Saudis	3,172.9	44.2	4,747.1	98.5
Non-Saudis	4,003.4	55.8	4,474.2	51.5
Total labour at government sector	916.2	12.8	988.0	100
Saudis	716.5	78.2	820.0	82.9
Non-Saudis	199.7	21.8	168.0	17.1
Total labour at private sector	6,260.1	87.2	8,233.3	100
Saudis	2,422.7	38.7	3,927.1	47.6
Non-Saudis	3,837.4	61.3	4,306.2	52.4

Source: Ministry of Planning, Seventh and Eighth Development Plans

that the main growth of the labour market comes from the private non-oil sector and this was forecasted to grow from 2,422 million Saudis in 1999 to 3,927 million by 2009 or a 62% increase. The overall *Saudization* ratio would rise from 44.2% in 1999 to 51.5% by 2009 for both the public and private sector as illustrated in Table 12.2.

According to the Ministry of Planning, the main growth rate for employment would be generated from the industrial, trade and service sectors, as illustrated in Table 12.3, while the agricultural and energy sectors would see the smallest labour gains.

Table 12.3 Sectoral structure of total labour force–Eighth Development Plan

	2004		2009		Change 2004–2009		
	Number (000)	%	Number (000)	%	Number (000)	%	Growth rate %
Agriculture	596.7	7.2	602.6	6.5	5.89	0.6	0.20
Non-oil mining and quarrying	17.8	0.2	18.6	0.2	0.88	0.1	0.97
Oil refining	20.4	0.3	21.3	0.2	0.90	0.1	0.87
Petrochemical industries	23.2	0.3	26.6	0.3	3.37	0.4	2.75
Other manufacturing industries	607	7.3	734.4	8	127.40	13.6	3.88
Electricity, gas and water	77.3	0.9	76.7	0.8	−0.64	−0.1	−0.17
Building and construction	1,585.2	19.1	1,772.4	19.2	187.18	19.9	2.26
Goods producing sectors	2,927.6	35.3	3,252.6	35.2	324.98	34.6	2.13
Trade, restaurants and hotels	1,137.1	13.7	1,417.5	15.4	280.31	29.8	4.51
Transport and communication	341.9	4.1	395.3	4.3	53.43	5.7	2.95
Financial services	47.4	0.6	53.1	0.6	5.77	0.6	2.33
Real estate services	291.9	3.5	316.4	3.4	24.51	2.6	1.63
Community and personal services	2,330	28.1	2,433.2	26.4	103.23	11.0	0.87
Service sectors	4,148.3	50.1	4,615.5	50.1	467.25	49.7	2.16
Total private sectors	7,075.9	85.4	7,868.1	85.3	792.23	84.3	2.15
Government services	1,105.4	13.3	1,236.9	13.4	131.49	14.0	2.27
Non-oil sectors	8,181.3	98.8	9,105	98.7	923.72	98.3	2.16
Crude oil and gas	100.5	1.2	116.3	1.3	15.72	1.7	2.95
Total labour	8,281.8	100.0	9,221.3	100.0	939.44	100.0	2.17

Source: Ministry of Planning

The data from the above two tables are from the Ministry of Planning and they are not explicit on how these forecasts are derived, nor on how they can be met by the requirements of the private sector. There is also no breakdown between male and female labour entrants. The reality in terms of Saudi non-oil private sector

Table 12.4 Planned and actual labour market structure: Saudis and non-Saudis

	2008 Actual		2009 Planned		Difference	
	Number of workers	% distribution	Number of workers	% distribution	Number of workers	% distribution
Total labour force	7,121,658	100	9,221,300	100	(2,099,642)	−29.5
Saudis	1,656,903	23.27	4,747,100	48.5	(4,581,197)	−27.6
Non-Saudis	5,464,755	76.73	4,474,200	51.5	990,555	18.1
Total labour govt. sector	899,711	12.63	988,000	100	85,289	9.8
Saudis	827,846	92.01	820,000	82.9	7,546	0.8
Non-Saudis	71,865	7.99	168,000	17.1	(96,135)	−135.2%
Total private sector	6,221,947	87.37	8,233,300	100	(2,011,353)	−32%
Saudis	829,057	13.32	3,927,100	47.6	(3,098,043)	−373%
Non-Saudis	5,392,890	86.68	4,306,200	52.4	1,086,690	20%

Source: Ministry of Planning, SAMA

employment has been somewhat different to the above official forecasts as illustrated in Table 12.4. It would seem that the government planners had optimistically projected a faster Saudi labour intake into the Saudi private sector of nationals, and at the same time there would be more replacement of foreigners, but the contrast between planned and actual is significant.

Table 12.4 illustrates that while the government had optimistically forecasted the increase in Saudi employment in the private sector by a massive 370%, the actual Saudi private sector labour force was 829,000 in 2008 as opposed to the forecasted 3.9 million. The Ministry of Planning seemed to have been on target for the government positions, especially for Saudis, as such positions have to be budgeted and approved beforehand as per civil service employment regulations, and there is more certainty and control over labour force entrants to the government sector. The policy of *Saudization* or the manner in which it has been applied has not, on the above private sector employment evidence, seemed to have met national goals. Before analysing this issue in greater detail later in the chapter, it is also important to analyse the distribution of manpower in the private sector by economic activity, as well as their educational level and professional classification as this might indicate some of the *Saudization* bottlenecks faced. Figure 12.2 illustrates all three factors.

Analysis of Fig. 12.2(a) by distribution of manpower in the private sector reveals that the bulk of workers, or nearly 75%, are in the construction, wholesale and retail and manufacturing sectors – areas that have been traditionally shunned by Saudi labour, although there is evidence that young Saudis are now willing to enter the wholesale and retail trade. The Saudi Arabian labour force – both national and foreign – is generally literate, with only around 14% being illiterate, mostly comprising foreign household maids and menial labourers, as illustrated in Fig. 12.2(b). Those holding diploma degrees and above are at a respectable 10%

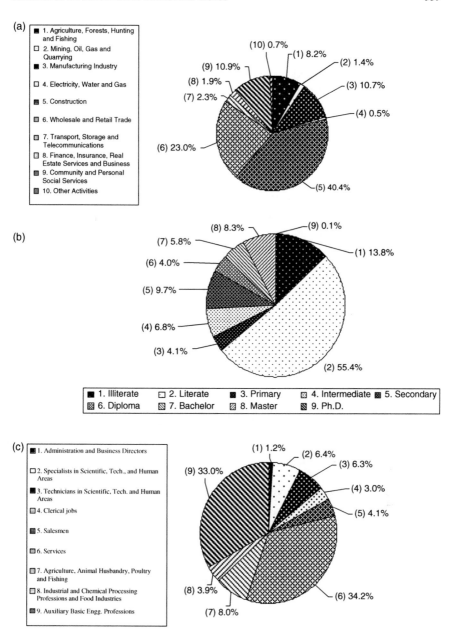

Fig. 12.2 (**a**) Distribution of manpower in the private sector by major economic activity during 2008; (**b**) Breakdown of labour force in the private sector by educational level in 2008; (**c**) Distribution of manpower in the private sector by major professions during 2008 (Source: SAMA)

of the total labour force, but still below OECD levels of 40%. Figure 12.2(c) illustrates that analysing the labour force by professional classification, around 67% are concentrated in the services and auxiliary basic engineering professions, followed by agro-business and specialists and technicians in scientific and technical areas. Agriculture and fishing and food processing accounted for around 8% of the workforce professionals' classification, despite the pressure of urbanization noted earlier in the chapter.

The capital-intensive nature of the oil industry means that there are relatively few workers employed in the sector, despite its importance for government revenue and export. There are fewer than 90,000 employed in the oil and gas industry in 2008, which accounts for a mere 1.4% of the total workforce, as Fig. 12.2(a) shows. The growth of jobs in the oil sector is also low, which implies that over the longer term the industry will account for a diminishing proportion of the total workforce. Even the ambitious schemes to expand the local industrial petrochemical base will not contribute significantly to employment unless substantial new employment is generated from the new industrial cities of Jubail II and III, which aim to attract secondary value-added industries, as well as the mega-economic cities discussed in the previous chapter, which aim to generate an additional 1.3 million new jobs between them over the coming decade.

One reason for the lower than forecasted rate of Saudi employment by the private sector is that the cost of job creation, especially in manufacturing, is relatively high as explored by Table 12.5, which calculates the investment per employee required for different manufacturing enterprises.

Table 12.5 Industrial and manufacturing employment and investment per employee (2008)

Sector	Number of licences	Investments (SR million)	Employment	Investment per job (SR'000)
Food and beverage	668	35.117	86,515	408
Textiles/clothing	155	4.840	22,238	221
Carpentry	52	0.784	3,932	261
Paper/printing	255	9.941	26,275	382
Chemical and petroleum	497	183.099	59,856	3,103
Rubber and plastics	444	11.531	39,740	296
Non-metals	679	48.169	69,478	698
Basic metals	296	35.349	42,377	841
Machinery and equipment	217	5.025	22,411	228
Construction metal products	288	7.247	26,230	279
Total industry average	4,167	359.533	466,661	771

Source: SAMA

While the overall industrial investment per worker is around SR 770,000, this is raised considerably by the high investment costs per employee in the chemical and petroleum sector, which stood at an average of SR 3,103,000 compared with SR 200,000–300,000 average per employee for most of the other manufacturing

Table 12.6 Average wage in Saudi Arabia during the period 1994–2008

	Saudis		Non-Saudis	
	Males	Females	Males	Females
1994	7,298	3,660	2,153	3,133
1995	7,896	3,864	2,142	3,016
1997	7,570	4,144	2,046	2,716
1998	7,473	3,812	1,934	2,740
2000	6,877	3,217	1,763	2,391
2001	6,684	3,151	1,710	2,403
2002	5,984	2,703	1,543	2,221
2008	7,650	3,100	1,650	2,480

Source: Ministry of Labour, SAMA

industries. This includes the cost of both Saudi and non-Saudi jobs, but the cost of the former is higher as illustrated in Table 12.6.

The "Duality" of the Saudi Wage Market

There was a long-term erosion in the average wage level of Saudis and non-Saudis, both male and female, but this reversed in the recent "boom" years from 2007. Table 12.6 illustrates the gradual decline in wage level from 1994 to 2008; non-Saudis (male and female) have been most affected.

The average wage level for a non-Saudi male is lower than his Saudi counterpart. This is due to the fact that a large number of non-Saudi labour have low-level skills and work in wage professions. Again, such low wage levels are a problem for potential *Saudization* and for Saudi entrants. There is anecdotal evidence that some Saudis are beginning to accept lower salaries in areas that were once deemed to be "beneath" them, such as restaurants, barbershops, porter services and others, but these are still rare. Wide variations are found in actual salaries: the banking, services, insurance, legal and accounting professions command high salaries and benefits that are comparable to, if not better than, similar positions in Europe or the USA. Similarly, the expatriate wage levels mask some extremely high salary levels for professionals and technical experts, whose tax-free compensation packages provide superior levels of earnings than similar jobs in their home countries. Overall though, decreased economic growth, volatile oil prices and government expenditures, competition for jobs and the private sector's desire to control labour costs have together tended to create a downward push on wage levels in the Kingdom. This is set to continue for the foreseeable future with erosion in the purchasing value of wages also affected by the more recent rise in domestic inflation as discussed in earlier chapters.

The "duality" of wages between Saudis and non-Saudis can be explained in terms of two distinct labour markets. This case was made by a Saudi economist, and it seems applicable to the wider GCC labour market (Al Sheikh, 2003).

Fig. 12.3 Duality of GCC
labour markets

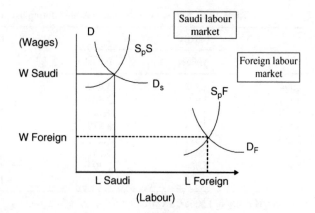

Figure 12.3 sets out the concept in terms of differentiated demand and supply for Saudi and non-Saudi labour markets. In the figure, D_s and S_pS stand for demand and supply for Saudi labour, while D_F and S_pF stand for demand and supply for foreign labour.

As pointed out earlier, there are wide differences in wage levels not only between Saudis and expatriates but also between different skill groups of expatriates. As such, the demand and supply for foreign labour in Saudi Arabia exhibits a greater degree of market segmentation and supply elasticity, leading to different wage levels amongst foreign workers. By supply elasticity we mean the responsiveness of the supply of labour to changes in the wage level. This is illustrated in Fig. 12.4.

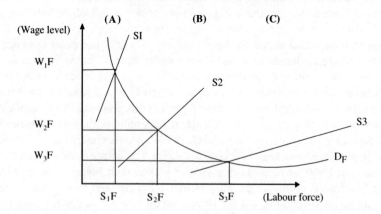

Fig. 12.4 Demand supply for expatriate labour in Saudi Arabia by market segmentation

Figure 12.4 shows that in segment (A), the supply of expatriate labour is relatively inelastic because of specialized technical or managerial skills, and as such, these foreign workers enjoy higher wages at W_1F levels. Segment (B) shows a relatively more elastic supply curve for foreign workers, including middle management, accountants, salesmen and others who command a lower salary level at W_2F, and

Saudis are more competitive over these positions in terms of similar skills and training. Segment (C) shows the wage level paid in the almost wholly elastic supply curve of manual and menial foreign labour at W_3F. A small adjustment in the supply of labour causes sharp movements to salary levels. Effective short-term *Saudization* policies should aim for job creation in segment (B) and eventual knowledge-based, high-value job migration to segment (A).

Although government planners in Saudi Arabia stress the role of the private sector in increasing employment for local citizens and reducing unemployment, there is no analysis of the workings of the labour market in the development plans. Other writers have raised some pertinent issues which are touched upon in the theoretical illustrations above. How responsive is the demand for labour to the expected wage rate, and what is the wage rate that would bring demand and supply into equilibrium in the job market? Are labour markets in Saudi Arabia excessively fragmented, with insufficient occupational and geographical mobility? Are the labour markets for Saudi Arabian and foreign workers completely segmented so that little competition exists between the two groups? Although answers may not be readily available given data limitations, there is little evidence that fundamental questions are really being asked (Wilson, 2003).

Saudization: A Viable Solution?

Saudi Arabia recognized very early the necessity to *Saudize* the workforce. In 1970, the government decreed that 75% of workers in all businesses operating in the country should be Saudi, and that they should receive at least 51% of the company's total salary payment (Wright, 1996). However, as Fig. 12.5 shows, the number of foreign workers steadily increased, reaching a peak of 5.392 million in 2008.

Figure 12.5 indicates that the number of foreign workers began to decline from 1995 from just over 5 million to 4.475 million by 2004, but then rose again to 5.392

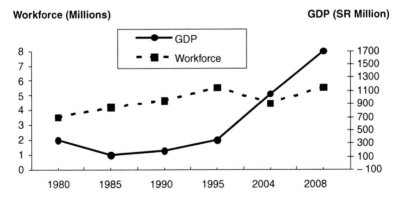

Fig. 12.5 GDP and expatriate workforce in Saudi Arabia 1980–2008 (Source: SAMA)

million by 2008. What is interesting is that the number of foreign workers continued
to rise over the period 1980–1995 despite erratic fluctuations in Saudi GDP and
reduced economic growth. One possible reason is the way the *Saudization* policy
itself works, with permits granted to Saudi companies and new permits only issued
as replacement to existing ones. As such, Saudi companies often hold onto their
foreign workers, fearful of losing their permits if they make their workers redundant,
and preferring cutting costs in times of recession by reducing workers' salaries, as
evidenced from the decline in average non-Saudi and Saudi salaries in Table 12.6.

One clarification is needed: sometimes data on "foreign workers" add together
actual workers and their dependents in the Kingdom. Thus, when figures of 6 million
expatriates or higher are mentioned, they would include 2.3 million dependents in
Saudi Arabia under the age of 18 (Al Najjar, 1998). Past that age, they cease being
dependents and are not granted residence visas.

The Government of Saudi Arabia hopes that manpower demand and supply projections, resulting from various schemes and administrative policies, will continue
to reverse the trend and ensure a majority Saudi labour force by 2020. Table 12.7
displays the government's own projections for the Eighth Plan period (2004–2009)
and its long-term perspective to 2020. By that year, the number of non-Saudi
workers will have been reduced by 2.25 million, to stabilize around 1.25 million.
The assumption is that no new foreign labour will enter the market.

However, as discussed earlier, these government assumptions seem overly optimistic, especially concerning private sector employment prospects. There are many

Table 12.7 Manpower demand and supply projections (1999–2020)

Description	Thousands			Average annual growth rate %	
	1999	2004	2020	Seventh Plan (2000–2004)	Long-term perspective (2000–2020)
1. Demand					
Government services	916.2	923.3	984.0	0.35	0.34
Crude oil and gas	98.9	100.4	127.0	0.30	1.20
Private sector	6,161.2	6,472.2	9,635.0	0.99	2.15
Total demand	7,176.3	7,504.9	10,746.0	0.90	1.94
2. Supply					
Saudi population	15,658.4	18,520.3	29,717.0	3.41	3.10
Saudi labour force	3,172.9	3,990.2	8,263.0	4.69	4.66
3. Demand/supply Balance					
Non-Saudi labour force	4,003.4	3,514.7	2,483.0	(2.57)	(2.25)

Source: Ministry of Planning

reasons why Saudi nationals are not taking certain jobs being carried out by expatriates.

The largest sources of employment in Saudi Arabia are in construction, retail trade and finance and real estate. The majority are non-Saudi Arabians. Most construction employment involves housing and commercial projects for the private sector. For the housing and commercial projects, large numbers of unskilled and semi-skilled workers are required, most coming from the Indian subcontinent. They are paid relatively modest wages for the long hours they work, but this keeps construction costs low. Few Arabian nationals are interested in jobs in the construction industry.

Given the increasing size of the Saudi Arabian market for consumer goods there has been a substantial expansion in retailing in recent years, which has created many employment opportunities. As all establishments have to be owned by local nationals, this ensures that large numbers of Saudis are absorbed; indeed, more are engaged in retailing than in any other private sector activity. In order to boost the employment of local nationals, the government has decreed that one-third of the workforce in retail establishments should be Saudi Arabian, but this is widely ignored. In the cheaper shops in the downtown areas that cater for migrant workers and local citizens with limited amounts of disposable income, most employees are from South Asia. In the more expensive stores, often run on a franchisee basis and selling branded products, many of the sales staff are from other Arab countries, but Saudi Arabian nationals are increasingly employed. In such upmarket establishments where quality matters, it is important to have sales staff who know the products and are able to converse with the customers; therefore, a knowledge of Arabic as well as English is important.

Some have argued that *Saudization* can be both a blessing and a curse for Saudi Arabia (Chadhury, 1989, Kapiszewski, 2001, Cordesman, 2003). The "blessing" is that inherent in Saudi Arabia's present dependence on legal (and illegal) foreign workers lies one solution: to create Saudi employment, theoretically, by expelling most of the foreign workers. The "curse" of the present dependence on foreign labour is that most of the non-Saudi jobs are the type, because of social values, that many young Saudis do not want.

The issue of *Saudization* and its effectiveness has received large attention, but the views are mixed, with some (Looney, 2004, Al Sultan, 1998, AlSheekh, 2001) being cautiously optimistic but only if certain fundamental labour and wage reforms are put into place, while others feel that demographic pressures will cause long-term problems if employment generation measures are not taken now (Toaijery, 2001, Abdul Rahman, 1987).

To some extent, the *Saudization* programme has been successful in replacing foreign workers with Saudi employees, but this has been primarily in the government sector where there is much more hiring control than in the private sector. Figure 12.6 illustrates the success of this government policy, which ensured that by 2008, the majority of employees in the government sector were Saudis.

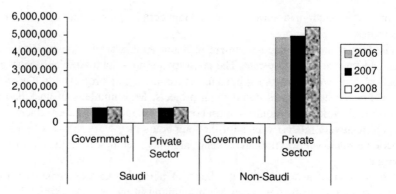

Fig. 12.6 Saudi and non-Saudi employment by government and private sector (2006–2008) (Source: SAMA)

Saudization: *Government Measures and Responses*

The Saudi government's *Saudization* measures have centred around key strategic goals:

1. Increase employments for Saudi nationals across all sectors of the domestic economy.
2. Reduce and reverse over-reliance on foreign workers.
3. Recapture and reinvest income which otherwise would have flowed overseas as remittances to foreign workers' home countries. Over the last 10 years expatriate workers in the Kingdom have remitted about SR 524 billion ($139 billion) over the period 1990–2008, according to SAMA. Increased levels of *Saudization* will ensure that such levels of remittances are reduced to the benefit of Saudi Arabia.

Figure 12.7 illustrates the significance of some of the remittances from Saudi Arabia to selected labour exporting countries.

Remittances have a paramount socio-economic impact in recipient countries, especially those dependent on foreign capital inflows. According to the World Bank, Saudi Arabia accounted for 50% of the Gulf region's total remittances between the period 2001 and 2008.

Unlike some of its neighbours in the Gulf, Saudi Arabia has not experienced a significant downturn in foreign workers, who accounted for 27% of the 24.8 million Saudi population in 2008. This trend is evident in remittance numbers. Expatriate workers in the kingdom sent home SR 78.6 billion ($ 20.9 billion) in 2008 – up 33% from the year earlier as the global economic crisis was in full swing.

Studies conducted on the level of remittance outflows and economic factors revealed that there is a significant positive relationship between the level of per capita GDP variable and that of remittance per-worker from the Kingdom (Abdelrahman, 2006). Remittances were seen to be pro-cyclical, with activity in the

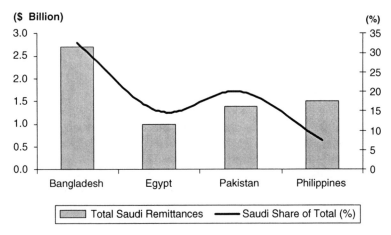

Fig. 12.7 Saudi remittances to key country destinations 2008 (Source: Central banks of respective countries)

Kingdom increasing during booms (such as in 2007 and 2008) and rising incomes, while receding during recessions and declining incomes. Wages also proved to be a significant positive determinant of the level of per-worker remittances, despite downward pressure on wages during recession years. What seems clear though is that the level of remittances has increased during the financial crisis years of 2008/ 2009 due to workers saving more for remittances and spending less in Saudi Arabia.

Given the strategic goals set out, the Saudi government has tried the following measures to speed up *Saudization*:

- Ensuring strict compliance with the resolutions and circulars regarding *Saudization* and enhancing the relevant implementation mechanisms.
- Enhancing the role of the Human Resources Development Fund (HRDF) to provide efficient support to *Saudization* programmes, through direct employment or training that ends with actual employment.
- Provide more information on vacant positions to Saudi job applicants and to employers about the characteristics of the unemployed national workforce.
- Continue to invigorate the role of the agencies responsible for the training and employment of the national workforce, and enhance the human and technological potentials of these agencies. Examples of the agencies referred to are: General Organization for Technical Education and Vocational Training (GOTEVT), labour offices of the Ministry of Labour, the National Organization for Cooperative Training organized by the GOTEVT, and the Human Resources Development Fund.
- Link foreign labour recruitment with *Saudization* policies. Ensure that the recruitment of foreign labour is restricted to job categories where the supply of national workforce is insufficient.
- Study the level of wages and adopt an adequate wage policy that ensures a balance between the employment of Saudis and the growth and profitability of the private sector.

The above are commendable goals if they can be achieved in what is essentially a free market economic system, and where the private sector operates on the basis of profit-maximizing principles, rather than state control.

Private Sector Saudization *Issues*

There seems to be some reluctance on parts of the private sector to hire Saudis to replace foreigners, despite government directives and regulations, as well as inducements and encouragements that will be explored in more detail below.

Some ascribe the reluctance to cultural attitudes towards work inherent in Saudi society. The fact is that because of negative attitudes about certain types of work among Saudis, there are many expatriates in the Kingdom, even though it is the only country in the GCC with a large enough population to carry out the country's development on its own (Looney, 1992, Nur Uthman, 1995). Additionally, the combination of importing foreign workers while offering generous state welfare benefits to nationals has reinforced this negative attitude towards work and created a vicious cycle that encourages Saudis to stay out of a large part of the job market. It is certainly hard to explain the staggering statistic from the Ministry of Labour that some 150,000 Saudis did not bother to return and complete formalities for guaranteed private sector jobs they had been assigned through the various labour offices over the past 4 years. The issue of work ethics has attracted some debate both from within and outside Saudi Arabia (Shatkin, 2002, Cordesman, 2003, Niblock, 1980).

That said, certain changes for the better have taken place. The younger generation has indicated its willingness to accept positions that have been traditionally rejected by their fathers, such as jobs at hotels, restaurants, barbershops and other direct services to customers.

However, there are several reasons for the private sector's resistance to *Saudization*. These are summarized in Table 12.8 and are based on the comments raised in the media by several Saudi industrial leaders.

As the private sector sees it, market forces drive at least part of the solution to these problems. Over time, Saudi nationals will need to be more realistic in their demands regarding wages and employment conditions.

Saudi government policy has largely focused on preventing, through quotas and higher fees, the employment of expatriates. This might not be the most appropriate policy at this stage of Saudi economic development, given the relative lack of skills in the Saudi labour force. However, the foreign workforce at the lower skill levels might never be completely *Saudized*, possibly because they add very little to overall national productivity. For example, in 2008 there were some 1.8 million foreign females in the Kingdom, with a large number working as housemaids. Most of these jobs are unlikely to be replaced by Saudi men or women, for cultural and social reasons, although it is interesting to note that according to press reports some Saudi women are now being placed in household day jobs with Saudi families.

Table 12.8 Private sector *Saudization* issues

Issues	Private sector justifications
1. Labour cost	• The relatively high cost of Saudi manpower, compared to foreign manpower, results in private sector reliance on imported cheap manual labour, deployed in labour-intensive occupations. This helps private sector profitability despite government attempts to increase expatriate costs (residency or *Iqama,* visa renewals, etc.)
2. Social and cultural perceptions	• Saudis are reluctant to take up and seriously pursue certain types of jobs, despite *Saudization* directives. For example, the forced *Saudization* of employees in the vegetable markets has failed. *Social status* is still important for young Saudis as it affects marriage and other social relations
3. Control over process of production	• Expatriate workers are easier to control and more disciplined than Saudis. Control is exercised through short-term employment contracts. In some cases, there are few legal obligations towards expatriates, who are prohibited from changing jobs without their sponsor's permission
4. Lack of social integration in multicultural work environment	• Local populations are reluctant to integrate into multicultural work environments, fearing that it might degrade their existing status
5. Job tenure	• It is more difficult to fire Saudi workers than foreign workers
6. Inadequate qualifications	• Saudi employees may have inadequate qualifications, a lack of good English or a non-technical background
7. Mobility	• Saudi workers are less mobile than foreigner workers; they are reluctant to change job locations

Similarly, there are about 800,000 foreign males who work in extremely menial, low-status jobs that will be hard to *Saudize* (SAMA). Turning *Saudization* theory into practice means to restructure much of the present Saudi labour market in order to create new types of knowledge-based, high-value jobs for young Saudis. Restructuring might help avoid fiascos such as the imposition of *Saudization* on complete sectors, like the markets of vegetable-sellers, travel agencies and gold-sellers, only to see results flounder later on when foreign labour was re-hired back to these sectors owing to lack of interest from Saudi labour (Arab News, June, 2003).

Regulating Foreign Labour

As we said earlier, opening up the Saudi economy to globalization and making it attractive to foreign direct investment (FDI) could cause conflict for the twin objectives of *Saudization* and liberalization. The Kingdom's aggressive *Saudization* policy could be seen as too negative for foreign companies that prefer to operate in an open labour market, one that is dictated by experience, qualifications and the needs of market supply and demand. Those foreign companies might refuse to comply with imposed *Saudization* quotas.

One area of impact from *Saudization* may be a reduction of FDI in the Kingdom. Foreign firms may feel not only that *Saudization* puts them at a disadvantage compared to their foreign competitors but also that the whole *Saudization* programme itself is unpredictable, with rules and quotas changing without warning. This element, combined with concerns over domestic terrorist violence, may drastically reduce FDI inflows. Concern over *Saudization's* impact on foreign investors likely underlines the Kingdom's decision to reduce the rate of tax on profit on foreign companies to 20% from 40% as discussed in the previous chapter.

The pace of *Saudization* decrees has picked up over the years. In the mid-1990s, a law was issued requiring private businesses employing more than 20 people to increase the Saudi nationals by 5% of the workforce every year. The current required rate of Saudi employees is 30%. The employment of foreigners in 22, mostly administrative, professions was banned. The Saudi government increased fees on the recruitment of expatriates, with the money going into a special fund set up to help "nationalize" jobs.

In January of 2003 the *Shoura* Council began to apply *Saudization* metrics to companies working in the Kingdom that are directly owned by Saudi Aramco as well as those implementing Aramco projects. The *Saudization* level of contractors must now be included in annual performance reports submitted by the Ministry of Petroleum and Mineral Resources. While this may increase the complexity of foreign competitive bids for oil and gas projects, from the council's perspective the measures should help towards achieving the country's national labour force interests.

In February 2003, the Saudi government decided to take an even more drastic step to reduce foreign workers in the Kingdom. Prince Naif bin Abdulaziz, the Interior Minister and Head of the Manpower Council, announced that 3 million expatriates were to be phased out from Saudi Arabia within a decade, and that the total number of expatriates must not exceed 20% of the Saudi population by 2013. This brings forward from 2020 to 2013 the "optimum" number of expatriates of 1.25 million that seems the government's preferred foreign labour target.

The surprise decision also stipulated a quota system for foreign nationalities in which no single nationality must exceed 10% of total expatriates.

This system, if implemented in full, will hit the Asian communities in Saudi Arabia particularly hard as illustrated in Table 12.9.

The Egyptians, Filipinos and Yemenis will also be affected, since they too represent a large percentage of the current workforce, especially when their dependents are included. Those least affected would be the small numbers of highly paid and professional expatriates from the USA and Europe. It is interesting to note the absence of the large numbers of Korean and Thai workers seen during the early 1980s' construction boom (Moon, Chung In, 1996).

Only time will tell how rigorously this announced quota system for nationality groups will be implemented, but it is more than likely that citizens of Arab states such as Egypt and Yemen will be granted some form of exemption. This is due to inter-Arab governmental sensitivities about the relatively high unemployment in the wider Arab world.

Table 12.9 Major expatriate communities in the GCC countries (estimates for various years, in thousands)

Expatriate communities	Bahrain 2004	Kuwait 2003	Oman 2002	Qatar 2002	Saudi Arabia 2004	UAE 2002
Indians	120	320	330	100	1,300	1,200
Egyptians	30	260	30	35	900	140
Pakistanis	50	100	70	100	900	450
Filipinos	25	70		50	500	120
Yemenis					800	60
Sri Lankans		170	30	35	350	160
Jordanians/Palestinians	20	50		50	260	110
Syrians		100			100	
Indonesians		9			250	
Sudanese					250	30
Bangladeshis		170	110		400	100
Turks					80	
Nepalese				70		
Iranians	30	80		60		40
Total expatriate population	275	1,329	570	500	6,090	2,410

Source: UNDP

Foreign workers in Saudi Arabia bring both positive and negative economic and social consequences to the Kingdom.

Expatriates contribute as both consumers and producers to the Saudi economy. While expatriate workers – especially those who are single – have a high propensity to save (Sinclair, 1988), and thus to transfer funds outside the Kingdom in remittances, the expatriate population as a whole spends a considerable amount of money within the Kingdom. They are a major source of income to Saudi-owned establishments, such as travel, luxury items, supermarkets and hotels. A drastic reduction in expatriate numbers will cause dislocation to some local businesses, unless increased Saudi spending patterns provide compensation.

A study prepared by the GCC Secretariat in Riyadh in 2003 called for encouraging expatriate workers in the Kingdom to bring their families in order to increase their spending within the country and to cut down overseas remittances. Another view is that government actions to *Saudize* interfere in business affairs and pose challenges, such as a loss of competitiveness in those labour-intensive industries which employ cheap labour. In addition to the purely economic ramifications, the presence of other diverse nationalities amongst an indigenous population often creates an intangible two-way benefit to both sides.

On the Saudi side, getting to know and working with many different national groups could enable Saudis to encounter and perhaps adopt the best possible work ethics and practices from amongst them, increasing their own productivity without changing basic Saudi social norms or customs. Outside visitors to the Eastern Province of the Kingdom often comment on how similar the attitudes of Saudis in that region are to American working attitudes. This is a function of the long-term involvement of American companies in the Eastern Province.

Because of the inherent conflict between the government's *Saudization* objectives and private sector interests, the state was obliged to issue the *Saudization* and quota decrees mentioned above, but sometimes the state has had to react pragmatically to private sector concerns and realities on the ground and amend some of its decrees.

Like any major policy initiative, *Saudization* clearly creates disturbances with some sectors of the economy affected more than others. The ultimate goal of development and higher growth comes with a cost in the form of short-term transitional disruption. It is too early to gauge the impact of *Saudization* on the economy, but there are two main concerns. First, many firms may feel that *Saudization* will reduce their competitiveness and for that reason may decide to leave the Kingdom for a more business-friendly environment. These would most likely be firms in the service sector. *Saudization* of jobs would likely cause a gain of business to other regional centres, particularly Dubai, with a reported 2,500 Saudi companies opening up shop in Dubai, rather than in the Kingdom (Looney, 2004).

Reacting to such private sector pressures, the Saudi Ministry of Labour announced in 2006 that *Saudization* rates for certain categories of jobs were being reduced from 30 to 10% after noticing few Saudis applied for them. The specific job categories covered bakers, tailors, blacksmiths, carpenters, aluminium foundry workers, laundry workers, heavy goods vehicle drivers, gas station attendants and workers engaged in similar activities. Any Saudi national though applying for such jobs will be granted preference.

Saudi Arabia is not the only one that is facing "localization" issues in replacing foreign workers with nationals; several solutions have been proposed and implemented in the GCC countries. One such proposal was in 2008 when some GCC countries suggested placing a "time limit" on foreign workers in their countries to preserve the demographic nature of countries such as the UAE, which who have a large number of expatriates to the local population, as will be examined in a later chapter. However, the proposals did not go far, as it soon became clear that there was no agreement if the "time limit" would apply to all foreigners regardless of the type of job they do, or to only non-skilled foreign workers, whose jobs, as discussed, some nationals preferred not to do.

The Kingdom of Bahrain, a member of the GCC, broke ranks with other members and during August 2009 took the bold step of scrapping entirely the private sector sponsorship system and replaced it by a government sponsorship system. Under the new Bahrain labour law, foreign workers would be directly sponsored by the Labour Market Regulatory Authority (LMRA) and would be free to move jobs without the consent of their previous employer. Bahrain would introduce a ceiling on expatriate workers allowed into the country, but henceforth market supply and demand forces would determine workers' movements between jobs and wage levels. The Bahrain move is being monitored closely by the other GCC countries to see how it will be controlled and the effect on national employment levels, but until then the other GCC countries, including Saudi Arabia, seem to be sticking to their sponsorship system under which employers do the sponsoring and which has come under criticism by human rights groups for placing workers at the mercy of their employers, who usually hold on to the foreign workers' passports.

An "Incentive-Based" *Saudization* Strategy

From the above review of the composition of the national economic sector and the various obstacles faced in the implementation of a meaningful *Saudization* policy, several lessons are learned:

(a) Developing new employment opportunities rather than substituting local workers for foreign workers is the only long-term solution to accommodate a growing national labour force.
(b) Training new entrants for likely job openings is the way to a successful national employment policy.
(c) The capital intensity of the oil sector makes it extremely difficult for that sector to create an adequate number of jobs for nationals and still remain competitive, especially in the petrochemical sector.

As such, instead of quotas and threat of punishment, *Saudization* should be implemented more through market forces and incentives, induced through an expanded and reformed education and national training programme which is addressed in the next chapter. *Saudization* should be implemented in a manner that provides new jobs for Saudi nationals through increased competitiveness and a strong and sustainable non-oil growth in the economy. Some analysis has been done on this using simplified economic demand and supply theory (Looney, 1994, Taecker, 2003, Smith, 2003).

The basic assumptions are as follows:

1. From the perspective of private sector firms, the demand for Saudi native workers is inversely related to the cost of their hiring and firing. It is also inversely related to the cost of employing low-skilled expatriate workers. As a reduction in the number of low-skilled employees likely reduces the marginal productivity of national workers, an increase in the cost of employing low-skilled workers would reduce the demand not only for these workers but also for Saudi workers.
2. If skilled expatriate workers are sufficiently substitutable with Saudi workers, then demand for Saudis should be positively related to the cost of employing skilled expatriates; increases in these costs would lead firms to reduce their demand for skilled expatriate workers and to substitute them with national workers.
3. The demand for Saudi workers is positively related to their level of human capital the stock of capital and technology, because increases in these factors should raise the return to employing an additional national worker.

4. The supply of national workers to the private sector should depend on the compensation relative to their reservation wage (the minimum wage one is willing to
   accept for their work). Reservation wages in turn are determined by the wage,
   social benefit and employment policies of the government. If the public sector
   provides relatively high wages, social benefits and job security to nationals, then
   the reservation wage and benefits will be relatively high for the private sector.

From these supply and demand considerations, several policies can be adopted
to increase job opportunities for Saudi workers in the private sector. According to
analysts, these may be grouped into three broad categories depending on whether
they directly affect (a) wages and employment costs, (b) acquisition of human capital or (c) investment in capital and technology (Looney, 2004). These policies are
structural and market-based, in contrast to quantitative measures, such as job quotas, which may adversely affect competitiveness and non-oil growth by raising costs
and limiting employment flexibility.

The Saudi government has been using direct subsidies to entice Saudis into jobs
through company training programmes. The Human Resources Development Fund
(HRDF) has been one such instrument of increasing the *Saudization* ratio in the
private sector. The HRDF's mission since its establishment in 2000 is simple: to
provide grants for qualifying, training and recruiting Saudis for work in the private sector. The HRDF pays private sector companies 75% of the salary of an
employee while he is under training, not exceeding SR 1,500 per month for a period
of 3 months, and 50% of the salaries of young Saudis for their first 2 years of
employments up to a maximum of SR 2,000 per month to encourage employment.
According to HRDF, it targeted the IT, construction and health sectors as part of
a new strategy to create 30,000 new jobs in these sectors (HRDF, 2008). The fund
is financed by a levy of SR 100 per expatriate worker in the Kingdom which is
included in the visa permit and renewals. Under the HRDF subsidy programme,
employers will be responsible for providing the necessary skills training, while the
employee will commit to completing the programme.

Since its establishment in 2000, the HRDF has expanded the scope of private sector support and now provides loans to private sector companies which are involved
in the training and human development sector in addition to providing technical and
administrative consultations in the field of national workforce training. The HRDF
also provides a student loan programme for Saudi college students at the undergraduate and diploma levels studying in the private sector, who cannot afford the tuition,
with repayment of the loan to be after graduation and commencement of work. To
date, around SR 150 million has been disbursed in this support category to needy
students. Table 12.10 summarizes the number of private sector companies supported
by HRDF subsidies and the *Saudization* results.

From Table 12.10, the HRDF's results were somewhat modest, with additional
target rate of 51% of new Saudi labour force to be added, but with an actual 38%
or under 40,000 new employees, after a 17% dropout rate from the programme.
The HRDF is trying to improve on the overall retention rate and minimize the
dropout ratio by conducting interviews with Saudi trainees to assess the reasons

Table 12.10 HRDF subsidy support programme: Saudi private sector companies (2002–2006)

Activity		Status/results
• Number of contracts signed with private sector companies	–	1,662
• Total number of employees working with these companies (including foreigners)	–	1,108,810
• Total number of Saudis working with these companies	–	204,237
• Percentage of Saudis employed before HRDF subsidy	–	18
• Total number of new Saudi jobs agreed between HRDF and private sector and %	–	104,269 (51%)
• Expected *Saudization* after HRDF subsidy	–	25%
• Actual number of new Saudis employed and %	–	39,923 (38%)
• Saudis dropped out and %	–	6,781 (19.6%)

Source: HRDF, 2008

for dropping out, and whether it was based on lack of "meaningful" training or job placement by the Saudi private sector employers, as there had been some criticism that some national companies had taken on Saudi trainees and new hires just to fill up *Saudization* quotas but provided little in terms of actual training or meaningful jobs for the young Saudis.

Labour Participation – A Model for New Entrants

Analysis of Saudi Arabia's future labour market is particularly difficult given the lack of precise data on the constitution of the current labour force. As such, researchers have to come up with a model that realistically captures labour entrant flow. This is important for planning an effective *Saudization* and for economic and educational planning.

The total number of the nation's labour force is illustrated below. This does not take account of expatriate labour entrants, as the entry and exit of the Kingdom's foreign (legal) workers can be controlled.

Figure 12.8 concentrates on the educational sector and its impact through providing new labour entrants. Like other societies, some Saudi youth drop out of the educational system at various stages, while others continue until graduation. Again, Saudi education data focus only on current school or higher education enrolment numbers and does not provide figures for dropouts.

From this, one can extrapolate the current level of labour force or job-seekers and the level of unemployment, focusing primarily on Saudi males for whom some government data exist. We shall use the base data from the Central Department of Statistics as well as our own estimates for Saudi student graduates and dropout rates.

Table 12.11 forecasts employment changes for Saudi males, for the period 2003–2013, based on the model of labour entrants developed in Fig. 12.8. We must emphasize at the outset that the approach taken to arrive at new job entrants, new

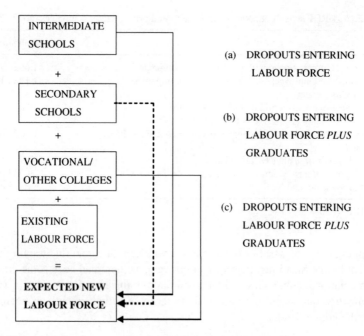

Fig. 12.8   Sources of new entrants into Saudi labour market (Saudis only)

job creation and the estimated unemployment levels is based on several assumptions and data that are possibly incomplete. Therefore, the estimates are liable to a wide margin of error. However, this is a first attempt to understand the dynamics of all these factors over the next decade.

Starting with the employment base level of 2003 based on Ministry of Planning data, we used male education data from the Ministry of Planning statistics for the year 2002. Students currently at the elementary school age 11 mark our starting point. We projected forward to 2013 for all these students in the education system, assuming a 5% dropout rate for intermediate schools, 10% for secondary education and 10% for higher education. The results appear as the male entrants to the market labour force in Table 12.11. We have also assumed that the private sector will be the major source of new job creation for the Saudi economy and that it will grow at levels of 3–5% p.a. over the next 10 years. The latest GDP actual growth rates and economic forecasts indicate that this is a reasonable estimation.

On the basis of an ever-increasing number of new male entrants into the labour force due to the demographic trends explained earlier, Table 12.11 highlights the possibility that Saudi male unemployment levels could reach 48% within a decade.

In summary, Saudi Arabia needs job creation and skills creation to ensure job growth. As discussed earlier, the job creation need will eventually be somewhat alleviated by the ability of the current *Saudization* programme to replace foreigners and employ some Saudis. However, as the data analyse only male labour entrants, the employment picture becomes even gloomier if female labour entrants are added.

Table 12.11 Employment developments from 2003 to 2013: Saudi Arabia (males only)

	2003[a]	2006	2008	2011	2013
Male entrants to market labour force	450,000	497,478	531,882	587,999	628,663
Private sector GDP growth (%)		4	4	5	3
Jobs created – new	150,000	167,107	182,481	207,221	224,130
Total male labour force	2,861,006	4,304,904	5,351,179	7,057,809	8,294,463
Employed[a]	2,417,720	2,900,007	3,257,951	3,854,130	4,293,770
Unemployed[a]	443,286	1,404,897	2,093,228	3,203,679	4,000,693
Employment rate (%)	84.51	87.37	60.88	54.61	51.77
Unemployment rate (%)	15.49	13.63	39.12	45.39	48.23
Total (%)	100.00	100.00	100.00	100.00	100.00

[a]2003 as base year

Source: Ministry of Planning, 19th Issue, Achievements of the Development Plans, 2002, pp. 300–301

Currently there are 2,602,000 female students at all levels of education compared with 3,065,000 males (SAMA, 2009). If one assumes one fifth of females wish to enter the labour market, then the forecasted combined unemployment levels for both sexes would be much higher.

Saudi Unemployment

Recently, there has been some more information released by Saudi Arabia about the level of official unemployment rates for Saudis and non-Saudis. According to SAMA's latest figures, the Saudi unemployment rate stood at 9.8% for 2008, compared with a peak of 12.0% in 2006. The comparable figures for non-Saudis were 0.4 and 0.8%, respectively (SAMA, 2009, p. 426). If the total workforce (Saudis and non-Saudis) is included, the unemployment level falls to 6.3% in 2006 and 5.0% in 2008, but this is not a good indicator, as foreigners are in the Kingdom to work and most are obliged by law to leave the country when their work permit expires. There are many foreign workers whose permits expire but who remain in the country as illegal workers and become as a class of disguised unemployment without being added to the official statistics.

The truth of the matter is that there is no precise way to measure the rate of Saudi unemployment; there is no "signing-up benefit" system similar to other countries that register those who are involuntarily unemployed and who are able and willing to take up jobs. From time to time, some figures are released about the number of

Saudi job-seekers registering with the Ministry of Labour offices, reported at around 155,000 for 2006 and at 500,000 levels for 2010 (Saudi Press Agency, 22 Jan. 2010).

At such, in the absence of a formal unemployment compensation scheme, unemployment numbers cannot be estimated through benefit claimants. For social reasons, many in Saudi Arabia do not count themselves as unemployed but being engaged in looking for a job while being dependent on their families. The Saudi *Majlis Al Shoura* Consultative Council presented proposals in January 2010 to King Abdullah to pay an unemployment allowance of SR 1,000 ($267) per month to the estimated 500,000 jobless Saudis mentioned in the press, as long as they are registered with the Ministry of Labour until they find a job.

This initiative breaks yet another social taboo in the Kingdom. There used to be a social stigma attached to accepting such unemployment benefits, and this complicated matters when trying to establish precise data on voluntary and involuntary unemployed. While unemployment rates may vary with each announcement, the greatest challenge remains the same: the labour force is increasing faster than the available jobs, based on the demographic structure of the Kingdom.

However, we must avoid confusing two issues: the number of job-seekers not working and the overall number of people of working age who are not working. The number of job-seekers, as a percentage of the overall population, is called the *labour participation rate*, and this is expected to be low for Saudi Arabia, given its very youthful demographic profile and low participation rate of females. This is illustrated in Table 12.12 comparing Saudi Arabia with other countries of the Gulf Cooperation Council and USA.

Table 12.12 Selected labour participation rates[a]: GCC countries 2007/2008 (%)

Country	Male (%)	Female (%)	Total (%)
Saudi Arabia	51.7	11.6	33.8
Kuwait	84.4	45.8	52.3
Qatar	94.9	49.4	91.7
UAE	89.4	41.9	54.9
Oman	76.9	24.6	36.6
USA	73.0	59.4	66.0

[a]Labour force as % of total population
Source: International Labour Organization (ILO)

Table 12.12 does indeed show that Saudi Arabia has a lower male and female participation rate than the rest of the GCC countries or a representative developed country such as the USA. Qatar had the highest participation rate, almost full employment for males at nearly 95%, while Qatari female participation was the highest in the GCC assisted by the economic and social transformation that is taking place in that Gulf country due to a boom in gas export revenue, backed by Qatar's third largest global gas reserves.

The growing unemployment numbers, whether official or voluntary, are having an impact on poverty levels in the Kingdom. Again, no official statistics exist on what constitutes a national poverty level, nor of the total number of those depending on social security assistance, but there are some official figures to illustrate the magnitude of the problem. According to figures released by the Ministry of Social Affairs in January 2010, there were 692,508 social security beneficiaries receiving monthly financial support of just under SR 1 billion a month in total, or an average of SR 1,400 per beneficiary (Al Tamimi, 2010). Recipients include orphans, disabled people and widows, as well as those with changed circumstances. Assuming that each recipient has a dependency ratio of 2, which is a conservative dependency ratio, then the number of Saudis dependent on monthly state support is around 2.1 million people or around 11.3% of an estimated 18.5 million Saudi population in 2010.

The issue of poverty is one of the concerns of the Saudi government, and the 2008 and 2009 national budgets allocated increased social security benefits. The government would bear, for a period of 3 years from 2010, 50% of the fees relating to passports, vehicle licences and ownership transfers and renewal of residence permits for domestic workers for those depending on domestic help, in effect reducing the level of indirect taxation for Saudi citizens.

Increasing the Labour Participation Rate: Oil Boom "Baby Boomers"

While there are no official data on the level of dropout rates in the Saudi education system, we believe that the average level of 5% that we used in our earlier analysis erred on the conservative side. Dropout rates calculated for the early 1980s averaged around 25% for all three educational sectors (Johany, 1986). Plentiful and easier job opportunities in those early "boom years" may well have contributed towards higher dropout and labour participation rates.

The situation will become more difficult as growth in the labour force exceeds population growth. There is likely to be a natural increase over time in the labour participation rate due to the demographic bulge of the "oil boom baby boomers" coming into the job market in greater numbers, as indicated in the following figures.

According to SAMA, there were 3.513 million male Saudis in the labour force, or around 19% of the total Saudi population of working-age Saudi males. What is clear from Fig. 12.9 is that unemployment is closely correlated with age groups: the younger age groups have the highest unemployment rates.

Thus, unemployment was 28% for Saudi males who are 20–24 years old, but only 9.8% for Saudis between 25 and 39. According to 2007 government data, the unemployment level for all Saudis over the age of 40 was almost non-existent at 0.9%. Again, this is a function of those who found employment more readily during the earlier "boom" period and held on to those jobs.

What is worrying for future employment trends is the large number of future job entrants in the 10–19 age group as illustrated in Fig. 12.9.

The non-Saudi expatriate population exhibits a different employment pattern as illustrated in Fig. 12.10, showing a greater unemployment pattern among the

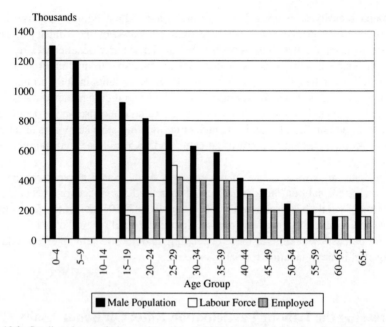

Fig. 12.9 Saudi male population and employed 2008 (male and female expatriates excluded) (Source: SAMA, Ministry of Planning)

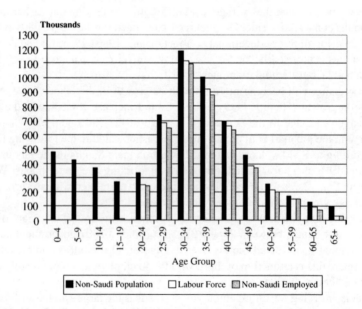

Fig. 12.10 Non-Saudi population and employed, 2008 (Source: SAMA, Ministry of Planning)

younger expatriates in the 20–24 and 25–29 age groups, with employment rates rising the older the expatriates are.

The main difference with the Saudi male population profile discussed earlier is in the 15–19 age group. According to SAMA, the total non-Saudi labour force was 4.281 million in 2008, with 4.260 million employed. Expatriates under the age of 19 are the dependents of foreign workers and are not expected to join the Saudi labour market. The younger expatriate workers tend to be unskilled, with low educational levels. In times of economic downturn, they are the vulnerable ones, more likely to be dismissed than the older, professional/technical fixed-contract term expatriates. Non-Saudi population data and employment patterns only cover those who are officially registered, and therefore do not include large numbers of illegal migrants, such as *Hajj* pilgrims who do not return to their countries, despite intensive efforts by the authorities each year to repatriate them. In economic terms, the illegal expatriates only manage to drive down the wage levels of low-paid legal workers. Government efforts to remove such illegal workers every year does not help *Saudization* much, as most Saudis would not take on their low-paid and menial jobs.

Education and Labour Participation Levels

The emphasis on education and increasing Saudi labour productivity has taken a centre stage in Saudi economic development and planning. The 2010 Saudi budget allocated SR 138 billion or 25% of total expenditure for human resource development, continuing the high expenditure pattern for this sector over the past few years. The aim is to ensure that the number and quality of Saudi job-seekers are enhanced with specific skills through training programmes for jobs needed in the labour market. Earlier in the chapter, we had analysed the breakdown of the labour force in the private sector by educational level for 2008, and it was noted that over 86% of the total population was literate, and those holding diplomas to higher degrees accounted for 10% of the total workforce. However, despite this massive investment in human resources, the number of those seeking jobs with a higher educational level has been increasing over the years, as illustrated in Table 12.13, while the numbers of job-seekers who are illiterate is declining.

Table 12.13 Breakdown of registered Saudi job-seekers by educational level (1997–2008)

Educational level	1997	2002	2006	2008
Illiterate	6,316	1,725	658	472
Literate	7,910	2,406	4,044	1,991
Primary school	16,943	13,187	18,097	24,691
Intermediate school	11,980	15,401	23,220	43,135
High school	10,083	27,217	44,571	50,411
Diploma	–	–	13,484	14,933
Bachelor	2,141	4,321	16,191	11,461
Higher education (Master/Ph.D.)	–	–	122	103
Total	55,373	64,257	120,387	147,197

Source: ARAMCO

While the number of job-seekers with intermediate and high school certificates has been growing the most rapidly, there is a worrying number of job-seekers holding diploma and bachelor degrees, although the 2008 boom year reduced their numbers but not the number of the overall job-seekers. In the following chapter, we will assess the effectiveness of the current Saudi educational system in terms of the quantity and quality of graduate output. However, given the young population age structure of the Kingdom and the forecasted numbers of higher education graduates in the coming years, there is concern that Saudi Arabia will start to exhibit a symptom of *structural unemployment amongst educated citizens.*

"Educated" Unemployed

Many developing countries have high rates of unemployment among their educated citizens. Though empirically well documented, the causes of this phenomenon have received little attention with the exception of Bhagwati and Hamada (1974), whose approach nonetheless fails to explain why educated unemployment is not common to all less developing countries (LDCs). In a recent paper, Fan and Stark (2007) propose a model in which educated unemployment is a result of the prospect of international migration. The authors argue that migration of educated workers is a "brain drain" for the developing countries and contrasts sharply with the pattern of unemployment in developed countries, where, in the latter, the unemployment rate and educational attainment are strongly negatively correlated. This was also confirmed by other authors' research in developed economies (Ashenfelter and Ham, 1979). For such developing non-resource-rich countries, "educated unemployment" is caused by the prospect of international migration. In a simple job-search framework an individual's reservation wage (minimum acceptable wage) in the labour market of the home country increases with the probability of working abroad. Workers who fail to obtain employment abroad are less likely to immediately search for work in their home countries but instead enter voluntary unemployment in order to engage in repeated attempts to secure foreign employment and contribute to the "brain drain."

However, international employment data show that unemployment rates for educated workers are high even in LDCs that do not export skilled labour. Both national and International Labour Organization (ILO) data show high unemployment levels among educated citizens in Saudi Arabia, a country with low out-migration rate. This combination of low out-migration and substantial skilled unemployment is particularly common among mineral- and fuel-exporting countries.

Though the unemployment of educated citizens is sometimes dismissed as a temporary problem with limited long-term consequences, it can create significant economic and social problems for resource-rich LDCs. As these countries struggle to escape the "resource curse" and develop their non-resource economies, educated unemployment is a considerable waste of valuable human capital. This may be a particular problem for countries that depend on fuel and mineral extraction industries,

which tend to be capital- and skilled labour-intensive. For these economies, educated unemployment may be another mechanism through which the resource curse
undermines the growth effects of human capital accumulation. In addition to being
an important economic development issue, high unemployment among educated
young people is also an international political concern. Policies aimed at addressing
this problem would therefore have potentially huge pay-offs in terms of national
economic performance and global political stability.

In Stark and Fan's model, workers become educated in order to make themselves
eligible for high-wage jobs overseas. They then remain unemployed in their home
country while searching for these jobs both because searching for an overseas job is
time-consuming and because experience gained in the home country is not valued by
firms in the high-wage country. A skilled-labour resource-rich sector may generate
educated unemployment in much the same way. In an oil-exporting country, for
example, workers may seek higher education in order to become qualified for jobs
in the oil industry, where wages are higher because of revenues from resource rents
and, if the industry is nationalized, revenue sharing by the government. However,
as even large fuel- and mineral-exporting industries tend to be capital-intensive,
job opportunities in this high-wage sector are limited. If applying for these jobs is
time-consuming and experience in other industries is not valued by the oil sector, a
fraction of these educated citizens may choose to remain unemployed while looking
for oil sector or government jobs, rather than accept employment in another industry.

The policy of *Saudization*, under the above model, would therefore be expected
to increase unemployment amongst educated citizens in the short term as they
search for oil/resource-based jobs, and further increase educated unemployment
in the medium term as citizens facing such a preferred hiring model decide to
become educated. The above has important policy implications for the Kingdom,
assuming those "educated unemployed" do not seek alternative jobs than their preferred resource-based or government sector jobs. If the resource industry is already
government-owned, as in Saudi Arabia, the government should avoid redistribut-
ing revenues through higher resource/public sector wages and instead allow the
manufacturing industry to benefit from the "educated unemployed" human capital, causing wages in that sector to rise and therefore removing the incentives for the
"educated unemployed" to remain unemployed.

Controlling the Public Sector "Free Ride"

Figure 12.11 shows the bias towards public, as opposed to private, sector employment by Saudis, indicating that by 2008 nearly 92% of all government employees
were Saudis, as opposed to around 13% in the private sector for the same year.

There are several reasons for this, including the security of tenure for government
jobs, a less demanding working environment and hours compared to the private sector as well as the relative disparity between public and public sector pay as illustrated
in Fig. 12.12.

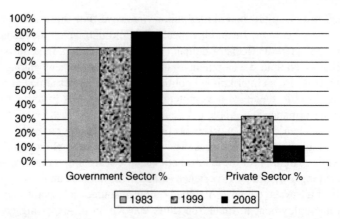

Fig. 12.11 Saudis employed in government and private sectors as % of total employment (1983–2008) (Source: SAMA)

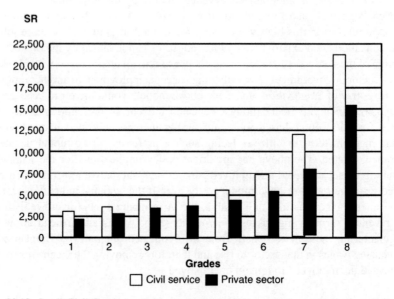

Fig. 12.12 Saudi Civil Service and private sector monthly wages by educational grade levels (average 2005–2008) (Source: Central Department of Statistics)

It shows that public sector pay and benefits are higher than those of the private sector at education levels one through eight, according to the government's civil service grades.

Government sector employees also benefited from the state's decision to include 5% inflation salary allowance which was added to the wages of public sector employees and retirees for 3 years from 2008, and which is estimated to have cost the government around SR 60 billion. Such salary price adjustments could become a fixture for future public sector pay rises which are inflation index-linked and more guaranteed than private sector salary scales, which depend upon individual company policies and personal negotiations between employer and employee. Continuing public sector salary increases run the risk of enticing too many Saudis to seek government jobs without similar increases in productivity and reinforce the cycle of "educated unemployed" analysed earlier.

Public sector salaries are often a signal to the rest of the economy and provide the private sector with a salary benchmark, but given that the majority of private sector employees are non-Saudis on fixed 2-year contracts, the discrepancy between public and private sector pay might increase.

The preponderance of employees in the government sector has come at a heavy price. Table 12.14 shows that the wage bill for 2008 stood at 27% of total government expenditures, as opposed to 25% for capital/investment spending during the same year.

Table 12.14 Government wage bill as % of government expenditure and oil revenue (1994–2008)

Year	Government wage bill as of percentage			Investment expenditure as % of total government expenditure (%)
	GDP (%)	Government expenditure (%)	Oil revenue (%)	
1994	18.0	51.1	91.5	14.0
1996	16.0	45.6	66.4	13.5
1999	23.0	56.0	98.6	9.0
2002	16.25	50.2	70.3	12.8
2007	8.5	27.1	22.4	25.5
2008	7.9	26.9	14.2	25.2

Source: SAMA, Ministry of Planning, National Accounts of Saudi Arabia

The wage bill has sometimes equalled or exceeded oil revenues, especially during times of falling oil prices. The Saudi government is attempting to rationalize this expenditure and has frozen hiring for certain government positions in a bid to direct more employment to the private sector. However, until the trend is significantly reversed, Saudi Arabia will continue to exhibit one of the world's highest government employment ratios to labour force and population. The high-wage policy for Saudis in the public sector has had some important economic implications. The successful policy of *Saudization* in the government sector has been accompanied at a financial cost, a function of the wage differential between Saudis and non-Saudis. Studies have shown that had the Saudi government maintained the same ratio of expatriates to Saudis in 1999 as in 1983, the national wage bill would have been 30% less than at current levels (Kapiszewski, 2001).

The large Saudi public sector wage bill is not necessarily reflected in the level of public sector performance. Some studies indicate that an overhaul of this sector's methods and procedures is necessary to improve productivity (AlJanoubi, 2002, Sharway, 2002). The level of *disguised unemployed* hidden in unproductive jobs within the public sector is high in the GCC countries. Studies estimate that disguised unemployment ranges from 40% for Kuwait to 14% for Bahrain (Cordesman, 2003).

Female Labour Participation

While the Kingdom has done well on its mission to completely eliminate gender disparity at all levels of education, despite the fact that girl's education was introduced relatively later than that of boys and as late as the 1960s, the participation rate of females in the total employment is much lower than for males as illustrated in Fig. 12.13.

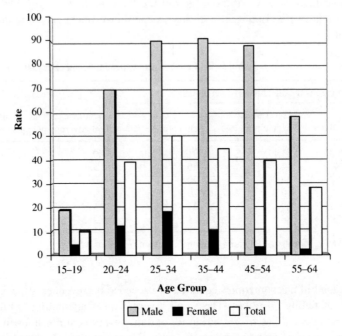

Fig. 12.13 Participation rates by gender and age group (2007) (Source: Ministry of Planning, SAMA)

The available data show that the highest female participation levels are in the 25–34 age group, followed by the 20–24 age group. With parental and family commitments, participation rate for the older age groups falls off or is completely negligible. This could be due to the fact that there were few job openings for females several decades ago, when it was not socially accepted that women seek jobs.

A mere 6.5% of the 3.95 million Saudi Arabian women aged between 19 and 49 were in formal employment in 2008, one of the lowest proportions in the world. This participation rate, however, is thought to underestimate the role of females in economic activities owing to two basic reasons: (a) while total employment statistics included those formally employed in the agricultural sector, females working in agriculture and other traditional occupations, however, are not included in the statistics; (b) the employment statistics do not yet take into account females employed in small, family-run businesses.

Although there are several factors that explain the low participation by females in economic activity, there is increasing interest in increasing the employment levels of females as economic and social development progresses. Development has created new social and economic conditions, which require higher participation by women in the labour market, in occupations that are compatible with the prevalent cultural norms and values. The belief remains widespread though out in the Kingdom that a wife neglects her duty of taking care of her husband and children if she decides to take up employment outside her home.

Expansion of female education has encouraged many females to join the labour force and seek employment. Most formally employed females in the Kingdom are working in the services sector, particularly in education, health and social services. This is illustrated in Fig. 12.14, which sets out participation rate by gender and educational achievement for Saudi nationals. It is noted in this regard that Saudi females' participation in the workforce is highest in the age group 25–34 holding graduate degrees (about 52%). It is clear that female participation rate in the workforce is directly proportional to educational attainment, moderated with marital status, where married women with children may prefer not to work outside the home.

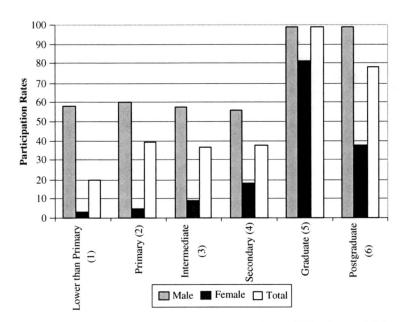

Fig. 12.14 Participation rates by gender and educational level (2007) (Source: Ministry of Planning, SAMA)

There is an urgent need to close the wide mismatch between educational qualifications of graduates, i.e. education system output, on the one hand and the needs of the labour market on the other. This issue, however, does effect the employment of all the national workforce – males and females but it has a greater impact on the latter due to reduced job opportunities and other social and cultural factors.

Work is sexually segregated in Saudi Arabia, with men, usually expatriates from South Asia, serving as secretaries for male managers rather than women as in the West, except for some international companies in their compounds and Saudi Aramco. Saudi Arabian women are unable to become nurses in hospital wards with male patients, and even in banks they are not permitted to work in the same offices as men or to deal directly with male clients. As women cannot drive, getting to work creates a problem, with women teachers having to rely on male relatives or paid male drivers to transport them to their schools. All this adds to the cost of being employed and deters women from entering the workforce.

However, research carried out in Saudi Arabia of a survey of women in the labour market showed that a majority of those employed were married, whereas the majority of those unemployed were single, as opposed to Western female participation models, but reconfirmed by the participation rate by gender and age group in Fig. 12.13. In that figure, the majority of Saudi female labour participants were in the elder age groups, and traditionally had already been married in Saudi Arabia by the age of 24 due to local customs and traditions. It seems somewhat evident from such field research carried out that work was not a prime concern in educational choices, as over 70% of women had chosen subjects likely to convey a high social status after graduation, whereas only 16% had considered the market needs of the private sector. Most women in Saudi Arabia, like their male counterparts, expressed a preference for public sector work, and most wanted employment in order to fulfil cultural and social needs rather than to support personal or family financial needs (Dosary, 2002, Doumato, 2001).

However, the issue of *Saudi female participation* cannot be effectively tackled until and unless women are more directly involved in Saudi nation-building. This matter is commanding attention inside Saudi Arabia. Indeed, no less a person than King Abdullah stated as early as 1999 when he was Crown Prince that "we will not allow any person to undermine the role of Saudi women or marginalize the active role they take for their religion or country... Saudi women have proven their ability to handle responsibilities with great success, whether through their principal duties as mothers or professionals. We look forward to women playing a major role in a way that will promote the interest of this nation on the basis of *Shariah* (Islamic law)" (Saudi Press Agency, 12 September 2003).

Statements of encouragement and support like those of the King Abdullah have galvanized women's groups to demand better treatment on the economic front. Saudi businesswomen have petitioned the *Majlis Al Shoura* for ways to facilitate their investment activities, so that they can play a greater role in the country's economic development. King Abdullah has reinforced his support for empowering Saudi women, the most recent public statement being in March 2010 when he opened the new session of the *Majlis Al Shoura* and said that Saudi women have participated along with men in all development programmes and he would pursue this agenda.

Women's economic issues and the speed of women's integration within Saudi society still meet strong resistance in the name of tradition and values. Despite the Saudi government's desire for change and reform on women's issues, some sources of resistance cannot be ignored. According to one of the Kingdom's well-known modernist officials, Prince Khaled Al Faisal, ". . . Saudi Arabia is probably the only country in the world where the government is pushing for reforms and the people are pulling back . . ." (Qusti, 2003).

Counting the Cost of Unemployment

Besides the social cost of unemployment, to which the government now openly admits, unemployment also gives rise to economic waste. The economic loss in output to society is known as "the potential output gap," and it has been statistically measured in more developed economies. One such measure is *Okun's Law,* pioneered by the U.S. economist Arthur Okun using data for the USA. This law states that each extra percentage point of cyclical unemployment is associated with about a 2% point increase or decrease in the output gap, measured in relation to potential output. Thus, for example, if cyclical unemployment increases from 1 to 2% of the labour force, the recessionary gap will increase from 2 to 4% of potential GDP. When actual output is below potential output, the resultant output gap is called a *recessionary gap.* When actual output is above potential output, it is called an *expansionary gap.*

Table 12.15 attempts to quantify, through applying *Okun's Law,* the potential loss of Saudi output for the period 1993–2008. There are no detailed statistics available on two major inputs: the actual rate of unemployed (signified as U) and the natural rate of unemployed (signified as U^*). The base year of 1993 was chosen as it coincided with the first official pronouncements on the existence of some level of Saudi unemployment.

Further, non-oil GDP at producer prices was used for the period. This was felt to provide a better estimation for GDP, given the oil sector's volatility and the uncontrolled external factors determining this component. The Saudi Arabian "natural rate of unemployment" (U^*) is based on the author's own estimation, taking into consideration Saudi extended family structures, where the kinship system looked after those who did not have a job or did not wish to enter the labour market, as well as the lower female participation rate examined earlier. As such, compared with other countries, the higher Saudi "*natural rate of unemployment*" cushions the impact of the actual rate of unemployment.

The results show a virtual doubling of the Saudi unemployment rate every 5–7 years, but at an accelerating pace, with sizeable losses in potential output in GDP. The assumed rate of unemployment begins to fall for the period 2006–2008, which saw high oil prices and rising surpluses and government work programmes and

Table 12.15   Saudi unemployment and potential GDP losses (1993–2008)

Year	Non-oil GDP at producer prices (SR billion) (Y) (1)	Unemployment rate % (U) (2)	% Natural rate of unemployment % (U^*) (3)	Output gap (%) (4)	Value of output gap (SR billion) (5)	Potential output (SR billion) (Y^*) (6)
1993	296.8	7	5	4	11.9	308.6
1994	304.1	8	6	4	12.2	316.3
1995	314.9	9	6	6	18.9	333.8
1996	328.9	9	7	4	13.2	342.1
1997	347.5	11	8	6	20.8	368.3
1998	351.8	12	9	6	21.1	372.9
1999	361.9	13	9	8	28.9	390.8
2000	379.6	15	10	10	37.9	417.5
2001	390.9	18	11	14	54.7	445.6
2002	402.6	20	12	16	64.4	467.0
2003	473.1	21	13	16	25.3	548.7
2004	514.7	22	13	18	92.6	607.3
2005	554.1	25	14	22	121.9	676.0
2006	603.8	28	15	26	156.9	760.7
2007	641.9	27	15	24	154.1	796.0
2008	685.8	25	15	20	137.2	823.0

Y = Real output; Y^* = Potential output; U = Unemployment rate; U^* = Natural rate of unemployment

Note: "Output gap" is measured by subtracting (3) from (2) and multiplying by a factor of 2 as per Okun's formula. The resultant % is multiplied to actual GDP (1) to arrive at the value of output gap in (5). Potential output (6) is derived from adding (1) with (5)

Sources: Author's own forecasts for (U^*); Central Department of Statistics, Media Reports, SAMA, 2002

expenditures. The GDP "losses" increase virtually every year and total SR 1,021 billion for the period 1993–2008 using the above assumptions. Our estimate for an unemployment level of 25% for 2008 is below the government's estimate of 31.7% for both genders, as reported in the media. If we were to err on the higher side, then the rate of unemployment increases, and potential output losses would be much higher for these years. However, more studies are needed that examine both the natural and real rate of unemployment in the Kingdom.

Saudi Labour Model: Unique to Saudi Arabia?

In this section, we argue that the Saudi labour model is different from conventional labour models, by introducing "Saudi-specific" interconnected socio-economic preconditions. These are as follows:

Continuous high economic growth: High and sustained economic growth rates were once thought to make it possible for the country to achieve full employment and at the same time to provide sufficient scope for the redistribution of oil wealth. This feeling of "well-being" permeated Saudi society at all levels and contributed to the high population growth rates we now witness. This labour model came under pressure in the period 1986–2002, but with higher oil prices and increased government expenditure from 2003 it gained a new lease of life although the 2008/2009 global financial crisis has caused some to rethink.

High oil prices: The oil export-led growth model was dependent on a high oil income compatible with the Saudi government's welfare spending and investment. Until the oil shocks of the mid-1980s and the period 1997–2002, the country seemed to believe that oil prices could rise forever and that OPEC was in control of market supply. Today, the government does not publicize the effects of high oil prices, arguing that they are temporary and could be harmful to Saudi interest in the long run. One aim of such a low-key public policy is to avoid building up higher expenditure expectations, based on "windfall gains" from higher oil prices that exceed forecasted revenues at lower oil price levels.

Availability of highly paid jobs in the public sector: In Saudi Arabia, private sector compensation is generally lower than compensation in the government sector. There is a widespread view that the government has better pay and benefits for Saudis than in the private sector. This has been borne out by government data on wage and compensation analysed earlier. This differs from most developed economies, where private sector pay generally outstrips the public sector, and is more in tune with economic productivity and measurable performance.

Conclusion: Expectations, Realism and Adaptation

The labour market in Saudi Arabia has changed because of internal population dynamics, as well as a breakdown of the old Saudi labour model. The policy of creating special privileges for nationals in the labour market has had additional adverse, long-term effects. For the younger nationals, it has meant growing up with the assumption that a standard of living higher than that of non-nationals is an inalienable right, irrespective of any personal contribution to the wealth and well-being of society as a whole. By guaranteeing positions in the public sector for their citizens, the authorities unintentionally engendered the notion that they were the universal benefactors of their citizens. Strong public signals are now being sent out that this will have to be changed, and that employment will be based on skill, education and productivity. The private sector has been arguing for this, rather than the arbitrary policies of *Saudization* of economic sectors.

While Saudi Arabia somewhat lags behind other GCC states, such as *Bahrain, Kuwait, Oman* and *UAE*, the increased employment of Saudi women is expected to continue in the near future. Among Saudi women there is a strong interest in working and in attaining an improved education. The government has also been willing to openly address this issue.

Increased participation of women in the labour market should be possible because of the spread of modern technology, which allows employees to be productively engaged electronically while remaining in protected places (for example, banking call centres). However, as we know from the low participation rate for women in the Saudi labour force, there is still some social pressure on them to accept the traditional housewife role and not to go out and work.

Current government policies to reduce foreign labour and encourage *Saudization* have had mixed results. It has been difficult to introduce and effectively manage the regulations restricting the number of expatriates, because the importation of foreign labour enjoys strong support from the powerful lobbies of trading and merchant families. Their fortunes have been built to a large extent on cheap expatriate labour. The sponsorship system of foreign workers or *kefalaa* artificially hinders market demand and supply forces, creating rigidities in certain sectors with surplus labour and supply shortages in others. This results in further importation of foreign labour under the sponsorship system. The government should consider a policy of gradually scrapping the sponsorship system after compensating those employers for the costs of sponsorship. These costs can be recouped from workers' wages on a pro-rata basis. In the short run, the Saudi government has decided to limit the number of new work visas they grant in order to curb new foreign labour entrants to the market and to create a Saudi "labour supply" pool. This has caused friction among some parts of the private sector, but the Saudi Minister of Labour Al Gosaibi had made this restrictive policy a central plank in his effort to direct Saudi labour to available jobs. The appointment in August 2010 of a new Labour Minister Adel Fakieh, with strong credentials in the private sector, following Al Gosaibi's death, is being closely watched to see if a new era of private sector cooperation will be established.

A new key concern has been growing evidence of a new pool of Saudi unemployed, the so-called "educated unemployed," which seems to be spurred on by the desire to take up resource-based or government jobs, driving citizens to acquire more education while adding to the pool of "educated unemployed."

The liberalization of labour policies could become an issue in the future following the Kingdom's accession to the WTO in 2005, with WTO provisions demanding that member states allow free movement of labour. This could involve scrapping local sponsorship laws. Furthermore, the *International Labour Organization* (ILO), of which Saudi Arabia is a member, may challenge the continuation of existing policies towards foreign workforces. The ILO has been urging Saudi Arabia, as well as other GCC countries, to accept basic International Labour Standards and to ratify relevant conventions relating to workers' rights. Saudi Arabia has successfully argued to maintain its *Saudization* policy following WTO accession, but this could act as deterrence for more FDI flows in the future if the *Saudization* quotas are strictly applied.

Summary of Key Points

- *The current state of the Saudi labour market and unemployment is becoming a major issue of concern to the Saudi government. Underlying causes are the relatively young age profile of the population, high fertility rates and a mismatch between Saudi labour entrants and market needs in terms of required skills.*
- Saudization *has become one tool by which the government aims to replace foreigners with Saudis, using a dual programme of incentives and visa restrictions for foreign workers.*
- *The private sector would be the main source of Saudi employment generation as government jobs become frozen at current levels for the next decade. Saudi employment in the private sector indicates that the* Saudization *policy has had mixed results, with only public utilities and finance achieving majority Saudi employment.*
- *Changing perceptions about culture and work ethics are important. Indications are that Saudi youth are beginning to be more realistic about their job expectations and adapt their skills to meet market needs. The private sector continues to raise issues of concern that need addressing before they increase the level of* Saudization*: labour costs, control over the process of production (with expatriate labour easier to control), Saudi job tenure, inadequate qualifications, mobility and lack of integration in a multicultural work environment.*
- *Both the private sector and the government are focusing on improving the education and skill base of job entrants. Saudi planning is becoming more focused on sector-specific employment goals.*
- *The issue of foreign labour needs to be addressed carefully and sympathetically, as the Kingdom is still in need of large numbers of skilled expatriates for the foreseeable future. The presence of other diverse nationalities amongst a local population can sometimes create a two-way intangible benefit to both sides.*
- *It is difficult to quantify precisely the current level of the Saudi labour force as not everyone registers for employment. As such, it is also difficult to calculate the precise number of unemployed Saudis. This is doubly difficult for Saudi female labour, where it is estimated that Saudi female labour participation levels are among the lowest in the world.*
- *Unemployment not only causes social problems and a rise in unemployment-related crimes but also has an economic cost to society. It is estimated that around SR 1,021 billion was lost in GDP "output gap" between 1993 and 2008 because of Saudi unemployment levels, using a simplified "Okun's Law" calculation for the output gap.*
- *The Saudi labour market is characterized by its "dual" nature for Saudis and non-Saudis in terms of differentiated demand and supply of labour for these two labour segments, as well as different supply and demand elasticities.*

Chapter 13
Education: A Tool for a Knowledge-Based Economy

All who have mediated on the art of governing mankind have been convinced that the fate of empires depends on the education of youth.

Aristotle

Learning Outcomes

By the end of this section, you would understand:

- *The growth in education expenditure to meet population needs*
- *Facing up to the globalization challenges*
- *The Saudi educational structure*
- *Moves to restructure the educational system*
- *Saudi education and market needs*
- *Options for change in the education structure*

Introduction

There are a number of reasons why education plays such a crucial role in Saudi Arabia: its young population, the influx of expatriate labour, the lack of natural resources besides exhaustible oil and a relatively new educational system. The major issue, however, is not the amount of expansion, but rather the orientation of the educational system. A major problem with this system is that it attributes high social prestige to university education, while underestimating the significance of technological and vocational education. It is widely, if unfairly, believed that only school dropouts and academically poor students enter technical training (Kibbi, 2002). This belief is further strengthened by employment policies which, until recently, encouraged an educational structure that offered priority employment opportunities in the government sector to university graduates, thus making technical and vocational education even less attractive and less socially desirable (The Economist, 1997).

M.A. Ramady, *The Saudi Arabian Economy*, DOI 10.1007/978-1-4419-5987-4_13,
© Springer Science+Business Media, LLC 2010

In development literature, the role of education in building "human capital" has been consistently highlighted. The positive role of higher education in the construction of knowledge-based economies and democratic societies is highly promoted by international organizations such as the World Bank (Larocque, 2002). These groups stress that higher education exercises a direct influence on national productivity, which in turn largely determines living standards and a country's ability to compete in the global economy. Investment in quality training and higher education generates major external benefits that are crucial for knowledge-driven economic and social development (World Bank, 2001).

Technological progress and the "diffusion" of scientific and technical innovations lead to higher productivity. That encourages improvement in all sectors of the economy. Higher skill levels in the labour force – an outcome of increased educational levels – and improved education permit workers to use new technology and boosts productivity. As such, the ability of any society to produce, select, adapt and commercialize knowledge is critical for sustained economic growth and improved living standards. In relation to its population, size and educational investment, Saudi Arabia has produced a negligible number of commercial patents, compared to other countries. Singapore, Malaysia and Korea have invested smaller amounts per capita in higher education than Saudi Arabia, but seem to have used it better to generate sustained economic growth. With Saudi Arabia's accession to the World Trade Organization (WTO), it faces both opportunities and threats stemming from changes in the global environment, specifically in the educational sector. In this regard, the Kingdom has been reassessing the educational sector's role in meeting national development objectives, both quantitatively and qualitatively.

Meeting the Globalization Challenges

Developing economies face significant new trends in the global environment, the most critical of which is the increasing importance of knowledge, the main driver of growth within this information and communication revolution (Salmi, 2003).

Today, economic growth is as much a process of knowledge accumulation as of capital accumulation. Firms in developed countries devote more and more of their investment to knowledge-based intangibles such as training, research and development, patents, licensing and design. The aim is to gain a competitive edge over others in the global economy. The same applies to countries as well as to companies; information and communication technologies (ICTs) speed up the flow of knowledge across boundaries.

However, joining the global knowledge-based economy brings with it both opportunities and threats. Some of these issues are highlighted in Table 13.1.

On the positive side, the role of higher education in the construction of knowledge-based economies and democratic societies is more influential than ever. On the negative side, the technological transformation of knowledge-based societies carries the real danger of a growing digital, and by implication economic, divide between nations.

Table 13.1 Opportunities and threats stemming from changes in the global environment

Change factor	Opportunities	Threats
Growing role of knowledge	• Possibility of leapfrogging in selected areas of economic growth • Resolution of social problems (food, security, health, water supply, energy, environment)	Increasing knowledge gap among nations
ICT revolution	• Easier access to knowledge and information	• Growing digital divide among and within nations
Global labour market	• Easier access to the expertise, skills and knowledge of professionals	• Growing brain drain and loss of advanced human capital
Political and social change	• Positive environment for reform • Spread of democracy	• Growing brain drain and political instability • Loss of human resources

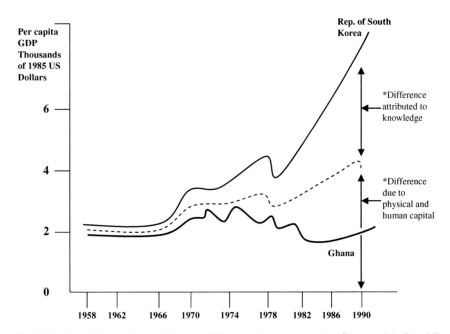

Fig. 13.1 Knowledge as a factor in income differences between countries: Ghana and the Republic of South Korea 1956–1990 (Source: World Bank (1999))

Figure 13.1 demonstrates how, according to World Bank studies, two countries – South Korea and Ghana – that had almost identical per capita GDP in 1957/1958 diverged in their economic growth paths by the late 1990s, owing to the pace of knowledge in their development.

Figure 13.1 illustrates the significant difference a knowledge-based development strategy makes to economic growth. Such knowledge-based development exercises a direct influence on national productivity, which largely determines living standards, as the per capita divergence between Ghana and South Korea confirms. This development approach supports knowledge-driven economic growth strategies and poverty reduction by (a) training a qualified and adaptable labour force, including scientists, professionals, technicians, teachers and business leaders; (b) generating new knowledge; and (c) building the capacity to access existing stores of global knowledge and to adapt that knowledge to local use (Salmi, 2002, Dukhayil, 2002, Larocque, 2002).

Analysis of global competitiveness amongst nations seems to indicate a high degree of correlation between the level of higher education and training and national competitiveness indexes. Saudi Arabia still lags behind other Middle East countries such as the United Arab Emirates and Qatar as illustrated in Fig. 13.2.

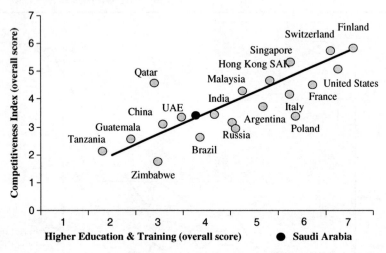

Fig. 13.2 Higher education training and competitiveness index – selected nations 2007 (Source: The Global Competitiveness Report)

According to studies conducted by the US-based Brookings Institute, there has been a gain of 13–30% in productivity because of increased investment in higher education, which comprises both diploma-level and tertiary- or university-level education (Global Competitive Report, 2007).

Education in Saudi Arabia

Education has been an important unifying and nation-building facilitator since the proclamation of the modern Kingdom of Saudi Arabia in 1932 to date (Al-Rasheed, 2002, Champion, 2003). Education advances nation-building by promoting greater social cohesion, trust in social institutions, national participation and appreciation of diversity in social class. These are the *positive externalities* of applying a national educational programme. Saudi Arabia's wealth in oil resources has provided the means for broader economic and national infrastructural development, including education. This natural desire to develop the nation's human resources has been undertaken with enthusiasm by successive rulers of the Kingdom who have taken a great personal interest in this area (Al-Rasheed, 2002).

Saudi Arabia has been able to build a large educational infrastructure within a short period of time because of the financial resources it derives from oil revenues. As discussed in earlier chapters, budgetary outlays on education had been steadily rising with SR 138 billion allocated in the 2010 budget, or 29% of total expenditure. The total amount planned for education and human resource development in the Ninth Development Plan 2010–2014 was SR 479.9 billion or 55% of total sector expenditures for the 5-year period (Ministry of Planning). As a comparison, the First Five-Year Plan for the period 1970–1974 forecasted education and human resources development at SR 7 billion or 20.6% of total expenditure. As a result of this consistent expenditure pattern, literacy rates and enrolment ratios at all levels have been increasing as illustrated in Fig. 13.3.

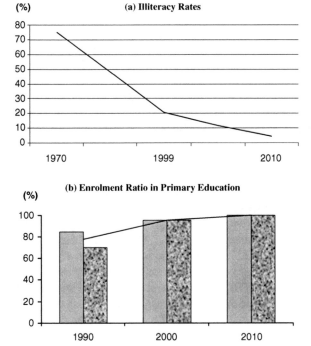

Fig. 13.3 Illiteracy and enrolment rates: Saudi Arabia (Source: Statistical Yearbook, Ministry of Planning, Eighth Development Plan)

As illustrated in Fig. 13.3, youth literacy rate reached 97.3% in 2010 and adult literacy stood at 79.8% for the same year according to the Ministry of Planning. Primary school enrolment ratio registered 100% for both males and females in 2010, compared with around 83% for males and 70% for females in 1990.

The Kingdom provides free education in its public schools, colleges and universities. Furthermore, the Seventh and Eighth National Development Plans made primary- and secondary-level education compulsory for both males and females. In addition the private sector has been assuming an increasing role in the provision of education, historically in primary and secondary education, and more recently in tertiary education with new private sector universities being established such as Prince Sultan University and Al Yamamah University in Riyadh and Prince Mohammed University in Alkhobar in the Eastern Province.

There is a growing imbalance between the quality and quantity of occupational expertise produced by the educational system and the occupational structure demanded by the economy, as reflected in the qualifications and expertise required by present and future employment opportunities. As will be discussed later, about two thirds of the total number of male and female students in higher education graduate with degrees in humanities and other fields that are not in great demand by the labour market. Consequently, the education policy is under continuous review and assessment, with the objective of tuning the system output to better match the needs of economic and social development.

The educational system is increasingly challenged by rapid scientific, technological and other developments, which requires a continuous review of the educational curriculum so it stays attuned to developments in the domestic market as well as to relevant international developments. This policy entails: (a) continuous enhancement of educational methodologies; (b) upgrading the educational environment; (c) strengthening the technical capabilities and performance of the educational system; (d) improving the technical capabilities of teachers, instructors and other educational professionals; and (e) enhancing educational governance and management. These issues will be explored in more depth later on in the chapter.

However, the information and communication revolution that is sweeping the globe is having a profound effect on Saudi Arabian society in the social, educational and economic spheres. It has not been lost upon the Saudi government that new communication technologies have had a positive economic impact on many developing countries, such as China, India, Malaysia and the nearby GCC countries, particularly Dubai and Bahrain. With the help of a relatively effective educational system, these countries have all successfully created information technology that allows them to compete in the global market. Dubai's "Internet City" is indeed a powerful model for Saudi Arabia. However, as Fig. 13.4 shows, there is still a wide divide between the distribution of Internet access and the world's population. The USA and Canada, with 5.1% of the world's population, account for 65% of Internet host sites, compared to around 6% of Internet sites for the developing countries, which have 80% of the world's population (World Bank, 2008).

Compared to World Bank reports as early as 2002, Saudi Arabia has made some significant progress on the spread of technology and information communication.

(i) Distribution of Internet hosts

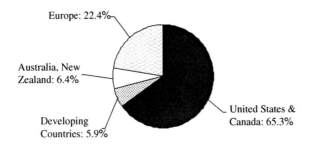

(ii) Distribution of world population

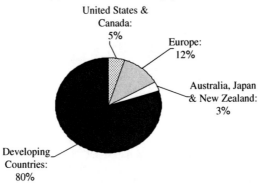

Fig. 13.4 Distribution of Internet hosts and world population, by region (2007) (Source: Data from International Telecommunications Union, the United Nations, World Bank, 2008)

Figure 13.5 indicates that the Kingdom was third in the GCC countries behind the UAE and Bahrain in terms of mobile telephone and Internet user penetration for 2008 and fourth by personal computer ownership.

Globalization, declining communication and transportation costs and the opening of borders combine to facilitate an increased movement of skilled people, leading to a global marketplace for the advanced human capital. In the twenty-first century marketplace, richer countries try in many ways to attract and retain the world's best-trained minds. For example, according to the World Bank, nearly 25% of the science and engineering students in US graduate schools come from other countries, and in 2000 the USA made available 600,000 new visas for immigrant scientists and engineers (World Bank, 2002).

In Saudi Arabia, the Ministry of Communications and Information Technology (MCIT) published, in 2005, its plan for ICT sector development. The vision for ICT sector development has called for the creation of a knowledge-based society that is

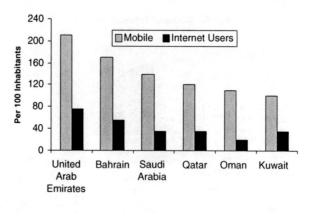

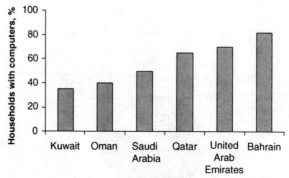

Fig. 13.5 (a) Mobile and Internet user penetration in GCC countries (2008) (Source: ITU World Telecommunication /ICT Indicators Database); (b) Percentage of households with computers, GCC countries (2008) (Source: ITU World Telecommunication /ICT Indicators Database)

able to produce, access, use and interact with the flow of latest information, thereby contributing to improving efficiency, productivity and the quality of products and services.

The following targets have been attached to the development plan:

- Raising direct foreign investments in ICT projects to US$500 million.
- Establishing a number of IT incubators and technology zones.
- Continuing review of government procedures to make them consistent with e-government best practice and provide government services on the Internet.
- Establishing a national gateway for e-government.
- Creating high administrative posts for IT in government agencies.
- Establishing a centre under the umbrella of the Chambers of Commerce and Industry to support greater use of ICT applications in the private sector.
- Issuing the e-transactions regulation.
- Opening up competition in fixed line services starting from 2006.
- Licensing additional operators to deliver mobile telephone services, which was achieved by 2010 with two other operators, Mobily and Zain, being licensed.

With its relatively high population growth and fluctuating economic wealth due to erratic oil revenues, Saudi Arabia faces challenges in the educational field that have wider implications for human development and economic growth (Looney, 1989). These challenges are summarized in Table 13.2.

Table 13.2 Summary of challenges facing Saudi Arabian education

Economic	Access
• Education spending comprises 29 percent of the national budget • High percent of Saudi males are unemployed while only 6% of Saudi females are in employment	• Population growth of 2.2% per annum • 50% of the population is under 18 years of age • The higher education sector cannot accommodate over 30% of the high school graduates • An estimated 636,000 students in higher education in 2010
Relevance	Quality
• New teaching methodology, materials and syllabi needed to meet the needs of the knowledge economy • There is a mismatch between skills development and labour market requirements • English-language instruction from primary school level is important	• High, though reducing, dropout and repetition rates • Wide variation in the ability of entrants at each education level • Lack of national capacity to assess educational quality and trends against comparable international data • Adaptability to worldwide information base

The summary table highlights the issues of relevance and quality facing the Saudi educational system today. The government has instigated several initiatives to address these issues by re-examining syllabuses and curriculum to ensure that they meet the requirements of a more technological oriented market, and English language is being introduced from an early age at junior schools. International benchmarking is now being established for accreditation in the sciences and social sciences by leading Saudi universities. Best practices are being introduced guided by the establishment of international "advisory boards," whose members often include distinguished academics from renowned US, European and Asian universities. King Fahd University of Petroleum and Minerals and King Abdulaziz University have set up such international advisory boards, whose members also include non-academic private sector international figures who have made exceptional contributions in their own countries. Other Saudi private sector universities have established strategic alliances with foreign universities for collaboration in teaching and student placements.

The above "spillover" best practice benchmarking will take time to assimilate as it involves a paradigm shift in the manner and mode of teaching and learning, especially in the higher education sector where experimentation with new ideas is often inhibited by faculty themselves. As such, current educational norms and values affect work ethic perceptions in Saudi society at large.

A survey of Saudi and US male undergraduate students showed that Saudi students in higher education placed greater emphasis on social, non-economic issues in their perception of potential benefits resulting from their studies. US students gave a lower priority to issues of status. The results are set out in Table 13.3.

This table of student perceptions basically reflects the values and attitudes of Saudi society, with higher emphasis placed on prestige and social mobility rather than on professional mobility and adaptation to knowledge-based economy (Wright et al., 1996).

However, there has been a noticeable change in the values and attitudes of some Saudi graduates over the past few years, which indicates a greater emphasis to gain more specialized qualifications as well as a desire to conduct varied undergraduate internships within and outside the Kingdom to acquire more competitive and international skills.

Table 13.3 Potential benefits from higher education: Saudi Arabian and US college students' perceptions

Benefits	Private issues	Public spillover	Saudi students	US students
Economic	• Higher salaries	Greater productivity	*M*	*H*
	• Employment security	National and regional development	*H*	*H*
	• Higher savings	Reduced reliance on government financial support	*L*	*H*
	• Improved working conditions	Increased consumption	*M*	*H*
	• Personal and professional mobility and advancement	Increased potential for transformation from low-skill industrial to knowledge-based economy	*M*	*H*
	• Leadership	Nation-building and development of leadership	*H*	*L*
	• Being a decision-maker	Affecting society's future	*H*	*L*
	• Improved personal status	Public standing and status	*H*	*L*
Social	• Conventionality	Rigid social customs	*M*	*L*
	• Healthier lifestyle and higher life expectancy	Improved health	*M*	*H*
	• Autonomy	Initiative culture	*L*	*H*
	• Working by self	Initiative culture	*L*	*H*

Note: H = High importance; M = Moderate importance; L = Low importance
Source: Survey of KFUPM students and US college students conducted during 2001/2002, Lawrence Shatkin

The Saudi Educational Structure

In quantitative terms, the growth in educational levels of both males and females in Saudi Arabia has been impressive on all counts. According to the World Bank (Diwan and Girgis, 2002) and the Saudi Ministry of Planning (Ministry of Planning, 2002), during the last decade alone, the average education level increased 27% or by more than 1.5–6.6 years on average. The implication for a rise in future productivity in the economy is positive, as World Bank research has tended to support the finding that a one-year rise in a nation's education level generates a 10% increase in GDP (Diwan and Girgis, 2002). However, this largely depends on the quality of education output that matches the needs of the economy. In Saudi Arabia, as we will examine later in this chapter, the largest number of students are taking undergraduate degrees in Islamic and social science studies, with engineering, sciences, education, the humanities and medicine being ranked the next most popular subjects. Women especially predominate in Islamic studies and education, while men do so in engineering, sciences and medicine, but as we will discuss, women are also making progress in the sciences, especially in medicine.

According to the latest data, illiteracy rates are now very low in Saudi Arabia and compare favourably with many developing and other Arab countries. Figure 13.6 sets out the level of educational attainment for Saudis, male and female, over the age of 10 for the year 2007. We note that Saudi male illiteracy stood at around 8% and female at 18%. According to commentators, most illiterates have usually been found in the older age groups (Wilson et al., 2003) as adult literacy programmes

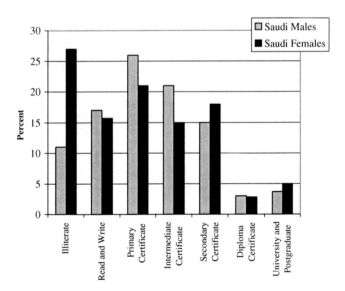

Fig. 13.6 Breakdown of Saudi population (10 years old and above) by educational status in 2007 (Source: Ministry of Planning, UNDP)

have only had a limited impact. The situation had marginally improved for such age groups by 2010.

What is of note from the above figure is that higher-level educational attainment is more prominent for females than for males, especially at the university and graduate level as explored in more detail in Table 13.4.

Table 13.4 showed that there were 2,276 million male and 2,125 million female students at the general education level in 2007. According to Ministry of Education, these students were served by a total of 25,473 schools, of which 12,865 were male and 12,608 for female. They were taught by 202,369 male and 218,074 female teachers, which gave Saudi Arabia a relatively low pupil/teacher and pupil/school ratios. These are illustrated in Table 13.5.

The ratios for Saudi Arabia compare favourably with most developed countries, and are far superior to developing countries. They corroborate the significant budgetary allocations for educational development highlighted earlier. In spite of such impressive statistics, there is still much room for educational development. Reservations as to the quality of Saudi education are commonplace, and hence the figures mask the issue of qualitative education delivery and the state of the teaching

Table 13.4 Saudi Arabia education enrolment and graduate levels by gender (2000–2007)

	2000		2007	
Educational level	Male ('000)	Female ('000)	Male ('000)	Female ('000)
Primary	1,117.5	1,108.4	1,125.5	1,118.7
Intermediate	564.4	471.7	609.3	535.2
Secondary	366.7	338.4	541.9	471.2
Intermediate diploma	25.6	28.1	124.9	38.0
Bachelor	201.9	227.3	275.2	488.1
Master	6.4	3.2	8.2	6.2
Ph.D.	1.3	0.7	1.7	1.6
Total	2,283.8	2,177.8	2,686.7	2,659.0

Source: SAMA

Table 13.5 Saudi pupil/teacher and pupil/school ratios 2000/2007

	2000	2001	2003	2007
Pupil/teacher ratio				
Male	13.7	13.1	13.3	11.2
Female	11.2	11.1	11.4	9.74
Pupil/school ratio				
Male	190.9	189.8	186.1	176.9
Female	186.1	184.5	179.4	168.5

Source: Ministry of Education, SAMA

profession at the general education level. According to surveys on this subject, the following were the major problems relating to teachers:

- Lack of expertise
- Poor commitment to the teaching profession
- Lack of teacher participation in setting curriculum, resulting in teacher apathy and low morale
- Low esteem of teachers in the eyes of society as a whole
- Teachers "moonlighting" for additional income

As for the curriculum, one study (Dukhayil, 2002) made the following criticisms:

- Repetition and duplication of information from year to year
- Too much material, forcing memorization rather than absorbing contents intellectually
- Unrelated to the modern age
- Outdated information, often relying on the translation and copying of other sources
- No attention to special students – whether gifted, talented or those with disabilities
- Weak English language and science curriculum
- Students taught to obey authority and discouraged from showing initiative and creativity

While there are undoubtedly highly committed, dedicated and professional teachers at all levels in Saudi Arabia, yet, according to an employers' survey, there has been a noticeable decline in the quality of student graduates' achievements, especially in higher education. Saudi private sector employers are beginning to voice some concern.

A recent survey of 280 female college students in *Dammam* (Mishkas, 2004) found that educational problems at colleges were still unresolved. Students cited "difficult curriculum, tough teachers, no choice in selecting their majors and lack of preparedness to handle research independently" as major factors. These issues, however, have not deterred Saudis from pursuing further education. Education is perceived as bringing economic and social advancement to those who continue to higher levels. This became clear in a 2000 survey of average monthly compensation for Saudis and non-Saudis who had attained different levels of education, and is set out in Table 13.6.

The survey also showed that compensation to Saudi males is, on average, twice that of Saudi females with the same education, and that compensation for Saudis is, on average, triple that of non-Saudis with the same level of education. The only exception is at the university and postgraduate levels, where it is twice the difference. The unequal compensation levels currently paid to Saudis and non-Saudis pose challenges for labour policy in the Kingdom, especially for the private sector,

Table 13.6 Average monthly compensation (SRs) of Saudis and non-Saudis by educational levels

	2000		2007	
Educational level	Saudi	Non-Saudi	Saudi	Non-Saudi
Illiterate	3,155	1,136	3,100	1,150
Read and Write	3,450	1,260	3,580	1,310
Primary School	4,600	1,378	4,750	1,390
Intermediate School	5,437	1,587	5,640	1,650
Secondary School	7,200	2,580	7,450	2,600
Intermediate School	6,810	2,880	6,970	3,100
University Graduate	10,893	10,856	12,900	11,100
Average (SR)	5,935	3,096	6,341	3,185

Source: Central Department of Statistics, SAMA

which is being forced into employing more Saudis under accelerated *Saudization* programmes.

For sustainable economic development to take place in Saudi Arabia, the educational system's output has to be geared towards the economy's current and future needs. Figure 13.7 is a flow chart of education and training provided in Saudi Arabia under the government's auspices.

The most significant expansion has been in the number of new universities opened in the Kingdom over the period 2005–2010, numbering 13, some of which were community college branches of existing Saudi universities such as Al Jouf and Hail, but others entirely new ones such as the 50,000 all-female Princess Noura bint Abdul Rahman University in Riyadh. The educational establishment flow chart illustrated in Fig. 13.7 does not take into account the new private sector universities and colleges that have opened up over the past decade and which include Prince Sultan University as well as Al Yamamah University in Riyadh and Prince Mohammed University in Alkhobar, while Jeddah boasts of the renowned Effat University and Dar Al Hikma College, as well as Jeddah Business College. All these private sector colleges teach in English and have international affiliations with international universities, as follows: Effat University (Duke University, Mount Holyoke, Georgetown, La Sorbonne), Dar Al Hikma (Fletcher Tufts, University of Colorado, University of California), Prince Sultan (INSEAD) and Prince Mohammed (University of Leeds, American University, Texas A&M, Curtin University of Australia). In a bold move, one of the Saudi female colleges – Effat University – has embarked on a programme to offer its students engineering degrees in association with Duke University of USA, to break away from the mould of only graduating females for teaching and social services jobs, severely restricting their access to the Saudi labour market.

At first glance, it would seem that the Kingdom caters for different types of educational needs, right through from kindergarten to university, as well as specialized

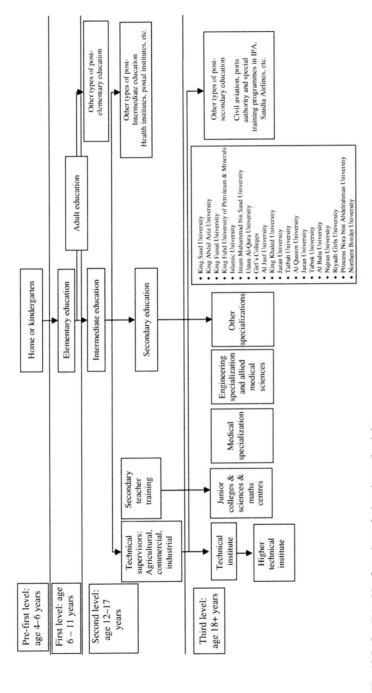

Fig. 13.7 Saudi Arabia: flow chart of education and training

technical and vocational institutes. Girls' education is catered for, albeit on a segregated basis from elementary level, and today girls account for just under 50%
of all students in general education, as we saw earlier in Table 13.4. The same
table also indicated a stronger desire for higher-level education by Saudi girls,
with some 488,000 undertaking a bachelor's degree as opposed to 275,000 male
students.

The phenomenon of higher enrolments for women's education is not particular
to Saudi Arabia: the rest of the Gulf Cooperation Council (GCC) member states
exhibit the same trends. It also seems to hold for other developed economies, as we
can see in Table 13.7, which shows gross higher education enrolment for the period
1980–1998 and a breakdown by gender for 1998.

Table 13.7   Gross higher education enrolment rates (%) – selected years 1980–1998 and by gender
1998

Country	1980	1985	1990	1995	1998 Total	Male	Female
Middle East							
Bahrain	5.0	12.8	17.7	20.0	25.0	19.0	30.0
Egypt	16.1	18.1	15.8	20.2	21.0	24.2	15.9
Jordan	13.4	13.1	16.1	16.0	17.9	26.3	29.4
Kuwait	11.3	16.6	12.5	19.2	19.3	14.6	24.0
Lebanon	30.0	27.8	28.9	27.0	27.0	27.2	26.8
Oman	0.5	0.8	4.1	5.3	8.0	9.0	7.0
Qatar	10.4	20.7	27.0	27.5	26.6	13.6	40.9
Saudi Arabia	*7.1*	*10.6*	*11.6*	*15.8*	*19.0*	*16.0*	*21.0*
UAE	3.1	6.8	9.2	11.0	13.0	15.2	19.8
Others							
Belgium	26.0	32.2	40.2	56.3	56.0	53.0	59.0
Canada	57.1	69.6	94.7	87.8	87.3	80.7	95.3
Ireland	18.1	22.3	29.3	39.6	48.0	44.0	52.0
Norway	25.5	29.6	42.3	58.6	65.0	55.0	77.0
UK	19.1	21.7	30.2	49.6	58.0	53.0	64.0
USA	55.5	60.2	75.2	80.9	81.0	70.6	91.8

Source: World Bank, Salmi (2003)

The level of female higher education enrolment in the USA and Canada of over
90% dwarfs that in other European countries, which ranges between 52 and 77%.
Within the GCC and other selected Arab countries, Oman scores a low of 7% while
Qatar is the highest at 41%. However, the gap between some Arab countries of the
GCC such as Qatar and Saudi Arabia and the developed countries has narrowed over
the 10-year period since 1998, with Saudi Arabia's female enrolment rate standing
at around 47% in 2008 (SAMA, 2009), more than doubling over the period.

Saudi Education and Employment

Changes in any educational system cannot be quick-fix solutions, as they must be responsive to social, economic and international labour pressures. Saudi Arabia cannot long ignore the need for a transformation from a state-led employment path to one that is driven by the labour market. In the current development phase, the absence of a unified labour market, where relative wages are set freely for both Saudis and non-Saudis, undermines a key signal about the real value of acquired skills. This can cause people to have less incentive to gain a market-responsive education (Schawb, K. 2003).

A new regulatory approach for the Saudi school system is needed to cope with the demands of the market place. Table 13.8 summarizes key areas where current government educational control needs to be either loosened or tightened, and is based on a comprehensive World Bank study of the Saudi educational system.

Table 13.8 A new regulatory approach for Saudi school education

Issue	Current approach to regulating education	Degree of control by government	Proposed approach to regulating education
Stakeholders' expectations	• Few expectations from stakeholders • Limited performance specifications	*From loose to tight*	• High expectations from stakeholders • Clear sector performance specifications
Teaching autonomy	• Prescriptive and input-based • Minimal autonomy for private schools	*From tight to loose*	• Output-based and freedom to innovate • Greater institutional autonomy
Accountability and performance assessment	• Weak accountability for results • Little performance measurement • Few sanctions for failures	*From loose to tight*	• Strong accountability for results • Information on academic results disclosed • Annual national assessment performance for all schools/students

Source: Based on a World Bank study for Saudi Arabia, 2000

The government of Saudi Arabia has sought advice from the World Bank and UNESCO in restructuring the education system of the Kingdom (Kibbi, 2002). Their aim is to ensure quality education that can meet the twin objectives of internal efficiency and desired learning outcomes. By internal efficiency we mean the ability of institutions to keep students enrolled and progressing in order to reduce dropout levels. By learning outcomes, we mean the extent to which systems produce graduates who possess the knowledge and skills required for effective participation in the economy. The desired outcome for both would be to link education with the world of work. How has Saudi Arabia performed?

The Saudi government has initiated some internal reform of the educational structure, especially at the elementary and intermediate levels. Their goal is to make the system more responsive to current world standards and to parents' demand for change. For example, the Saudi government has now approved English-language instruction from an earlier age at schools, following internal debate on the subject. English will now be taught from sixth grade (12 years) rather than seventh grade (13 years) starting in 2003/2004 (Abdulgafour, 2003).

The Saudi cabinet decision in August 2003 to introduce English at an earlier age also included the commitment to "improve the teaching of English at intermediate and secondary levels by updating curricula, enhancing the competence of teachers and using modern technologies."

Because of the perception that the public educational system does not provide a wide career choice, there is now a thriving sector of private education in Saudi Arabia. The private delivery and finance of education provides a significant means through which the government can, in a cost-effective way, address the twin challenges of improving quality and expanding access. But in order to maximize the private sector's substantial potential for growth, the Saudi government needs to adopt a different approach to regulating the private pre-university educational sector. At the same time, it must safeguard the broader public interest in education.

This experiment in private higher education will be watched with great interest to see if such universities will produce the kind of graduates that the labour market needs. They will also observe how the private institutions will affect existing state universities.

The Saudi government is also aware that expenditure on education must be allocated in an efficient manner in order to produce an output compatible with the economy's future needs. In the higher education sector alone, the Eighth Development Plan (2004–2009) envisages a total of 730,000 new entrants to the different higher education institutes, while some 392,000 graduates are expected over the same period.

To assess whether the massive investment in education has brought about the desired output of graduates, we look at the breakdown of graduates by specific specialization in Table 13.9.

Teacher education, social sciences and religious studies accounted for nearly 60% of total university graduates during the period 1990–1995, although this declined to around 53% by 2000. The largest change occurred for courses in the computer sciences; these saw their share of graduates double from 7.4% in the period between 1990 and 1995 to 14.6% in the years between 1995 and 2000. Engineering remained steady at around 9% of all university graduates.

The situation in terms of graduates in the "hard sciences" had not changed over the period 2001–2004. According to the Ministry of Planning, there were 199,000 university graduates over that 4-year period, of whom 66% were female or 131,340. While no breakdown was provided by gender for each of the field of specializations, it was revealed that the following were the broad areas of graduate specialization:

Table 13.9 Saudi Arabia: New entrants to the labour force by level of education (1990–2000)

Highest level of education completed	1990–1995				1995–2000			
	Male	Female	Total	%	Male	Female	Total	%
University (Total)	*38,300*	*30,300*	*68,600*	*30.5*	*73,800*	*40,900*	*114,700*	*32.9*
➤ Engineering	4,700	0	4,700	2.0	10,100	0	10,100	2.9
➤ Natural Sciences	4,100	4,700	8,800	3.9	10,000	5,500	15,500	4.4
➤ Medical Sciences & Health	2,300	1,000	3,300	1.4	5,500	2,600	8,100	2.3
➤ Statistics, Math, Computer Sciences	3,000	2,100	5,100	2.3	12,700	4,100	16,800	4.8
➤ Economics and Business	3,700	1,600	5,300	2.4	2,600	700	3,300	0.9
➤ Social Sciences	8,600	10,400	19,000	8.5	9,000	12,800	21,800	6.3
➤ Teacher Education	5,400	5,200	10,600	4.7	8,000	4,500	12,500	3.6
➤ Religious Study	6,500	5,300	11,800	5.3	15,900	10,700	26,600	7.6
Junior colleges Technical (total)	*7,400*	*0*	*7,400*	*3.3*	*12,800*	*0*	*12,800*	*3.7*
➤ Industrial	5,700	0	0		N/A			
➤ Commercial	1,700	0	0		N/A			
Secondary school (Total)	*139,500*	*9,000*	*148,500*	*66.2*	*209,600*	*11,500*	*221,100*	*63.4*
➤ General Education	103,100	7,500	110,600	49.1	172,000	8,900	180,900	51.9
➤ Technical and Vocational	36,400	1,500	37,900	17.1	37,600	2,600	40,200	11.6
Total	185,200	39,300	224,500	100	296,200	52,400	348,600	100

Source: Ministry of Planning, Seventh Development Plan

- *Science and technology* (including science, engineering, medicine and agriculture) – 12.5% or 24,875 graduates
- *Administration and Sociology* (including business administration, economics, accounting, sociology and psychology) – 66.4% or 132,136 graduates
- *Islamic studies and Shariah* – 9.3% or 18,507 graduates
- *Humanities* (including history, languages and art) – 11.8% or 23,482 graduates

To overcome the deficiency in science graduates and meet the growing need of the private sector for technical and vocational college graduates, the Kingdom has embarked on an ambitious programme to expand technical colleges. Table 13.10 illustrates the growth in both technical colleges and student numbers under the auspices of the General Organization for Technical Education and Vocational Training (GOTEVT).

Table 13.10 Technical education at institutions of the General Organization for Technical Education and Vocational Training (2008)

	Number of new students	Total number of students	Number of graduates (2007)	Number of institutes
• Technological colleges				
Diploma level	38,048	61,549	12,426	35
Bachelor level	724	1,337	N/A	N/A
• Girls higher technological institutes	2,111	3,031	N/A	9
• Vocational training centres	11,663	17,430	10,707	57
Total	52,546	83,347	23,133	101

N/A: not available
Source: SAMA

Technical and vocational training seems to have become more popular over the years, as in 2002 the total number of graduates stood at 16,000 compared with 23,000 in 2007, while the number of new students was 31,000 in 2002 compared with just over 52,000 in 2007. Over the period, the number of vocational institutes rose to 101 compared with 83 in 2002. What is interesting from Table 13.9 is that while there was not a single female vocational training institute in 2002, by 2008 there were 9 with a total female enrolment of just over 3,000 girls. More social taboos were being broken in the Kingdom, as some females have decided that it was probably easier to enter the labour market by acquiring a technical and vocational qualification than a university degree. As there have been no female graduates from this sector by 2010, this social and educational experiment will be keenly watched to assess its success in attracting Saudi females to women-only manufacturing facilities being set up. What makes this transition to open up vocational and technical training to Saudi females even more remarkable, given the conservative social attitudes of Saudi society, is that publicly funded education for girls began only in 1960, 7 years after the first school for boys opened (Doumato, 2003). It is the need to work, the need to help support a family, in which Saudi women are finding the incentive to change the facts on the ground.

Restructuring the Saudi Education System

The results of the past decades' educational transformation in the Kingdom have been impressive, at least on paper. The real question is whether the inherent structural imbalances in the output of graduates can be sustained, or whether a fundamental reform of the whole educational system is needed.

Change must also occur at the higher education level. The transformation of domestic economics and international education flows are powerful forces for change in Saudi Arabia. Higher education will face the necessity to competitively deliver competent and relevant educational programmes that meet society's needs

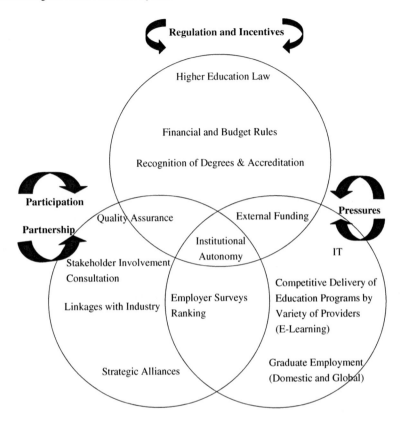

Fig. 13.8 Forces for change in higher education (Adapted from The World Bank 2000)

and achieve international accreditation. Figure 13.8 sets out some of these major forces for change that impact on the higher education sector. Given rising student numbers and budgetary constraints, there will be a growing need for higher education to forge links with industry and external independent financing.

Most universities in developing countries seem to function at the periphery of the international scientific community, unable to participate in the production and adaptation of knowledge necessary to confront their countries' most important economic and social problems (Larocque, 2002). One growing issue is their lack of access to the global knowledge pool and the international academic environment. This situation is often compounded by cumbersome administrative rules and bureaucratic procedures. In many countries, the ministries of higher education determine staffing policies, budgetary allocations and the number of student admissions; the universities have little say about the number of positions, level of salaries and promotion of their staff.

Such total government control is the most extreme scenario. For Saudi Arabia, the truth lies somewhat more in the middle. The Ministry of Higher Education still has a powerful influence, but the Saudi universities are gaining a larger degree of independence concerning educational and staff issues (Dukhayil, 2003). The 2003 cabinet reshuffle granted greater autonomy to the Saudi university rectors. But until universities acquire further institutional autonomy, they will be hampered by a cumbersome government bureaucracy that is slow to react to the competition that Saudi universities face from private sector higher education colleges and universities.

Recognizing a potential niche in this area, the GCC state of Bahrain (population 766,000) authorized the establishment of eight new private sector universities. Their obvious target market is Saudi Arabia. All new private universities in Bahrain, the United Arab Emirates (UAE) and Qatar have established strong strategic alliances and supra-national links with worldwide centres of academic excellence. In the case of Qatar, several prominent foreign universities have opened branches in the "Education City" of Qatar Foundation, such as Carnegie Mellon University, Weil Cornell Medical College, Virginia Commonwealth University, Texas A&M, Georgetown University of Foreign Service and Northwestern University. This makes their degrees more recognizable and attractive than those from Saudi universities. The issue of degree credibility, accreditation and degree equivalency will become major concerns if private universities proliferate, as a result of both altruistic and profit motives. The focus of teaching in these new Gulf universities is on computer sciences, natural sciences and business management. The fact that they are also co-educational, with both sexes taught together, expands opportunities for Saudi female students, especially those who wish to pursue a broader range of disciplines than Saudi Arabia offers, while still living and studying in societies that are culturally compatible to the Kingdom.

Looking Towards the Future

The interplay among a variety of elements – erratic oil revenues, demographic trends, a rigid educational system and low labour productivity – has deeply affected the direction of development outcomes in Saudi Arabia in the past few decades. Population has grown faster than oil revenue in some years and labour productivity has not kept pace with private sector market forces. In order to compensate for this "oil drag," labour productivity, and hence educational standards, will have to rise significantly in the next decade. The educational levels of both males and females in Saudi Arabia have demonstrated impressive improvement by world standards, but the 20-year boom of current education patterns and job creation is now under strain.

Because of these factors, Saudi Arabia is opening up, especially in the education sector, where a revised curriculum and educational approach are needed to ensure Saudi Arabia can compete in the global environment. Saudi Arabia has set the right general priorities in education, but its goals and means are not yet adequate to solving the problem. A mismatch remains between educational output, quality and the needs of the Saudi labour market. Some have argued that the Kingdom is giving undue attention to "education push" rather than "job pull" in the private sector (Cordesman, 2003). This criticism ignores to some extent the recognition by

Table 13.11 Saudi government education development plan recommendations and outcomes

Recommendations	Outcomes
• Establishing new channels and patterns of higher education such as open universities and distance learning	• Achieved in both areas
• Improving the internal efficiency of the universities by reducing number of years for students to graduation	• Process is underway with universities reporting on achievements to the Ministry of Higher Education
• Encouraging the private sector to establish private universities and colleges	• Achieved – new colleges and universities opened such as Prince Sultan University, Prince Mohammed University, Institute of College of Business Administration and Dar Al-Faisal University
• Establishing more effective coordination between research centres and development centres, so that the producers and users of national technological solutions are linked	• Several initiatives to establish technology cities and science parks e.g., Jeddah Bio-Technology, Dhahran Techno Valley at KFUPM, science parks at King Saud University and King Abdulaziz University
External efficiency	
• Matching the output of the education system with the requirements of economic and social development to meet needs of the labour market	• Partially achieved as there is still mismatch between graduate specialization and market needs
• Sending 5,000 students on scholarships abroad	• Target exceeded as 70,000 Saudi students have gone overseas under the King Abdullah scholarship starting from 2006
• Establish National Authority for Academic Evaluation and Accreditation and ensure Saudi universities obtain international accreditation	• Achieved and many Saudi universities have obtained international accreditation, such as AACSB and ABET

Saudi planners for the need for fundamental reforms to education, to align its output with private sector needs. Some of the government's recommendations, as set out in the Eighth Development Plan (2004–2009), illustrate its priorities. These are summarized in Table 13.11.

An analysis of the policy recommendations and achievements indicates that, with the exception of the external efficiency of matching graduate output with labour market needs, most of the other policy objectives have been achieved. Since 2006, the number of Saudi students sent overseas for further education or undergraduate degrees under the King Abdullah Scholarships reached 70,000 by 2010. The initial emphasis had been on science and science-related subjects, but other subjects were soon approved and Saudi students were placed in many countries such as China, Australia, New Zealand, South Korea and Malaysia besides the usual placement countries such as the USA, UK, Germany and France. The King Abdullah Scholarship plan also had another long-term objective: opening up to the outside world and establishing a means of dialogue amongst nations to promote moderation, which King Abdullah continuously stresses in his public statements.

Curriculum development plans in the Kingdom were accelerated after the events of September 11, 2001 and the violence within Saudi Arabia following the Riyadh bombings of May 2003. In addition, the GCC countries publicly endorsed such educational reforms at their GCC summit meeting in Kuwait in December 2003. Education and other reform issues took centre stage at national dialogue forums held in Riyadh and *Makkah* in 2003 and early 2004 under the auspices of the then Crown Prince Abdullah, who was presented with the *Makkah* forum's recommendation to "root out extremism, immediate reform of academic curricula, and more freedom of media" (Abdulghafour, 15 January 2004).

The academic accreditation programme initiated by nearly all Saudi universities, whether public or private, has been successful. The most common accreditation has been the International Association to Advance Collegiate Schools of Business (AACSB) and Accreditation Board for Engineering and Technology (ABET). In pursuit of this, there are a range of plans in place: to include private sector participants in the continuous review of curricula to ensure that proposed academic trends are commensurate with the actual needs of the market; to improve training in advanced technology; and to develop a national plan for the use of information technology and of information sources, including databases.

In Pursuit of Academic Excellence: Establishing World-Class Universities

According to World Bank studies, there are four complementary roles of strategic dimensions that can guide countries in the transition to a knowledge-based economy: an appropriate economic and institutional regime, a strong human capital base, a dynamic information infrastructure and an efficient national innovation system (World Bank, 2002).

Tertiary education is central to all four pillars of this framework, but its role is particularly crucial in support of building a strong human capital base and contributing to an efficient national innovation system. Tertiary education helps countries build globally competitive economies by developing a skilled, productive and flexible labour force and by creating, applying and spreading new ideas and technologies. A recent global study of patent generation has shown, for example, that universities and research institutes, rather than firms, drive scientific advances in biotechnology (Cookson 2007).

Within the tertiary education system, research universities play a critical role in training the professionals, high-level specialists, scientists and researchers needed by the economy and in generating new knowledge in support of national innovation systems. In this context, an increasingly pressing priority of many governments is to make sure that their top universities are actually operating at the cutting edge of intellectual and scientific development. The same applies to Saudi Arabia as will be explored further below, exemplified by the establishment of the King Abdullah University of Science and Technology (KAUST), which is set on shaping the direction of how Saudi scientific research and international collaboration should be established.

There are many important questions to ask about the widespread push towards world-class status for universities around the world. Why is "world-class" the standard to which a nation should aspire to build at least a subset of its higher education system? Might many countries be better served by developing the most locally relevant system possible, without concern for its relative merits in a global comparison? Is the definition of "world-class" synonymous with "elite Western" and therefore inherently biased against the cultural traditions of higher education in non-Western countries? There are many factors that lead to the creation of a world-class university.

In the past decade, the term "world-class university" has become a catch phrase, not simply for improving the quality of learning and research in university education but also, more importantly, for developing the capacity to compete in the global higher education marketplace through the acquisition, adaptation and creation of advanced knowledge. With students looking to attend the best possible universities that they can afford, often regardless of national borders, and with governments keen on maximizing the returns on their investments in universities global standing is becoming an increasingly important concern for institutions around the world (Williams and Van Dyke 2007). The paradox of the world-class university, however, as Altbach has succinctly and accurately observed, is that "everyone wants one, no one knows what it is, and no one knows how to get one" (Altbach 2004, 2005).

Becoming a member of the exclusive group of world-class universities is not achieved by self-declaration; rather, elite status is conferred by the outside world on the basis of international recognition. Until recently, the process involved a subjective qualification, mostly that of reputation. For example, Ivy League universities in the United States such as Harvard, Yale or Columbia, the Universities of Oxford and Cambridge in the United Kingdom and the University of Tokyo have traditionally been counted among the exclusive group of elite universities, but no direct and rigorous measure was available to substantiate their superior status in terms of outstanding results such as training of graduates, research output and technology transfer. Even the higher salaries captured by their graduates could be interpreted as a signalling proxy as much as the true value of their education.

With the proliferation of league tables in the past few years, however, more systematic ways of identifying and classifying world-class universities have appeared. Although most of the best-known rankings purport to categorize universities within a given country, there have also been attempts to establish international rankings. The two most comprehensive international rankings, allowing for broad benchmark comparisons of institutions across national borders, are those prepared by the Times Higher Education Supplement (THES) and Shanghai Jiao Tong University (SJTU).

To compare the international stature of institutions, these league tables are constructed by using objective or subjective data (or both) obtained from the universities themselves or from the public domain. The THES ranking selects the top 200 universities in the world. First presented in 2004, the methodology for this ranking focuses most heavily on international reputation, combining subjective inputs (such as peer reviews and employer recruiting surveys), quantitative data (including the numbers of international students and faculty) and the influence of the faculty (as represented by research citations). Operating since 2003, SJTU uses a methodology that focuses on objective indicators exclusively, such as the academic and research performance of faculty, alumni and staff, to identify the top 500 universities in the world. The measures evaluated include publications, citations and exclusive international awards such as Nobel Prizes and Fields Medals.

Some researchers have highlighted serious methodological limitations of any rankings exercise (Salmi and Savoyan, 2007, Liu and Cheng, 2005) but acknowledge that world-class universities are recognized in part for their superior output in terms of well-qualified graduates who are in high demand on the labour market, and in conducting leading-edge research published in top scientific journals, as well as contributing to technical innovations through patents and licenses.

Table 13.12 lists the top 20 world universities as ranked by the THES and SJTU for 2008, and it is notable for the absence of Middle East universities, while Fig. 13.9 sets out the geographical distribution of these top-ranked universities.

Table 13.12 Top 20 Universities in THES and SJTU world rankings 2008

Rank	THES	Rank	SJTU
1	Harvard University	1	Harvard University
2	Yale University	2	Stanford University
3	University of Cambridge	3	University of California, Berkeley
4	University of Oxford	4	University of Cambridge
5	California Institute of Technology	5	Massachusetts Institute of Technology (MIT)
6	Imperial College London	6	California Institute of Technology
7	University College London	7	Columbia University
8	University of Chicago	8	Princeton University
9	Massachusetts Institute of Tech. (MIT)	9	University of Chicago
10	Columbia University	10	University of Oxford
11	University of Pennsylvania	11	Yale University
12	Princeton University	12	Cornell University
13	Duke University	13	University of California, Los Angeles
14	Johns Hopkins University	14	University of California, San Diego
15	Cornell University	15	University of Pennsylvania
16	Australian National University	16	University of Washington, Seattle
17	Stanford University	17	University of Wisconsin, Madison
18	University of Michigan	18	University of California, San Francisco
19	University of Tokyo	19	University of Tokyo
20	McGill University	20	Johns Hopkins University

Source: THES 2008; SJTU 2008

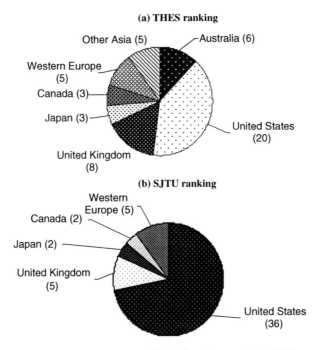

Fig. 13.9 Geographical distribution of world-class universities (top 50 in 2008)

While there were no Arab universities in the top 100 ranked universities in the 2008 THES list, they were represented in the lower rankings, with King Fahd University of Petroleum and Minerals ranked the highest Arab institution at 338th position for 2008, and improving its ranking to 266th position in the 2009 THES ranking. The latest 2009 rankings had a surprise new Saudi ranking of 247 for King Saud University, which was not ranked in the top 500 in the 2008 THES survey. For 2009, the American University of Beirut was ranked at 351, the United Arab Emirates University at 374, Cairo University in the 401–500 list and King Abdulaziz University in Jeddah ranked in the 501–600 category (THES, 2010).

The reasons for the lower rankings of Arab institutions, although Saudi Arabia did relatively well compared to other Arab countries, are due to many factors, some of which are low innovation output and quality, as opposed to quantity of research output. These are illustrated in Figs.13.10 and 13.11.

As Fig. 13.11 illustrates, the number of patents for Middle East countries was negligible compared to Asian countries such as Hong Kong, China, India and Malaysia, while Fig. 13.11 also indicates that despite credible output in terms of the number of articles published, Arab countries are below the world average in terms of relative citations which is the quality benchmark.

A notable attempt has been made to propose some manageable definition of what constitutes a world-class university which concentrates on the following

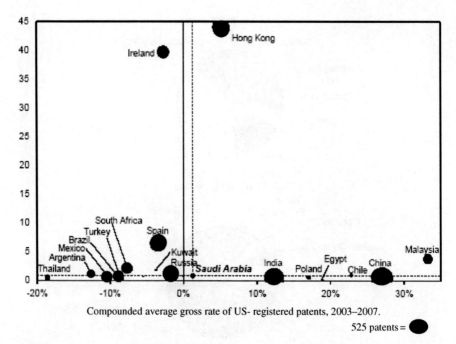

Compounded average gross rate of US- registered patents, 2003–2007.

525 patents =

Fig. 13.10 Innovation output of selected countries' average US patents per 1 million population (2003–2007) (Source: USPTO (2008), EIU (2008))

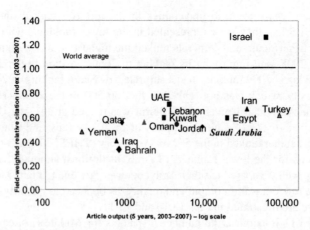

Fig. 13.11 Middle East: research article outputs – quantity vs. quality (Note: citations shown as field-weighted relative index) (Source: Higher Education Policy Institute, UK, 2009)

factors which meet the need to have an output involving highly sought graduates, leading-edge research and commercialized technology transfer (Salmi, 2009):

(i) a high concentration of talent, both faculty and students;
(ii) abundant resources to offer a rich learning environment to conduct advanced research; and
(iii) favourable governance features that encourage strategic vision, innovation and flexibility, and that enable institutions to make decisions and manage resources without being encumbered by bureaucracy.

KAUST: A New Saudi Education Paradigm

In the past, the role of governments in nurturing the growth of world-class universities was not a critical factor, and world-class universities such as those listed in the THES ranking grew to prominence as a result of incremental progress over many decades, and often centuries, such as Oxford and Cambridge universities. Today, however, with rapid globalization, technological changes and mobility of knowledge and labour, it is unlikely that a world-class university can be rapidly created without a favourable policy environment and a direct government initiative and support if only because of the high costs involved in setting up advanced and specialized cutting-edge research facilities and capacities, and "jump-start" the process.

Research carried out by the World Bank and others (World Bank, 2002, Salmi, 2009, Alden and Lin, 2004, Altbach, 2004) reveals that three basic strategies can be followed to establish world-class universities:

• Governments could consider upgrading a small number of existing universities that have the potential of excelling (picking winners).
• Governments could encourage a number of existing institutions to merge and transform into a new university that would achieve the type of synergies corresponding to a world-class institution (hybrid formula).
• Government could create new world-class universities from scratch (clean-slate approach).

Each of the above approaches has their advantages and disadvantages, and these are summarized in Table 13.13.

The establishment of a world-class university requires strong leadership, a bold vision of the institution's mission and goals and a clearly articulated strategic plan to translate the vision into concrete targets and programmes. The establishment of King Abdullah University of Science and Technology (KAUST) seems to fit all the above criteria as evident from Table 13.12 if the Kingdom wishes to "jump-start" its presence into the top ranked world-class universities, while nurturing and upgrading the existing institutions which are beginning to make their mark such as KFUPM and King Saud University.

Table 13.13 Costs and benefits of strategic approaches for establishing world-class universities and Saudi Arabian applicability

Conditions	(A) Upgrading existing institutions	(B) Merging existing institutions	(C) Creating new institutions	Saudi applicability
Ability to attract talent	Difficult to renew staff and change the brand to attract top students	Opportunity to change the leadership and to attract new staff; existing staff may resist	Opportunity to select the best (staff and students); difficulties in recruiting top students to "unknown" institution; need to build up research and teaching traditions	(A) Salary scales are fixed and difficult to adjust for prominent hiring (B) Not common as such institution is established by Royal Decree (C) Viable option: KAUST model
Costs	Less expensive	Neutral	More expensive	Government funding not an issue
Governance	Difficult to change mode of operation within same regulatory framework	More likely to work with legal status different from that of existing institutions	Opportunity to create appropriate regulatory and incentives framework	(A) Difficult to change mode of operation (B) Same regulations could apply (C) New model and policy
Institutional culture	Difficult to transform from within	May be difficult to create a new identity out of distinct institutional cultures	Opportunity to create culture of excellence	(A) Has been tried but results are patchy (B) Not tried (C) KAUST model applicable
Change management	Major consultation and communication campaign with all stakeholders	Normative, approach to educate all stakeholders about expected norms and institutional culture	"Environmentally adaptive" approach to communicate and socially market the new institution	(A) Slow process with internal resistance (B) Not tried (C) New approach and procedures are at the core of KAUST model

Source: Adapted from Jamil, 2009

King Abdullah University of Science and Technology received in September 2009 its first batch of 400 students selected from different parts of the world ahead of its official opening on 23 September 2009, which fell on the 79th anniversary of Saudi Arabia's National Day. It is a bold plan that many around the world are watching closely to assess whether the grand dream can translate into an engine of change in how modern scientific research results can benefit all mankind, just as the results of the early Islamic universities passed on the torch of learning of the ancient Greeks and Egyptians to future generations.

KAUST has long been the brainchild of King Abdullah and he invited several world leaders to attend the grand opening of this international research university which is his dream project and in which he takes great personal interest, often dropping in unannounced to evaluate the progress of construction. Born out of the barren desert, KAUST is now a reality and is located in *Thuwal*, a village on the Red Sea, about 80 km north of Jeddah. King Abdullah first announced his plan to establish the world-class university during a reception given to him by the people of Taif on 23 July 2006. "The establishment of this university has been a living idea in my mind for more than 25 years and I thank God for helping us to realize it," the King said during KAUST's groundbreaking ceremony in October 2007. To make the dream a reality, nothing has been spared to make it a truly global player in terms of research and scientific breakthrough. The King has guaranteed that his dream lives on by ensuring that KAUST is self-funded through one of the most generous endowments of over $10 billion, so as not to depend on the vagaries of state funding.

The emphasis is unambiguous – scientific research and application to complement the humanities bias of some of the major Saudi universities, with the exception of King Fahd University of Petroleum and Minerals, which emphasized science and engineering since its establishment by Saudi Aramco to meet that giant oil company's needs. Saudi Aramco has once again acted as the midwife of a Saudi university, as it was empowered by King Abdullah to manage the overall KAUST project and bring its unmatched project management skills to complete the project on time. KAUST will offer master's and doctoral degrees in all major theoretical and applied sciences.

Specialized research centres, in collaboration with the best international universities and scientific brains, are a hallmark of KAUST. To serve its students, KAUST has recruited highly qualified and experienced faculty members from both sexes from 80 countries as KAUST is also a co-educational institute, a first for Saudi Arabia and a bold experiment that is being closely watched by both opponents and proponents of this model of learning. Its students come from Saudi Arabia and other Gulf and Arab states, Europe, America, East Asia and South Africa and have been offered generous King Abdullah Scholarships to live and study in Saudi Arabia, to dispel some of the image of a secluded and closed Kingdom. Its first president is a highly respected non-Saudi academic from Singapore, again a first for a Saudi university.

KAUST offers master's and doctoral degrees in applied mathematics and computational science, bioscience, chemical and biological engineering, chemical science, computer science, earth science and engineering, electrical engineering, environ-mental science and engineering, marine science and engineering, materials science and engineering and mechanical engineering.

The MS degree offered by the university will take 18 months to complete, and will be offered to both traditional full-time students and part-time students including industry-sponsored students on semester-long company leaves. The Ph.D. degree, which is a 3–4-year post-master's degree, involves original research at a KAUST research centre.

To support and drive KAUST's research agenda, the university has identified four primary strategic research thrusts and several interdisciplinary *research centres* that will apply science and technology to problems of human need, social advance-ment and economic development. The KAUST strategic research thrust areas are as follows:

1. Resources, energy and environment
2. Biosciences and bioengineering
3. Materials science and engineering
4. Applied mathematics and computational science

To meet its objectives, KAUST has established nine research centres and their selection was based on strategic goals that meet the following criteria:

- Ability to advance fundamental knowledge in science and engineering
- Relevance of research thrusts and centres to the existing industries in Saudi Arabia
- Development of future, knowledge-based industries
- Social and economic needs of Saudi Arabia
- The potential regional and international impact

As of 2010, the nine research centres include the following – Catalysis Research, Clean Combustion, Solar and Alternative Energy, Water Desalination, Plant Stress Genomics and Technology and Red Sea Science and Engineering. As discussed in earlier chapters, the Kingdom is now stressing the importance of renewable, espe-cially solar, energy, and the research in water desalination is particularly important given the eminent position of the Kingdom in this sector.

One of the aims of King Abdullah is to foster international understanding, fol-lowing the events of September 11, 2001 and Saudi Arabia's international image. Speaking at the groundbreaking ceremony, King Abdullah emphasized how the new university would serve as a bridge between cultures and nations and a lighthouse of knowledge. He said KAUST would help Saudi Arabia to have a world-class inde-pendent scientific research centre and act as a scientific base as well as a driving force for the national economy. As a new *"Bayt Al-Hekma"* (house of wisdom), KAUST will be a beacon of hope and reconciliation and will serve the people of the Kingdom and benefit all the peoples of the world in keeping with the teachings of the *Holy Qur'an*, which explains that "God created mankind in order for us to come to know each other," the King said (Saudi Press Agency, September 2009). It will certainly spur the other Saudi universities to adapt to higher peer standards.

Conclusion

The emphasis on qualitative education is now recognized by Saudi intellectuals and others but it will be a hard transition for the younger generation to make. Without change, Saudi youth will be competing in a highly sophisticated market with under-developed skills, causing frustration and resentment (Birks and Sinclair, 1980, World Bank, 1995, Yamani, 2000). Their inherited deference to patriarchal author-ity means the young blame employers and turn to the government for solutions. They definitely prefer government employment, when available. There are encour-aging signs of more realistic attitudes towards job searches and the educational needs of the market, but the task is still an uphill one. However, the Government of Saudi Arabia is tackling other major internal reform issues, in addition to educa-tion, with a new realism and openness. This sense of increased candour and decisive action gives rise to genuine optimism. The emphasis on a knowledge-based society is receiving greater attention and the tertiary sector especially is being gradually overhauled either through internal processes and change or through the creation of world-class research and teaching institution such as KAUST, which should set an international benchmark for its peers. However, such long-term visions are closely correlated with the country's overall economic and social development, and the ongoing changes and other reforms at the lower levels of the education system to build up an integrated national education programme are just as important.

Summary of Key Points

- *Financial resources have enabled Saudi Arabia to build a large educational infrastructure for both males and females in a short period of time. Expenditure on education is now a major item in budgetary expenditures and rising. The gov-ernment is aware that education plays a crucial role in economic development and in meeting the demands of the globalization age.*
- *Saudi Arabia faces several challenges in its education policies, namely providing relevant education to meet the needs of a modern society, as well as providing quality education that is adaptable to worldwide education changes.*
- *In terms of the quantity of education output, the Kingdom has done well in com-parison with other developing countries in pupil/teacher and pupil/school ratios. There are inherent weaknesses in terms of low output of higher education science and vocational and technical graduates.*
- *Female higher level education has grown rapidly. Currently females outnumber males at the undergraduate and postgraduate levels. Saudi females can now take*

science-based subjects, which previously were only available to male students, but technical education is still restricted to males.

- *To meet enrolment shortages in government-owned schools, the Kingdom has encouraged the provision of education through privately owned education institutions which have seen a remarkable growth in the number of students enrolled.*
- *The issue of Saudi education and meeting the employment requirements of the private sector is one of the immediate concerns. The Saudi education system is being pressed to deliver a varied educational programme that is of high quality, relevant to societies' needs and internationally recognized.*
- *The interplay between erratic oil revenues, high demographic trends, a rigid educational system and low Saudi labour productivity has affected the direction of development outcomes in Saudi Arabia. Education was driven by "education-push" rather than "jobs-pull" in the private sector. This is changing, as recent government budgetary allocations for different higher education establishments indicate that new priorities are now being set out.*
- *The Kingdom has established a new world-class university, KAUST, that will contribute towards creating applied research to the benefit of Saudi Arabia, as well as spur changes and reforms in other Saudi educational establishments.*

Chapter 14
Saudi Arabia's Global Relations: GCC and Beyond

When your neighbour's house is on fire, your own property is at risk.

Horace

Learning Outcomes

By the end of this section, you would understand:

- *Saudi Arabia's evolving global economic relations*
- *The objectives for establishing the GCC*
- *The different settings of the GCC member states*
- *Facing up to economic diversification and integration*
- *The importance of oil and gas to the GCC*
- *The lack of progress on industrial diversification*
- *The GCC financial sector and regulatory framework*
- *The GCC capital markets*
- *GCC trade patterns*
- *Demographics and the GCC labour markets, and the issue of expatriate labour*
- *New evolving strategic economic partners: China and India*

Introduction

Over the past three decades, the Kingdom has deepened its economic, political and military relationships with its immediate neighbours in the Gulf Cooperation Council, and most recently has expanded its economic and geopolitical relationship with key emerging global economic powers, specifically China and India. The Kingdom has ensured that its existing multifaceted relationship with other European countries and the USA is still maintained on an amicable basis, but as explored in

M.A. Ramady, *The Saudi Arabian Economy*, DOI 10.1007/978-1-4419-5987-4_14, © Springer Science+Business Media, LLC 2010

a previous chapter, it has become noticeable that Saudi trade flows, especially in energy and energy-related products, are now moving towards the Asian economies, rather than towards the USA and Europe. This new openness to the rest of the world has been due to several factors, economic and political, and have been largely driven by King Abdullah bin Abdulaziz. They have their roots in the Saudi experience in the establishment of the Gulf Cooperation Council (GCC), which provided the Kingdom with the mechanism and framework of bilateral and multilateral negotiations, as well as the Kingdom's accession to the World Trade Organization in 2005 which opened up new international market opportunities, such as China and India.

The Rationale for Regional Blocks

Before analysing the establishment of the GCC block and its achievements to date, it is important to examine the rationale for establishing regional blocks so as to establish a benchmark for the GCC's achievements.

A nation's most natural trading and investment partners are its immediate neighbours, whether for the ASEAN, EU or NAFTA blocs. A nation's economic growth and prospects can be greatly enhanced by a prosperous regional grouping that can complement each other. Such groupings can not only provide a large, growing and accessible market for local firms, especially for companies with limited international experience, but also make them feel more comfortable in dealing with neighbouring countries that have same linguistic or social affinity and similarity such as the GCC countries. National productivity can be greatly enhanced through regional coordination of economic policies instead of negotiation on a bilateral basis with larger blocs, and as such, being a member of a regional bloc, creates a greater weight in international relations. Table 14.1 summarizes the perceived benefits accruing from regional membership in upgrading competitiveness for its members.

The First Milestone: The GCC

On 25 May 1981, in Abu Dhabi, the Charter creating the *Gulf Cooperation Council* (GCC) was signed by the Heads of State of these Arab Gulf countries: Bahrain, Oman, Kuwait, Saudi Arabia, Qatar and United Arab Emirates. The objectives of the GCC, as stated in its founding charter, are to effect coordination and interconnection between member states in all fields, so as to achieve unity between them, and to deepen and strengthen relations and cooperation between their peoples in various fields. The GCC is further charged with formulating similar regulations in most areas of national concern. The comprehensive list includes economic and financial affairs, agriculture, industry, commerce, customs, communications, education, culture, social and health affairs, information and tourism. In addition, the GCC aims to encourage cooperation by the private sector (Nakhleh, 1986, Ramazani, 1988).

Table 14.1 Regional bloc membership competitiveness upgrading benefits

Business environment	Macroeconomic policies	Political institutions and governance
Improving efficiency and interconnectivity of transportation infrastructure Enhancing regional communications Creating an efficient energy network Linking financial markets Opening the movement of students for training or higher education Eliminating trade and investment barriers within the region Simplifying and harmonizing cross-border regulations, paperwork and visas Coordinating antitrust and competition policies Harmonizing environmental and energy standards Harmonizing product safety standards Establishing reciprocal consumer protection laws Opening government procurement within the region	Coordinating macroeconomic policies Regional development banks – or central bank Coordinated capital requirements Coordinated monetary policy intervention or policy signed	Sharing best practices in government operations Creating regional institutions Dispute resolution mechanisms Harmonizing economic statistics Developing a regional position with international organizations Having one voice on international issues of importance to bloc

Source: Adapted from Porter (2010)

Since 1981, the GCC has managed to assemble a few joint efforts in various fields. In defence, a joint military force called "Peninsular Shield" was established with headquarters in *Hafr Al Batin* in Saudi Arabia (Ramazani, 1988). On the economic front, on 1 January 2003, a common customs and tariffs policy was agreed that set tariffs at 5% among all member states. This had been preceded in 1982 by a Unified Economic Agreement, and in 1984 by the establishment of the Gulf Investment Corporation (GIC). In the same year, the Gulf Standards Organization was created when the Saudi Arabian Standards Organization was transformed into a regional body serving all the GCC countries. The GCC Commercial Arbitration Centre was created in December 1993 to settle trade disputes among GCC citizens or between GCC citizens and foreigners.

Administratively, the GCC is managed through the Secretariat General, head-quartered in Riyadh, and headed by a Secretary-General, who is appointed by the Supreme Council for a 3-year term, renewable only once. The Supreme Council is the GCC's highest authority and is composed of the member states. As will be discussed later in the chapter, while the GCC member states may share interests and social characteristics, there are also differences between the individual member countries in many fields, despite the hopes of those who signed the original establishment charter.

Since 1981, the GCC has evolved into a powerful economic bloc in its own right, with strong negotiating authority with other economic blocs, such as the European Union (EU) (Devlin, 1996). The EU and the GCC signed an Economic Cooperation Agreement in 1988 which laid the framework for the elaboration of a bilateral free trade agreement between the two regional blocs, with formal negotiations beginning in 1990, but until March 2010 it has not been concluded. In June 2009, the GCC signed a free trade agreement with the four-member European Free Trade Association comprising Switzerland, Norway, Iceland and Liechtenstein – countries that had not joined the European Union. The GCC–EU negotiations seemed to have stalled because of GCC accusations that lobby groups representing European petrochemicals and aluminium industries are stalling the talks, and could have also been a reason for the Kingdom's search for alternative markets for its petrochemical products in Asia.

States of the GCC: The Setting

Any analysis of the GCC must take into consideration the member states themselves. Half a century ago, all of the six countries that make up the present GCC were poor; some were very thinly populated and had a loose central government (Beblawi, 1984, Niblock, 1980). All were pushed into modernity by oil and they were left scrambling to find their own way to manage their sudden riches. Each country has had to cope with more extreme social upheavals and dramatic changes than anywhere in living memory. They had no blueprints or common guidance on which to fall back (Fahim, 1995, Netton, 1986). They now face the fastest population growth rates in the world and the most rapid urbanization; at the same time they are dealing with some of the effects of the biggest tide of *managed* worker immigration in recent history.

First and foremost, the majority of the GCC states are fairly small. Their total area is under 1 million square miles, ranging from the smallest, Bahrain (260 square miles), to the largest, Saudi Arabia (approximately 865,000 square miles). The six states are primarily desert with minimal rainfall, so they are not self-sufficient in agriculture. Food security is a real issue and one major challenge is to secure future food independence.

In terms of population, the GCC states face significant problems, including for some the small size of their native population, their large foreign workforce, a shortage of trained national workers and dependency on a narrow source of income and economic base. Economic diversification is now an imperative, but different countries of the GCC have achieved different degrees of success (Devlin, 1996, Erian, et al., 1997).

According to researchers on the GCC (Erian, et al., 1997), the bloc's economies passed through several distinct phases, which can be summarized as follows:

(i) *Extending the Expansion Phase 1981–1985*: This phase focused on expanding the physical and social infrastructure and on diversifying the economic base, given the historically high oil prices. There was expenditure on development projects, especially petrochemical projects. Sizeable foreign reserves and budget surpluses were built up during this period.

(ii) *Consolidation Phase 1986–1989*: This period witnessed lower oil prices, which contributed to imbalances in the budgets. There were reductions in some capital project expenditures, but current expenditures remained high. Budget deficits increased as did drawdowns on external reserves. Fiscal consolidation differed significantly across GCC states, reflecting the varied successes of economic diversification measures.

(iii) *The First Gulf Crisis 1990–1991*: The Iraqi invasion of Kuwait in August 1990 put pressure on government budgets and external reserves, despite higher oil prices. This period was characterized by an erosion of investment income, sharp declines in oil exports and the high costs of restructuring and rebuilding Kuwait after the liberation.

(iv) *Rehabilitation Period 1992–1994*: GCC countries emerged financially weaker from the first Gulf crisis and Kuwait suffered from human and economic dislocation. The period was characterized by oil market weakness and a slowdown in world economies. Budget deficits increased in most GCC countries, to reach over 10% of GDP despite lower capital expenditures and foreign borrowing for some GCC countries.

(v) *Adjustment and Reforms 1995–till date*: GCC financial imbalances were reduced, helped by increased oil prices and economic diversification. Non-oil revenues increased, employment policies were geared towards private sector needs and inflation remained modest. Despite the second Gulf crisis of 2003 and the Iraq War, the GCC countries continued their internal economic and social reforms in the fields of education, administration and politics. This period also witnessed the accession of many GCC countries to the WTO and adjustment to globalization issues as well as fallout from the global financial crisis of 2008/2009 and the debt restructuring problems faced by Dubai, an emirate in the United Arab Emirates and a member state of the GCC. The issue of "localization" or increasing the number of nationals in the local workforce was also an emerging issue in this period.

This period also witnessed further concrete efforts at inter-GCC economic consolidation with reduction in customs duties to 5% and some progress made on joint defence issues. The groundwork for full monetary union by 1 January 2010 was laid out but not implemented for a common GCC currency by the set deadline. The movement of citizens between GCC countries was streamlined, as well as the granting of inter-GCC banking licences.

The GCC in a "Snapshot"

Tables 14.2 and 14.3 offer a snapshot view of the main social, demographic and economic indicators of the six GCC member states. Table 14.2 sets out the social indicators; one is immediately struck by the relatively young population profile of all the GCC countries, with a large percentage of the population under 14 years of age. Oman and Saudi Arabia have the highest percentage in this age group, and the UAE has the lowest at 19%, but this still outstrips other developed countries (World Bank, Global Development Prospects).

Table 14.1 also shows that the region as a whole has one of the highest population growth rates. The UAE and Qatar lead the way at 4.9 and 6.0%, respectively.

Table 14.2 GCC Countries: population, labour force and social indicators (1997 or most recent year)

	Bahrain	Kuwait	Oman	Qatar	Saudi Arabia	UAE
Demographic indicators						
Population (millions)	1.1	3.4	2.9	0.8	24.2	5.6
Aged 0–14 (% of total)	27.3	17.8	31.6	22.5	33.9	19.5
Aged 15 and over (% of total)	72.7	82.2	68.4	77.5	66.1	80.5
Population growth (%, 1997–2008 average)	2.0	3.10	4.7	6.0	2.2	4.9
Population gender ratio (men:women)	57:43	56:44	53:47	63:37	55:45	63:37
Age dependency ratio[a]	0.6	0.6	1.0	0.5	0.9	0.5
Urban population (% of total)	90	97	32	94	82	92
Labour force indicators						
Total labour force (millions)	0.35	1.68	0.66	0.09	7.58	2.56
Males (% of total)	76.8	77.6	75.3	69	84.5	86.5
Females (% of total)	23.2	22.4	24.7	31	15.5	13.5
Labour force growth (%, 1993–1999 average)	2.3	−1.6	5.2	3.9	3.3	3.9
Participation rate (%)	54	49	25	52	33	46
Unemployment %	4.0	0.7	8.0	–	13.0	2.3
Social indicators						
School enrolment (%)						
Primary	100	100	90	100	100	100
Secondary	100	100	65	99	95	75
Tertiary	30	30	15	40	35	35
Adult literacy rate (%)	92	90	45	80	80	82
Population per physician	760	650	1,200	667	749	1,208
Access to safe water (% of population)	100	100	85	100	93	98
Life expectancy at birth (years)	76	78	70	76	73	79
Infant mortality rate (per 1,000 live births)	19	11	18	18	20	16

[a]Population under the age of 15 and over the age of 65 as a share of the total working-age population
Sources: World Bank, Social Indicators of Development, UNDP, Human Development Report, Arab World Competitiveness Report

Bahrain, with relatively higher literacy, education enrolment and labour participation rates, registered the lowest population growth rate of the GCC at 2.0% p.a.

According to Table 14.1, all GCC countries have an imbalance of males to females; Oman has a 53:47 ratio, but the UAE shows the most imbalance at 63:37, highlighting the recent trend amongst UAE nationals to marry from outside. All GCC countries are largely urbanized – the GCC average is around 78%.

Oman is the exception at 32% urbanization, reflecting the relative importance of agriculture in that more geographically diverse country. Most members of the labour force are male, but both Kuwait and Bahrain show high female participation rates of around 23%, respectively, reflecting the relatively more advanced status of female labour participation in these two countries since early independence days, but they have been overtaken by Qatar where female participation in all sectors of Qatari society has accelerated rapidly over the past decade, since Sh. Hamad bin Khalifa Al Thani assumed power.

While school enrolment is high for all the GCC countries, Kuwait, Qatar and Bahrain have the highest ratios at all levels of education. Bahrain leads the way with 92% adult literacy. Saudi Arabia reached 80% level adult literacy by 2007, up from 63% in 1995.

In terms of life expectancy, Saudi Arabia was the lowest at 73 years, and Kuwait and UAE were the highest, a reflection of the evolution of widespread national health programmes in these countries. This has resulted in a lower infant mortality rate for both countries, in contrast with Saudi Arabia, which had the highest at 20 deaths per 1,000 live births.

Figure 14.1 illustrates the significant share that Saudi Arabia has in the total GCC GDP for 2008, dwarfing all the other five member states, with a share of just under 50%.

While Saudi Arabia might dwarf the other GCC members in terms of its GDP, the other economic indicators highlighted in Table 14.3 reveal some interesting country differences. In terms of GDP per capita, it is Saudi Arabia that is at the lower end

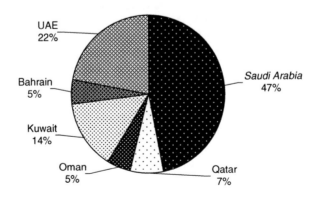

Fig. 14.1 Country share of total GCC GDP: 2008 (Source: SAMA)

Table 14.3 GCC countries: economic indicators 2008

	Bahrain	Kuwait	Oman	Qatar	Saudi Arabia	UAE
Nominal GDP ($ billion)	18.5	148.8	53.1	104.6	468.8	239.5
Real GDP growth (%)	6.1	6.3	6.2	16.4	4.4	7.4
GDP per capita ($)	18,810	35,930	19,480	65,060	18,700	43,350
Inflation (%)	7.0	10.8	12.5	15.1	9.9	14.0
Imports ($ billion)	14.6	26.1	16.7	21.2	100.6	116.6
Exports ($ billion)	16.9	88.8	33.3	53.2	313.3	180.9
Current account ($ billion)	1.3	59.5	4.8	18.3	134.0	28.7
Government balance (% of GDP)	2.7	30.8	4.2	9.6	33.6	12.2
Oil and gas reserves (Billion boe)	1.6	112.7	11.8	174.7	308.8	135.9
Oil sector (% of nominal GDP)	33	55.8	47.2	62.1	56	34.4
Net foreign assets ($ billion)	3	295	23	100	403	272
External debt to GDP ratio (%)	157	25	16	87	23	76
Cross-border foreign claims/GDP (%)	70	21	25	51	12	67
Ease of doing business (2009) (1 = best, 178 = worst)	20	61	65	39	13	33
Global competitiveness ranking	37	30	38	31	35	37
Rating (S&P)	A	AA–	A	AA–	AA–	AA

Sources: GCC central banks, IMF, World Bank

of the GCC league table at around \$18,000 for 2008, while Qatar's GDP per capita dwarfed others at around \$65,000, followed by the UAE at \$42,000 levels.

According to Table 14.3, all GCC countries show positive trade balances and current account surpluses for 2008; the largest trade surpluses were registered for Saudi Arabia, Kuwait and the UAE. Inflationary trends were on the rise for all GCC countries during 2008, with the highest inflation levels registered in Qatar and the UAE which were driven by their construction-led boom, while Bahrain's inflation was the lowest at 7%. The UAE's high inflation level is also a reflection of the more open economy as the UAE, particularly the emirate of Dubai, has a large volume of trade with the rest of the world compared to its population size of 5.6 million, and yet imports of \$116.6 billion in 2008 compared with imports of \$100.6 billion for Saudi Arabia with a population of 24.2 million.

Saudi Arabia had the largest net foreign assets of the GCC countries at around \$403 billion for 2008, followed by Kuwait and Abu Dhabi of the UAE. In terms of sovereign country credit rating, Standard & Poor's gave the highest rating to Abu Dhabi (AA) with Saudi Arabia, Qatar and Kuwait all at AA– and Bahrain and Oman at A. The Kingdom's rating was due to the improved macroeconomic situation, especially in 2007 and 2008.

In terms of external debt, all GCC countries showed varying degrees of external debt levels. The figure for Bahrain is unusually high compared with the other GCC countries at 157% of external debt to GDP ratio, but includes the private debt data, and if these are excluded then the Bahrain ratio falls to around 7%. Qatar's external debt resulted from its international borrowing for massive gas-related projects, while the UAE's debt includes borrowing by the smaller emirates of *Sharjah* and *Dubai* for their construction and energy-related projects. The Saudi external debt is not officially classified as direct sovereign borrowing by the state, but rather non-recourse borrowing by semi-governmental organizations, without guarantees from the Kingdom of Saudi Arabia, a prime example being the 2010 syndicated loan facility of around $10 billion raised by Saudi Aramco from local and international banks for the Saudi-Aramco-Total Refinery (SATORP), despite the global financial crisis fallout.

In all the GCC countries, the government sector plays an important role in the economic fortunes of the member states through its expenditures, and the government balance as percent of the GDP was high for Saudi Arabia at 33% followed by Kuwait at 31% compared with the lower ratios of the other GCC states which had a more diversified economic base such as Bahrain and Oman.

Social and economic indicators confirm that the GCC countries experienced an enviable boom from the mid-1970s to mid-1980s; then, from 2002 to 2008, an economic prosperity touched every facet of life in these countries, fuelled by a rise in oil prices and revenues. A whole infrastructure for social and public services, industrial development and education was created within a few years. However, fluctuating oil revenues from the mid-1980s, energy competition from other oil producers and uneven world economic growth began to affect the GCC countries. Doubts crept in about the general soundness of certain economic policies they were following. The crash of the unofficial Kuwaiti stock market (*Souk Al Manakh*) in 1984 was a great shock to both Kuwait and the other Gulf states, and involved close to $100 billion; it was followed by a regional and global crisis accentuated by Dubai's announcement in November 2009 to restructure some loans. This triggered a search for a sounder financial and economic footing for the GCC member states to ensure that such episodes do not affect the painstaking financial and economic progress that had taken place, especially for the more "open" economies of the GCC such as the UAE (Dubai) and Bahrain that had built up offshore financial centres.

Economic Diversification and Economic Integration

The aspiration to achieve economic productivity in order to reduce an overwhelming dependence on oil revenues was one of the main driving forces behind the concept of GCC economic integration in 1981 (Askari, et al., 1997, Abdulkerim, 1999). Some have argued that a collapse of the oil boom may slow down the process of economic integration but this did not materialize as all GCC countries emerged relatively stronger from the earlier oil price falls.

All of the GCC states, except Bahrain, have large oil reserves and therefore a longer time to develop their non-oil productive capacity before oil runs out. This fact does not, however, affect their determination to reduce their dependence on oil as soon as possible (Askari, et al., 1997, Erian and Cyrus, 1997). The economies of the GCC hold a large segment of the known world oil reserves as well as substantial gas reserves as illustrated in Table 14.4, which also sets out the continuing importance of oil revenues for some GCC countries.

Table 14.4 GCC hydrocarbon indicators 2008

	Bahrain	Kuwait	Oman	Qatar	Saudi Arabia	UAE	Global share %
A. Proven oil reserve (Billion barrels)	0.12	101.5	5.3	15.2	262.9	97.8	45
B. National gas reserves (Billion cubic meters)	102	1,784	690	25,466	7,570	6,091	22.8
C. Export of crude oil ('000 barrels/day)	0.1	1,738	592.7	703	7,321	2,334	20
D. Gross oil exports revenues ($ billion)	0.3	57.2	14.9	15.4	207.1	60.7	N/A
E. Contribution of the energy sector to GDP (%)	13.3	78	48.9	55	60.7	35.8	N/A

Sources: GCC Secretariat, OPEC, OAPEC, BP

The economies of the GCC hold around 45% of known world oil reserves, nearly 23% of gas reserves and around 20% of world crude exports. As Table 14.4 illustrates, despite economic diversification efforts, some are still heavily reliant on the energy sector as a major contributor to their GDP. Kuwait, Saudi Arabia and Qatar have the heaviest reliance, with nearly 80% of the Kuwaiti GDP contributed by the oil sector, while the lowest is Bahrain which has negligible oil and gas reserves.

Saudi Arabia has the largest oil reserves (55% of the total) in the GCC, as well as the third largest gas reserves at around 18%. The Qatari gas reserves are the third largest in the world, after Russia and Iran, and account for 61% of total GCC gas reserves. Unlike Saudi gas production, which is associated gas (produced as a by-product of oil production), Qatar gas production is mostly non-associated (Mabro, 2002).

Qatar's oil reserves have been depleting and today Qatar exports around 450,000–500,000 barrels per day or nearly 4% of total GCC exports. For Qatar, gas is now the driving force of the economy.

While Bahrain has some oil reserves, the level is negligible. Bahrain was one of the first oil exporters of the GCC in the 1920s, but now depends mainly on services as the main support of its economy. The UAE and Kuwait have approximately the same oil reserves, but the UAE's gas reserves are the second largest in the GCC, slightly ahead of Saudi Arabia's.

Given the importance of the hydrocarbon sector to the GCC, how successful have the countries concerned been in diversifying their economies away from dependency on energy revenue?

To some extent, the GCC has succeeded, as the contribution of the oil sector to the GDPs of the respective countries has been diminishing from the mid-1970s to date, as Table 14.5 illustrates. The figures in Table 14.4 for 2008 are somewhat biased due to the high oil prices seen in that year which reached $147 a barrel, and it is important to analyse a longer time period to assess whether oil dependency has been reduced or not.

Table 14.5 Contribution of the oil sector to GDP 1977–2005 (%)

Country	1977	1986–1990	1996–1998	1992–2002	2003–2005
Bahrain	27	12.8	16.8	21.5	23.6
Kuwait	61	37.2	38.7	45.5	45.9
Oman	61	47.2	37.7	24.9	30.9
Qatar	68	34.7	38	35.3	29.1
Saudi Arabia	63	28.9	34.4	24.7	36.4
UAE	59	38.1	28.2	16.6	79.7

Sources: ESCWA and the League of Arab States, Statistical Indicators of the Arab World for the Period 1970–1979, ESCWA, Statistical Abstract of the ESCWA Region, 17th and 19th issues, 1999, GCC central banks' annual reports

In Table 14.5, we note that from around 60% levels in 1977, the contribution of the oil sector fell to under 40% for Saudi Arabia in the pre-oil boom period of 2003/2005. The UAE's oil contribution was the lowest at under 20% due to the non-oil service sector boom in Dubai and the other emirates in the UAE, while Kuwait's oil sector contribution to GDP continues to be the highest amongst the GCC countries.

In each of the GCC countries, the dependency on oil revenues as the main source of government revenues makes it difficult to chart a long-term economic policy, given oil price fluctuations and ever-changing trends (Oweiss, 2000).

Assuming stable government revenues against the GCC's high population growth rates, the per capita income could shrink for most member states and the standard of living could decline over time. For that reason, economic diversification in their non-oil GDP is encouraging.

Population growth projections for the GCC countries indicate an expected increase of 55% over the 15-year period 2000–2015 (World Bank Population Conference, April, 1999). Unless oil prices increase by the same ratio, per capita income will decline and budget deficits will increase. Per capita expenditures on health, education and general welfare must be reduced unless other measures are taken, and at the same time labour productivity must be increased. Studies have shown that labour productivity in the GCC contributed 9–11% of overall growth, which contrasts with industrialized nations, where their levels are at 75% (Oweiss, 2000). The main source of growth, then, comes from natural resources.

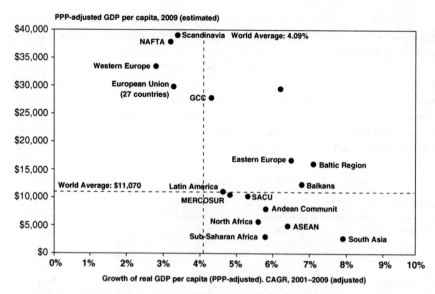

Fig. 14.2 Comparative performance of GDP growth rates for selected regional groupings (2001–2009) (Source: Porter, 2010, Economist Intelligence Unit, 2009)

Figure 14.2 illustrates the comparative performance ranking for the GCC against other regional blocs in terms of growth in real GDP per capita, adjusted for purchasing power parity (PPP), on a compounded annual growth rate for the period 2001–2009.

What Fig. 14.2 highlights is that while some individual GCC members' per capita incomes are amongst the highest in the world (Qatar and Kuwait), yet the GCC as a regional bloc is below the European Union with its 27 countries, in terms of both PPP-adjusted GDP per capita and growth in real GDP per capita, and far behind the North American Free Trade Association (NAFTA) and Scandinavia.

One major aspect of higher regional ranking is the perception of ease or difficulty of doing business in a country. Table 14.6 examines the individual GCC countries overall ranking in the ease of doing business and the benchmarks achieved for the specific criteria.

From Table 14.6, Saudi Arabia is ranked the highest in the GCC, with a world ranking of 13 compared with Oman's lowest ranking at 65. The high ranking for Saudi Arabia has come as a surprise to many observers who had believed that the UAE would rank higher, but it ranked at 33, below Bahrain which ranked at 20. The analysis of various indicators used to come up with the overall ease of doing business ranking reveals wide variances amongst the GCC countries, with the UAE leading in the trading across borders category owing to its open economy and Dubai's eminent position as a Gulf trading port and hub, while Saudi Arabia scoring high in starting a business, registering property, getting credit and protecting investors categories. Bahrain's high ranking was due to a perceived advantage

Table 14.6 Ease of doing business: GCC countries' 2009 rankings

Country	Ease of doing business	Starting a business	Dealing with licences	Employ. workers	Regist. property	Getting credit	Protect. investors	Paying taxes	Trading across borders	Enforcing contracts	Closing a business
Saudi Arabia	*13*	*13*	*33*	*73*	*1*	*61*	*16*	*7*	*23*	*140*	*60*
Bahrain	20	63	14	13	22	87	57	13	32	117	26
UAE	33	44	27	50	7	71	159	4	5	134	143
Qatar	39	68	28	68	55	135	93	2	41	95	33
Kuwait	61	137	81	24	89	87	77	11	109	113	69
Oman	65	62	130	21	20	127	93	8	123	106	66

Source: Global Competitiveness Report, Global Economic Forum, 2009

in the following categories: dealing with licences, employing workers and closing a business. The decision to scrap the local sponsorship system and replace it with a government sponsorship of foreign workers discussed in a previous chapter has earned Bahrain positive ranking in the employing of workers category, while Saudi Arabia's ranking in this category was the worst in the GCC.

Diversifying the Economic Base

Some progress is being made on the manufacturing front in the various GCC countries, in an effort to diversify and create value-added economic growth, especially from hydrocarbon-related industries as analysed earlier for Saudi Arabia in the energy sector. Table 14.7 illustrates the growing share of manufacturing in the GCC's GDP.

Table 14.7 GCC: Value added by manufacturing sector to GDP 1980–2008 ($ billion and % of GDP)

Country	1980	1991	1998	2008
Bahrain	558 (18.0%)	517 (11.2%)	788 (12.7%)	1,705 (12.8%)
Kuwait	1,609 (5.9%)	536 (3.0%)	3,009 (11.9%)	5,866 (7.2%)
Oman	45 (0.8%)	390 (3.4%)	669 (4.7%)	2,566 (8.2%)
Qatar	410 (5.2%)	852 (12.4%)	718 (7.4%)	3,582 (8.4%)
Saudi Arabia	6,555 (4.2%)	9,559 (8.1%)	12,542 (9.7%)	29,522 (9.3%)
UAE	1,142 (3.8%)	2,661 (7.8%)	5,500 (11.8%)	16,663 (12.2%)

Sources: ESCWA, SAMA, UNDP

Saudi Arabia dominates the GCC manufacturing sector and manufacturing now accounts for just under 10% of the Saudi GDP, almost double the level of 1980. Other GCC countries that have also made significant progress in this sector have been Oman, which took its manufacturing contribution to GDP from a negligible 0.8% in 1980 to 8% in 2008, as well as the UAE, where manufacturing now accounts for around 12% compared to under 4% in 1980.

Kuwait's manufacturing base was severely disrupted and damaged during the 1991 Iraq war and Liberation of Kuwait, but the manufacturing contribution now stands at around 7%, as Kuwait, unlike other GCC countries, has concentrated more on services which accounts for around 52% of its GDP (World Bank, 2009).

The next set of figures illustrates the structure of the GCC countries' manufacturing base in terms of sector distribution, investment flows and the distribution of the labour force by the various manufacturing industries.

Total investment in manufacturing sector in the GCC reached nearly $160 billion in 2008, compared to $90 billion in 2001, employing some 972,000 workers compared with 623,000 in 2001, and operating 12,300 factories of different sizes (GOIC, 2009). What Fig. 14.3(b) reveals, however, is that the emphasis has been on capital-intensive industries dating from the early days of the GCC countries, as over

(a) By different manufacturing sector firms   (b) By Investment

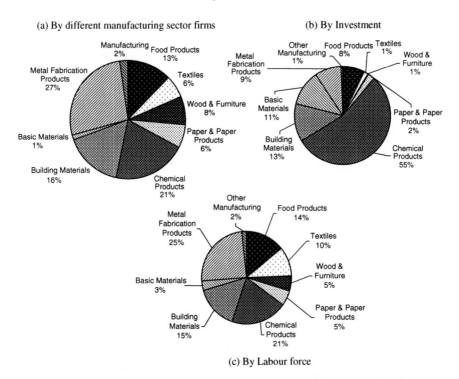

(c) By Labour force

Fig. 14.3 GCC manufacturing sector breakdown (2008) (**a**) by different manufacturing sector firms; (**b**) by investment; (**c**) by labour force (Source: Gulf Organization for Industrial Consulting, GOIC, 2009)

54% of the total investments are in the capital-intensive chemical industry which employs around 20% of the total labour force, as illustrated in Fig. 14.3(c).

The capital-intensive bias of GCC industries still persists despite the fact that smaller firms are the ones that employ a larger number of workers, as illustrated in Fig. 14.4.

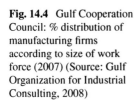 **Fig. 14.4** Gulf Cooperation Council: % distribution of manufacturing firms according to size of work force (2007) (Source: Gulf Organization for Industrial Consulting, 2008)

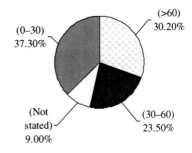

The distribution of workers in these categories shows that nearly 61% of workers were employed in small-sized manufacturing firms of less than 60 employees, with nearly 40% working in companies having less than 30 employees. This reinforces the argument of those advocating small- and medium-sized enterprises (SMEs) as an important employment mechanism for the GCC, especially in countries with high unemployment levels. However, as will be discussed in more detail later in this chapter, the fact that the majority of the labour force in GCC manufacturing is foreign labour has tended to ease pressure on the larger capital-intensive national industries, as they tend to have a higher percentage of the (fewer) labour force, but the national workforce in such companies tend to be better paid. This reinforces the argument put forward in the previous chapter about preferences for such national resource-based jobs, leading to "educated unemployed" nationals who do not wish to enter the lower-paid manufacturing jobs.

A breakdown of the ongoing projects in the various GCC countries reveals that construction plays an important role in the number of projects, but petrochemical-related industries and refining are important sectors, especially in Saudi Arabia, Qatar and Oman, as illustrated in Fig. 14.5.

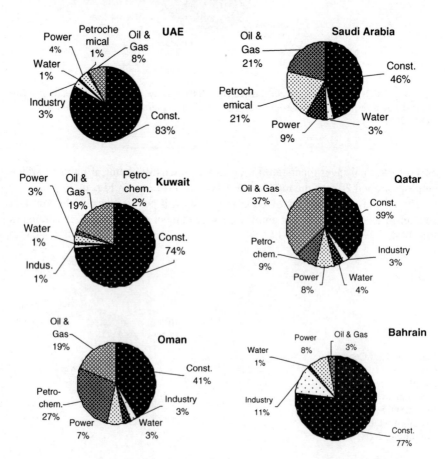

Fig. 14.5 GCC Projects: Share by Country and Sector (2009) (Source: MEED Projects)

The UAE has the lion's share of GCC projects, by value $865 billion, representing 45% of all projects, followed by Saudi Arabia with $468 billion or nearly 25%. Bahrain has the smallest project value share at $33 billion.

Declining costs and new techniques in mining engineering have contributed towards reduced costs in upstream development (exploration and production) worldwide, which will help to boost non-OPEC and OPEC hydrocarbon production because of reduction in costs.

The GCC countries will continue to benefit from technological improvements in upstream development. Also in their favour is their role as large reserve and low-cost producers, and a geographic location that is convenient for meeting the future growing energy demands of the world's fastest growing regions: South East Asia, China and India.

Each GCC country, to one extent or another, is embarking on either upgrading or expanding its upstream industry. Table 14.8 sets out the largest projects currently under way in this sector.

The number and value of ongoing and planned upstream oil and gas projects in the GCC is impressive, with Qatar and Saudi Arabia leading in the mega project league, especially in Qatar's gas-related developments, a result of GCC countries' attempt to expand their market share, with an eye to entering the environmentally friendly energy sector. Kuwait is the exception; its projects are mainly in oil development projects. Bahrain is missing altogether from this list of projects, for the island kingdom diversified its economy by concentrating on non-hydrocarbon industries and services.

The development of these upstream projects will enable the GCC countries to expand their downstream (by-product) operations and ensure diversification into end-user petrochemical industries. This will generate high-value jobs, skills for their citizens and a more stable revenue source compared to unpredictable income from oil and gas.

The GCC Financial Sector: Surviving the Global Turmoil

Over the past decade, the thriving GCC financial system has become integrated with international markets. Several countries, such as Bahrain and Dubai, have established themselves as world financial centres with numerous foreign financial institutions operating there. This brought about both benefits and threats of contagion if affected by global financial crisis, as happened with Dubai during 2009. In one form or another, domestic bank intermediation has led to increased deposits and a large capital base. Bank productivity has improved through the acquisition of new technology, and their profits have been enhanced through developing consumer-based services. GCC central banks have strengthened domestic regulations and bank supervision, especially around the problem of money laundering.

With the exception of Bahrain and Dubai, competition in most countries has been relatively limited to domestic banks, by applying restrictions to bank licensing and foreign participation. In January 2004, Kuwait reversed a long-standing policy and agreed to allow foreign banks to open branches there (Haddadin, 2004). There has

Table 14.8 Selected major upstream oil and gas projects in the GCC 2009

Country	Project	Cost ($million)	Scope of work	Status
(a) Saudi Arabia				
Saudi Aramco	Khurais Field Development	3,000	Full field development	Gas project
Saudi Aramco	Eastern Province Straddle Plant	1,100	Construction of 800 million cu. ft/day plant to handle NGL	Jacobs engineering, in production
Saudi Aramco	Haradh Gas Plant Expansion	400	Increasing capacity by 500,000 cu. ft/day	In production
Saudi Aramco	Hawiyah Gas Plant Expansion	400	Increasing capacity by 800,000 cu. ft/day	Jacobs Engineering, in production
Saudi Aramco-Total	Refinery Jubail	10,000	Refinery capacity 400,000 b/d to process Arabian heave crude	2013 commissioning of plant
Saudi Aramco-Sumitomo Petro Rabigh	Petro-Chemical	10,000	World's largest integrated petrochemical complex	Ethylene/propylene contractor–Foster Wheeler ethylene process technology shows Stone & Webster operation since 2008
Saudi Aramco	Ras Tanura refinery/ petrochemical complex	N/A	Upgrade of existing refinery capacity by 400,000 bpd and building of new petrochemical complex	At FEED stage, completed 2009, production 2013
(b) Qatar				
Qatargas II	Trains 4 and 5	12,000	Two trains of 7.8 million tons/year each	Chiyoda doing downstream feed, while McDermott upstream. First gas production in 2008
Rasgas III	Trains 5 and 6	12,000	Two trains started of 7.8 million tons/year each	Qatar Petroleum and Exxon Mobil. First gas 2008/2009
QP/Royal Dutch/Shell	Ras Laffan GTL Plant	5,000	140,000 barrel/day	First production started 2008/2009
QP/DEL	Dolphin Gas Pipeline	3,500	120 km pipeline	Gas pipeline to Dubai operational

Table 14.8 (continued)

Country	Project	Cost ($million)	Scope of work	Status
(c) UAE				
GASCO/ ADCO	NGL feed gas	2,300	Additional volumes of NGL/gas	Tenders submitted
ADMA/OPCO	Umm Shaif gas re-injection	1,200	600 million cu. ft./day gas	Company selection
ADNOC	District gas grid	380	Construction of new LPG train on Das Island	Chiyoda
GASCO	Habshan gas expansion	350	350 million cu. ft./day train	Fluor Daniel
(d) Kuwait				
KPC	Project Kuwait	7,000	Doubling oil production from fields to 900,000 barrel/day	International oil companies
KOC	Flow lines replacement	800	Replacement of flow lines	Operational
KOC	Water disposal	150	Western oilfields	Operational
(e) Oman				
PDO	Haweel Phase II gas injection	850	Construction of gas injection in seven fields	AMEC operational
PDO	48 in. loop	350	265 km gas pipeline	Operational
PDO	Kawther Field development	250	Gas field development	New gas project

Source: Middle East Economic Digest

been some success by banks originating in the GCC to establish branches in other GCC countries. For example, Saudi Arabia has already given three licences to banks registered in Bahrain, Kuwait and UAE – Gulf International Bank (GIB), National Bank of Kuwait (NBK) and Emirates Bank, respectively.

The domestic capital markets still lack depth and diversification. In a number of cases, equity investment and financing continue to face supply constraints, while listing and trading also experience restrictions (Azzam, 1998, Bakheet, 1999).

Like any other evolving financial sector worldwide, the GCC financial system will face challenges in the future. There continues to be potential re-emergence of government deficits and government borrowing from commercial banks, and these pose a long-term problem of "crowding out" private sector credit. At the same time, governments are exhorting the private sector to assume more responsibility through diversified economies (Seznec, 1995).

The pursuit of economic liberalization and privatization by many countries of the GCC will ensure that the GCC financial sector plays a role in mobilizing private financing for large investment projects in many infrastructure areas. In addition, external competition, a by-product of globalization, will push GCC banks to meet an increased demand for more varied financial services by a younger and more financially sophisticated population (Sheikh, 1999).

The Regulatory Framework

The six GCC countries have adopted open economic systems with free movement of capital and fixed exchange rate systems. Table 14.9 compares the exchange rate and capital restrictions of the individual member states. For exchange rate arrangements, all the GCC states are pegged to another currency – in this case to the US dollar with the exception of Kuwait which has introduced a basket of currency peg. They all have forward exchange markets with prices calculated on the premium or discount of such forward prices, based on the interest rate differential between local and US dollar interest rates. In nearly all cases, local currencies exhibit small interest premiums over comparable US dollar rates.

The sharp fall in the value of the US dollar in the 2003/2004 and 2007/2009 periods is beginning to cause some concern amongst oil producers, as well as the GCC states themselves. Their cost of non-dollar imports rises, adding to current account pressure.

Table 14.9 shows that, with the exception of Oman, there were virtually no controls on current payments and transfers, and even in Oman's case these controls were on payments for "invisible" transactions on current transfers. Qatar and Bahrain, followed by the UAE, instituted the fewest controls on capital transactions, and Kuwait had the most controls. All GCC states avoided controls on liquidation of direct foreign investment, in a bid to create a more liberal and open economy. Liberalization of the financial services sector requires a reduction of direct financial market intervention, especially when they do not address market imperfections. An open and

Table 14.9 The Gulf Cooperation Council: exchange rate and capital restrictions

Index	Saudi Arabia	UAE	Bahrain	Qatar	Oman	Kuwait
Exchange rate arrangement						
Currency	SR	UAE dirham	Bahrain dinar	Qatar riyal	Omani riyal	Kuwait dinar
Exchange rate structure	Unitary	Unitary	Unitary	Unitary	Unitary	Mixed currency
Classification	Conventional pegged	Conventional pegged	Conventional pegged	Conventional pegged	Conventional pegged	Conventional pegged
Exchange tax	No	No	No	No	No	No
Exchange subsidy	No	No	No	No	No	No
Forward exchange market	Yes	Yes	Yes	Yes	Yes	Yes
Controls on current payments and transfers						
Arrangements for payments and receipts	No	No	No	No	No	No
Control on payments for invisible transactions and current transfers	No	No	No	No	Yes	No
Proceeds from exports and/or invisible transactions	No	No	No	No	No	No
Capital controls						
Capital market securities	Yes	Yes	Yes	No	Yes	Yes
Money market instruments	Yes	Yes	No	No	No	Yes
Collective investment securities	Yes	Yes	No	No	No	Yes
Derivatives and other instruments	Yes	No	No	No	No	Yes
Commercial credit	Yes	No	No	No	No	No
Financial credit	Yes	No	No	No	No	No
Direct investment	Yes	Yes	Yes	Yes	Yes	Yes
Liquidation of direct investment	Yes	Yes	Yes	Yes	No	No
Real estate transactions	Yes	Yes	Yes	No	Yes	Yes
Personal capital movement	Yes	No	Yes	Yes	No	No
Provisions specific to commercial banks	Yes	Yes	Yes	No	Yes	Yes
Provision specific to institutional investors	No	No	No	No	No	No

Source: World Economic Forum "Arab World Competitiveness Report"

efficient financial market, will, *ceteris paribus*, positively affect the savings and investment environment and improve the domestic allocation of resources.

Since the accession to the WTO by all the GCC countries and the internal economic and structural reforms undertaken, especially to make FDI more attractive to foreign investors, the number of exchange and capital restrictions has either been amended or totally removed, and an analysis of Table 14.9 shows Saudi Arabia in good light in this respect and this could have also been a contributing factor for its high ranking in the ease of doing business global table and the highest ranking in the GCC.

Despite having roughly similar foreign exchange regimes and capital controls in place, not all the GCC central banks have used similar monetary policies. Some have increased their reliance on open market instruments to try to control money supply and interest rates. Table 14.10 summarizes the main GCC central bank instruments.

Table 14.10 GCC central banks' main operating instruments

Bahrain	Open market operations (purchase/sales of government securities, *repos* of government securities); open market-type operations (outright sales in the primary market); central bank lending operations (overdraft window, overnight lending)
UAE	The UAE central bank relies mainly on purchases of foreign exchange and swap facility in central bank certificates of deposit
Qatar	Same as UAE, plus a discount window facility
Saudi Arabia	*Repo* operations in government and reverse *repos* for liquidity investments; foreign exchange swaps and government deposits with banks
Oman	Mixture of FX purchase/sales and discount window
Kuwait	Same as Bahrain; central bank of Kuwait also has a "liquidity scheme" in the form of 1-month deposits with the central bank

Source: Annual reports, IMF

With the exception of the Saudi Arabia Monetary Agency (SAMA), all the other GCC central banks are in a position to support their commercial banks through overnight lending, discount window facilities or certificates of deposits. SAMA tries to overcome this lending and borrowing prohibition in its Charter of Establishment (Abdeen and Shook, 1984) through open market operations by using *repos* (with banks selling part of their securities to SAMA) and *reverse repos* (banks placing liquidity with SAMA). During the global financial crisis of 2007/2008, virtually all the GCC central banks intervened to support their national banks by providing liquidity injections, FX swaps and, above all, sent out signals of confidence to the general public by agreeing to guarantee commercial bank deposits.

The GCC regulatory authorities have, in general, tended to err on the side of prudence and conservatism in regulating the commercial banking and financial sectors. The outcome, other than the Kuwaiti *Souk Al Manakh* fiasco in the early 1980s and the more recent collapses of unregulated financial companies in Qatar (Al Medinah Investments) and Saudi Arabia (Eid, Juma'a Companies), has resulted in the emergence of a highly profitable, well-capitalized and diversified GCC commercial banking sector.

The banking sector is a vital one for the development of any economy, and the GCC banking sector is no exception. Figure 14.6 sets out major banking indicators for the GCC countries. An analysis of these is quite revealing: In terms of the distribution of GCC bank assets, the Saudi banking industry dominates the other countries and accounts for around 41% of total assets, followed by the UAE banking sector.

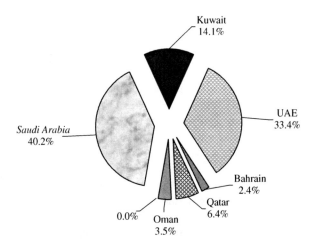

Fig. 14.6 GCC countries' distribution of GCC banks private sector assets (2007): banking sector indicator (Source: GCC Secretariat, GOIC)

In terms of the ratio of banking assets to GDP, Kuwait had the highest level at around 125% for 2006, with Oman the lowest at 44%. The Gulf average was 94%. According to surveys, Japanese banks had a higher ratio at 167%, while UK banks excelled at 390%. US banks were at 90%. Lower banking assets to GDP indicate the existence of larger informal financial economies, ones that are still outside the formal banking sector.

GCC banks' assets totalled around US$288 billion at the end of 2007, with the Saudi share at slightly over US$115 billion. However, in terms of return on assets, Bahraini, Omani and UAE banks outperformed Saudi, Qatari and Kuwaiti banks. According to GOIC, Bahraini and Omani banks also showed the best return on equity, while Saudi, Kuwaiti and UAE banks followed next.

Using a three-bank *concentration ratio*, the GCC banking sector demonstrates a high level of concentration. Kuwait's three-bank concentration for 2008 was nearly 78%, while for Qatar it was around 82%. Studies of Saudi Arabia indicate approximately 50% for the top three banks, which were the National Commercial Bank (NCB), Samba and Riyad Bank. NCB accounted for 17% of the total bank assets of SR 1,594 billion at year-end 2009.

The most extreme case of bank asset concentration was in Qatar, where the largest bank (Qatar National Bank) accounted for slightly less than 70% of total Qatari bank assets.

Development of Offshore and Islamic Banking

In the GCC, Bahrain has since 1975 been the pioneer in the development of off-shore banking units (OBUs) (Bisisu, 1984). The principal condition imposed on OBUs was a prohibition from engaging in any individual or corporate business with Bahrain residents, without the specific permission of the *Bahrain Monetary Agency*. The reason for this was simple: Bahrain wanted to diversify its economy and take advantage of the increased flow of oil revenues that needed fast access to banks in the main financial markets. Besides Bahrain, both Dubai and Abu Dhabi have attempted to create rival financial centres, but the Bahrain Monetary Agency has acquired a reputation as one of the most solid supervising bodies in the GCC.

Dubai, however, seems to be the more energetic and embarked on further developing its economy with a series of "free zones" that it is now extending to the services sector. These include Dubai Internet City and Dubai Media City, but in 2004 it launched the biggest of them all: Dubai International Financial Center (DIFC). The DIFC is a major competitor to Bahrain's financial industry, although it will be based on Western financial concepts and not on *Islamic Shariah*.

What made DIFC attractive were its free zone status and its aim to bridge the "financial space" between western Europe and East Asia. Financial institutions applied for licences in a whole range of financial services sectors such as investment banking, corporate and private banking, capital markets including derivatives and commodity trading as well as insurance and reinsurance services. Firms operating out of the 110 acre free zone are eligible for benefits such as zero tax rates on profits, 100% foreign ownership and no restriction on foreign exchange or repatriation of capital. Unlike "offshore" tax havens, the DIFC seemed to boast of a unique advantage over others in the Gulf in that it was also a fully fledged "onshore" capital market comparable to other leading financial centres such as Hong Kong, London and New York. Dubai seemed unbeatable but others were having a go.

Bahrain decided to challenge Dubai's role and has conceived its own Bahrain Financial Harbour on a somewhat more modest scale than Dubai's. Created as a distinctive new architectural landmark to replace the older office space that has served Bahrain's financial services community, the financial centre includes the Harbour House, Towers, Harbour Mall and Harbour House, once again combining real estate projects and financial office space, with leisure opportunities thrown in. In its regulatory approach, however, Bahrain has decided to complement rather than to take Dubai head on.

Bahrain has adopted a lower, no-nonsense approach and marketed its regulatory oversights strength as a safe banking environment that boasts of a financially skilled and educated local population, good communications and a recognized Islamic finance niche player rivalling that of Malaysia. The attraction of the nearby Saudi market was a big draw. The less frenetic pace of life and the business culture of Bahrain have attracted both regional as well as Saudi institutions, which have found it convenient and cost-effective to penetrate the lucrative Saudi market and yet benefit from the wide range of expertise available in the island kingdom of Bahrain.

Other Gulf states have also decided to throw their financial hat into the ring. From a backwater in the Gulf in the 1970s and 1980s, the state of Qatar is today undoubtedly a major Gulf economic tiger, propelled by a self-confidence based on growing revenue surpluses from gas sales. Not to be outdone by the existing financial centres, Qatar established its own Qatar Financial Centre (QFC) as a financial and business hub to tap into the projected $140 billion of Qatari-led investments over the next 5 years. Qatar seems to have examined the DIFC model well, as the QFC incorporates some elements of the Dubai model such as the ability to engage in both onshore and offshore business, as well as 100% ownership by foreign companies and full remittance of profits outside Qatar. To ensure international best practice, Qatar is promising to establish an independent judiciary comprising civil and commercial centres and regulatory tribunals, with the QFC Regulatory Authority acting as an independent financial regulator.

The OBU industry, however, is also subject to unstable economic conditions in the GCC. Its growth potential has been reduced significantly by increasing competition from domestic banks in the region, especially in Saudi Arabia, as well as the greater ease by which international banks have been able to access the GCC markets from their head offices without having a physical presence in the OBUs. As such, Bahrain, especially, has concentrated on trying to create a niche financial market for itself in the Islamic banking sector.

Islamic banking is gradually gaining more acceptance and credibility in the various Gulf countries. Since its origins in the mid-1960s, it has grown not just in the Gulf but worldwide (Archer and Karim, 2002, Abdeen and Shook, 1984, MEED, 2001). According to these sources, the Islamic banking community is worth some US$100 billion and growing by 10–15% per annum. With rising demand for Islamic products, conventional banks in the GCC have begun to offer products that are compatible with Islam. Bahrain sees itself as a pioneer in this field, both in terms of a strong and respected regulatory and supervisory authority (the Bahrain Monetary Agency) and also in Islamic accounting practices. No other GCC state has as many Islamic banks and financial institutions as those registered to operate in Bahrain, with 30 institutions at the last count. These include four full commercial banks, three OBUs, 20 investment banks, one representative office and two other financial service providers (BMA 2009).

With Saudi Arabia's membership in the World Trade Organization (WTO), all GCC states have become members of that organization. Potentially, this presents both opportunities and threats to existing banks. Less efficient banks with high operating costs are likely to suffer international competition. There is some fear that the entry of foreign banks, such as those that have entered into Saudi Arabia, as well as the new banking law in Kuwait authorizing foreign banks will lead to foreign banks dominating the GCC banking industry. Some have welcomed this, especially in Kuwait, which unlike other GCC states did not have a foreign bank presence. It is felt that the presence of "foreign banks in Kuwait, with their expert administration, abilities and resources, will improve the performance and the patterns of spending by local banks" (Haddadin, 2004). One way forward is for GCC banks to merge, creating institutions with large capital bases, which, combined with their better knowledge of local markets, could help them to effectively compete with foreign banks. The 2007/2008 global financial crisis has certainly led to some discussion on this aspect, but the only move in this direction has been in the UAE which has seen some national banks merge due to the financial difficulties faced by Dubai during the crisis. One example of this was the merger of Emirates Bank International and National Bank of Dubai in 2007 to form Emirates NBD, the largest bank in Dubai with a market capitalization of $11.3 billion and assets of $45 billion (Central Bank of UAE, 2007). The merged bank has branches in Saudi Arabia, Qatar and Britain and representative offices in India, Iran and Singapore.

The GCC Capital Markets

Equity markets in the GCC are expanding, as scope for private enterprise is increasing and demand for equity investment is rising (Azzam, 1998). Table 14.11 shows that Saudi Arabia's equity market is by far the largest in the GCC in terms of capitalization, and, indeed, the largest in the Arab world.

As illustrated in Table 14.11, the UAE has two stock markets, one in Abu Dhabi (ADX market), and the other in Dubai (DFM market), with Abu Dhabi being the largest in terms of capitalization. With the exception of Oman, the majority of GCC capital markets are at nearly 100% of the ratio to their GDP with the most active being Kuwait and Saudi Arabia reflected by their higher price/earnings ratios.

The financial sector has a heavy weighting in all the GCC capital markets, reaching nearly 80% in Bahrain and in the 70s levels for Qatar and Dubai – all competing as financial centres as explained earlier. In Saudi Arabia the financial sector weighting in the *TADAWUL* index is around 45%, followed by around 24% for basic materials, industry and telecoms.

Earlier in this chapter, we considered how the GCC countries adopted policies to ensure that their markets were open to investors, at first from the GCC and later from non-resident foreigners, but some like Kuwait do not allow non-foreign investors.

However, in common with Saudi Arabia, GCC equity markets exhibit few traded companies and low turnover ratios when compared with stock markets in industrial countries and other rapidly growing emerging markets. The GCC equity markets face a number of constraints: there are insufficient brokers and market-makers, and foreign access is generally restricted to GCC nationals or using swap facilities for non-residents such as in the Saudi market. Only Oman and Bahrain markets are free to foreign entry, but these are restricted to GCC residents and foreign residents in their countries.

There is substantial scope in most GCC countries for further development of capital markets, including securities, money markets and stock exchanges. The range of instruments available to borrowers and savers could be expanded further, as borrowers switch from traditional banking instruments to equity and marketable securities. Ultimately, all the GCC countries are aiming to open up their markets to foreign investors, for the amount of foreign direct investment (FDI) to the region has been

Table 14.11 GCC stock market by capitalization, % of GDP, P/E ratios and sector weighting (June 2009)

Stock market capitalization

	$billion	% of GDP	P/E
Saudi	333	90	16.2
UAE	102	47	9.3
Abu Dhabi	68	52	9.2
Dubai	34	39	9.5
Kuwait	93	93	13.4
Qatar	80	94	11.7
Oman	18	33	12.1
Bahrain	17	101	9.4
GCC	*643*	*77*	*13.2*

Sector weight in GCC stock market indices

	Financials	Telecom	Industry
Saudi	45.3	8	10.8
UAE	54.8	27.7	8
ADX	43.9	39	5.5
DFM	76.5	5	13
Kuwait	42.3	3.4	24
Qatar	71.4	0.0	25.9
Oman	51.7	9.5	23
Bahrain	79.2	14.6	1.8

	Basic Material	Cons. Goods	Cons. Services
Saudi	23.9	4.2	3.9
UAE	1.7	0.8	3.4
ADX	2.6	0.9	2.3
DFM	0.0	0.0	5.5
Kuwait	3.7	5.1	10.9
Qatar	0.0	0.2	2.4
Oman	0.6	2.6	1.7
Bahrain	0.0	0.4	4.0

Source: Bloomberg, CMA

less relative to their economies. The GCC capital markets are indeed at a crossroads (Seznec, 1995). Qatar announced in 2004 that foreigners, both individuals and companies, could deal in its stock market as long as they did not hold more than 25% of a firm's issued capital.

Several countries have implemented capital market reforms and introduced new regulations to ensure that capital markets are better served through independent authorities. Some examples are Saudi Arabia's new Capital Market Law of 2003 and those of the UAE, Bahrain and Oman the same year. These regulatory changes will take time to bear fruit, as reforms are also needed in legal and commercial laws to ensure foreign participation on an equal footing (Seznec 1995, Azzam, 1998). The proposed Saudi mortgage law in 2010 is one such move in "financial deepening" of the Saudi capital market.

From 2007 onwards, the pace of debt security issuance in the GCC countries picked up, despite the global financial crisis that broke out, and Table 14.12 illustrates the diversity of issuers, both for traditional and *Shariah*-compliant bonds or *sukuks*.

From Table 14.12, we note the significant amounts raised through *sukuks*, especially by Saudi corporations such as Saudi Basic Industries Corporation (SABIC), which tapped the markets twice in 2007 and 2008. Given the increased perception of global credit risk in 2007, investors preferred issues in local currencies, whether in SR or UAE dirhams as illustrated in Table 14.12. The share of dollar-denominated *sukuks* fell from 69% in 2007 to 14% in 2008. In the conventional bonds, the global marine and port operator DP World and Abu Dhabi National Energy Company (TAQA) raised the largest amounts of funds in 2006–2008 for financing major

Table 14.12 Top 10 *sukuk* and conventional bond issues in the GCC 2007–2010

Issuer	Sukuk	Country	Year	Issue ($ million)	Currency
(A) Top 10 *sukuk* issues					
Nakheel Dev. Ltd.	Ijarah	UAE	2006	3,520	USD
Ports Customs and Free Zone Corp.	Musharakah	UAE	2006	3,500	USD
Aidar Funding Ltd	Mudarabah	UAE	2007	2,530	USD
Saudi Basic Industries Corp.	Al istithmar	Saudi Arabia	2007	2,133	SAR
JAFZ Sukuk Ltd.	Musharakah	UAE	2007	2,043	AED
DP World Sukuk Ltd.	Mudarabah	UAE	2007	1,500	USD
Saudi Electricity Co.	Ijarah	Saudi Arabia	2007	1,333	SAR
Saudi Basic Industries Corp.	Al Istithmar	Saudi Arabia	2008	1,333	SAR
Dubai Sukuk Centre	Mudarabah	UAE	2007	1,250	USD
Aider Sukuk Funding (No. 2) Ltd	Ijarah	UAE	2008	1,021	AED
Saudi Electricity Co.	Ijarah	Saudi Arabia	2010	1,870	SAR

Issuer	Industry	Country	Maturity year	Issue year	Amount (5 million)
(B) Top 10 conventional bond issues					
DP World	Corporate	UAE	2037	2007	1,748
TAQA	Corporate	UAE	2012	2007	1,500
TAQA	Corporate	UAE	2036	2006	1,500
RAS LAFFAN LNG 5	Corporate	Qatar	2020	2005	1,400
Emirates Airlines	Corporate	UAE	2013	2006	1,380
DP World	Corporate	UAE	2037	2007	1,115
Dubai	Sovereign	UAE	2013	2008	1,088
TAQA	Corporate	UAE	2016	2006	1,000
ABU DHABI COM BK	Corporate	UAE	2010	2005	1,000
TAQA	Corporate	UAE	2013	2008	999

Source: NCB Capital Research

global acquisitions and refinancing old debt. DP World became the first issuer to list both conventional and Islamic debt securities on the Dubai International Financial Exchange and its *sukuk* made financial history as being the first convertible instrument in the Islamic finance market. However, the increasing issuance of *sukuks* has led to some debate amongst Islamic scholars as to the complete *Shariah* compliance of such instruments.

The basic *sukuk* structures involve an underlying asset, which is used to generate revenues needed for payouts to the *sukuk*-holders. However, many Islamic scholars objected to *sukuks* structured in ways that effectively replicate conventional bonds with capital guarantees and a predictable yield. This is seen as contravening the *shariah* ban on *riba*, which essentially means using money – as opposed to a real asset – to generate revenue. Common structures, especially ones based on *ijarah* (or lease) structures, offer guarantees to buy back the underlying assets at their original value while offering a fixed rate of return. It has been customary to price *sukuks* by offering a mark-up on LIBOR or some other benchmark interest rate.

A new Accounting and Auditing Organization for Islamic Financial Institutions (AAOIFI) rule in 2008 challenged the prevailing practices on a number of counts. In particular, the organization believes that structures that fail to transfer the ownership of the collateral to the holders were not true *sukuks*. In numerous instances, the *sukuk*-holders were only nominal owners of the assets. Moreover, in some cases, the *sukuk*-holders did not have any effective recourse to the underlying assets, as the collateral in question was not expected to be sold or bought. The AAOIFI rejected the practice of issuing guarantees on the resale value of the underlying collateral, stipulating instead that some type of market-determined price must be used. This suggests that the value of *sukuks* can vary in response to changing market conditions as the value of the underlying assets changes. This is quite different from the conventional bond paradigm and takes *sukuks* much closer to the *Shariah* principle of genuine risk sharing.

Despite the AAOIFI ruling, the Gulf markets saw increased interest in *sukuks* from both individual and institutional investors and the ruling was a welcome intervention that was also seen as part of an ongoing process intended to introduce greater standardization in the *sukuk* market, as it reduces costs and fragmentation of the *sukuk* market.

The GCC capital markets are still evolving and below are some recommendations for further developments:

First, there is a greater need for effective disclosure. Information and analysis on local companies and stock markets would provide investors with a reliable database, through which companies listed on the Gulf stock markets would maintain a higher level of public disclosure than present. This would comply with international accounting standards.

Second, an independent regulatory body needs to be established. While there are presently GCC regulations to prohibit price manipulation, monitoring and enforcement mechanisms in these markets are not very effective. The stock price movements are often turbulent, but with no apparent specific economic cause. Insider trading penalties should be enforced; family or affiliated group share holdings should be restricted.

Third, it is essential to deepen current stock markets by listing privately held, family-owned companies, which seem to be the mainstay and backbone of the Gulf economies (Field, 1985, Fahim, 1995). Given their economic significance in terms of investment, employment and GDP contribution, it is essential that the more successful family-owned businesses should go public, on the assumption that the founding family retains some stake. This will increase the size of the market and provide liquidity and depth. The problems faced by prominent Saudi family companies such as the Saad and Gosaibi groups in 2009 provided an added urgency in the matter.

Fourth, the GCC stock markets should be linked. Some positive steps have already been taken, such as the UAE-based Arab Monetary Fund (AMF) linking six Arab stock markets in a database that can facilitate inter-Arab and GCC investment. Stock markets in Kuwait, Jordan, Bahrain, Tunisia, Oman and Morocco are linked into this AMF Arab markets database, which lists 377 companies. In 1995, the Bahrain and Oman stock markets were linked, making cross-buying and selling possible. Kuwait, Jordan and Qatar have all expressed an interest to join. This linking can facilitate government sales of sovereign securities in such cross-linked markets, increasing the amounts that can be borrowed and helping to deepen the capital markets.

Fifth, there is a need for specialist investment banks in the GCC. Such financial institutions would provide stronger financial analysis, underwriting of shares' issue, flotation of shares to the public and market-making functions. They could advise GCC companies on the optimum mix of debt and equity borrowing, on pricing levels and on the timing for coming into the market. They could inform Gulf corporations about how to obtain international credit ratings from institutions such as Moody's and Standard & Poor.

Sixth, the GCC countries must not slow their efforts at economic and financial integration, if they are to have a powerful voice in international affairs. Debate surrounds the issue of the adoption of a common or unified currency for the region by 1 January 2010, a date that came and went with no agreement on a common currency as will be examined later. Article 22 of the GCC Council Summit Unified Agreements states that "Member States shall seek to coordinate their financial, monetary and banking policies and enhance cooperation between monetary agencies and central banks, including the endeavour to establish a joint currency in order to further their desired economies" (GCC Secretariat, 2001). The unified Gulf currency, whatever it may be called – *riyal, dirham* or *dinar* – could emerge as one of the major currencies of the Arab world and should help ease remittances between one country and another, and boost the development of the GCC capital markets.

Much needs to be done beforehand, however, especially in achieving harmony and agreement between the GCC member states on acceptable levels of budget deficits, inflation, monetary and fiscal policies. These are matters that the European

Union member states also had to deal with before establishing their single currency, the euro, and still are causing problems in the eurozone as seen during the turbulence of 2010.

GCC Trade: Non-Regional Bound

The trade composition of GCC countries can best be described as "asymmetrical": exports are concentrated largely in crude oil and petroleum products, while imports are more diversified. This situation means that GCC countries are vulnerable to pricing developments in international commodity markets – oil in particular, over which the GCC countries have limited control.

The GCC economies are amongst the most open in the world, with no foreign exchange controls and relatively low tariff and quota protection. Figure 14.7 illustrates the geographical distribution of GCC foreign trade for 2007, and it demonstrates that the major export markets are Japan, China, South East Asia, European Union (EU) and USA. The EU tended to dominate imports, with around 32% of total, while South East Asia, China, USA and Japan followed in importance.

Inter-GCC trade is still small relative to the rest of the world, with exports accounting for under 5% and imports at around 8% for 2007.

The GCC faces a very different world economy than that only 20 years ago. Trade with South East Asia and Europe has now become much more significant,

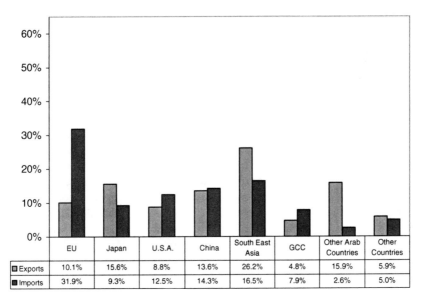

	EU	Japan	U.S.A.	China	South East Asia	GCC	Other Arab Countries	Other Countries
▢ Exports	10.1%	15.6%	8.8%	13.6%	26.2%	4.8%	15.9%	5.9%
▪ Imports	31.9%	9.3%	12.5%	14.3%	16.5%	7.9%	2.6%	5.0%

Fig. 14.7 Geographical distribution of GCC foreign trade in 2007 (%) (Source: Gulf Organization for Industrial Consulting)

while trade with the USA is declining. International exchange rate adjustments have had a major impact on import sourcing, and the fixed exchange rate policies of the GCC, closely tied to the US dollar, have affected the value of imports due to the sharp fall in the US dollar during 2002/2003 and 2007/2008.

Even more striking is the lack of meaningful diversity in the pattern of GCC exports. This is illustrated by Fig. 14.8.

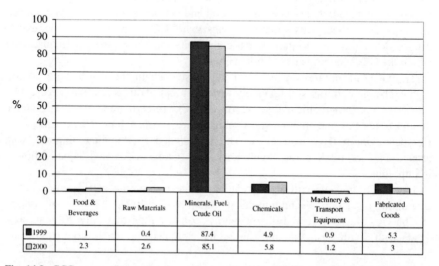

	Food & Beverages	Raw Materials	Minerals, Fuel. Crude Oil	Chemicals	Machinery & Transport Equipment	Fabricated Goods
■1999	1	0.4	87.4	4.9	0.9	5.3
□2000	2.3	2.6	85.1	5.8	1.2	3

Fig. 14.8 GCC commodity exports by major commodities (%) (Source: Gulf Organization for Industrial Consulting, 2002, 2009)

Analysis of the major commodity exports over the period 1999–2007 indicates that, with the exception of a rise in petrochemical exports, there have been modest changes in the composition of GCC exports. Analysis of exports by broad clusters for the individual GCC countries reveals the predominance of oil and gas products for all the GCC countries with the exception of Bahrain which has a more diversified export base. This is illustrated in Fig. 14.9.

The picture of GCC exports by commodity confirms what we noted earlier: that crude oil, minerals and fuel accounted for around 85% of total exports, followed by chemicals. The process of economic diversification within the GCC seems to have had a much greater impact on domestic consumption patterns than on export diversification. The reason is simple: comparative advantage. The policy of export specialization based on comparative advantage has served the GCC well in the short run. The development of petrochemicals and energy-related industries made economic sense in terms of comparative advantage. But in the long term, GCC companies that aspire to compete internationally must establish cost control, effective marketing and product differentiation to help them to open up export markets.

Export Share of Total

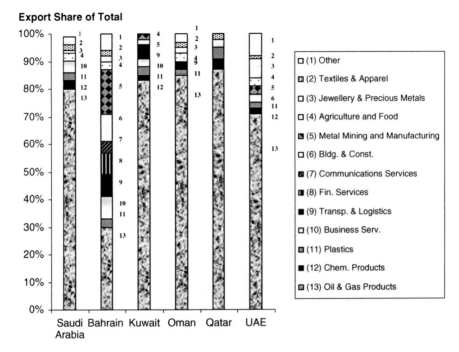

Fig. 14.9 GCC: Share of total exports by broad cluster for individual countries (2007) (Source: GOIC, GCC Secretariat Riyadh)

GCC Demographics and the Labour Market

The GCC countries have one of the highest population growth rates in the world, but the presence of a large percentage of expatriates in virtually all the GCC countries is also another striking feature of the GCC. How they manage this large expatriate workforce and implement a policy of "localization" or replacement of foreign workers with nationals will be one of the most important issues the GCC will face in the future. The issue is often discussed at two levels. First is the number of expatriates and their dependents as a percentage of the total population, which is a strategic demographic issue. Second is the number of foreign workers, particularly in the private sector, as a percentage of the total labour force, which is an employment issue. Because of the sensitivity of the two issues, especially for GCC countries with large expatriate population or labour force, GCC population statistics and national and expatriate labour participation rates are notoriously difficult to obtain for several reasons: the differing estimates provided by national governments and the irregularity of population consensus and of the breakdown by nationals and expatriates. Figure 14.10 attempts to illustrate both aspects – breakdown by population and by labour force using the most available national and GCC data.

Table 14.11 reveals that the UAE has a high ratio of foreigners to total population at nearly 64% but seemed totally dependent on foreign labour, as the expatriate

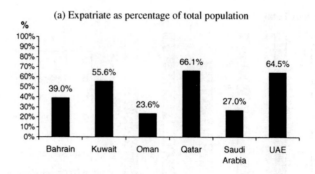

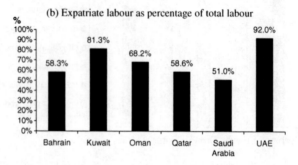

Fig. 14.10 GCC demographics and labour force (2003 or latest); (**a**) Expatriate as percentage of total population; (**b**) Expatriate labour as percentage of total labour (Source: World Bank, ESCWA, World Health Organization)

labour represented 92% of the total workforce for that country, compared with 51% for Saudi Arabia. Kuwait also evidenced a high foreign labour dependency ratio as did surprisingly Oman at nearly 70%, despite the economic diversification efforts in that country. One reason for the relatively high foreign labour participation rate is that from their boom days some GCC countries have followed a common development strategy that was characterized by high labour imports.

As in Saudi Arabia, the labour markets in the GCC countries are segmented along several dimensions: between public and private sectors, nationals and non-nationals and skilled and unskilled labour. In some GCC countries, unemployment is also beginning to rise, but for some countries such as Qatar and the UAE, it is still a relatively recent phenomenon of a largely frictional (in-between jobs) and voluntary nature. However, in the years ahead, labour market conditions are expected to tighten as the number of nationals entering the labour force grows. This is coupled with a situation in which some GCC governments can no longer act as employers of first and last resort because of budgetary considerations.

Given the preference for nationals to work in the government sector in the GCC, foreign workers tend to be employed in the private sector in manufacturing, construction and services. Policies such as the *kafala* or sponsorship system in the GCC have heightened structural dependence on foreign labour, in fact insulating foreign labour from economic downswings in the national economies. This phenomenon of *kafala* has been commented upon (Longva, 1997, Qudsi, 1977) and is one cause of the unusual occurrence of recurring foreign labour unemployment at the same time as labour shortages for the same skills. This is due to the inability of free "non-*kafala*" labour market demand and supply forces to operate effectively and was one of the major reasons that prompted Bahrain to scrap its private sector sponsorship laws in August 2009 and replace it with a government sponsorship and free mobility of foreign labour.

One aspect of foreign labour in the GCC states that attracts most attention is the size of worker remittances, which local commentators argue is detrimental to the GCC economies. In terms of volume, the figures for remittances are substantial. Data shows that the outflow of workers remittances has been rising over the period 1975–1995, with some slight falls in various years due to economic downturn (Birks and Sinclair, 1992). The total amount of remittances now accounts for around 22–25% of the combined GDP of the GCC countries (Chadhury, 1989, 1997, Sinclair, 1988).

As unemployment is virtually non-existent in Qatar, there is no formal labour market strategy, while Saudi Arabia, Bahrain and Oman have implemented *Saudization, Bahrainization* and *Omanization* plans to replace foreigners with nationals. Kuwait has policies to achieve the creation of a specific number of jobs for their nationals; these include raising the cost of expatriate labour and upgrading the skills of nationals. As for the UAE, there are no formal plans covering all the federation, but the Dubai Strategic Development Plan aims to increase the share of nationals in Dubai's labour force from 7 to 10% by raising labour force participation and facilitating the employment of nationals in the private sector.

The relatively limited amount of inter-GCC labour migration seems surprising 29 years after the GCC's establishment. With the exception of Bahraini skilled and semi-skilled labour working in Saudi Arabia's Eastern Province, and some Omani labour working in the UAE, there is little evidence to date of inter-GCC labour mobility. Such inter-GCC labour flows could overcome some of the perceived negative social aspects of non-Gulf labour (Atiyyah, 1996, Girgis, 2002, ESCWA, 1993).

Labour market issues are one of the key policy challenges for the GCC countries. They all recognize that such issues are closely linked to other structural policies related to economic efficiency and to the role of the private and public sectors. As such, policies to increase the flexibility of the labour market are now being defined in a broader framework that includes structural budget reforms and privatization to shoulder the burden of national job creation. These are all long-term structural policies. To create jobs for nationals in the short run, GCC countries, to various degrees, will apply employment quotas, percentage restrictions on foreign labour and administrative directives. None of the above measures can substitute for human resource development that aims to match the skill profile of national labour with the present and future requirements of the private sector. Qatar, Dubai and Bahrain, and, to a lesser extent, Oman, have shown that it can be done and other GCC states are now embarking on upgrading their educational systems to cope with a knowledge-based economic future.

GCC Monetary Union: A Long and Hard Road

During the GCC summit of December 2001, the GCC member countries signed an economic agreement that laid out some specific steps that would need to be taken in order to establish a GCC monetary union by 1 January 2010. That date came and passed and today the prospects of a unified Gulf currency, one of the decisions taken at that 2001 summit, seem more remote than ever due to several events. In December 2006, Oman decided to opt out of the GCC monetary union and this was followed in May 2007 by Kuwait declaring that it would abandon the Kuwait dinar peg to the US dollar in favour of a peg to an undisclosed currency basket, in effect reverting to the exchange rate system that Kuwait had from 1975 to December 2002.

In May 2009, the GCC rulers agreed that the location of a GCC monetary council – the proposed forerunner of a GCC central bank – will be located in Riyadh, Saudi Arabia. This prompted the UAE to formally withdraw from the GCC common currency plans in November 2009. The more recent decisions came against the background of the global financial crisis of 2008 and 2009, which shifted some of the discussions of the proposed GCC common currency to the issue of a unified GCC currency and its peg against a declining US dollar value.

The UAE's decision to opt out stems from far more than an emotional reaction to losing the location of the GCC central bank to Riyadh, but more on a deep-seated belief that a conservative regulatory regime based on Saudi Arabia's dominance and influence on the unified CCC central bank would dash the UAE's, and specifically Dubai's, continued belief in an open economy model, which in turn might threaten that emirate's future expansion as a global financial hub.

Nevertheless, the UAE's decision caught everyone by surprise and is causing the remaining members of the project – Saudi Arabia, Bahrain, Qatar and Kuwait – to go back to the drawing board and ask what sort of unified GCC central bank will now emerge.

Given that both Oman and the UAE have withdrawn, should a unified currency still be pursued? Some might argue that this can be done, and they point to Europe's experience (SAMBA, 2009, Rutledge, 2009). When the UK opted out of the European monetary union, the European Central Bank and the euro common currency, it still remained a member of the European Union and was left with the choice of perhaps joining later. In addition, the UK has participated in all EU-related economic issues. So can the GCC live with a model of four-plus-two, giving the UAE and Oman the space and the time to reconsider their decisions, as they indicated they might when they opted out?

Having said that there would appear to be some doubts within the remaining states still committed to the project. Will the UAE's decision end the momentum towards a unified currency? The Kuwaitis already have adopted a managed peg for the dinar. However, Qatar, Saudi Arabia and Bahrain still have their currencies pegged to the US dollar. But if the decision ultimately is taken to peg a unified GCC currency to the dollar, will this cause Kuwait also to opt out?

In all probability for the immediate future, the unified currency is a low priority, and it is doubtful any of the remaining members of the project will wish to pursue this vigorously. Instead, they might adopt a wait-and-see policy – to judge the dollar's position over the coming years and how the international financial crisis will work out in terms of global financial and economic power, as well as the problems faced by the euro in 2010.

Monetary union does not necessarily mean a common currency. The union, for example, could concern itself with harmonizing regulatory policies and risk management practices throughout the GCC, and work towards the deepening of economic ties. In this way, even those that have opted out of the common currency project can still participate (Rutledge, 2009).

The terms "monetary union" and "currency union" are often used interchangeably but viewed properly; monetary union is a broad-ranging process of economic and financial integration, and the end result of such a successful monetary union is a well-functioning common market for the regional bloc.

Some significant progress has been made since the establishment of the GCC bloc in the field of harmonization of domestic and external policies, in liberalizing inter-regional trade and capital movements, but there still remain some impediments for full labour and capital movements.

Once again the European Union (EU) model stands out, as the experience of this bloc suggests that there are some key ingredients necessary for a monetary union to lead to an efficient common market. This centres on the free movement of goods, labour and capital and each of these has had a chequered history in the GCC.

While the 1 January 2008 launch of the GCC common market went a long way in codifying all previous agreements, especially in provision of equality for Gulf citizens in investment, real estate ownership, tax treatment, stock ownership and company formation, other aspects such as a full and free labour mobility remains slow. In the GCC, the issue of labour mobility is viewed on two levels – one concerning Gulf nationals and the other concerning expatriate labour.

Theoretically national labour mobility should be the easier of the two to resolve. This becomes more important for the GCC's monetary union because in the absence of a more flexible exchange rate regime and an independent monetary policy away from the USA, because of the peg to the dollar, a high degree of GCC national labour mobility will allow some countries to absorb labour in times of shortages and others to export labour in times of economic recession. This would allow the GCC economy as a whole to adjust to labour market inefficiencies and maintain relatively full employment. The slow progress on this front has been mired up with social customs and traditions as well as unofficial barriers to the employment of other GCC citizens in the government sector, which is often seen as a preserve for each country's nationals (Rutledge, 2009).

This is where the expatriate labour market can play a safety valve role for macroeconomic stabilization across the whole Gulf if expatriate labour is allowed to move more freely. Bahrain is the first country of the GCC to have taken the bold decision to scrap its sponsorship system effective from August 2009 and to place it under a single government ministry. The Bahrain decision does not imply a full and free flow of labour into Bahrain, as the new sponsorship system would form part of a broader initiative to place a ceiling on the number of expatriate workers in Bahrain. In effect, domestic supply and demand for labour would set the ceiling for the number of foreign labour allowed to work in Bahrain.

The other GCC countries are not immune to similar pressure to change their sponsorship system as there has been growing support from some Gulf Cooperation Council governments to introduce some form of "time limits" on the residency of expatriates, while Saudi Arabia has also announced that it might consider setting up specialized private sector companies sponsoring foreign labour in place of a myriad of individuals, citizens and companies (Saudi Press Agency, 2009).

Another area where monetary union can help is in accelerating the free movement of goods and building on the existing customs union. This stipulated a common GCC external tariff of 5% and elimination of all intra-GCC tariff and non-tariff barriers and introducing common regulations and procedures. Once again, progress has been patchy with some countries undermining this unified stance by entering into unilateral free trade agreements (FTAs), especially with the USA. This poses a question – what would happen to US goods entering one GCC country with an FTA agreement, such as Bahrain, when these goods enter another non-FTA GCC country and face a tariff levy? The answer is that a stronger monetary union would force the GCC to negotiate as a bloc with other bodies, such as the ongoing discussions with the EU discussed earlier in this chapter, rather than take unilateral action.

One bright spot of GCC economic integration seems to have been in capital mobility which assisted some economies who are net capital importers in times of economic slowdown and helped to reduce inter-GCC economic imbalances. For inter-GCC capital mobility to take effect, there has to be even more harmonization and adoption of similar regulatory operating frameworks that are perceived to be investor-friendly and cost-efficient and possessing a credible oversight role to protect the financial sector in times of international crises. A stronger monetary union could play this role.

However, to achieve a viable monetary union, there has to be what is termed "policy convergence" amongst member states. Again the EU monetary union is the one that the GCC countries agreed to with slight modifications. These involved several factors that need to be achieved prior to the formation of any single currency and they are low and stable rates of inflation, broadly aligned interest rates, stable individual exchange rates, moderate fiscal deficits and a sustainable (and stable) level of public debt. The economic and political problems that were faced by several members of the EU in 2010, such as Greece and Portugal, testify to the policy convergence criteria on member states and the effect on the larger group from economic and financial divergence of a few weaker members. Table 14.13 illustrates the various convergence criteria and how the GCC members fared as of 2009 against the criteria.

Table 14.13 reveals that most of the GCC member states met the convergence criteria in 2009, with the exception of the inflation target for Qatar and the UAE which experienced relatively high inflation levels as discussed elsewhere in this chapter,

Table 14.13 Monetary union convergence criteria: Maastricht and GCC comparative analysis (2008)

Criterion	Maastricht	GCC	GCC Compliance*
Exchange rates	Fluctuations within normal margins for 2 years; no devaluation against any other member state's currency	Long-term stability of GCC exchange rates means that this criterion has not been an issue	N/A
Foreign reserves	No such criterion	To cover 4 months of imports	Bahrain ✗ Qatar √ Oman √ Kuwait √ KSA √ UAE √
Interest rates	Long-term rates must not exceed a margin of 2% points over the average of the three lowest-inflation members	As Maastricht but for short-term rates (3 months)	Bahrain √ Oman √ Kuwait √ UAE √ Qatar √ KSA √
Inflation rates	Must not exceed more than 1.5% points of the average of the three lowest-inflation members	As Maastricht	Bahrain √ Qatar ✗ Kuwait √ KSA √ Oman √ UAE ✗
Fiscal deficits	Must not exceed 3% of GDP	As Maastricht when OPEC basket oil price is $25/b or more	Bahrain √ KSA ✗ Kuwait √ UAE √ Qatar √ Oman √
Government debt	Must not exceed 60% of GDP	As Maastricht	Bahrain √ Oman √ UAE √ Kuwait √ KSA √ Qatar √

Note: √ = criteria met; ✗ = criteria not met
Source: Adapted from Rutledge, 2009

while Saudi Arabia's 2009 budget deficit of 3.3% to GDP ensured it did not meet the fiscal deficit criteria, but the margin was just outside the 3% target levels and follows several years of healthy budget surpluses for the Kingdom as discussed in an earlier chapter.

To Peg or Not to Peg against the Dollar?

One of the critical decisions in the formation of a monetary union is the choice of an appropriate exchange rate regime for the single currency. The member countries of the Gulf Cooperation Council agreed in 2003 to peg their currencies to the US dollar and to maintain the parity until the establishment of the GCC monetary union in 2010. A decision on the exchange rate regime for the single GCC currency was to be made then. Although the choice of the US dollar peg as the external anchor for monetary policy served the countries of the GCC well for many years in maintaining macroeconomic stability, rising inflationary pressures, especially in the period 2007–2008, continuing depreciation of the US dollar against major currencies and differing economic cycles and policy needs to that of the anchor country (the United States) have raised questions about whether the peg to the dollar remains appropriate, and therefore would be appropriate for the GCC monetary union.

The standard criterion for determining the optimal exchange rate regime is macroeconomic and financial stability in the face of real or nominal shocks. Ideally, the exchange rate regime chosen should yield external and internal stability, preserve monetary credibility and international competitiveness and reduce balance sheet risk and transaction costs. In applying these criteria to the GCC, however, it is necessary to take account of the dominant influence of the oil sector in GDP, exports and government revenue; the labour market structure; and the ability of these countries to pursue domestic goals of inflation and growth if they had monetary policy independence.

The GCC face four main options for their unified currency should they decide to proceed on this issue. These are as follows:

- pegging to the US dollar
- managed floating
- pegging to a basket of currencies
- pegging to the export price of oil

Table 14.14 summarizes the major advantages and disadvantages of each option for the GCC countries.

Although good arguments can be made for adopting a more flexible exchange rate policy after a monetary union, particularly in order to be able to use monetary policy as a stabilization tool, there are equally valid arguments in favour of maintaining the current currency peg to the US dollar as illustrated in Table 14.14. Specifically, the peg to the US dollar allows the region to reduce volatility in the exchange rate and in capital flows that could result from nominal shocks (such as continuing geopolitical risks and oil price volatility unrelated to fundamentals), provides a credible and easily understood anchor for monetary policy and simplifies trade and financial transactions, accounting and business planning. A more flexible exchange rate regime would allow the countries to adjust to real shocks better than under a fixed exchange rate regime, but the structural and institutional characteristics of the GCC countries, the challenge of choosing an alternative nominal anchor and the need to implement a number of financial reforms and decision-making processes to operationalize a floating regime suggest that moving to a float is more of a longer-term option. The intermediate regime of a basket peg can be a useful way to introduce some flexibility in the exchange rate and to reduce the adverse effects of swings among values of major currencies, but at the same time would not yield monetary independence. Furthermore, it would also be less easily understood and hence potentially less able to anchor expectations. Pegging to the export price of oil

Table 14.14 GCC: pros and cons of possible exchange rate regimes for a unified currency

Exchange rate regime	Pros	Cons
1. Fixed dollar peg	■ Provides a credible and easily understood anchor for monetary policy and simplifies trade and financial transactions and business planning ■ Provides certainty about the future ■ Labour market flexibility can support international competitiveness ■ Preferred by major oil exporters	■ No flexibility to adjust to real shocks ■ Imports monetary policy from USA not appropriate to local needs ■ Dollar weakness can be easily transmitted to domestic prices – imported inflation triggering price-wage spirals, generation of low interest rates and increased risk of asset price bubbles
2. Managed floating	■ Ability to use monetary policy to smooth business cycles, by absorbing real shocks (negative or positive change in terms of trade) and more appropriate to globalization trends ■ Potential to increase competitiveness of non-oil sector	■ Institutional weaknesses may inhibit adoption of either inflation targeting or monetary targeting ■ Possibility of large and frequent FX intervention in face of large swings in oil prices ■ Complicates budgetary accounting and business planning
3. Peg to oil prices	■ Would allow real exchange rate to move in line with price of the dominant export	■ Rising oil prices would mean real appreciation of currency, damaging competitiveness of non-oil sector ■ Would introduce greater volatility in the exchange rate, leading to lower government revenues and higher government debt
4. Basket peg	■ Useful "halfway" solution offering some nominal flexibility to contain shocks, while retaining main anchor properties of a fixed peg ■ Can help in short term to contain imported inflation	■ Does not give monetary independence and would not address the management of oil price volatility or increase of liquidity arising from high oil prices ■ Undisclosed basket (such as Kuwait's) could invite speculation and complicate future business planning

(PEP) delivers automatic accommodation to terms-of-trade shocks, but that could transmit significant volatility to other sectors of the economy.

From the above arguments for and against pegging, it would seem that the GCC countries would remain by and large anchored to the US dollar, despite the perceived long-term erosion in the value of the US currency, and this dollar peg has been strongly defended by new SAMA Governor Dr. Mohammed Al-Jasser on more than one occasion *as the right policy* to follow (Saudi Press Agency, February 2010). In March 2010, Dr. Jasser was appointed as the first Chairman of the GCC Monetary Council with the Bahraini Central Bank Governor as the Deputy Governor. As such, and given this strong backing from the GCC's largest economic power, the most plausible prospective exchange rate regime for any proposed GCC common currency would be the US dollar peg and any new GCC central bank would inherit a well-functioning anchor and associated monetary framework that the participants understand and is straightforward to administer without attracting speculative pressure as happened when the euro was launched on 1 January 1999 until the new European currency found its market price. GCC policy-makers wish to avoid such speculative pressure in the birth of any future unified GCC currency.

Thinking West but Moving East: Saudi Arabia's New Strategic Partnerships

There has been undoubtedly a blossoming of relationship between the world's major oil producer Saudi Arabia with the emerging Asian manufacturing and service powers, China and India. It was not lost on many observers that the first official overseas state visit of King Abdullah bin Abdulaziz on succession as King in August 2005 was to China and to India in January 2006 rather than to the more traditional Western allies. The Saudi monarch's visit was reciprocated when Chinese President Hu Jintao visited the Kingdom in April 2006 to further cement the relationship, and laid the foundation of further strategic cooperation between the two countries. Senior visits to the Kingdom were also carried out by Indian statesmen, the last being the visit by Indian Prime Minister Manmohan Singh in February 2010 when the two countries signed the "Riyadh Declaration," ushering in a new era of strategic relationship.

What is at stake for all three countries is extremely significant in geopolitical energy terms. The issue of security of oil supply and demand is important for all as they diversify energy partners. Expanding the capacity of their respective private sectors to deal with each other is also an important strategic goal. The heart of the matter remains, however, a sustainable energy alliance.

What is remarkable about the new-found relationship with China is that the People's Republic of China and the Kingdom of Saudi Arabia established diplomatic relations only in 1990.

Oil and energy issues have moved to the top of China's agenda as it seeks to assert its role as a great economic power, and to assure itself of reliable energy partners to feed its unmatched economic growth. The Middle East, Saudi Arabia in particular, is the source of such energy supply. Over the past few years, China and Saudi Arabia have increased the scope and size of bilateral energy-related cooperation besides seeing the size of bilateral trade rising sharply as illustrated in Table 14.15 which analyses imports and exports from Saudi Arabia to both China and India over the period 1984–2008.

From Table 14.15, we note that Saudi Arabia enjoys a substantial trade surplus in both its relations with China and India, with imports from China now accounting for 11% of total imports in 2008, making China the Kingdom's the second largest trading importing partner after the USA. This compares with the almost negligible

Source: SAMA

Table 14.15 Saudi trade with China and India 1984–2008 ($ million)

Year	Exports to China	Imports from China	Exports to India	Imports from India
1984	6.4	183.4	1,119	265.9
1991	92.2	625.0	1,094	292.5
1998	328.0	958.0	1,622	815.1
2002	2,885.3	1,718	3,931	2,630
2006	15,957	8,710	17,098	3,074.4
2008	27,987	12,677	22,744	4,803.2
(2008) % to total Saudi export/imports	8.9	*11.0*	7.2	4.2

amounts of trade both ways in the early 1990s. Exports to India have been traditionally higher than for China, but by 2008, Saudi exports to China had overtaken
those to India as well as imports from China. Despite the fall in ranking compared
to China, India was Saudi Arabia's sixth largest trading partner in 2008.

Energy Security at the Heart of Asian Relationships

China consumed an estimated 7.8 million barrels per day (bbl/d) of oil in 2008,
making it the second largest oil consumer in the world behind the United States.
During that same year, China produced an estimated 4.0 million bbl/d of total oil
liquids, of which 96% was crude oil. China's net oil imports were approximately
3.9 million bbl/d in 2008, making it the third largest net oil importer in the world
behind the United States and Japan. IEA forecasts that China's oil consumption
will continue to grow with oil demand reaching 8.2 million bbl/d in 2010. This
anticipated growth of over 390,000 bbl/d between 2008 and 2010 represents 31%
of projected world oil demand growth in the non-OECD countries for the 2-year
period. By contrast, China's oil production is forecast to remain relatively flat at 4
million bbl/d in 2009. According to Oil & Gas Journal (OGJ), China had 16 billion
barrels of proven oil reserves as of January 2009.

The gap between China's growing oil consumption needs and its domestic production is illustrated in Fig. 14.11, which highlights the growing import needs of
that country.

To meet China's oil import needs, the country has tried to diversify its sources of
imports from as many countries as possible.

The Middle East remains the largest source of China's oil imports, although
African countries also contribute a significant amount to China's oil imports.
According to FACTS Global Energy, China imported 3.6 million bbl/d of crude
oil in 2008, of which approximately 1.8 million bbl/d (50%) came from the Middle
East, 1.1 million bbl/d (30%) from Africa, 101,000 bbl/d (3%) from the Asia-Pacific

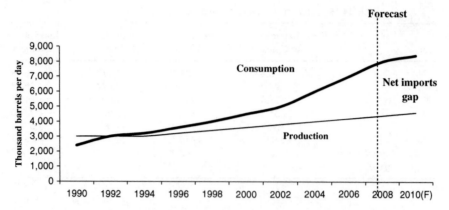

Fig. 14.11   China's oil production and consumption, 1990–2010 (forecast) (Source: IEA, 2009)

region and 603,000 bbl/d (17%) came from other countries. A similar pattern is evident in import data from the first 5 months of 2009 as illustrated in Fig. 14.12 for 2008 and January–May 2009. In 2008, Saudi Arabia and Angola were China's two largest sources of oil imports, together accounting for over one third of China's total crude oil imports.

But it is not on the energy front alone that Saudi-Sino relations are being built. During President Hu's visit in 2006, a number of accords were signed in security, defence, health, trade and youth matters. There were discussions about establishing a Chinese strategic oil reserve in south-east China with Saudi supplies of around 31 million barrels, which again makes eminent sense given the possibility of a breakdown of Iranian oil supplies to China due to Iranian–US tensions in 2010. In other major developments, Saudi Aramco and Sinopec, China's top refiner and petrochemical producer, signed memorandums of understanding to increase trade cooperation as well as reviewing Sinopec's gas exploration activities in the Saudi *Al-Rub AlKhali* (Empty Quarter). At the same time, Saudi Basic Industries Corp. (SABIC) discussed with their Chinese counterparts plans to establish a $27 billion refinery and petrochemical project in north-eastern China. It is now obvious to the major petrochemical players of the world that, with both Saudi Arabia and China having acceded to the WTO, the only viable competitive route open to multinational companies is to enter Saudi Arabia as a major petrochemical producer. In this way, they can ensure competitive supplies to their domestic markets, as well as feed China's growing petrochemical needs from their Saudi Arabia operations.

However, it is the increasing economic and investment ties at the private sector level that is gathering pace between the two countries. The private sectors of Saudi Arabia and China have come of age. The Chinese, while operating under a benign centralized economy, to all intents and purposes are working on a free market basis. The Chinese government started the legal process of establishing the conditions for private oil companies to engage in oil exploration, which until now has been monopolized by the three giant state-owned companies – PetroChina Com. Ltd.,

2008 Total 3,568

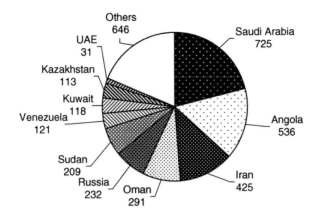

2009 (Jan–May) Total 3,505

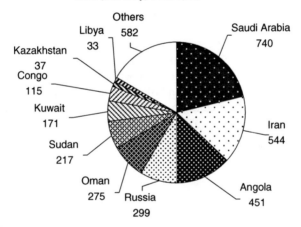

Fig. 14.12 China's crude oil imports by source (thousand barrels per day) (Source: FACTS Global Energy, 2009)

the offshore oil producer CNOOC Ltd. and Sinopec. The Saudi private sector has now matured enough to be able to source strategic investment partners of choice away from more traditional trading partners in the Western world. The opening up of such strategic sectors of the Chinese economy should provide opportunities for Saudi private sector companies to establish advanced technology, primarily offshore and oil exploration joint venture companies.

Discussions are under way in many areas that will be of benefit to both private sectors in the fields of finance and banking, petrochemicals, cement production and electronics. It is somewhat surprising that there are no Chinese or Saudi banks operating in each other's country to intermediate in the growing trade flows. The possibility of a Saudi–Chinese bank being established soon is very likely, as some Saudi banks are making a bold step to open branches, or acquire existing banks in the Far East, as was announced by the Al-Rajhi Bank's Malaysian expansion plans.

Obstacles do remain, however, including language barriers, business attitudes, methods of dealing with the outside world as well as a lack of transparency in information and data on potential investment projects. These barriers are being gradually reduced through regular contacts and visits by Saudi businessmen who are now travelling in greater numbers to the East these days, rather than to the West for investment opportunities and making business contacts.

Saudi–Indian Relations: Technology and Trade

The Kingdom and India share long trading and cultural links, as India is also home to about 170 million Muslims, the world's second biggest Muslim population after Indonesia. As analysed in earlier chapters, Indian expatriates represent around 20% of Saudi Arabia's expatriate population, many of whom have made Saudi Arabia their home for many years. Indian companies, especially in high technology and IT, have established joint venture projects or established a presence in their own name following Saudi Arabia's WTO accession. According to the Saudi Arabian General Investment Authority (SAGIA), there are more than 200 Indian companies in Saudi Arabia with FDI investment of around SR 4 billion. The most recent Saudi–Indian economic agreements have concentrated on renewable energy research, including solar energy, as well as potential Saudi investment in India's agriculture sector.

Conclusion

Half a century ago, all six of the countries that make up the modern-day Gulf Cooperation Council were poor, mostly thinly populated and loosely governed. All were pushed into modernity by oil wealth and left trying to find their way in a fast-changing world. All had to cope with some of the most radical social changes the world had ever seen in such a condensed period of time, including the world's fastest population growth rates, the most rapid urbanization and the biggest tide of managed labour migration. The consequences are still being felt today. Political events in the region, including the turmoil of wars and the problems of domestic terrorism, have affected the GCC. However, with small but concrete steps, the GCC has steadily solidified the 1981 union. Economic issues are high on the summit agendas, as are educational reforms aimed at reformulating school curricula to promote moderation and critical thinking among the young.

Undoubtedly, the GCC countries and citizens face many challenges in this new millennium. The success of the GCC to date has been based on the social, economic and cultural similarities of the member states. Diversity in membership might bring divisiveness.

However, it is more important to ensure that the GCC becomes open and accessible to the ordinary citizens of the member states so that they understand the objectives of the GCC and how it affects their lives. More coordination is needed to get this message across to those in the fields of economics, finance, commerce, education, communication and education. To date, the ordinary GCC citizen is not fully informed about the GCC and its structure, or about transnational opportunities for all its citizens in terms of jobs, mobility and economic opportunities. The GCC countries are facing issues common to all in terms of finding jobs for their young population and in managing their expatriate labour force. The GCC monetary union is being assembled, albeit with four members, after the opting out of Oman and the UAE from the common currency, but other aspects of the GCC common market are proceeding.

At the same time, the governments of the GCC are embarking on internal economic, political and social reforms with far-reaching consequences for their citizens.

Each state of the GCC is moving ahead at its own pace of reform and change. Inaction is no longer an option. It is a measure of statesmanship to balance change with taking care not to alienate those who are feeling most threatened. Such a balance will ensure that the GCC family survives as a stronger political and economic entity in the twenty-first century. Saudi Arabia is also developing new global strategic alliances with China and reinvigorating existing ones with countries such as India as it seeks to diversify its global competitive trading strengths in the Asian markets. This will become a more prominent feature of Saudi economic and foreign policy in the new millennium.

Summary of Key Points

- *The GCC was established to effect coordination and interconnection between its six founding member states in 1981 in the economic, social and political fields.*
- *The GCC economies face similar structural problems and are dependent on few revenue sources. The period since 1981 saw the GCC go through several phases including a consolidation phase, several crisis phases relating to the Gulf wars and the current adjustment and reform phase.*
- *The GCC countries adopt open, free market economic philosophies and are committed to economic and social reforms to meet the aspirations of their largely young population.*
- *Economic diversification and economic integration have now assumed great importance for all GCC countries in various degrees of success, as oil and gas revenue dependency is still high. Bahrain and Dubai have achieved some measurable degree of diversification into non-oil services.*
- *The diversification of the GCC manufacturing base has been erratic due to the size of the domestic national markets. There is continued emphasis on hydrocarbon projects in the major GCC energy producers.*

- *The GCC financial sector witnessed rapid development and integration with international markets and both Bahrain and Dubai have established themselves as world financial centres. Capital markets are being developed to tap national private sector capital back into GCC projects. Full monetary union that was planned for 2010 is not materializing, especially for the Gulf common currency.*
- *GCC countries' international trade is still "asymmetrical," with exports highly concentrated largely in crude oil and petroleum products while imports are more diversified. This means that the GCC economies are vulnerable to pricing developments in international commodities. Trade between the GCC countries is still limited.*
- *Internal demographics and composition of the population of the GCC countries are causing some concern because of the imbalance between nationals and expatriates in some GCC countries. The UAE has the highest percentage of foreign workers at 77% of total population, followed by Qatar and Kuwait. The lowest is for Saudi Arabia at 25%. All GCC countries are currently re-examining their foreign labour force policies. Some have adopted "localization" as a means of employing nationals, with* Saudization, Omanization *and* Bahrainization *being the most prominent.*
- *Saudi trade relations with China and India have grown rapidly and both countries are now major strategic economic allies of the Kingdom.*

Part VII
Conclusion

Chapter 15
The Challenges Ahead

Reforms begin at home and stay there.

Anonymous

So Rich and Yet So Poor

The pace and tempo of change in Saudi Arabia has accelerated. For the last 30 years, modern economic history has seen few national changes as rapid and turbulent as those that have affected Saudi Arabia. They have transformed the desert Kingdom beyond recognition. For better or for worse, the Kingdom and its citizens have to live with the consequences of decisions taken in earlier days, and press on to meet the growing list of challenges facing the country in the new millennium. Sitting on top of a quarter of the world's proven oil reserves, Saudi Arabia attracts both envy and fear of its economic potential. However, no other country, some analysts would argue, is so rich and yet so poor. Despite massive oil reserves, its per capita income is below those of its neighbours in the GCC; the country is beset by a rising tide of population growth and the spectre of growing unemployment. Despite many discussions about diversification and public exhortations to the private sector, the Kingdom is still reliant on two main exports: crude oil and energy-related petrochemical products.

Domestic issues are now paramount, including much needed economic and social reforms, along with better management of citizen's expectations. The structural reforms in the legal, economic and government organs of state over the past few years, especially since the succession of King Abdullah to the throne in 2005, have boosted international interest in the Kingdom, but there continues to be a strong need for additional reforms on a number of levels. These include an accelerated strengthening and modernization of the country's legal framework, particularly in areas of business and commercial law; aligning the objectives of the country's rapidly increasing educational institutions with the needs of the growing private sector; and further enhancing the efficiency of the public sector through fiscal reforms aimed at rationalizing government expenditure to avoid another bout of increased government debt burden, especially if oil prices remain weak in the face of global economic

M.A. Ramady, *The Saudi Arabian Economy*, DOI 10.1007/978-1-4419-5987-4_15,
© Springer Science+Business Media, LLC 2010

recovery uncertainties. Further measures that Saudi Arabia needs to address are in increasing the overall level of institutional transparency so as to ease both domestic and foreign investors concerns with respect to potential economic risk. Some important strides have been made in the Saudi capital market to make it one of the better regulated markets in the region that has now allowed foreign investors to participate while ensuring regulatory oversight is not compromised. Saudi Arabia is not standing still and in 2010, the Capital Market Authority authorized the first exchange-traded funds or ETFs which will allow non-resident foreign investors to trade in it. This will open the Saudi capital market even more to foreign investors without exposing it to speculative "hot money" flows. However, going forward, there is still a need for increasing the depth, stability and sophistication of the domestic financial markets by fostering an even higher degree of transparency, a greater involvement by institutional, as opposed to individual, investors and deeper bond markets. The introduction of a Saudi Mortgage Law will add depth to the Saudi capital market with the possibility of a government "Fannie Mae" type of company being set to buy mortgages from financial institutions and to inject liquidity to the real estate market. This will deepen the sector and provide a safer channel for investment, with the proposed government company in effect becoming the primary purchaser of eligible home loans from institutional issuers and having the mandate to securitize these loans into mortgage-backed securities and sell them to investors through Islamic *sukuks* or bonds and create a liquid secondary market. Studies in the real estate sector point to a large untapped market, especially for affordable middle- to low-income housing, which, if added to the ongoing mega projects, adds to an estimated $730 billion real estate market over the next decade.

Managing Expectations and Reforms

The sequencing of reforms and change is also an important issue to Saudi policy-makers, so that it is not seen as competition between external and domestic reform. Experiences of some developing countries with reforms, especially those of the former Soviet bloc, showed us that it can be destabilizing to move forward too quickly on the external agenda, leaving domestic reforms behind.

The pace of change can be quickened or slowed to suit a particular country's social, religious and political evolution. It must maintain a harmonious relationship with the above factors, for otherwise there will be a widening gap between actual changes and reforms and the expectations of the citizens.

While some sections of society might feel aggrieved that they have not shared in the prosperity that their elder brothers and fathers enjoyed during the boom years of the 1970s and early 1980s, there is a new dawn of realism within Saudi society that times have indeed changed. King Abdullah has been instrumental in signalling that Saudi society will henceforth be more caring for the unfortunate elements in society and encompassing all sections without creating large disparities. Young Saudis have begun to lower their expectations of high salaries, automatic government tenure and minimal education levels in order to obtain jobs.

The spectre of unemployment, coupled with the younger generation's higher education levels, especially amongst females, has also brought about a change in social attitudes towards having large families.

Saudi Arabia's young population holds great potential for the future, but will the job opportunities be there? Over the past 30 years, the Saudi population has grown at an average annual rate of about 3.75%, compared to 1.83% for other developing countries and 0.47% for industrial nations, although female education and life style expectations have brought the birth rate down to 2.3% levels. As a result, Saudi Arabia now has one of the youngest populations in its peer group. Among Saudi nationals, who account for about 75% of the total population, close to 48% are 19 years old or younger. The dependency ratio in Saudi Arabia, which stands at around 69% among Saudi nationals and 55% for the population as a whole, is higher than that of other high- to middle-income countries. This along with the fact that a large proportion of Saudi women do not participate in the workforce explains why no more than 23% of Saudi citizens are actively employed or seeking employment. The official unemployment rate stands at about 10% although this is disputed. Notwithstanding the possibility that the actual rate of unemployment may be even higher, one needs to also consider the potential for significant underemployment among working Saudi nationals. Relatively well-compensated and less-demanding government jobs may be accentuating labour market inefficiencies by reducing the incentive for nationals to join the private sector, reinforcing what we have termed "educated unemployed" amongst Saudi nationals.

The substitution of Saudi nationals for expatriates through the government's so-called *Saudization* program may provide partial relief, but in the long term the whole basis of *Saudization* as an employment generation tool has to be reassessed as actual Saudi employment in the private sector has been completely out of line with government-planned projections.

The degree of success in generating sustainable levels of new employment will be the central measure by which any future Saudi administrative and economic reforms will be judged. *Saudization* can be a two-edged sword. The government's natural desire to replace foreigners with Saudis to resolve a growing unemployment problem needs to be tempered with long-term consequences to the private sector. These might include reduced efficiency, lower productivity, higher costs and economic slowdown should *Saudization* be unwillingly enforced. The model has to be more of a "partnership," exemplified by the commendable results of the Saudi banks' *Saudization* experience. Both foreign bank partners and the Saudi community benefited in terms of profitability, skill transfer, productivity and product innovation.

The issue of foreign workers and how they are treated and replaced must be approached with care and caution. This could become one of the most contentious issues in the years ahead. Most books on the economy of Saudi Arabia have tended to discuss this matter in purely statistical terms. They have neglected to delve more deeply, beyond the numbers, to assess the potential economic implications should the policy of *Saudization* be mishandled. A rushed policy of *Saudization* could bring about a reduction in both actual and potential Gross Domestic Product, if expatriate workers feel threatened and begin to voluntarily "withdraw" part of their labour input and create economic inefficiencies. As discussed, all the GCC countries are facing similar problems, with the exception of high-income but low-population countries such as Qatar and Kuwait. Bahrain has been the most progressive by being the first to abolish the so-called "*kafeel*" or private sponsorship of foreign workers and replacing it with government sponsorship, and enabling foreign workers free to move between jobs at wages set by market demand and supply forces. The Kingdom is studying variations of the Bahraini decision, but maintaining the status quo is not a long-term option in face of a mismatch between domestic labour supply and private sector labour requirements.

The presence of these expatriates has undoubtedly brought about most of Saudi Arabia's material benefits. Many voices, including some from the government, have argued that expatriate workers are valued guests and will be protected as such. This was especially expressed during the tense period of the third Gulf War and domestic terror acts. This spirit needs to be nourished, if a successful and willing handover of responsibilities and technical skills to Saudi labour is to occur as part of the *Saudization* process. At the same time, any significant exodus of skilled expatriate labour will bring forward the day when qualified Saudis take responsibility in their own country, either through skill transfer or "learning by doing."

Social Cohesion and Poverty Reduction

The Kingdom has stated that it has met nine out of the eleven United Nations Millennium Development goals, with eradication of poverty being the most important goal left. As discussed in this book, it may come as a surprise to many that there exist elements of poverty amongst segments of Saudi society. According to data provided by the Saudi government to the United Nations, the number of Saudi nationals who earn less than $2 a day was 1.63% of the population, or approximately 300,000 citizens. There are a further 400,000 families which spend less than SR 3,800 or $1,000 a month and which represent around 19% of the population according to the office of the National Strategy to Combat Poverty. The Saudi government is now embarking on social assistance programmes by providing social security benefits, subsidized housing and vocational and technical training for low-income families, and free education grants for children from such deprived families. Domestic philanthropy and employment generation programmes by socially responsible Saudi companies such as the impressive "*Bab Rizq*" programme of Abdullateef Jameel Group are set to increase by example in the future.

Since his succession, King Abdullah has set a trend for more devolution of power to the legislative arm of the Saudi government, which will continue in the foreseeable future, until the balance between appointed and elected *Shoura* Council membership reflects the different social, tribal and regional strata of the Kingdom. This has already been carried out by the Gulf Cooperation Council State of Qatar, which held a referendum in April 2003 to approve a new national constitution.

Evolution and consensus-building, the hallmarks of Saudi government, are key to allowing for economic planning and stability.

It is within this tradition for consensual change that the municipal elections took place in Saudi Arabia, with half of the candidates elected by eligible Saudi males, and half appointed by the government. It was an important first step in the commitment for change and reform by the Saudi government and it will be interesting to observe which economic powers are devolved to the regional Municipal Councils, especially in the allocation of expenditures and the increase in future service tariffs and rates. After all, each region will try to attract domestic and international inward investment based on the region's perceived economic strengths and comparative advantages.

It is not only on the domestic front that Saudi Arabia has embarked on a more embracing social charter but in international affairs also the Kingdom has taken the lead in promoting interfaith dialogue with the first global interfaith dialogue held in Madrid in 2008 and a follow-up in Geneva in 2009. The Saudi government also took the unprecedented decision to allow the establishment of a private human rights group in 2003, and elevated the government's own Human Rights Commission to ministerial rank with independent investigative authority in the 2009 cabinet reshuffle by King Abdullah.

The Challenges Ahead

The Kingdom is evolving. On the privatization front, the programme has moved ahead in some significant sectors and the next few years will witness a more invigorated privatization programme in some key sectors such as water, aviation as well as banking and government procurement. The successful privatization of the Saudi mining company *Maaden* has opened up the mining sector to Saudi and foreign private sector partnership, and the Kingdom will also emphasize more public–private partnership (PPP) in the coming years, especially in the mega cities' construction projects. These new mega cities will reduce pressure on the large urban centres and create regional economic hubs and new clusters around key industries to provide regional economic diversity. In the financial sector, the Kingdom has earned international credit at the way it has managed to steer the Saudi financial sector without having it affected by the global financial crisis fallout. The Saudi family businesses sector will become a focus of government oversight, with more transparency and corporate governance required as a condition for remaining private, following the wake-up call this important economic sector had after the financial debacles of the Saad and Al Gosaibi groups during 2009. The Kingdom will play a more high-profile role in such international organizations such as the G20, as well as multilateral institutions as the International Monetary Fund and the World Bank. Saudi Arabia will continue with its conservative surplus investment policies, without diversifying too much from traditional US financial securities, and the small Sovereign Wealth Fund (*Sanabel*) it set up will concentrate on value-added international investments that can attract technology transfer and job creation to the Saudi economy.

Job creation is, and will continue to be, one of the major policy objectives of the Saudi government in the foreseeable future. More attention needs to be given to small- and medium-sized enterprises (SMEs), for they are more attractive in terms of job creation on an SR-to-SR investment comparative basis than larger corporations.

This will help diversify the economy, reduce dependence on oil price volatility and create a new breed of private sector entrepreneurs to drive the economy forward. A step has been taken with increased allocation for SME loans through the Saudi Credit Bank and government guarantees through Saudi commercial banks. More support for this sector is forecasted in the future, especially in building up "industrial clusters" around key industries such as petrochemicals where the Kingdom has a comparative advantage and can duplicate the experiences of other countries such as Japan which have successfully integrated SMEs with large corporations in Japan and are attempting to do the same through their Saudi Aramco–Sumitomo Petro Rabigh petrochemical complex in Saudi Arabia.

Foreign direct investment (FDI) will still be a prime focus for the Kingdom, but the future emphasis will be on qualitative FDI partnerships and foreign company licensing rather than on quantitative monetary inflows. More emphasis and priority will be given to companies that bring technology and expertise in areas such as IT, renewable energy (especially solar), food security and water desalination and recycling. Through the efforts of the Saudi Arabian General Investment Authority (SAGIA), the burden of doing business in the Kingdom has been reduced and SAGIA is confident that the general and specific government administrative and bureaucratic reforms will ensure that Saudi Arabia sits at the high table of the "top ten" nations in terms of global competitiveness and ease of doing business. While most commentators had shrugged off such ambitions as mere wishful thinking, yet by 2010 the Kingdom had outperformed other more fancied Middle East and GCC countries in its global ranking as discussed in this book. The key is to maintain the reform process across all sections of the Saudi government infrastructure.

Given the erratic nature of Saudi revenues, dependent on the vagaries of oil prices, there has been some discussion about setting up an "oil stabilization fund" by the Kingdom to be used when oil price falls as an emergency reserve. This could materialize in the next few years, but the issue is establishing transparent guidelines on the mechanisms of drawdown and oversight process. The Norwegian experience in managing such reserves could be one such guideline.

Regional and International Relations

Tensions in the Gulf between the USA and Iran over the issue of nuclear energy have propelled the Gulf Cooperation Council into closer economic and political cooperation. The impetus for "strength through unity" has translated itself more on the political front, and Saudi Arabia was fully supported by the GCC countries during the brief conflict between Saudi forces and Yemeni irregulars known as "*houthis*" during 2010. On the economic front, there were some advances made in terms of a full customs union by 2005, but the GCC single currency and monetary union planned for 2010 took a setback when Oman and the UAE opted out of the former. While Riyadh was finally chosen as the seat of the monetary union, the predecessor of a GCC central bank in 2009, there are doubts whether a unified GCC currency will materialize. Saudi Arabia hopes that emphasis on a more invigorated monetary union involving labour, goods and capital movement between the GCC states can be the cornerstone of cementing GCC ties at the practical level that affects ordinary GCC citizens, and has left the door open for Oman and the UAE to rejoin the union at a later date.

On the broader international stage, Saudi Arabia will continue with its policies of acting as a mediator and arbitrator in inter-Arab and Muslim nation affairs, as the Kingdom enjoys moral authority due to the location of Islam's two holiest sites *Makkah* and *Madinah*, as well as the Kingdom hosting the Organization of Islamic Conference (IOC) and the Islamic Development Bank (IDB) and supporting both organizations morally and materially.

The Kingdom will continue to "look East" in its international trade orientation, and over the coming years there will be a significant increase in the economic and political relationship with China and other Asian countries such as India and Malaysia. Saudi Arabia is also expanding its relationship elsewhere, and trade ties with Brazil and Russia are also expanding, exemplified by high-level state visits to both countries. Building up a viable strategic food reserve for Saudi Arabia also underlies some of the international strategic alliances, with India and Brazil expressing interest to cooperate with Saudi Arabia in this vital sector.

Education: Quality, Not Quantity

The Saudi government has recognized the need for qualitative educational policies leading to a knowledge-based economy. This will be the way forward to provide its citizens with the technical skills necessary to meet the challenges of a more competitive IT-driven world economy. The creation of the new Ministry of Communication and Information Technology points in the right direction. From being behind most other Middle East nations in terms of Internet access, today the Kingdom has one of the fastest growing Internet penetration rates in the world.

In order to foster practical and industry-related applied research, Saudi universities must be encouraged to adopt policies that would facilitate industry secondment with international and Saudi enterprises. The cross-fertilization of ideas will provide a pool of talented Saudi educationalists who have had practical experience within industry and can generate solutions that give such industries a competitive manufacturing edge. The envisaged large-scale privatization of many Saudi public sector organizations will require the services of pragmatic and capable "captains of industry" to manage them.

Such university/industry cross-placements can be the breeding ground for future technical managers.

The establishment of science parks in collaboration with universities as well as the establishment of industrial cities and technology parks in Riyadh, Dhahran and Jeddah by the government indicates the seriousness with which research and development and their scientific applications are now being taken. At the same time, the 2008 and 2009 budget allocations sent an unmistakable signal that science-based education and technical training would, from now on, be the focus of expenditure. The establishment of the King Abdullah University of Science and Technology (KAUST) was a landmark decision in that path, and promises to change the operating landscape of how higher education is carried out in the Kingdom besides possibly placing one Saudi university in the top 10 ranked international universities in the coming decade.

In order to ensure a match between educational sector output and private sector needs, the government and various private sector organizations have been having a closer dialogue on assessing future skill needs. Over the next few years, it is expected that the private sector will take the lead and establish privately owned universities and other specialized educational institutions. Their goal will be to meet the needs of the market and to compensate for shortfalls due to budgetary constraints in student placements in Saudi government universities. It is important for the Saudi government to implement an appropriate quality control oversight process, along with a course and degree accreditation system. This will raise confidence among parents, students and employers regarding the output of such private institutions.

Women's Issues Will Be Important

King Abdullah has made a personal point of openly meeting and greeting female Saudi professionals during his various tours of private and public corporations, and has taken Saudi businesswomen along on international state visits. The message is clear: female participation in all aspects of Saudi working life is encouraged, within the confines of Saudi social customs and norms. These symbolic gestures have helped to speed up Saudi society's acceptance of women's participation in more activities and areas than hitherto allowed. The idea of women members of the *Majlis Al Shoura* or of women in cabinet positions is no longer inconceivable as evidenced when the first Saudi female deputy ministerial-level appointment was made for female education affairs. Qatar has shown the way with the appointment of its first female cabinet minister in 2003 followed by Oman, Bahrain and the UAE during 2004.

The participation of relatively educated women will have an economic impact on productivity, consumption and reduction in foreign workers' remittances, for women could replace some expatriate workers in assembly line, clerical, administrative, IT and customer support work areas. This would have been inconceivable only 20 years ago. Female participation in the national economy is now a major factor in terms of investment, diversity and scope of employment, with females playing a prominent role in the various Chambers of Commerce and Industry. Since 2005, the momentum to grant Saudi women more economic and social rights has gathered pace and women are now allowed to use their own picture IDs to make transactions with banks and other government bodies, as well as opening stock trading accounts without using male relatives or intermediaries. The value of investments held by Saudi women is substantial, reportedly around SR 8 billion in the retail, services and SME sector and having 43,000 commercial registrations in their own name, and around SR 45 billion in bank deposits. More professions are being opened for women, including the legal profession, with women lawyers representing female clients in courts, and women appointed as senior representatives of the Kingdom in overseas missions.

Despite the above changes, the vast majority of employed women continue to be concentrated in the public sector as teachers, lab technicians, doctors, administrators, social workers and professors, but plans are underway to set up a women's police academy and positions as immigration officers. In the private sector, the most sought after jobs for those with higher education have been in the banking and insurance sector and Saudi Aramco has been a significant employer of Saudi female professionals at all levels of the organization. What was notable over the past few years was the readiness of Saudi female students to enrol in female technical and vocational colleges and to consider what had been thought of as "menial jobs" open only to foreign female workers. As females enter the Saudi labour market in the future in ever increasing numbers, as evidenced by the fact that females now outnumber males at the undergraduate bachelor's level, there will be increased pressure to accommodate women in the Saudi labour market.

Fuller female participation in society, while respecting religion, social customs and traditions, will be a positive economic force in the future of the Kingdom.

Stake in Society

In the final analysis, as numerous models of economic development and growth illustrate around the world, self-sustained economic development and "take-off" can only come from within society; called the endogenous or internal factor, it can be sparked by education, innovation, productivity or social cohesion.

For Saudi Arabia, one such element for ensuring private sector "take-off" is the re-emergence and strengthening of the "middle classes" and other professional elements in society. At the same time, the professional middle class has acquired a wide range of specialist education and transferable skills, and it is not inconceivable that Saudi professionals will seek employment abroad as engineers, bankers, doctors and lawyers, thus reversing, in a small way, a cycle of labour import to Saudi Arabia.

This has already begun in the banking, media, medical and legal professions, and can be considered a natural evolution of economic development. It will bring the Kingdom valuable invisible exports and added international skills.

The emergence of grass-roots volunteer experience at the individual and primarily youth level was an important phenomenon that was triggered by the Jeddah floods and large loss of life in December 2009. Saudi citizens gained valuable experience in how to manage such crisis situations and in fact outperformed official government bodies by the speed and efficiency of their relief work. Institutionalizing and building upon such local citizen's action groups could help to bring about Saudi social cohesion and ensure accountability in government services.

Like other countries, Saudi Arabia is painfully discovering that only through its own sweat, toil, exertions and nation-building will it find its rightful place in the world and dispel the unfounded label of the "Kingdom of inertia." Many observers have been surprised by the pace, diversity and scale of change to date, especially since King Abdullah's succession in 2005. The hope is that it will continue to do so in the future, as the well-being of the Saudi economy has implications reaching far beyond its shores.

Bibliography

Abalkhail, Mohammed. "The Role of Fiscal Policy in Realizing the Vision". Centre for Economic and Management Studies. *Future Vision of Saudi Arabia*. Riyadh, Oct. 2002.

Abdeen, Adnan and Shook, Dale. *"The Saudi Financial System in the Context of Western and Islamic Finance"*. New York, NY: John Wiley & Sons, 1984.

Abdelrahman, M.A. "The determinants of foreign worker remittances in the Kingdom of Saudi Arabia". *King Saudi Univ.*, Vol. 18, Admin. Sci. (2), pp. 93–121, Riyadh, 2006.

Abdul Ghafour, P.K. "GCC Weighs Sales Tax". *Arab News*. 23 October 2004.

Abdelkarim, Abbas. *"Oil, Population Change and Social Development in the Gulf: Some Major Trends and Indicators"*. New York, NY: St. Martins Press. Inc., 1999.

Abdullatif, Ahmed. "Future Role of Banking Sector". Shoura Council. *Future Vision of Saudi Arabia*. Riyadh, Oct. 2002.

Abdul Rahman, O. *"The Dilemma of Development in the Arabian Peninsula"*, London: Croom Helm Ltd, 1987.

Abdulqadir, A. *"Saudization* in Civil Service". Vice Minister Civil Service. *Future Vision of Saudi Arabia*, Riyadh. Oct. 2002

Abed, G., Nuri Erbas, S. and Guerami, B. "The GCC Monetary Union: Some Considerations for the Exchange Rate Regime". *IMF Working Paper* No. 03/66, 2003.

Abir, Mordechai. *"Saudi Arabia in the Oil Era: Regime and Elites, Conflict and Collaboration"*. London: Croom Helm, 1988

Abir, Mordechai. *"Saudi Arabia: Government, Society and the Gulf Crisis"*. London: Routledge, 1993.

Ackert, Lucy, Bryan, C. and Deaves, R. "Emotion and Financial Markets". *Economic Review.* Second Quarter, 88, p.33, 2003

Adelman, M.A. *"The Genie out of the Bottle: World Oil Since 1970"*. Cambridge, MA and London: MIT Press, 1995.

Agarwal, J.P. "Determinants of foreign direct investment: a Survey". *Weltwirtschaftliches Archieve*, Vol. 116, 1980.

Agence France Presse. "Saudi Cabinet endorses Islamic Insurance Law". *AFP*. 15 July 2003.

Aghion, P. and Griffith, R. *"Competition and Growth: Reconciling Theory and Evidence"*. Cambridge, MA: MIT Press, 2007.

Ahmad, Mahmoud. "Move to Employ Women in Factories Welcomed". *Arab News*. 13 March 2003.

Aissaoui, Ali. "The Oil Price Dimension of Global Energy Security – Does Saudi Arabia's Price Preference Matter?" *Economics & Research Arab Petroleum Investments Corporation (APICORP)*, 25 September 2009.

Aitken, Brian, Gordon H. Hanson and Ann E. Harrison "Spillovers, foreign investment, and export behaviour". *Journal of International Economics*, Vol. 43, pp. 103–132, 1997.

Akeel, Maha. "Saudi Businesswomen Go Off Beaten Track". *Arab News*, 18 March 2003.

Akeel, Maha. "Dialogue Forum Ends Amid Heated Debate", *Arab News*, Jeddah, 15 June 2004.

Al-Aali, A. "Obstacles facing Saudi Arabian food and chemical exporters", *International Journal of Commerce and Management*, Vol. 5, No. 3, pp. 17–31, 1996.

Alden, J. and Lin, G. *"Benchmarking the Characteristics of a World-Class University: Developing an International Strategy at University Level"* Leadership Foundation for Higher Education, London, 2004.

Alfaisal, Turki, HRH. "Evolution of the Constitution of Saudi Arabia", *St. Antony's College Oxford University Lecture*, 2007.

Ali Sheikh, Rustum. *"Saudi Arabia and Oil Diplomacy"*. New York, NY: Praeger, 1976.

Ali, Abdulrahman Yousef, Al. "Saudi Arabian export strategy: A micro-level analysis". in J. Wright, (ed.), *Business and Economic Development in Saudi Arabia*. London: Macmillan, pp. 152–169, 1996.

Almana, Aisha Mohamed. *"Economic Development and its Impact on the Status of Women in Saudi Arabia"*. (Ph.D. Dissertation). Boulder, CO: University of Colorado, 1981.

Alqahtani, S.S. "The extent of adequacy of higher education output to the labour market needs: exploratory study of King Saud University and Riyadh private sector", *Journal of Public Administration*, Vol. 38, No. 3, October 1998.

Alrumaihi, F.A. "Science and Technological Cooperation among the Gulf Cooperation Council Countries", Ph.D. Thesis (*University of Manchester*), 1994.

Al Sadoun, A. "The Impact of Saudi Arabia's Accession to WTO on Petrochemical Industries", *Arab News*, Jeddah, 12 Dec 2005.

Alsahlawi, M. "The Real Prospect of Non-OPEC Oil Supply", *The Journal of Energy and Development*, Vol. 18, No. 2, 1995.

Alsahlawi, M.A. "An Alternative Oil Pricing Currency And OPEC's Foreign Assets", *The Journal of Energy and Development*, Vol. 33, No. 1, 2009.

Alsheekh, S.A. "Demography movement in the Kingdom of Saudi Arabia and its effect on the labour market and economic growth", *The Saudi Economic Journal*, No. 5, Spring 2001.

Al Sultan, A. *"Saudization* of labour market in Kingdom of Saudi Arabia: dimension, obstacles and suggested remedies", *Journal of Public Administration*, Vol. 38, No. 3, October 1998.

Al Tamimi, Sultan. "Saudis on the Dole Up by 1.39%". *Arab News*. Jeddah. 28 January 2010.

Altbach, P. "A World-Class Country without World-Class Higher Education: India's 21st Century Dilemma". *International Higher Education* (40, Summer): 2005.

Altbach, P. "The Costs and Benefits of World-Class Universities". *Academe 90* (1 January–February), 2004.

Altoaijery, "Demography studies determine the future of economic and social problems", The Saudi Economic and Social Problem, *The Saudi Economic Journal*. No. 5. Spring, 2001.

Andersen, Norman. *"The Kingdom of Saudi* Arabia". London: Stacey International, 1996

Anderson, J.E. and van Wincoop, E. "Trade costs", *Journal of Economic Literature* Vol. 42, No. 3, pp. 691–751, 2004.

Arab Banking Corporation. *"The Arab Economies"*. 4th Revised Edition. Bahrain: Arab Banking Corporation, 1994.

Arab News. "Top 100 Saudi Companies – 2001: Ranked by Sales, Assets and Employees". *Jeddah*, 2002.

Arab News. "The Impact of Saudi Arabia's Accession to WTO on Petrochemical Industries" 12 December 2005.

Archer, Simon. and Karim, Abdel-Rifaat. *"Islamic Finance, Innovation and Growth"*. Euromoney Books and AAOIFI, London, 2002.

Arthur, J.B. "Effects of human resources systems on manufacturing performance and turnover". *Academy of Management Journal*, Vol. 437, pp. 670–687, 1994.

Ashenfelter, O. and Ham, John. "Education, unemployment, and earnings". *Journal of Political Economy*. Vol. 87, No. 5, pp. 99–116, 1979.

Askari, Hossein. "Saudi Arabia's economy: oil and the search for economic development". *Contemporary Studies in Economic and Financial Analysis. No. 67*. Greenwich, CT: Jai Press, 1990.

Askari, Hossein, Vahid, Nowshirvani. and Mohamed, Jaber. "*Economic Development in the GCC: The Blessing and the Curse of Oil*". Greenwich, ConnecticuT: JAI Press, 1997.

Atiyyah, H.S. "Expatriate acculturation in Arab Gulf countries". *Journal of Management Development*; Vol. 15, No. 5 pp. 37–47, 1996.

Auty, R.M. "The transition from rent-driven growth to skill-driven growth: recent experience of five mineral economies". In: Maier, J., Chambers, B., Farooq, A. (eds.) *Development Policies in Natural Resource Economies*. Cheltenham: Edward Elgar, 1999.

Auty, R.M. "*Resource Abundances and Economic Development*". Oxford: Oxford University Press, 2001.

Awaji, Ibrahim, Al. "Bureaucracy and development in Saudi Arabia: The case of local administration". *Journal of Asian and African Studies*, Vol. 24, No. (1–2), pp. 49–61, 1989.

Azzam, H. "*Development of Capital Markets in the Gulf*". Gulf International Bank B.S.C., Bahrain, 1988.

Azzam, H. "*The Emerging Arab Capital Markets*". New York, NY: Kegan Paul International, 1997a.

Azzam, H, "Preparing for a Global Future". *The Banker*. Vol. 47, pp. 72–76, 1997b.

Azzam, H. "Saudi Arabian Economy: The Outlook for 1998". *Saudi Economic Survey*, April 8 and 15, 1998.

Azzam, H. "*The Arab World: Facing the Challenges of the New Millennium*". IB Tauris, London, 2002.

Baadi, Hamad, Al. "*Social Change, Education, and the Roles of Women in Arabia*". (Ph.D. Dissertion) Palo Alto, CA: Stanford University, 1982.

Bakheet, Beshir. "Developing GCC Stock Markets: The Private Sector Role". *Middle East Policy*. Vol. 6, No. 3, pp. 72–77, February 1999.

Baland, J.-M. and Francois, P. "Rent-seeking and resource booms". *Journal of Development Economics*. Vol. 61, pp. 527–542, 2000.

Baldwin, R. and Forslid, R. "Trade Liberalization with Heterogeneous Firms", *CEPR Discussion Paper N° 4635*, London: CEPR, 2004.

Barney, J.B. and Wright, P.M. "On becoming a strategic partner: the role of human resources in gaining competitive advantage", *Human Resources Management*, Vol. 37, pp. 31–46, 1998.

Bashir, Abdulwahab. "Saudis Told to Learn New Things, Develop New Habits", *Arab News*. 4 June 2004.

Bashir, F, Al. "*A Structural Econometric Model of the Saudi Arabian Economy, 1960–1970*". New York, NY: Wiley, 1977.

Bassam Fattouh. "The Oil Market through the Lens of the Latest Oil Price Cycle", *Oxford Institute for Energy Studies*. Presentation at Saudi Association for Energy Economics. 23 January 2010.

Batlay, Grais, W. and Sendan E. "Financial Sector Reforms: International Experience and Issues for Saudi Arabia". World Bank. *Future Vision of Saudi Arabia*. Riyadh, Oct. 2002.

Bazai, Hamad, Al. "Privatization – A Prelude to Government Projects Reform". Ministry of Finance and National Economy. *Future Vision of Saudi Arabia.*, Riyahd, 2002.

Beblawi, Hazem. "*The Arab Gulf Economy in a Turbulent Age*". London: Croom Helm, 1984.

Beblawi, Hazem. "The Rentier State in the Arab world". *Arab Studies Quarterly.* Vol. 9 No. 4, (Fall), pp. 383–398, 1987.

Beck, R. and Kamps, A. "Petrodollars and Imports of Oil Exporting Countries". Working Paper Series 1012, European Central Bank, 2009.

Bernstein, H. (ed.). "*Underdevelopment and Development*". Harmondsworth: Penguin Book, 1973.

Bhagwati, J. and Brecher, R.A. "National welfare in an open economy in the presence of foreign-owned factors of production", *Journal of International Economics*, Vol. 10, No. 1, pp. 103–115, 1980.

Bhagwati, J. and Srinivasan, T.N. "Trade and poverty in poor countries", *The American Economic Review*, Vol. 92, No. 2, pp. 180–183, 2002.

Bhagwati, J.N. and Hamada, K. "The brain drain, international integration of markets for professionals and unemployment: a theoretical analysis", *Journal of Development Economics*, Vol. 1, No. 1. pp. 19–42, 1974.

Bhala, Raj. "Saudi Arabia, the WTO and American Trade Law and Policy". No. 38. The International Lawyer. pp. 741–812. Fall 2004.

Birks, J.S. and Sinclair, C.A. *"Arab Manpower: The Crisis of Development"*. New York, NY: St. Martin's Press, 1980.

Birks, J.S. and Sinclair, C.A. "Repatriation, remittances and reunions: What is really at stake for Arab countries supplying labor to the Gulf Cooperation Council States?" in Charles E. Davies (ed.), *Global Interests in the Arab Gulf*. New York, NY: St. Martin's Press, 1992.

Bisisu, Adnan. "Offshore Banking in Bahrain". Bahrain Chamber of Commerce and Industry, 1984.

Blakely, James, R. "The Oweiss Demand Curve". *Blakely's Commodity Review*. Vol. 1, No. 1, pp. 1–8 May, 1983.

Blondal, S. and Christiansen, H. "The Recent Experience with Capital Flows to Emerging Markets Economies". *Economics Department Working Paper*. 211 OECD, Paris, 1999.

Boase, Roger. *"Islam and Global Dialogue"*. Burlington, VT: Ashgate Press, 2005.

Bolbol, A. and Omran, M. "Arab Stock Markets and Capital Investment". *Arab Monetary Fund Papers. No. 8*, Feb. 2004.

Borensztein, E. and Lee, J.W. "How Does Foreign Direct Investment Affect Economic Growth?" *NBER Working Paper* No. 5057, 1995.

Bottazzi, L. and Peri, G. "The international dynamics of R&D and innovation in the long run and in the short run", *The Economic Journal*, Vol. 117, pp. 486–511, March 2007.

Bourbakri, N. and Cosset, J. "The Financial and Operating Performance of Newly Privatized Firms: Evidence from Developing Countries". Mimeo Laval University, 1997.

Bourland, Brad. *"The Saudi Economy under the changing global context"*. Saudi American Bank. *Future Vision of Saudi Arabia*, Riyadh, Oct. 2002.

Bourland, Brad. *"The Saudi Economy: 2001 Performance and Forecast"*. Saudi American Bank, Riyadh.2001,

Bourland, Brad. *"The Saudi Economy: Mid-year 2003"*. Saudi American Bank, Riyadh. August 2003.

Branstetter, L.G. "Are knowledge spillovers international or international in scope? Micro econometric evidence from the U.S. and Japan", *Journal of International Economics*. Vol. 53, No. 1, pp. 53–79, 2001.

Brown, G. and Sarkozy, N. "Oil prices need government supervision", Opinion, *Wall Street Journal*, 8 July 2009.

Buch, C. Kleinert, J. Lipponer, A. Toubal, F. "Determinants and effects of foreign direct investment: evidence from German firm-level data". *Economic Policy*, pp. 51–110, January 2005.

Buhulaiga, Ihsan. "Challenges and Prospects of the Saudi Labor Market". *Arab News*. 20 January 2004.

Buiter, W.M. "Economic, Political, and Institutional Prerequisites for Monetary Union among the Members of the Gulf Cooperation Council", *CEPR Discussion Paper* No. 6639, 2008.

Burtless, Gary, Robert Z. Lawrence, Robert E. Litan and Robert J. Shapiro. *"Globaphobia: Confronting Fears about Open Trade"*, Washington, DC: Brookings Institution, Progressive Policy Institute. Twentieth Century Fund, 1998.

Business Software Alliance. *"Sixth Annual BSA-IDG Global Software 2008 Piracy Study"*, DBA–IDC. May 2009.

Campbell, C.J. "Peak Oil: An Outlook on Crude Oil Depletion", http://www.mbendi.co-zai/indy/oilg/p0070.htm., Oct. 2000.

Carden, W.M. "Boom Sector and Dutch Disease Economics: Survey and Consolidation". Oxford Economic Paper. 36, 1984.

Carter, J.R.L. *"Merchant Families of Saudi Arabia"*. London: Scorpio Books, 1984.

Central Department of Statistics. *"Employment and Wages-2000"*. Ministry of Planning. Riyadh, 2001.

Central Department of Statistics. *"National Accounts of Saudi Arabia, 2000 & 2001 Indicators"*. Ministry of Planning. Riyadh, 2002.

Central Department of Statistics. *"Statistical Yearbook 2002"*. Ministry of Planning. Riyadh, 2003.

Chadhury, Kiren Aziz. "The price of wealth: business and state in labor remittance and oil economies". *International Organization*. Vol. 43, pp. 101–45. Winter 1989.

Chadhury, Kiren Aziz. *"The Price of Wealth: Economies and Institutions in the Middle East"*. Ithaca, NY: Cornell University Press, 1997.

Chalk, N.A., Treichel, V. and Wilson, J. *"Financial Structure and Reform"*. Building on Progress: Reform and Growth in the Middle East and North Africa, 1996

Chalk, N.A., El-Erian, M.A., Fennel, S.J., Kireyev, A.P. and Wilson, J.F. "Kuwait: from reconstruction to accumulation for future generations". *IMF Occasional Paper*, 150, Washington, IMF, 1997.

Champion, Daryl. *"The Paradoxical Kingdom: Saudi Arabia and the Momentum of Reform"*. C. Hurst and Co. UK, 2003.

Chang, E.C., Cheng, J.W. and Khorana, A. "An examination of herd behavior in equity markets: an international perspective", *Journal of Banking and Finance*, Vol. 24, No. 10, pp. 1651–1699, 2000.

Chenery, H. *"Structural Change and Development Policy"*. London: Oxford University, 1979.

Christie, W.G. and Huang, R.D. "Following the pied piper: do individual returns herd around the market?" *Financial Analyst Journal*, July–August 1995, pp. 31–37, 1995.

Clarke, Thomas (ed.) *"International Privatization: Strategies and Practices"*. Berlin and New York, NY: Walterde Giruyter, 1994.

Clarke, Thomas and Pitelis, Christos (eds.) *"The Political Economy of Privatization"*. London and New York, NY: Routledge, 1995.

Cleron, Jean-Paul. *"Saudi Arabia 2000: A Strategy for Growth"*. London: Croom Helm, 1978.

CMA. *"Annual Report 2008"*, Capital Market Authority, Riyadh, www.cma.gov.sa.

Cohen, W.M. and Levinthal, D.A. "Innovation and learning: The two faces of R&D", *The Economic Journal*, Vol. 99, No. 397, pp. 569–596, 1989.

Cookson, C. "Universities Drive Biotech Advancement", *Financial Times Europe*, May 7, 3, 2007.

Cordesman, A.H. *"After the Storm: The Changing Military Balance in the Middle East"*. Boulder, CO: Westview, 1993.

Cordesman, A.H. "Saudi Arabia: *Guarding the Desert Kingdom*". Boulder, CO: Westview, 1997.

Cordesman, A.H. *"Saudi Arabia Enters the 21st Century"*. New York, NY: Praeger, 2003.

Cornelius, Peter (ed.). "The Arab World Competitiveness Report 2002–2003". *World Economic Forum*. Oxford: Oxford University Press, 2003.

Council of Saudi Chambers of Commerce and Industry. "CSCCI Creates Office for SME's". *CSCCI*. Riyadh. 14 March 2004.

D'Souza, Juliet and William Megginson. "The Financial and Operating Performance of Privatized Firms During the 1990s". Mimeo, Department of Finance, Terry College of Business, The University of Georgis, Athens, GA, 1998.

Dabbagh, A, Al. "Mining in the Kingdom and its Role in Economic Diversification". *MAADEN. Future Vision of Saudi Arabia*, Riyadh, Oct. 2002.

Dagdeviren, M. "Revisiting privatization in the context of poverty alleviation". *Journal of International Development*, Vol. 18, pp. 469–488, 2006.

Daghsh, Muna. "Family Companies have SR 250 billion in Investments", *Arab News*, Jeddah, 2 April 2004.

Dahel, R. and Laabas, B. "The behaviour of stock prices in the GCC markets". Working paper 99, *Economic Research Forum*. Vol. 17, No. 17, 1999.

Dailami, Mansour. *"OPEC: Twenty Years and Beyond"*, London: Croom Helm Ltd, 1982.

Deardorff, A.V. "Weak links in the chain of comparative advantage", *Journal of International Economics*, Vol. 9, pp. 197–209, May 1979.

Devarajan, S., Go, D.S. and Li, H. "Quantifying the Fiscal Effects of Trade Reform", Working Paper No. 2162, *World Bank*, Washington DC., 1999.

Devenow, A. and Welch, I. "Rational herding in financial economics", *European Economic Review*, Vol. 40, pp. 603–615, 1996.

Devlin, Julia (ed.). *"Gulf Economies: Strategies for Growth in the 21st Century"*. Washington, DC: Georgetown University, 1996.

Diwan, Ishac and Girgis, Maurice. "Labour Force Issues and Employment Strategies: A Strategic Vision for Saudi Arabia". World Bank. *Future Vision of Saudi Arabia*. Riyadh, Oct. 2002.

Dosary, Adel, S, Al. *"Localization of Jobs in the Saudi Labor Market* (Saudization) *Strategies: Implementation Mechanisms through a Multiple Track Approach"*. 4th Annual Saudization Conference, Jeddah, 2002.

Doumato, Eleanor Abdella. "Women and the Stability of Saudi Arabia". *Middle East Report.* No. 171, pp. 34–37, July–August, 1991.

Doumato, Eleanor Abdella. "Between Breadwinner and Domestic Icon?". in Souad Joseph and Susan Slyomovics (ed.) *Women and Power in the Middle East*. Philadelphia, PA: University of Pennsylvania Press, 2001.

Doumato, Eleanor Abdella. "Education in Saudi Arabia: Gender, Jobs and the Price of Religion". in Doumato, E and Poususney, M. (ed.). *Women and Globalization in the Arab Middle East – Gender, Economy and Society.* New York, NY: Lynne Reinmer, Inc., 2003.

Doumato, Eleanor Abdella and Posusrey, Marsha. "Women and Globalization in the Arab Middle East". in *Gender, Economy and Society*. New York, NY: Lynn Reinmer, Inc., 2003.

Dukhayil, Abdulaziz, A, Al. "Higher Education Outputs and their Compatibility with Future Development Requirements in the Kingdom". KFUPM. *Future Vision of Saudi Arabia*, Riyadh, Oct. 2002.

Dukheil, Abdulaziz, M, Al. *"The Banking System and its Performance in Saudi Arabia"*. London: Saqi Books, 1995.

Dukheil, Abdulaziz, M, Al. "Impact of dollar depreciation on Saudi economy". *Saudi Commerce and Economic Review.* Dammam. No 118. pp. 12–14, Feb 2004.

Economist Intelligence Unit. *"Country Profile: Saudi Arabia, 2001–2002"*. London: Economist Intelligence Unit, 2003.

Edwards, Robert (ed.). *"The GCC Demographic Report 1998"*. Dubai, MERAC, 1998

EFG-Hermes. "Profitable Growth at a Price: Analysis of Saudi Banks". *EFG-Hermes.* Cairo.14 Aug. 2003.

Ehteshami, A. "The politics of participation in the oil monarchies". in Najem, Tom and Hetherington, Martin (ed.) *Good Governance in the Middle East Oil Monarchies*. London: Routledge Curzon, 2003.

Eichengree, B. "International Lending in the Long Run: Motives and Management", in Richard Levich (ed.) *Emerging Market Capital Flows*. Boston, MA: Kluwer Academic Publishers, 1998.

Eltony, M, Nazy. *"Can an Oil Based Economy be Diversified? A Case study of Kuwait"*. Kuwait: Arab Planning Institute, 2000.

Emirates Centre for Strategic Studies and Research. "Privatization and Deregulation in the Gulf Energy Sector". *ECSSR*. Abu Dhabi, UAE, 1999.

Erian, Mohamed A, El. and Cyrus Sassanpour. "GCC's Macroeconomic Strategies: Towards the 21st Century", in Devlin, Julia (ed.) *Gulf Economies: Strategies for Growth in the 21st Century*. Washington D.C.: Georgetown University, 1997.

ESCWA. *"Arab Labor Migration to the Gulf: Size, Impact and Major Policy Issues"*. Amman, United Nations Economic and Social Commission for Western Asia (ESCWA), 1993.

ESCWA. *"Bi-Annual ESCWA Session"*. Beirut, Lebanon. United Nations Economic and Social Commission for Western Asia. (ESCWA). April 2003.

Essayyad, M., Ramady, M. and Al Hejji, M. "Determinants of bank profitability of petroleum economy: the case of Saudi Arabia". *Petroleum Accounting and Financial Management Journal.* Vol. 22. No. 3. pp 69–101. Fall/Winter 2003.

Fadel, Fida, Al. "Technological Incubators". UNESCO. *Future Vision of Saudi Arabia*. Riyadh, Oct. 2002.

Fahim, Mohammed, Al. *"From Rags to Riches: A Story of Abu Dhabi"*. London, Center for Arab Studies, 1995.

Falvey, R., Foster, N. and Greenaway, D. "Intellectual property rights and economic growth", *Review of Development Economics*, Vol. 10, No. 4, pp. 700–719, 2006a.

Fan, C.S. and Stark, O. "International Migration and Educated Unemployment". *Journal of Development Economics*, Vol. 4–6, pp. 847–859, 2007.

Faroqui, Mahmoud. *"Islamic Banking and Investment"*. New York, NY: Kegan Paul International, 2002.

Farsi, Fouad, Al. *"Saudi Arabia: A Case Study in Development"*. London: Routledge and Kegan Paul International, 1982.

Farsi, Fouad, Al. "Saudi *Arabia"*. LBC Information Services, 2001.

Fayez, Khalid. "Future Role for Banks and Saudi Financial Markets Under the Globalization of the Economy". *Future Vision of Saudi Arabia*. Riyadh, Oct. 2002.

Fidelity Investments. "Annual Report" Boston, MA, 2006.

Field, Michael. *"The Merchants: The Big Business Families of Saudi Arabia and the Gulf States"*. Woodstock, N Y: Overlook Press, 1985.

Fisher, G., Hughes, R. Griffin, R. and Pustay, M. "International Business: managing in the Asia-Pacific", *Pearson Education*. Australia, 2006.

Gelb, A.H. et al. *"Oil Windfalls: Blessing or Curse?"*. New York, NY: Oxford University Press, 1998.

Gently, B. (ed.). *"Private Capital Flows and the Environment: Lessons from Latin America"*, Cheltenham, Edward Elgar Publishing, 1998.

Ghantus, Elias T. *"Arab Industrial Integration: A Strategy of Development"*. London: Croom Helm, 1982.

Ghazanfar, Ali Khan. "World's Largest Islamic Financing Deal Concluded". *Arab News*, Jeddah, 27 Sept. 2004.

Girgis, Maurice. "National Versus Migrant Workers in the GCC: Coping with Change", in Handoussa, Heba and Zafirris Tzannatos, *"Employment Creation & Social protection in the Middle East and North Africa"*. Cairo, Egypt: The American University in Cairo Press, 2002.

GOIC. "*Annual Report 2008*", Gulf Organization for Industrial Consulting, Doha, Qatar, 2009.

Gould, D.M. and Gruben, W.C. "The role of intellectual property rights in economic growth", *Journal of Development Economics*, Vol. 48, No. 1996, pp. 323–350, 1996.

Graham, E.H. "Foreign Direct Investment in the World Economy". *IMF Working Paper.* WP/95/59.1995

Grubel, H.G. "Intra-industry specialization and the pattern of trade", *The Canadian Journal of Economics and Political Science* Vol. 33, No. 3, pp. 374–388, 1967.

Gulf Cooperation Council (GCC). *"The Unified Economic Agreement"*. Riyadh, Saudi Arabia: *Gulf Cooperation Council Secretariat*, Riyadh, 1981.

Gupta, A. "A Vision for Export Promotion in Saudi Arabia". World Bank. *Future Vision of Saudi Arabia*, Riyadh, Oct. 2002.

Gupta, K.L. *"Financial and Economic Growth in Developing Countries"*. London: Croom Helm, 1984.

Gylfason, T. "Natural resources, education, and economic development". *European Economic Review*, Vol. 83, pp. 76–87, 2001.

Gylfason, T., Herbertsson, T. and G. Zoega. "A mixed blessing: natural resources and economic growth". *Macro Economic Dynamics*. Vol. 3, pp. 204–225, 1999.

Haddadin, H. "Kuwait to Open Banking Sector". *Reuters*, 13 January 2004.

Hafni, Zainals. "Involving Saudi Women in Nation Building". *Al-Sharq Al-Awsat*. 21 August 2003.

Haidar, Saeed. *"Saudization*: The Objective is Clear, the Means are Not". *Arab News*, 13 July 2003.

Hamed, Osama. "Foreign labour, currency substitution and economic stability in Gulf Cooperation Council countries". *Arab Economic Journal*, No. 9, 1997.

Hammoudeh, S. and Choi, K. "Behaviour of GCC stock markets and impacts of US oil and financial markets", *Research in International Business and Finance*, Vol. 20, No. 1, pp. 22–44, 2006.

Harrison, Ann. "Determinants and Consequences of Foreign Investment in Three Developing Countries", in Mark Roberts and James Tybout, (eds.), *Industrial Evolution in Developing Countries*. New York, NY: Oxford University Press, 1997.

Hegelan, A, Al and Palmer, M. "Bureaucracy and Development in Saudi Arabia", in Niblock, T and Wilson R. (ed.). *The Political Economy of the Middle East*. Vol. 5. pp. 1–22, Cheltenham: Edward Elgar, 1999.

Helpman, E., Melitz, M.J. and Yeaple, S.R. "Exports versus FDI with heterogeneous firms", *American Economic Review*, Vol. 94, No. 1, pp. 300–316, 2004.

Heneman, R.L., Tansky, J.W. and Michael, S. "Human resources management practices in small and medium-size enterprises: unanswered questions and future research perspective", *Entrepreneurship, Theory & Practice*, Vol. 25, No.1, Fall 2000.

Hijab, Nadia. *"Woman Power: The Arab Debate on Women at Work"*, Cambridge: Cambridge University Press, 1988.

Hoekman, B., Maskus, K.E. and Saggi, K. "Transfer of Technology to Developing Countries: Unilateral and Multilateral Policy Options", *Policy Research Working Paper No. 3332*, Washington, D.C.: The World Bank, 2004b.

Holayan, Eissa. "Bill Gates and our Philanthropists". OKAZ. 20 December. 2003.

Holden, David and Johns, Richard. *"The House of Saud"*. London: Sidgwick and Jackson, 1981.

Hollis, Rosemary. *"Oil and Regional Developments in the Gulf"*. London: The Royal Institute of International Affairs, 1998.

Hubbert, M. King. "Energy and power: the energy resources of the earth", *Scientific American*, pp. 60–70, Sept. 1971.

Humaid, Abdulwahid, Al. "Labour and *Saudization* Policies". Manpower Council. *Future Vision of Saudi Arabia*. Riyadh, Oct. 2002.

Hunter, Shireen. *"Gulf Cooperation Council: Problems and Prospects"*. Washington DC: Center for Strategic and International Studies, 1984

Husseini, Saleh, Al. "Diversification of Industrial Sector". Ministry of Industry and Electricity. *Future Vision of Saudi Arabia*. Riyadh, Oct. 2002.

Iktissad Wal-Aamal, Al. (Economics and Business). *"Special Issue on Saudization"*. Riyadh, March 1997.

International Monetary Fund. *"Financial Systems and Labor Markets in the Gulf Cooperation Council Countries"*. Washington, DC: Middle Eastern Dept., International Monetary Fund, 1997.

International Monetary Fund. "Improvements in global financial system hinge on transparency and management of risk". Survey, 5 September, 110, 1999.

Iqbal, M. and Wilson, R. (eds.). *"Islamic Perspectives on Wealth Creation"*, Edinburgh: Edinburgh University Press, 2005.

Islami, A. Reza, S. and Rostam Mehraban Kavoussi. *"The Political Economy of Saudi Arabia"*. Seattle, WA: Department of Near Eastern Languages and Civilization, University of Washington, 1984.

Jalal, Mahsoun, B. *"The Industrialization Option and the Role of the National Industrialization Company in its Implementation"*. Riyadh: Middle East Press, 1985.

Janoubi, S., Al. "Level of Performance in the Saudi Public Sector". Institute of Public Administration. *Future Vision of Saudi Arabia*. Riyadh, Oct. 2002.

Jasser, Sulaiman, Al. "Developing the Financial Sector for Better Economic Growth". SAMA. *Future Vision of Saudi Arabia*. Riyadh, Oct. 2002.

Jasser, Sulaiman, Al and Banafe, Ahmed. "Monetary Policy Investments and Procedures in Saudi Arabia". *Saudi Arabian Monetary Agency* (SAMA). Riyadh, 2003.

Johany, Ali, D. *"The Myth of the OPEC Cartel: The Role of Saudi Arabia"*. New York, NY: John Wiley, 1982.

Johany, Ali D., Michel Berne and Wilson Mixon, Jr. *"The Saudi Arabian Economy"*. Baltimore, MD: John Hopkins University Press, 1986.

Joseph, Suad and Slyomovics, Susan. *"Women and Power in the Middle East"*. Philadelphia, PA: University of Pennsylvania Press, 2001.

Kanovsky, Eliyahu. "The Economy of Saudi Arabia: Troubled Present, Grim Future". *The Washington Institute for Near East Policy Papers*, 1994.

Kapiszewski, Andrzej. *"Nationals and Expatriates, Population and Labor Dilemma of the Gulf Cooperation Council States"*. Reading, MA: Garnet Publishing Limited, 2001.

Karl, Terry Lynn. *"The Paradox of Plenty: Oil Booms and Petro-States"*. Berkeley and Los Angeles: University of California Press, 1997.

Kate, W.T. and Geuns, L.V. "The Future of the World's Oil Supply", *European Energy Review*, July–Aug. 2008.

Keller, W. "Geographic localization of international technology diffusion", *The American Economic Review*, Vol. 92, No. 1, pp. 120–142, 2002.

Kemp, M.C. "The Gains from International Trade". *Economic Journal*, 72. pp. 803–819, 1962.

Kemp, R. *"Privatization: The Provision of Public Services by the Private Sector,"* Jefferson, NC, USA; and London, UK: McFarland & Co., 2007.

Khalaf, M. "Third National Dialogue Forum-Diary of a Woman". *Arab News*. 25 Jun 2004.

Khazindar, Abid. "Combating Rising Crime". OKAZ. 30 December. 2003.

Khemani, R.S. "Fostering Diversification and Competitiveness; Strategies and Options for the Kingdom of Saudi Arabia". World Bank. *Future Vision of Saudi Arabia*, Riyadh, Oct. 2002.

Khoshhal, Khader. "Investment Behavioral Decision Making – A Case Study of the Saudi Stock Market". *Unpublished MBA Project Dissertation*. King Fahd University of Petroleum and Minerals. June 2004.

Khoury, Nabil and Moghadam, Valentine. *"Gender and Development in the Arab World: Women's Economic Participation Patterns and Policies"*. London: Zed Books, 1995.

Kibbi, Jamal, Al. "Using knowledge for Development in Saudi Arabia". World Bank. *Future Vision of Saudi Arabia*. Riyadh, Oct. 2002.

Kim, Y. "Causes of capital flows in developing countries". *Journal of International Money and Finance*, Vol. 19, pp. 235–253, 2000.

Knauerhase, Ramon. "The economic development of Saudi Arabia: an overview". *Current History*, pp. 6–10, 32–34, January 1977.

Knight, M. "Developing Countries and the Globalization of Financial Markets" *World Development*. 26(7), pp. 1185–1200, 1998.

Kofman, Eleonore and Gillian Youngs. *"Globalization: Theory and Practice"*. London: Printer, 1996.

Krimly, Rayed. "The political economy of adjusted priorities: Declining oil revenues and Saudi fiscal policies". *Middle East Journal*. Vol. 53, No. 2, (Spring), pp. 254–267, 1999.

Kugler, Maurice. "Spillovers from foreign direct investment: Within or between Industries?" *Journal of Development Economics*, Vol. 80, No. 2. pp. 444–477, 2006.

Kurdi, Usamah, Al. "A Future Vision for the Development of Small and Medium Enterprises". Council of Saudi Chambers of Commerce. *Future Vision of Saudi Arabia*. Riyadh, Oct. 2002.

Kuruvilla, S. "Linkages between Industrialization Strategies and Industrial Relations/Human Resources Policies: Singapore, Malaysia, the Philippines, and India," *Industrial and Labour Relations Review*, Vol. 49, pp. 635–657, July 1996.

Kuwaiz, Abdullah, El. "OPEC and the International Oil Market: The Age of Realism". *OPEC Review*. Oxford 10, No.4. Winter. 393–408, 1986.

Lackner, Helen. *"The House Built on Sand: A Political Economy of Saudi Arabia"*. London: Ithaca Press, 1978.

Lall, S. and Streeten, P. *"Foreign Investment, Transnational and Developing Countries"*. Boulder, CO: Westview Press, 1977.

Larocque, Norman. "Future of Higher Education: International Trends". World Bank. *Future Vision of Saudi Arabia*. Riyadh, Oct. 2002.

Lathom, Michael. "Education Reform: Trends and Lessons Learned". World Bank. *Future Vision of Saudi Arabia*. Riyadh, Oct. 2002.

Lee, Kuan Yue. *"The Singapore Story: The Memoirs of Lee Kuan Yeu"*. Singapore, Times Edition Pte, 1988.

Liu, N.S.C. and Cheng, Y. "The Academic Ranking of World Universities: Methodologies and Problems". *Higher Education in Europe* 30, pp. 127–136, 2 July 2005.

Liu, X., Siler, P., Wang, C. and Wei, Y. "Productivity spillovers from foreign direct investment", *Journal of International Business Studies*. Third Quarter, pp. 407–425, 2000.

Longva, Anh Nga. *"Walls Built on Sand: Migration, Exclusion and Society in Kuwait : Keeping migrant workers in check: The Kafala sytem in the Gulf"*. Boulder, CO: Westview Press, 1997.

Looney, R. *"Saudi Arabia's Development Potential"*. Lexington, MA: Lexington Books, 1982.

Looney, R. "Saudi Arabia's Development Strategy: Comparative Advantage versus Sustainable Development," *Orient*. 75–96. March 1989.

Looney, R. *"Economic Development in Saudi Arabia: Consequences of the Oil Price Decline"*. Greenwich, CT: Jai Press, 1990.

Looney, R. "Factors Affecting Employment in the Arabian Gulf Region, 1975–1985". *International Journal of Social Economics*. Vol. 19. pp. 72–86, 1992

Looney, R. *"Manpower Policies and Development in the Persian Gulf Region"*, New York, NY: Praeger, 1994.

Looney, R. *"Saudization* and Sound Economic Reforms: Are the Two Compatible?". *Strategic Insights*. Vol. 3, No. 2, 2004.

Lumsden, Philip. "Dealing with the problems of localization", *Middle East Economic Digest*, Vol. 37, No. 10, pp. 46–48, 1993.

Mabro, Robert. "Strategic Consideration for Gas Development in Saudi Arabia". Oxford Institute for Energy Studies. *Future Vision of Saudi Arabia*. Riyadh, Oct. 2002.

Mahdi, Kamil A. "Aspects of higher education in the Arab Gulf", in K.E. Shaw (ed.), *Higher Education in the Gulf: Problems and Prospects*. Exeter: Exeter University Press, 1997

Malik, Monica. "The Role of the Private Sector", in Wilson, Rodney, A. Salamah, M. Malik and A. Rajhi. *"Economic Development in Saudi Arabia"*. Routledge Curzon. pp. 126–138, 2004.

Mallakh, Ragaei, El. *"Saudi Arabia: Rush to Development"*. London: Croom Helm, 1982.

Mallakh, Ragaei, El and Mallakh, Dorothea, El. *"Saudi Arabia: Energy, Developmental Planning, and Industrialization"* Lexington, MA: Lexington Books, 1982.

Marboli, Leopold. "Strategic Consideration for Mining Sector Development in Saudi Arabia". World Bank. *Future Vision of Saudi Arabia*, Riyadh, Oct. 2002.

Markham, Ian and Ozdenur, Ibrahim. *"Globalization, Ethics and Islam"*. Burlington, VT: Ashgate Press, 2005.

Masmoudi, M. "The Arab World and the Information Age: Promises and Challenges". in *"The Information Revolution and the Arab World: Its Impact on State and Society"*. *The Emirates Centre for Strategic Studies and Research*. Abu Dhabi. pp. 120–140, 1998.

Masood, Rashid. *"Economic Diversification and Development in Saudi Arabia"*. Sargam, 1989.

McHale, Thomas. "Saudi Oil Policy and the Changing World Energy Balance". *International Research Center for Energy and Economic Development*. Colorado. Occasional Paper. No. One. 1986.

Megginson, W., Nash, R., and Van Randenborgh, M. "The Financial and Operating Performance of Newly Privatized Firms: An International Empirical Analysis". The Journal of Finance, Vol. XLIX, No. 2, June 1994.

Merrell Foster, Leila. *"Saudi Arabia"*. Scholastic Library Publishing, London, 1996.

Mettale, Thomas. *"Saudi Oil Policy and the Changing World Energy Balance"*. Institute Research Centre for Energy and Economics, 1987.

Michael, E.P. "Competitiveness and the State of Entrepreneurship in Saudi Arabia". *Harvard Business School*, 27 January 2009.

Ministry of Industry and Electricity. "Industrial Statistical Report for 1996 and 1998". Riyadh, April 1998.

Ministry of Planning. *"Private Establishments Survey, Volume I, Summary Report"*. Riyadh, 2000.

Ministry of Planning. *"Seventh Development Plan, 2000–2004"*, Riyadh. 2000.

Ministry of Planning. *"Achievements of the Development Plans: 1970–2000, Facts and Figures"*, Riyadh. 2002

Ministry of Planning. *"Eighth Development Plan, 2004–2009"*, Riyadh. 2004.

Mishkas, Abeer. "Failing Students". *Arab News*. 17 February 2004.

Mitchell, John and Steven, Paul. *"Funding Dependence – Had Choices for Oil Exploration Centre"*, Chatham House, UK, 2008.

Mofleh, Ibrahim, Al. "Promoting Direct Foreign Investment Development and Export Promotion". Saudi Fund for Development. *Future Vision of Saudi Arabia*, Riyadh, Oct. 2002.

Molives, Donald. *"The Economy of Saudi Arabia"*. New York, NY: Praeger, 2001.

Moody's. "Middle East: Resurgent Inflation Sharpen fiscal and Political Risks". Moody's Investor Services, June 2008.

Moon, Chung. In "Korean Contractors in Saudi Arabia: Their Rise and Fall", *Middle East Journal*. Vol. 40, No. 4, Autumn, 1986.

Morris, M.H., Marks, A.S., Allen, N.S. and Perry, J. "Modeling Ethical Attitudes and Behavior under Conditions of Environmental Turbulence". *Journal of Business Ethics*. Vol. 15, pp. 1119–1130, 1996.

Mughni, Haya. *"Women in Kuwait: The Politics of Gender"*. London: Sagi Books, 2001.

Mundell, R.A. "International trade and factor mobility", *The American Economic Review*, Vol. 47, No. 3, pp. 321–335, 1957.

Naggar, Said, El. *"Financial Policies and Capital Markets in Arab Countries"*. Washington: International Monetary Fund, 1994.

Najem, Tom and Hetherington, Martin (ed.). *"Good Governance in the Middle East Oil Monarchies"*. London: RoutledgeCurzon, 2003.

Najjar, Baquer Salman, Al. *"Population Policies in the Countries of the Gulf Cooperation Council"*. New York, NY: St. Martin's Press Inc, 1998.

Nakhleh, Emile A. *"The Gulf Cooperation Council"*. New York, NY: Praeger Publishers, 1986.

Naomi, Sakr (ed.). *"Women and Media in the Middle East"*. I.B. Tauvis, 2004.

Nashashibi, Hikmat, "The Role of Arab Capital Markets in Investing the Financial Surpluses", *Middle East Banking Finance*. Arab Press Service, Vol. 3, pp. 195–208, 1983.

National Commercial Bank (NCB). "The Mutual Funds Market in Saudi Arabia". *The NCB Economist*. Second Quarter, 2000.

National Commercial Bank (NCB). "The Evolving role of Financial Institutions in the New Decade". *NCB*. Jeddah. First Quarter 2001a.

National Commercial Bank (NCB). "What is Monetary Policy and Fiscal Policy? How does it work in the U.S. and Saudi Arabia?". *Saudi Economic Review*. Third/Fourth Quarter, 2001b.

Nazir, H. "The Role of Public-Private Partnership in Realizing Vision". Nazer Group. *Future Vision of Saudi Arabia*, Riyadh, Oct. 2002.

Netton, Ian Richard. *"Arabia and the Gulf: From Traditional Society to Modern States"*. London: Croom Helm, 1986

Newberry, David. "Oil Prices, Cartels, and the Problem of Dynamic Inconsistency". *Economic Journal*, Vol. 91, No. 363, pp. 617–646, September 1981.

Niblock, Tim. *"Social and Economic Development in the Arab Gulf"*. London: Croom Helm, 1980.

Niblock, Tim, (ed.). *"State, Society, and the Economy in Saudi Arabia"*. London: Croom Helm, 1982.

Nojaidi, A, Al. "Experience and Vision in Foreign Investment Development and Export Promotion". Saudi Fund for Development and Export Promotion – A SABIC Perspective. SABIC. *Future Vision of Saudi Arabia*. Riyadh, Oct. 2002.

Noreng, Oystein. *"Crude Power: Politics and the Oil Market"*. I.B. Tauris. London, 2006.

Nur Uthman. *"The Labor Force in GCC Countries: Present and Future"*, Secretariat-General of the Arab Gulf Cooperation Council, 1995.

O'Sullivan, Edmund. *"Saudi Arabia"*. MEED, London, 1993.

OPEC Secretariat, *OPEC Annual Statistical Bulletin*, 2007, Vienna, 2008.

Organization of Petroleum Exporting Countries (OPEC). *Annual Reports*. Various Years. Vienna.

Osama, Abdul Rahman. *"The Dilemma of Development in the Arabian Peninsula"*. London: Croom Helm, 1987.

Osmundsen, P. "Is oil supply choked by financial market pressures?", *Energy Policy*, Vol. 35, pp. 467–474, 2007.

Ostapski, S.A., Oliver, J. and Gonzales, G.T. "The legal and ethical components of executive decision making: a course for business managers". *Journal of Business Ethics*. Vol. 15, pp. 571–579, 1996.

Oweiss, Ibrahim M. "Economics of Petrodollars," in Haleh Esfandiari and A.L. Udovitch (ed.) *The Economic Dimensions of Middle Eastern History"*. pp. 179–197. Princeton, NJ: Darwin Press, 1990.

Oweiss, Ibrahim M. "The Arab Gulf Economies: Challenges and Perspectives". *The Emirates Center for Strategic Studies and Research*. Abu Dhabi, 2000.

Owen, Roger and Pamuk Sevket. "A History of Middle East Economies in the Twenty First Century". *IB Tauris*, 1998.

Parra, Franscisco. "Oil Politics: A Modern History of Petroleum". *IB Tauris*, 2004.

Patrick, H.T. "Financial Development and Economic Growth in Underdeveloped Countries". *Economic Development and Cultural Change*. Vol. 14. No. 2 pp. 174–177, 1996.

Porter, M. "Competitiveness and the State of Entrepreneurship in Saudi Arabia". Harvard Business School. 27 January 2009.

Porter, M. "Regions and Competitiveness: Implications for Saudi Arabia". Global Competitiveness Forum. Riyadh, 26 January 2010.

Porter, M.E. *"The Competitive Advantage of Nations"*, New York, NY: The Free Press, 1990.

Power, Colin. "Higher education: Future vision". Paper presented at the Riyadh Conference on Higher Education, 22–25 February 1998.

Presley, John, R. *"Guide to the Saudi Arabian Economy"*. London: Macmillan, 1989.

Quandt, William B. *"Saudi Arabia in the 1980s: Foreign Policy, Security, and Oil"*. Washington, DC: Brookings Institution, 1982.

Qudsi, Sulayman, Al. "Labor Market Policies and Development in GCC: Does International Policy Consistency Matter?", in Julia Devlin (ed.). *Gulf Economies: Strategies for Growth in the 21st Century* Center for Contemporary Arab Studies. Washington, DC: Georgetown University, 1977.

Qusti, Raid. "Dictates of Tradition". *Arab News*. 9 July 2003.

Radwan, Ismail. "Small and Medium Enterprise Development: A Vision for Action in Saudi Arabia". World Bank. *Future Vision of Saudi Arabia*, Riyadh, Oct. 2002.

Raj Bhala. "Saudi Arabia, the WTO, and American Trade and Policy" *The International Lawyer*, Vol. 38, No. 3, Fall 2004.

Ramady, M., Sahlawi, M., Al. "Education as a force for economic change in an oil based economy: a case study of Saudi Arabia". *Journal of Energy and Development*. Vol. 30. No. 2. Spring 2005.

Ramady, M. "Government finances: a case study of Saudi Arabian budgetary reforms". *Business & Economics Society International*. Anthology 2004.

Ramady, M.A. "Evolving Banking Regulation and Supervision: A Case Study of the Saudi Arabian Monetary Agency (SAMA). *International Journal of Islamic and Middle East Finance and Management*, Vol. 2, No. 3, pp. 235–250, 2009.

Ramazani, R.K. *"The Gulf Cooperation Council: Record and Analysis"*, Charlottesville, VA: University Press of Virginia, 1988.

Ranis, G. and Fei, J.C.H. "Development Economics: What Next?" In: Ranis, G., and Schultz, T.P. (eds) *The State of Development Economics: Progress and Perspectives*. Cambridge: Basil Blackwell, 1988.

Rasheed, M, Al. *"A History of Saudi Arabia"*. Cambridge: Cambridge University Press, 2002.

Reuters. "Moody's Annual Credit Opinion on Saudi Arabia Shows High Government Financial Strength: A1 Rating". 16 February 2009.

Richard, Alan and Waterbury, John. *"A Political Economy of the Middle East: State, Class, and Economic Development"*. Boulder, CO: Westview Press, 1990.

Richard, Frederick. "Future Strategy for the Industrial Sector 2020". UNIDO. *Future Vision of Saudi Arabia*, Riyadh, Oct. 2002.

Riyad Capital. "Economic Briefing Riyad Bank", Jan. 10, 2010.

Rofail, Maged. "The Economic Impact of Broadening and Deepening the Saudi Stock Market". *Unpublished MBA Dissertation*. King Fahd University of Petroleum and Minerals. June 2003.

Romer, P.M. "Endogenous technological change", *The Journal of Political Economy*, Vol. 98, No. 5, S71–S102, 1990.

Romer, Paul. "The Origins of Endogenous Growth". *Journal of Economic Perspectives*. pp. 3–22. Winter, 1994.

Rostow, Walt, W. *"The Stages of Economic Growth: A Non-Communist Manifesto"*. Cambridge University Press, 1960.

Rostow, Walt, W. *"Economic Growth"*. Oxford: Oxford University Press, 1970.

Rugh, William. "Emergence of a new middle class in Saudi Arabia". *The Middle East Journal*, Vol. 27, No. 1, pp. 7–20, 1973.

Rutledge, Emile. *"Monetary Union in the Gulf"*, New York, NY: Routledge, 2009.

Sachs, J.D. and Warner, A.M. "The curse of natural resources". *European Economic Review*. Vol. 45, pp. 827–838, 2001.

SAGIA. "Approved Foreign Companies to Sponsor Their Own Employees". Riyadh, May, 2002.

SAGIA (Saudi Arabian General Investment Authority). "Women Only Industrial City Planned in Riyadh". *SAGIA*. 13 June 2004.

SAGIA (Saudi Arabian General Investment Authority). "Jeddah Economic Forum Opens with Active Saudi Women Participation". *SAGIA*. 18 January 2004.

SAGIA (Saudi Arabian General Investment Authority). "Future of SME's". *SAGIA*. 8 March 2004.

SAGIA (Saudi Arabian General Investment Authority). "Jeddah to have First Industrial City for Women". *SAGIA*. 3 June 2004.

Sajini, Ismail. "Effects of WTO on Small and Medium Enterprises". *Arab News*. 19 January 2004.

Salah, Ahmed. "Economic Impact of joining WTO". Ministry of Planning. *Future Vision of Saudi Arabia*. Riyadh, Oct. 2002.

Salmi, Jamil. "Constructing Knowledge Societies: New Challenges for Tertiary Education". World Bank. *Future Vision of Saudi Arabia*. Riyadh, Oct. 2003.

Salmi, Jamil. *"The Challenge of Establishing world-Class Universities"*, World Bank, 2009.

Salmi, J. and Saroyan, A. "League Tables as Policy Instruments: Uses and Misuses". *Higher Education Management and Policy*, Vol. 19, No. 2, pp. 24–62, 2007.

SAMBA Financial Group. *"The Saudi Economy at Mid-year 2004"*. August 2004.

SAMBA Financial Group. *"The Saudi Economy: 2003 Performance, 2004 Forecast"*. Riyadh. February 2004.

SAMBA. *"GCC Monetary Union: Progress to Date and Outstanding Issues"*, SAMBA, Riyadh, May 2009.

Samii, M., Rajamanickam, M. and Thirunavkkararasu, A. "Euro Pricing of Crude Oil: An OPEC's Perspectives". International Business Research, Southern New Hampshire University, Manchester, NH. January 2004.

Samuelson, P.A. "The gains from international trade", *Canadian Journal of Economics and Political Science*, Vol. 5, No. 2, pp. 195–205, 1939.

Sanabary, Nagat, El. "Female education in Saudi Arabia and the reproduction of gender division". *Gender and Education*. No. 2, 1994.

Sandwick, J.A. (ed.). *"The Gulf Cooperation Council: Moderation and Stability in an Interdependent World"*. Boulder, Co: Westview Press, 1987.

Saravia, Edgar. "Regulation and Competition". World Bank. *Future Vision of Saudi Arabia*. Riyadh, Oct. 2002.

Sarma, S.N. "An Analysis of Seasonality in GCC Stock Markets", *ICFAI Journal of Applied Finance*, Vol. 13, No. 5, pp. 28–36, 2007.

Sassanpour, Cyrus, *"Policy Challenges in the Gulf Cooperation Council Countries"*. Washington, DC: International Monetary Fund, 1996.

Saudi Arabia Ministry of Education. *"Education in the Kingdom of Saudi Arabia within the Last Hundred Years"*. Riyadh: Ministry of Education, 2001.

Saudi Arabian Monetary Agency (SAMA). *"A Case Study on Globalization and the Role of Institution building in the Financial Sector in Saudi Arabia"*. Riyadh. February 2004.

Saudi Arabian Monetary Agency (SAMA). *Thirty-Nine Annual Report*, 2003, *Fortieth Annual Report*, 2004, *Forty Fifth Annual Report*, 2009.

Saudi Aramco. "Master Gas System". *Saudi Aramco*, 2003.

Saudi Aramco. "Facts and Figures 2008". *Saudi Aramco, 2009.*

Saudi Press Agency. "Crown Prince Abdullah makes Historic Visit to Russia". Riyadh. 2 September 2003.

Saudi Press Agency. "Kingdom Announces Regulations for Municipal Elections". Riyadh. 10 August 2004.

Saudi Press Agency. "Government to Increase Subsidies on Basic Foodstuffs to Combat Inflation". Riyadh. 18 May 2008.

Saudi Research and Marketing "Top 100 Saudi Companies 2007". *Arab News*, Jeddah, Dec. 2007.

Sayigh, Yusif. *"The Arab Economy: Past Performance and Future Prospects"*. Oxford: Oxford University Press, 1982.

Seznec, Jean-Francois. *"The Financial Markets of the Arabian Gulf"*. London: Croom Helm, 1987.

Seznec, Jean-Francois. "The Gulf Capital Markets at a Crossroads. *"Columbia Journal of World Business*, Vol. 30 (Fall), pp. 6–14, 1995.

Seznec, Jean-Francois. "WTO and the dangers to Privatization: An analysis of the Saudi Case". *SIPA*. Columbia University, 2002.

Shaban, A.R., Asaad, R. and Al-Qudsi, S. "The Challenges of Employment in the Arab Region". *International Labour Review*, Vol. 134, pp. 65–82, 1995.

Sharway, A. "In search of Better Performance in the Public Sector". Institute of Public Administration. *Future Vision of Saudi Arabia*, Riyadh, Oct. 2002.

Shatkin, Lawrence. "The world of work as viewed from Saudi Arabia". *Unpublished Research Mimeo.* Dec. 2002.

Sheikh, F, El and Abdelrahman, A, El. *"The Legal Regime for Foreign Private Investment in Saudi Arabia"*. Cambridge: Cambridge University Press, 2003.

Sheikh, Said. "Structure of Gulf Banking and effects of Globalization and Financial Liberalization". *The NCB Economist*. Issue No. 2. Vol. 9, March/April 1999.

Sinclair, C.A. "Migrant workers' remittances in the Arab world: scale, significance and prediction", in B.R. Pridham (ed.), *The Arab Gulf and the Arab World*, London: Croom Helm, 1988.

Singh, H. and Jun, K. "Some New Evidence on Determinants of Foreign Direct Investment in Developing Countries". *Policy Research Working Paper.* 1531, World Bank, Washington DC, 1995.

Sirageldin, I. and Al-Ebraheem, Y. "Budget deficit, resource gap and human resource development in oil economics", in Sirageldin, I (ed.). *Population and Development in the Middle East and North Africa: Challenges for the Twenty-First Century*. Working Paper, Baltimore, MD: John Hokins University, 1999.

SJTU (Shanghai Jiao Tong University). *Academic Ranking of World Universities 2008*. Retrieved September 30, 2008, from http://www.arwu.org!rank2008/EN2008.htm., 2008.

Smith, Grant. *"Saudization*: Development and Expectations Management". *Saudi American Forum*, 31st October 2003.

Solow, Robert. *"Price Expectations and the Behavior of the Price Level"*. Manchester University Press, Manchester, 1970.

Soufi, Wahib Abdulfattah and Mayer, Richard. *"Saudi Arabian Industrial Investment: An Analysis of Government-Business Relationship"*. Quorum Books, 2002

Speakman, John. "Privatization and Private Sector Participation in Infrastructure: A Vision for Saudi Arabia". World Bank. *Future Vision of Saudi Arabia*, Riyadh, Oct. 2002.

Stevens, Paul John. "The Interaction Between Oil Policy and Industrial Policy in Saudi Arabia", in Ragaei El Mallakh and Dorothea H. El Mallakh (ed.) *Saudi Arabia: Energy, Development Planning, and Industrialization*, pp. 27–45. Lexington, MA: Lexington Books, D.C., 1982.

Sturm, M., Strasky, J., Adolf, P. and Peschel, D. "The Gulf Cooperation Council Countries: Economic Structures, Recent Developments, and Role in the Global Economy", *European Central Bank Occasional Paper* No. 92, 2008.

Sugair, Ali. "Saudi Credit Bank and Small and Medium Sector Support Performance". *Future Vision of Saudi Arabia*. Riyadh, Oct. 2002.

Suhaimi, Jammaz. "Consolidation, Competition, Foreign presence and systematic Stability in the Saudi Banking Industry". SAMA. Riyadh, 2002.

Swiss-ReSigma. "World Insurance in 2008", *Swiss Re Insurance*, Zurich, 2009.

Taecker, K. "Myths and Realities about Unemployment in Saudi Arabia", *Saudi American Forum* 30 March 2003.

Taher, Nahed. "Saudi Arabian Budget and Challenges of Sustainable Growth", *Arab News*, Jeddah, 22 December 2003.

The Economist. *"Gulf citizen, no qualifications, seeks well-paid job"*. Vol. 343, No. 8012, p. 41, 1997.

THES. *"The Times Higher Education World University Rankings 2008"*, Retrieved September 30, 2008, from http://www.timeshighereducation. co.uk/hybrid.asp?typeCode=243&pubCode=1. 2008.

THES. *"Times Higher Education Supplement: Top 500 Universities 2009"*. The Times Newspaper Publication. London, 2010.

Thirwall, A.P. *"Growth and Development"*. London: Macmillan, 1994.

Todaro, M. *"Economic Development"*. London: Longmans, 1994.

Towajri, H.A. Al. *"The labor market in Saudi Arabia: family effects, compensating wage differentials, and selective bias"*. Ph.D. Thesis, University of Oregon, 1992.

Trivedi, P. "In Search of Better Performance of Public Sector: Vision for improving Public Sector efficiency in the Kingdom of Saudi Arabia". World Bank. *Future Vision of Saudi Arabia*, Riyadh, Oct. 2002.

United Nations. *"Millennium Development Goals Report for the Kingdom of Saudi Arabia 2002"*, UN Riyadh, 2002.

UNCTAD. *World Investment Report, 1999, 2000, 2008–2009*.

United Nations Development Program (UNDP). *"Arab Human Development Report 2002"*. New York, NY: United Nations Development Program/Arab Fund for Economic and Social Development, 2002.

Ventura, J. "Growth and interdependence", *The Quarterly Journal of Economics*, Vol. 112, No. 1, pp. 57–84, 1997.

Warde, I. *"Islam and Economics"*. Edinburgh: Edinburgh University Press, 2005.

Whelan, John, (ed.). *"Saudi Arabia"*. London: MEED, 1981.

Williams, R. and Van Dyke N. "Measuring the International Standing of Universities with an Application to Australian Universities" *Higher Education*, Vol. 53, pp. 819–841, 6 June 2007.

Wilson, J.S.G. *"Banking and Structure: A Comparative Analysis"*. London: Croom Helm, 1986.

Wilson, Rodney. *"Banking and Finance in the Arab Middle East"*. London: Macmillan, 1983.

Wilson, Rodney. *"Economic Development in the Middle East"*. London: Routledge, 1995.

Wilson, Rodney, "Saudi Arabia: WTO Membership," *Oxford Analytica Daily Brief*. May 14, 1997.

Wilson, Rodney. "The Changing Composition and Direction of GCC Trade". *The Emirates Center for Strategic Studies and Research*. Abu Dhabi, 1998.

Wilson, Rodney. "Good International Governance: Implications for Saudi Arabia's Political Economy", in Najeim, T. *"Good Governance in the Middle East Oil Monarchies"*. London: RoutledgeCurzon, 2003.

Wilson, Rodney, Malik, Monica, Al-Salamah, A. and Al-Rajhi, A. "*Economic Development in Saudi Arabia*". London: RoutledgeCurzon, 2003.

Winters, L.A. and Yusuf, S. "Dancing with Giants: China, India, and the Global Economy", Washington D.C.: The World Bank and Institute of Policy Studies, 2007.

Woodward, Peter. "*Oil and Labour in the Middle East-Saudi Arabia and the Oil Boom*". New York, NY: Praeger, 1988.

World Bank. "*A Population Perspective on Development in the Middle East and North Africa*". Washington, DC.: World bank, August 1994.

World Bank. "*Will Arab Workers Prosper or Be Left Out in the Twenty-First Century?*" Washington, DC: World Bank, 1995.

World Bank. "*Global Development Finance*". Washington, 2001.

World Bank, "*Constructing Knowledge Societies: New Challenges for Tertiary Education*", Washington, DC: World Bank. Retrieved December 2, 2008, from http://go.worldbank.org/ N2QADMBNI0. 2002.

World Bank. "Global Economic Prospects 2008: Technology Diffusion in the Developing World", Washington: World Bank, 2008.

World Bank. *Global Development Prospects*. Various editions.

World Bank. *World Development Indicators*. Various editions.

World Economic Forum (ed.) Schwals, Klaus. "*The Arab World Competitiveness Report 2002–2003*". New York, NY: Oxford University Press, 2003.

World Trade Organization (WTO). "*World Merchandise Exports by Region and Selected Economy, 1980, 1985, 1990, 1995, and 1991–2001*". www.wto.org

World Trade Organization (WTO). "*World Trade in 2000: Overview*". www.wto.org

Wright, Jr. J.W. with Hani Khashoggi and Christopher Vaughn. "Labor Constraints on Saudi Business Development" in J.W. Wright, Jr (ed.), *Business Development in Saudi Arabia*. London: Macmillan, 1996.

Wright, Jr. J.W. "*Business and Economic Development in Saudi Arabia*", London: Macmillan Press Ltd, 1996.

WTO. "*International Trade Statistics 2007*", Geneva: WTO, 2007.

WTO. "*World Trade Report 2008: Trade in a Globalizing World*", WTO, Geneva, 2009.

Yamani, Mai. "The New Generation in the GCC: the case of Saudi Arabia", in Rosemary Hollis (ed.), "*Oil and Regional Developments in the Gulf*". London: The Royal Institute of International Affairs, 1998.

Yamani, Mai. "*Changed Identities: The Challenge of the New Generation in Saudi Arabia*". London: The Royal Institute of International Affairs, 2000.

Yamani, Zohair. "Oil-fired growth: Export-led development in Saudi Arabia, 1960–1990", Ph.D. Thesis. *University of Nebraska*. January 1, 1994.

Young, A. "Learning by doing and the dynamic effects of international trade", *The Quarterly Journal of Economics*, Vol. 106, No. 2, pp. 369–405, 1991.

Yusuf, S. and Nabeshima, K. "*How Universities Promote Economic Growth*", Washington DC: World Bank, 2007.

Zamil, A, Al. "Petrochemicals Industry in the Kingdom: Past, Present and Future". Al Zamil Group. *Future Vision of Saudi Arabia*. Riyadh, Oct. 2002.

Zamil, Abdullah. "Manufacturer's Message: *Saudization* Insight from Zamil Air Conditioners Experience". First Contractors Saudization Forum, Saudi Aramco, Dammam. 22 December 2003.

Zamil, Ahmed, Al. "Future of Labour Market in the Kingdom after a Generation". Ministry of Labour and Social Affairs. *Future Vision of Saudi Arabia*. Riyadh, Oct. 2002.

Zarouk, Jamal. "Prospects for Expansion of Trade in Services in the Saudi Economy". World Bank. *Future Vision of Saudi Arabia*. Riyadh, Oct. 2002.

Zulficar, M. "*Women in Development: A Legal Study*". New York, NY: UNICEF. January 1995.

Index

Note: The locators followed by 'f' and 't' refers to figures and tables cited in the text.

Lightning Source UK Ltd.
Milton Keynes UK
19 October 2010

161567UK00002B/1/P